America's National Anthem

America's National Anthem

"The Star-Spangled Banner" in U.S. History, Culture, and Law

John R. Vile

An Imprint of ABC-CLIO, LLC

Santa Barbara, California • Denver, Colorado

Library of Congress Cataloging-in-Publication Data

Names: Vile, John R., author.
Title: America's National Anthem : "The Star-Spangled Banner" in U.S.
   History, Culture, and Law / John R. Vile.
Description: Santa Barbara, California : ABC-CLIO, An Imprint of ABC-CLIO,
   LLC, [2021] | Includes bibliographical references and index.
Identifiers: LCCN 2020006125 | ISBN 9781440873188 (hardcover) | ISBN
   9781440873195 (ebook)
Subjects: LCSH: Baltimore, Battle of, Baltimore, Md., 1814—Juvenile
   literature. | Star spangled banner (Song)—Juvenile literature. | United
   States—History—War of 1812—Flags—Juvenile literature. | National
   songs—United States—History and criticism—Juvenile literature. | Key,
   Francis Scott, 1779-1843—Juvenile literature. | Flags—United
   States—History—19th century—Juvenile literature.
Classification: LCC E356.B2 V55 2020 | DDC 973.5/2—dc23
LC record available at https://lccn.loc.gov/2020006125

ISBN: 978-1-4408-7318-8 (print)
       978-1-4408-7319-5 (ebook)

25 24 23 22 21   1 2 3 4 5

This book is also available as an eBook.

ABC-CLIO
An Imprint of ABC-CLIO, LLC

ABC-CLIO, LLC
147 Castilian Drive
Santa Barbara, California 93117
www.abc-clio.com

This book is printed on acid-free paper ∞

Manufactured in the United States of America

Dedicated to those brave citizens who are determined to see that America remains "the home of the free."

Contents

Alphabetical List of Entries

Guide to Related Topics

ALTERNATIVES TO "THE STAR-SPANGLED BANNER"

Alternatives to the National Anthem

"America the Beautiful"

"Battle Hymn of the Republic"

"Columbia, the Gem of the Ocean"

"God Bless America"

"Hail Columbia"

"Hail to the Chief"

"My Country, 'Tis of Thee" ("America")

National Anthem Contest

Regional Appeal

"Stars and Stripes Forever, The"

"This Land Is Your Land"

"When the Warrior Returns"

"You're a Grand Old Flag"

ANTHEMS OF OTHER ENTITIES AND NATIONS

Confederate National Anthem

"God Save the Queen"

"La Marseillaise"

Latino National Anthem

Liberian National Anthem

"Lift Every Voice and Sing"

Mennonite National Anthem

Mexican National Anthem

"O Canada"

Panamanian National Anthem

Philippine National Anthem

Songs of the U.S. Armed Forces

State Songs and Anthems

ARTISTIC DESCRIPTIONS AND DEPICTIONS

Advertising

"Birth of the Star-Spangled Banner, The"

By Dawn's Early Light

Carr, Thomas

Cartoons and the National Anthem

"Chesapeake: Summer of 1814"

Collectibles and Souvenirs

Copyright

"Defence of Fort M'Henry"

Early Printings

Everson, Joe

Flag Is Full of Stars, The

Murals

"O'er the Ramparts"

Paintings of the Bombardment of Fort McHenry

"Steamroller Music Box"

Very Visionary Star-Spangled Sidewalk

"View of the Bombardment of Fort McHenry"

Visual Arts

Wyeth, N. C.

COMPOSERS AND AUTHORS

Clague, Mark

Holmes, Oliver Wendell, Sr.

Key, Francis Scott

Smith, John Stafford

Sousa, John Philip

CRITICS AND SUPPORTERS OF "THE STAR-SPANGLED BANNER"

Cheatham, Kitty

Holloway, Mrs. Reuben Ross

Linthicum, John Charles

Ripley Cartoon

Stetson, Augusta E.

GENRES

Anthem

Drinking Song

Hymn

Parodies

GROUPS

Abolitionists

African Americans

American Sign Language

Children

Immigrants

Jehovah's Witnesses

LGBTQ Community

Native American Indians

Veterans

Women

HISTORIC CONNECTIONS

Baltimore, Maryland

Fort McHenry

Fort McHenry Visitor and Education Center

Francis Scott Key House

Indian Queen Hotel (Baltimore)

National Peace Jubilee

Star Spangled Music Foundation

Star-Spangled Banner Flag

Star-Spangled Banner Flag House

Star-Spangled National Historic Trail

Very Visionary Star-Spangled Sidewalk

INDIVIDUALS

Abdul-Rauf, Mahmoud

Anacreon

Armistead, George

Atlee, E. A.

Barr, Roseanne

Beanes, William

Broyhill, Joel

Carr, Thomas

Cheatham, Kitty

Clague, Mark

Cochrane, Alexander Inglis

Everson, Joe

Feliciano, Jose

Ferguson, Stacy Ann ("Fergie")

Franklin, Aretha

Gaye, Marvin

Hendrix, Jimi

Holloway, Mrs. Reuben Ross

Holmes, Oliver Wendell, Sr.

Houston, Whitney

Kaepernick, Colin

Key, Francis Scott

Linthicum, John Charles

Madison, James

Monroe, Lucy

Nicholson, Joseph Hopper

O'Connor, Sinead

Patty, Sandi

Pickersgill, Mary Young

Ross, Betsy

Ross, Robert

Skinner, John Stuart

Smith, John Stafford

Smith, Samuel

Sonneck, Oscar George Theodore

Sousa, John Philip

Stetson, Augusta E.

Stravinsky, Igor

Svejda, George J.

Tomlinson, Ralph

Tracy, Benjamin Franklin

Trump, Donald J.

Wilson, Woodrow

Wyeth, N. C.

LAWS, CUSTOMS, AND REGULATIONS RELATED TO "THE STAR-SPANGLED BANNER"

Code for the National Anthem

Congress and "The Star-Spangled Banner"

Copyright

English Language and "The Star-Spangled Banner"

First Amendment

Military Regulations

National Anthem Day

Pledge of Allegiance

Political Theory

Presidential Campaigns

Public Schools

Sheldon v. Fannin (1963)

Singing the National Anthem in Public Spaces

"Star-Spangled Banner, The," Official Version

State and Municipal Laws and Ordinances

POPULAR CULTURE

Advertising

Cartoons and the National Anthem

Collectibles and Souvenirs

Commemorations of "The Star-Spangled Banner"

Fireworks

Knowledge of the National Anthem

Madama Butterfly

Movie Theaters

Murals

National Anthem Project

Patriotic Holidays

Patriotism

Places of Worship

Popular Opinion

Presidential Campaigns

Public Schools

Radio, Television, and Satellite Transmissions

Sports Events

Star-Spangled Banner Pageant

Star-Spangled Banner: Anthem of Liberty

Visual Arts

PRECURSORS TO "THE STAR-SPANGLED BANNER"

"Adams and Liberty"

"Defence of Fort M'Henry"

"Hymn for the Fourth of July, 1832"

"To Anacreon in Heaven"

"When the Warrior Returns"

SCHOLARSHIP AND THEORY

Clague, Mark

Criticisms and Defenses of "The Star-Spangled Banner"

Knowledge of the National Anthem

National Anthem Project

Nationalism versus Internationalism

Patriotism

Political Theory

Scholarship

Slavery

Sonneck, Oscar George Theodore

Svejda, George J.

Unity

SONGS RELATED TO "THE STAR-SPANGLED BANNER"

"Battle of Baltimore, The"

"Battle of the Wabash, The"

"Yankee Doodle"

WAR

Civil War

Confederate National Anthem

German-American Composers during
World War I

Military Regulations

Smith, Samuel

Songs of the U.S. Armed Forces

Veterans

Vietnam War

War and the National Anthem

War of 1812

Wilson, Woodrow

World Wars I and II

Preface

This is the fourth consecutive reference book on iconic American symbols that I have written for ABC-CLIO. The other three have dealt successively with the U.S. flag, the Declaration of Independence, and the Liberty Bell.

Just as the Liberty Bell has a written inscription and was designed to appeal to the ear, so too the words of the national anthem are set to music. Like all three of the previous symbols about which I have written, the national anthem has a long history, which was forged in the crucible of a single dramatic battle and yet continues to influence Americans' perception of themselves and the world.

Although not all nations have a specific moment in which they declared their independence in a formal written document or a specific national symbol that is equivalent to the American Liberty Bell, most have both flags and anthems. One of the beauties of America is that the anthem is actually an amplification of the flag and the ideals for which it stands, which is further validated with the pledge to the flag that many of us have recited since childhood.

I do not intend for this work to be a comparative study, but in attempting to explicate America's national anthem, I have found it helpful to discuss a number of other national anthems, especially those in the North American continent or in nations with specific links to the United States. Moreover, it is important to recognize that there were quite a number of alternatives to the anthem, and even after Congress designated "The Star-Spangled Banner" as the national anthem, there are other songs that evoke similar patriotic emotions. I have thus detailed quite a number of alternatives that might have become the anthem or that are sometimes used in its place or as supplements of sorts to "The Star-Spangled Banner."

It took more than one hundred years for Congress to designate a particular set of words written by Francis Scott Key to express national ideals as the nation's official anthem, without designating a specific arrangement. One of the most fascinating aspects of the anthem is the manner in which modern performers have sought to put their own musical interpretations on this anthem, at times even using the medium of languages other than English. On some of these occasions, listeners have reacted with scorn to what they perceive to be performers' self-conscious efforts to garner attention for themselves, but others citizens have expressed greater appreciation for the national anthem and its sentiments when it has been dressed in different musical garb. In all of these cases, however, at least some debate has raged over the merits of the performance in question for the simple reason that people possess a wide range of musical tastes.

For more than a century before Congress adopted "The Star-Spangled Banner," critics complained that it was too militaristic, too anglophobic, and too difficult to sing, and yet, especially since Congress officially recognized the tune, both it and its referent—the American flag—have served as unifying symbols. Although I suspect that both the national anthem and the flag that it highlights will largely continue to fulfill this role, it is clear that recent controversies over whether to stand, sit, or kneel during the playing of the national anthem and/or the raising of the American flag show that both symbols sometimes reveal discord as well. With my own background in constitutional law and with my particular respect for the First Amendment, I find myself in the position of being able to respect individuals who salute the flag and stand for the anthem as well as those who respectfully express their dissent over current policies or aspects of American society by sitting or kneeling during the national anthem. I have therefore tried to document and explain these sentiments and the most prominent occasions where they have been evidenced, with due sensitivity to the sentiments of all the participants.

There is something challenging about living in a nation where individuals have the freedom to regard expressions of respect for the flag or the anthem as expressions of support for specific laws, policies, or societal attitudes. As an educator, I like the idea that whatever choice individuals make, they do thoughtfully and with a willingness to explain their point of view in a manner that respects the rights of others.

If I could choose from among the many inspiring lines of "The Star-Spangled Banner," I would not choose the lofty reference to "broad stripes and bright stars" or the description of America as "the land of the free and the home of the brave" or even the motto "In God is our trust," but rather the line in the fourth verse that says, "Then conquer we must, when our cause it is just." At least in my mind, this verse recognizes that our nation deserves to prevail, not in every conflict we enter or in every policy that we enforce, but in those cases, which I hope are the large majority, "when our cause it is just."

If I have interpreted this meaning correctly, however dear and revered the nation may be, it achieves greatness by adhering to ideals and pursuing policies that would adorn any nation or people who pursues them freely and bravely.

Acknowledgments

I am grateful to all those who have helped with this project, including Kevin Hillstrom, Tessa Somberg, and Robin Tutt at ABC-CLIO. Thanks also to Dr. Stephen Smith, associate dean of the College of Liberal Arts at Middle Tennessee State University, for helping to find an author for an essay on the music aspects of "The Star-Spangled Banner"; Pam Middleton in the Interlibrary Loan Office of the Walker Library at Middle Tennessee State University; and Hailey Clark, a student aide who helped me proofread the manuscript.

I remain grateful to colleagues and family members who patiently listened to my stories and served as sources for entries for this encyclopedia, including a wife and grandson who accompanied me on a trip to Fort McHenry in Baltimore, Maryland. Gregory R. Weidman and Tim Ertel at the Fort McHenry National Monument and Historic Shrine also provided information about their book and archival holdings. Various members of the Honors College staff further helped me through various computer issues associated with this project.

Dr. Rebekka King at Middle Tennessee State University helped me locate an episode of *Hood Adjacent* featuring "The Star-Spangled Banner," while Amy Harris-Aber provided information about Mennonites and the national anthem. I am also grateful to Dr. Joseph Morgan, who penned an introductory chapter.

Introduction

As reference librarians and others who keep track of such things may know, this is the fourth in a series of books that I never intended to be a series but that has taken on a momentum of its own.

I started the project, innocently enough (at least in my own mind), when agreeing to write an encyclopedia on the American flag. Although I was hardly new to the writing of encyclopedias, I initially viewed the flag book as a stand-alone work that covered what I considered to be a fascinating and multidimensional topic that would interest a wide variety of audiences.

My own graduate training was in political theory, which taught me the importance of symbols, but I found that writing about a specific symbol was a way of bringing such theory down to earth and associating it with the history of a particular nation. Before long I was totally absorbed in the task of exploring the rich history and meanings of the flag.

After completing the American flag encyclopedia I found myself pondering a similar volume on the Declaration of Independence. Having already written in other contexts on the U.S. Constitution, I knew that the Declaration was a seminal document in American history—and that a book-length treatment would allow me to examine the noble sentiments that it expressed and the ways in which the Constitution was deeply ingrained in American symbolism and its understanding of itself.

For many years I have visited local schools, particularly during Constitution Week, to discuss the American Founding. I did so not only because I thought the topic was so important but also because I found it challenging to take abstract principles and complicated institutions and explain them to children. As much as any experiences I have had, these presentations helped teach me the way that symbols not only stimulate the intellect but also the emotions. I quickly learned that any time I mentioned that Independence Hall, where the Constitution and Declaration of Independence were proposed, was near where the Liberty Bell was displayed, children began raising their hands and blurting out such questions about the bell as "Who made it?," "When did it crack?," "Why did it crack?," "What is it made of?," "What does it sound like?," "How tall is it?," and the like. Those experiences provided the inspiration for an encyclopedia devoted to the Liberty Bell.

This at last brings me to this book, which surveys a symbol of America that has become the subject of particularly intense debate over the last several years. One of the fascinating aspects of "The Star-Spangled Banner," which is fairly distinctive, is that it not only serves as an anthem, or symbol, for the nation, but it also references another such symbol that preceded it—the American flag. It is thus, to use scholarly jargon, "metasymbolic."

"THE STAR-SPANGLED BANNER" AS A SYMBOL

Although "The Star-Spangled Banner" appears to have increased in popularity over time and been especially popular during times of war, it is difficult to know how to rank it in terms of national symbols. Carlos Abril notes that a poll taken in 2002 showed that it was "the third most recognizable symbol of the United States, behind the U.S. flag and the Statue of Liberty" (2007, 76). By contrast, numerous studies suggest that many Americans cannot identify the name of the national anthem and still fewer know even the words to the first stanza.

In addition to encountering the song in school, Americans are most likely to hear the song at sports events. Indeed, it has been humorously suggested that some children think the last words of the anthem are "Play Ball!" There is continuing debate as to whether the anthem has become overexposed. Although it seems clear that those who sit or take a knee during the anthem are not so much protesting the anthem as they are a policy or policies (typically racism and/or police brutality) that they associate with governing authorities, recent protests do raise the question as to whether a symbol that was once meant to unite has lost some of its power to do so. One of the virtues of the American anthem as a symbol, however, is the fact that the first verse both begins and ends with a question that encourages citizens not simply to ask whether the flag still flies but to reflect on whether it still flies over a specific kind of land, namely one that is the "land of the free and the home of the brave."

VICES AND VIRTUES OF "THE STAR-SPANGLED BANNER"

Although Francis Scott Key wrote "The Star-Spangled Banner" in 1814, Congress did not officially declare it to be the national anthem until 1931. Prior to this time, presidential orders had established "The Star-Spangled Banner" for a number of military uses, but debates about declaring it the national anthem, which was heavily influenced by proponents of the anthem from Maryland, its state of birth, have continued even after Congress made it official.

I have not written this volume with the purpose of either defending or opposing the use of Francis Scott Key's song as the national anthem, but I have tried to present arguments both for and against it as fairly as I could. As discussed below, the song vividly captures a critical moment in U.S. history and has both sophisticated language and an elegant tune. Some object that the tune was borrowed from England (a criticism that also applies to "My Country, 'Tis of Thee"); some still think of it as a "drinking song" (although it was hardly the kind of song one typically associates with a pub); and some, who concentrate on a verse (the third) that is rarely sung and even less remembered, fear that it might be racist or sexist. For others, the song still effectively evokes patriotic feelings that they remember as early as grade school.

With a fairly limited vocal range, I can still whistle or hum the tune much more easily than I can sing it, particularly in public gatherings, like our graduations, where I prefer to have an accomplished singer perform it alone or lead the audience rather than trying to struggle to reach the high notes on my own. I have great admiration for those who can capture the explosive majesty of its verses.

One virtue of the song, which I did not initially appreciate, was the manner in which it so vividly captures a critical moment in U.S. history. Perhaps the song would be even better had Francis Scott Key been at Valley Forge or at Yorktown when the nation was securing its initial independence, or at Gettysburg when the Union was being saved. It is important to remember, however, that many Americans who lived in 1814, including those like Key who had initially opposed the War of 1812, literally viewed the conflict as a second American revolution that would establish once and for all whether the former colonies would be independent or whether they would revert to the control of the mother country.

Were it common to sing all four verses, I would undoubtedly squirm a bit during the notorious third verse, although I've also gained enough perspective to understand that it's fairly common to consider invaders of one's native land with the same contempt that Key and his contemporaries did. Moreover, what research I have done on other anthems suggests that our anthem is less militaristic than many, including some, such as "La Marseillaise," that are often identified as superior. Prior to studying the fourth verse, I don't believe that I knew it was the apparent origin of one of the nation's mottos, "In God We Trust," but there is certainly something positive to be said on behalf of a song that celebrates both a nation's flag and its motto.

The United States has a representative, or republican, system in which Congress is considered to be the first branch of government, and the fact that Congress adopted the anthem and the president affirmed this decision strongly suggests that, at least in 1931, it had sufficient support among the American people to express their aspirations. Anyone contemplating challenging the exalted status of the anthem has the task of proposing an alternative, and if one ever emerges, it is likely to be from a crisis situation similar to the one that prompted Francis Scott Key to write "The Star-Spangled Banner" rather than from a scholar's study.

SONG AND MEMORY

When I was a child, I spent a year in Costa Rica as my parents learned Spanish in preparation to be missionaries to Peru. After health interfered with these plans, I returned to the United States with a Spanish vocabulary of probably two hundred to three hundred words, few of which I now remember. Among the few sentences that I do remember (but did not learn to spell) were the words to "Jesus Loves Me" in Spanish, which I still enjoy singing, although I have learned that I didn't apparently remember the song as originally written. In the Honors College at Middle Tennessee State University, we have a Center of Accelerated Language

Acquisition (CALA) that uses songs and movement to convey languages. As I have studied "The Star-Spangled Banner" and other patriotic songs, I have come to an increased appreciation for the power of music to touch emotional chords that can either steel citizens to rise to the defense of their countries or, as in totalitarian countries, be utilized for less noble chauvinistic ends.

In his classic work on the flag, Dr. George J. Svejda quotes the Latin aphorism *Amoris patriae nutrix, carmen*, which means "Song is the nurse of patriotism" (2005, 223). Edward Delaplaine recounts the saying, "Let me write the songs of a people, and I care not who make their laws" (1944/1945, 17). Students of political philosophy will remember the attention that Plato directed in his *Republic* to the types of music that he would permit in his city in speech. In 1869, the Reverend Elias Nason of Massachusetts wrote that "a patriotic song is an enchanted key to memory's deepest cells; it touches secret springs, it kindles sacred flames in chambers of the soul unvisited by other agencies. It wakes to life ten thousand slumbering chords and makes them thrill and pulsate—just as if some loving angel's finger touched them—to the God-given sentiment of liberty" (Hildebrand 2014, 253).

One of the lessons I have taken from some usual renditions of the anthem is that there is probably no single tune that can unite everyone, and renditions that seem novel to one generation are sometimes celebrated by the next. I think Americans should take pride in the fact that the government has yet either to prescribe a particular way of singing the national anthem or to have forbidden the singing of rivals. I further think the nation is a richer place for having a variety of patriotic songs, some of which may sometimes be as appropriate, if not more so, than the officially designated anthem.

ORIGINS OF THE ANTHEM

Although the origins of the tune were largely lost in time until the twentieth century, it is now fairly firmly established that the music was the work of John Stafford Smith and that Ralph Tomlinson of the London Anacreontic Society put words to the song that then became the society's constitutional song. For about twenty-five years before Francis Scott Key used the tune for "The Star-Spangled Banner," it was widely parodied in England and in the United States. Indeed, Key had himself written words to this tune entitled "When the Warrior Returns" prior to writing what is today's national anthem.

Whereas the origin of many lyrics is lost in the mists of time, it is easy to trace the origin of "The Star-Spangled Banner" to events associated with the War of 1812. This war, which has sometimes been called the Second War for Independence, began in 1812 in reaction to trade policies that Great Britain and France had imposed on American shipping as they warred with one another. The British especially became associated with the policy of stopping American ships on the high seas and taking, or "impressing," sailors whom they suspected had deserted from the British navy. Some of the members of Congress who advocated war with Britain also saw the conflict as an opportunity to take Canada, where British forces had seemed to be encouraging attacks by their Native American allies on U.S. settlers.

The war was deeply divisive. New Englanders had already suffered economically from U.S.-imposed embargoes unsuccessfully designed to secure concessions from Britain and France, and the war further hindered shipping and commerce, except in cities like Baltimore where privateering under letters of marque proved lucrative. Francis Scott Key, a fairly prominent Maryland attorney, was among members of the Federalist Party who had initially opposed the war, in which Americans suffered as many defeats as they did victories. American hopes of capturing Canada proved particularly illusory, with America not only failing to gain new territory but barely saving its own military reputation by a few successful skirmishes on the Great Lakes.

As Napoleon was exiled to Elba and the British were able to send more ships and troops to America, they succeeded in winning a battle against American militiamen at Bladensburg and then attacking and burning most public buildings in the nation's capital, including the Capitol Building and the White House. Although the British could point to previous American attacks on the Legislative Assembly in York (today's Toronto), this was a more than disproportionate response that threatened the new nation's independence as well as its third largest city.

British troops passing through Upper Marlborough had spent some of their time at the home of Dr. William Beanes, whom they may incorrectly have thought (perhaps because of his own representations) was actually a Scottish citizen. In any event, after they left to burn Washington and returned through his town, he was among those who called authorities to arrest some British stragglers who were making a nuisance of themselves. After one of them escaped back to British lines, the British subsequently arrested Beanes, treated him harshly, and put him aboard a British ship to transport him for a trial in Canada, for what the British considered to be his duplicity, if not treason. Francis Scott Key was enlisted to secure his release and went with Colonel John S. Skinner under a flag of truce to meet with Admiral Alexander Cochrane and General Robert Ross (the latter of whom would die in skirmishes at North Point). Reports suggest that the British remained suspicious of Beanes and what they perceived to be his lack of good faith. They eventually decided to release him not so much because they thought he was innocent but because the American delegates had provided evidence that Americans had humanely treated wounded British soldiers whom they had left in Maryland. Because the American emissaries on behalf of Dr. Beanes were privy to British preparations for the attack on Fort McHenry (the prelude to the attempt to capture Baltimore), the British did not permit the Americans to leave until after the attack, which they witnessed aboard their own ship.

Key and his companions helplessly witnessed a bombardment of the fort by numerous British ships knowing that the fate of Baltimore, and perhaps the nation itself, was in the balance. Throughout the night Key caught sight of the storm flag that was waving above the fort, but as shelling ceased, he had no way of knowing how the battle had gone until he witnessed the huge flag that Major George Armistead had ordered from Mary Pickersgill as it flew above the fort the next morning. Scott Sheads has noted, "Nowhere in our history, save perhaps the raising of the flag upon Iwo Jima during World War II, has a historic event so centered upon the nation's flag. The sight of the flag over Fort McHenry during the 1814 bombardment, and the poem that immortalized it, gives the story 'folkloric proportions'" (1995, 101). Apparently writing notes from his ship on the back of a letter, Key wrote out the words to "The Star-Spangled Banner" as he stayed overnight at the Indian Queen Motel. Shortly thereafter it was printed as a broadside, under the title "The Defence of Fort M'Henry," and later in newspapers and songsters.

EVOLUTION OF THE SYMBOL

By the time Key wrote "The Star-Spangled Banner," there were already a number of American songs that evoked strong patriotic emotions. Although one could question whether it rose to the dignity of an anthem, "Yankee Doodle," which dated in America at least as far back as the French and Indian War and through the Revolutionary War, was a favorite in which Americans played into British stereotypes by portraying themselves a yokels who nonetheless often outwitted their foes.

A more anthem-like song was Joseph Hopkinson's "Hail Columbia," which he authored in 1798, borrowing from an earlier tune known as "The President's March." In time, it would be joined by another song "Columbia, the Gem of the Ocean," which was likely borrowed from British sources.

In 1831, Samuel Francis Smith composed "My County, 'Tis of Thee," also known as "America," which became quite popular. So too was Katharine Lee Bates's "America the Beautiful." It had been inspired by her trip to the World's Columbia Exposition in Chicago in 1893 as well as a trip to Colorado to teach, where she had seen Pikes Peak.

Largely because "The Star-Spangled Banner" lauded the flag, it became fairly exclusive to the North during the Civil War. The war also witnessed the composition of the "Battle Hymn of the Republic," which was especially popular in the North, and the elevation of "Dixie," which while written in the North, became fairly popular in the South.

Although none of these songs, or those that followed, were elevated to the status of national anthem, military forces began the day, starting in the 1890s, by playing "The Star-Spangled Banner" on bases. In 1931, during the presidency of Herbert Hoover, Congress finally designated it as the official national anthem. Even before this, the anthem was played to represent the United States at Olympic Games and, increasingly, at domestic sports events.

DOES THE ANTHEM REMAIN A SYMBOL OF UNITY?

As indicated above, the bicentennial of the national anthem brought renewed celebrations of and scholarly attention to the song, but it did not obliterate criticism. Yet, despite the fact that the anthem lauded the defense of the homeland rather than aggressive action, some critics still associated the song with American militarism, while others, focusing on the largely forgotten third verse, feared that it drove a wedge between the United States and Great Britain and that it was racially and sexually tainted by its reference to slaves and to "freemen."

As renditions of the anthem became more ubiquitous, especially at sports events, it remained unclear how many people knew the words or pondered the lyrics. It became increasingly common for music stars to sing the tune in new genres that sometimes disquieted those who first heard them. Many African Americans have embraced "Lift up Your Voice and Sing" as a black national anthem, while partisans of the right embrace Lee Greenwood's "I'm Proud to Be an American," and those on the left have embraced Woody Guthrie's "This Land Is My Land." Just as song preferences sometimes define and divide generations, so too it sometimes seems as though the national anthem is a touchstone for those who largely support and those who largely oppose U.S. policies.

The flag has become a symbol that is sometimes burned or desecrated by protestors, and so too has the anthem as individuals, especially athletes, increasingly sit or take a knee during renditions, typically in protest of perceived police brutality against African Americans. Politicians, in turn, stir this emotional pot for political gain, which results in still further division.

As I write, it is impossible to know whether the anthem, like the flag, has been claimed by those who support and oppose U.S. policies du jour or whether the anthem is capacious enough to be embraced by those of differing political persuasions. At least for now, both major political parties appear to honor the flag and the anthem that celebrates it.

HOW THIS BOOK IS ORGANIZED

Just as we have certain expectations with respect to a song designated as a national anthem, so too we have certain expectations about a book, like this one, that aims to explicate U.S. history, culture and law. Although I have avoided the word encyclopedia in the title, I have tried to make this volume into an encyclopedic treatment of a limited topic, namely the song that is designated as the U.S. national anthem. As explained earlier, although there is clearly some overlap, I have designed this volume to describe the anthem rather than the flag, except insofar as knowledge of the anthem also requires knowledge of the flag.

I have organized this book, again consistent with other reference books with which I am familiar, as a series of individual essays that generally range from about 250 to 3,000 or so words and are arranged in alphabetical order. A table of contents so lists the individual essays. Each essay contains references to related entries and sources and suggestions for further reading about the subject of the essay.

I have composed a guide to related topics for those who are looking for organizing themes. Major categories include other pieces of patriotic music that were considered for anthem status; discussions of anthems of other nations on the North American continent, or closely related to the United States, or by subgroups within the population; artistic depictions of the events and individuals connected to the anthem; and composers and authors with similar relationships. I have included entries on individuals and events that led to the congressional decision to adopt "The Star-Spangled Banner" as the national anthem; a discussion of the anthem and related musical genres; groups and other individuals with ties to the anthem; related laws, customs, and regulations; criticism, parodies, and performances of the anthem; and specific phrases within the song. Many of the entries relate to the mutual influences of the anthem and U.S. culture. I also list a number or precursors to the anthem, protests involving the anthem, and publications. I highlight various historic sites connected to the anthem, related tunes, the setting of the anthem, and its connection not only to the War of 1812 but also to other wars in U.S. history.

As much as I want to help researchers, my hope is that the national anthem remains a subject of general interest and that some may simply enjoy perusing the volume as citizens. I doubt that many individuals will choose to read alphabetically through the volume, but I think that many citizens, particularly those who regard themselves as patriots, will find multiple subjects that pique their interests whether at a public library or from their own personal copies.

American government has evolved over time, but there is reason to fear that some of the common trust that bound Americans together has been eroded and that partisanship is relatively high. As a people, we seem much more impatient with existing flaws than we once were and much more willing to entrust the man owoman of the day with increased powers, but I believe that what unites us is still stronger than what divides us.

I realize that the anthem has itself become something of a Rorschach test dividing those who believe that the nation has largely achieved freedom for all and those who are convinced that it has fallen far short of this goal. Still, I take some heart in believing that the current anthem, while largely describing a specific historic event, also articulates American aspirations that the nation remain free and the hope that Americans will have sufficient citizen virtue, especially bravery, to preserve this. I certainly remain appreciative of those who risk their lives to defend American values. Although born in war, the anthem celebrates a battle that was defensive. Moreover, the final verse of the anthem, almost as much as a prayer as a song, hopes for "vict'ry and peace." As long as Americans long for the victory of freedom, and seek peace, I think that the anthem, and the flag that it celebrates, will continue to unite us.

Further Reading

Abril, Carlos R. 2007. "Functions of a National Anthem in Society and Education: A Sociocultural Perspective." *Bulletin of the Council for Research in Music Education*, no. 172 (Spring): 69–87.

Delaplaine, Edward S. 1944/1945. "Francis Scott Key and the National Anthem." *Records of the Columbia Historical Society* 50th Anniversary Volume: 13–26.

Hildebrand, David K. 2014. "Bicentenary Essay: Two National Anthems? Some Reflections on the Two Hundredth Anniversary of 'The Star-Spangled Banner' and Its Forgotten Partner, 'The Battle of Baltimore.'" *American Music* 32 (Fall): 253–71.

Sheads, Scott S. 1995. *Fort McHenry*. Baltimore: Nautical & Aviation Publishing Company of America.

The National Anthem: Performance, Ritual, and Music

Joseph E. Morgan

Ever since Congress designated "The Star-Spangled Banner" as our national anthem in 1931, it has remained an important tradition within the cultural consciousness of citizens of the United States. From a civilian perspective it is typically performed at the beginning of most sporting events—whether professional, collegiate, or grade school—and certainly before every baseball game, as well as opening seasons for orchestras. In the military context, ever since President Woodrow Wilson ordered it in 1918, the anthem has been performed at military and naval occasions. At these occasions the performance of the national anthem has sought to blend the secular with the sacred in a patriotic space of devotion.

There is a somewhat sophisticated ritual involved in the anthem's performance. From the moment it is initiated by public announcement: "Ladies and Gentlemen, please stand for the singing of our national anthem," expectations immediately kick in for both performer and audience in a carefully organized expression of national identity. Audience members, for example, are expected to adhere to specific protocols described by the federal code:

(a) Designation.—The composition consisting of the words and music known as the Star-Spangled Banner is the national anthem.
(b) Conduct During Playing.—During a rendition of the national anthem—
   (1) when the flag is displayed—
      (A) individuals in uniform should give the military salute at the first note of the anthem and maintain that position until the last note;
      (B) members of the Armed Forces and veterans who are present but not in uniform may render the military salute in the manner provided for individuals in uniform; and
      (C) all other persons present should face the flag and stand at attention with their right hand over the heart, and men not in uniform, if applicable, should remove their headdress with their right hand and hold it at the left shoulder, the hand being over the heart; and

(2) when the flag is not displayed, all present should face toward the music and act in the same manner they would if the flag were displayed. ("Patriotic and National Observances," 36 U.S.C. § 301)

For athletes on the field, the *Game Operations Manual* of the National Football League (NFL) lays out some of their requirements:

> The National Anthem must be played prior to every NFL game, and all players must be on the sideline for the National Anthem. During the National Anthem, players on the field and bench area should stand at attention, face the flag, hold helmets in their left hand, and refrain from talking. The home team should ensure that the American flag is in good condition. It should be pointed out to players and coaches that we continue to be judged by the public in this area of respect for the flag and our country. Failure to be on the field by the start of the National Anthem may result in discipline, such as fines, suspensions, and/or the forfeiture of draft choice(s) for violations of the above, including first offenses. (Fitzpatrick 2017)

The NFL's wording and edicts of possible punishment reflect recognition of the symbolic importance of the national anthem in American society.

In addition to honoring national ideals, this well-prescribed ritual has provided a powerful and highly visible event by which people have engaged in what has come to be known as "anthem protests" in order to register their dissatisfaction or anger with one aspect or another of American society. As early as 1917, the *St. Louis Star* and *St. Louis Times* reports that one member of a local YMCA who said "I'll never enlist" was "forced to salute the regiment's officers and then put out of the building because he refused to stand when the First Regiment Band had played 'The Star Spangled Banner'" ("Y.M.C.A. Boys"). That same year, at the trial of activist and anarchist Emma Goldman, a band four stories below the courtroom performed "The Star Spangled Banner" and the whole court rose, except for Goldman and her supporters. The judge responded harshly, ordering the deputies to "eject all, except the defendants, who refuse to stand—and don't let them back into the court again" ("Reds Turned Out at Trial of Emma" 1917). Those who refused to stand "made a quick exit or were given a little treatment by the Deputies" ("Reds Turned Out").

In subsequent decades, renditions of the national anthem also became occasions for African American civil rights activists to publicly express their unhappiness with racial discrimination and their perception that the United States is not living up to its stated ideals of equality and democracy. These forms of protest have ranged from medalists raising their fists from an Olympic podium during the playing of the national anthem, as happened in 1968, to professional and amateur athletes "taking a knee" at various sporting events during the 2010s to protest police violence against people of color.

Historically, however, the singing of the anthem has usually proven to be a powerful catalyst for bringing Americans together. Whether the performance at ground zero or Buckingham Palace after the attacks on 9/11, or the performance on the USS *Arizona* on the morning of December 7, 1941, that was interrupted by the Japanese attack on Pearl Harbor, the anthem remains a touchstone for a shared national identity.

Key to this shared identity is the audience participation that has been one of the expectations of the performance since the very beginning. "The Star Spangled Banner" was already a well-known patriotic tune when the band performed it at the 1918 World Series in Chicago during the seventh-inning stretch:

> The yawn was checked and heads were bared as the ball players turned quickly about and faced the music. Jackie Fred Thomas of the U.S. Navy was at attention, as he stood erect, with his eyes set on the flag fluttering at the top of the lofty pole in right field. First the song was taken up by a few, then others joined, and when the final notes came, a great volume of melody rolled across the field. It was at the very end that the onlookers exploded into thunderous applause and rent the air with a cheer that marked the highest point of the day's enthusiasm. (Barbash and Andrews 2016)

This famous series, in which Babe Ruth pitched a shutout for Boston, was fraught with difficulties, especially with the players coming under criticism from "people wondering why they [the players] were on the ballfield rather than the battlefield" (Barbash and Andrews 2016). When the series returned to Boston, the song was performed again, but at the beginning of the game instead. That rendition is usually cited as establishing the now-entrenched, nationally recognized tradition of playing the anthem before athletic competitions and other events.

Of the requirements for the audience in the public ritual, perhaps the most difficult aspect is actually singing the tune. This difficulty is bound up with the song's creation, which is based on a melody written for the wealthiest people of London in 1775 and, under different verses, became a popular pub staple (Leepson 2014). The author of the text to the anthem, Francis Scott Key, knew the melody well; indeed, on the first broadsheet he published seven days after writing the lyrics on September 14, 1814, he indicated the musical accompaniment thusly: "Tune—Anacreon in Heaven."

The composition of "To Anacreon in Heaven" is generally attributed to John Stafford Smith (1750–1836), an English composer, church organist, and early musicologist. The venue for which he wrote the tune, the Anacreontic Society of England, was a subscription-based club for men of high social rank that would meet on Wednesday nights to consume fine dinners and give "concerts of the best performers in London," who would then become honorary members of the society ("History of the Anacreontic Society" 1780). The song, then, was written by a man with a great deal of musical training for a group of well-educated men, many of whom probably enjoyed a large measure of musical training.

The range of the tune, slightly more than one and a half octaves, and its tendency to leap from one note to the next, makes it quite difficult to sing for amateur voices—if begun too low, sopranos and tenors will have difficulty with the lowest notes, but if begun too high, altos and basses will have difficulty with the highest notes. An amateur voice typically cannot reach too far beyond an octave, while for a trained voice a two-octave range is common. Further, when sung by an amateur, the leaps in the melody often result in the tune ending in a different key from the one in which it began. For trained voices, it is a matter of making the range fit in their register so that the most important high notes can be sung, especially at the climactic, penultimate phrase with the text "over the land of the free." Here, the highest note of the song is expected to be held under a fermata (a musical notation for a pause of unspecified length) and even belted out the way perhaps a bunch of drunk, yet vocally trained Englishmen, might have.

Another important aspect of the performance of the national anthem is the requirements of the soloist. As a melody whose lyrics were first quite bawdy for the day, it certainly leads to interpretive challenges. For example, while lyrically the ascent in the melody to the highest note at "the rockets' red glare" might make musical sense, historically there is nothing about Anacreon's original lyrics that would seem to indicate a rocketing ascent. Here the music doesn't describe the words, but, oddly, Key's ingenious lyrics make a metaphor of the music.

However, the real problems created for the performer emerged in the earliest performances of the anthem when the tune switched genres from a drinking song to a national anthem. As part of a genre, the anthem has been described as "a Protestant sacred choral composition, of 16th-century British origin, usually a setting of English prose from the Scriptures" (Daniel, Wienandt, and Sampsel 2013). But the anthem wasn't accepted as a mainstream patriotic genre until after the French Revolution, when nationalist and patriotic fervor became a matter of survival for Western European nations in the face of Napoleon's army. This patriotism rose to a religious fervor, so it is only appropriate that a public display of patriotism would be coupled with a religious sentiment. Along with the religious sentiment, an expectation came, too, of a certain gravitas or reverence in performance. The result is that even today performers will face criticism if their interpretation strays too far from the melody as written or if the performance strikes listeners as too casual or irreverent.

Further, like anthems that are sung in church, one of the primary purposes of the performance of the national anthem is to achieve audience participation. Adherence to the melody as written and as typically performed is the surest way to guarantee the audience will be willing to sing too. As a nationalistic expression, the purpose of national symbols is to allow citizens to enter into a shared patriotic experience; with an anthem, what better way than to let them sing?

References

Barbash, Fred, and Travis M. Andrews. 2016. "A Brief History of 'The Star-Spangled Banner' Being Played at Games and Getting No Respect." *Washington Post*, August 30. https://www.washingtonpost.com/news/morning-mix/wp/2016/08/30/a-brief-history-of-the-star-spangled-banner-being-played-at-games-and-getting-no-respect.

Daniel, Ralph T., Elwyn A. Wienandt, and Laurie J. Sampsel. October 16, 2013. "Anthem." *Grove Music Online*. https://www-oxfordmusiconline-com.

Fitzpatrick, Alex. 2017. "Does the NFL Require Players to Stand for the National Anthem?" *Time*, September 25. https://time.com/4955704/nfl-league-rulebook-a62-63-national-anthem-rule.

"History of the Anacreontic Society." 1780. *Gentlemen's Magazine* 50:224. https://babel
.hathitrust.org/cgi/pt?id=hvd.hw2945&view=1up&seq=244.

Leepson, Marc. 2014. *What So Proudly We Hailed: Francis Scott Key, A Life.* New York:
Palgrave/Macmillan.

Mindock, Clark. 2019. "Taking a Knee: Why Are NFL Players Protesting and When Did
They Start to Kneel?" *Independent*, February 4. https://www.independent.co.uk
/news/world/americas/us-politics/taking-a-knee-national-anthem-nfl-trump-why
-meaning-origins-racism-us-colin-kaepernick-a8521741.html.

"Patriotic and National Observances, Ceremonies, and Organizations: National Anthem."
36 U.S.C. § 301. https://www.govinfo.gov/content/pkg/USCODE-2018-title36/pdf
/USCODE-2018-title36-subtitleI-partA-chap3-sec301.pdf.

"Reds Turned Out at Trial of Emma." 1917. *New York Sun*, July 7, 4. https://www.news
papers.com/clip/7116037/reds_turned_out_at_trial_of_emma_the/.

Spander, Art. 2006. "A Moment in Time: Remembering an Olympic Protest." *CBS College Sports*, February 24. http://www.cstv.com/sports/c-track/stories/022406aas
.html.

"Y.M.C.A. Boys Force a Slacker to Salute." 1917. *St. Louis Star and Times*. https://www
.newspapers.com/clip/7116016/the_st_louis_star_and_times/.

ABOUT THE CONTRIBUTOR

Dr. Joseph E. Morgan is an assistant professor of music at Middle Tennessee State University. He earned his degrees at the University of Pittsburgh; the University of Maryland, College Park; and Brandeis University. He has written *Carl Maria von Weber: Oberon and Cosmopolitanism in the Early German Romantic* (2014) and *Experiencing Carl Maria von Weber: A Listener's Companion* (2017), both published by Rowman and Littlefield, and he has coedited a collection of essays entitled *Tyranny and Music*, published by Lexington Press in 2017.

Timeline

1626
The Dutch national anthem, known as the "Wilhelmus" and believed to be the world's oldest, is composed.

1761
James Lyons publishes *Urania, or a Choice Collection of Psalm-tunes, Anthems, and Hymns*, the first published version of "God Save the King" in America.

1766
Approximate date of the founding of the London Anacreontic Society.

1776
Thirteen American colonies declare their independence from Great Britain.

1777
Congress adopts a law on June 14 (today's Flag Day) designating that the design of the U.S. flag will include both stars and stripes.

1778
First publication of "To Anacreon in Heaven," which becomes the tune for "The Star-Spangled Banner."

1779
Birth of Francis Scott Key.

1783
Treaty of Paris ends the Revolutionary War.

1787
A convention meeting in Philadelphia drafts the U.S. Constitution.

1789
The new U.S. Constitution goes into effect.

1791
The states ratify the first ten amendments, which become known as the Bill of Rights.

1795

Congress adds two stars and two stripes to the U.S. flag to mark the admission of Kentucky and Vermont into the Union.

1798

Robert Treat Paine writes a song entitled "Adams and Liberty" to the same tune that Francis Scott Key will later use for "The Star-Spangled Banner."

Joseph Hopkinson writes "Hail Columbia."

1800

First apparent use of the name Fort McHenry.

1801

Thomas Jefferson is selected as president, marking the transition of the office from a Federalist (John Adams) to a Democratic-Republican.

1802

Francis Scott Key marries Mary Tayloe Lloyd, who went by the name of Polly.

1805

Francis Scott Key authors "When the Warrior Returns" to honor American heroes returning from war in Tripoli. It is set to "To Anacreon in Heaven."

1806

Future Supreme Court Justice Roger Taney marries Key's only sister.

1807

The British capture the *Chesapeake* and take sailors they believe to be British deserters.

The United States enacts an Embargo Act designed to apply pressure on France and Britain and avoid war by embargoing American ships from trading with them.

1812

The United States declares war on Great Britain in what becomes known as the War of 1812, and sometimes as the Second American Revolution. Despite some U.S. naval victories, attempts to invade Canada prove to be disastrous.

1813

Major George Armistead commissions Mary Pickersgill to make the huge flag that later becomes known as the Star-Spangled Banner.

1814

The British defeat Americans at the Battle of Bladensburg and burn most public buildings in the nation's capital, including the Capitol Building and the White House. The United States torches its own navy yard to keep it out of the hands of the British.

Francis Scott Key writes "The Defence of Fort M'Henry," which later becomes "The Star-Spangled Banner," after observing the American flag flying in the wake of the British shelling of the fort in an unsuccessful attempt to capture Baltimore.

The War of 1812 officially ends with the Treaty of Ghent, but forces in America do not find out until after the Battle of New Orleans.

1815

Americans commanded by General Andrew Jackson gain a victory over the British in New Orleans.

Baltimore holds its first Defenders' Day commemoration at which it laid the cornerstone for the fifty-two-foot Battle Monument. The monument takes ten years to complete and later becomes part of the seal of Baltimore in 1827.

1817

President James Monroe inspects the troops and facilities at Fort McHenry.

1818

Congress reduces the number of stars on the flag back to thirteen but then adds new stars for additional states, raising the number to twenty.

1819

Americans in France celebrating U.S. independence give a toast to the Star-Spangled Banner that was likely accompanied by singing. If so, this may have been the first such rendition of the hymn at a gathering on foreign soil.

1824

U.S. Revolutionary War hero the Marquis de Lafayette visits Fort McHenry on October 24, and the Star-Spangled Banner is raised above the fort to commemorate the event.

1828

Andrew Jackson is elected U.S. president. Francis Scott Key is appointed to his so-called "kitchen cabinet."

Baltimore erects an eight-foot marble statue in honor of George Armistead, who had commanded Fort McHenry during the British attack of 1814.

1831

Samuel Francis Smith composes "My Country, 'Tis of Thee" to the tune of "God Save the King."

1832

Francis Scott Key composes his "Hymn for the Fourth of July 1832."

1833

President Jackson appoints Francis Scott Key as U.S. attorney for Washington.

The Battle Monument honoring defenders of Fort McHenry is completed and dedicated in downtown Baltimore.

1839

The first known harmonization (for three voices) of "The Star-Spangled Banner" is published.

1843

U.S. flags are lowered to half-mast for the death of Francis Scott Key.

1856

Tom Thumb sings "The Star-Spangled Banner" to an audience in Cleveland while dressed as General Winfield Scott.

1857
Reverend Henry V. D. Johns publishes *Poems of the Late Francis S. Key, Esq.*

1858
Baltimore reinters the remains of Daniel Wells and Henry Gough McComas, who were believed to have fired the shots that killed General Robert Ross during the Battle of North Point, at Ashland Square where a monument was erected in their honor.

1859
Key's widow, Polly, dies at the age of 74.

1860
Abraham Lincoln is elected as first Republican president.

1861
Attempted secession of Southern states leads to Civil War.

Julia Ward Howe pens the words to the "Battle Hymn of the Republic."

George Armistead Appleton, the grandson of George Armistead, is arrested as a Southern sympathizer; Frank Key Howard, the editor of a pro-Southern newspaper, is also arrested and held at Fort McHenry.

Oliver Wendell Holmes, Sr., pens another verse to "The Star-Spangled Banner" in which he anticipates freedom for the slaves.

1862
The first documented performance of "The Star-Spangled Banner" at a baseball game held in Brooklyn, New York.

1864
The words "In God We Trust" first appear on a U.S. coin.

1865
The Civil War ends with a victory for the North, and the Thirteenth Amendment abolishes involuntary servitude.

A band plays "The Star-Spangled Banner" as the American flag is raised once again over Fort Sumter.

President Abraham Lincoln is assassinated.

1866
Francis Scott Key's remains are removed from St. Paul's Episcopal Church in Baltimore and moved to Mount Olivet Cemetery in Frederick, Maryland.

1869
Boston hosts a National Peace Jubilee, in which ten thousand people sing "The Star-Spangled Banner" to the accompaniment of an orchestra of one thousand members.

1872
Yellowstone is designated as America's first national park.

1873

Baltimore completes a twenty-one-foot obelisk to commemorate Daniel Wells and Henry Gough McComas.

1876

John Philip Sousa composes an orchestral fantasia that includes "The Star-Spangled Banner" and other patriotic songs for U.S. centennial celebrations of the Declaration of Independence in Philadelphia called the International Congress.

1887

George Balch composes a pledge to the U.S. flag.

Thomas Edison invents the phonograph, which will make recordings of "The Star-Spangled Banner" possible.

1888

The Francis Scott Key Monument, which portrays him sitting beneath a marble shrine topped with a figure of Lady Liberty and an American flag, is dedicated in the Golden Gate Park in San Francisco.

1889

The U.S. Secretary of the Navy Benjamin Franklin Tracy orders that "The Star-Spangled Banner" be played at morning flag raisings and "Hail Columbia" at the retiring of the colors.

President Benjamin Harrison attends the opening day of a week of events commemorating the attack on Fort McHenry that concluded with a reenactment of the bombardment of the fort.

1890

Tracy orders the U.S. Marine Band to play "The Star-Spangled Banner" at the end of its performances.

1892

The Massachusetts governor issues a proclamation on the four hundredth anniversary of the birth of Christopher Columbus and the eighty-second birthday of Samuel Smith that all children in the state should sing "America."

School children mark Columbus Day with a new pledge to the flag composed by Francis Bellamy.

1893

Navy regulations are changed to mandate playing of "The Star-Spangled Banner" at both morning and evening flag events.

1894

The Congregationalist publishes "America the Beautiful" for the first time.

William Welch, the last known soldier who survived the bombardment of Fort McHenry, dies.

1895

Army regulations specify the playing of "The Star-Spangled Banner" at the evening lowering of the colors.

1896

John Philip Sousa writes "The Stars and Stripes Forever."

1897

John Philip Sousa gives the first performance of "The Stars and Stripes Forever."

1898

A monument is dedicated at Mt. Olivet Cemetery in Frederick, Maryland, portraying Francis Scott Key.

War with Spain leads to an increase in nationalism that results in the American acquisition of foreign colonies.

John Philip Sousa's band is recorded playing "The Star-Spangled Banner."

1899

James Weldon Johnson writes "Lift Every Voice and Sing," which is set to music by his brother John Rosamond Johnson and later designated as the official song of the National Association for the Advancement of Colored People before being later described as the black national anthem.

President Benjamin Harrison attends the opening day of a weekend of events marking the seventy-fifth anniversary of Defenders' Day, which marks the anniversary of the Battle of Baltimore.

1903

The U.S. Navy issues an order requiring sailors to stand at attention while "The Star-Spangled Banner" is played.

1905

Hiram Cronk, the oldest living veteran of the War of 1812, dies at the age of 105 in Ava, New York.

1906

The first performance of George Washington, Jr., by George M. Cohen previews "You're a Grand Old Flag."

1907

The Francis Scott Key Association is formed to purchase the Key homestead in Georgetown and convert it into a museum.

1908

Maryland proclaims September 12, Defenders' Day, as an official state holiday in honor of the successful defense of Fort McHenry and the writing of "The Star-Spangled Banner."

The Francis Scott Key House was opened in Georgetown, Virginia, but was closed by 1912.

1910

The Mormon Tabernacle Choir releases a recording of twelve hymns and patriotic songs, including "America."

1911

President William Taft and his wife march to the tune of "The Star-Spangled Banner" while celebrating their twenty-fifth wedding anniversary at the White House.

1912

Congressman George Edmond Foss of Illinois introduces the first bill within Congress to designate "The Star-Spangled Banner" as the national anthem.

The last military unit to be posted for coastal defense leaves Fort McHenry.

The flag known as the Star-Spangled Banner is donated to the Smithsonian Institution.

1914

The Edison Film Company publishes a two-reel dramatization entitled "The Birth of the Star-Spangled Banner," which was written by J. W. Blake and directed by George A. Lessey.

President Woodrow Wilson establishes June 14 as Flag Day.

A monument to George Armistead, who commanded U.S. forces during the British bombardment of Fort McHenry, is unveiled at the fort on the centennial of that battle.

Maryland commemorates the centennial of "The Star-Spangled Banner" with eight days of celebration from September 6 to September 13. Festivities include the creation of a huge human flag of school children at Fort McHenry, fireworks, and carrying the original flag through Baltimore.

1916

President Woodrow Wilson proclaims "The Star-Spangled Banner" as the national anthem for the armed forces.

President Wilson issues the first presidential proclamation of Flag Day.

President Wilson signs the law creating the U.S. Park Service.

The city of Baltimore adopts an ordinance prohibiting the use of "The Star-Spangled Banner" in medleys or ragtime performances.

1918

"The Star-Spangled Banner" is played during the seventh inning of the first game of the World Series between the Chicago Cubs and the Boston Red Sox.

Mrs. Reuben Ross Holloway, the president of the Maryland United States Daughters of 1812, joins Congressman J. Charles Linthicum of Baltimore in seeking to get Congress to designate "The Star-Spangled Banner" as the national anthem.

Kitty Cheatham publishes a pamphlet arguing against the adoption of "The Star-Spangled Banner" as the national anthem.

Columbia Records releases a recording of "The Star-Spangled Banner" as sung by Margaret Woodrow Wilson, the president's daughter, to benefit the Red Cross.

1922

On Flag Day, President Warren G. Harding is broadcast by radio (the first time a U.S. president has been so heard) dedicating a forty-foot statue of Orpheus outside Fort McHenry as a memorial to Francis Scott Key.

1923

The Francis Scott Key Bridge is opened across the Potomac River.

1924

The Olympics begins the practice of playing the national anthem of the winners of athletic events.

1925

The U.S. Navy Band is formed.

Fort McHenry is designated as a national park.

1928

A chorus of girls from more than twenty different countries sing "America the Beautiful" to Katharine Lee Bates at the annual Convention of the National Education Association in Minneapolis, Minnesota.

1929

The Great Depression begins.

1931

Congress declares "The Star-Spangled Banner" to be the U.S. national anthem.

A bronze tablet honoring Francis Scott Key is unveiled at the National Cathedral in Washington, DC.

1932

Congress adopts a resolution commending the singing of "My Country, 'Tis of Thee" on Independence Day to celebrate its centennial.

Ferde Grofe writes an orchestral score for "September 13, 1814," later known as the "Ode to the Star-Spangled Banner," which is performed at Radio City Music Hall.

1933

Fort McHenry is transferred to the National Park Service.

1938

Kate Smith does her first rendition on the radio of "God Bless America" by Irving Berlin.

1939

Fort McHenry is designated as a National Monument and Historic Shrine.

1940

The U.S. Supreme Court rules in *Minersville School District v. Gobitis* that children who do not salute the flag in public schools can be expelled.

Woody Guthrie writes "God Blessed America," which later becomes "This Land Is Your Land."

1941

Japanese planes attack Pearl Harbor, Hawaii, leading to U.S. entry into World War II.

The practice of playing "The Star-Spangled Banner" before major league baseball games resumes.

Igor Stravinsky draws criticism for a new arrangement of "The Star-Spangled Banner."

1942

Miss Lucy Moore sings "The Star-Spangled Banner" for the two thousandth time.

The original Star-Spangled Banner flag that inspired Francis Scott Key is moved to the Shenandoah National State Park for safekeeping for two years during World War II.

A U.S. Coast Guard Training Site is dedicated at Fort McHenry.

Elton Britt records "There's a Star-Spangled Banner Waving Somewhere," which went on to become a gold record.

Riots break out in Klamath Falls, Oregon, when a group of Jehovah's Witnesses refuse to stand as a sound truck blasts "The Star-Spangled Banner" into one of their meetings.

1943

In *West Virginia State Board of Education v. Barnette*, the U.S. Supreme Court reverses its earlier decision upholding compulsory flag salutes.

1945

The famous photograph, later commemorated in bronze, of U.S. Marines raising the U.S. flag above Mount Suribachi at Iwo Jima is taken.

World War II ends with an Allied victory over the Axis powers lead by Germany and Japan.

Neil Swanson publishes *The Perilous Fight*.

1947

Francis Scott Key's house is demolished in order to provide access to a bridge named in his honor.

1948

The United States issues a three-cent stamp in Francis Scott Key's honor.

President Harry S. Truman officially authorizes the U.S. flag to fly perpetually over Fort McHenry during both day and night.

1949

Congress adopts, and President Truman signs, a law authorizing June 14 as National Flag Day.

A mock bombardment and fireworks display is held at Fort McHenry to commemorate V-J Day (Victory over Japan) and Defenders' Day.

1954

The Maryland Historical Society unveils the original draft of "The Star-Spangled Banner" at an event commemorating the 140th anniversary of its composition.

Congress votes to add the words "under God" to the Pledge of Allegiance.

1955

President Dwight D. Eisenhower presented a medal to Irving Berlin for writing "God Bless America" and other works.

1958

Archaeologists working at Fort McHenry discover the oak timbers that supported the original flagpole at Fort McHenry.

1959

A replica of the original flagstaff is dedicated at Fort McHenry and becomes a focus of future commemorative events, including the first official raising of the forty-nine-star flag marking the entry of Alaska into the Union.

1960

Fort McHenry hosts the first raising of the fifty-star flag to mark the entry of Hawaii into the Union.

A four-cent stamp is issued to honor Francis Scott Key.

1963

Syncon II, a communications satellite, receives "The Star-Spangled Banner" and transmits it back to earth.

A U.S. district court decides in *Sheldon v. Fannin* that a school cannot expel students who refuse to stand for the playing of the national anthem because of religious convictions.

1964

A new visitors' center opens at Fort McHenry to commemorate the sesquicentennial of the attack on the fort and the writing of "The Star-Spangled Banner."

1965

Singer Robert Goulet forgets some of the words of "The Star-Spangled Banner" when performing for the heavyweight title fight between Cassius Clay (Mohammad Ali) and Sonny Liston at Lewistown, Maine.

A group of volunteer marines called the Fort McHenry Tattoo begins performing a thirty-five-minute evening ceremony at Fort McHenry that incorporates maneuvers and music, including "The Star-Spangled Banner."

1967

Visitors who have been told that the U.S. flag always flies over Fort McHenry are startled to find the flag not flying over the fort, which was, at the time, one of the few places authorized to fly the flag twenty-four hours a day. They subsequently discover that the flagpole had just been painted and authorities were waiting for it to dry.

On March 31, 1967, English military officials visit the Air and Space Museum of the Smithsonian Institution and donate a Congreve rocket, like those used to attack Fort McHenry. As the officials noted, this time the fuse was not lit.

1968

Jose Feliciano's folk-rock rendition of "The Star-Spangled Banner" in Detroit at a World Series game between the Tigers and the St. Louis Cardinals drew considerable criticism.

Both civil rights leader Martin Luther King, Jr., and U.S. Senator Robert Kennedy are assassinated.

Miss Aretha Franklin's "soul" rendition of the anthem at the Democratic National Convention in Chicago elicits criticism.

African American sprinters Tommie Smith and John Carlos hold their hands in a Black Power salute as they receive medals at the Mexico City Olympics during the playing of the U.S. national anthem.

1969

Jimi Hendrix performs an electrified rendition of "The Star-Spangled Banner" at the Woodstock Music and Art Fair in New York.

George F. Svejda first issues his *History of the Star Spangled Banner from 1814 to the Present*.

1971

An antiwar comedy show by Donald Sutherland, Jane Fonda, and others includes a skit about individuals who refuse to stand for the national anthem.

1972

Sprinters Wayne Collett and Vince Matthews are expelled from the Munich Olympics after they strike poses during the playing of the national anthem.

1974

In his last public performance, Irving Berlin performs "God Bless America" at the White House for returning Vietnam prisoners of war.

1976

The United States celebrates the bicentennial of the beginning of the Revolutionary War and the writing of the Declaration of Independence.

1977

The Francis Scott Key, or Outer Harbor, Bridge, which spans the Patapsco River, is dedicated.

The Pride of Baltimore, a reproduction of a Baltimore clipper ship, is commissioned on May 1.

1980

The Canadian Parliament adopts "O Canada" as its national anthem.

1983

Marvin Gaye gives a unique performance of "The Star-Spangled Banner" at an NBA All-Star Game in California.

1986

An ABC broadcast of Sandi Patty's rendition of "The Star-Spangled Banner" for the centennial of the Statue of Liberty brings widespread acclaim and introduces her to a much wider audience.

1987

The United States names John Philip Sousa's "The Stars and Stripes Forever" as the official march of the United States.

The United States celebrates the centennial of the writing of the U.S. Constitution.

1989

President George H. W. Bush attends the 175th anniversary celebrations at Fort McHenry of the Battle of Baltimore and the writing of "The Star-Spangled Banner" and calls for a constitutional amendment banning flag desecration.

1990

Comedian Roseanne Barr draws criticism for her parody-like rendition of "The Star-Spangled Banner" between rounds of a doubleheader at San Diego's Jack Murphy Stadium.

Sinead O'Connor refuses to perform at the Garden State Arts Center in Holmdel Township, New Jersey, until it agrees not to play the national anthem.

1991

Whitney Houston gives a rousing rendition of the national anthem at Tampa Stadium for Super Bowl XXV.

1996

Chris Jackson (Mahmoud Abdul-Rauf) of the Denver Nuggets is suspended by the National Basketball Association after refusing to stand during the playing of the national anthem.

2001

Irvin Molotsky publishes *The Flag, the Poet and the Song: The Story of the Star-Spangled Banner.*

Terrorists strike the World Trade Center and other targets killing thousands of civilians. Members of Congress gather on the steps of the Capitol to sing "God Bless America."

Whitney Houston releases her powerful rendition of "The Star-Spangled Banner."

Queen Elizabeth II allows her troops to play "The Star-Spangled Banner" at the Buckingham Palace in a tribute to American victims of the 9/11 terrorist attacks.

2005

The Music Teachers National Association launches "The National Anthem Project: Restoring America's Voice," an effort to promote knowledge about and performances of "The Star-Spangled Banner."

2006

U.S. Senator Lamar Alexander (R, TN) introduces a resolution in the Senate that would require the national anthem only be sung or recited in English.

2008

Jazz musician Rene Marie is asked to sing "The Star-Spangled Banner" at Denver's State of the City Address, and she chooses instead to sing the black national anthem, "Lift Every Voice and Sing," to the tune of "The Star-Spangled Banner."

The New York Philharmonic Orchestra, directed by Lorin Maazel, performs the American and South Korean national anthems at a concert in North Korea.

2010

Maryland issues a license plate with a likeness of Fort McHenry to commemorate the bicentennial of the War of 1812. This is replaced in 2016 with a likeness of the state flag.

Goshen College in Indiana, which has ties to the Mennonite Church, whose members do not salute the flag, decides to play "The Star-Spangled Banner" for the first time at a baseball game, but after concerns that the words were too militaristic (Mennonites are pacifists) only an instrumental version is played.

2011

The National Park Service opens a new visitor and education center at Fort McHenry.

2012

The U.S. Mint releases Star-Spangled Banner coins. The gold coins depict a naval battle scene on one side and words from Key's song against a flag on the other. The silver coins have a picture of Lady Liberty waving a flag of fifteen stars and fifteen stripes and Fort McHenry in the background on one side and a modern U.S. flag on the other.

The Cleveland Institute of Art commissions Dave Cole to build the "Steamroller Music Box," which plays "The Star-Spangled Banner."

2014

Celebrations mark the bicentennial of "The Star-Spangled Banner."

President Barack Obama visits Fort McHenry.

The Baltimore Symphony Orchestra performs Grofe's "Ode to the Star-Spangled Banner."

The U.S. Postal Service releases a Star-Spangled Banner Forever Stamp depicting a flag against a background of fireworks to acknowledge the bicentennial of the song.

Marc Ferris publishes *Star-Spangled Banner: The Unlikely Story of America's National Anthem.*

The Smithsonian displays a copy of Key's lyrics to "The Star-Spangled Banner" along with the flag that inspired it.

Janine Stange of Long Island, New York, completes her goal of performing "The Star-Spangled Banner" in all fifty states with an appearance in Tennessee, to be followed by a further rendition in Baltimore on the two hundredth anniversary of its writing.

2015
Mark Clague and Andrew Kuster publish the *Star Spangled Songbook*.

2016
Colin Kaepernick of the San Francisco 49ers kneels in protest during the playing of the national anthem before a game with the San Diego Chargers in San Diego to protest what he believes to be police mistreatment of African Americans.

Donald J. Trump, who is very critical of athletes who take a knee during the playing of the national anthem, is elected as U.S. president.

Star Swain of Tallahassee, Florida, becomes a Facebook and YouTube sensation after she sings an impromptu rendition of "The Star-Spangled Banner" at the Lincoln Memorial.

A guard at the National September 11 Memorial & Museum in Manhattan, New York, asks a group of middle school students to cease their rendition of "The Star-Spangled Banner" on its plaza, apparently because they had not secured a permit to do so.

2017
In September, the Francis Scott Key Monument in Baltimore is splashed with red paint and the words "Racist Anthem," but it is quickly restored and surrounded by a fence.

2018
Jose Feliciano performs the national anthem at a naturalization ceremony at the Smithsonian's National Museum of American History.

Travelers passing through the Nashville International Airport spontaneously begin singing "The Star-Spangled Banner" to a group of children of fallen service members who were being honored with a trip to Disney World.

Accompanied by a ukulele, Willie K. sings the national anthem to a new tune at a football game at the University of Hawaii.

2019
Gladys Knight sings the national anthem for Super Bowl LIII in Atlanta, Georgia.

Abdul-Rauf, Mahmoud

In 1996, Mahmoud Abdul-Rauf (1969–), a high-scoring guard for the Denver Nuggets NBA basketball team, became a figure of considerable controversy. The source of the controversy was his statement in an interview that he had been staying in the locker room for the last sixty games or so during the playing of "The Star-Spangled Banner" because of his Muslim faith. He told a reporter that he saw the American flag as "a symbol of oppression, of tyranny, so it depends on how you look at it. I think this country has a long history of that. If you look at history, I don't think you can argue the facts. You can't be for God and for oppression. It's clear in the Qu'ran" (Grewal 2007, 115). The National Basketball Association (NBA) subsequently suspended him indefinitely without pay. He responded to the suspension by declaring, "My beliefs are more important than anything. If I have to give up basketball, I will" (Grewal 2007, 113).

Although many members of the public assumed from his name and his dark skin that Abdul-Rauf was a Muslim immigrant, he had, in fact, grown up as Chris Jackson in Gulfport, Mississippi. The son of a single mother, he had used basketball and his newfound Muslim faith to overcome Tourette's syndrome. He starred at Louisiana State University from 1988 to 1990 before joining the Denver Nuggets as the third overall pick in the 1990 NBA draft.

Abdul-Rauf's decision not to participate in the national anthem prompted criticism from both the African American and American Muslim communities. Some Muslim immigrants who commented on the situation explained that Muslims were expected to respect the symbols of their nations and that they could do so without worshipping them. Hakeem Olajuwon, a Nigerian Muslim who was a star player for the Houston Rockets, thus explained: "In general, Islamic teachings require every Muslim to obey and respect the law of the countries they live in. You know, that is—that is Islamic teachings. You know, to be a good Muslim is to be a good citizen" (Grewal 2007, 115).

After sitting out a game (which cost him just over $34,000), Abdul-Rauf agreed to stand and pray silently on the court during the playing of the anthem. Fans continued to be critical, however, and the Nuggets traded Abdul-Rauf to the Sacramento Kings before the 1996 season. He played with Sacramento until 1998, whereupon he signed a contract to play in Europe. He spent the next several years playing in leagues around the world before retiring in 2011.

Abdul-Rauf's example may have provided inspiration to Colin Kaepernick and other African Americans who have taken a knee during performances of the national anthem to protest social conditions in the United States.

See also: Kaepernick, Colin; Sports Events.

Further Reading

Araton, Harvey. 2017. "From the N.B.A., a Cautionary Tale on National Anthem Pro-
    tests." *New York Times*, November 6. https://www.nytimes.com/2017/11/06/sports
    /basketball/anthem-nba-abdul-rauf-kaepernick.html.
Grewal, Zareena. 2007. "Lights, Camera, Suspension: Freezing the Frame on the Mah-
    moud Abdul-Rauf-Anthem Controversy." *Souls* 9 (2): 109–22.

Abolitionists

Like the affirmation in the Declaration of Independence that "all men are created
equal" and entitled to the rights of "life, liberty, and the pursuit of happiness," the
description of America as "the land of the free" in "The Star-Spangled Banner"
was in obvious conflict with the institution of chattel slavery.

Abolitionists, who generally advocated immediate slave emancipation, were
aware of these discrepancies between America's stated ideals and its daily realities and sought to exploit them. In 1836, the American Anti-Slavery Society published a broadside entitled "Slave Market of America," which included nine
engravings, each followed by an explanation. The engraving of the reading of the
Declaration of Independence was entitled "The Land of the Free," while that of
the U.S. Capitol, which was flying two U.S. flags, was entitled "The Home of the
Oppressed" (Asch and Musgrove 2017, 75; Hogan 2015).

In 1844, E. A. Atlee published in an abolitionist newspaper a poem entitled "Oh
Say, Do Your Hear?" that parodied "The Star-Spangled Banner," not simply by
using the same melody but by using lyrics that emphasized the brutality and evil
of slavery. The last two lines of the poem, which was reprinted in other antislavery
publications, proclaimed (Clague 2016):

> And our star spangled banner at half mast shall wave
> O'er the death-bed of Freedom—the home of the slave.

In 1861 Oliver Wendell Holmes penned an additional verse to "The Star-
Spangled Banner" designed for those who anticipated that the Civil War would
bring an end to slavery (Veltman 2017):

> When our land is illum'd with Liberty's smile,
> If a foe from within strike a blow at her glory,
> Down, down, with the traitor that dares to defile
> The flag of her stars and the page of her story!
> By the millions unchain'd who our birthright have gained
> We will keep her bright blazon forever unstained!
> And the Star-Spangled Banner in triumph shall wave
> While the land of the free is the home of the brave.

See also: African Americans; Atlee, E. A.; Parodies; Slavery.

Further Reading

Asch, Chris Myers, and George Derek Musgrove. 2017. *Chocolate City: A History of Race and
    Democracy in the Nation's Capital.* Chapel Hill: University of North Carolina Press.

Clague, Mark. 2016. "Abolitionist Star Spangled Banner—'Oh Say, Do You Hear?' (1844)." *Star Spangled Music*, September 3. Star Spangled Music Foundation. http://starspangledmusic.org/abolitionist-star-spangled-banner-oh-say-do-you-hear-1844.

Dunaway, David King. 1987. "Music and Politics in the United States." *Folk Music Journal* 5:268–94.

Hogan, Liam. 2015. "Slave Market of America: An Anti-Slavery Broadside (1836)." *Medium*, July 21. https://medium.com/@Limerick1914/slave-market-of-america-an-anti-slavery-broadside-1836-1b6bc7f37e03.

Veltman, Chloe. 2017. "Why We Should Sing 'The Star-Spangled Banner's' Obscure Fifth Verse." *KQED*, March 2. https://www.kqed.org/arts/12822853/why-we-should-sing-the-star-spangled-banners-obscure-fifth-verse.

"Adams and Liberty"

In 1798, Robert Treat Paine, the son of a signer of the Declaration of Independence, composed a song for the Massachusetts Charitable Fire Society on its fourth anniversary. Entitled "Adams and Liberty," the song was called "the anthem of the Federalist Party" (Fischer 2005, 172). It consisted of nine verses and was designed to laud the Adams administration. The song was written during one of the most partisan periods in American history, an era in which Federalists (led by John Adams) were generally sympathetic to Great Britain and rival Democratic-Republicans (led by Thomas Jefferson and James Madison) generally favored France in the ongoing war between the two European powers. It was a time when both parties looked at the other with suspicion, in the belief that if their party opponents were truly committed to the national interest, they would share a common vision rather than be in a rival faction.

The poem was set to the music of "To Anacreon in Heaven," which is the tune that Francis Scott Key later appropriated for "The Star-Spangled Banner." As with some future contenders to be the national anthem, the first verse refers to Americans as "Ye sons of Columbia," with Columbia being a common designation at the time for America. Wishing that the nation might increase in peace and that it might combine "the glory of Rome, and the wisdom of Greece," the last two lines of the verse, which became a chorus for each subsequent stanza, proclaimed (Paine, "Adams and Liberty"):

And ne'er shall the sons of Columbia be slaves,
While the earthy bears a plant, or the sea rolls its waves.

With a view toward disruptions of shipping and trade at sea by both Britain and France, the second verse decried any attempt to hurl "the trident of Commerce . . . to incense the legitimate powers of the ocean." At the same time, it warned that "should pirates invade, / Though in thunder arrayed, / Let your cannon declare the free charter of trade."

In the third verse, Paine claimed, "The fame of our arms, of our laws the mild sway, / Had justly ennobled our nation in story" and charged that "the dark clouds of faction" had "obscured our young day." Similarly, in the fourth verse, Paine contrasted the dove living in peace under the U.S. Constitution with the bloodletting of the French Revolution.

The fifth verse warns "the vassals of Europe in arms" of "the fire of the flint," which is strengthened by adherence to law, while the sixth suggests that Americans would sooner destroy all their forests than allow a foreign foe to rule victorious. Similarly, the next verse warns against "Anarch's pestilent worm" and pledges to defend "our altars and laws."

The penultimate verse refers to the nation's affection for "Freedom's temple" and cites the example of George Washington. The last verse refers specifically to Adams.

> Her pride is her Adams; Her laws are his choice,
> And shall flourish, till Liberty slumbers for ever.

Musicologist Richard S. Hill believes that Paine's composition did much to make the tune "To Anacreon in Heaven" popular in America (1951, 192).

By 1801, Democratic-Republicans had composed their own song, "Jefferson and Liberty," which was also set to the same tune. Ironically, it too referred derisively in its sixth verse to "the thun-der of fac-tion" (Clague and Kuster 2015, 70). It featured the same chorus as the song lauding Adams.

Francis Scott Key, who wrote "The Star-Spangled Banner," had been a southern Federalist who had opposed American entry into the War of 1812 as well as Northern talk of secession. He was likely familiar with "Adams and Liberty." Historian Fischer believes that the beauty of "The Star-Spangled Banner" is that Key "took the song of a political party that in 1814 was identified with peace and sectionalism and made it a hymn to martial courage and national unity" (2005, 172).

See also: Key, Francis Scott; Presidential Campaigns.

Further Reading

Clague, Mark, and Andrew Kuster, eds. 2015. *Star Spangled Songbook: A History in Sheet Music of "The Star-Spangled Banner."* Ann Arbor, MI: Star Spangled Music Foundation.
Fischer, David Hackett. 2005. *Liberty and Freedom*. New York: Oxford University Press.
Gray, Myron. 2017. "A Partisan National Song: The Politics of 'Hail Columbia' Reconsidered." *Music & Politics* 11 (Summer): 1–20.
Hill, Richard S. 1951. "The Melody of 'The Star-Spangled Banner' in the United States before 1820." In *Essays Honoring Lawrence C. Wroth*, edited by Lessing J. Rosenwald Collection (Library of Congress), 151–92. Portland, ME: Anthoensen Press.
Paine, Robert Treat. 1798. "Adams and Liberty." *Poem of the Week.org.* http://www.potw.org/archive/potw233.html.

Advertising

In 1907, in the case of *Halter v. Nebraska*, the U.S. Supreme Court upheld a Nebraska anti-flag desecration statute that was designed to maintain the dignity of the American flag by prohibiting its use in advertising. In view of subsequent interpretations of the First Amendment that have expanded its legal parameters, it is quite unlikely that the Supreme Court would uphold a similar law today. Indeed, given the flag's identification with the colors red, white, and blue, with such symbols as Uncle Sam, and even with such comic book figures as Captain America and Wonder Woman, it would be difficult to frame a law that would be able to define and regulate "desecration" with precision.

As early as the composition of "Adams and Liberty" in 1798, it was common to set a song lauding a political figure or candidate to the melody of what is commonly recognized as "The Star-Spangled Banner." Numerous political campaigns subsequently employed the same tune on behalf of their own candidates, and eventually it became the musical backdrop for television and radio advertising as well. Whatever the purpose of its use—whether to sell the public on a candidate or a Fourth of July sale on appliances or clothing—these efforts reflected a recognition that the song was closely associated with patriotism and American identity among most members of the public.

The federal government has recognized these associations as well. A report first published in 2015 revealed that the U.S. Department of Defense had split some $5.4 million among fourteen National Football League (NFL) teams for pregame activities celebrating the U.S. flag and anthem. This apparently did not count the cost of military jet flyovers, which could cost as much as $450,000 each.

In 2014, Coca-Cola unveiled an advertisement for the Super Bowl that featured individuals singing "America the Beautiful" in different languages. Although apparently lauded by many liberals, it provoked outrage among some conservatives, a number of whom apparently thought the song was the national anthem (Feloni 2014).

In recent years, Colin Kaepernick and other athletes have garnered widespread attention and criticism for deciding to take a knee during the playing of the national anthem at NFL games. This did not stop Nike from running an advertisement in 2018 encouraging viewers to "Believe in something. Even if it means sacrificing everything. Just Do It." Although the Nike advertisement led to a boycott of the athletic shoe and apparel company, it also apparently resulted in increased sales (Abad-Santos 2018).

Earlier that same year, Marsha Blackburn, a successful Republican candidate for a U.S. Senate seat in Tennessee, launched a series of radio advertisements encouraging individuals to stand for the playing of the national anthem (Ebert 2018). The NFL apparently rejected an application by American Veterans to place an advertisement at the Super Bowl encouraging fans to do so. Spokesman Brian McCarthy explained the league's position by saying that the game-day program "is designed for fans to commemorate the game, players, teams and the Super Bowl" and that "it's never been a place for advertising that could be considered by some as a political statement" (Starnes 2018).

See also: "Adams and Liberty"; Barr, Roseanne; Houston, Whitney; Kaepernick, Colin; Presidential Campaigns; Sports Events.

Further Reading

Abad-Santos, Alex. 2018. "Nike's Colin Kaepernick Ad Sparked a Boycott—and Earned $6 Billion for Nike." *Vox*, September 24. https://www.vox.com/2018/9/24/17895704/nike-colin-kaepernick-boycott-6-billion.

Becker, Sam. 2018. "The Crazy Amount of Money the Military Gives to the NFL." *CheatSheet*, June 11. https://www.cheatsheet.com/money-career/amount-money-military-gives-nfl.html/.

Ebert, Joel. 2018. "As Super Bowl Looms, Blackburn Launching Radio Ads Encouraging Standing during National Anthem." *Tennessean*, January 25. https://www.tennes sean.com/story/news/politics/2018/01/25/super-bowl-blackburn-launching -radio-ads-encouraging-people-stand-during-national-anthem/1067052001/.

Feloni, Richard. 2014. "Coke Had Americans Singing 'American the Beautiful' in Different Languages and a Bunch of People Hated It." *Business Insider*, February 2. https://www.businessinsider.com/coke-super-bowl-america-the-beautiful -ad-2014-2.

Halter v. Nebraska, 205 U.S. 34 (1907).

Starnes, Todd. 2018. "NFL Rejects Veterans Group's Super Bowl Ad Urging People to Stand for the Anthem." *Fox News*, January 23. https://www.foxnews.com/opinion /nfl-rejects-veterans-groups-super-bowl-ad-urging-people-to-stand-for-the -anthem.

African Americans

In contrast to Canada, its neighbor to the north, the United States does not have a bilingual national anthem. Although there are many songs that express U.S. patriotism, "The Star-Spangled Banner" is intended to unite all citizens in love of country.

From the beginning, however, there have been questions as to whether the song, now designated as the national anthem, applies equally to all Americans. The song was written by a lawyer, Francis Scott Key, who owned slaves, opposed abolitionists, and favored a plan to recolonize freed slaves back in Africa. This helps explain why, in September 2017, vandals defaced a statue of Francis Scott Key in a Baltimore park with red paint and slogans that included "Racist Anthem" (Olson 2017).

In their day, abolitionists rightly parodied "The Star-Spangled Banner" for its lofty references to the "land of the free." They might further question whether God would enable the nation to continue to conquer when the final verse of the anthem linked such conquest to occasions "when our cause it is just." When many abolitionists envisioned the "stars and stripes," they thought not so much of the American flag as of the beatings and lashings that slaves received from their masters (Vile 2018, 304–7). Oliver Wendell Holmes, Sr., added a fifth verse to "The Star-Spangled Banner," often recorded in postbellum editions of the song, that proclaimed, "By the millions unchain'd who our birth-right have gain'd, / We will keep her bright blazon forever unstain'd" (Clague and Kuster 2015, 224–25). Former slaves undoubtedly remembered that "Dixie," the lyrics of which painted a picture of African American longing to be back in the South, had been a type of unofficial anthem for the Confederate States of America, which had sought to perpetuate slavery.

Not only does "The Star-Spangled Banner" refer specifically to "freemen," but after saying that "their blood has wash'd out their foul footstep's pollution," in the most problematic verse of "The Star-Spangled Banner" (the third), Key further opined, "No refuge could save the hireling and slave / From the terror of flight or the gloom of the grave." The most common interpretation of this passage is that it applies to British mercenaries (the hirelings) and members of the Corps of

Colonial Marines, which consisted of American slaves who had volunteered to fight for the British in exchange for their freedom. Using this interpretation, Key was wishing for the death of those slaves who were attempting to achieve their own freedom. Walter Olson (2017) of the Cato Institute, however, argues that the term slave also "meant someone such as a soldier, official, or laborer who served for money rather than from some more durable loyalty such as to family or nation."

After the adoption of the Thirteenth Amendment, which eliminated slavery in 1865, and the Fourteenth Amendment, which extended citizenship to all persons born or naturalized in the United States in 1868, the country moved closer to being a true "land of the free," in the exultant words of "The Star-Spangled Banner." Another important step in that regard came with the Supreme Court's landmark decision in *Brown v. Board of Education* (1954) that began the process of ending racial segregation in the United States. These advances, however, were not sufficient to neutralize decades of institutional racism and racial violence in the Jim Crow South and other parts of the country. Moreover, many racial disparities remain in America today in income, education, health, and other basic measures of quality of life. In recent years a number of black athletes, most notably Colin Kaepernick, the former quarterback for the San Francisco 49ers football team, have knelt during the playing of the national anthem in protest over these inequities. Kaepernick has been especially concerned over incidents in which white police officers have shot unarmed African American suspects. As a result, some African Americans have embraced the song "Lift Every Voice and Sing," which specifically invokes the history of slavery in the United States, as a type of black national anthem.

See also: Kaepernick, Colin; Key, Francis Scott; "Lift Every Voice and Sing"; "O Canada"; Sports Events.

Further Reading

Bass, Amy. 2002. *Not the Triumph But the Struggle: The 1968 Olympics and the Making of the Black Athlete.* Minneapolis: University of Minnesota Press.

Clague, Mark, and Andrew Kuster, eds. 2015. *Star Spangled Songbook: A History in Sheet Music of "The Star-Spangled Banner."* Ann Arbor, MI: Star Spangled Music Foundation.

Olson, Walter. 2017. "History of the National Anthem: Is 'The Star-Spangled Banner' Racist?" *National Review*, September 15. https://www.cato.org/publications/com mentary/star-spangled-banner-racist.

Redmond, Shana L. 2015. "Indivisible: The Nation and Its Anthem in Black Musical Performance." *Black Music Research Journal* 35 (Spring): 97–118.

Schwarz, Jon. 2016. "Colin Kaepernick Is Righter Than You Know: The National Anthem Is a Celebration of Slavery." *The Intercept,* August 28. https://theintercept.com /2016/08/28/colin-kaepernick-is-righter-than-you-know-the-national-anthem-is -a-celebration-of-slavery.

Staples, Brent. 2018. "African-Americans and the Strains of the National Anthem." *New York Times*, June 9. https://www.nytimes.com/2018/06/09/opinion/african-ameri cans-national-anthem-protests.html.

Vile, John R. 2018. *The American Flag: An Encyclopedia of the Stars and Stripes in U.S. History, Culture, and Law.* Santa Barbara, CA: ABC-CLIO.

Alternatives to the National Anthem

Although Congress designated "The Star-Spangled Banner" as the national anthem in 1931, some individuals continued to think that the words and poetry were too complex, the tune too difficult, and the language too militaristic. The seldom-sung third stanza has also been criticized for being too warlike. In part because they had such a strong constituency in Maryland and surrounding states, Francis Scott Key's words ultimately prevailed, but this has not stopped detractors from suggesting alternative songs that were present when Congress adopted the anthem. In addition, several songs composed since 1931 have been touted as better choices for a national anthem.

One of the former songs, which is variously designated by its first verse "My Country, 'Tis of Thee" or simply as "America," was written by a Samuel Francis Smith in 1831 when he was a student at Andover Seminary in Newton, Massachusetts. Although the tune is simple and easy to sing, Smith did not originally realize that the musical arrangement, which he had taken from a German hymnbook, was actually that of "God Save the Queen," which is the anthem of Great Britain—the country against which American colonists took up arms to secure their independence. This fact made it highly unlikely that Smith's song would generate sufficient support to be designated as the official U.S. anthem.

A song that preceded both "America" and "The Star-Spangled Banner" was "Hail Columbia," which was written by Joseph Hopkinson in 1798. It was set to the tune of "The President's March," which had been composed for George Washington's inauguration and referenced the Revolutionary War. One disadvantage of Hopkinson's composition was that although the term "Columbia" was widely used in the nineteenth century to refer to the young American nation, it gradually fell into disuse as an alternative term for the United States.

Another very popular song, which was particularly easy to sing, was "Yankee Doodle," the tune for which appears to have been homegrown in America, perhaps as early as King George's War. The ironic lyrics of the song—which appear to have been the work of many authors and describe Americans mocking themselves in apparent hopes to appear as rubes and thus confirm British assessments of them—made it a popular song, but those same words were also widely seen as too lowbrow and insufficiently dignified for most affairs of state.

At the beginning of the Civil War, Julia Ward Howe used the music to "John Brown's Body" to craft the "Battle Hymn of the Republic." This song was soaked in Biblical imagery and was clearly more favored in the North during the Civil War than in the South, which used "Dixie" as something of an unofficial anthem.

In 1895, a Wellesley professor named Katharine Lee Bates published "America the Beautiful," the words for which had been largely inspired by her trips to the World's Columbia Exposition in Chicago and to Pikes Peak in Colorado. It puts great emphasis on the beauty of the U.S. landscape.

Although Irving Berlin wrote his first version of "God Bless America" in 1918 while he was a serviceman in the U.S. Army, it did not attract wide attention until 1938, when singer Kate Smith sang an updated version of the song—also composed by Berlin—on a national radio broadcast. The song would likely have been a strong competitor for recognition as America's national anthem had it been available in 1931. In fact, some people continue to believe that "God Bless America" is the superior song and should replace "The Star-Spangled Banner."

In 1940 folk singer Woodie Guthrie published "This Land Is Your Land," partly in reaction to the religious language and triumphalism that he thought "The Star-Spangled Banner" anthem represented. Although Guthrie's song is quite singable (and, like "America the Beautiful," evokes a variety of American landscapes), his criticisms of the free enterprise system virtually assured that it would never receive the necessary support to replace "The Star-Spangled Banner" as the nation's official anthem.

More recently, Lee Greenwood's "God Bless the USA" has become an increasing popular song, the chorus of which is close to Bates's classic in its call for "God [to] bless the USA." "Lift Every Voice and Sing" is a song that has sometimes been described as an unofficial black national anthem in light of its enduring popularity among African Americans. Although Native Americans tend to show strong support for "The Star-Spangled Banner," many tribes also have their own anthems.

See also: African Americans; "America the Beautiful"; "Battle Hymn of the Republic"; Confederate National Anthem; Congress and "The Star-Spangled Banner"; Criticisms and Defenses of "The Star-Spangled Banner"; "God Bless America"; "God Save the Queen"; "Hail Columbia"; "Lift Every Voice and Sing"; "My Country, 'Tis of Thee" ("America"); Native American Indians; "Yankee Doodle."

Further Reading

Elson, Louis C. 1900. *The National Music of America and Its Sources*. Boston: L. C. Page.

Peithman, Stephen. 2014. "America's Five National Anthems." *Capital Public Radio*, July 4. http://www.capradio.org/music/classical/2014/07/04/americas-five-national-anthems-1.

Rissier, Tyler. 2014. "The Story Behind 'The Star-Spangled Banner': A Q&A with Author Marc Ferris." *American Songwriter*, December 2. https://americansongwriter.com/2014/12/star-spangled-banner-qa-marc-ferris.

Shellnutt, Kate. 2018. "Make Worship Patriotic Again? The Top 10 Songs for Fourth of July Services." *Christianity Today*, June 29. https://www.christianitytoday.com/ct/2018/june-web-only/make-worship-patriotic-again-top-10-songs-fourth-of-july.html.

"America" (see "My Country, 'Tis of Thee")

"America the Beautiful"

Although it was not designated as the national anthem, one of the songs that has been dear to many generations of Americans is "America the Beautiful." It was written by Katharine Lee Bates (1859–1929), who was both a graduate of and an English professor at Wellesley College in Wellesley, Massachusetts.

In 1893 Bates was invited to teach drama at Colorado College in Colorado Springs. On the way, she made stops at Niagara Falls and at the World's Columbia

Exposition. While in Colorado she took a trip to Pikes Peak, where she was so inspired that she took out pencil and paper and wrote the draft of what was to become "America the Beautiful." After making a number of emendations, she published the first edition of the poem in the July 4, 1895, issue of the *Congregationalist*.

Sometime later, Clarence A. Barbour, a Baptist minister who thought that the poem should be set to music, uncovered the song "Marterna" (also known as "O Mother Dear, Jerusalem") with a musical arrangement that fit the words. This song had, in turn, been composed by Samuel Ward, a church musician, who had written it after he and his family took a trip to Coney Island, New York. Barbour successfully matched the melody to the words of "America the Beautiful" in 1888 in a publication called *Parish Choir*.

Neither Bates nor Ward earned any money for their creations. Bates further refused to join those who favored making the song the national anthem.

The first verse, as revised, was most closely linked to Bates's experience on Pikes Peak, where she would have viewed not only the "purple mountain majesties" but also the grains growing on the distant plains:

O beautiful for spacious skies,
For amber waves of grain.
For purple mountain majesties
Above the fruited plain!
America! America!
God shed his grace on thee
And crown thy good with brotherhood
From sea to shining sea!

In analyzing the lyrics, Lynn Sherr, who wrote a book on the subject, asks, "Who but a child of the seacoast would see Kansas wheat growing in 'waves'? And later define the scope of the continent by its waters?" (2001, 74, 76). Musicologist Mark Pedelty observes that, like "God Bless America" and "This Land Is Your Land," the words "represent America not only as a nation, but also as nature" (2012, 49).

The second verse emphasized the Puritan founders of both Massachusetts and America, with whom Bates connected to America's march of freedom. The end of this stanza is a type of prayer:

O beautiful for pilgrim feet
Whose stern impassioned stress
A thoroughfare of freedom beat
Across the wilderness!
America! America!
God mend thine every flaw,
Confirm thy soul in self-control,
Thy liberty in law!

The third verse further ties America's current freedom to its forebears' patriotism and their self-sacrifice:

O beautiful for heroes proved
In liberating Strife.
Who more than self their country loved
And mercy more than life!
America! America!
May God thy gold refine
Till all success be nobleness
And every gain divine!

The final verse, with its reference to "alabaster cities," is probably a reference to the white buildings that Bates had observed at the Columbian exposition. Its final two lines repeat those of the first stanza in aspirational verse with the line "Undimmed by human tears" as applicable to heaven as to earth:

O beautiful for patriot dream
That sees beyond the years
Thine alabaster cities gleam
Undimmed by human tears!
America! America!
God shed his grace on thee
And crown thy good with brotherhood
From sea to shining sea!

Because of its age and its close association with Baltimore, whose politicians strongly supported its adoption, "The Star-Spangled Banner" had something of a running start in the contest to be designated as the national anthem, but in 1926, the National Hymn Society was among the groups that wanted "America the Beautiful" to receive the honor. One of the supporters of this movement said, "It expresses the highest and deepest emotions of patriotism, not in any spirit of militant aggress and world-conquering imperialism, but with a profound gratitude and affection for the country, the government, and the traditions that have made us what we are" (Sherr 2001, 88).

Even after adoption of "The Star-Spangled Banner" as the national anthem, there have been some attempts to replace it with "America the Beautiful." In 1985, Representative Andy Jacobs, Jr., a Democrat from Indiana, introduced such a resolution in Congress. A similar resolution, introduced by Republican Representative Margaret Heckler, who represented the district that included Wellesley, also failed. It is doubtful that Bates would have cared. Writing to a newspaper about making her song the national anthem she responded, "[A]s to making it the national anthem, I am personally more than content with the heart-warming reception the song . . . has already had . . . I am glad to have it go as far as popular goodwill carries it. As for 'pushing' it or 'urging' it or striving to have it 'supplant' something else, nothing could be more at variance with my constant attitude toward it nor more averse to my temperament" (Sherr 2001, 93).

The song remains beloved. President Lyndon B. Johnson cited the words of the song shortly after becoming president upon the assassination of President John F. Kennedy. Pope John Paul II referred to the song during his visit to the United States in 1979. Al Gore mentioned it in his concession speech after the contested 2000 presidential election (Sherr 2001, 72).

The song has been commemorated by a plaque on Pikes Peak, and another plaque in the Grace Episcopal Church in Newark recognizes Samuel Augustus Ward for composing the tune. There is a full-size statue of Bates on the library lawn at Falmouth, Massachusetts, where she was born, and the students at Wellesley sing "America the Beautiful" at each graduation (Sherr 2001, 103).

See also: Alternatives to the National Anthem; Congress and "The Star-Spangled Banner."

Further Reading

Collins, Ace. 2003. *Songs Sung Red, White, and Blue: The Stories Behind America's Best-Loved Patriotic Songs.* New York: HarperCollins.

Pedelty, Mark. 2012. *Ecomusicology: Rock, Folk, and the Environment.* Philadelphia: Temple University Press.

Sherr, Lynn. 2001. *America the Beautiful: The Stirring True Story Behind Our Nation's Favorite Song.* New York: Public Affairs.

American Sign Language

It has become increasingly common to have a sign language interpreter at public ceremonies or speeches to aid members of the audience who are deaf. Beginning in 1992, for example, an American Sign Language interpreter has signed the national anthem at annual Super Bowl football games (Schmitt 2017, 131). However, at least one writer has expressed concern that broadcasting such translations in a bubble on the bottom of television screens furthers "the perception of sign language as an accommodation for a minority who have a handicap, as opposed to a full-fledged language of artistic expression" (Schmitt 2017, 132).

Professor Carlos Abril, who focuses on sociocultural issues in music education, attended a concert in 2006 that featured "an orchestra, choir, and over one dozen students from a school for the deaf, who translated the text into American Sign Language" (2007, 74). He concluded, "This translation of the text did not change the essence of the song, signing merely facilitated communication with a different segment of the population. In so doing, those members of our society were welcomed into the song's fold" (74).

See also: English Language and "The Star-Spangled Banner."

Further Reading

Abril, Carlos R. 2007. "Functions of a National Anthem in Society and Education: A Sociocultural Perspective." *Bulletin of the Council for Research in Music Education*, no. 172 (Spring): 69–87.

Schmitt, Pierre. 2017. "Representations of Sign Language, Deaf People, and Interpreters in the Arts and the Media." *Sign Language Studies* 18 (Fall): 130–47.

Anacreon

Anacreon (c. 570–c. 485 BC) was a Greek poet from Teos, an ancient Greek city on an island off the coast of what is today Turkey that was once part of twelve cities that were part of the Ionian League. Anacreon was associated with the court of Polycrates, the tyrant of Samos, which was known for its sweet muscat wine.

Anacreon was the inspiration for "To Anacreon in Heaven," the constitutional song of the London Anacreontic Society, a group of high-society gentlemen who listened to musical performances and feasted together. The song was first published in 1778 and written by one of the Anacreontic Society's early presidents, a lawyer named Ralph Tomlinson. He positively portrayed Anacreon for his poetic ability "to entwine, the myrtle of Venus [the goddess of love] with Bacchus's [the god of alcoholic beverages and revelry] Vine." The tune of this constitutional song, which has been attributed to the otherwise relatively unknown Englishman named John Stafford Smith, in turn became the tune for "The Star-Spangled Banner."

Poetic tastes vary from one era to another, and Anacreon's star has waned since the time that "To Anacreon in Heaven" and "The Star-Spangled Banner" were composed, but he was one among a number of poets who had praised drinking and intoxication and who was quite popular in the seventeenth and eighteenth centuries, when contemporaries ranked him with such other Greek poets as Hesiod and Pindar (Berry 1970, 132). His poems were "written in the manner of *skolia*, or songs to be sung during the symposium that followed a Greek dinner" (Montgomery 1948, 30). One scholar has observed, "His philosophy . . . is hedonistic, a natural development of the cultured, luxury-loving society of a wealthy tyrant's court" (Berry 1970, 133). He was known for being able to evoke an image or phrase that, while not "metaphysical," was "simply clever, just ingenious enough to be right" (133).

Although deeply admired by his contemporaries, less than two hundred lines of his poetry remain today. At the time of the Anacreontic Society, however, there was a much larger corpus of "Anacreontea," or "poems in the style of Anacreon" (Berry 1970, 134), typically of somewhat lesser quality, that were also attributed to him. Moreover, it was common for educated gentleman of the time to seek either to translate his poems or imitate their meter. One commentator, Tom Mason, thus observed, "The story of Anacreon is an extraordinary literary phenomenon. It is the history of a ghost-poet, a poet who did and did not exist but who had an enormous influence on European poetry" (Roth 2000, 314).

Although some have criticized "The Star-Spangled Banner" for celebrating a military victory and thus being too warlike, others have noted that it is not nearly as martial as other national anthems and not easily used as a marching song. Perhaps this is because it continues to reflect, at least in part, its origin as a poem connected to love and wine, which has itself been another point of criticism.

See also: Criticisms and Defenses of "The Star-Spangled Banner"; "To Anacreon in Heaven."

Further Reading

Berry, Edmund. 1970. "The Poet of Love and Wine." *Mosaic: An Interdisciplinary Critical Journal* 3 (Winter): 132–43.

Montgomery, Henry C. 1948. "Anacreon and the National Anthem." *Classical Outlook* 26 (December): 30–31.
Roth, Marty. 2000. "'Anacreon' and Drink Poetry; or, the Art of Feeling Very Very Good." *Texas Studies in Literature and Language* 42 (Fall): 314–45.

Anthem

Long before Congress recognized Francis Scott Key's song "The Star-Spangled Banner" as the national anthem, it was widely sung and/or performed for numerous occasions, particularly those involving matters of state. It would likely have remained popular even had Congress not so designated it.

One obvious question that has arisen concerns is the actual meaning of the word "anthem." Interestingly, not only do some states have more than one anthem, but some also simply designate them as songs.

The word appears to be derived from the Greek word *antiphona*, and the Saxon *antefn*, which originally referred to what Dr. George Svejda, who wrote an important study for the National Park Service, has described as "a liturgical practice involving alternate singing between two choirs" (2005, 265). Historically, the precise form appears chiefly to have developed in England. A student of this account of origin notes, however, that it had a variety of meanings:

1. a song with words
2. a song of praise or glorification (as "National Anthem")
3. usually performed by a choir with or without soloists as opposed to soloists without choir
4. a choral work with or without accompaniment
5. intended for use in a worship service as a nonliturgical piece of concerted vocal music as opposed to a setting of a portion of the mass, such as a "Kyrie" or a "sanctus," etc.
6. a thorough-composed piece as opposed to a hymn, chorale, or pslam tone in which the same music is used for several different stanzas or verses
7. an independent work as opposed to a portion of an oratorio, passion, or cantata.
8. A work which derives its inspiration and thematic material solely from its text (often scriptural) without being based on a hymn tune, chorale, or plainsong with the exception of the very earliest anthems in a motet style. (Otte 1978, 16)

According to Svejda, the word "anthem" has been employed since the sixteenth century to refer to musical pieces "of sacred or patriotic character, involving an element of gladness or praise" (2005, 269). After defining a hymn as "a song of praise," and an anthem as originating from "a song performed in a responsorial fashion," another scholar says, "An anthem as well as a hymn is a song of praise made for communal singing" (Fornas 2012, 149–50). Professor Yu Chen ties the anthem to "the Ancient Greek tradition of praising the deities" and says, "It is consistent with the view that the nation-state is sacred and serves as an altar to praise that 'sacredness'" (2010, 2).

Journalist Alex Marshall (2008) has identified four types of anthems: (1) the traditional European hymns or military marches, (2) "folk anthems based on traditional melodies," (3) "the Arab fanfare" common in Middle Eastern countries and consisting of little more than a trumpet flourish, and (4) the Latin American "epic anthems." In a study of the European anthem, which is largely based on the "Ode to Joy" in Ludwig van Beethoven's Ninth Symphony, Fornas further notes, drawing from Malcolm Boyd, that national anthems can be divided into five main categories, the first two of which are most common:

> (a) Hymns with a solemn pace and melody (for instance the British "God Save the Queen" or the European anthem); (b) marches (such as the French "La Marseillaise"); (c) operatic tunes (exemplified by El Salvador and some other Latin American countries); (d) folk tunes (mainly used in Asia, for instance by Japan and Sri Lanka); and (e) fanfares without text (found in Kuwait, the United Arab Emirates, and other oil states in the Middle East). (2012, 150; Boyd 1980, 46–47)

Although the American national anthem is not Fornas's focus, "The Star-Spangled Banner" and most other national anthem alternatives that Congress considered would appear to fit the first category. Exceptions would likely be "Yankee Doodle," which would more likely be characterized as a folk tune, and "You're a Grand Old Flag," which is a march. The song "We Shall Not Be Moved" is a folk song, with origins in religious revivals, that has long been used as an anthem in the U.S. labor movement (Spener 2016).

It is notable that whereas some national anthems, most notably those of Great Britain, pay homage to a monarch or a national founder, the United States directs praise to the national flag. Boyd observes, "National anthems are the equivalent in music of a country's motto, crest or flag" (1980, 46).

Anthems may also represent international movements as well as nations. "The Internationale," written by Eugene Pottier in 1871, has been a rallying point for socialists since the nineteenth century, although it was also used for a time by the Soviet Union. In a much different vein, African Americans demonstrating for civil rights often used "We Shall Overcome" and "We Shall Not Be Moved" to rally supporters.

See also: Congress and "The Star-Spangled Banner"; State Songs and Anthems; "Yankee Doodle"; "You're a Grand Old Flag."

Further Reading

Boyd, Malcolm. 1980. "National Anthems." In *New Grove Dictionary of Music and Musicians*, 46–70. London: Macmillan.

Chen, Yu. 2010. "An Empirical Study of Hispanic American National Anthems." University of Texas at Austin. http://lanic.utexas.edu/project/etext/llilas/ilassa/2010/chen.pdf.

Fornas, Johan. 2012. *Signifying Europe*. Bristol, UK: Intellect.

Johnson, Latrise P., and Elizabeth Eubanks. 2015. "Anthem or Nah? Culturally Relevant Writing Instruction and Community." *Voices from the Middle* 23 (December): 31–36.

Marshall, Alex. 2008. "And the Winning Anthem Is." *The Guardian*, August 10. https://www.theguardian.com/music/2008/aug/11/olympics2008.

Otte, Paul R. 1978. "The English Anthem." *Choral Journal* 18 (April): 16–24, 26–28.

Spener, David. 2016. *We Shall Not Be Moved / No nos moveran: Biography of a Song of Struggle*. Philadelphia: Temple University Press.

Svejda, George J. 2005. *History of the Star Spangled Banner from 1814 to the Present.* Honolulu, HI: University Press of the Pacific. First published in 1969 by Division of History, Office of Archeology and Historic Preservation, U.S. Department of the Interior, National Park Service.

Anti-British Sentiments

One of the past criticisms of "The Star-Spangled Banner" was that it exhibited animus against the British. Fortunately, the only part of the song that lends itself readily to such an interpretation is the third stanza, which is rarely sung today:

> And where is that band who so vauntingly swore,
> That the havoc of war and the battle's confusion
> A home and a country should leave us no more?
> Their blood has wash'd out their foul footstep's pollution.
> No refuge could save the hireling and slave
> From the terror of flight or the gloom of the grave.
> And the star-spangled banner in triumph doth wave
> O'er the land of the free and the home of the brave.

A more common contemporary criticism of this verse is its reference to the "hireling and slave," but the phrase probably refers not to chattel slaves but to mercenaries or slaves to whom the British had promised freedom in exchange for their service in fighting against fellow Americans.

Early Americanist David Hildebrand (2014) has further pointed out that, in contrast to "The Battle of Baltimore," which also described the events surrounding the British invasion and even made fun of the British commander who was killed, Key's "The Star-Spangled Banner" does not mention England, or English generals, by name. People familiar with the background of the song know that Key was speaking of British invaders, but his sentiments do not appear to be directed against the English specifically but rather against any group that would seek to invade the country.

It is, notable, however, that as early as 1824, an otherwise obscure American gentleman named George Spowers composed an alternate verse designed to show that the United States and Britain were now friends:

> But hush'd be that strain! They our Foes are no longer;
>   Lo Britain the right hand of Freindship extends,
> And Albion's fair Isle we behold with affection
>   The land of our Fathers—the land of our Friends!
>   Long, long may we flourish, Columbia and Britain,
>   In amity still may your children be found.
> And the Star-spangled Banner and Red Cross together
> Wave free and triumphant the wide world around!

In analyzing this verse, musicologist Oscar Sonneck observed that the stanza was "well-meant but objectionable, because it, too, drags our national hymn into foreign politics" (1914, 96). Today, the term "Red Cross" also seems an odd description for the Union Jack, but at the time it referred to the red cross of England's patron saint, Saint George, which was one of the Union Jack's underlying symbols.

In any event, Spowers's verse does not appear to have secured popular favor. Despite fears raised during World War I that "The Star-Spangled Banner" might strain relations with Britain, a key war ally, the song did not emerge as a point of contention during the Great War—or, for that matter, during World War II or the number of subsequent lesser conflicts in which the United States and Britain stood together.

A better-known suggested addition was a verse proposed by Oliver Wendell Holmes, Sr., which was designed to celebrate the fact that the United States had emancipated the slaves. Some African Americans have preferred to express such sentiments in "Lift Every Voice and Sing" rather than by adding an additional stanza.

See also: Criticisms and Defenses of "The Star-Spangled Banner"; "Lift Every Voice and Sing"; Lyrics of "The Star-Spangled Banner"; Pickersgill, Mary Young; Slavery; Smith, Samuel.

Further Reading

Hildebrand, David K. 2014. "Bicentenary Essay: Two National Anthems? Some Reflections on the Two Hundredth Anniversary of 'The Star-Spangled Banner' and Its Forgotten Partner, 'The Battle of Baltimore.'" *American Music* 32 (Fall): 253–71.

"The National Anthem." 2006. Boy Scouts Merit Badge Activity. Semanic Scholar. https://pdfs.semanticscholar.org/fb87/ebcdca3a6f450f164c0133a4625a21da168b .pdf.

Sonneck, Oscar George Theodore. 1914. *"The Star Spangled Banner" (Revised and Enlarged from the "Report" on the Above and Other Airs, Issued in 1909).* Washington, DC: Government Printing Office (Library of Congress).

Armistead, George

George Armistead (1780–1818) was one of the individuals who was arguably most responsible for inspiring "The Star-Spangled Banner." Born in Caroline County, Virginia, in 1780, he served in the military for much of his relatively short life. He spent from 1802 to 1807 at Fort Niagara, after which he was transferred to Fort McHenry in Baltimore before returning to Fort Niagara. There he distinguished himself in a battle against the British at Fort George in May of 1813 and brought back captured British flags to President Madison, who then appointed him as the commander of Fort McHenry.

In addition to acquiring cannons for the Fort, Armistead was responsible for ordering two flags from Mary Pickersgill. One was a smaller storm flag that likely flew during much of the Battle of Baltimore, during which British ships attacked Fort McHenry, and the other was a gigantic forty-two-by-thirty-foot American flag.

Closely allied with Samuel Smith, the U.S. senator and major general who did so much to prepare Baltimore for possible attack by British forces during the War of 1812, Armistead commanded about one thousand troops during the British bombardment of Fort McHenry. Although his cannons could not reach British ships through much of the battle, he directed a withering attack when British vessels approached within range. During the rest of the battle, he continued to fire from time to time to indicate that he and his men were still defending the fort. As the British ceased their barrage, Armistead had his men raise the giant American flag that he had purchased from Mary Pickersgill. This is likely the flag that Francis Scott Key observed just before writing "The Star-Spangled Banner."

Almost immediately after the battle, Armistead developed a fever and was bedridden. He finally was able to issue a report on the engagement in a letter to the incoming Secretary of War and future president, James Monroe, on September 24, 1814. In the letter, he commended naval lieutenant Newcomb, who commanded nearby Fort Covington, for his actions. Calculating that the British had lodged somewhere in the range of fifteen hundred to eighteen hundred shells at Fort McHenry during a twenty-five-hour bombardment, he was able to report that American losses were four dead and twenty-four wounded. He noted "that every officer and soldier under my command did their duty to my entire satisfaction" (Armistead 1814).

President James Madison promoted Armistead to brevet lieutenant colonel, and he remained as commander of Fort McHenry until his death of apparent heart problems in 1818. The Star-Spangled Banner flag that is now housed at the Smithsonian Institution came down through his custody and that of his family. It is on display at the Smithsonian, which also displays a large silver bowl shaped like a British bomb, a silver tray, and goblets. The set was produced by Thomas Fletcher and Sidney Gardiner of Philadelphia and bears the following inscription: "Presented by a number of the citizens of Baltimore to Lieutenant Colonel George Armistead for his gallant and successful defense of Fort M'Henry during the bombardment by a large British Force, on the 12th and 13th September 1814 when upwards of 1500 shells were thrown; 400 of which fell within the area of the Fort and some of them of the diameter of this Vase" (Wood 1967, 151).

In responding to this presentation on May 11, 1816, Armistead expressed his appreciation while also sharing the credit with his troops:

> As the offering of free born citizens, cherishing the pure principles of independence and civil liberty, it is the richest boon that could be bestowed upon a soldier emulous of fame: As much I am proud to receive it, and glory in this opportunity of transmitting to my posterity, so distinguished a mark of a country's gratitude; giving thereby, to that country, an undisputed claim to their talents and exertions in support of that free and happy constitution and laws, under which we live. I do not claim to myself an excessive right to this rich reward; great merit is due to the officers and soldiers with whom it was my good fortune to be associated, in the important occasion you have sought to commemorate; and to their united, cordial and patriotic exertions, aided by the interposition of Divine Providence, in a great measure do we owe the safety and prosperity of our beloved city. (Sheads 1999, 65–66)

In 1828, Baltimore dedicated an eight-foot marble monument to Armistead, which was decorated with military emblems. After it fell into disrepair, it was replaced in 1882 by a fourteen-foot-high memorial at Eutaw Place that was moved in 1886 to Federal Hill, where it remains. In 1914 a bronze statue of Armistead executed by Edward Berge was dedicated at Fort McHenry during the National Star-Spangled Banner Centennial Celebrations (Shead 1999, 29–30).

See also: Baltimore, Maryland; Fort McHenry; Key, Francis Scott; Star-Spangled Banner Flag.

Further Reading

Armistead, George. 1814. "Official Account of the Bombardment of Fort McHenry. Copy of a Letter from Lieut. Colonel Armistead, to the Secretary of War." Smithsonian National Museum of American History (website). https://amhistory.si.edu/stars-pangledbanner/pdf/TRANSCRIPT%20Official%20Account%20of%20the%20Bombardment%20of%20Fort%20McHenry.pdf.

Sheads, Scott S. 1999. *Guardian of the Star-Spangled Banner: Lt. Colonel George Armistead and the Fort McHenry Flag.* Baltimore: Toomey Press.

Smith, Gene A. 1999. "Armistead, George." In *American National Biography*, edited by John A. Garraty and Mark C. Carnes, 1:596–98. New York: Oxford University Press.

Wood, Elizabeth Ingerman. 1967. "Thomas Fletcher: A Philadelphia Entrepreneur of Presentation Silver." *Winterthur Portfolio* 3:136–71.

Atlee, E. A.

One of the disturbing aspects of "The Star-Spangled Banner" is the fact that the third verse disdainfully refers to the slaves and hirelings that the British employed during the War of 1812. This points to the sad reality that Francis Scott Key was a slaveholder and that enslaved African Americans of that era had a better chance of gaining their freedom by joining the invading British armies than in securing it from fellow countrymen.

On July 22, 1844, a man named E. A. Atlee published a scathing new version of Key's song, called "Oh Say, Do You Hear?" in an abolitionist newspaper called *Signal of Liberty.* William Lloyd Garrison later published the same poem in the September 13, 1844, edition of *The Liberator* (Clague 2016). Atlee's grim and angry parody is titled a "New Version of the National Song" and contains four verses, each with vivid imagery. Each of the first three verses ends, like Key's anthem, with "O'er the land of the free and the home of the brave."

The first verse concentrated on the brutality inflicted on American slaves:

Oh say, do you hear, at the dawn's early light,
The shrieks of those bondmen, whose blood is now streaming.
From the merciless lash, while our banner in sight
With its stars, mocking freedom, is fitfully gleaming?
Do you see the back bare? Do you mark every score
Of the whip of the driver trace channels of gore?
And say, doth our star-spangled banner yet wave
O'er the land of the free, and the home of the brave?

The second verse, directly mimicking some of Key's language, shifts the scene from ships of war to those carrying slaves:

On the shore, dimly seen thro' the mists of the deep,
Where Africa's race in false safety reposes,
What is that which the breeze, o'er the towering steep,
As it heedlessly sweeps, half conceals, half discloses?
'Tis a slave ship that's seen, by the morning's first beam,
And its tarnished reflection pollutes now the stream:
'Tis our star-spangled banner! Oh! When shall it wave
O'er the land of the free, and the home of the brave!

The third verse emphasizes how victory for American troops will not benefit enslaved African Americans:

And where is the band, who so valiantly bore
The havoc of war, and the battle's confusion,
For Liberty's sweets? We shall know them no more:
Their fame is eclipsed by foul Slavery's pollution.
No refuge is found on our unhallowed ground,
For the wretched in Slavery's manacles bound;
While our star-spangled banner in vain boasts to wave
O'er the land of the free, and the home of the brave!

The last verse, like Key's, mentions God, while suggesting that a flag that only symbolizes freedom for its white population should be at half-mast (a sign of mourning). This juxtaposition is furthered by the jarring reference in the last line to "the death-bed of Freedom" and the description of America as "the home of the slave":

Shall we ne'er hail the day when as freemen shall stand
The millions who groan under matchless oppression?
Shall Liberty's shouts, in our heaven-rescued land,
Ne'er be shared by the slave in our blood-guilty nation?
Oh, let us be just, ere in God we dare trust;
Else the day will o'er take us when perish we must;
And our star-spangled banner at half mast shall wave
O'er the death-bed of Freedom—the home of the slave.

Muisicologist William Robin observed that "The Star-Spangled Banner" has long been a contested symbol, as evidenced by NFL quarterback Colin Kaeper-nick's refusal to stand as it was being played before football games during the 2016 season. Robin further observed that in 1861, Oliver Wendell Holmes, Sr., proposed adding the following lines to Key's song, which was increasingly being used during Union flag raisings:

By the millions unchained who our birthright have gained
We will keep her birth blazon forever unstained;
And the star-spangled banner in triumph shall wave
O'er the land of the free, and the home of the brave.

See also: African Americans; Key, Francis Scott.

Further Reading

Clague, Mark. 2016. "Abolitionist Star Spangled Banner—'Oh Say, Do You Hear?' (1844)." *Star Spangled Music*, September 3. Star Spangled Music Foundation. http://starspangledmusic.org/abolitionist-star-spangled-banner-oh-say-do-you -hear-1844.

Robin, William. 2016. "Colin Kaepernick and the Radical Uses of 'The Star-Spangled Banner.'" *New Yorker*, August 29. https://www.newyorker.com/culture/culture -desk/colin-kaepernick-and-the-radical-uses-of-the-star-spangled-banner.

Wilson, Christopher. 2016. "Where's the Debate on Francis Scott Key's Slave-Holding Legacy?" *Smithsonian Magazine*, July 1. https://www.smithsonianmag.com /smithsonian-institution/wheres-debate-francis-scott-keys-slave-holding-legacy -180959550.

Baltimore, Maryland

No city is more closely tied to "The Star-Spangled Banner" than Baltimore, Maryland. It was the prize that the British were seeking when they attacked Fort McHenry during the War of 1812, and its successful defense inspired Francis Scott Key to write the famous song that became America's national anthem.

Maryland was one of the original thirteen colonies, but it was the last to ratify the Articles of Confederation due to concerns about being dominated by the larger states, which were claiming huge swaths of western lands. Maryland had also served as the site of the Annapolis Convention, which had issued the call for the Constitutional Convention of 1787 that formulated the U.S. Constitution in Philadelphia. One of Maryland's delegates had been James McHenry, who later served as Secretary of War and for whom Fort McHenry was later named.

Maryland was founded by Cecil Calvert, the second Lord Baltimore, who had been given a grant of land to the colony by Charles I to exercise broad rights equivalent to that which a number of English bishops held over palatinates in England (Martinez 2008–2010). Although Lord Baltimore was a Roman Catholic, he had pursued a policy of religious toleration to encourage immigration by Protestants, who in time would declare the Anglican Church to be the state's official church. During the War of 1812, Lord Baltimore's namesake city supported churches of eleven different denominations (Gelles 2015, 53).

The city of Baltimore, which had been incorporated in 1796, grew rapidly in size during the nation's early decades. Its population expanded from six thousand residents in 1776 to forty-six thousand people in 1810 (Head 2015, 65), by which time it was the nation's third largest city, not far behind Philadelphia but about half the size of New York. It was divided into eight wards and had a bicameral system of government in which the lower house was composed of two popularly elected representatives from each ward and the upper house of one representative from each ward selected by electors, with a mayor constituting the city's chief executive (Gelles 2015, 37).

The city was a particular irritant to the British because it was the birthplace and production site of the Baltimore clipper, a schooner rig that was known as the fastest of its day. During the War of 1812, the U.S. Navy was small, and the nation relied on privateers to whom it granted so-called "letters of marque" to attack British shipping. The owners and crew of these vessels were motivated not only by patriotism but also by the lure of prize cargoes. Even after the war ended, many of these individuals shifted their business to prey on Spanish shipping on the authority of letters of marque from countries in South America seeking their freedom from Spanish colonial rule (Lewis 1981).

During the War of 1812, the *London Times* accordingly referred to the city as a "nest of pirates" (Sheads 1995, 17). The city had numerous flour mills that processed wheat from western Maryland (Johnston and Pilling 2014, 1). Ken Iglehart (2012) says that most city residents owed their livelihoods to shipping. The population included about ten thousand free blacks, the largest in any U.S. city of the day, as well as native-born whites and immigrants from England, Ireland, and Scotland (Iglehart 2012). The city also included French refugees from Nova Scotia and Santa Domingo with continuing ties to France and its colonies (Hickey 2012, 52).

Although the city was dominated by members of the Democratic-Republican Party, it was also the home to Alexander Hanson's *Federal Republican*, which was a highly partisan Federalist paper. It became the target of several acts of mob violence, the last of which in late July of 1812 resulted in injuries to several of its supporters, including the editor, Richard Henry Lee, and Brigadier General James M. Lingam, the latter of whom died from his wounds. This bloody attack became something of a cause célèbre throughout the nation among those opposing the war (Vile 2015, 134).

The attack on Fort McHenry, which began on September 13, 1814, and continued through the early hours of the next day, came after American militiamen suffered defeat in the Battle of Bladensburg on August 24, 1814, and the British torched most of the public buildings in Washington, DC. The British attempt to attack Baltimore by land, however, had suffered severe setbacks after American snipers killed General Robert Ross in a battle at North Point. On September 12, 1814, Fort McHenry and the city itself had benefited from preparations that Senator Samuel Smith, who commanded Maryland's third militia division, had made the previous year in anticipation of an attack (Cassell 1969). Merchants paid militiamen to defend the city, knowing that if the British made it to the city, everyone's property would be in jeopardy.

The British attack on Fort McHenry involved two-hundred-pound bombs and Congreve rockets, which not only posed threat to life and limb but the sound and sights of which must have been terrifying. Baltimore's *Salem Gazette* wrote, "The attack on Fort McHenry, by nearly the whole British fleet, was distinctly seen from Federal Hill and from the tops of houses which were covered with men, women, and children. The night of Tuesday and the morning of Wednesday until about 4 o'clock presented the awful spectacle of shot and shells, and rockets, shooting and bursting through the air. . . . As the darkness increased, the awful grandeur of the scene augmented" (Iglehart 2017).

Francis Scott Key, who had been watching the battle from a ship, did not initially know whether the cessation of British gunfire signaled the end of the attack or an American surrender. "The Star-Spangled Banner" reflected his joy in seeing the U.S. flag flying above the fort at daybreak, meaning that the British had retreated and Baltimore remained secure.

In 1916, the city of Baltimore adopted an ordinance that attempted to regulate the manner in which "The Star-Spangled Banner" would be performed. The ordinance stirred considerable controversy. Among other provisions, it prohibited the song from being played as a dancing or exit march (Rall 2015).

Maryland congressmen (most notably John C. Linthicum) and members of patriotic organizations across the state (especially Mrs. Reuben Ross Holloway of the Maryland Society of the United Daughters of the War of 1812) were among the earliest and most persistent advocates of designating "The Star-Spangled Banner" as the national anthem. Both the city of Baltimore and the state of Maryland recognize September 12 as Defenders' Day with celebrations meant to commemorate the successful defense of Fort McHenry. Defenders' Day, in fact, has been an official state holiday since 1908 (Donahue 2013, 100). Baltimore's proud stand during the War of 1812 was noted by other Americans as well. During an 1827 visit to the city, President John Quincy Adams gave a toast in which he called Baltimore "the Monumental City" and said, "May the days of her safety be as prosperous and happy as the days of her danger have been trying and triumphant" (Johns Hopkins, n.d.).

Fort McHenry and associated sites such as the Star-Spangled Banner House and the Baltimore house of Mary Pickersgill, who supervised the sewing of the Star-Spangled Banner flag that flew over Fort McHenry, continue to lure tourists to Baltimore. The flag itself, which inspired Key to write "The Star-Spangled Banner," is one of the prime attractions at the Smithsonian's National Museum of American History in Washington, DC.

Baltimore is the home to many monuments as well. Construction of its Battle Monument began in 1815 on the first anniversary of the celebration of the battles of North Point and Fort McHenry. The fifty-two-foot monument, which took ten years to complete, is the city's official emblem and is portrayed on its flag. Constructed by French American architect Maximilian Godefroy (1765–c. 1838) on a base designed to resemble an Egyptian sarcophagus, the monument sits on eighteen layers of marble to symbolize the eighteen states in the Union at the time (Johns Hopkins, n.d.). The shaft of the monument is a Roman fasces with a ribbon recording the names of all the Americans soldiers who died at Fort McHenry during the attack. The monument is capped by a depiction of Lady Baltimore, created by Antonio Capellano of Italy, wearing a crown of victory and holding a laurel wreath in one hand and a ship's rudder in the other. Twice restored, she has since been moved to the Maryland Historical Society and replaced with a concrete replica that can better withstand the elements.

See also: "Battle of Baltimore, The"; Fort McHenry; Holloway, Mrs. Reuben Ross; Linthicum, John Charles; Ross, Robert; Star-Spangled Banner Flag House; War of 1812.

Further Reading

Cassell, Frank A. 1969. "Baltimore in 1813: A Study of Urban Defense in the War of 1812." *Military Affairs* 33 (December): 349–61.

Donahue, Alice D. 2013. "*The Star-Spangled Banner* Weekend, September 7–9, 2012." *Public Historian* 35 (February): 100–4.

Gelles, Aunaleah V. 2015. "Commemorating the Defense of Baltimore, 1815–2015." Master's thesis, University of Maryland, Baltimore County.

Head, David. 2015. *Privateers of the Americas: Spanish American Privateering from the United States in the Early Republic.* Athens: University of Georgia Press.

Hickey, Donald R. 2012. *The War of 1812: A Forgotten Conflict.* Bicentennial edition. Urbana: University of Illinois Press.

Iglehart, Ken. 2012. "200 Years: The War of 1812." *Baltimore Magazine.* https://www
.baltimoremagazine.com/2012/6/1/200-years-the-war-of-1812.

Johns Hopkins, n.d. "Battle Monument." Explore Baltimore Heritage (website). https://
exp.ore.baltimoreheritage.org/items/show/2.

Johnston, Sally, and Pat Pilling. 2014. *Mary Young Pickersgill: Flag Maker of the Star-
Spangled Banner.* Bloomington, IN: AuthorHouse.

Lewis, Walker. 1981. "John Quincy Adams and the Baltimore 'Pirates.'" *American Bar
Association Journal* 67 (August): 1010–14.

Martinez, Albert J., Jr. 2008–2010. "The Palatinate Clause of the Maryland Charter,
1632–1776: From Independent Jurisdiction to Independence." *American Journal
of Legal History* 50 (July 6): 305–25.

Morley, Jefferson. 2012. *Snow-Storm in August: Washington City, Francis Scott Key, and
the Forgotten Race Riot of 1835.* New York: Doubleday.

Rall, Laura. 2015. "You May Have Been Illegally Singing the National Anthem Your
Whole Life." *Star Spangled Music* (blog). Star Spangled Music Foundation,
December 4. http://starspangledmusic.org/you-may-have-been-illegally-singing
-the-national-anthem-your-whole-life.

Sheads, Scott S. 1986. *The Rockets' Red Glare: The Maritime Defense of Baltimore in
1814.* Centreville, MD: Tidewater.

Sheads, Scott S. 1995. *Fort McHenry.* Baltimore: Nautical & Aviation Publishing Company of America.

Smith, Herbert C., and John T. Willis. 2012. *Maryland Politics and Government.* Lincoln:
University of Nebraska Press.

Vile, John R. 2015. *The Wisest Council in the World: Restoring the Character Sketches by
William Pierce of Georgia of the Delegates to the Constitutional Convention of
1787.* Athens: University of Georgia Press.

Barr, Roseanne

The last fifty years have witnessed the rise of a number of unusual, highly publicized renditions of "The Star-Spangled Banner" at public events. These performances have ranged from Jose Feliciano's folk rendition at a World Series game in
1968 and Jimi Hendrix's distortion-heavy electric guitar performance of the song
at the Woodstock rock concert in 1969 to Whitney Houston's rousing performance
at the 1991 Super Bowl.

There is general agreement, however, that none have been as notoriously unsuccessful as the performance by comedian Roseanne Barr (1952–) on July 25, 1990,
at San Diego's Jack Murphy Stadium between games of a baseball doubleheader
between the San Diego Padres and the Cincinnati Reds. Barr had achieved fame
as the irreverent, wisecracking star of *Roseanne*, a working-class comedy that ran
on the ABC network from 1988 to 1997. The comedian-actress was not known for
her singing, but there is still debate as to whether she sang the national anthem
purposely off-key or whether she simply got off-key and attempted to play to the
audience. The situation was exacerbated when she put her fingers in her ears,
probably to block the audio delay. As she continued singing off-key, the crowd
began booing loudly. As she finished, instead of walking quietly away, Barr
attempted to get a laugh by grabbing her crotch and spitting. Whether this was an
attempt to mock the stereotypical behavior of baseball players on the field or a

hostile response to the crowd was unclear. Whatever her motivation, the coarse gesture further exacerbated the crowd's negative reaction to what many considered to be a disgraceful and insulting performance. Opera singer Robert Merrill, who often performed the anthem at Yankee Stadium, later likened the performance to a flag burning (Collins 2018).

For her part, in a press conference on July 27, 1990, Barr said, "I'm not going to apologize for doing it, because I feel like it was the wrong choice for all of us to make. But not anybody anticipated (the reaction) would be this negative . . . You can all take this as fun or you can act like this is the worst thing committed by an American. I went down there with the best intentions. We thought it would be a fun, positive thing . . . I'm sorry I didn't sing so good. How much more can I say?" (Collins 2018).

By contrast, President George H. W. Bush remarked, "My reaction is, it's disgraceful. A lot of people in San Diego said the same thing" (Collins 2018). Steve Rippley, the first-base umpire, noted, "I don't think you should be a comic with the national flag and the national song" (Collins 2018). Barr's rendition has given birth to the so-called Roseanne Rule, which is "If you're a public figure, don't mock 'The Star-Spangled Banner' ever, ever, ever, ever, ever, ever" (Montgomery 2008).

The criticism leveled at Barr did not derail her namesake television show, however. ABC rode out the controversy and *Roseanne* ran for several more seasons, broadcasting its final episode in 1997. ABC revived Barr's television show in 2018 at a time when Barr was identifying herself as a supporter of President Donald J. Trump. The network canceled the show, however, after Barr tweeted a comment about Valerie Jarrett, an advisor to former President Barack Obama, that was widely considered to be crude and racist.

See also: Sports Events.

Further Reading

Collins, Cory. 2018. "Roseanne Barr's National Anthem: An Oral History of the Barr-Bungled Banner." *Sporting News*, May 29. http://www.sportingnews.com/us/mlb/news/roseanne-barr-national-anthem-video-padres-reds-oral-history-25th-anniversary/jf1o4z9qe1ai13ot11z0w58cl.

Kenney, Kirk. 2015. "Roseanne Barr's Anthem Still Anathema." *San Diego Union-Tribune*, July 24. https://www.sandiegouniontribune.com/sports/padres/sdut-roseanne-barr-butcher-padres-anthem-25th-years-ago-2015jul24-htmlstory.html.

McKenna, Dave. 2008. "The Other National Anthem." *Washington City Paper*, September 26. https://www.washingtoncitypaper.com/arts/theater/article/13036334/the-other-national-anthem.

"Battle Hymn of the Republic"

Of all the songs in the American repertoire, only one has become known as its "battle hymn." The song, sometimes incorrectly attributed to William Steffe, a South Carolinian who had later settled in Philadelphia, was actually adopted from "Say, Brothers, Will You Meet / On Canaan's Happy Shore." Described as "a Southern camp-meeting spiritual," this song was first published by the Methodist circuit rider Stith Mead in a hymnbook in 1807 under the title "Grace Reviving in the Soul" (Stauffer 2015, 124). In its original form, it was structured as a call-and response with the question, "O brothers will you meet me, On Canaan's happy shore?" met with the response, "By the grace of God I'll meet you, On Canaan's happy shore." The chorus intoned:

> We'll shout and give him glory, we'll shout and give him
>   glory,
> We'll shout and give him glory, for glory is his own

Before becoming the "Battle Hymn of the Republic," the song underwent a metamorphosis into lyrics that would remain popular throughout the Civil War, namely "John Brown's Body." One of the catalysts to the Civil War was a raid by John Brown and his sons (who had previously been active in Kansas) on the federal arsenal at Harper's Ferry, Virginia (now West Virginia), in an attempt to spark a slave uprising. After he was captured and hanged, Brown became a martyr for the antislavery cause.

The Second Battalion, which was also known as the Tiger Regiment, was garrisoned in Boston at the start of the war. It included a Scottish immigrant who was also named John Brown. His comrades, with whom he had formed a choral group, used to tease him about how he could be John Brown when Brown's body was "mouldering in the grave" (Stauffer 2015, 128). After the Tigers merged with the Massachusetts Twelfth Regiment, it adopted the John Brown song as its anthem, to an arrangement by C. B. March, which C. S. Hall, a Boston abolitionist, published in 1861. The verses that praised Brown as "a soldier in the army of the Lord," proclaimed, "His soul's marching on!" (Stauffer 2015, 130). Despite a jaunty beat, the lyrics were fairly coarse.

In November 1861, Julia Ward Howe (1819–1910), a poet and social activist who was married to Samuel Gridley Howe, a member of the U.S. Sanitary Commission, visited troops in Washington, DC. She joined them in singing "John Brown's Body" when her Unitarian minister James Freeman Clarke encouraged her to write more appropriate words for the song. That evening, tucked away in a room in Washington, DC's Willard Hotel, she wrote out the lyrics to the "Battle Hymn of the Republic."

Drawing from the Bible's book of Revelation and other scriptural passages (Snyder 1951), as well as from "an extensive popular culture in which biblical imagery was omnipresent" (Fahs 2001, 79), Howe launched the song with the following famous lines:

> Mine eyes have seen the glory of the coming of the Lord:
> He is trampling out the vintage where the grapes of wrath are stored;
> He has loosed the fateful lightning of His terrible swift sword:
> His truth is marching on.

In February, 1862, the *Atlantic Monthly* published this version on its front page.

The song, which is one of the most religious songs that are sometimes sung in a secular setting, takes its imagery of the winepress of wrath and "the fateful lightning of His terrible swift sword" from Revelation 14. This book, which has been interpreted as describing God's judgment on the wicked at the end of times, is particularly appropriate because it reflected the manner in which many individuals interpreted the Civil War in apocalyptic terms, the conclusion of which they hoped would, like God's final judgment of the world, bring about a new age of peace and prosperity (Stauffer 2015, 134).

Although Howe was a Unitarian, the last verse would have special appeal to a wide range of Christians. It proclaimed:

In the beauty of the lilies Christ was born across the sea,
With a glory in his bosom that transfigures you and me:
As he died to make men holy, let us die to make men free,
While God is marching on.

Black Union soldiers sometimes varied the text, as in the following verse:

We are done with hoeing cotton, we
    Are done with hoeing corn,
We are colored Yankee soldiers, as
    Sure as you were born;
When Massa hears us shouting, he will think 'tis Gabriel's horn,
As we go marching on.

Professor John Stauffer, who coauthored a book on the subject, observes that Howe's song was at once "a heroic song, an inspirational song, a revenge song, and a comradeship song" (2015, 136). Although chiefly sung by Northern soldiers, many of whom also continued to sing "John Brown's Body," the song gained wider acceptance in the 1880s as the nation sought reconciliation. As Stauffer explains, "Southerners, too, believed that they had fought for God and freedom" (139). The University of Georgia later adopted the song as its fight song, and the Progressive Party adopted the tune to "The Song of Armageddon," which it used as its campaign song. Theodore Roosevelt wanted the "Battle Hymn of the Republic" to be adopted as the national anthem. The song was a favorite of evangelists Billy Sunday and Billy Graham as well as of civil rights leader Dr. Martin Luther King, Jr., who quoted the first verse in a speech at the Alabama capital in March 1965 (Stauffer 2015, 140–41). It has special appeal among those who believe they are fighting for a holy cause, and it is commemorated by carvings on seven pillars in the Lincoln Bay of the National Cathedral in Washington, DC. The African American singer Mahalia Jackson, who was active in the civil rights movement, did much to popularize the song with her varied renditions (Collins 2003, 58–61).

Arguing that it has become a kind of "unofficial anthem" for America, Stauffer offers several reasons for its popularity. He believes that by distinguishing "us" and "them," it makes the song a natural one to adopt in wartime. He further argues that it exemplifies American civil religion, that it has been "immensely adaptable," that it "exploits the millennialist strain in American culture," that it is "aspirational," and that it "is a musical masterpiece" (2015, 144–45).

Dr. Grant Shreve, a freelance writer, notes that the opening line of the "Battle Hymn of the Republic" is engraved on the base of a statue by Donald Harcourt De Lue (1897–1968) called "The Spirit of American Youth Rising from the Waves" at the Normandy American Cemetery and Memorial in Coleville-sur-Mer, France. This cemetery is the final resting place for more than ninety-three hundred American servicemen who were killed at the decisive Battle of Normandy during World War II. Shreve observes, "De Lue's use of the poem's line transforms into a testament to the promises of internationalism after World War II" (2017).

Yet another inspiriting song that arose from the Union side during the U.S. Civil War was "The Battle Cry of Freedom," which was written by Chicago music publisher George Frederick Root in 1861. Urging fellow citizens to "rally round the flag" while "shouting the battle cry of freedom," the song was particularly effective in encouraging men to enlist for the war effort (Lyons 1942, 53–57; Spofford 1904, 234).

Howe wrote another song entitled "Child's American Hymn," which lauds America as a "country of the free." Praising American "fathers from beyond the sea," in its third and final verse, it notes that the nation "yields her space to ev'ry race" (McConathy et al. 1946, 201).

See also: Alternatives to the National Anthem.

Further Reading

Collins, Ace. 2003. *Songs Sung Red, White, and Blue: The Stories Behind America's Best-Loved Patriotic Songs.* New York: HarperCollins.

Fahs, Alice. 2001. *The Imagined Civil War: Popular Literature of the North and South, 1861–1865.* Chapel Hill: University of North Carolina Press.

Gamble, Richard M. 2019. *A Fiery Gospel: The Battle Hymn of the Republic and the Road to Righteous War.* Ithaca, NY: Cornell University Press.

Lyons, John Henry. 1942. *Stories of Our American Patriotic Songs.* New York: Vanguard Press.

McConathy, Morgan, Mursell, Bartholomew, Bray, Miessner, and Birge. 1946. *New Music Horizons.* Fifth book. New York: Silver Burdett.

Meacham, Jon, and Tim McGraw. 2019. *Songs of America: Patriotism, Protest, and the Music That Made a Nation.* New York: Random House.

Sanders, Mary. 2016. "A Mighty Fortress Is Our Battle Hymn of the Republic: Episcopal Liturgy and American Civil Religion in the National Prayer Service on 14 September 2001." *Anglican and Episcopal History* 85 (March): 63–86.

Shreve, Grant. 2017. "The Long, Winding History of the 'Battle Hymn of the Republic.'" *JSTOR Daily Newsletter*, October 20. https://daily.jstor.org/the-long-winding-history-of-the-battle-hymn-of-the-republic.

Snyder, Edward D. 1951. "The Biblical Background of the 'Battle Hymn of the Republic.'" *New England Quarterly* 24 (June): 231–38.

Spofford, Ainsworth R. 1904. "The Lyric Element in American History." *Records of the Columbia Historical Society* 7:211–36.

Stauffer, John. 2015. "'The Battle Hymn of the Republic': Origins, Influence, Legacies." In *Exploring Lincoln: Great Historians Reappraise Our Greatest President*, edited by Harold Holzer, Craig L. Symonds, and Frank J. Williams, 123–45. New York: Fordham University Press.

Stauffer, John, and Benjamin Soskis. 2013. *The Battle Hymn of the Republic: A Biography of the Song That Marches On.* New York: Oxford University Press.

"Battle of Baltimore, The"

The 1814 Battle of Baltimore was a pivotal point in U.S. history, especially since it came soon after the trauma caused by the British burning of the nation's capital. It is hardly surprising that "The Star-Spangled Banner," originally entitled the "Defence of Fort M'Henry," was not the only song commemorating the occasion.

About two months after the British fleet retreated from its assault on Baltimore, John Gruber and Daniel May of Hagerstown, Maryland, published a collection of patriotic songs called the *National Songster*. Immediately preceding "The Star-Spangled Banner" in the collection was another song, entitled "The Battle of Baltimore," which has now largely faded from public memory. Just as the song that followed was set to a popular melody ("To Anacreon in Heaven"), so too "The Battle of Baltimore" was set to the tune of another popular song of the day, namely "Yankee Doodle."

Dr. David K. Hildebrand of the Colonial Music Institute has analyzed and compared both "The Star-Spangled Banner" and "The Battle of Baltimore." He believes that the success of the one that was later designated as the national anthem can be attributed in part to the fact that it had greater appeal among Maryland's upper classes, who would hardly characterize it simply as a common drinking song. He further points out that whereas "To Anacreon in Heaven," upon which the "Star-Spangled Banner" was based, had "a complex metrical structure . . . the meter for 'Yankee Doodle' offered only six or seven syllables per line—just four lines per verse—and the chorus clearly repeated throughout verbatim" (Hildebrand 2014, 254, 259).

The result is that "unlike the thoughtful, reflective verses by Key, 'The Battle of Baltimore' is descriptive, unfolding chronologically through its inner eleven verses, each much shorter than Key's four. They are crammed with blunt factual information, rather than descriptive imagery" (Hildebrand 2014, 261). Whereas "The Battle of Baltimore" names and mocks British commanders (even referencing the fact that the body of General Ross, who died, was taken to Nova Scotia in gallons of rum), "The Star-Spangled Banner" does not even identify the enemy as British. Hildebrand believes it is thus fitting that "one became the official anthem (as of 1931)—a widely known, upper-class composition, perhaps even hymn-like. The other, arguably one of many possible contenders, is an unofficial, lower-class, anonymous and mostly forgotten parody to a melody considered by many today as childish." Nonetheless, Hildebrand reports that the tune "Yankee Doodle" was the selection that the band of Fort McHenry chose to accompany the flag raising on the morning after the British left the harbor (Hildebrand 2014, 264).

Whereas Francis Scott Key's composition focuses chiefly on the American flag, "The Battle of Baltimore" notably did not. It referred instead in the first verse to "the song of Glory" and in the chorus to the beating of a drum. (For full lyrics, see Hildebrand 2014, 266).

A songster published in 1817 added an additional stanza to "The Star-Spangled Banner," which at least one writer believes may have been written by Francis Scott Key himself. The stanza was a fiting complement to "The Star-Spangled

Banner" in that it focused on the Battle of New Orleans, which had followed the Battle of Baltimore. The lines, which included a number of alternate spellings, were as follows:

Hail Jackson, Coffee and all the brave band
Who gallantly foiled the foes last "Demonstration,"
Who, formed in firm phalanx, resistless did stand
Between their loved homes and the war's desolation:
Long shall Britian deplore the terrific roar
Of Tennesee Rifles on New-Orleans shore,
Where the Star Spangled Banner in triump still waves
In proudest defiance of Britain's vile Slaves.

Another song dealing with the War of 1812 entitled "The Battle of North Point" appeared in the *American Songster* of 1851 and was set to the same tune. Like "The Battle of Baltimore," it was filled with allusions to various British partici-pants, with particular focus on General Ross, who had been killed in his attempt to invade Baltimore. Referring to his boast that he would dine in Baltimore on the evening of his attack, the last lines of the fourth of five verses noted that:

When lo, their *first* fire brought down great Goliath;
He went down to dine with his aged grandsire;
To dine in our city determined was he
Or else dine in hell, so there let him be.

See also: "To Anacreon in Heaven."

Further Reading

Hildebrand, David K. 2014. "Bicentenary Essay: Two National Anthems? Some Reflec-tions on the Two Hundredth Anniversary of 'The Star-Spangled Banner' and Its Forgotten Partner, 'The Battle of Baltimore,'" *American Music* 32 (Fall): 253–71.

Lawrence, Vera Brodsky. 1975. *Music for Patriots, Politicians, and Presidents: Harmo-nies and Discords of the First Hundred Year*s. New York: Macmillan.

Svejda, George J. 2005. *History of the Star Spangled Banner from 1814 to the Present.* Honolulu, HI: University Press of the Pacific. First published in 1969 by Division of History, Office of Archeology and Historic Preservation, U.S. Department of the Interior, National Park Service.

"Battle of the Wabash, The"

One early collection of patriotic songs that included "The Star-Spangled Banner" was published by G. E. Blake of Philadelphia. The song in the collection that appeared immediately before Francis Scott Key's famous piece was called "The Battle of the Wabash: A Patriotic Song." It was written by Joseph Hutton, most likely in 1812, published in 1814, and was specifically designated as being set to the tune of "To Anacreon in Heaven"—the same music that Key had appropriated for "The Star-Spangled Banner."

As the title of Hutton's song suggested, it was designed to commemorate the disaster of a well-known battle by the Wabash River in the Northwest Territory that had taken place in 1791. There General Arthur St. Clair and his forces had been overwhelmed by a superior army of Native Americans. The Battle of the Wabash was one of the greatest early victories of Native American tribes in their struggle against U.S. forces.

The song consisted of five verses. The first, comparing the Native Americans to wild lions, described their surprise attack and ended with the following lines, repeated twice:

> But the laurel shall e-ver con-ti-ue to wave,
> And glory thus bloom o'er the tomb of the brave.

Subsequent verses of the song ended in the same fashion. The next two also mention specific American officers whom "their banners defended" against their foes. The fourth and fifth verses attempt to console the American officers, ironically designated as chiefs, by highlighting the ideals for which they were fighting. The fourth thus says:

> Ye chiefs of the Wabash, who gallantly fought,
>   And fearlessly heard the dread storm of war rattle;
> Who lived to see conquest so terribly bought,
>   While your brothers were slain in the uproar of battle,
>   Still fearless remain,
>   And though stretched on the plain,
> You shall rise on the records of Freedom again.

Similarly, the fifth verse extolls the sacrifices of the American troops:

> Ye sons of Columbia when danger is nigh,
>   And Liberty calls round her standard to rally;
> For your Country, your wives, and your children, to die,
>   Resolve on your foes, in stern valour to rally [possibly sally];
>   Every hero secure,
>   That his fame shall endure,
> 'Till eternity, time in oblivion immure [confine];
>   For the laurel shall e-ver con-ti-nue to wave,
>   And glory thus boom o'er the tomb of the brave,
>   But the laurel shall e-ver con-ti-une to wave,
>   And glory thus bloom o'er the tomb of the brave.

The song is notable not only for being patterned on the same tune as "The Star-Spangled Banner," but for its invocations of the waving laurel (a symbol of victory); for its references, however generic, to "banners"; and for the manner in which the concluding verses of each stanza reference "the tomb of the brave," which is similar in phrasing to "the home of the brave."

See also: "To Anacreon in Heaven."

Further Reading

Hutton, Joseph. 1814. "The Battle of the Wabash: A Patriotic Song." Lester S. Levy Sheet Music Collection. Johns Hopkins, Sheridan Libraries and University Museums. https://levysheetmusic.mse.jhu.edu/collection/000/004.

Beanes, William

Although it is common knowledge that Francis Scott Key was inspired to write "The Star-Spangled Banner" after watching the bombardment of Baltimore's Fort McHenry during the War of 1812 from a nearby ship, the circumstances that led him to be aboard the ship that night are less known.

Key was there as an emissary to secure the release from British custody of Dr. William Beanes, a friend who lived just outside Upper Marlborough in Prince George's County, Maryland. Beanes was born in 1749 and probably received his education from private tutors, such as learning how to practice medicine by interning with a neighborhood doctor. He married Sarah Hawkins Hanson, the niece of John Hanson, the president of the First Continental Congress, and treated American soldiers who were wounded during the Revolutionary War. He was one of the founders of the Medical and Chirurgical Faculty of Maryland and served as the first senior warden to the Trinity Protestant Episcopal Church in Upper Marlborough. Beanes lived in an elegant house outside Upper Marlborough called Academy Hill, owned a number of farms and a gristmill, and was highly regarded by his neighbors.

As British Major General Robert Ross passed through Upper Marlborough on his way to attack the U.S. capital, he used Beanes's house on August 22 and 23 as his headquarters and even held a council of war there with Rear Admiral George Cockburn. At a time when considerations of class may sometimes have linked people from different nations, Beanes apparently regarded his visitors as fellow gentlemen and treated them with respect, perhaps in part in an effort to protect his own property and slaves during the conflict. It is unclear whether Beanes led them to believe that he was a Scottish immigrant rather than a native-born citizen, whether he expressed his own opposition to the war, or whether the British simply assumed this from the fact that he was a member of the Federalist Party, whose members had largely taken an antiwar position (Magruder 1919, 221). It also seems impossible to establish on the basis of existing evidence whether Beanes entered into some formal agreement with his guests not to engage in any hostile acts against British soldiers, or whether the British simply assumed that his service as host called for such continuing respect.

In any event, as Ross's soldiers retreated back to their ships after burning the Capitol Building on August 24, a number of them, perhaps stragglers, apparently showed up and began either acting in a rowdy fashion or appropriating local property. Beanes joined with his cousin, Robert Bowie, a former state governor, to authorize the soldiers' arrest and imprisonment. After one apparently escaped and brought the news to Ross, the British commander had Beanes arrested about midnight and put on board ship, apparently with the idea of transporting him to Halifax, Nova Scotia, for trial. Perhaps thinking that they had been betrayed, Ross and Cockburn treated him disrespectfully both in arresting him and while he was aboard their ship.

After receiving authorization from President Madison, Francis Scott Key subsequently joined administration representative John S. Skinner under a flag of truce to reach the British ship where Beanes was held. Even after they agreed to release Beanes, the British commanders made it clear that they were not doing so because they thought he was deserving of freedom but because Americans had provided medical treatment to wounded British soldiers left behind. Chief Justice Roger Taney noted in a letter that the British "did not seem to regard him, and certainly did not treat him, as a prisoner of war" (Magruder 1919, 219). Taney elaborated further and said, "He was in the forward part of the ship among the sailors and soldiers. He had not had a change of clothes from the time he was seized; was constantly treated with indignity by those around him and no officer would speak to him. He was treated as a culprit and not as a prisoner of war and this harsh and humiliating treatment continued until he was placed on board the cartel" (Magruder 1919, 219).

General Ross sent a letter specifically indicating that he released him "not from any opinion of his own merit" but because letters he had received from wounded British troops indicated that that they had been humanely treated (Conner 1979, 227). Whatever their misgivings, however, the British transferred Beanes to the ship of truce during the bombardment of Fort McHenry.

However the British might have felt about Beanes, his countrymen remained firmly convinced that he had acted in the affair as a gentleman. As part of the centennial celebrations of "The Star-Spangled Banner," the tombs of Dr. Beanes and his wife were restored and surrounded by an iron fence and six columns, which are surmounted by cannon balls (Meyer 1995, 43). It contains two tablets. Both feature a waving American flag, one with some of the lyrics from "The Star-Spangled Banner." One plaque says, in all capital letters (Magruder 1919, 226):

On the site of the
MARLBOROUGH HIGH SCHOOL
Stood the residence of
DR. WILLIAM BEANES
Here General Ross Made his Headquarters
August 22, 23, 1814
On His March to Bladensburg and
Washington, Here Dr. Beanes Was Made
A Prisoner for Instigating the Arrest
Of Marauders from the British Army.

It Was to Secure His Release that
FRANCIS SCOTT KEY
Visited the British Fleet and Being
Detained During the Bombardment
Of Fort McHenry Was Inspired
By Its valiant defense to Write
The American National Anthem.
This Tomb Was Restored by the Public School
Children of Prince George's County
Assisted by the National Star-Spangled Banner
Centennial Commission
Under the Auspices of the Star-Spangled
Banner Society of
Prince George's County
1914

A second plaque, also in capital letters, reads as follows:

Within These Walls Rest the Remains
Of
WILLIAM BEANES
1749–1828
PRINCE GEORGE'S COUNTY
PHYSICIAN, PLANTER, PATRIOT
Served on the Committee of Prince
Georgians to Carry Into Effect
The Resolutions Adopted by the
FIRST CONTINENTAL CONGRESS
Surgeon in the General Hospital,
Philadelphia during the Revolutionary
War. First Senior Warden of
Trinity Church, Marlborough
This Tablet is Place by the
Medical and Chirurcical Faculty of Maryland
To commemorate One of Its Most Distinguished
Founders and Organizers
1914

The burial site was further repaired in 1985.

See also: Key, Francis Scott; War of 1812.

Further Reading
Conner, Eugene H. 1979. "Notes and Events." *Journal of the History of Medicine and Allied Sciences* 34 (April): 224–32.

Magruder, Caleb Clarke, Jr. 1919. "Dr. William Beanes, the Incidental Cause of the Authorship of the Star-Spangled Banner." *Records of the Columbia Historical Society* 22:207–25.

Meyer, Sam. 1995. *Paradoxes of Fame: The Francis Scott Key Story*. Annapolis, MD: Eastwind.

"Birth of the Star-Spangled Banner, The"

On August 28, 1914, the Edison Film Company released an historical drama, consisting of approximately two thousand feet of film, entitled "The Birth of the Star-Spangled Banner." Written by J. W. Blake and directed by George A. Lessey, it would have had subtitles and was likely accompanied by live music in many theaters. Most of the cast appeared to consist of actors playing military personnel and their aides.

The film was a mixture of fact and fiction. As it begins, President James Madison has sent his aide, Captain Potter, with the original copy of the Declaration of Independence to secure it at Fort McHenry—in point of historical fact, Secretary of State James Monroe had sent this to a home in Leesburg, Virginia (Vile 2019, 215). In the film, Potter stops on his journey at the home of Dr. William Beanes. He and Beanes's daughter, hiding behind a screen, learn of British plans to attack the fort. Potter is able to escape with this news, but he apparently incriminates Beanes in the process, and British authorities take the doctor into custody. President Madison, in turn, sends an aide and Francis Scott Key to negotiate for Beanes's release, during which they witness the battle that became the subject of "The Star-Spangled Banner."

According to the summary of the script in an Edison Film Company publication called *The Kinetogram*, "This film is a masterpiece of dramatic production which will bring every good American out of his seat, and make him cheer till his throat is hoarse" (Mashon 2014).

Even before this film, Dr. George Svejda , a leading scholar of "The Star-Spangled Banner," believes that "the development of the phonograph contributed heavily to the increased popularity of the Star Spangled Banner" (2005, 357). He notes that the Edison Concert Band had recorded the anthem on a two-minute standard cylinder as early as 1896, that Frank Stanley recorded it on a similar cylinder in 1897, and that the U.S. Military Band recorded it on yet another in 1910 (2005, 357–58). He points out that Edison Diamond Disc Records subsequently issued records by the New York Military Band sometime about May 1914, by Thomas Chalmers in June 1914, and by Anna Case in May 1917 (2005, 358).

See also: Beanes, William; Key, Francis Scott; War of 1812.

Further Reading

Mashon, Mike. 2014. "The Birth of the Star-Spangled Banner (Edison, 1914)." *Now See Hear! The National Audio-Visual Conservation Center Blog*, September 11. Library of Congress. https://blogs.loc.gov/now-see-hear/2014/09/the-birth-of-the -star-spangled-banner-edison-1914.

Svejda, George J. 2005. *History of the Star Spangled Banner from 1814 to the Present.* Honolulu, HI: University Press of the Pacific. First published in 1969 by Division of History, Office of Archeology and Historic Preservation, U.S. Department of the Interior, National Park Service.

Vile, John R. 2019. *The Declaration of Independence: America's First Founding Document in U.S. History and Culture.* Santa Barbara, CA: ABC-CLIO.

Black National Anthem (see "Lift Every Voice and Sing")

"Bombs Bursting in Air"

Two of the most memorable images in "The Star-Spangled Banner" are those of "the rockets' red glare, the bombs bursting in air" during the British naval attack on Fort McHenry during the War of 1812. The rockets referenced in Francis Scott Key's lyrics to the song were so-called Congreve rockets, which emitted a distinctive red trail when they were fired. These British weapons would have been especially terrifying to militiamen who had never before encountered such weapons. They seem to have been especially effective at the Battle of Bladensburg in terrifying militiamen, whose defeat opened up the U.S. capital to attack.

Although contemporary Americans probably think of bombs being dropped from planes, those to which Francis Scott Key referred were being launched from ships. Rather than the cannonballs that one might typically associate with such battles, the bombs launched from aboard mortars on British ships would actually have been fired, as depicted in contemporary prints, in an arc and would have either exploded, as "The Star-Spangled Banner" described, "in [the] air" above Fort McHenry or after they landed. It is believed that the British launched somewhere between fifteen hundred and eighteen hundred bombs and rockets during their attacks on Fort McHenry. Many missed their mark, however, and one bomb that penetrated the storage area of a huge supply of gunpowder failed to ignite, thus sparing the fort's defenders from an horrific explosion. Such luck might have been furthered by the storm that raged most of the night of the shelling.

Most of the bombs fired were approximately the size of a modern basketball. Two years after the battle, the citizens of Baltimore presented Colonel George Armistead, who had commanded Fort McHenry, with an engraved thirteen-inch silver punch bowl and goblets that were made in the design of such a bomb and held by figures shaped like eagles. This set is now displayed at the Smithsonian Institution along with the Star-Spangled Banner flag (Cole and Sheads 2001, 20).

See also: Armistead, George; Fort McHenry; "Rockets' Red Glare."

Further Reading
Cole, Merle T., and Scott S. Sheads. 2001. *Images of America: Fort McHenry and Baltimore's Harbor Defenses.* Charleston, SC: Arcadia.

Broyhill, Joel

Joel Broyhill (1919–2006) served eleven terms in the U.S. House of Representatives for Virginia, from 1952 to 1974. Prior to his election to Congress, he served in World War II (rising to the rank of captain) and joined his father's real estate company. Best known for opposing the 1954 U.S. Supreme Court decision mandating racial desegregation in public schools in *Brown v. Board of Education*, Broyhill was also known for his opposition to federally subsidized housing and antipoverty legislation (Hevesi 2006).

Broyhill sought the congressional adoption of an official musical version of "The Star-Spangled Banner." It is not clear whether he was aware of earlier attempts by the National Education Association to achieve such uniformity early in the twentieth century, but Broyhill introduced his initial bill on the subject in 1955 (H.R. 341) and a revised version in 1958. It is apparently the first such bill ever to contain musical notes, and much as though it were a biblical translation, it was labeled as:

"U. S. A. NATIONAL ANTHEM
"THE STAR-SPANGLED BANNER
"REVISED STANDARD VERSION BY PAUL TAUBMAN

It marked changes, presumably from the first version Broyhill had introduced, in brackets (TRNL's Content, Context & Capacity Project 2012).

Congress never adopted this law, and performers have continued to experiment with new arrangements and genres.

See also: Controversial Performances; Flubbed Performances; "Star-Spangled Banner, The," Official Version.

Further Reading

Hevesi, Dennis. 2006. "Joel T. Broyhill, 86, Congressman Who Opposed Integration, Dies." *New York Times*, October 4. https://www.nytimes.com/2006/10/04/washing ton/04broyhill.html.
TRLN's Content, Context & Capacity Project. 2012. "O Say, Can You See?" Facebook, November 26. https://www.facebook.com/trlnccc/photos/a.404504509596658 /444431442270631/?type=3.

By Dawn's Early Light

One of the most iconic portrayals of the dawn in which Francis Scott Key observed the Star-Spangled Banner waving from the ramparts of Fort McHenry is an oil painting on canvas that was painted by Edward Percy Moran (1862–1935), probably in 1912. It depicts Key standing on board the side of a ship and beckoning with his right hand toward the flag flying in the distance. The canvas is in the collection of the City Hall Paintings of the Baltimore City Life Museum Collection. Although praising the "spirit" of the picture, historians Mark Clague and Andrew Kuster (2015) believe it is inaccurate in painting Key aboard a British rather than an American ship and in positioning the ships too close to Fort McHenry.

The Philadelphia-born son of an American artist, Moran painted a variety of American historical scenes, many of which depicted flags. These include a painting entitled *The Birth of Old Glory*, which he painted around 1917 and fancifully portrays Betsy Ross and her daughter presenting a flag to George Washington and three other men.

See also: Key, Francis Scott; Star-Spangled Banner Flag.

Further Reading

Clague, Mark, and Andrew Kuster, eds. 2015. *Star Spangled Songbook: A History in Sheet Music of "The Star-Spangled Banner."* Ann Arbor, MI: Star Spangled Music Foundation.

Moran, Edward Percy. [1912?]. *By Dawn's Early Light*. Painting. https://theartstack.com /artist/edward-percy-moran /dawn-s-early-light-1.

By Dawn's Early Light, by Edward Percy Moran, depicts Francis Scott Key on a ship looking at the flag during the Battle of Baltimore, his inspiration for writing "The Star-Spangled Banner." (Library of Congress)

Carr, Thomas

The first known arrangement of "The Star-Spangled Banner" was published by Thomas Carr (1780–1849) in Baltimore in 1814. Just under the title "THE STAR SPAN-GLED BANNER" was a misprint identifying it as "A PARIOTIC SONG," which suggests that it may have been somewhat hastily printed. Carr listed the song as having been "Printed and Sold at CARR'S Music Store, 56 Baltimore Street" (see photograph of original in Clague and Kuster 2005, xxiii). A note at the bottom of the first page notes that it was "adpd. And arrd. By T.C.," which would have referred to Thomas Carr.

Thomas Carr's daughter, Mary Jordan Carr Merryman, later observed, "Mr. Key brought his manuscript to Mr. Carr and requested him to put it to Music . . . Mr. C. was a Professor and Publisher of Music. He kept a large Musical Establishment in the City, was favorably, and well known. He had recourse to the best English works and tried several subjects and both concluded on this one and what other composition could have been better adapted for it?" (Redway 1932, 152–53).

Carr came from a family that had long been involved in musical publishing. His father, Joseph Carr, had come to America with him shortly after his brother Benjamin had made the journey. Joseph and Thomas set up shop in Baltimore while Benjamin had businesses in both Philadelphia and New York. The Carrs chiefly focused on British tunes, with the exception of "American patriotic songs, which the new nation demanded to express its new patriotism and its new partisanships" (Redway 1932, 152). In 1806, Thomas married Milcah Merryman from a prominent Baltimore family, and they both died on the same day forty-three years later.

Thomas's father, Joseph, founded and published the *Musical Journal*, which his son Benjamin edited. He served for thirteen years as the organist of Christ Church in Baltimore and passed away in 1819 at the age of eighty (Redway 1932, 154). Sometime in 1822, Thomas appears to have either sold or abandoned his music store in Baltimore and gone to Philadelphia, where he published some of his brother Benjamin's compositions. In 1840, he wrote political songs for the Whig Party.

Benjamin Carr (1768–1831), who had studied under Dr. Samuel Arnold and Charles Wesley while in England, appears to have been the most talented member of the family. He is believed to have published the first editions of both "Yankee Doodle" and "Hail Columbia," the latter initially under the title of "The New Federal Song." (Redway 1932, 156). Benjamin also composed the *Federal Overture*, which has been described as "a medley of popular, Federalist, and French Revolutionary songs," that included "Yankee Doodle" (Riordan 2011, 179).

See also: Early Printings; "Hail Columbia"; Writing of "The Star-Spangled Banner"; "Yankee Doodle."

Further Reading

Clague, Mark, and Andrew Kuster, eds. 2015. *Star Spangled Songbook: A History in Sheet Music of "The Star-Spangled Banner."* Ann Arbor, MI: Star Spangled Music Foundation.

Filby, P. William. 1976. "Music in the Maryland Historical Society." *Notes* 32 (March): 503–17.

Redway, Virginia Larkin. 1932. "The Carrs, American Music Publishers." *Musical Quarterly* 18 (January): 150–77.

Riordan, Liam. 2011. "'O Dear, What Can the Matter Be?' The Urban Early Republic and the Politics of Popular Song in Benjamin Carr's *Federal Overture*." *Journal of the Early Republic* 31 (Summer): 179–227.

Cartoons and the National Anthem

One indication of a symbol's pervasiveness is the number of times that it is referenced in popular culture. Just as such symbols as the American flag, the Statue of Liberty, the Liberty Bell, the writing and signing of the Declaration of Independence, and the U.S. Constitution are often the subjects of political cartoons, so too are references to the national anthem.

Some people believe that a 1929 cartoon by Robert L. Ripley, of *Ripley's Believe It or Not* fame, influenced the congressional decision to adopt "The Star-Spangled Banner" as the national anthem in 1931. A cartoon published in the *[Baltimore] Sun* on March 5, 1931, just after this recognition, pictured what George Svejda, who worked at the Library of Congress, described as a "puzzled" Uncle Sam asking, "I Wonder If They'll Make Me Learn The Words Now?" (2005, 340).

Since then, cartoonists of a wide range of backgrounds, from creators of popular strips to editorial cartoonists, have created numerous cartoons on the subject, many related to contemporary controversies.

Occasional cartoons have also related specifically to the writing of "The Star-Spangled Banner." Cartoonist Roy Delgado, for example, composed an illustration showing a friend of Francis Scott Key advising the author of the anthem: "My advice, Francis, is to cut the 'Oh say can you see . . .' part and just go with the last three stanzas." Similarly Glenn and Gary McCoy show a publisher telling Key, "Let's stick with your original 'Star Spangled Banner,' and pretend there never was this dance-remix version."

Many of the cartoons are fairly generic. Ironically, some use the song as a cover for misbehavior or to refer to marital discord. A cartoon by George Price shows a man returning home to a wife with a rolling pin in her hand as he waves the flag and says, "But first, our national anthem." Another by Jack Ziegler, which is probably taken from the 1950s when television broadcasters ended their day by playing "The Star-Spangled Banner," shows a woman with suitcases in hand explaining to her husband who is in bed watching television, that "the reason I'm singing the national anthem, Steve, is that I'm signing off now." In a similar vein, a cartoon published by Sofia Warren in *The New Yorker* shows individuals around a hospital bed with one person explaining, "He didn't have any last words. He just sang the national anthem and then went blank." Yet another by Charles Barsotti shows an individual about to speak (probably before a congressional committee) saying, "On the advice of counsel, Senator, I'd like to sing 'The Star-Spangled Banner.'" In a somewhat more risqué version, a man tells an undressed woman in bed with him, "But first, our national anthem."

Some cartoons are directed either to the lack of knowledge of the lyrics or the inability of many people to sing the anthem. In a cartoon by Michael Shaw that depicts a baseball game, an announcer says, "Please stand and join us in half-assing your way through our national anthem," while another has a teacher asking her students, "Who knows the words to the theme song of the United States?" A cartoon by Lindsay Foye shows two figures on a pier with one asking, "How old were you before you discovered our football club song wasn't the national anthem?" Although it is not in the form of a cartoon, the satirical magazine, *The Onion*, published a story proclaiming that a study by historians at Boston University found that 85 percent of Americans did not know the original dance moves to the anthem ("New Study Finds" 2012).

A fair number of cartoons poke fun at the number of times the anthem is played and the etiquette that surrounds such performances. A cartoon by Joseph Farris thus shows a husband announcing to a couple at a card table that "before we start our bridge game, Emily will sing the National Anthem." As members of a firm stand and salute the flag in a cartoon by Roy Delgado, one says, "I know government contracts saved us, but I still don't think we should have to hear the national anthem every morning." In another Delgado cartoon, as several men salute a women holding a phone, one says, "I wish you'd get rid of that National Anthem ringtone." Another cartoon by Hugh Brown portrayed a woman preparing to sing the national anthem before a hanging.

Cartoons sometimes apply the words, or new versions of the words of the anthem, to contemporary issues. Focusing on immigration, Mark Winger shows the face of President Trump like a red, white, and blue flag and a sidebar that rephrases the anthem to let incoming immigrants know that they will soon be leaving, following the standard "Oh, say can you see / By the dawn's early light" with:

As you arrive in this country,
To be told you're just leaving!

Likely reflecting contemporary concerns about federal budget deficits, Rex May (a cartoonist also known by the name "Baloo") crafted a cartoon in which a king tells his subjects, "Let's just say that our new national anthem is 'We Ain't Got a Barrel of Money.'" Many other cartoonists, meanwhile, have created works that focus on the American flag, the subject of the "Star-Spangled Banner." Steve Greenberg, for example, drew a political cartoon that portrays women with "Me Too" on their shirts taking a knee to a flag with the symbol of a male in the canton and red stripes that read "Sexism, Leering and Catcalls, Groping, Sexual Assault, Unwanted Contact, Sexual Harassment, [and] Using Power to Coerce Sex."

Not surprisingly, a number of recent cartoons related to Colin Kaepernick and others who have chosen to sit or take a knee during the playing of the national anthem have been published as well since 2016, when Kaepernick first took that action to protest racism and police violence against minorities in American society. A cartoon by Ramses Morales Izquierdo shows a kneeling football player being stabbed in the back with knives from the Nazis, the Ku Klux Klan, and President Trump. Cartoonist Jerry King portrays two athletes, one with "Rich" and the other with "Athletes" on their jerseys, taking a knee as one says to the other, "After we protest how oppressed we are, let's take my private jet back to my mansion so I can show you my latest sports car." Bringing the issue back to personal relations, cartoonist Tim Cordell shows a man on a knee planning to propose to his girlfriend who says, "How disrespectful!" In a cartoon by Denis Rano, a seated President Trump, who did not serve in the U.S. military, responds to the question "They're playing the anthem, why aren't you standing?" with "Darn bone spurs are killing me!"

Other cartoons about sports and the national anthem relate to the quality of the renditions of the anthem prior to games. Cartoonist Steve Moore thus has an announcer say, "And now, please stand and join us as a complete amateur butchers our national anthem." In a Jeff Stahler cartoon, one apparent member of Congress asks another, "Are you supporting Obama's position or were you just lip-syncing?"

A number of cartoonists poke fun at "O Canada," "God Save the Queen," or other anthems. In another Baloo cartoon, a scribe is speaking with a knight: "I'm writing a national anthem for the King—what rhymes with 'William of Orange'?"

With this kind of creativity, one can only imagine what cartoonists might have done had Congress adopted "Yankee Doodle" as the national anthem!

See also: Ripley Cartoon; Sports Events.

Further Reading

Cartoon Stock (website). https://www.cartoonstock.com.
Daily Dose. n.d. "March 3, 1931: 'The Star Spangled Banner' Finally Becomes the Official National Anthem for the United States." http://www.awb.com/dailydose/?p=1949.
"New Study Finds 85% of Americans Don't Know All the Dance Moves to National Anthem." 2012. *The Onion*, July 4. https://www.theonion.com/new-study-finds-85-of-americans-dont-know-all-the-danc-1819573602.
Rinaldi, Sierra. n.d. "10 Things You Didn't Know About 'The Star-Spangled Banner.'" *Readers' Digest.* https://www.rd.com/culture/star-spangled-banner-national-anthem-facts.
Svejda, George J. 2005. *History of the Star Spangled Banner from 1814 to the Present.* Honolulu, HI: University Press of the Pacific. First published in 1969 by Division of History, Office of Archeology and Historic Preservation, U.S. Department of the Interior, National Park Service.

Cheatham, Kitty

Of all the critics of adopting "The Star-Spangled Banner" as the national anthem, few were as passionate as Kitty Cheatham (1864–1946). She expressed her fierce opposition to the proposal in a statement that was first published in the *New York*

American singer and actress Katherine "Kitty" Cheatham (1864–1946) in 1916. (Library of Congress)

Times on June 22, 1918, and then as a pamphlet published later that year. One reason that her objections may have been more effective than those of other contemporary opponents is that Cheatham reveled in her own patriotic forebears, including settlers at the famous Jamestown Colony (the first permanent English settlement in North America), the grandparents of George Washington, a general (Archibald Cheatham) who fought side-by-side with Andrew Jackson at the Battle of New Orleans, a father (Richard Cheatham) who served as mayor of Nashville, Tennessee, and a cousin and brother who were serving in the military during World War I when she published her declaration.

Cheatham was a musician and actress who had studied in New York, Paris, and Berlin and performed throughout the world. She was especially known for entertaining children and is credited with introducing African American folk songs to European audiences (Martin 2017). In contrast to some critics of "The Star-Spangled Banner," she had sung the song before thousands of people. In her critique, she observed that she had done so "because I refrain from depriving any man of what he has accepted as his highest symbol of patriotism," although in doing so, "my nobler self sternly rebukes me with 'to thine own self be true.'" (Cheatham 1918, 4). Moreover, Cheatham, who was a member of the Christian Science Church, was clearly motivated by high ideals. In 1920, she published a book entitled *America Triumphant under God and His Christ*.

Cheatham, who liberally sprinkled her critique with passages from scripture and high-minded speeches from President Woodrow Wilson, had a number of concerns about Francis Scott Key's song. One centered on the fear that the anthem would drive a wedge between the United States and its British ally. She thus observed, "It behooves the people of America not to 'linger in an age that is dead and gone.'" Continuing, she said that "the 'bombs bursting in air and rockets' red glare' of a dead past can no longer disrupt Anglo-Saxon unity, nor continue its schismatic influence against ultimate world-wide unity—universal divine democracy—which is fast appearing in the dawn of a new era." Cheatham argued that "the light of truth and brotherly love" had "guided the fathers of our infant nation and the creators and signers of our Declaration of Independence, just as clearly as the star in the East two thousand years ago, led the wise men to the cradle of Christ Jesus, the Son of God, the Light of the world" (Cheatham 1918, 8, 11). She believed that an appearance of a nova in the constellation of Aquila on June 8, 1918, was another sign of Christ soon coming to earth and that America should be prepared for it.

Cheatham continued by arguing that such preparation for spiritual liberty was not furthered by singing "an old English drinking song" to "heathen gods and goddesses." She also asserted, "While I would not detract from the spirit of patriotism which incited Francis Scott Key to write his verses, and set them to this music, we need to remember that we are advancing at a tremendous rate of spiritual unfoldment. The law of progress is divine and immutable." She believed such fulfillment was hindered by the militarism of widely recognized songs like "The Star-Spangled Banner," the "Battle Hymn of the Republic," and "John Brown's Body." In correspondence that she attached to her main essay, Cheatham observed, "The music [of the Star-Spangled Banner] is an old English drinking song and its influence keeps active the intoxication of the material senses. The words are a tribute to a pagan idolater whose poisonous vine of 'myrtle of Venus and Bacchus's vine' must be mentally uprooted and ultimately forever cast out of the Anglo-Saxon consciousness" (Cheatham 1918, 5, 14, 21, 36).

Observing that American had achieved independence in 1776 and had freed the slaves in 1865, she looked forward to "a new Declaration of Independence, emancipation from *mental* slavery, as humanity discerns, through spiritual understanding a Creator who is divine, universal Life and Love" (Cheatham 1918, 22).

In attaching letters that she had written to individuals who had both supported and critiqued her stance, Cheatham further advanced the argument—without providing any evidence for the claim—that the effort to encourage the adoption of "The Star-Spangled Banner" was part of the "German propaganda" effort to sow division between the United States and Great Britain (Cheatham 1918, 27).

Responding to those who believed that "The Star-Spangled Banner" could not be changed because it was too entrenched as an institution, she said, "'The Star-Spangled Banner' is not our official anthem and therefore is not a national institution. It is an excrescence—an illegitimate branch that has been engrafted on the holy roots of our national consciousness. It is a blot on our escutcheon and in no way represents us in this momentous hour" (Cheatham 1918, 41). Cheatham was particularly concerned that the song was being taught to children, especially incoming immigrants. She noted that she rose "in righteous indignation against the inoculation of the childhood of this nation, with the mental poison of hatred, autocracy, fear, animality—the warring animus that this song expresses" (49).

One problem that opponents to "The Star-Spangled Banner" have faced is choice of an alternative. Cheatham apparently favored a song entitled "Our America," which had been written by Alice Morgan Harrison (Cheatham 1918, 55–56). This song, first published in 1916, contained eight verses:

America, America, thou gavest birth
To light that lighteth all the earth.
    God keep it pure!

We love that onward leading light;
We will defend it with our might;
    It shall endure.

America, America, our love of thee
Is freemen's love of Liberty,
    The Spirit-blest,
Which holds high happiness in store,
When Right shall reign from shore to shore,
    From East to West.

America, America, thy seer-graved seal
Foretells the perfect Commonweal
    Of God-made men;
Its eagle with unwearied wings
Is symbol of the thought-seen things
    Of prophets's ken.

America, America, on-pressing van
Of all the hopes of waking man,
    We love thy flag!—
Thy stately flag of steadfast stars,
And white, close held to heart-red bars,
    Which none shall drag!

America America, in thee is found
Manasseh's tribe, to Ephraim bound.
    By Israel's vow,
Whose destiny is heaven-sealed;
Far-spreading vine in fruitful field.
    God's planting, thou!

America, America, faith-shadowed land,
Truth dwells in thee, and Truth shall stand
    To guard they gate.
Thy planted seed of potent good
Shall grow to world-wide brotherhood,
    Man's true estate.

America, America, the God of love,
Whose name is ev'ry name above,
    In thy defense.
'Tis thou must lead the longing world
From phantom fears to Love's unfurled
    Omnipotence.

When the Committee of the Judiciary of the U.S. House of Representatives held hearings in January 1930—hearings that would eventually result in approval of a resolution to adopt "The Star-Spangled Banner" as the national anthem—a petition with five million signatures, including the support of twenty-five of the forty-eight governors, was presented in support of the resolution. Cheatham was the sole witness in solid opposition. She argued that although the president had the power to specify regulations respecting what hymn the military could designate as an anthem, he had no similar power to make such a decision on behalf of the people of the United States as a whole.

See also: Criticisms and Defenses of "The Star-Spangled Banner"; War and the National Anthem.

Further Reading

Cheatham, Kitty. 1918. *Words and Music of "The Star-Spangled Banner" Oppose the Spirit of Democracy which the Declaration of Independence Embodies: A Protest; [including] Correspondence, Protest in Defense of Children, Excerpts from Letters.* N.p.

"Legislation to Make 'The Star-Spangled Banner' the National Anthem." 1930. Hearings before the Committee on the Judiciary, House of Representatives, Seventy-First Congress, Second Session on H.R. 14. Washington, DC: Government Printing Office.

Martin, Sarah Jackson. 2017. "Katherine 'Kitty' Cheatham." In *Tennessee Encyclopedia*, October 8. http://tennesseeencyclopedia.net/entries/katherinecheatham.

"Chesapeake: Summer of 1814"

In anticipation of the bicentennial of the writing of "The Star-Spangled Banner," Michael Bandolfi (1956–) of Boston composed a cantata entitled "Chesapeake: Summer of 1814." It was premiered by the Reno Philharmonic Orchestra and Chorus directed by Laura Jackson.

As its title suggests, the cantata was designed to tell the story of the Chesapeake Campaign during the War of 1812. This campaign witnessed the ignominious defeat of U.S. forces at the Battle of Bladensburg on August 14, 2014, the torching of the U.S. Capitol by British forces later that day, and the subsequent successful defense of Fort McHenry, which Francis Scott Key witnessed and commemorated in song.

The cantata opens with premonitions of "The Star-Spangled Banner" followed by renditions of "Rule Britannia" and "Hail Columbia," as well as "Mrs. Madison's Minuet." The latter tune is designed to emphasize the first lady's narrow escape from British troops at the White House.

British confidence in eventual victory in the conflict is expressed in "See, the Conqu'ring Hero Comes!" as well as "God Save the King." The later song is, however, counterposed against "Yankee Doodle." As the cantata mimics the British bombardment of Fort McHenry, a prisoner asks whether the flag is flying, and Key proclaims, "Wait! The sun has found it . . . The Stars and Stripes still fly!" ([Clague] 2013). The piece ends as tenors sing "The Star-Spangled Banner."

See also: "God Save the Queen"; "Hail Columbia"; War of 1812; "Yankee Doodle."

Further Reading

[Clague, Mark] Usmusicscholar. 2013. "Star Spangled Cantata—Michael Gandolfi's
    *Chesapeake: Summer of 1814." O Say Can You Hear: A Music History of Ameri-
    can's Anthem* (blog), March 9. https://osaycanyouhear.wordpress.com/2013/03/09/
    star-spangled-cantata-michael-gandolfis-chesapeake-summer-of-1814.

Children

Educators often consider socialization into American values as one of their
responsibilities, especially for children who may have immigrated to the United
States from other countries. One common approach in this regard is to teach children "The Star-Spangled Banner" and other patriotic songs. A schoolteacher writing in 1942 recalled that he and other students at his school in New York City not
only had to learn the words to "The Star-Spangled Banner" but also the punctuation for a citywide contest (Aronson 1942, 107–8). Kitty Cheatham was among
critics of "The Star-Spangled Banner" who opposed it in part because she thought
its sentiments were too warlike and too dismissive of the British to be taught to
children.

At the 1914 centennial celebrations of the Battle of Baltimore and the writing of
the anthem, a sculpture by J. Maxwell Miller was unveiled that depicted a boy and
a girl holding a scroll that reads, "To commemorate the centennial of the writing
of the Star-Spangled Banner, the pupils of the public schools of Baltimore have

At the Bicentennial Living American Flag Celebration held at Fort McHenry in Baltimore, Maryland, in 2014, students donned red, white, and blue to form a living flag.
(Jay Baker/Flickr)

erected this memorial upon Hampstead Hill where in September, 1814, the citizen soldiers of Maryland stood ready to sacrifice their lives in defense of their homes and country" (Miller 2018, 23). Similarly, thousands of children were assembled at Fort McHenry at centennial and bicentennial celebrations in 1914 and in 2014 for a living flag display. An extensive survey of American children in the second through sixth grades has revealed that "songs about our country" were popular at all these grade levels (Blyler 1960, 14).

Because it has a one-and-a-half-octave range, the national anthem is more difficult to teach and learn than some other songs, and its words are considerably more complex than such tunes as "My Country, 'Tis of Thee" or "America the Beautiful." Nonetheless, in 2018 the American Public Education Foundation sponsored a nationwide sing-along on the anniversary of the 9/11 terrorist attacks encouraging children across the country to sing "The Star-Spangled Banner" at the same time.

Because the song is so difficult to sing, children sometimes make headlines when they master it. In September 2018, a seven-year-old girl named Malea Emma Tjandrawidjaja gave a rousing rendition of the national anthem at a Los Angeles Galaxy soccer game against the Seattle Sounders ("Video" 2018). It was so powerful that some participants called her the most valuable player. In December 2018, a three-year-old boy named Drake Winslow, although lacking in enunciation, sang the anthem before a Syracuse University women's basketball game (Li 2018).

In what is believed to be a first, seven-year-old child prodigy Abigail Huang of Winter Garden, Florida, played a piano rendition of "The Star-Spangled Banner" before a December 23, 2018, NBA game featuring the Orlando Magic and the Miami Heat (Cardona 2018). Earlier that year, Ridge Brown, an autistic high school senior who had never before publicly played his guitar, gave a flawless performance of the song at a pep rally at Ironwood High School in Glendale, Arizona (Lear 2018). In December 2018, meanwhile, travelers spontaneously stopped at the Nashville International Airport to sing "The Star-Spangled Banner" to a group of school children of fallen service members who were being honored by the Gary Sinise Foundation with a trip to Disney World.

See also: Cheatham, Kitty; Public Schools; Singing the National Anthem in Public Spaces.

Further Reading

Abril, Carlos R. 2007. "Functions of a National Anthem in Society and Education: A Sociocultural Perspective." *Bulletin of the Council for Research in Music Education*, no. 172 (Spring): 69–87.

Aronson, Julian. 1942. "P.S. 2 Won the War: Back in 1917 We Pupils Memorized the National Anthem and Sold War Stamps in the Office Buildings." *Clearing House* 17 (October): 107–9.

Blyler, Dorothea. 1960. "The Song Choices of Children in the Elementary Grades." *Journal of Research in Music Education* 8 (Spring): 9–15.

Cardona, Carolina. 2018. "This 7-Year-Old Girl Is a Natural-Born Pianist." *Click Orlando*, December 10. https://www.clickorlando.com/news/this-7-year-old-girl-is-a-natural -born-pianist.

Kogan, Judith. 2016. "As Patriotic Songs Lose Familiarity in Public Schools, Do They Still Hold Value?" *Weekend Edition*, National Public Radio, July 3. https://www .npr.org/2016/07/03/484563018/as-patriotic-songs-lose-familiarity-in-public -schools-do-they-still-hold-value.

Lear, Justin. 2018. "His Rendition of the 'Star-Spangled Banner' Blew Away the Audience and Shattered Stereotypes." *CNN*, April 12. https://www.cnn.com/2018/04 /12/health/star-spangled-banner-performance-trnd/index.html.

Li, Johanna. 2018. "3-Year-Old Wows Basketball Fans With 'Star-Spangled Banner' Rendition." *Inside Edition*, December 18. https://www.insideedition.com/3-year-old -wows-basketball-fans-star-spangled-banner-rendition-49349.

McCrea, Nick. 2015. "National Anthem to be Sung in Schools across US on 9/11." *Bangor Daily News*, September 5. https://bangordailynews.com/2015/09/05/news/nation /national-anthem-to-be-sung-in-schools-across-us-on-911.

Miller, Marla R. 2018. "The U.S. Flag in America's Historic-House Museums." In *The American Flag: An Encyclopedia of the Stars and Stripes in U.S. History, Culture, and Law*, edited by John R. Vile, 19–32. Santa Barbara, CA: ABC-CLIO.

"Video: 7-Year-Old Girl Crushes National Anthem at LA Galaxy Game." 2018. *ABC 7 Eyewitness News*, September 24. https://abc7.com/sports/video-7-year-old-crushes -national-anthem-at-la-galaxy-game/4328455.

Civil War

Francis Scott Key was inspired to write "The Star-Spangled Banner" after observing the flag flying over Fort McHenry after the British bombardment on September 13–14, 1814, during the War of 1812. War often nourishes national identification with its symbols, and no war in American history has been more traumatic than the Civil War (1861–1865). It erupted as eleven Southern states chose to leave the Union in the wake of the election of Abraham Lincoln, the first Republican president, who was committed both to stopping the expansion of slavery and preserving the Union.

Although Southerners somewhat reluctantly abandoned both the anthem and the American flag upon pledging their allegiance to the Confederacy in 1861, there is general agreement that the war did much to increase interest in "The Star-Spangled Banner" among Union troops who had the advantage of flying under the flag (with additional stars) that the song had originally celebrated. "The Star-Spangled Banner" was translated into German in an apparent effort to help recruitment among German immigrants (Morris 2018).

In one of the more comprehensive reviews of the role of the flag in the Civil War, Dr. George Svejda (2005) of the National Park Service documents numerous instances in which individuals or bands have played or sang "The Star-Spangled Banner." These range from a band playing the song at the raising of the flag over Fort Sumter on December 27, 1860, to the singing of the anthem as the flag was raised once again at the fort at the end of the war on April 14, 1865 (Svejda 2005, 163, 200). At a rally on January 5, 1861, at National Hall in Philadelphia there were "loud cries for 'The Star Spangled Banner,' 'Give us the glorious old Star Spangled Banner again,' and 'the band in the gallery struck up 'The Star Spangled Banner,' which was listened to in breathless silence, and vociferously applauded at its conclusion" (164).

In a much more personal story, a northern woman who asked what she could do to help the cause was told that she could sing to wounded soldiers. After singing "The Star-Spangled Banner" to one such soldier, she found that even though his case was thought to be hopeless, he revived during the singing as he "drank in every note like so much nectar" (McWhirter 2012, 102).

The song was part of the inauguration ceremonies for Lincoln, and it was featured at recruiting events for the Union, at grammar schools, and at churches for the duration of the war. It was a favorite of Union military bands, whose members sometimes played it as men marched into battle or in celebration of military victories. While many such performances were planned, others were spontaneous. After a Union victory at Fort Macon, North Carolina, on April 16, 1862, for instance, "an old man with a long white beard, leaped upon the ruined rampart with a silver bugle in his hand, and joyously blew the notes of 'The Star-Spangled Banner'" (Svejda 2005, 184).

As in the previous decades, performances of "The Star-Spangled Banner" were especially ubiquitous at Independence Day celebrations. In 1861, Oliver Wendell Holmes, Sr., penned an extra verse to "The Star-Spangled Banner" that expressed support for African American emancipation. Holmes's version was widely printed.

Because Congress had not yet chosen an official anthem for the United States when the Civil War erupted, "The Star-Spangled Banner" vied with such other songs as "Hail Columbia," "Yankee Doodle," "John Brown's Body," "Battle Hymn of the Republic," and "America." A National Anthem Contest failed to provide a single substitute. For their part, Southerners adopted "Dixie" as a kind of unofficial anthem, but they were also fond of "The Bonnie Blue Flag" and other airs.

See also: Confederate National Anthem; Holmes, Oliver Wendell, Sr.; National Anthem Contest; Popular Opinion; War and the National Anthem; War of 1812.

Further Reading

Davis, James A. 2010. "Music and Gallantry in Combat during the American Civil War." *American Music* 28 (Summer): 141–72.

McWhirter, Christian. 2012. *Battle Hymns: The Power and Popularity of Music in the Civil War.* Chapel Hill: University of North Carolina Press.

Morris, Athina. 2018. "Today in History: 'The Star Spangled Banner' Becomes the National Anthem." *WFLA*, March 3. https://www.wfla.com/national/today-in -history-the-star-spangled-banner-becomes-the-national-anthem/1030603400.

Stone, James. 1941. "War Music and War Psychology in the Civil War." *Journal of Abnormal and Social Psychology* 36 (October): 543–60.

Svejda, George J. 2005. *History of the Star Spangled Banner from 1814 to the Present.* Honolulu, HI: University Press of the Pacific. First published in 1969 by Division of History, Office of Archeology and Historic Preservation, U.S. Department of the Interior, National Park Service.

Clague, Mark

One of the individuals who has done the most to analyze and understand "The Star-Spangled Banner" and to combat various myths that surround it is Mark Clague, an associate professor of musicology in the School of Music, Theatre &

Dance at the University of Michigan as well as the school's associate dean for academic and student affairs. Clague earned his bachelors of music and his bachelors of art degrees at the University of Michigan and his master's and PhD degrees from the University of Chicago. He has also served as the board president of the Star Spangled Banner Music Foundation

In 2014, which marked the bicentennial of Francis Scott Key's creation of "The Star-Spangled Banner," Clague and Jamie Vander Broek curated an exhibition entitled *Banner Moments: The National Anthem in American Life*, which displayed various artifacts that illumined the anthem. It is available for schools, libraries, and museums at StarSpangledMusic.org.

Clague teamed with Andrew Kuster to compile and edit the *Star Spangled Songbook* (2015), which presents a history of the anthem through a collection of sheet music, with Clague writing historical introductions to major sections of the book. A companion CD entitled *Poets & Patriots* provides renditions of the songs. Clague has also edited a book about Alton Augustus Adams, Sr., the first black bandmaster of the U.S. Navy.

Clague may be best known for posting a series of posts explaining the history of "The Star-Spangled Banner" and refuting various "mythconceptions" about it. He writes under the name usmusicscholar. He has also written longer scholarly works, including a discussion of Jimi Hendrix and his renditions of "The Star-Spangled Banner" that was published in 2014 in the *Journal of the Society for American Music*.

See also: Hendrix, Jimi; Star Spangled Music Foundation.

Further Reading

Blackstone, Jerry, Mark Clague, and Andrew Thomas Kuster. 2014. "A Star-Spangled Bicentennial: A Conversation with Jerry Blackstone, Mark Clague, and Andrew Kuster." *Choral Journal* 54 (April): 6–17.

Clague, Mark, ed. 2008. *The Memoirs of Alton Augustus Adams, Sr.: First Black Bandmaster of the United States Navy.* Berkeley: Univeristy of California Press.

Clague, Mark. 2014. "'This Is America': Jimi Hendrix's Star Spangled Banner Journey as Psychedelic Citizenship." *Journal of the Society for American Music* 8: 435–78.

Clague, Mark, Jerry Blackstone, Andrew Kuster, and Dave Schell. 2014. *Poets & Patriots: A Tuneful History of "The Star-Spangled Banner."* 2 compact discs. Ann Arbor, MI: Star Spangled Music Foundation. http://starspangledmusic.org/poets-patriots-recording-project.

Clague, Mark, and Andrew Kuster, eds. 2015. *Star Spangled Songbook: A History in Sheet Music of "The Star-Spangled Banner."* Ann Arbor, MI: Star Spangled Music Foundation.

Cochrane, Alexander Inglis

Alexander Inglis Cochrane (1758–1832), the son of a Scottish member of Parliament, enlisted in his youth in the Royal Navy and subsequently saw combat in America both during the Revolutionary War and the War of 1812. After fighting in the Napoleonic Wars and serving in the Dutch West Indies, he became a vice admiral and was chief commander of the British forces in America during the War of 1812.

Cochrane had a deep hatred for Americans, whom he referred to as "a whining, canting race, much like the spaniel and require the same treatment—[they] must be drubbed into good manners" (Vogel 2013, 57). His hatred may have been fueled in part by the death of his older brother during the siege of Yorktown in the final battle of the Revolutionary War. Shortly before the attack on Fort McHenry during the War of 1812, Cochrane and Major General Robert Ross had dined aboard the HMS *Tonnant* with Francis Scott Key and John Skinner, who had come to negotiate the release of Dr. William Beanes, an American who had been taken into custody by British forces.

Cochrane, who had planned the attack on Washington, DC, that preceded the attack on Fort McHenry, had also transported Ross and others to the attack on Baltimore, which Cochrane intended to burn to the ground (Vogel 2013, 259). After his fleet failed to capture Fort McHenry, Cochrane participated in the subsequent Battle of New Orleans. Despite the British defeat at New Orleans, he was promoted to admiral and later served as commander in chief of Plymouth until his retirement.

See also: Ross, Robert; War of 1812.

Further Reading

"Alexander Cochrane." n.d. War of 1812, Biography. American Battlefield Trust. https://www.battlefields.org/learn/biographies/alexander-cochrane.

Vogel, Steve. 2013. *Through the Perilous Fight: From the Burning of Washington to the Star-Spangled Banner; The Six Weeks That Saved the Nation.* New York: Random House.

Code for the National Anthem

After "The Star-Spangled Banner" became the national anthem of the United States, official recommendations were adopted related to its performance. Many of these were set forth in a 1946 report by a National Anthem Committee that was created by the Music Educator's National Conference in 1942, which adopted the "Code for the National Anthem" ("Our National Anthem" 1946).

Stressing that "the message of the Anthem is carried largely in the text," the committee said that "it is essential that emphasis be placed upon the singing rather than the instrumental performance" ("Our National Anthem" 1946, 40). The committee recommended that men should remove their hats and stand facing the flag or the person leading the performance of the song. It also recommended that members of a band or orchestra stand, if possible, while accompanying the song.

Although the committee thought that "it is not in good taste to make or use sophisticated concert versions of the national anthem, as such," it did accept the practice of "incorporating the Anthem, or portions of it, in extended works for band, orchestra, or chorus" ("Our National Anthem" 1946, 40). Whereas the original key of the song was in B-flat, the committee recommended that A-flat be the standard for mixed singing.

Title 36 of the U.S. Code, Section 301, further specifies that when the flag is present during a rendition, members of the military (especially those in uniform) should give a military salute at the first note, that civilian men should remove their hats, and that others should hold their right hands over their hearts. When the flag is not displayed, individuals should face toward the music in the same manner as they would if the flag were present.

Legislation has been proposed from time to time at the state level to further standardize the playing and observance of the national anthem. Massachusetts has a law, of dubious constitutionality, that is designed to prohibit dance and other versions of the anthem. Congress has failed to adopt proposals introduced in the 1950s by Congressman Joel Broyhill of Virginia designed to standardize the anthem's musical score.

See also: Broyhill, Joel; Congress and "The Star-Spangled Banner."

Further Reading
"Our National Anthem." 1946. *Music Educators Journal* 32 (June): 40.
"Patriotic and National Observances, Ceremonies, and Organizations: National Anthem."
    36 U.S.C. § 301. https://www.govinfo.gov/content/pkg/USCODE-2018-title36/pdf
    /USCODE-2018-title36-subtitleI-partA-chap3-sec301.pdf.

Collectibles and Souvenirs

For better or worse the American flag is frequently used in advertising, and there is a virtually unlimited number of postcards, prints, glass and porcelain figurines, and the like related to it. Similarly, there are numerous souvenirs related to the Declaration of Independence, especially on occasions of its major commemorations (1876, 1926, 1976). In addition to numerous replicas of the Liberty Bell (including full-size replicas that may still be purchased for about $75,000), there are numerous items connected to the fairs and expositions that it visited from 1885 to 1915.

Individuals interested in collecting souvenirs related to "The Star-Spangled Banner" apart from its representation of the U.S. flag have more limited options. The Kaufmanm & Strauss Company of New York produced a tin plate that was distributed by the C.D. Kenny Company to commemorate the centennial of Key's writing of the anthem. The center portrays a picture of a bronze plaque with the dates 1814 and 1914 on either side of the top, with a coin-shaped portrayal of Francis Scott Key in the center right wrapped in a red, white, and blue flag and laurel. The bottom of the plate portrays two contemporary flags, while the four verses of the anthem are printed between three other flag shields and embraced by a blue rim with many white stars. It seems likely that other such souvenirs would have been sold for commemorations in 1914 and 2014. In 1972 the Fostoria Glass Company issued a limited-edition crystal plate depicting Key looking toward the flag over Fort McHenry surrounded by a musical score with some of the words of the anthem around the side.

Defenders' Day has been celebrated in Baltimore since 1815, and historically those festivities have produced a variety of ribbons, medallions, and other materials related to these ongoing commemorations. Not surprisingly, schedules or programs of these events have typically focused on Key's famous song. The program cover for the 1914 centennial event featured a striking image of a woman clad in white and carrying a flag in one hand and a laurel wreath in the other.

The U.S. Postal Service has long used a flag, and later simply wavy lines, to cancel stamps. Although proponents did not succeed in getting them to issue a stamp in 1914 to commemorate the centennial of the writing of "The Star-Spangled Banner," Baltimore was given permission to use a special cancellation that read "National Star Spangled Banner Centennial—Baltimore Sept. 1914" (Boggs 1938, 8). In 1948, the United States issued its first stamp honoring Francis Scott Key. It pictures his likeness in an oval between two flags, one with fifteen stars and the other with forty-eight, above his printed name and a sketch of his house in the bottom left. One first day of issue envelope contains a similar picture of Key in a rectangular frame above the words "Honoring Francis Scott Key, Author of Our National Anthem." In 2014, the United States issued a Forever Stamp highlighting individuals below a massive flag defending Fort

This commemorative plate, on display at Fort McHenry, was created in 1964 to celebrate the sesquicentennial (150th anniversary) of the writing of "The Star-Spangled Banner." (Jim The Photographer/Flickr)

McHenry during the War of 1812. There are, of course, numerous stamps depicting the U.S. flag, including a fifteen-cent stamp specifically depicting the Fort McHenry flag with the words "The Land of the Free. The Home of the Brave."

Other mementos include postcards that portray Key or various memorials that have been made to him, menus from the Francis Scott Key Hotel, and a wide variety of political cartoons that reference Key or his famous song. There is an Uncle Sam bobblehead that, when equipped with two double-A batteries, apparently sings the national anthem.

In addition to sheet music for "The Star-Spangled Banner," collectors of vinyl records might further seek signature recordings of the anthem. Collectors might also seek out a number of coins and medals like those of gold and bronze that were struck in 1914 by the National Star-Spangled Banner Centennial Commission (Magruder 1919, 225). In 1964, the Francis Scott Key Memorial Foundation in Frederick, Maryland, issued a souvenir half-dollar for the New York World's Fair that depicted the memorial at Key's gravesite and the words "O'ER THE LAND OF THE FREE AND THE HOME OF THE BRAVE" on one side and the Star-Spangled Banner flag flying above Fort McHenry on the other.

In 2012, the United States minted coins to raise money for the forthcoming bicentennial of the writing of "The Star-Spangled Banner." The silver version of the one-dollar coin (which, of course, cost considerably more) depicted Lady Liberty waving the fifteen-star and fifteen-stripe flag against the backdrop of Fort McHenry, while the reverse focused on the stars in the flag's canton. The gold coin, designated as a five-collar coin (but again, worth much more) depicted a battle scene on the obverse, or heads side, and on the reverse were printed the words "O say can you see" in Key's handwriting against a flag backdrop (Vogel 2012). Those looking for a far less expensive coin might seek out the quarter, minted as part of the America the Beautiful series and dated 2013, that depicts the American flag flying over Fort McHenry during a bombardment.

A bronze medal that appears to be from the 1930s depicts Fort McHenry, and a sterling charm depicts Key looking from a ship at the American flag flying over Fort McHenry. There are a number of souvenir spoons of Baltimore, including at least two with pictures of the Battle Monument (Rainwater and Felger 1977, 80–81), and numerous collectibles tied specifically to Fort McHenry.

There are some advertisements, like the 1958 full-page insurance advertisement by the John Hancock Life Insurance Company that shows a picture of Key looking at the bombardment of Fort McHenry. High-end collectors might look for autographs by Francis Scott Key and/or of individuals who worked to make his song the national anthem. Old prints or maps related to the Battle of Baltimore or the War of 1812 more generally would also enhance most collections.

Collectors would be ill-advised to seek souvenirs in other ways, such as the pen and inkwell that Key used to write "The Star-Spangled Banner" that were recovered from a prior theft from a museum in 1978.

See also: Cartoons and the National Anthem; Commemorations of "The Star-Spangled Banner"; Early Printings; Key, Francis Scott; Writing of "The Star-Spangled Banner."

Further Reading
Boggs, Winthrop S. 1938. "Music and Stamps." *Musical Quarterly* 24 (January): 1–10.
Magruder, Caleb Clarke, Jr. 1919. "Dr. William Beanes, the Incidental Cause of the Authorship of the Star-Spangled Banner." *Records of the Columbia Historical Society* 22:207–25.
"Memorabilia of Francis Scott Key Recovered after a Museum Theft." 1978. *New York Times*, February 14, p. 26.
Rainwater, Dorothy T., and Donna H. Felger. 1977. *American Spoons: Souvenir and Historical*. N.p.: Everybodys Press.
Vogel, Steve. 2012. "The Battle for Star-Spangled Coins." *Washington Post*, March 5. https://www.washingtonpost.com/blogs/federal-eye/post/star-spangled-coins -released/2012/03/02/gIQAz3TgnR_blog.html.

"Columbia, the Gem of the Ocean"

One of the patriotic songs that was popular during the nineteenth century and considered for designation as America's national anthem was a song written by actor Thomas A'Becket in 1843 at the request of singer David T. Shaw, who was looking for a tune that would bring audiences to their feet (Collins 2003, 70–71).

The resulting song, "Columbia, the Gem of the Ocean" (sometimes published under the title "Columbia, the Land of the Brave"), appears to have been based on a similar song, "Britannia, the Pride of the Ocean," which had been composed the prior year by Stephen Joseph Meany and set to words by Thomas E. Williams (Grattan 1915, 159). This would explain why the term "gem," which was sometimes applied to islands, might now be attributed to only part of the North American continent. Like "The Star-Spangled Banner," "Columbia, the Gem of the Ocean" referred to "the home of the brave and the free." Instead of identifying the U.S. flag as a star-spangled banner, the song refers to "the red, white, and blue," a term that, while often applied to the U.S. flag, could equally apply to the British Union Jack.

One indication of the continuing influence of the song is the manner in which parts of it have been appropriated by other composers of patriotic songs. Scholar David Thurmaier has demonstrated how Charles Ives (in his song "The Fourth of July") and other songwriters used short fragments of the song in their works (Thurmaier 2014, 52).

See also: Congress and "The Star-Spangled Banner"; Star-Spangled Banner Flag.

Further Reading

Collins, Ace. 2003. *Songs Sung Red, White, and Blue: The Stories Behind America's Best-Loved Patriotic Songs.* New York: HarperCollins.

"Columbia the Gem of the Ocean." 2002. Song-Collection. Library of Congress. https://www.loc.gov/item/ihas.200000004.

Flood, W. H. Grattan. 1915. "'Britannia, the Pride of the Ocean': Origin of the Song and Tune." *Musical Times* 56 (March 1): 159.

Thurmaier, David. 2014. "'When Borne by the Red, White, and Blue': Charles Ives and Patriotic Quotation." *American Music* 32 (Spring): 46–81.

Commemorations of "The Star-Spangled Banner"

One of the reasons that "The Star-Spangled Banner" proved popular from its inception was that it commemorated a victory in a bitterly fought conflict—the War of 1812—that had contained as many defeats for the United States (particularly in its futile efforts to conquer British-controlled Canada) as triumphs. On September 12, 1815, a year after the attempted invasion of Baltimore by British forces had begun, Baltimore celebrated what became known as Defenders' Day. In 1908, the state declared September 12 to be an annual state holiday.

In a history thesis, Aunaleah Gelles noted that thousands of people, many with memories of the battle still fresh on their minds, showed up for the first Defenders' Day commemoration, which she described as "pious and solemn" (2015, 15). She also wrote that this attitude of "gratitude and reverence" continued throughout the nineteenth century, including the Civil War, when Fort McHenry held Frank Howard Key, the grandson of the anthem's author and the editor of a pro-Southern newspaper, as a prisoner. In 1864 the mayor of Baltimore urged citizens to display flags on the fiftieth anniversary of the bombardment (Sheads and Lunz 1998, 306).

For the one hundredth anniversary of the writing of "The Star-Spangled Banner" in 1914, the city of Baltimore decorated homes and storefronts with flags. (*Baltimore Sun* file photo)

In 1889, the city marked the seventy-fifth anniversary of the defense of Fort McHenry and the writing of "The Star-Spangled Banner." The event was attended by President Benjamin Harrison and included "a 15,000-person parade, battle reenactments, and a rendition of 'The Star-Spangled Banner' performed by a 415-piece band and a chorus 500 voices strong" (Gelles 2015, 68). It also included "an 'auto parade,' a carnival of electric lights, a military ball, an outdoor concert, fireworks over Fort McHenry, a display of visiting ships in the harbor, and schoolchildren forming a human flag" (69).

As might be expected, centennial celebrations, which were held from September 6–13 in 1914, were even more extravagant. During a time when delegates from Philadelphia had been accompanying the Liberty Bell on tours throughout the country, in early 1914 Baltimore Mayor James Preston visited sixteen states and twenty-two cities to promote the celebration of the anthem (Gelles 2015, 19). The eight days of festivities were respectively designated as "Patriots' Day, Industrial Day, Francis Scott Key Day, Fraternal Orders' Day, Municipal Day, Army and Navy Day, Star-Spangled Banner Day, and Peace Day" (19). A chorus of five thousand people and a band of sixty instrumentalists performed for fifty thousand people, while six thousand school children created a human flag at Fort McHenry, which also witnessed a display of fireworks and a speech by then Secretary of State William Jennings Bryan (19–20). Congress spent $50,000 to refurbish its oldest frigate, the USS *Constitution,* which it stationed in the city for the celebration (O'Connell 1914, 68), while the Smithsonian Institution restored the flag that inspired Francis Scott Key (Miller 2018, 23).

The year 1914 also witnessed the unveiling of a number of commemorative tablets and the creation of the Centennial Monument in Patterson Park, which included a sculpture by J. Maxwell Miller depicting two children holding a scroll that reads, "To commemorate the centennial of the writing of the Star-Spangled Banner, the pupils of the public schools of Baltimore have erected this memorial upon Hampstead Hill where in September, 1814, the citizen soldiers of Maryland stood ready to sacrifice their lives in defense of their homes and their country" (Miller 2018, 23). The city and state also used the occasion to highlight the suitability of "The Star-Spangled Banner" as the national anthem.

Although the dedication took place on Flag Day in 1922, rather than on Defenders' Day, President Warren G. Harding traveled to Fort McHenry to attend the unveiling of a statue of Orpheus as the Francis Scott Key Memorial. His accompanying address was the first presidential address to be carried on national radio. In 1942, another live broadcast described the induction of new recruits into the armed services and the dedication of a new Coast Guard Training Station at the fort. In 1954, the Maryland Historical Society unveiled the earliest known copy of "The Star-Spangled Banner" sheet music as part of an exhibition on the War of 1812 (Sheads and Lunz 1998, 310–11).

The 175th anniversary celebrations held in 1979 featured eight days of celebration that included the composition and performance of a musical drama entitled "O'er the Ramparts," a performance by the U.S. Naval Academy Band, a parade of ships, and fireworks (Grauer 1989). It was also tied to a fund-raising effort for the preservation of Fort McHenry.

Bicentennial celebrations, dubbed the Star-Spangled Spectacular, were held from September 10–16 in 2014, with the purpose not only of highlighting the city and state's role in the War of 1812 but also for promoting tourism. School students formed another human flag at Fort McHenry, while the navy's Blue Angels flight demonstration squadron gave an air performance, and ships joined in a so-called "Star-Spangled Sailabration." There was also a televised pop concert and a fireworks display over the harbor. Forward Analytics issued a report estimating that 1.43 million visitors attended the events, about 1.2 million of whom were Maryland residents. It further estimated that in return for $4.57 million in operating expenses, the city reaped $96.5 million in economic benefit (Gelles 2015, 24).

These events combined a desire to express community pride with that of educating the public about historical events and generating tourism dollars for the city and state economies. All these aims were also augmented when the National Park Service opened its $15 million visitor and education center at Fort McHenry in 2011. As one scholar noted, these celebrations of the Battle of Fort McHenry and Key's subsequent authorship of "The Star-Spangled Banner" have "shaped public memory of the battle into a demonstration of triumph instead of a period of dread" (Gelles 2015, 33).

While early celebration included both the Battle at North Point and the defense of Fort McHenry, later celebrations have emphasized the latter over the former, which has largely fallen victim to development.

See also: Baltimore, Maryland; Collectibles and Souvenirs.

Further Reading

Breig, James. 2014. "1914 Speech Saluted 'Star-Spangled Banner.'" Gettysburg Flag Works, August 21. https://www.gettysburgflag.com/blog/history-lessons/1914 -speech-saluted-star-spangled-banner.

Dennis, Matthew. 2014. "Reflections on a Bicentennial: The War of 1812 in American Public Memory." *Early American Studies* 12 (Spring): 269–300.

Donahue, Alice D. 2013. "*The Star-Spangled Banner* Weekend, September 7–9, 2012." *Public Historian* 35 (February): 100–4.

Fahs, Alice. 2001. *The Imagined Civil War: Popular Literature of the North and South, 1861–1865.* Chapel Hill: University of North Carolina Press.

Gelles, Aunaleah V. 2015. "Commemorating the Defense of Baltimore, 1815–2015." Master's thesis, University of Maryland, Baltimore County.

Grauer, Neil A. 1989. "Seeking the Old Glory of Fort McHenry." *Washington Post*, September 7. https://www.washingtonpost.com/archive/local/1989/09/07/seeking-the-old-glory-of-fort-mchenry/3bf272e6-a8ae-4dfd-89a5-2c32147e8244.

Miller, Marla R. 2018. "The U.S. Flag in America's Historic-House Museums." In *The American Flag: An Encyclopedia of the Stars and Stripes in U.S. History, Culture, and Law,* edited by John R. Vile, 19–32. Santa Barbara, CA: ABC-CLIO.

O'Connell, Frank A. 2014. *National Star-Spangled Centennial Baltimore, Maryland, September 6 to 13, 1914.* Baltimore: National Star-Spangled Banner Centennial Commission.

Plitt, Amy. 2014. "Why Baltimore Is Extra Patriotic This 4th of July." *Conde Nast Traveler,* June 30. https://www.cntraveler.com/galleries/2014-06-30/celebrate-star-spangled-banner-bicentenntial-all-summer.

Sheads, Scott S., and Anna von Lunz. 1998. "Defenders' Day, 1815–1998: A Brief History." *Maryland Historical Magazine* 93 (Fall): 301–15.

Sullivan, Patrick. 2013. *Fort McHenry National Monument and Historic Shrine: Administrative History.* New South Associates Technical Report 2256. Stone Mountain, GA: New South Associates for the National Park Service.

Confederate National Anthem

During the American Civil War (1861–1865), the Union had no officially designated national anthem—although "Hail Columbia," "The Star-Spangled Banner," and "Yankee Doodle" were so popular in the North that the South Carolina legislature outlawed them when the state seceded (McWhirter 2012, 60). Although some Southerners did try to claim "The Star-Spangled Banner" for their own since Francis Scott Key had been from Maryland and most of his descendants allied with the South during the conflict, Southerners also composed songs like "Farewell to the Star Spangled Banner" and "Farewell to Yankee Doodle" that expressed their renunciation of those songs (McWhirter 2002, 61). Notably, there were some songs, such as St. George Tucker's "The Southern Cross" (first published in 1861), that were composed to the same musical arrangement as "The Star-Spangled Banner." Tucker's opening lines asked "Oh say can you see through the gloom and the storm, More bright for the darkness, that pure constellation?" (Fahs 2001, 71). Similarly, another song set to the same tune and entitled "The Flag of Secession" began:

> O, say can't you see, by the dawn's early light,
>   What you yesterday held to be vaunting and dreaming?
> The Northern men routed, Abe Lincoln in flight,
>   And the Palmetto flag over the Capitol streaming. (71)

As with the Union during the war, however, Southern forces never settled on an official anthem. Over the course of the conflict, however, several songs emerged that were often used to promote Southern unity. Curiously, one such song was the

French "La Marseillaise," a stirring marching song admired on both sides of the Mason-Dixon Line. The song was especially popular in New Orleans, which America had acquired as part of the Louisiana Purchase of 1803, and among Southern idealists (Stone 1941, 545), although some Southerners thought that it promoted anarchy. Moreover, Southern forces played this song as federal forces surrendered at Fort Sumter and when first flying the Confederate flag over Richmond, Virginia (McWhirter 2002, 62). Sheet music was issued under both the titles of "The Virginian Marseillaise," composed by F. W. Rosier, and "The Southern Marseillaise" by A. E. Blackmar (63).

Published by the composer in Richmond in 1862, this rare illustrated sheet music cover is titled "Our National Confederate Anthem." It features a Confederate soldier who is down on one knee holding a large flag with the words "God save the South." (Library of Congress)

The song perhaps best recognized as a potential national anthem for the Confederate States of America was "Dixie," but it too was admired in the North, with President Lincoln reputedly claiming that it was among his favorites (Hutchison 2007, 603). Indeed, when a crowd gathered around the White House after the Union capture of the Confederate capital of Richmond, Virginia, in the war's final days, Lincoln came out and told the assembled people: "Gentlemen, I cannot make a speech to-night. I rather feel like hearing music. I want to hear my favorite old tune, *Dixie*. I always did love *Dixie*; and the attorney-general says that we may have it; for *Dixie*, gentlemen, is now our own by right of conquest" (Nason 1869, 69).

Although many Southerners may have been unaware of the fact, this song had, moreover, been written by Daniel Decatur Emmett of Ohio, the author of another famous folk song called "Old Dan Tucker." Emmett had written "Dixie" for a traveling minstrel show in 1859, where it was often sung by individuals in blackface. The song received a boost in the Confederate states when the Prussian bandleader Herman E. Arnold played the song on February 18, 1861, at President Jefferson Davis's inauguration in Montgomery (McWhitter 2002, 66). The song became especially popular among Southern troops.

As originally penned, "Dixie" was written in an exaggerated African American dialect and purported to express the sentiments of a former slave living in the

North and looking back wistfully over his time as a Southern slave (McWhirter 2002, 69):

> I Wish I was in de land ob cotton,
> Old times dar am not forgotten
> Look away! Look away! Look away! Dixie Land.
> In Dixie Land whar I was born in,
> Early on one frosty mornin',
> Look away! Look away! Look away! Dixie Land.

The lines went on to describe how the slave mistress had married "Will de Weaber," whom it described "a gay deceiber" for his apparent belief that he would outlive her and inherit her property. Emmett later reputedly said that, had he realized the use Southerners would make of it, "I will be damned if I'd have written it!" (McWhirter 2002, 70). McWhirter believes that the song may have been "rooted in Confederate apprehension over slave loyalty" (70).

Just as the tune of "The Star-Spangled Banner" appropriated an earlier tune, so too there were some variations on "Dixie," the most important of which was written in 1861 by General Albert Pike, who tried to convert the song from African American dialect to a call to arms. In what was sometimes called the "War Song," he thus wrote (McWhirter 2002, 72):

> Southrons, hear your country call you
> Up! Less worse than death befall you!
> To arms! to arms! To arms! In Dixie!
> Lo! All the beacon fires alighted,
> Let all hearts be now united!
> To arms! To arms! To arms! In Dixie."

There were also Northern versions of the song, one of the most interesting by Frances [better known as Fanny] J. Crosby (1820–1915), a noted Christian hymn writer, entitled "Dixie for the Union." It was first published in 1861. The first verse was as follows (Hutchison 2007, 618):

> On! Ye patriots to the battle
> Hear Fort Moultrie's cannon rattle
> Then away, then away, then away to the fight!
> Go meet those Southern Traitors with iron will
> And should your courage falter boys
> Remember Bunker Hill
> Hurrah! Hurrah! Hurrah!
> The stars and stripes forever!
> Hurrah! Hurrah! Our Union shall not sever!

One puzzling aspect of "Dixie" was the origin of the title. One theory was that the term was named after a slaveholder named Dix whose land was reputed to be a type of paradise. Another associated it with a nickname for Louisiana, but the most common explanation was that it derived from the Mason-Dixon Line that separated Maryland and Pennsylania (McWhirter 2012, 69). Another explanation is that the term derived from an African American character in minstrel shows who was called "Dixie," which became a nickname for African Americans, and thus for the Southern states where they were most heavily concentrated (Nathan and Emmett 1949, 75–76).

Yet another candidate for an anthem for the Confederate States of America was a song authored by Harry Macarthy (1834–1888) entitled "The Bonnie Blue Flag." It originated after the president of the Mississippi Secession Convention was presented with a blue flag with a white star to the cheers of "Hurrah for the bonnie blue flag!" (McWhirter 2002, 73). Macarthy popularized the song, which contained the names of each of the seceding states, in emotional performances for Southern troops, but the song encountered two problems. Although it shared the distinction with "The Star-Spangled Banner" of focusing on a flag, the "bonnie blue flag" it described was not actually a flag that the Confederate states adopted. Moreoever, Macarthy claimed British citizenship to avoid the draft and eventually returned to England rather than serve in the Southern army. Like other songs of the day that came to be identified with one side or the other in the Civil War, Macarthy's composition was sometimes parodied in the North. A Union soldier from Iowa named J. L. Geddes, for example, wrote one such parody (McWhirter 1919, 96):

> We treated you as brothers until you drew the sword,
> With impious hands at Sumter you cut the silver cord,
> So now you heard our bugles we come the sons of Mars
>   [the Roman god of war]
> We rally round the brave old flag, that bears the Stripes and Stars.

There were similar problems with the song "Maryland, My Maryland," which was written by James Ryder Randall, a Confederate sympathizer from Baltimore who was teaching in Louisiana when the war began. His song reflected his unrealized hope that Maryland would eventually join the Confederacy. Other tunes that had some popularity within the South included "God Save the South," which was written by George Henry Miles under the pen name Ernest Halpin, and was actually published in Virginia under the heading of "Our National Confederate Anthem." As a battle hymn it was something of a counterpart to Julia Ward Howell's "Battle Hymn of the Republic." A similar song by James Pierpont was entitled "We Conquer or Die" (McWhirter 2002, 82).

Ellen Key Blunt, a daughter of Francis Scott Key who was living in England, initially pled for unity but ultimately ended up writing a song entitled "The Southern Cross" as federal officials suppressed the Baltimore newspaper that published it. One of its stanzas proclaimed (Bonner 2002, 64):

> With tearful eyes, but steady hand,
> We'll tear its stripes apart,

And fling them like broken fetters
Which will not bind the heart.
But we'll save our stars of glory
In the might of his sacred sign
Of Him who has fixed forever
Our Southern Cross to shine.

See also: Congress and "The Star-Spangled Banner."

Further Reading

Bonner, Robert E. 2002. *Colors and Blood: Flag Passions of the Confederate South.* Princeton, NJ: Princeton University Press.

Davis, James A. 2005. "Hearing History: 'Dixie,' 'Battle Hymn of the Republic,' and Civil War Music in the History Classroom." In *Music and History: Bridging the Disciplines*, edited by Jeffrey H. Jackson and Stanley C. Pelkey, 200–19. Jackson: University Press of Mississippi.

Davis, James A. 2019. *Maryland, My Maryland: Music and Patriotism during the American Civil War.* Lincoln: University of Nebraska Press.

Fahs, Alice. 2001. *The Imagined Civil War: Popular Literature of the North and South, 1861–1865.* Chapel Hill: University of North Carolina Press.

Hutchinson, Coleman. 2012. *Apples and Ashes: Literature, Nationalism, and the Confederate States of America.* Athens: University of Georgia Press.

Hutchison, Coleman. 2007. "Whistling 'Dixie' for the Union." *American Literary History* 19 (Autumn): 603–28.

McWhirter, Christian. 2012. *Battle Hymns: The Power and Popularity of Music in the Civil War.* Chapel Hill: University of North Carolina Press.

Nason, Elias. 1869. *A Monogram on Our National Song.* Albany: Joel Munsell.

Nathan, Hans, and Daniel Decatur Emmett. 1949. "Dixie." *Musical Quarterly* 35 (January): 60–84.

Stone, James. 1941. "War Music and War Psychology in the Civil War." *Journal of Abnormal and Social Psychology* 36 (October): 543–60.

Congress and "The Star-Spangled Banner"

On March 3, 1931, the U.S. Congress adopted a law to designate "The Star-Spangled Banner" as the national anthem, and President Herbert Hoover signed it that same day. Far earlier, however, Francis Scott Key's famous composition had become an important part of some American patriotic traditions. Beginning in 1889, for example, U.S. Navy Secretary Benjamin Franklin Tracy had specified that the song be played at morning flag raisings, and other military officials had added to these regulations in the interim. None, however, had the authority to designate the song as the national anthem, even though as early as 1900 a writer referred to "The Star-Spangled Banner" as just that: "above all others, [it] may claim to be the national hymn of America" (Elson 1900, 192).

Critics, however, charged that the song was too militaristic, that it was too hostile to the English people, that it was based on the music of a foreign song, and that it was difficult to sing. Moreover, there were a number of possible rivals for national anthem status, including "America the Beautiful," "My Country, 'Tis of Thee," and "Battle Hymn of the Republic." In 1910 Congressman William W.

Griest of Pennsylvania introduced a concurrent resolution that provided for the publication of one thousand copies of a report by Oscar George Theodore Sonneck on a number of these tunes (Svejda 2005, 322).

Congressman George Edmund Foss of Illinois appears to have introduced the first congressional resolution for making "The Star-Spangled Banner" the national anthem on July 24, 1912. However, Congressman J. Charles Linthicum of Maryland appears to have been the most consistent congressional supporter. He introduced his resolution to formally designate Key's song as the country's official anthem in January 1913, and he continued to do so on an annual basis until the bill finally succeeded in getting congressional approval in 1931. He was also an advocate for designating Fort McHenry as a national monument.

Numerous members of Congress introduced resolutions to make "The Star-Spangled Banner" the national anthem in the intervening years, with some attributing the music to John Stafford Smith, and others to Samuel Arnold. They received encouragement from Mrs. Reuben Ross Holloway, the president of the Maryland Society of the United Daughters of the War of 1812, as well as the corresponding secretary Mrs. James B. Arthur. The Daughters of the American Revolution, the Daughters of the American Colonists, and the American Legion supported the resolutions. Congressman Emanuel Celler of Brooklyn, New York, and Senator Millard E. Tydings of Maryland were also strong supporters.

After noting that music critic Richard Grant White had observed in 1861 that the words of "The Star-Spangled Banner" were "almost descriptive, and of a particular event . . . they paint a picture, they do not embody a sentiment," journalists Joss Fong and Estelle Caswell (2018) further observed that "the descriptive, localized content of 'The Star-Spangled Banner' meant that it had something that its competitors ('America, the Beautiful,' 'Hail, Columbia') lacked: A constituency." Although the anthem remains national, it continues to have particular resonance in Baltimore and in Maryland more generally. Investigative reporter Jefferson Morley (2013) has argued that it also had strong support among those who had continued to sympathize with the Confederate cause and who saw adoption of the anthem as a way of acknowledging Southern contributions. Citing a resolution from the Baltimore City Council, another writer observed that "unlike 'America the Beautiful,' 'The Star-Spangled Banner' has a hometown" (Sherr 2001, 91).

One impetus for the adoption of "The Star-Spangled Banner" as the national anthem was an event that took place in 1929. At that time, a newly elected member of the Erie City Council in Pennsylvania opened one of its meetings by singing "The Internationale," which is claimed as an anthem by socialists (Morley 2012, 252). This was seen as an outrageous provocation by many Americans who took issue with socialist criticisms of America's economic system of free enterprise.

Faced with questions as to whether "The Star-Spangled Banner" was too difficult to sing, supporters had recruited Mrs. Elsie Jorrs-Reilley to sing before the congressional committee considering the proposal. As she was singing, she was joined by Mrs. Grace Evelyn Boldin of Baltimore who was in the audience, with apparent good effect (Svejda 2005, 338).

On April 27, 1931, a dinner celebrating the designation of "The Star-Spangled Banner" as the nation's official anthem was held at the Mecca Temple ballroom in New York City. Over five hundred guests, including politicians and representatives of various patriotic groups, attended the event, which included a speech by Congressman Linthicum (Svejda 2005, 411–12). The National Society United States Daughters of 1812 held another ceremony on Flag Day of 1931 to mark the congressional resolution, in which Congressman Linthicum presented Mrs. Reuben Ross Holloway with the pen that President Hoover had used to sign the bill (Svejda 2005, 412). Some groups in attendance refused to march, however, when Boy Scouts carried not only the American and Maryland flags but also that of the Confederacy (Svejda 2005, 413).

In the 2010s, national anthem scholar Marc Ferris of Greenwich, Connecticut, sought the help of Representative Jim Himes of Connecticut's Fourth Congressional District to declare March 3, the date that President Hoover signed the national anthem bill into law, as National Anthem Day (Dunne 2015).

Other individuals have suggesting replacing the current anthem with another. The task of doing so is a formidable one, however. Advocates of such a course of action would have to secure majorities in both houses of Congress (or supermajorities in the case of a presidential veto) for such a law (Hunter-Hart 2017). Given the strong affinity that many Americans have for "The Star-Spangled Banner," such an effort would be enormously difficult to accomplish.

See also: Anthem; Baltimore, Maryland; Criticisms and Defenses of "The Star-Spangled Banner"; Drinking Song; Holloway, Mrs. Reuben Ross; Linthicum, John Charles; Singing "The Star-Spangled Banner."

Further Reading

Dunne, Susan. 2015. "Greenwich Author Says 'Star-Spangled Banner' Deserves a National Anthem Day." *Hartford Courant*, March 2. https://www.courant.com /entertainment/arts/hc-star-spangled-banner-book-0303-20150302-story.html.

Elson, Louis C. 1900. *The National Music of America and Its Sources*. Boston: L. C. Page.

Fong, Joss, and Estelle Caswell. 2018. "Does the USA Need a New National Anthem?" *Vox*, July 4. https://www.vox.com/2018/7/4/17531950/national-anthem-star-spangled -banner-hard-to-sing.

Hunter-Hart, Monica. 2017. "Could the United States Actually Change Its National Anthem?" *Inverse*, June 29. https://www.inverse.com/article/33437-how-could-the -united-states-change-its-national-anthem.

Knox, Felicity. 2014. "The Fight for the Anthem." *Towson University* History, TU Special Collections and University Archives, June 30. https://wp.towson.edu/spcoll/2014 /06/30/the-fight-for-the-anthem.

Morley, Jefferson. 2012. *Snow-Storm in August: Washington City, Francis Scott Key, and the Forgotten Race Riot of 1835*. New York: Doubleday.

Morley, Jefferson. 2013. "Star-Spangled Confederates: How Southern Sympathizers Decided Our National Anthem." *Daily Beast*, July 4. https://www.thedailybeast .com/star-spangled-confederates-how-southern-sympathizers-decided-our -national-anthem.

NPR Staff. 2013. "For 'Star-Spangled Banner,' a Long Road from Song to Anthem." *Morning Edition*, National Public Radio, July 4. https://www.npr.org/2013/07/04 /198418605/for-star-spangled-banner-a-long-road-from-song-to-anthem.

Sherr, Lynn. 2001. *America the Beautiful: The Stirring True Story Behind Our Nation's Favorite Song.* New York: Public Affairs.

Sonneck, Oscar George Theodore (compiler). 1909. *Report on "The Star-Spangled Banner," "Hail Columbia," "America," "Yankee Doodle."* Washington, DC: Government Printing Office (Library of Congress).

Svejda, George J. 2005. *History of the Star Spangled Banner from 1814 to the Present.* Honolulu, HI: University Press of the Pacific. First published in 1969 by Division of History, Office of Archeology and Historic Preservation, U.S. Department of the Interior, National Park Service.

Congreve Rockets (see "Rockets' Red Glare")

Contests (see National Anthem Contest)

Controversial Performances

Like the American flag that it highlights, performances of "The Star-Spangled Banner" may evoke different emotions in different citizens. School children might not fully understand the words. Veterans might remember their years of service in the military. African Americans and other racial minorities may wonder whether they share in the full rights of citizenship. Athletes might find that their thoughts about the flag are overshadowed by anticipation and/or anxiety about the game that awaits them. And performers may wonder whether they are up to the task of singing the song in the public arena.

Congress has never enacted legislation adopting a specific arrangement of the national anthem, and even if such a law were adopted, it would probably conflict with the free speech clause of the First Amendment to the U.S. Constitution. Because it stands for the nation as a whole, however, audiences might consider unduly individualistic renditions of the anthem as inappropriate attempts at self-glorification rather than as celebrations of collective identity.

Although there were controversies during World War I as to whether conductors could decide whether or not to play the anthem at concerts, most controversies over individualistic performances of the anthem appear to have occurred within the last fifty years.

One criticism that came from an earlier time was directed at Russian-born conductor Igor Stravinsky when in 1941 he premiered an orchestral arrangement of the anthem in which he varied traditional chords and harmonies. Although he was seeking American citizenship and was devoted to the United States, his foreign birth undoubtedly contributed to suspicions about his intentions.

The year 1968, which was marked by demonstrations against the war in Vietnam and the assassinations of Dr. Martin Luther King, Jr. and Senator Robert Kennedy, provided occasions for at least two controversies related to performances of "The Star-Spangled Banner." Singer Aretha Franklin became involved in the fray after she sang a soulful version of the anthem at the 1968 Democrat National

Convention in Chicago. That political convention, however, became far better known for an unrelated "police riot" that erupted when police attacked antiwar demonstrators outside the convention hall. Later that fall, Puerto Rican singer and guitarist Jose Feliciano encountered even greater criticism after he sang a soulful Latin jazz version of the song at a World Series game. The facts that Feliciano was invited to perform at a Detroit Tigers baseball game in 2010 and by the Smithsonian Institution to perform at Flag Day in 2018 indicates that much of the initial negative reaction dissipated over time.

One of the most memorable and controversial versions of "The Star-Spangled Banner" was played on electronic guitar by rock musician Jimi Hendrix at the Woodstock music festival in Woodstock, New York, in August 1969. Hendrix's fiery, distortion-heavy instrumental rendition of the song conjured up sounds of rockets and bombs described in Key's lyrics, and it diverted into "Taps" at one point in what many took to be criticism of the war in Vietnam. Many rock-and-roll historians and critics now regard the performance as a classic.

Marvin Gaye gave a highly individualistic and soulful performance of the national anthem at a 1983 All-Star Game that, while criticized in some quarters for sexualizing the song, has been largely lauded. In 2000, Faith Hill was lauded by at least one news outlet for putting some "giddyap" into her somewhat hurried version of the anthem for Super Bowl XXXIV (Reich 2000).

In 2018, Stacy Ann Ferguson, better known as Fergie, was criticized for a bluesy rendition of "The Star-Spangled Banner" at an NBA All-Star Game. Her version caused some players and members of the audience to try to suppress their laughter.

Few have had kind words for comedian Roseanne Barr's off-key performance of the national anthem at a baseball game in 1990—or for her decision to compensate for her bad singing by grabbing her crotch, an expression of crass humor that was widely denounced as inappropriate for the occasion.

Some renditions of the anthem, like that of Whitney Houston at the 1991 Super Bowl, are regarded as classics not for their individuality but for the way that they were able to unite the nation at a time of conflict—in Houston's case ten days after the launching of Operation Desert Storm to liberate Kuwait from Iraq's occupation. Mark Anthony Neal, a professor of black culture at Duke University, observed that "she turned the song into a pop hit and brought a level of musicality to the song that argued for the right of African Americans to claim it" (2019). Some performers, such as Lucy Monroe (the "Star-Spangled Soprano" who was especially active during World War II), have established their reputations largely around their skillful performances of the song.

See also: Barr, Roseanne; Feliciano, Jose; Ferguson, Stacy Ann ("Fergie"); Flubbed Performances; German-American Composers during World War I; Hendrix, Jimi; Houston, Whitney; Monroe, Lucy; "Star-Spangled Banner, The," Official Version; Stravinsky, Igor.

Further Reading

Clague, Mark. 2014. "'This Is America': Jimi Hendrix's Star Spangled Banner Journey as Psychedelic Citizenship." *Journal of the Society for American Music* 8:435–578.

Neal, Mark Anthony. 2019. "Gladys Knight Has Earned the Right to Sing the National Anthem at the Super Bowl." *CNN*, January 21. https://www.cnn.com/2019/01/21 /opinions/gladys-knight-super-bowl-national-anthem-neal/index.html.

Nix, Naomi. 2012. "Perfect Anthem? Dream On." *Chicago Tribune*, January 24. https://
www.chicagotribune.com/news/ct-xpm-2012-01-24-ct-talk-national-anthem-0124
-2-20120124-story.html.

Reich, Howard. 2000. "Faith Hill Puts Some Giddyap into National Anthem." *Chicago
Tribune*, January 31. https://www.chicagotribune.com/news/ct-xpm-2000-01-31
-0001310175-story.html.

Copyright

Modern authors and composers of musical works typically seek a copyright, which is designed to provide incentives to produce such pieces by protecting them from uncompensated uses of their work. After citing the need "to promote the Progress of Science and useful Arts," Article I, Section 8 of the U.S. Constitution thus grants Congress the power of "securing for limited Times to Authors and inventors the exclusive Rights to their respective Writings and Discoveries" (Vile 2015, 45).

Congress's initial copyright laws, first enacted in 1790, did not extend copyright protection to musical composition. Francis Scott Key, the author of "The Star-Spangled Banner," who likely considered his composition as a gift to the nation, neither applied for a copyright nor received any royalties for his composition. Nor did Thomas Carr, whose firm published the first known sheet music edition of the work (Svejda 2005, 114). Indeed, after noting that "instead of copyrighting their publications of the Star Spangled Banner, the Carrs claimed their right of ownership in notations printed at the bottom of the second page," musicologist Svejda observed that "often Carr did not receive credit from other publishers who copied and reprinted his revision of the song" (2005, 203). An intellectual property website by Sean Patrick Suiter, Chad W. Swantz, and their associates further observes that "since the song was declared the national anthem of the United States, the copyright became public domain to all U.S. citizens and enterprises" (Suiter Swantz IP 2017). This is immediately followed with the reservations that "mechanical, publishing, and performance rights may still apply."

This caveat indicates that one could not record a specific performance of the anthem and market this recording for a profit. Suiter and Swantz thus observed that "when the National Anthem is sung, broadcast, or recorded during a televised National Football League (NFL) game, the NFL owns the mechanical, performance, and publishing rights for that specific performance. The same rules apply to anthems sung by other organizations such as Major League Baseball (MLB), National Basketball Association (NBA), etc."

See also: Key, Francis Scott.

Further Reading

Cananaugh, Ray. 2016. "The Star-Spangled Banner: An American Anthem with a Very British Beginning." *Guardian*, July 4. https://www.theguardian.com/music/2016/jul/04/star-spangled-banner-national-anthem-british-origins.

Suiter Swantz Intellectual Property. 2017 "Who Owns the Copyright to the National Anthem?" https://www.suiter.com/the-national-anthem-and-copyright.

Svejda, George J. 2005. *History of the Star Spangled Banner from 1814 to the Present.* Honolulu, HI: University Press of the Pacific. First published in 1969 by Division of History, Office of Archeology and Historic Preservation, U.S. Department of the Interior, National Park Service.

Vile, John R. 2015. *A Companion to the United States Constitution and Its Amendments.* 6th ed. Santa Barbara, CA: Praeger.

Criticisms and Defenses of "The Star-Spangled Banner"

Even though "The Star-Spangled Banner" has been the nation's official anthem since Congress declared it such in 1931, and even though the military was already treating it as such years before, the song, which obviously has many defenders, nonetheless remains subject to a number of long-repeated criticisms.

Musical critic Carl Wilson (2014) focuses on three major criticisms, the first of which is that "it is elitist, in both source and form." This criticism, which is in tension with earlier criticisms that the tune was that of an "English drinking song," is based on the fact that the tune was borrowed from an elite gentleman's club in England that had used it for "To Anacreon in Heaven," which was its constitution song. Far from a local pub, the group was composed of elites, and the tune was often sung by its finest singers.

A second criticism is that the song is militaristic; although it arguably pales in comparison to such other "national fight songs" as "La Marseillaise" of France (Page 1996). Ironically, Francis Scott Key, who wrote the song, was at the time a Federalist who had opposed American entry into the war, but he had come to the defense of his native land and state when the British had invaded. The song contains vivid images of "rockets' red glare" and "bombs bursting in air," but both images are those of enemy weaponry rather than American. Kitty Cheatham, who often made presentations to children, went to great lengths to criticize the ill effects of such lyrics as "Their blood has wash'd out their foul footstep's pollution" and references in the third verse to "the hireling and slave" who faced "the terror of flight or the gloom of the grave," but it is rare to hear renditions that include them, and which, after all, were directed against those who were invading American soil. What seems militaristic to one group might well seem inspiring to another.

Although the author of an editorial in the *New York Times* had little positive to say about the anthem, he found criticisms that the anthem was warlike to be "less than compelling" in part because of its cadence. After observing that "'The Star-Spangled Banner' is not in the standard march time of 4/4 and therefore is incapable of encouraging anyone—except perhaps a battalion of ballet dancers—into battle," he cited an early *Times* editorial to say that a "national anthem, if it is anything, is a symbol of allegiance, like the flag, but allegiance has hardly any meaning until a country goes to war. It other times, it is hardly more than a stamp on a passport" (Rips 1986).

Military bands began regularly playing the tune long before Congress declared it to be the national anthem. Military personnel, who often identify closely with the flag, might also find the words to be especially meaningful, particularly the final line of each verse that identifies the United States as "the land of the free and the home of the brave." For better or worse, the song that serves as the American national anthem directs most of its attention to the flag, which is a national symbol, rather than to abstract principles, other than perhaps that of "freedom." Almost as if fulfilling the prophecy of the song, the official motto of the United States, "In God We Trust," is quite similar to that of the verse "In God is our trust" in the anthem, and to the words "under God," which Congress added to the Pledge of Allegiance in 1954. To date, court decisions have recognized both phrases as acceptable examples of ceremonial deism rather than as violations of the establishment clause of the First Amendment.

Wilson (2014) raises the further criticism that "the words are incomprehensible," accusing the song of being "full of half-thoughts interrupted by tangents that complete themselves three lines later on." He tries to find some redemption by observing that this presents an "advantage," namely that of making it "open-endedly available to reinterpretation."

This accusation is generally tied to the criticism that the song is simply too difficult to sing, especially by lay audiences, which is similar to the first criticism that it is too elitist. Wilson (2014) notes at one point that what might be "elitist" to one person might be "aspirational" to another. Enough performers are honored to be asked to sing the song that some organizations actually have competitions to decide who shall be chosen.

Some individuals have objected specifically to the term "star-spangled," which they regard as too trivial a way to describe the national banner. Citing the manner in which the last two lines of each stanza were better than the rest, Richard Grant White still exclaimed, "But even in regard to this, who cannot but wish that the spangles could be taken out, and a good honest flag be substituted for the banner!" (1861, 19).

Another concern that critics have raised, especially those writing during World War I before the song became the congressionally authorized anthem, was that the song might encourage anglophobic sentiments at a time when the United States was allied with Britain against Germany and its allies. There is relatively little evidence, however, that most Americans or British interpret the song in such a partisan fashion. Moreover, this criticism is somewhat balanced by the criticism that the song in inappropriate because it was expropriated from a British tune, rather than from an American one.

An additional criticism is that "The Star Spangled Banner" would be better if it focused more on national sentiments or ideals than on a specific event. Richard Grand White, who served on a commission to solicit a new anthem, thus observed that the words of the anthem "are almost entirely descriptive, and of a particular event. Such lines as these have not a sufficiently general application for a national hymn; they paint a picture, they do not embody a sentiment" (1861, 18). Similarly, Lucia Ames Mead, who thought Congress had no business elevating one national tune over another, complained that whereas "The Star-Spangled Banner" was "an occasional poem commemorating a stirring episode in one of our wars," other hymns "appeal to those universal experiences and broad, noble sentiments which touch the deepest emotions of all classes of people at all times, whether in peace or war" (1921, 400). By contrast, Mark Clague believes that "what makes the

Banner work as an anthem is Key's affinity for philosophical abstraction; he writes about justice and truth and bravery and courage and God's trust and perseverance and all of these idealistic things. He offers a vision for the future of the nation, not a narration of the present" (Blackstone, Clague, and Kuster 2014, 13).

Katherine Meizel has observed that Irving Berlin's "God Bless America" and Lee Greenwood's "God Bless the USA" often serve "substitutional or supplemental roles in contests that might conventionally call for the official national anthem" (Meizel 2006, 499). "My Country, 'Tis of Thee" is another song that is often used for children or those without the musical range needed to sing the official anthem.

One of the reasons that "The Star-Spangled Banner" was ultimately chosen was that it had a solid constituency of congressmen from Maryland and surrounding states who wanted to adopt it as the national anthem, whereas support for other songs was more diffuse. Writing more than twenty-five years before Congress designated "The Star-Spangled Banner" as the national anthem, Ainsworth Spofford offered a summary of criticism and defenses:

> Is "The Star-Spangled Banner" of Francis S. Key a fit composition to be regarded as a national song? It is objected to it that the lines are too long, that it is difficult to sing it in tune, and that it is too local, in describing a particular event, whereas a national song should be broadly general in character. On the other hand, it is claimed that it is original, elevated, and inspiring, full to the brim of patriotic feeling. The melody admits of solo, duet and chorus. Its spirit fitly represents a free nation, full of energy and exulting hope. It is martial enough for a battle hymn, as it was born amid the bursting of the shells, and the thunder of the guns; and its closing verse and grand choral lines fit it in a good degree for a national anthem in time of peace. (1904, 214)

See also: Cheatham, Kitty; Congress and "The Star-Spangled Banner"; Drinking Song; "La Marseillaise"; "To Anacreon in Heaven."

Further Reading

Blackstone, Jerry, Mark Clague, and Andrew Thomas Kuster. 2014. "A Star-Spangled Bicentennial: A Conversation with Jerry Blackstone, Mark Clague, and Andrew Kuster." *Choral Journal* 54 (April): 6–17.

Mead, Lucia Ames. 1921. "A Vigorous Protest." *Journal of Education* 94 (October): 399–400.

Meizel, Katherine. 2006. "A Singing Citizenry: Popular Music and Civil Religion in America." *Journal for the Scientific Study of Religion* 45 (December): 497–503.

Morley, Jefferson. 2013. "Star-Spangled Confederates: How Southern Sympathizers Decided Our National Anthem." *Daily Beast*, July 4. https://www.thedailybeast .com/star-spangled-confederates-how-southern-sympathizers-decided-our -national-anthem.

Page, Tim. 1996. "National Fight Songs." *Washington Post*, July 28. https://www.wash-ingtonpost.com/archive/lifestyle/style/1996/07/28/national-fight-songs /012f9c4b-c0f7-4413-b5aa-e809d884f76b.

Rips, Michael D. 1986. "Freedom, in Song and Literature: Let's Junk the National Anthem." *New York Times*, July 5, 23.

Spofford, Ainsworth R. 1904. "The Lyric Element in American History." *Records of the Columbia Historical Society* 7:211–36.

White, Richard Grant. 1861. *National Hymns: How They Are Written and How They Are Not Written. A Lyric and National Study for the Times.* New York: Rudd & Carleton.

Wilson, Carl. 2014. "Proudly Hailed: 'The Star-Spangled Banner' Is Militaristic, Syntactically Garbled, and Impossible to Sing. It's Perfect." *Slate*, July 3. https://slate .com/culture/2014/07/the-star-spangled-banner-four-reasons-it-shouldnt-be-the -national-anthem-but-always-will-be.html.

"Defence of Fort M'Henry"

The first printing of what is today known as "The Star-Spangled Banner," a copy of which is owned by the Maryland Historical Society, was published as a one-page broadside, either by the Baltimore *American and Commercial Daily Advertiser* or by a print shop owned by Benjamin Edes, under the title of the "Defence of Fort M'Henry." Recollections differ on whether the verses were delivered by Joseph Nicholson, Rebecca Nicholson, Francis Scott Key, John Stuart Skinner, or perhaps more than one of them (Leepson 2014, 65). It included only the lyrics, but an accompanying note indicated that the lyrics were set to the music of "To Anacreon in Heaven." The broadside also included an account of the song's creation:

> The annexed song was composed under the following circumstances—A gentleman had left Baltimore, in a flag of truce for the purpose of getting released from the British fleet, a friend of his who had been captured at Marlborough.—He went as far as the mouth of the Patuxent, and was not permitted to return lest the intended attack on Baltimore should be disclosed. He was therefore brought up the Bay to the mouth of the Patapsco, where the flag vessel was kept under the guns of a frigate, and he was compelled to witness the bombardment of Fort M'Henry, which the Admiral had boasted that he would carry in a few hours, and that the city must fall. He watched the flag at the Fort through the whole day with an anxiety that can be better felt than described, until the night prevented him from seeing it. In the night he watched the Bomb Shells, and at early dawn his eye was again greeted by the proudly waving flag of his country. ("Defence of Fort M'Henry" 1814)

Arguably, one of the most fascinating aspects of this printing is that it did not identify Francis Scott Key by name. English Professor Kim McMullen suggests that this has a larger significance: "'The Defense of Fort M'Henry' becomes the deed and charter of the discursive field at the center of one version of an emerging American mythos, and so powerful is the originary narrative Key devises that its militaristic patriotism can be heard to articulate and justify parts of the national autobiography into the present" (McMullen 1990, 415).

See also: Early Printings; Fort McHenry; Key, Francis Scott; Nicholson, Joseph Hopper; "To Anacreon in Heaven"; War of 1812; Writing of "The Star-Spangled Banner."

Further Reading

"Defence of Fort M'Henry." 1814. Maryland Historical Society. http://www.mdhs.org /digitalimage/defence-sic-fort-mhenry.

Leepson, Marc. 2014. *What So Proudly We Hailed: Francis Scott Key, A Life.* New York: Palgrave/Macmillan.

McMullen, Kim. 1990. "The Fiction of Correspondence: 'Letters' and History." *Modern Fiction Studies* 36 (Autumn): 405–20.

Defenders' Day (see Commemorations of "The Star-Spangled Banner")

"Dixie" (see Confederate National Anthem)

Drinking Song

From January 1, 1920, through December 5, 1933, the Eighteenth Amendment to the U.S. Constitution prohibited the sale and consumption of alcoholic beverages. It is therefore not surprising that when Congress was considering whether to designate "The Star-Spangled Banner" as the national anthem, one of the criticisms against it was that it had originated as a drinking song.

In point of fact, the original words to a poem written by Ralph Tomlinson entitled "To Anacreon in Heaven," and later set to music by an English composer named John Stafford Smith, had been prepared for the Anacreontic Society (Lichtenwanger 1977). It was a gentleman's club of amateur musicians that met first at a London coffeehouse on Ludwig Hill and later at the Crown and Anchor Tavern (Hildebrand 2005, 258) to drink and feast together after concerts. Tomlinson had served as the president of the society, which designated the composition as its constitutional song. The song itself was dedicated to Anacreon of Teos (c. 570–c. 485 BC), a Greek poet who was known as a poet of wine and love. Celebrating Venus, the goddess of love, and Bacchus, the god of wine, the closing verse read: "And besides, I'll instruct you like me, to entwine, / The Myrtle of Venus with Bacchus's Vine" (Hildebrand 2014, 261).

Professor Mark Clague reported that an Internet search of the phrase "The Star Spangled Banner is a drinking song" in the early 2010s produced more than fifty thousand hits, but he noted that such results require a great deal of qualification (Clague 2014). He was particularly concerned about connecting the song, which was typically sung by a single gifted performer (often to the accompaniment of a harpsichord), to a barroom song. In addition to noting that the Anacreontic Society was a leading social club, Clague noted that it was not until the latter part of the nineteenth century that individuals called the song a "drinking song." He further pointed out that even those references were to two parodies entitled "The New Bibo" and "Jack Oakum in the Suds," both of which "may have functioned less as 'drinking songs' than morality tales urging moderation" (Clague 2014). American prohibitionists would later draft their own versions of the tune to convey a similar message.

Clague believes that one appeal of "The Star-Spangled Banner" may be that Americans actually take pride in the fact "that an upstart and democratic people with a can-do 'Yankee Doodle' spirit could rise above their elite European ancestors to transform a ragtag colony into a nation due international respect. Similarly, the anthem as drinking song narrative offers the image of an always unified, sonorous, and fun-loving people as substitute for the nation's more discordant history of struggle to find community across boundaries of race, class, ethnicity, and gender" (Clague 2014).

See also: Abolitionists; Anacreon; Clague, Mark; Criticisms and Defenses of "The Star-Spangled Banner"; Smith, John Stafford; "To Anacreon in Heaven"; Tomlinson, Ralph.

Further Reading

Clague, Mark. 2014. "To Be or Not: Is 'The Star-Spangled Banner' Really Based on an Old English Drinking Song?" *Musicology Now* (blog), January 30. American Musicological Society. http://musicologynow.org/2014/01/to-be-or-not-is-star -spangled-banner.html.

Hildebrand, David K. 2014. "Bicentenary Essay: Two National Anthems? Some Reflections on the Two Hundredth Anniversary of 'The Star-Spangled Banner' and Its Forgotten Partner, 'The Battle of Baltimore,'" *American Music* 32 (Fall): 253–71.

Lichtenwanger, William. 1977. "The Music of 'The Star-Spangled Banner': From Ludgate Hill to Capitol Hill." *Quarterly Journal of the Library of Congress* 34 (July): 136–70.

Montgomery, Henry C. 1948. "Anacreon and the National Anthem." *Classical Outlook* 26 (December): 30–31.

Muskal, Michael. 2014. "'Star-Spangled Banner': Anthem Was Once a Song of Drinking and Sex." *Los Angeles Times*, September 13. https://www.latimes.com/nation /nationnow/la-na-nn-star-spangled-banner-200-anniversary-20140912-story.html.

Early Printings

The first publication of the words to the song "The Star-Spangled Banner" was apparently a broadside (a single page sheet suitable for posting) published by the Baltimore *American and Commercial Daily Advertiser*, probably on September 17, which, coincidentally, would have marked the day that delegates to the U.S. Constitutional Convention had signed the U.S. Constitution in 1787 (Svejda 2005). It was published under the title "Defence of Fort M'Henry" and was preceded with the following description:

> The annexed song was composed under the following circumstances—A gentleman had left Baltimore, in a flag of truce for the purpose of getting released from the British fleet, a friend of his who had been captured at Marlborough.—He went as far as the mouth of the Patuxent, and was not permitted to return lest the intended attack on Baltimore should be disclosed. He was therefore brought up the Bay to the mouth of the Patapsco, where the flag vessel was kept under the guns of a frigate, and he was compelled to witness the bombardment of Fort McHenry, which the Admiral had boasted that he would carry in a few hours, and that the city must fall. He watched the flag at the Fort through the whole day with an anxiety that can be better felt than described, until the night prevented him from seeing it. In the night he watched the Bomb Shells, and at early dawn his eye was again greeted by the proudly waving flag of his country. ("Defence of Fort M'Henry" 1814)

Since there is continuing dispute as to whether the work was composed primarily as a poem or a song, it may be significant that the broadside both identified the piece as a "song" and, just before the lyrics, it included the heading "Tune—ANACREON IN HEAVEN." The only two known copies of this work, one thousand copies of which were likely printed, are held in the Library of Congress and at the Maryland Historical Society. The text appears to have been set by Samuel Sands, an apprentice printer to the paper (Miller 2014). The paper republished this broadside as a newspaper article on page 2 of its September 21, 1814, issue, again with no mention of Francis Scott Key's name (Svejda 2005, 85).

The first time the song was printed as part of a regular newspaper appears to have been on September 20, 1814, when the *Baltimore Patriot & Evening Advertiser* published it on the first day it resumed publication after the attacks (Svejda 2005, 84). The newspaper editor referred to the work as a "beautiful and animated effusion" that was "destined long to outlast the occasion, and outlive the impulse, which produced it" (Svejda 2005, 84). The editor also indicated that the poem should be sung to the tune of "Anacreon in Heaven."

On June 15, 2017, the Christie's auction house sold two pages of the September 21, 1814, edition of this paper for $35,000 (it had been estimated to bring from $8,000 to $12,000) at a New York auction of "Fine Printed Books & Manuscripts Including Americana and the Eric C. Caren Collection." Referring to the British commander who had died during the attempted invasion of Baltimore, the issue of the paper that Christie's sold had observed that "it is certain their commander in chief, Gen. Ross, has paid for his cheaply earned laurels at the Capitol, with the forfeiture of his life at Baltimore. It is also well ascertained, that the invaders sustained a loss in the last affair, beyond all comparison greater than the loss of Americans in both. If they make another attempt, it will be a desperate one, and desperately will they be met. For '—The star-spangled Banner in triumph shall wave. O'er the Land of the Free and the Home of the Brave.'"

The song was published, each time under the title "The Defence of Fort M'Henry," in the *Frederick-Town Herald* on Saturday, September 24, 1814; by the Washington *Daily National Intelligencer* on Monday, September 26, 1814; by the Georgetown *Federal Republican* on September 27, 1814; by the New York *National Advocate* on September 17, 1814; by the *Boston Patriot* on September 18, 1814; by Richmond, Virginia's *Enquirer* on September 28, 1814; by *The Republican: And Savannah Evening Ledger* on October 4, 1814; by the *New-Hampshire Patriot* on October 11, 1814; and by the *Federal Gazette and Baltimore Daily Advertiser* on October 14, 1814 (Svejda 2005, 85–87). Senior music specialist Ray White of the Library of Congress also noted that the Washington *National Intelligencer* had published the words on September 17, 1814 (Miller 2014). None of these papers listed Francis Scott Key as the author of the song's lyrics.

Thomas Carr of Baltimore is believed to have published the first sheet music edition—at Key's request—on October 16, 1814 (Miller 2014). As of 2010, there were only eleven known copies of this edition. Christie's auction house sold the only known private copy to a phone bidder for $506,500 in December 2010.

At least fifteen sheet music editions of "The Star-Spangled Banner" were published in Baltimore, Boston, New York, and Philadelphia from 1814 until 1843, with a Carr edition of 1821 being notable for being the first to accompany the music with an engraving of the bombardment of Baltimore. At least sixty-nine editions of the sheet music had been published by 1864 and the first London edition was published in 1853 (Miller 2014).

The *Analectic Magazine* appears to have been the first magazine to publish the work, doing so in November 1814. It observed, "These lines have been already published in several of our newspapers; they may still, however, be new to many of our readers. Besides, we think that their merit entitles them to preservation in some more permanent form than the columns of a daily paper" (Svejda 2005, 88).

Among the most prized copes of "The Star-Spangled Banner" are those that were handwritten or signed by Francis Scott Key. One, believed to be the original, is owned by the Maryland Historical Society (Filby 1976, 510). Key signed at least two others about twenty-five years later. These include an autographed copy that he gave to Louis J. Cist in 1840, which was acquired by the Library of Congress in the 1941–1942 fiscal year (Svejda 2005, 429) and a copy that Key gave to General

George Keim in 1842, which Keim's son subsequently gave to the Pennsylvania Historical Society in Philadelphia (Svejda 2005, 430). Georgetown University owns a copy that Key autographed in 1842 for the father of Mrs. J. A. Nunn, and Key autographed another, which may have been a lithograph, for a White House gardener named James Mahar. The whereabouts of yet another copy (possibly spurious and known to scholars as the Howard copy) remains unknown (Svejda 2005, 430).

See also: Carr, Thomas; Key, Francis Scott.

Further Reading

Blanck, Jacob. 1966. "The Star Spangled Banner." *Papers of the Bibliographical Society of America* 60 (Second Quarter): 176–184.

Christie's. 2017. "THE STAR SPANGLED BANNER – *Baltimore Patriot & Evening Advertiser*, Baltimore: Munroe & French, No. 54 South Street, 21 September 1814." June 15, Sale 14376, Lot 274. https://www.christies.com/lotfinder/Lot/the -star-spangled-banner-baltimore-patriot-6-details.aspx.

"Defence of Fort M'Henry." 1814. Maryland Historical Society. http://www.mdhs.org /digitalimage/defence-sic-fort-mhenry.

Filby, P. William. 1976. "Music in the Maryland Historical Society." *Notes* 32 (March): 503–17.

Filby, P. W., and Edward G. Howard (compilers). 1972. *Star-Spangled Books: Book, Sheet Music, Newspapers, Manuscripts, and Persons Associated with "The Star-Spangled Banner."* Baltimore: Maryland Historical Society.

"First Edition of Star Spangled Banner Given to Library." 1968. *The Quarto* 80 (March): 1. https://clements.umich.edu/wp-content/uploads/2019/09/quarto1st-80.pdf.

Levy, Lester S., and James J. Fuld. 1970. "Unrecorded Early Printings of 'The Star Spangled Banner.'" *Notes* 27 (December): 245–51.

Miller, Cait. 2014. "Printing 'The Star-Spangled Banner.'" *In the Muse* (blog), Library of Congress, September 15. https://blogs.loc.gov/music/2014/09/printing-the-star -spangled-banner.

Svejda, George J. 2005. *History of the Star Spangled Banner from 1814 to the Present.* Honolulu, HI: University Press of the Pacific. First published in 1969 by Division of History, Office of Archeology and Historic Preservation, U.S. Department of the Interior, National Park Service.

Vaughn, Ashley. 2010. "Auction of First Edition of 'Star Spangled Banner' Tops $500,000." *CNN*, December 3. http://www.cnn.com/2010/US/12/03/new.york.star.spangled .banner/index.html.

Early Recordings

It was impossible to distribute musical recordings until Thomas Edison invented the phonograph in 1877 and created the Edison Phonograph Company in 1887. Early recordings were made on wax cylinders and give insight into the way that "The Star-Spangled Banner" was often played in the late nineteenth century. A recording by John Philip Sousa's band from 1898, for example, plays the song at a slow, deliberate pace, probably in hopes of emphasizing its majesty.

One of the earliest vocal recordings of the "Star-Spangled Banner," believed to date to about 1899, featured George J. Gaskin, a tenor, and was produced by the Columbia Phonograph Company on cylinder #4101. Yet another, by bass singer

Frank C. Stanley, was published by RCA Recording sometime between 1904 and 1908. Margaret Woodrow Wilson, the president's daughter, performed a recording of "The Star-Spangled Banner" in 1918.

It was not until the development of microphones that it was possible to replace band music with vocal performances of the anthem at large sports events. For better or worse, observers often assert that modern renditions seem intended to highlight the performer more than the anthem itself.

In January 2013, the University of Michigan's American Music Institute made what it called a "world premiere" recording of the national anthem by attempting to replicate the way that it would have been played and sung shortly after it was published in 1814.

See also: Sousa, John Philip; Sports Events.

Further Reading

"History of the Cylinder Phonograph." n.d. Inventing Entertainment: The Early Motion Pictures and Sound Recordings of the Edison Companies. Library of Congress. https://www.loc.gov/collections/edison-company-motion-pictures-and-sound-record ings/articles-and-essays/history-of-edison-sound-recordings/history-of-the-cylin der-phonograph.

"The Star Spangled Banner." n.d. National Jukebox, Library of Congress. http://www.loc .gov/jukebox/recordings/detail/id/8141.

"'The Star-Spangled Banner' Original 1814 Version (High Definition)." 2013. YouTube, January 13. https://www.youtube.com/watch?v=lvVtFD9Na0I.

"'The Star-Spangled Banner' Early Recorded Version circa 1899 George J. Gaskin, Rare Cylinder." 2014. YouTube, December 14. https://www.youtube.com/watch?v=MN -0rBVoGxI.

"A World Premiere Recording of 'The Star-Spangled Banner'?" 2013. *Star Spangled Music* (blog), Star Spangled Music Foundation, January 18. http://starspangled music.org/a-world-premiere-recording-of-the-star-spangled-banner.

English Language and "The Star-Spangled Banner"

The music to the "The Star-Spangled Banner" was written by an Englishman and the lyrics were written by an American. In 2006, a number of Latin pop stars stirred up controversy with the release of "Nuestro Himno," which in Spanish means "our anthem" (Montgomery 2006, 1). Supporters saw the anthem they performed as a way for Spanish-speaking Americans to show their patriotism, but critics charged that it was a rejection of assimilation in the nation to which they had immigrated. For example, Pedro Biaggi, the host of a popular Hispanic radio station in Washington, DC, declared, "It's not for us to be going around singing the national anthem in Spanish. . . . We don't want to impose, we don't own the place. . . . We want to be accepted" (Montgomery 2006, 1). Similarly, Juan Carlos Ruis, the coordinator of the National Capital Immigration Coalition, said, "It's part of the process to learn English" (Montgomery 2006, 3).

One complicating fact was that while the first verse remained "relatively faithful" to the lyrics, other verses contained phrases like "we are equal, we are brothers" that were not in Key's original (Montgomery 2006, 2).

Some of the criticisms of the song, however, were regarded in some quarters as reflections of xenophobia. Columnist Michelle Malkin, for example, referred to the Spanish version as "The Illegal Alien Anthem." George Taplin, who directed the Virginia Chapter of the Minuteman Civil Defense Corps, thought that the Spanish version was a challenge to national sovereignty and argued, "I believe it should be in English as it was penned" (Montgomery 2006, 2). In May of 2006, President George W. Bush said that he thought the anthem should be sung in English, even though his own inauguration had been graced with a Spanish pop version of the song. Shortly after Bush's statement, U.S. Senator Lamar Alexander of Tennessee introduced a resolution proposing that "The Star-Spangled Banner" only be sung or recited in English (Abril 2007, 69). Even when individuals of Hispanic descent perform the national anthem in English, however, they sometimes receive racist feedback (Rodriguez 2013).

Scholars, meanwhile, have pointed out that translating the anthem from English is nothing new. Sociologist Carlos R. Abril observed that "the song was translated into German in an 1894 version called 'Das Star-Spangled Banner,'" and in 1919, "the U.S. Bureau of Education commissioned a Spanish version . . . called 'La Bandera de las Estrellas'" (Abril 2007, 74). Moreover, it was common for U.S. allies to translate "The Star-Spangled Banner" into their own languages, as did Tomas Garrigue Masaryk, the president of Czechoslovakia, after the fall of the Austro-Hungarian Empire in 1918 (Junior Research Seminar 2016). It is also not uncommon for the song to be accompanied by an individual using American Sign Language for those in the audience who might be hearing impaired. One writer noted, "We freely translate our most sacred religious texts into the vernacular because few of us can read the original Hebrew, Aramaic, Greek, Sanskrit, Arabic, or Latin with any degree of understanding. There's no reason to build an English-only bubble around our civic documents. After all, it's not a common English language, but commonly shared ideals, laws and culture, that provide the glue holding American society together" (Baron, n.d.).

In 1943, Dr. Avrom Aisen (Asen) translated "The Star-Spangled Banner" into Yiddish to commemorate the one hundredth anniversary of Francis Scott Key's death. In 1945 the U.S. State Department asked Latin American composer Clotilde Arias (1901–1959) to provide a Spanish translation of the national anthem as part of America's "Good Neighbor Policy," an approach to foreign affairs instituted by President Franklin D. Roosevelt to promote better relations with Latin America (Saez 2012). It is entitled "El Pendon Estrellado" and has been recorded.

In 1918, A. F. Geyser published a Latin version of "The Star-Spangled Banner" entitled "Vexillum Stellatum," which was presumably designed for the classroom. The last two lines of the first verse are translated as "*stellatumne vexillum Volans tegit nos, patriam liberam fortiumque domos?*" (1918, 191).

One advantage that "The Star-Spangled Banner" has over some other patriotic songs, most notably "My Country, 'Tis of Thee," is that it does not contain references to "my native country" or "land where my fathers died," which might seem to exclude immigrants (Hahner 2017, 113). Moreover, those who did not yet understand the English language would be less likely to understand the meaning of what they were singing if they were simply to memorize the words in English (Hahner 2017, 115).

See also: Criticisms and Defenses of "The Star-Spangled Banner"; Immigrants; Knowledge of the National Anthem.

Further Reading

Abril, Carlos R. 2007. "Functions of a National Anthem in Society and Education: A Sociocultural Perspective." *Bulletin of the Council for Research in Music Education*, no. 172 (Spring): 69–87.

Aisen (Asen), Avrom. 1943. "The Star Spangled Banner in Yiddish." Museum of Family History. http://www.museumoffamilyhistory.com/yw-ssb.htm.

Baron, Dennis. n.d. "Jose Can You See? The Controversy over the Spanish Translation of the Star-Spangled Banner." http://www.english.illinois.edu/-people-/faculty /debaron/essays/anthem.html.

Geyser, A. F. 1918. "The Star-Spangled Banner / Vexillum Stellatum." *Classical Weekly* 11 (April 22): 191.

Hahner, Leslie A. 2017. *To Become an American: Immigrants and Americanization Campaigns of the Early Twentieth Century.* East Lansing: Michigan State University Press.

Junior Research Seminar. 2016. "The National Anthem Effect on 'The Star Spangled Banner.'" Music in Twentieth Century American History, Villanova University. https://historyrocks.library.villanova.edu/music-history/national-anthem.

Montgomery, David. 2006. "An Anthem's Discordant Notes." *Washington Post*, April 28. http://www.washingtonpost.com/wp-dyn/content/article/2006/04/27/AR200604 2702505.html.

Rodriguez, Cindy Y. 2013. "Mexican-American Boy's National Anthem Sparks Racist Comments." *CNN*, September 16. https://www.cnn.com/2013/06/12/us/mexican -american-boy-sings-anthem/index.html.

Saez, Diana. 2012. "Singing 'El Pendon Estrellado.'" *O Say Can You See?* (blog), Smithsonian National Museum of American History, September 26. http://american history.si.edu/blog/2012/09/singing-el-pend%C3%B3n-estrellado.html.

Salomone, Rosemary C. 2010. *True American.* Cambridge, MA: Harvard University Press.

"'The Star-Spangled Banner'—ASL Translation." 2011. YouTube, September 19. https:// www.youtube.com/watch?v=CFPpJzLCs98.

Everson, Joe

The national anthem is one of many national symbols that honor the nation's flag. Just as Francis Scott Key's lyrics to the anthem proclaimed his joy in seeing the flag waving over Fort McHenry after an intense British bombardment during the War of 1812, so too one of the most iconic photographs in U.S. history was that of U.S. Marines raising the flag over Mount Suribachi during the battle for Iwo Jima during World War II.

Joe Everson, who was raised in Midland, Michigan, attended Northland International University in Dunbar, Wisconsin, where he also participated in singing. He subsequently moved to Greenville, South Carolina, where he drove a truck and set up an art gallery.

Seeking a way to combine his art with his musical interests, Everson developed an unusual performance that combined "The Star-Spangled Banner" with the iconic raising of the flag at Iwo Jima. "While singing the national anthem," noted one account, "Everson completes a painting based on the iconic image of U.S. soldiers raising the flag on Iwo Jima during World War II. Throughout most of the song, Everson's canvas is turned upside down, so the image isn't entirely recognizable until the song's final lines. That's when Everson spins the canvas 180 degrees on the easel and adds the painting's final touch—the red and white stripes of the flag—in a single broad stroke" (Pietras 2017). He has been invited to perform at numerous events since his debut at a game featuring the professional hockey team known as the Greenville Swamp Rabbits in March 2016. On July 4, 2018, he made a well-received appearance on *Fox & Friends,* which caused sales of his other paintings to skyrocket.

Everson has said that his art stems from a deep patriotism. He observed that "When everything was said and done, the flag's still there." Speaking of the national anthem, he observed that "to me, that's what it will always represent . . . men dying at the time to keep the flag raised. And the closest thing we had image-wise that was a little more current was the flag raising of Iwo Jima" (Pietras 2017).

See also: Star-Spangled Banner Flag; War and the National Anthem.

Further Reading

"'Bob Ross Meets Frank Sinatra.'" n.d. Joe Everson Art. https://www.joeeverson.com/about.

Bradley, James, and Ron Powers. 2000. *Flags of Our Fathers*. New York: Bantam.

Pietras, Emily. 2017. "Oh, Say, Can You See—And Hear—The Patriotic Art of Joe Everson?" *Greenville Journal*, June 20. https://greenvillejournal.com/arts-culture/oh-say-can-see-hear-patriotic-art-joe-everson.

Feliciano, Jose

Although Congress has never specified an "official" version of the national anthem, most Americans are most familiar with hearing the words to the tune that John Stafford Smith composed. This is the melody commonly taught in school music programs.

In 1968, a twenty-three-year-old blind singer named Jose Feliciano (1945–) who had immigrated to New York from Puerto Rico was invited by broadcaster Ernie Harwell to sing "The Star-Spangled Banner" to open game five of the World Series at Detroit's Tiger Stadium, which was hosting the St. Louis Cardinals. Sitting on a stool with his guide dog Trudy, Feliciano played his acoustic guitar and presented a Latin jazz version of the song—or what he described as "a gospel, soulful version" (Cantor-Navas 2018), which he hoped would "show my appreciation to America for what they had done for me" (Bates 2017). Offended by the way that many people would clap during other renditions of the national anthem, Feliciano decided that he would perform in a way that would require people to pay attention (Handel 2018).

Listeners did pay attention but not in the manner that Feliciano had anticipated. In a year that had witnessed the assassinations of civil rights leader Dr. Martin Luther King, Jr., and U.S. Senator Robert Kennedy of New York, many viewers interpreted the mellow, stripped-down performance by the long-haired, sunglasses-wearing Feliciano as "part of the Vietnam war protests" (George 2018).

In addition to receiving boos from many fans at the stadium, many television viewers called in to NBC television to complain about Feliciano's "'hippie' version of 'The Star-spangled Banner'" (Cantor-Navas 2018). After many American radio stations stopped playing his best-known song at that point in his career, a cover version of the Doors song "Light My Fire," Feliciano began touring in other countries. Moreover, RCA Records launched a single of the anthem that peaked at fiftieth on the charts (Davis 2017). In 1970, the experience apparently also led him to release one of his most popular songs "Feliz Navidad [Happy, or Merry, Christmas]," as a bilingual song rather than solely in Spanish (Cantor-Navas 2018).

In addition to preparing the way for far more radical reinterpretations of "The Star-Spangled Banner," Feliciano's performance led Susan Omillian, who was only fourteen at the time, to establish a fan club. Eleven years later they were married.

At the request of Ernie Harwell, the Detroit Tigers invited Feliciano back to the stadium to perform "The Star-Spangled Banner" on May 10, 2010. Fifty years after his initial performance in Detroit, Feliciano also was invited to perform at Flag Day at the Smithsonian's National Museum of American History, where he sang for a naturalization ceremony. At the ceremony, in which he donated the Concerto Candelas guitar on which he had first played the anthem, he said, "I have no regrets, though I was the first artist to stylize the national anthem, and I got a lot of protests for it. I have no regrets. America has been good to me. I'm glad that I'm here" (George 2018).

See also: Sports Events.

Further Reading

Bates, Karen Grigsby. 2017. "A Different National Anthem, Before the Nation Was Ready for It." November 20 NPR. Npr.org/sections.codeswitch/2017/11/02/560948130/a-different-national-anthem-before-the-nation-was-ready-for-it

Cantor-Navas, Judy. 2018. "Jose Feliciano to Sing 'Star-Spangled Banner,' Donate Guitar at Smithsonian Citizenship Ceremony: Exclusive." *Billboard News*, June 6. https://www.billboard.com/articles/columns/latin/8459567/jose-feliciano-sing-star-spangled-banner-donate-guitar-smithsonian-citizenship-ceremony.

Davis, David. 2017. "The World Series National Anthem That Infuriated America." *Deadspin*, October 6. https://deadspin.com/the-world-series-national-anthem-that-infuriated-americ-1819151571.

George, Alice. 2018. "For 50 Years, Jose Feliciano's Version of the National Anthem Has Given Voice to Immigrant Pride." *Smithsonian Magazine*, June 15. https://www.smithsonianmag.com/smithsonian-institution/for-50-years-jose-felicianos-soulful-take-national-anthem-given-pride-immigrant-pride-180969380.

Handel, Craig. 2018. "Jose Feliciano Paid a Price When He Sang National Anthem 50 Years Ago, but He Has No Regrets." *News Press*, October 5. https://www.news-press.com/story/entertainment/2018/10/05/jose-feliciano-paid-price-when-he-sang-national-anthem-1968/1514370002.

Ferguson, Stacy Ann ("Fergie")

Stacy Ann Ferguson (1975–), who used to sing with the popular rock band The Black Eyed Peas, is better known by her fans as Fergie. At an NBA All-Star Game in 2018 she rendered one of the more controversial contemporary renditions of "The Star-Spangled Banner" with a sultry tune that extended the rendition to two and a half minutes. Reporters for the Associated Press (2018) observed, "Although Fergie was on pitch, her tempo, musical accompaniment and sexy delivery were not exactly typical for a sporting event or a patriotic song." It further characterized the audience reaction as a combination of "varying levels of bemusement and enthusiasm" (Associated Press 2018).

Fergie responded to the criticism of her rendition by saying, "I've always been honored and proud to perform the national anthem and last night I wanted to try something special for the NBA. I'm a risk taker artistically, but clearly this rendition didn't strike the intended tone. I love this country and honestly tried my best" (Associated Press 2018).

See also: Flubbed Performances; Gaye, Marvin; Singing "The Star-Spangled Banner."

Further Reading

Associated Press. 2018. "Fergie Responds to 'Star-Spangled Banner' Criticism: 'I Honestly Tried My Best.'" *Newsday*, February 20. https://www.newsday.com/entertainment/celebrities/fergie-star-spangled-banner-nba-1.16863493.

Kreps, Daniel. 2018. "Watch Fergie's Disastrous National Anthem at NBA All-Star Game." *Rolling Stone*, February 29. https://www.rollingstone.com/music/music-news/watch-fergies-disastrous-national-anthem-at-nba-all-star-game-203023.

Fireworks

One of the primary images of "The Star-Spangled Banner" is that of "the rockets' red glare, the bombs bursting in air." Accordingly, one little-touted advantage of the song is that it lends itself to fireworks displays that often accompany Flag Day and Independence Day celebrations across the United States (as well as celebrations of Defenders' Day in Maryland).

Since fireworks, which were invented in China, preceded the use of bombs and rockets in warfare, it seems unlikely that most individuals viewing such displays are reminded of war so much as of celebration. Because the canton of the U.S. flag itself symbolized the birth of a new political constellation, many observers believe that it seems particularly appropriate that fireworks direct attention to the heavens.

Largely for reasons of safety, many modern fireworks displays take place on or over the water. This provides a further reminder that the official anthem celebrating the flag was itself composed after a British naval bombardment of a U.S. fort.

Major fireworks displays have been used on many historic occasions, including at Fort McHenry to commemorate the seventy-fifth anniversary of its bombardment and the writing of "The Star-Spangled Banner" in 1889, to commemorate the centennial of these events in 1914, to celebrate V-J Day and Defenders' Day in 1945, and for bicentennial celebrations in 2014.

See also: Commemorations of "The Star-Spangled Banner"; "Rockets' Red Glare"; Star-Spangled Banner Flag.

Further Reading

Shalev, Eran. 2011. "'A Republic Amidst the Stars': Political Astronomy and the Intellectual Origins of the Stars and Stripes." *Journal of the Early Republic* 31 (Spring): 39–73.

Sullivan, Patrick. 2013. *Fort McHenry National Monument and Historic Shrine: Administrative History.* New South Associates Technical Report 2256. Stone Mountain, GA: New South Associates for the National Park Service.

First Amendment

The First Amendment to the U.S. Constitution states, "Congress shall make no law respecting an establishment or religion, or prohibiting the free exercise thereof; or abridging the freedom of speech, or of the press, or the right of the people peaceably to assemble, and to petition to the government for a redress of grievances." The amendment was proposed as part of the first ten amendments (now known as the Bill of Rights) that the first Congress proposed in 1789 and that the requisite number of states ratified in 1791. These amendments were largely adopted in reaction to concerns expressed by those who had opposed adoption of the U.S. Constitution. These critics of the proposed Constitution, known as Anti-Federalists, feared that it made the new government too powerful. In time, after the 1868 adoption of the Fourteenth Amendment and its mandate that all Americans be provided "due process of law," courts began to apply the provisions of the Bill of Rights not only to Congress and other branches of the national government, but also to the states. The courts paid particular attention to defending the First Amendment but also noted that the amendment does not cover actions by private individuals other than from government. Thus, absent some kind of other contractual obligation, a private employer does have the right to restrict the speech and other First Amendment rights of employees (Paulson 2017).

In 1931, the U.S. Congress recognized "The Star-Spangled Banner" as the national anthem, and subsequent legislation passed by Congress has established guidelines of proper behavior during the playing or singing of the anthem. Largely because of the First Amendment, however, these laws carry no penalty for violations. This has not stopped some politicians, President Donald J. Trump in particular, from criticizing athletes who have decided to "take a knee" as a form of social protest rather than stand during renditions of the anthem. Trump and other critics of protest actions during the national anthem have called on organizations to fire such players, but neither the president nor representatives of other branches of government have the authority to do so themselves.

U.S. Supreme Court decisions related to saluting the flag provide considerable guidance as to individual rights in this area. Thus in *West Virginia State Board of Education v. Barnette* (1943), the court reversed an earlier decision made in *Minersville School District v. Gobitis* (1940) and ruled that public schools could not require individuals who had objected for religious reasons to salute the flag. Although not commending the practice, subsequent decisions in *Texas v. Johnson* (1989) and *United States v. Eichman* (1990) further upheld the First Amendment right of protestors to burn the U.S. flag.

State and federal legislators have sometimes introduced legislation to require performers to use a particular musical arrangement of the "The Star-Spangled Banner," to limit the singing of the anthem to English, to prevent parodies of the anthem, and the like. Constitutional experts, however, believe that all of these restrictions would likely fail existing First Amendment standards.

In what are known as "limited public forums," the government can limit the time, place, and manner of speech. Governments can thus limit performances of the anthem and other songs or performances at times and places (for example, on public highways or thoroughfares or in classrooms during regular classes) that might pose hazards or inconveniences, but they cannot under current doctrine single out certain types of speech, like the anthem, for special privileges.

The last verse of "The Star-Spangled Banner" says, "And this be our motto: 'In God is our trust.'" The United States does frequently employ the related phrase "In God We Trust" as well as "E Pluribus Unum" ("From Many, One") as its mottos. Supreme Court decisions have consistently refused to concern itself with such acts of ceremonial deism, or generic references to God, which the justices apparently do not believe rise to the level of "establishing" either religion in general or (despite the motto's apparent monotheism—belief in a single God) in favoring one particular version of religion over another (Epstein 1996). In *Sheldon v. Fannin* (1963), a U.S. district court specifically rejected the idea that the national anthem should be excluded from public schools as an unconstitutional "establishment" of religion. It said, "The singing of the National Anthem is not a religious but a patriotic ceremony, intended to inspire devotion to and love of country. Any religious references therein are incidental and expressive only of the faith which as a matter of historical fact has inspired the growth of the nation" (774).

In *McCreary County v. American Civil Liberties Union of Kentucky* (2005), however, the U.S. Supreme Court invalidated a display of the Ten Commandments at two Kentucky courthouses that included copies of other documents along with the lyrics to "The Star-Spangled Banner." The court struck down the displays not because of these lyrics but out of concern that the "primary intent" of the overall display was to advance religion (as found in the Ten Commandments) in violation of the establishment clause.

See also: Code for the National Anthem; English Language and "The Star-Spangled Banner"; Singing the National Anthem in Public Spaces; Sports Events.

Further Reading

Buhi, Jason. 1919. "A National Anthem Debate Led America to Reaffirm Freedom of Speech. Hong Kong Should Take Note." *South China Morning Post*, January 15. https://www.scmp.com/comment/insight-opinion/hong-kong/article/2181966/national-anthem-debate-led-america-reaffirm.

Cohen, David S. 2017. "What the Supreme Court Says about Sitting Out the National Anthem." *Rolling Stone*, October 6. https://www.rollingstone.com/politics/politics-features/what-the-supreme-court-says-about-sitting-out-the-national-anthem-199512.

Epstein, Steven B. 1996. "Rethinking the Constitutionality of Ceremonial Deism." *Columbia Law Review* 96 (December): 2083–174.

McCreary County v. American Civil Liberties Union of Kentucky, 545 U.S. 844 (2005).

Napolitano, Andrew. 2017. "Is Taking a Knee Protected Speech?" *RealClearPolitics*, October 12. https://www.realclearpolitics.com/articles/2017/10/12/is_taking_a_knee_protected_speech_135235.html.

Paulson, Ken. 2017. "NFL Protests: Your Boss Can Tell You to Stand for the Anthem. Trump Can't." *First Amendment Encyclopedia*, Free Speech Center, Middle Tennessee State University, October 2. https://mtsu.edu/first-amendment/post/57/nfl-protests-your-boss-can-tell-you-to-stand-for-the-anthem-trump-can-t.

Sheldon v. Fannin, 221 F. Supp. 766 (D. Ariz. 1963).

Texas v. Johnson, 491 U.S. 397 (1989).

United States v. Eichman, 496 U.S. 310 (1990).

Williams, Susan. 1991. "Content Discrimination and the First Amendment." *University of Pennsylvania Law Review* 139 (January): 615–730.

First Public Performance

The first known singing of "The Star-Spangled Banner" came within a month of its composition by Francis Scott Key. It took place at the Holliday Street Theater in Baltimore, Maryland, on the evening of Wednesday, October 19, 1814. A playbill by the Warren & Wood Company, which announced the performance of "Count Benyowsky," further announced that "after the play, Mr. Hardinge will sing a much admired song, written by a gentleman of Maryland, in commemoration of the gallant defence of Fort M'Henry, called the Star-Spangled Banner" (Filby and Howard 1972, 62, 90). An additional playbill, announcing the performance of "The Fortress" for November 12, 1814, further noted that J. Hardinge would be singing "The Star-Spangled Banner" for the "2nd time here" after the play (Filby and Howard 1972, 62, 90).

Ferdinand Durang, who had arrived in Baltimore with his brother Charles in a regiment of Pennsylvania volunteers after the attack on Fort McHenry but who had played with a theatrical company during this time, later claimed to have been the first to sing the song. There is, however, no contemporaneous record that would support this claim by Durang, who later wrote *The Philadelphia Stage from the Year 1749 to the Year 1855* (which was serialized in Philadelphia's *Sunday Dispatch* in 1855) (Filby and Howard 1972, 15–16, 61–62).

See also: Key, Francis Scott.

Further Reading

Filby, P. W., and Edward G. Howard (compilers). 1972. *Star-Spangled Books: Book, Sheet Music, Newspapers, Manuscripts, and Persons Associated with "The Star-Spangled Banner."* Baltimore: Maryland Historical Society.

Flag Is Full of Stars, The

The Flag Is Full of Stars is a colorful painting executed by Dale Gallon in 1989 that depicts American soldiers at Fort McHenry hoisting the flag that inspired Francis Scott Key to write "The Star-Spangled Banner" above the fort on the morning of September 14, 1814. Gallon, who lives in Gettysburg, Pennsylvania, is a graduate of the Art Center College of Design in Los Angeles, California, who taught for a time at the University of California at Long Beach.

Most of his more than three hundred paintings have been of Civil War scenes. Gallon's painting of Fort McHenry shows scores of men gathered on the ramparts with smoke (possibly from the nation's capital) rising from the background.

Limited edition prints of Gallon's painting were sold in 1994 to help launch the capital campaign for the new visitor and education center at Fort McHenry (Badger 1994).

See also: Fort McHenry; Fort McHenry Visitor and Education Center; Paintings of the Bombardment of Fort McHenry; Star-Spangled Banner Flag; "View of the Bombardment of Fort McHenry"; Visual Arts.

Further Reading

Badger, Sylvia. 1994. "Jim McManus Honored for His Service to Humanity." *Baltimore Sun*, September 9. http://www.baltimoresun.com/news/bs-xpm-1994-09-1994 252019-story.html.

"Dale Gallon: The Artist That Brings You the History!" n.d. Dale Gallon website. https://www.gallon.com/about-gallon/bio.

Flubbed Performances

As renditions of "The Star-Spangled Banner," especially at ball games, have become increasingly common, performers have encountered two criticisms. One is that they have taken too many liberties with the tune of the anthem by performing it in nontraditional ways. This criticism has been applied to performers as diverse as Igor Stravinsky, Jimi Hendrix, and Jose Feliciano. Other criticisms include performers unintentionally flubbing the lines and others having inadequately practiced or an inability to master the full musical range of a song, which is generally considered to be difficult to sing and is typically sung a cappella.

Examples are undoubtedly legion but have included many top stars. Although he won on *American Idol*, then eighteen-year-old Scott McCreery got off on the wrong foot at the first game of the 2011 World Series after first restarting the song due to a microphone malfunction and then accidentally singing "No Jose" instead of "oh say" (Effron and Marikar 2012). Cyndi Lauper of "Girls Just Wanna Have Fun" ended up singing "as our flag was still streaming" when performing for the U.S. Open in Flushing, New York, that same year, and Christina Aguilera, a judge for *The Voice*, also botched some of the lyrics in her 2011 performance at the Super Bowl (Effron and Marikar 2012). Keri Hillson forgot some of the words while singing before an NBA game involving the Los Angeles Lakers and the Atlanta Hawks.

Steven Tyler, a frontman for Aerosmith, was booed at the NFL playoff game between the New England Patriots and the Baltimore Ravens in 2012 for failing to hit the high notes. Scholar Mark Clague, who was more sympathetic than some of Tyler's critics, noted, "What people don't like is that he screeched the national anthem, but that's Steven Tyler's voice and that's his passion" (Nix 2012).

Even singers who come prepared might receive criticism. Thus, country music star Luke Bryan was criticized for reading the words of the anthem off his hand for the Major League Baseball All-Star Game in 2012. He responded, "I had a few key words written down to insure myself that I wouldn't mess up. I just wanted to do my best. I promise it was from the heart" (Effron and Marikar 2012).

Sometime performers manage to mangle both the words and the tune. In assessing the ten worst performances of the anthem, the staff of Billboard thus described the performance of Dominican singer Kat DeLuna at a 2008 football game as "a spectacular failure." They explained, "She tries too hard to hit the notes that only a rarefied circle of divas can, then takes us on a painfully bumpy roller coaster ride of vocal runs. She half-forgets the lyrics. She completely botches the last note. And she does it all with the swagger of something [sic] who believes she's positively killing it. When a chorus of boos erupts at the end, it's far too little, too late" (2018).

There is general agreement that another one of the most disastrous performances of all time was the one by comedian Roseanne Barr at a baseball game at San Diego's Jack Murphy Stadium in 1990. Apparently unable to hit the high notes required, Barr tried to redeem the situation with humor, but probably unintentionally came across as disrespectful.

See also: Barr, Roseanne; Feliciano, Jose; Ferguson, Stacy Ann ("Fergie"); Franklin, Aretha; Hendrix, Jimi; Stravinsky, Igor.

Further Reading
Billboard. 2018. "10 Worst National Anthem Performances Ever." *Billboard News*, February 2. https://www.billboard.com/articles/list/513562/10-worst-national-anthem-performances-ever.
Effron, Lauren, and Sheila Marikar. 2012. "Why Is 'The Star Spangled Banner' So Hard to Sing?" *ABC News*, July 11. https://abcnews.go.com/Entertainment/celebrities-flubbed-national-anthem-star-spangled-banner-hard/story?id=16756113.
Gavilanes, Grace. 2018. "Fergie Wasn't the First: The Most Controversial National Performances." *People*, February 19. https://people.com/music/controversial-national-anthem-performances.
Nix, Naomi. 2012. "Perfect Anthem? Dream On." *Chicago Tribune*, January 24. https://www.chicagotribune.com/news/ct-xpm-2012-01-24-ct-talk-national-anthem-0124-2-20120124-story.html.

Fort McHenry

The writing of "The Star-Spangled Banner" is closely associated with the huge U.S. flag that Francis Scott Key saw waving over Fort McHenry, a military outpost along the coast of Maryland, on the morning of September 13, 1814, when the garrison came under attack from British forces. The fort, which has long since lacked any strategic significance, began on the site of a five-sided star-shaped earthen redoubt (fortification) dug before the actual beginning of the Revolutionary War. The compound was expanded between 1794 and 1805 and became part of the nation's original coastal defense network (Sullivan 2013, 1, 4). It is located on a peninsula near the point where the Patapsco River splits just south of the Baltimore harbor.

Originally dubbed Fort Whetstone, but later renamed after James McHenry, who had served as a representative to the Constitutional Convention of 1787 from Maryland and later as Secretary of War, the fort was one of sixteen harbor defenses that Congress authorized on March 20, 1794, with the adoption of an "Act to Provide for the Defense of Certain Ports and Harbors in the United States." Fort McHenry was largely designed by Jean Foncin in an effort to protect upper and lower water batteries. In addition to containing forty cannons, "the redoubt enclosed a central parade ground bounded by a powder magazine, cistern, two enlisted men's barracks, two officer quarters, and flagstaff" and was protected on its east, north, and west sides by "a dry moat and earthen counterscarp" (Sullivan 2003, 7).

The fort was strengthened in 1813 with improvements that included "the construction of a brick-faced, rectangular ravelin [outwork of fortifications] to protect the Star Fort's sally port [secure entryway] entrance" (Sullivan 2013, 8). At the time of the British bombardment in September 1814, the fort was commanded by Major George Armistead. Through most of the attack, the guns of the fort were unable to reach the British ships, which were about two miles away, but the Congreve rockets and bombs that the British ships launched proved almost equally inaccurate. In an especially fortunate development for defenders of the fort, one British bomb that made it inside the powder magazine (the fort's

Fort McHenry, in Baltimore, Maryland, is the place where Francis Scott Key observed that the "flag was still there" and wrote the words to "The Star-Spangled Banner" following an engagement with the invading British during the War of 1812. (Library of Congress)

gunpowder storage building) did not explode. If that bomb had detonated, the entire fort might have been wiped out. British ships approached closer to the fort after one of their shells took out a cannon and resulted in a number of American casualties, but the defenders of the fort were able to beat them back. Batteries also effectively prevented a force of more than one thousand men from using the cover of night to reach and scale the walls of nearby Fort Covington (Armistead 1814).

The fort was further strengthened after the British retreated in 1814 and again from 1829 to 1839. As the Civil War approached, Maryland remained loyal to the Union. The state, though, contained a large contingent of Confederate sympathizers, some of whom attacked federal troops as they passed through Baltimore. Captain John C. Robinson dissuaded a group of Confederate sympathizers from attacking the Fort by threatening to attack Baltimore in reprisal (Sullivan 2013, 12). Union forces used the fort as a prison during the war, even holding one of Francis Scott Key's grandsons during the conflict.

Toward the end of the nineteenth century, the chief defenses of Baltimore were shifted to Fort Carroll, about seven miles south of Baltimore Harbor (Sullivan 2013, 14). During this period, Fort McHenry largely became known for its celebrations of Defenders' Day each September. In 1912, the last members of the military left the post and Baltimore quickly converted the space into a park. The park, in fact, was the site of centennial celebrations of the British attack and the writing of "The Star-Spangled Banner" in 1914, a mere two years after the last contingent of soldiers left the fort.

During World War I, the national government resumed control over the site, stationed regiments there, and surrounded the installation with hospital buildings, which were not closed until 1921. In 1925, Congress adopted a law designating the fort as the first to memorialize the War of 1812, and it was formally dedicated in 1928 (Sullivan 2013, 28). In 1939, the park became the Fort McHenry National Monument and Historic Shrine, the only such site to be so doubly dedicated (Sullivan 2013, 32).

Considerable restoration work took place during the New Deal, although the U.S. Coast Guard used the facilities as a training site for more than twenty-eight thousand men during World War II (Sullivan 2013, 42). From that time forward, the site has been largely dedicated as a place of commemoration and remembrance. A new visitor center was dedicated on July 4, 1964, but that was later superseded by a larger and more modern Visitor and Education Center that opened its doors in 2011. In addition to containing a museum of historical displays, a gift shop, and educational and office spaces, it contains an auditorium with a glass wall from which shades are drawn so that visitors can view the Star-Spangled Banner Flag after watching a film about its history.

Due to its enduring association with the creation of "The Star-Spangled Banner," Fort McHenry has largely overshadowed memorials and commemorations of the Battle of North Point of September 12, 1814, which thwarted the British land attack on Baltimore. Grants have also provided support to the Star-Spangled Banner Flag House and other sites within the vicinity that are related to the War of 1812 and Francis Scott Key's authorship of the national anthem.

On July 2, 1948, President Harry S. Truman designated Fort McHenry as the first site at which the U.S. flag would be flown twenty-four hours a day. Other sites also connected to the American flag or the U.S. military have since been designated. There is no law prohibiting displays of the American flag at night, although the U.S. flag code recommends that flags be illuminated in such circumstances.

See also: Armistead, George; Baltimore, Maryland; "Battle of Baltimore, The"; Fireworks; Fort McHenry Visitor and Education Center; Paintings of the Bombardment of Fort McHenry; Star-Spangled Banner Flag; Star-Spangled Banner Flag House; "View of the Bombardment of Fort McHenry."

Further Reading

Armistead, George. 1814. "Official Account of the Bombardment of Fort McHenry. Copy of a Letter from Lieut. Colonel Armistead, to the Secretary of War." Smithsonian National Museum of American History (website). https://amhistory.si.edu/stars pangledbanner/pdf/TRANSCRIPT%20Official%20Account%20of%20the%20 Bombardment%20of%20Fort%20McHenry.pdf.

Howard, Hugh. 2012. "War of 1812: Big Night in Baltimore." *HistoryNet*, January 6. https://www.historynet.com/war-of-1812-big-night-in-baltimore.htm.

National Park Service. n.d. "Archeological Treasures at Fort McHenry." https://www.nps .gov/fomc/learn/historyculture/upload/Archeological%20Treasures.pdf.

Robbins, Karen E. 2013. *James McHenry, Forgotten Federalist.* Athens: University of Georgia Press.

Sheads, Scott S. 1995. *Fort McHenry.* Baltimore: Nautical & Aviation Publishing Company of America.

Sullivan, Patrick. 2013. *Fort McHenry National Monument and Historic Shrine: Administrative History.* New South Associates Technical Report 2256. Stone Mountain, GA: New South Associates for the National Park Service.

Fort McHenry Visitor and Education Center

Fort McHenry remains the primary site for visitors interested in learning about the circumstances surrounding Francis Scott Key's writing of "The Star-Spangled Banner." Visitors interested in the history of the site generally go to the Visitor Center and Education Building that was opened on March 3, 2011. It is operated by the National Park Service.

The current two-story, 17,200-square-foot center replaced an earlier visitor center that was completed in 1964 but proved inadequate for the number of tourists (Sullivan 2013, 125). The current facility includes a lobby, a gift shop, exhibit galleries with displays on the War of 1812, and a theater with glass windows that open at the end of a short film to the Star-Spangled Banner flag flying over Fort McHenry.

The outside of the building is largely made of brick and zinc panels that appear to evoke the stars of the flag. The architects explain, "The two curved walls of the building reflect the dynamic nature of the flag and all it represents, while the juxtaposition of the walls—clad in distinct materials—invokes the meanings behind the flag's stripes. Brick, strong and solid, expresses the hardiness and valor represented by the red stripes, while the thin and more delicate zinc façade expresses the purity and innocence represented by the white" (GWWO Architects, n.d.).

The building of the new center also included the installation of panels in the path to, and the area encompassed by, the fort itself.

See also: Baltimore, Maryland; Fort McHenry; War of 1812.

Further Reading

GWWO Architects. n.d. "Fort McHenry Visitor & Education Center." https://www .gwwoinc.com/projects/fort-mchenry-visitor-education-center.

Sullivan, Patrick. 2013. *Fort McHenry National Monument and Historic Shrine: Administrative History.* New South Associates Technical Report 2256. Stone Mountain, GA: New South Associates for the National Park Service.

Francis Scott Key House

For most of his adult life, Francis Scott Key, the author of "The Star-Spangled Banner," lived in a house in Georgetown, Virginia. The house was located near the end of Bridge Street (later designated as M Street) and had originally been built by a merchant named Thomas Clarke. The elegant house rose two and a half stories above the ground in the front and three and a half stories in the back, which sloped toward the Potomac River. The home featured brick chimneys at either end and a gabled roof. There were also a number of surrounding buildings, including a coach house and a smokehouse.

Key and his family moved into the house sometime between 1805 and 1808 and remained until about 1820. They left when a portion of their backyard fell victim to the construction of the new Chesapeake and Ohio Canal, although Key apparently continued to use a wing of the house for his law office (Mackintosh [1981], 2–4). The house was subsequently used as a hotel and a restaurant. By 1895, it was advertising sodas for five cents a glass. Its owners had painted the words "The Key Mansion" across its facade (Mackintosh [1981], 4).

Shortly thereafter, a group of prominent citizens, including Admirals George Dewey and Winfield Scott Schley, who had distinguished themselves in the Spanish-American War, formed the Francis Scott Key Memorial Association to create a lasting memorial in Key's memory. In time they enlisted the support of Charles H. Weisgerber, who had promoted the Betsy Ross House in Philadelphia. They opened the Key house to tourists in 1908, but when it failed to attract many visitors, they converted the house back to commercial use. In about 1912–1913, the house was significantly modified for this use. Changes included alteration of the front facade and the demolition of a wing and a chimney. Weisgerber purchased some of the doors, sashes, and other materials during this time and moved them to Philadelphia and Berlin, New Jersey (Mackintosh [1981], 5, 6). In 1931, the national government acquired the house and surrounding properties with the intention of clearing and landscaping them to enhance the Potomac shoreline visible from the Francis Scott Key Bridge, which had been completed in 1923.

Although there was some interest in restoring the house, supporters encountered difficulty in getting money and over questions about whether enough of the original structure remained to make such restoration feasible. One of Key's great grandsons wrote a letter in which he indicated that even if the building could be restored on site, "it will not be the old building, nor will it be the house Key lived in with his family, nor the floors upon which he walked, nor the windows through which he looked, nor the doors through which he entered, nor the roof that sheltered him and his family" (Mackintosh [1981], 7). Key's furnishings had long since been disbursed. In such circumstances, tourists visiting the homes of other famous Americans might wonder about their own authenticity.

As other buildings on the block were demolished for a highway ramp that was justified in part as a way of furthering military preparedness by increasing access to the Pentagon, there was some talk of reconstructing the house, or what was left of it, on another site. The house was dismantled and its remains were moved to a storage area. With the support of U.S. Senators Robert A. Taft of Ohio and Millard Tydings of Maryland, as well as U.S. Representative J. Glenn Beall of Maryland, Congress adopted legislation to provide for a Francis Scott Key National Monument on a new site in 1947, but President Harry S. Truman never signed the bill. In time, what was left of the building's original materials disappeared, leading to some indignant headlines. An employee of the National Park Service who has done the most extensive research on the house concluded, however, that the failure to reconstruct the house was not as big a loss as some have charged. He observed that "the replica would have been a new structure masquerading as old"

(Mackintosh [1981], 13). He further pointed out that Key did not compose the national anthem in the house and that the house is unnecessary to an understanding of Key's life and work, which is commemorated at many other sites. Baltimore is the home of the Star-Spangled Banner Flag House, but that building is the former residence of Mary Pickersgill, who designed the flag that inspired Key to write "The Star-Spangled Banner."

See also: Key, Francis Scott; Star-Spangled Banner Flag House.

Further Reading

Mackintosh, Barry. [1981] "The Loss of the Francis Scott Key House: Was It Really?" National Park Service Integrated Resource Management Applications Portal. https://irma.nps.gov/DataStore/DownloadFile/469096.

Miller, Marla R. 2018. "The U.S. Flag in America's Historic-House Museums." In *The American Flag: An Encyclopedia of the Stars and Stripes in U.S. History, Culture, and Law*, edited by John R. Vile, 19–32. Santa Barbara, CA: ABC-CLIO.

Franklin, Aretha

In addition to highlighting sports events, school programs, Defenders' Day (Baltimore), Independence Day, Flag Day, and other patriotic holidays, "The Star-Spangled Banner" is often sung at partisan political events, especially national nominating conventions, where members of political parties attempt to demonstrate their wider love of—and deep loyalty to—their country.

It was not therefore unusual when Aretha Franklin (1942–2018), who would later be designated as "the Queen of Soul," performed the anthem for the Democratic National Convention meeting in Chicago on August 26, 1968. Her unconventional rendition, however, probably heightened perceived generational differences among her listeners, both on the convention floor and the world outside the hall (Stanton 2018). The year had been a traumatic one for America, marked by the assassinations of Dr. Martin Luther King, Jr., and U.S. Senator Robert Kennedy, both of whom had questioned the increasingly unpopular war in Vietnam. The Democratic convention itself became better known for the police attacks on antiwar protestors on Chicago's streets than for its nomination of Hubert H. Humphrey, who was eventually defeated by Republican Richard M. Nixon.

Franklin did make one minor mistake in wording, which she recovered while getting near the end of the stanza, but the main complaints she elicited centered on her injection of soul into the song. This may have been heightened among some listeners who resented the fact that an African American woman was singing.

Journalist Timothy Burke (2018) observed that the criticisms bore several common threads: "first, the scare-quotes around 'Soul' (or more coded words like 'jive' or 'bop'), and the implication—in some cases more overt than others—that the 'disrespect' shown by Aretha Franklin to this nation's flag, its anthem, and indeed the country itself was representative of the Democratic Party's (or, alternatively, African Americans') attitudes toward the same."

Later that October, Jose Feliciano received similar criticism for his Latin jazz delivery of "The Star-Spangled Banner" at a World Series game in Detroit. A year later, Jimi Hendrix presented his own electrified version of the national anthem at the famous Woodstock music festival in New York.

As appreciation for a more personalized approach to the national anthem increased, Franklin was invited to sing the anthem at a number of other events, including President Barack Obama's inauguration in 2009. She became known for lengthening the song beyond most others by drawing out her vocalizations of some lyrics. Although the average time to sing the anthem is one minute and fifty-seven seconds, in a Thanksgiving Day performance in 2016 at Ford Field in Detroit, Michigan, before an NFL game between the Detroit Lions and Minnesota Vikings she gave a rendition that lasted four minutes and fifty-five seconds (Resnikoff 2016).

See also: Feliciano, Jose; Hendrix, Jimi.

Further Reading

Burke, Timothy. 2018. "When Aretha Franklin's 'Star-Spangled Banner' Drew a Torrent of Racial Abuse." *Daily Beast*, August 18. https://www.thedailybeast.com/when-aretha-franklins-star-spangled-banner-drew-a-torrent-of-racial-abuse.

Resnikoff, Paul. 2016. "Aretha Franklin Plays the Longest National Anthem in U.S. History." *Digital Music News*, November 25. https://www.digitalmusicnews.com/2016/11/25/aretha-franklin-longest-national-anthem.

Stanton, Zack. "When Aretha Franklin Rocked the National Anthem." 2018. *Politico*, August 16. https://www.politico.com/magazine/story/2018/08/16/aretha-franklin-controversial-national-anthem-219364.

Gaye, Marvin

Marvin Gaye (1939–1984) presented one of the most memorable performances of "The Star-Spangled Banner" on February 13, 1983, at the NBA All-Star Game at The Forum in Inglewood, California. Gaye, who had just released his hit song "Sexual Healing," for which he would soon win a Grammy Award, had sung the anthem at a number of previous NBA games. He had been recruited by Lon Rosen, the director of promotions for the Lakers, after Rosen's first choice—pop star Lionel Richie—had declined the invitation.

Gaye, who arrived on stage in a suit and dapper sunglasses, sang to a simple drumbeat and in a different pitch than usual renditions of the anthem. He also infused his performance of the song with a heavy rhythm and blues sensibility. Gaye received a standing ovation from the capacity crowd when he was done, although the reaction from viewers across the nation was mixed. One interpretation embraced by Gaye biographer David Ritz was that Gaye's "performance offered a social commentary and revealed the singer's soul" (Croatto 2013). It may have also been something of "an inside joke: Here's a funky, distinctively black version that's representative of what's on the court" (Croatto 2013). The rendition is so well known that it later became the subject of a poem by Jeff Fallis published in *The Iowa Review,* a prestigious literary journal.

Fourteen months after Gaye's famous performance, however, his life was cut short. Struggling with substance abuse issues and mental illness, Gaye moved into his parents' house in Washington, DC, in the early fall of 1983. Tensions quickly escalated between the singer and his father, a stern disciplinarian with whom Gaye had always had a difficult relationship. On April 1, 1984, his father fatally shot the singer in a domestic dispute at the home. He later pled no contest to a voluntary manslaughter charge and received a six-year suspended sentence and five years of probation.

See also: Sports Events.

Further Reading

Croatto, Pete. 2013. "The All-Star Anthem." *Grantland*, February 16. http://grantland
 .com/features/the-marvin-gaye-national-anthem.

Fallis, Jeff. 2004/2005. "Marvin Gaye Sings 'The Star-Spangled Banner.'" *Iowa Review*
 34 (Winter): 81–82.

Greene, Andy. 2014. "Flashback: Marvin Gaye Reimagines 'The Star-Spangled Banner'
 in 1983." *Rolling Stone*, February 13. https://www.rollingstone.com/music/music
 -news/flashback-marvin-gaye-reimagines-the-star-spangled-banner-in-1983
 -117710.

Tinsley, Justin. 2018. "The Players' Anthem: When Marvin Gaye Sang 'The Star-Spangled Banner' at the 1983 All-Star Game." *The Undefeated*, February 13. https://the undefeated.com/features/marvin-gaye-the-star-spangled-banner-1983-nba-all -star-game-players-anthem.

German-American Composers during World War I

Although some athletes have stirred considerable controversy in recent years over their decision to kneel rather than stand during the playing of the national anthem, they are hardly the first to be criticized for such actions.

Prior to World War I, numerous musicians and composers had immigrated to the United States from Germany and Austria. Many became members of some of the nation's premier bands and orchestras. Karl Muck (1859–1940), who became the conductor of the Boston Symphony Orchestra, was among those who had not yet become a U.S. citizen. At the time, William Starr Myers, who was undoubtedly attempting to boost national pride, had said in a lecture at the Brooklyn Institute of Arts and Sciences that "The Star-Spangled Banner" expressed nobler sentiments than Beethoven's Ninth Symphony while Edwin Warfield, an ex-governor of Maryland, would soon declare that the song "will be sung when other symphonic works are long forgotten" (Bowler 2007, 411).

Muck's orchestra was scheduled to perform in Providence, Rhode Island, on October 30, 1917, nearly seven months after the United States had entered World War I against Germany. Prior to the Rhode Island concert, orchestra manager Charles Ellis and founder Major Henry Lee Higginson turned down a request to play "The Star-Spangled Banner," which they considered to be better suited to a military band than an orchestra. Although they had not consulted Muck, who said that he would have been willing to play it, some newspapers began a vituperative campaign against Muck that eventually led to a police raid on his house. That raid revealed a cache of love letters from a nineteen-year-old Boston heiress, which included numerous expressions of anti-American sentiments. Muck, who had canceled a concert in Baltimore after being threatened with violence, was eventually incarcerated with other German immigrants suspected of disloyalty in a camp at Fort Oglethorpe, Georgia. As World War I continued, many orchestras across the United States refused to perform German works, while some states banned the teaching of the German language in schools (Vacha 1983).

Another composer of German heritage, Ernst Kunwald (1868–1939) from Austria, directed the Cincinnati Symphony Orchestra. He experienced similar difficulties when he announced from a stage that "you all know where my heart and sympathies lie. They are on the other side, with my country, but I will play your anthem for you" (Bowles 2007, 417). He too was held at Fort Oglethorpe, although he was permitted to have a Steinway piano brought in and put together an orchestra there. Far more sullen during his incarceration, Muck nonetheless led the orchestra on one occasion in what witnesses later described as a stellar performance.

At the end of the war, Kunwald, who was Jewish, returned to Germany but later moved to Vienna when Hitler came to power. Muck also returned to Germany and eventually accepted the Order of the Golden Eagle from Hitler. When he died in 1940, the members of the Boston Symphony Orchestra stood in a final tribute (Bowles 2007, 430).

Frederick Stock (1872–1942), the German director of the Chicago Symphony, bought Liberty Bonds and took other measures to show his loyalty during the war. He also composed and conducted a pro-American "March and Hymn to Democracy," which the Chicago Symphony performed on a number of occasions.

See also: War and the National Anthem.

Further Reading

Bowles, Edmund A. 2007. "Karl Muck and His Compatriots: German Conductors in America during World War I (and How They Coped)." *American Music* 25 (Winter): 405–40.

Mugmon, Matthew. 2014. "Patriotism, Art, and 'The Star-Spangled Banner' in World War I: A New Look at the Karl Muck Episode." *Journal of Musicological Research* 33:4–26.

Tischler, Barbara L. 1986. "One Hundred Percent Americanism and Music in Boston during World War I." *American Music* 4 (Summer): 164–76.

Vacha, J. E. 1983. "When Wagner Was Verboten: The Campaign against German Music in World War I." *New York History* 64 (April): 171–88.

Warfield, Patrick. 2018. "Educators in Search of an Anthem: Standardizing 'The Star-Spangled Banner' during the First World War." *Journal of the Society for American Music* 12:268–316.

"God Bless America"

Irving Berlin's song "God Bless America" was not introduced to the American public until after Congress had recognized "The Star-Spangled Banner" as the national anthem in 1931, but the song became so popular that some of its supporters have favored replacing the current anthem with it.

"God Bless America" was originally composed by Berlin (1888–1989), a Russian Jewish immigrant, for a Broadway musical entitled *Yip! Yip! Yaphank!*, which Berlin wrote during World War I. Berlin put the song aside, though, because he did not think that it fit the rest of the musical. In the meantime, he was establishing himself as one of the nation's greatest songwriters with such famous and beloved songs as "White Christmas," "Puttin' On the Ritz," and "There's No Business Like Show Business."

Years later, when contralto singer Kate Smith (1907–1986) was seeking a new song to sing for an Armistice Day broadcast, she asked Berlin for ideas. He gave her the song that he had previously composed, which Smith promoted on *Kate Smith Speaks* on CBS. There she described it as "one of the most beautiful compositions ever written, a song that will never die" (Kaplan 2018). She performed the song later that same night, on November 24, 1938, on the *Kate Smith Hour.* Smith's rendition was an instant sensation—so much so, in fact, that some Americans began to lobby for Berlin's song to replace "The Star-Spangled Banner" as the national anthem.

Smith herself resisted replacing the existing anthem. In 1940, she actually recorded an album with "The Star-Spangled Banner" on one side and "God Bless America" on the other (Collins 2003, 89). She later sang "God Bless America" in the 1943 film *This Is the Army*.

Like Smith, Berlin opposed replacing "The Star-Spangled Banner." He said, "A national anthem is something that develops naturally through age, tradition, historic significance and general recognition. We've got a good national anthem. You can't have two" (Kaplan, 2018). Berlin also resisted efforts by the two major political parties to expropriate the song for partisan purposes rather than to highlight the nation as a whole.

In the 1970s the Philadelphia Flyers hockey team alternated "The Star-Spangled Banner" and "God Bless America" with Smith receiving a standing ovation when she sang the latter before more than seventeen thousand fans on October 11, 1973 (Collins 2003, 89). Berlin also sang the song, his last such performance honoring prisoners of war from Vietnam at a ceremony at the White House in 1974. Canadian singer Celine Dion gave additional resonance to the song when she sang it shortly after the 9/11 terrorist attacks of 2001 in a concert that had been organized to aid victims and their families.

Both Berlin and Smith donated the proceeds of the song to the Boy Scouts and Girl Scouts. Still, at a time when there were widespread fears of both Jews and immigrants, racist critics sometimes portrayed Berlin both as a money-grubber and as the leader of a Jewish conspiracy to subvert America.

The song, written like a prayer, is among the most religious of America's national songs. In contrasting "God Bless America" to "America the Beautiful," one scholar observed, "Berlin's song puts more emphasis on a heavenly presence and divine blessing. We, the people, are exceptional. 'America the Beautiful' humbly asks for God's 'grace,' whereas 'God Bless America' has a palpable sense of Manifest Destiny and a triumphant tone from title to final refrain. It is American exceptionalism made manifest in song" (Pedelty 2012, 51).

The opening lines, which appear originally to have been spoken rather than sung, anticipated the coming of World War II with its reference to "storm clouds" gathering across the sea. It further stresses the virtue of "a land that's free." Its reference to mountains and prairies "to the oceans white with foam" bear some similarity to the symbols in "America the Beautiful." Like "The Star-Spangled Banner," the song contrasts the "night" with "a light from above." The idea of America as a "home, sweet home" is particularly poignant coming from an immigrant. Folk singer Woodie Guthrie (1912–1967) was among those who thought that "God Bless America" was too religious and too self-congratulatory, and he composed "This Land Is Your Land" in partial response to it (Pedelty 2012, 51–52).

In April 2019, the New York Yankees baseball team and the Philadelphia Flyers hockey teams both decided to stop playing renditions of Smith's "God Bless America" before any of their games. They did so in response to revelations that she had also recorded "That's Why Darkies Were Born" in 1931, in which African Americans were said to have been born to pick cotton. She had also recorded "Pickaninny Heaven" in 1933, which portrayed African American orphans dreaming of a magical place where they could eat "great big watermelons" (Criss and

Martin 2019). The Philadelphia Flyers subsequently removed a statue outside their arena that they had erected in her honor a year after her death in 1986 (Criss, Martin, and Levenson 2019).

See also: "America the Beautiful."

Further Reading

Collins, Ace. 2003. *Songs Sung Red, White, and Blue: The Stories Behind America's Best-Loved Patriotic Songs.* New York: HarperCollins.

Criss, Doug, and Jill Martin. 2019. "Sports Teams Dump Kate Smith's 'God Bless America' because of Her Racist Songs." *CNN,* April 29. https://www.cnn.com/2019/04/19/us/kate-smith-yankes-flyers-god-bless-america-song-dropped-trnd/index.html.

Criss, Doug, Jill Martin, and Eric Levenson. 2019. "The Philadelphia Flyers Remove a Statue of Kate Smith over Her Racist Songs." *CNN,* April 21. www.cnn.com/2019/04/21/us/philadelphia-flyers-kate-smith-statue/index.html.

"God Bless America." n.d. Irving Berlin (website). Irving Berlin Music Company. http://www.irvingberlin.com/god-bless-america.

Kaplan, James. 2018. "The Complicated DNA of 'God Bless America,'" *New York Times,* November 9. nytimes.com/2018/11/09opinion/irving-b, , ,

Pedelty, Mark. 2012. *Ecomusicology: Rock, Folk, and the Environment.* Philadelphia: Temple University Press.

"God Save the Queen"

The lyrics to "The Star-Spangled Banner" stand out in greater relief when they are compared to the national anthem of the nation from which the United States secured its independence. The British anthem, widely recognized but never officially designated as the national anthem, is titled "God Save the Queen [or King]." It is sung to the same tune as "My Country, 'Tis of Thee," which is one reason why that latter song was not chosen as the U.S. anthem.

The British song dates as early as 1619 and may have been written by a songwriter named John Bull, although the link has not been definitively established. Just as Britain and other nations within the British Commonwealth of Nations often feature pictures of the monarch, who serves as the symbolic head of state, on coins and postage stamps (the United States does not give this honor to any living individual), so too the British anthem focuses on the monarch. By contrast, the anthem of the United States, which rejected a hereditary monarch for an elected president, highlights the flag (Svejda 2005, 68). By comparison to "The Star-Spangled Banner," which references a specific historical event, the words of "God Save the Queen" are much more generic, focusing on the person wearing the crown, who will vary from one era to another.

Prior to the publication of Thomas Paine's *Common Sense* in January 1776, even most Americans who hated British policies and questioned the right of Parliament to enact taxes on them had remained loyal to the king. "God Save the King" was first published in America by James Lyon in 1761 as part of a collection entitled *Urania, or a Choice Collection of Psalm-tunes, Anthems, and Hymns* (Branham and Hartnett 2002, 23).

Perhaps because the monarch is also head of the Church of England (and Scotland), each of the three verses evokes God. The first verse is as follows:

God save our gracious Queen,
Long live our noble Queen,
God save the Queen:
Send her victorious
Happy and glorious,
Long to reign over us:
God save the Queen.

Whereas American presidents serve as both heads of government (the role performed in Britain by the prime minister) and symbolic heads of state, the British monarch fulfills only the latter function. Monarchs are thus said to "reign" rather than to "rule." The words "victorious" and "glorious" are perhaps the best rhymes within the song.

The second verse of the British anthem equates the enemies of the United Kingdom with the enemies of God, and calls upon God for salvation:

O Lord, our God, arise,
Scatter thine enemies,
And make them fall
Confound their politics,
Frustrate their knavish tricks,
On thee our hopes we fix:
God save us all.

Interestingly, this is the only verse that does not specifically mention the monarch.

Almost as if to remedy this omission, the last verse returns to her majesty:

Thy choicest gifts in store,
On her be pleased to pour;
Long may she reign:
May she defend our laws,
And ever give us cause
To sing with heart and voice
God save the Queen.

Prior to the time that Americans appropriated the tune of "God Save the Queen" for "My Country, 'Tis of Thee," Americans had parodied the tune for their own purposes. Thus, in 1779, the *Pennsylvania Packet* published the following:

God save the Thirteen States!
Long rule the United States—
    God save our States!

Make us victorious,
Happy and glorious,
No tyrants over us,
    God save our States!
We'll fear no tryants nod,
Nor stern oppression's rod,
    Till fame's no more,
Thus Liberty, when driven
From Europe's states, is given
A safe retreat and haven
    On our free shore.

Richard Byrd, a lawyer and actor who worked at SBAl-AM radio station and served as a spokesman for the Patriots of Fort McHenry that helped organized the 175th anniversary celebration of the writing of "The Star-Spangled Banner," explained the significance of the British national anthem when he said, "If we'd lost the Battle of Baltimore, we might be singing 'God Save the Queen' instead of 'The Star-Spangled Banner'" (Grauer 1989).

Although the U.S. national anthem highlights the flag instead of the chief executive, the song "Hail to the Chief," which was inspired by Sir Walter Scott's *Lady of the Lake*, has been used when the president arrives for ceremonial occasions since the presidency of Andrew Jackson (Kirk 1997, 133). "Hail Columbia" has been designated as the song to honor the U.S. vice president.

See also: "Hail to the Chief"; "My Country, 'Tis of Thee" ("America").

Further Reading

Branham, Robert James and Stephen J. Hartnett. 2002. *Sweet Freedom's Song: "My Country 'Tis of Thee" and Democracy in America*. New York: Oxford University Press.

Grauer, Neil A. 1989. "Seeking the Old Glory of Fort McHenry." *Washington Post*, September 7. https://www.washingtonpost.com/archive/local/1989/09/07/seeking-the -old-glory-of-fort-mchenry/3bf272e6-a8ae-4dfd-89a5-2c32147e8244.

Kirk, Elise K. 1997. "'Hail to the Chief': The Origins and Legacies of an American Ceremonial Tune." *American Music* 15 (Summer): 123–36.

Scholes, Percy A. 1954. *God Save the Queen! The History and Romance of the World's First National Anthem*. New York: Oxford University Press.

Song and Praise. n.d. "God Save the Queen Lyrics." https://www.songandpraise.org/god -save-the-queen-hymn.htm.

Spofford, Ainsworth R. 1904. "The Lyric Element in American History." *Records of the Columbia Historical Society* 7:211–36.

Svejda, George J. 2005. *History of the Star Spangled Banner from 1814 to the Present*. Honolulu, HI: University Press of the Pacific. First published in 1969 by Division of History, Office of Archeology and Historic Preservation, U.S. Department of the Interior, National Park Service.

"Hail Columbia"

"Hail Columbia" was one of several songs that were considered to be a type of national anthem until Congress specifically gave this honor to "The Star-Spangled Banner" in 1931. "The Star-Spangled Banner" appears to have exceeded it in popularity only after the Civil War, during which time it was aided by its close association with the U.S. flag that flew over Union forts and troops throughout the conflict (Clague and Kuster 2015, 132).

"Hail Columbia" was written by Joseph Hopkinson (1770–1842). He was the son of Francis Hopkinson, a signer of the Declaration of Independence who served on a committee to design the Great Seal of the United States and who was most responsible for the design of the flag. A notable individual in his own right, Joseph Hopkinson was a Federalist lawyer who served as both a member of the House of Representatives from Philadelphia and as a judge on the U.S. District Court for the Eastern District of Pennsylvania.

Just as Francis Scott Key would borrow the musical arrangement for "The Star-Spangled Banner," so too Hopkinson borrowed the music for his song—in his case from Philip Phile (1734–1793), a German composer. Phile had in 1789 written the music to "The President's March" for the inauguration of President George Washington.

Hopkinson wrote "Hail Columbia," which was originally called the "New Federal Song," at the request of the singer and actor Gilbert Fox. He was scheduled to sing at a theater in Philadelphia in 1798 at a time when Democratic-Republicans and Federalists were deeply divided over whether the nation should be aligned with France or with Great Britain, which were warring with one another, and at a time when theater performances could pit members of rival parties against one another (Riordan 2011). Hopkinson carefully crafted words that he hoped would bring the audience together by highlighting their ancestors' patriotism. In presenting the song to George Washington, Hopkinson said, "I trust that we that are young will keep in view the constancy, the courage and the invincible patriotism of our fathers, and prove ourselves worthy of the rich inheritance they have achieved for us" (Coleman 2015, 616).

In a letter to Rufus W. Griswold dated August 24, 1840, Hopkinson further explained that his object in writing the song, had been "to get up an American spirit which should be independent of, and above the interests, passion and policy of both belligerents, and look and feel exclusively for our honour and rights" (Coleman 2015, 617). The song succeeded so well that the audience asked Fox for multiple encores, and after a second performance two days later attended by President Adams, Americans lined the street after the concert to join in the singing (Collins 2003, 103).

At the time the song was written, the term Columbia (derived from Christopher Columbus, the Italian explorer who had famously landed in the Caribbean in 1492) was used as a name for America. The opening verse of the song flashed back to those revolution-minded patriots who had won American independence from the British:

Hail Columbia, happy land!
Hail, ye heroes, heav'n-born band,
Who fought and bled in freedom's cause,
Who fought and bled in freedom's cause,
And when the storm of war was gone
Enjoy'd the peace your valor won.
Let independence be our boast,
Ever mindful what it cost;
Ever grateful for the prize,
Let its altar reach the skies.

This first verse, as well as each of the four subsequent verses, were followed by a chorus that emphasized the hope that continued unity might bring about peace and safety:

Firm, united let us be,
Rallying round our liberty,
As a band of brothers joined,
Peace and safety we shall find.

The second verse calls upon "immortal patriots" to defend their "rights" and their "shore" against rude foes who would "Invade the shrine where sacred lies / Of toil and blood, the well-earned prize." Much as "The Star-Spangled Banner" would proclaim the hope that the nation's cause would be just and that "in God is our trust," so too, the second verse of "Hail Columbia" affirmed:

In Heaven's we place a manly trust,
That truth and justice will prevail,
And every scheme of bondage fail.

The third verse concentrated on the memory of George Washington, who had guided the nation through both war and peace. The concluding verse similarly extolled the current president (John Adams) as "the rock on which the storm will break." The concluding two lines, which seem reminiscent of a speech by Patrick Henry at St. John's Church in Richmond, Virginia, in which he had been quoted as saying, "Give me liberty, or give me death," proclaimed that:

His steady mind, from changes free,
Resolved on death or liberty.

However the song might have united theatergoers, it was the subject of some of the partisan rancor that it had been intended to overcome. Benjamin Franklin Bache (1769–1798), the editor of the Democratic-Republican *Aurora*, thus denounced the song as a partisan stunt. He charged that the theater audience had been composed of "all the British merchants, British agents, and many of our Congress tories [who] attended to do honour to the occasion" (Coleman, 2015, 619).

Before the decision to switch to "Hail to the Chief," Hopkinson's song served as the president's anthem. It is now used to introduce the vice-president and is preceded by four ruffles and flourishes.

See also: Alternatives to the National Anthem; Congress and "The Star-Spangled Banner"; Sousa, John Philip.

Further Reading

Clague, Mark, and Andrew Kuster, eds. 2015. *Star Spangled Songbook: A History in Sheet Music of "The Star-Spangled Banner."* Ann Arbor, MI: Star Spangled Music Foundation.

Coleman, Billy [William]. 2017. "Guest Post: Patriotism, Partisanship, and 'The Star-Spangled Banner': A View from the Early Republic." *The Junto*, September 28. https://earlyamericanists.com/2017/09/28/guest-post-patriotism-partisanship-and -the-star-spangled-banner-a-view-from-the-early-republic.

Coleman, William. 2015. "'The Music of a Well Tun'd State': 'The Star Spangled Banner' and the Development of a Federalist Musical Tradition." *Journal of the Early Republic* 35 (Winter): 599–629.

Collins, Ace. 2003. *Songs Sung Red, White, and Blue: The Stories Behind America's Best-Loved Patriotic Songs*. New York: HarperCollins.

Gray, Myron. 2017. "A Partisan National Song: The Politics of 'Hail Columbia' Reconsidered." *Music & Politics* 11 (Summer): 1–20.

"Hail Columbia." https://www.liveabout.com/thmb/tQGn2tGS6t7W_3TruBlbwiGFp9w= /768x0/filters:no_upscale():max_bytes(150000):strip_icc():format(webp)/hail columbia-58b058ca3df78cdcd8805b39.jpg.

Riordan, Liam. 2011. "'O Dear, What Can the Matter Be?' The Urban Early Republic and the Politics of Popular Song in Benjamin Carr's *Federal Overture*." *Journal of the Early Republic* 31 (Summer): 179–227.

Sonneck, Oscar George Theodore (compiler). 1909. *Report on "The Star-Spangled Banner," "Hail Columbia," "America," "Yankee Doodle."* Washington, DC: Government Printing Office (Library of Congress).

"Hail to the Chief"

Although the United States rejected hereditary monarchy when it declared its independence, it did settle on a single rather than a plural national executive, which gives the individual holding the office a unique position within American government. The U.S. Marine Band, often designated as the "president's own band," almost always plays "Hail to the Chief" when the president enters a room on formal occasions.

The song was adopted from a theater production of Sir Walter Scott's *Lady of the Lake*. It was first performed in the United States at a theater in Philadelphia on January 1, 1812, and first published by G. E. Blake of Philadelphia between 1812 and 1814 (Kirk 1997, 125). Although the individual portrayed in Scott's play was a Scottish chieftain, Sir Roderick Dhu, who opposed the king of Scotland, it was first used on February 22, 1815, to honor the memory of George Washington and the recent treaty that ended the War of 1812 under the title "Wreaths for the Chieftain" at Stone Chapel in Boston.

The year 1829 marked the first time that the song was used to honor a living president, namely Andrew Jackson. The tune began to be regularly played for the president during the administration of John Tyler (1841–1845) and his successor James K. Polk, who served from 1845 to 1849. It has been classified by Elise Kirk, along with "The Star-Spangled Banner," as "our nation's oldest ceremonial melody" (1997, 133).

The music was composed by James Sanderson (c. 1769–c. 1841) of London's Surrey Theatre. The original words (Kirk 1997, 130) were:

Hail to the Chief who in triumph advances!
Honour'd and bless'd be the evergreen Pine!
Long may the tree in his banner that glances
Flourish, the shelter and grace of the line!
While e'ry Highland glen
Sends our shout back again,
     Roderigh Vich Alpine Dhu, ho! iero!

The current words typically used in the song today were written by Albert Gamse in 1900 (Stilwell 2018). They make a point of indicating that the president was "chosen" or "selected" as the nation's commander rather than being born into the role:

Hail to the Chief we have chosen for the nation,
Hail to the Chief! We salute him, one and all.
Hail to the Chief, as we pledge cooperation
In proud fulfillment of a great noble call.
Yours is the aim to make this grand country grander,
This you will do, that's our strong, firm belief.
Hail to the one we selected as commander,
Hail to the President! Hail to the Chief!

President Chester A. Arthur, who served as president from 1881 to 1885, so hated the song that he called upon John Philip Sousa to replace it. Sousa's "Presidential Polonaise" did not catch on, however, and future presidents reverted back to "Hail to the Chief." But presidents have also chosen other songs to be played upon their arrival on certain occasions, from the University of Michigan fight song "Hail to the Victors" (a favorite of president and former Michigan football player Gerald R. Ford) to country singer Lee Greenwood's "God Bless the USA" (selected by President Donald J. Trump) (Stilwell 2018).

"Hail to the Chief" is simply a song in honor of the president and "The Star-Spangled Banner," which focuses on the flag, is used as the U.S. national anthem.

In comparing "Hail to the Chief" with "The Star-Spangled Banner," one scholar observed that both acquired their significance during the War of 1812, and like the song that became the national anthem, "Hail to the Chief" is both "a colorful reflection of American life" and "a valued patriotic tradition" (Kirk 1997, 133–34).

Prior to the advent of "Hail to the Chief," presidents were often introduced to the tune of "Hail Columbia," the latter of which is now used to announce the arrival of the vice-president at formal occasions.

See also: "God Save the Queen"; "Hail Columbia"; War of 1812.

Further Reading

Gonyea, Don. 2017. "'Hail to the Chief': Fanfare Sought by Some Presidents, Avoided by Others." *Weekend Edition*, National Public Radio, March 4. https://www.npr.org /2017/03/04/518333087/hail-to-the-chief-fanfare-sought-by-some-presidents -avoided-by-others.

Kirk, Elise K. 1997. "'Hail to the Chief': The Origins and Legacies of an American Ceremonial Tune." *American Music* 15 (Summer): 123–36.

Stilwell, Blake. 2018. "How 'Hail to the Chief' Became the Presidential Anthem." *We Are the Mighty*, November 7. https://www.wearethemighty.com/history/hail-chief -presidential-anthem.

Hendrix, Jimi

Jimi Hendrix (1942–1970) was an African American rock performer. A fiery guitarist and singer, Hendrix carved out a reputation as a tremendous concert act. This became particularly true after his electrifying performance of "The Star-Spangled Banner" at the Woodstock concert in New York in 1969, which was memorialized in a film the following year. Hendrix used distortion effects to emphasize the sounds of rockets and bombs, sometimes combined with the playing of "Taps," which emphasized the horror of war at a time when increasing numbers of young people were protesting the Vietnam War.

Scholar Mark Clague observed that responses to Hendrix's performance of the "Star-Spangled Banner" have varied from music journalist Charles Shaar Murray's assessment that the song "is probably the most complex and powerful work of American art to deal with the Vietnam War," to rock journalist Charles Cross's statement that for Hendrix, the performance was "a musical exercise, not a manifesto," to Pete Johnson's view that it was "meaningless and constitutes the cheapest kind of sensationalism" (Clague 2014, 435).

Hendrix's performance at Woodstock, which he had preceded by making a sign of peace with his hand, is his best known, but it was only one of many renditions that he had given using "The Star-Spangled Banner." Hendrix had been a member of the 101st Airborne Division before seeking a discharge so that he could pursue his musical career. After spending some time in London to jump-start his musical career, he came back to the United States with a more critical eye about American military action in Vietnam. Ultimately, Clague believes that Hendrix's rendition was a challenge not only to America's participation in the war in Vietnam but also to what he considered to be the political apathy of many of his concertgoers.

Pushing back against interpretations of Hendrix's rendition as "a 'burning of the American flag,' a 'hate-filled guitar solo,' 'a searing, mind-blowing rendition,' a 'dismemberment of "The Star Spangled Banner,"'" and the 'triumphal deconstruction of the American Dream,'" Clague asserted that the performance also "contains a core of hope, that it is a celebration of possibility inspired by the Woodstock festival itself" (Clague 2014, 461).

See also: Vietnam War.

Further Reading

Christgau, Robert. 2019. "Jimi Hendrix's 'Star-Spangled Banner' Is the Anthem We Need in the Age of Trump." *Los Angeles Times,* August 13. https://www.latimes.com /entertainment-arts/music/story/2019-08-13/jimi-hendrixs-star-spangled-banner -is-the-anthem-we-need-in-the-age-of-trump.

Clague, Mark. 2014. "'This Is America': Jimi Hendrix's Star Spangled Banner Journey as Psychedelic Citizenship." *Journal of the Society for American Music* 8:435–578.

Cush, Andy. 2016. "Remember When Jimi Hendrix Protested the National Anthem on a National Stage?" *Spin,* September 12. https://www.spin.com/2016/09/remember -when-jimi-hendrix-protested-the-national-anthem-on-a-national-stage.

Holloway, Mrs. Reuben Ross

Of all the individuals who lobbied for the adoption of "The Star-Spangled Banner" as the official national anthem, none appears to have been more important, or more colorful, than Ella Virginia Houck Holloway (1862–1940). Better known as Mrs. Reuben Ross Holloway, she wanted no greater distinction than to be called "citizen." Beginning in 1918, she helped persuade U.S. Representative John Charles Linthicum of Maryland to introduce resolutions in Congress to elevate the song to anthem status. She also lobbied for passage of a teachers' oath bill, which was designed to prevent teachers from conveying communist doctrines to their students.

Characterized as "a civic gadfly," Holloway was known for accenting her imposing figure with a beaver hat and plume that apparently rose a foot above her head. She apparently once said, "The general contours of my hat and the Constitution of the United States must remain unchanged" (Rasmussen 2000). Opposed to what she considered to be liberal activism within the Episcopal Church of which she was a member, she walked out of what she considered to be inappropriately liberal sermons so frequently that she eventually stopped attending.

Holloway also served as head of the Maryland Society of the United Daughters of the War of 1812. She opposed national alcoholic prohibition, women's suffrage, and recognition of communist Russia while favoring a strong military, a daily family salute to the flag, and standing for "The Star-Spangled Banner." When she was asked what she would do if she were sitting in the bathtub when she heard the national anthem, she replied, "Young man, I stand when I hear 'The Star-Spangled Banner'" (Rasmussen 2000). She was known for patrolling the streets of Baltimore not only for improper displays of the flag but also for newsstands selling magazines with pictures of nude women, which she sought to ban ("Mrs. Holloway, Patriot, Is Dead" 1940).

A plaque was placed in her honor on March 25, 2006. A collection of her papers is found in the archives at the Fort McHenry National Monument and Historic Shrine.

See also: Congress and "The Star-Spangled Banner."

Further Reading
"Mrs. Holloway, Patriot, Is Dead." 1940. *Baltimore Sun*, December 1, p. 20.
National Society United States Daughters of 1812. n.d. "Mrs. Reuben Ross Holloway." https://usdaughters1812.org/mrs-reuben-ross-holloway.
Rasmussen, Frederick N. 2000. "She Wrapped Her Life in the Flag." *Baltimore Sun*, July 8. http://articles.baltimoresun.com/2000-07-08/features/0007080044_1_ross-hollo way-star-spangled-banner-reuben-ross.

Holmes, Oliver Wendell, Sr.

Oliver Wendell Holmes, Sr. (1809–1894) was a well-known physician and man of letters who may be best known for a poem he wrote when he thought the warship USS *Constitution* (dubbed "Old Ironsides" after having been so victorious during the War of 1812) was about to be scuttled. He is also the father of Oliver Wendell Holmes, Jr., who was one of America's most influential Supreme Court justices.

In 1861, Holmes penned an additional verse to "The Star-Spangled Banner" designed for those who anticipated that the Civil War would bring an end to slavery. It was printed in many songbooks of its day and is sometimes still considered to be a fifth stanza (Shafer 2013):

When our land is illum'd with Liberty's smile,
If a foe from within strike a blow at her glory,
Down, down, with the traitor that dares to defile
The flag of her stars and the page of her story!

By the millions unchain'd who our birthright have gained

We will keep her bright blazon forever unstained!
And the Star-Spangled Banner in triumph shall wave
While the land of the free is the home of the brave.

At the time Holmes was writing, the central goal of President Abraham Lincoln in waging war against the Confederate South was to preserve the Union. Over time the nation increasingly began to believe that Lincoln had been right in proclaiming that the nation could not forever remain half slave and half free, and uncompensated slave emancipation became a goal of the war. Slavery was eventually ended via the Thirteenth Amendment, which the requisite number of states ratified in 1865. This amendment helped eliminate the hypocrisy of a slave-holding nation declaring itself the "land of the free."

See also: Abolitionists; African Americans; Parodies; Presidential Campaigns; Slavery; War of 1812.

Further Reading

Shafer, Leah. 2013. "Francis Scott Key and the Complex Legacy of Slavery." *A Blog of History*, U.S. Capitol Historical Society, June 14. https://uschs.wordpress.com/tag /oliver-wendell-holmes.

Veltman, Chloe. 2017. "Why We Should Sing 'The Star-Spangled Banner's Obscure Fifth Verse." *KQED*, March 2. https://www.kqed.org/arts/12822853/why-we-should -sing-the-star-spangled-banners-obscure-fifth-verse.

Houston, Whitney

Among the many renditions of "The Star-Spangled Banner" at athletic events, the performance by singer and actress Whitney Houston (1963–2012) at the 1991 Super Bowl remains one of the most memorable. The performance obtained much of its force from the fact that it took place just ten days after the United States launched Operation Desert Storm to free Kuwait from a military invasion by neighboring Iraq and its dictatorial leader, Saddam Hussein. Houston saw her performance, which was widely praised, as a way of uniting the nation in the face of uncertainty. "It was an intense time for a country. A lot of our daughters and sons were overseas fighting," she recalled. "We needed hope, you know, to bring our babies home and that's what it was about for me, that's what I felt when I sang that song, and the overwhelming love coming out of the stands was incredible" (Kooijman 2013, 76).

The drama of Whitney's rousing rendition of the anthem was enhanced by the presence of a gigantic U.S. flag in the middle of the field and four F-16 jets that flew over the stadium at the end of the performance. Subsequently released as a single, Houston's rendition reached number 20 on Billboard's Hot 100, with another later release including "America the Beautiful" reaching number 6 (Kooijman 2013, 78–79).

An engineer later disclosed that although Houston was singing live, she was singing into a dead microphone, and television viewers were hearing a non-live prerecorded version (Kerr-Kineen 2017).

See also: Sports Events.

Further Reading

Kerr-Kineen, Luke. 2017. "How Whitney Houston's Iconic National Anthem Set-off a Pointless Controversy." *For the Win* (blog), *USA Today Sports*, February 2. https:// ftw.usatoday.com/2017/02/whitney-houston-national-anthem-video-super-bowl -51-2017.

Kooijman, Jaap. 2003. *Fabricating the Absolute Fake: America in Contemporary Pop Culture*. Netherlands: Amsterdam University Press.

Hymn

Although "The Star-Spangled Banner" has been America's official national anthem since 1931, it was long described as a hymn and continues to fit that genre. Moreover, that terminology explains in part why there are continuing questions about whether it is chiefly a poem or a song.

A hymn is traditionally understood to be a song in praise of God or a nation—with the flag largely symbolizing the nation in "The Star-Spangled Banner." Songwriter and former music director Bobby Gilles observed that a hymn can also be described as "a kind of poem set to music. . . . Most song lyrics are not really meant to be taken as poetry" whereas most hymns began as poems and were later set to music (Gilles 2012). He further observed, "Hymns often contain more words than contemporary popular songs, but each line is metrically precise." In what he admitted may sound like a "pedantic" distinction, he also noted that "classic hymns did not contain choruses."

One rhetorical advantage of referring to "The Star-Spangled Banner" as a hymn is that it somewhat mutes the criticism that it was derived from an old drinking song, namely "To Anacreon in Heaven." Moreover, Francis Scott Key was an amateur poet and labeled some of his other works as hymns, most notably his "Hymn for the Fourth of July."

See also: Anthem; Congress and "The Star-Spangled Banner"; Drinking Song; "Hymn for the Fourth of July, 1832"; "In God Is Our Trust"; "To Anacreon in Heaven."

Further Reading

Gilles, Bobby. 2012. "What Makes a Worship Song a Hymn?" *My Song in the Night* (blog), October 1. https://mysonginthenight.com/2012/10/01/what-makes-a-worship-song-a-hymn.

Riley, A. C. D. 1907. "Respect to Our National Hymn." *Journal of Education* 65 (May 2): 495.

"Hymn for the Fourth of July, 1832"

Although Francis Scott Key was an attorney, he was also an amateur poet. He was quite religious and had considered becoming an Episcopal priest. Although most of his poems described people he had known, he also wrote a few as hymns. He wrote one such hymn for Independence Day in 1832, almost twenty years after he penned "The Star-Spangled Banner." Whereas the song that became the national anthem did not invoke God until the fourth and final stanza, where it suggested that the national motto should be "In God is our trust," Key's hymn of 1832 is pervasively religious and is more oriented toward God than to either the nation or its flag.

The first verse of is fairly representative:

BEFORE the Lord we bow—
　　The God who reigns above,
And rules the world below,
　　Boundless in power and love.
　　　　Our thanks we bring,
　　　　　In joy and praise,
　　　　　Our hearts we raise
　　　　To heaven's high King.

The second verse thanks God for blessing the nation with "peace and rest" (Key 1857, 94). The next two verses evoke America's founders. Verse 3 thus notes that "Our fathers sought thee, Lord! / And on thy help relied" (95). It further attributed the nation's "victory" and freedom to God's power (95). Similarly, the opening line of the fourth verse refers to "God of our sires" and ends with the hope that the nation might be God's "fixed abode": "Be thou our God! / Thy people we!" (95).

The next verse, which focuses on the nation's physical beauty, expresses sentiments quite close to those that Katharine Lee Bates echoed in "America the Beautiful." Key thus wrote:

> May every mountain height,
>   Each vale and forest green,
> Shine in thy word's pure light,
>   And its rich fruits be seen!

The sixth verse moved from the nation to the earth, imploring it to "Cast down they pride, / Thy sin deplore, / And bow before / The crucified" (97). The seventh and final verse expresses the hope that when God returns, "our native land, / From all its rending tombs" will "Send forth a glorious band!" to sing God's praises (97).

See also: "America the Beautiful"; Hymn; "In God Is Our Trust"; Key, Francis Scott.

Further Reading

Key, Francis Scott. 1857. "Hymn for the Fourth of July, 1832." In *Poems of the Late Francis S. Key, Esq., Author of "The Star-Spangled Banner,"* edited by Henry V. D. Johns, 94–97. New York: Robert Carter & Brothers.

Immigrants

America is largely a nation of immigrants who have added incredible strength, vitality, and diversity to the country. Throughout much of American history, however, some native-born Americans of northern European descent have feared the influx of immigrants and their alleged foreign ideologies and values. In addition to establishing residency, new citizens must take a test to ascertain their civic knowledge. Under the Fourteenth Amendment, which the states ratified in 1868, individuals who are born in the United States become citizens as a result of such birth, even if their parents are immigrants.

Especially in the wake of immigration from non-English-speaking countries, communities have used their schools to inculcate a love of America in immigrants. This goal was a driving force behind the adoption of the pledge to the flag in the late nineteenth century as well as in teaching songs like "The Star-Spangled Banner," "America," and others that are viewed as embodying American values.

Many naturalization ceremonies include the singing or performance of the national anthem as part of the ceremony, which involves a renunciation of prior citizenship in order to become an American. A British writer has asserted that naturalized Americans, like members of the U.S. armed forces, are among those who most value the national anthem. He wrote, "They hear the song's final line about 'the land of the free and the home of the brave' and it motivates them, pushes them to take on two jobs, or to study late into the night. These are people for whom the American Dream really matters; who, unlike me, are convinced of its truthfulness" (Marshall 2015, 93). Calling Francis Scott Key, who wrote "The Star-Spangled Banner," "America's first great ad-man for helping create that dream," he further notes that "that simple phrase has driven people to travel thousands of miles, to risk everything, just to be part of a country. It is the greatest boast a country has ever had" (Marshall 2015, 93).

The seventh and final episode of a pageant held in Madison, Wisconsin, in 1914 to commemorate the centennial of Key's creation of "The Star-Spangled Banner" featured groups of children dressed in the folk costumes of their nations of origins. Pageant instructions noted that "at the conclusion . . . they all stand with hands clasped, thus showing that in America the German, the English, the French, the Irish, the Italian, the Greek, the Jew, the Norwegian, the Swede, and all other nationalities represented, have become united into the American with all of the old-world prejudices forgotten" (Rockwell 1914, 37).

See also: "Land of the Free and the Home of the Brave"; "My Country, 'Tis of Thee" ("America").

Further Reading

Abril, Carlos R. 2007. "Functions of a National Anthem in Society and Education: A Sociocultural Perspective." *Bulletin of the Council for Research in Music Education*, no. 172 (Spring): 69–87.

Baer, John W. 1992. *The Pledge of Allegiance: A Centennial History, 1892–1992.* Annapolis, MD: Free State Press.

Branham, Robert James, and Stephen J. Hartnett. 1996. "'Of Thee I Sing': Contesting 'America.'" *American Quarterly* 48 (December): 623–52.

Ellis, Richard J. 2005. *To the Flag: The Unlikely History of the Pledge of Allegiance.* Lawrence: University Press of Kansas.

Marshall, Alex. 2015. *Republic or Death! Travels in Search of National Anthems.* London: Random House.

Rockwell, Ethel T. 1914. *Star-Spangled Banner Pageant: Staged in the Capitol Park at Madison, Wisconsin, in Celebration of the One-Hundredth Anniversary of the Writing of This National Song by Francis Scott Key.* N.p.: Ethel Theodora Rockwell.

Salomone, Rosemary C. 2010. *True American.* Cambridge, MA: Harvard University Press.

"In God Is Our Trust"

The last stanza of Francis Scott Key's song "The Star-Spangled Banner" is the most religious in terms of tone and imagery, and it appears to be designed as a prayer (Meyer 1995, 13). In full, the verse says (Svejda 2005, 468):

> O! Thus be it ever, when freemen shall stand
> Between their loved home and the war's desolation!
> Blest with victory and peace, may the heav'n rescued land
> Praise the Power that hath made and preserved us a nation.
> Then conquer we must, when our cause it is just,
> And this be our motto: "In God is our trust."
> And the star-spangled banner in triumph shall wave
> O'er the land of the free and the home of the brave!

The verse thus attributes the victory to God, but, somewhat humbly, it only expects such help "when our cause it is just."

Key was a religious man. In a letter from October 5, 1814, to his friend John Randolph of Roanoke about his experiences during the bombardment of Fort McHenry and his fears for nearby Baltimore's safety if the British won that battle, Key wrote, "I hope I shall never cease to feel the warmest gratitude when I think of this most manifest deliverance. It seems to have given me a higher idea of the 'forbearance, long-suffering & tender mercy' of God than I had ever before conceived. Whether this gentle paternal chastisement we have been suffering will be sufficient for us is yet to be seen" (Svejda 2005, 67).

Key helped found—and served in leadership positions—in a number of Episcopal churches. He also was active in the Sunday school movement, which was especially interested in bringing religious education to western settlers. He was a lifetime member of the American Sunday School Union, which supported the spread of Sunday schools (Roach 2018).

Key is hardly the first songwriter to invoke God, but his language has the merit of suggesting that a nation can only fully expect God's help when it acts justly. Key's hope that the nation's motto shall be "In God is our trust" has largely been fulfilled. It began with the adoption of the phrase "In God We Trust" on selective U.S. currency beginning in 1864 and on all currency beginning in 1957 (though some took a number of years to implement). Such currency typically also contains the phrase "E Pluribus Unum" ("From Many, One").

In 1954, Congress voted to add the words, "under God," to the Pledge of Allegiance in an attempt to distinguish the values of the nation from those of the Soviet Union and its communist allies. In 1956, it further officially adopted the words "In God We Trust" as the nation's official motto.

Although the First Amendment to the U.S. Constitution prohibits the "establishment" of religion, U.S. courts have upheld the use of the phrase as an act of ceremonial deism while allowing students and others who might have religious objections to the pledge to refrain from participating. In *Sheldon v. Fannin* (1963), a U.S. district court judge specifically denied a claim that singing the national anthem in schools constituted an establishment of religion. The judge thus observed that "the singing of the National Anthem is not a religious but a patriotic ceremony, intended to inspire devotion to and love of country. Any religious references therein are incidental and expressive only of the faith which as a matter of historical fact has inspired the growth of the nation" (774).

It is typical for presidents and other public officials to end speeches with the words "May God bless America." The phrase recognizes that the dominant religions in America are monotheistic, although it might on this account be less appealing to American Hindus, who believe in multiple gods, or American atheists who do not believe in any higher spiritual power. Most monotheistic religions portray God as the sovereign creator of the universe, and a deity whose will shall ultimately prevail. In America, this doctrine was often connected to the idea that the nation had a special destiny, as in expanding geographically to the Pacific Ocean, or in overcoming its foreign foes.

Ethnomusicologist Katherine Meizel has observed that two other songs, "God Bless America" by Irving Berlin (which borrows, in part, from "America the Beautiful") and "God Bless the USA" by Lee Greenwood, both with highly religious themes, have become "substitutional or supplemental roles in contexts that might conventionally call for the official national anthem" (Meizel 2006, 499). Pointing in part to performances of these songs on the television program *American Idol*, in which the audience democratically helps select the winners, she further associates both songs with attempts not only to express faith and devotion to America but also to its capitalistic system.

In 1931, a special brass tablet designed by Philip E. Frohman and sponsored by the District of Columbia Society of the United States Daughters of 1812 was unveiled at the Washington Cathedral. Featuring a rising sun over Fort McHenry (which gives it something of the appearance of a mosque) under two U.S. flags, one with fifteen stars and stripes and another with forty-eight stars and thirteen stripes, the tablet is dedicated, in all capital letters, to:

FRANCIS SCOTT KEY
Author of the Star-Spangled Banner
August 9, 1780–January 11, 1843

The plaque quotes from the fourth stanza:

And This Be Our Motto: "In God Is Our Trust."
And the Star-Spangled Banner in Triumph Shall Wave,
O'er the Land of the Free and the Home of the Brave.

See also: First Amendment; Key, Francis Scott; *Sheldon v. Fannin* (1963).

Further Reading

Epstein, Steven B. 1996. "Rethinking the Constitutionality of Ceremonial Deism." *Columbia Law Review* 96 (December): 2083–174.

Fisher, Louis and Nada Mourtada-Sabbah. 2002. "Adopting 'In God We Trust' as the U.S. National Motto." *Journal of Church and State* 44 (Autumn): 671–92.

Gehrz, Chris. 2017. "A (Brief) Religious History of the Star-Spangled Banner." *Pantheos*, September 26. https://www.patheos.com/blogs/anxiousbench/2017/09/religious -history-star-spangled-banner.

"In God We Trust. 1892." *American Journal of Numismatics, and Bulletin of the American Numismatic and Archaeological Society* 26 (April): 83.

Krythe, Maymie. 1968. *What So Proudly We Hail: All About Our American Flag, Monuments and Symbols.* New York: Harper & Row.

Meizel, Katherine. 2006. "A Singing Citizenry: Popular Music and Civil Religion in America." *Journal for the Scientific Study of Religion* 45 (December): 497–503.

Meyer, Sam. 1995. *Paradoxes of Fame: The Francis Scott Key Story.* Annapolis, MD: Eastwind.

Roach, David. 2018. "Writer of 'Star Spangled Banner' Helped Evangelize West thru Sunday School Movement." *God Reports* (blog), July 4. https://blog.godreports .com/2018/07/writer-of-star-spangled-banner-helped-evangelize-west-thru-sunday -school-movement.

Sheldon v. Fannin, 221 F. Supp. 766 (D. Ariz. 1963).

Svejda, George J. 2005. *History of the Star Spangled Banner from 1814 to the Present.* Honolulu, HI: University Press of the Pacific. First published in 1969 by Division of History, Office of Archeology and Historic Preservation, U.S. Department of the Interior, National Park Service.

Indian Queen Hotel (Baltimore)

The primary subject of "The Star-Spangled Banner" is the large flag that Francis Scott Key observed flying over Fort McHenry after the British bombardment of the fortress on September 13–14, 1814. Although he jotted down notes about the battle while still on the ship from which he viewed it, Key is believed to have written the complete draft of all four verses after his release from British custody on September 16 while staying at the Indian Queen Hotel in Baltimore. Key's manuscript does not include a title, and his song was first published under the title "The Defence of Fort M'Henry" on the next day.

Key had arrived by land on September 16 at the Indian Queen Hotel, which was located at the corner of Hanover and Baltimore Streets and owned by John Gadsby (1766–1844), an English immigrant. On September 29, 1809, a visitor named Samuel Breck had observed that the inn was "in a style exceeding anything that I recollect to have seen in Europe or America. The inn is so capacious that it accommodates two hundred lodgers, and has two splendid billard-rooms, large stables and many other appendages. The numerous bed-chambers have call bells, and the servants are more attentive than in any public or private house I ever knew" (Baltimore 1814).

Gadsby had established his reputation as a hotelier at Alexandria's City Hotel, which he had run from 1796 to 1808 and had hosted prominent American founding fathers. That establishment is now known as Gadsby's Tavern Museum, and it featured special exhibits related to the writing of Key's anthem during bicentennial celebrations in 2014 (Williams 2014).

The Maryland Historical Society owns the manuscript that Key is believed to have authored at the Indian Queen.

See also: Baltimore, Maryland; Key, Francis Scott.

Further Reading

Baltimore 1814 (website). https://1814.baltimoreheritage.org/tag/indian-queen-tavern.

Williams, Liz. 2014. "Where Did Francis Scott Key Write the Song that Became Our National Anthem?" *O Say Can You See?* (blog), Smithsonian National Museum of American History, June 12. http://americanhistory.si.edu/blog/2014/06/where-did -francis-scott-key-write-his-famous-lines.html.

Jehovah's Witnesses

Jehovah's Witnesses are a religious group that was founded by Charles Taze Russell (1852–1916) in the 1870s in expectation of the imminent return of Christ to earth. They grew from the Watch Tower Society, which Russell founded in 1881 as a vehicle for producing and distributing religious tracts.

In addition to departing from orthodox Christianity in a number of ways, the Witnesses are known for their pacifist beliefs (and hence their historical nonparticipation in the military draft), for refusing to accept blood transfusions, and for refusing to salute the American flag, which they consider to be a form of idolatry in violation of the first of the Ten Commandments. They also are known for their fervent door-to-door witnessing.

The Jehovah's Witnesses stance in opposition to standing for the national anthem or saluting the U.S. flag has involved them in frequent controversies. A Supreme Court decision in *Minersville School District v. Gobitis* (1940), which ruled that the children of Witnesses were required to participate in compulsory flag-salute ceremonies in their schools, led to considerable violence against the Witnesses. A riot even broke out in Klamath Falls, Oregon, in 1942 after a group of Jehovah's Witnesses refused to stand after a sound truck began blaring "The Star-Spangled Banner" into their meeting place (LaLande 2018).

Citing the freedoms of expression guaranteed by the First and Fourteenth Amendments, the U.S. Supreme Court subsequently overturned its *Minersville* decision requiring compulsory flag salutes in *West Virginia State Board of Education v. Barnette* (1943). A U.S. district court decision in Arizona subsequently made it clear in *Sheldon v. Fannin* (1963) that schools could not force children to stand for the national anthem.

See also: First Amendment; *Sheldon v. Fannin* (1963).

Further Reading

LaLande, Jeff. 2018. "Jehovah's Witnesses Riots, 1942." *Oregon Encyclopedia*. Last updated March 17, 2018. https://oregonencyclopedia.org/articles/jehovah_witness_riots_of_klamath_falls_1942.

Newton, Merlin Owen. 1995. *Armed with the Constitution: Jehovah's Witnesses in Alabama and the U.S. Supreme Court, 1929–1946*. Tuscaloosa: University of Alabama Press.

Peters, Shawn Francis. 2000. *Judging Jehovah's Witnesses: Religious Persecution and the Dawn of the Rights Revolution*. Lawrence: University Press of Kansas.

Smith, Chuck. 2001. "The Persecution of West Virginia Jehovah's Witnesses and the Expansion of Legal Protection for Religious Liberty." *Journal of Church and State* 43 (Summer): 539–77.

Kaepernick, Colin

Colin Kaepernick (1987–) was a quarterback for the San Francisco 49ers in the National Football League (NFL) who garnered significant attention when, during the 2016 preseason, he began sitting (and later kneeling on one bended knee) during the pregame playing of "The Star-Spangled Banner" as a way to protest racial injustice in the United States.

The son of a white woman and an African American man who was adopted by a white couple, Kaepernick played for the University of Nevada and was drafted by the 49ers in 2011. Kaepernick became a star quarterback, showcasing dual-threat capabilities as both a runner and passer. He became a free agent in 2016 after his protests, however, and has not been picked up by another team. Most observers believe that the refusal of NFL teams to consider him for even a backup quarterback spot on their rosters is due to the controversy that surrounds his national anthem protest actions.

Kaepernick's protest came at a time when there were a number of well-publicized police shootings of unarmed African Americans. Kaepernick thus explained, "I'm not going to stand up to show pride in a flag for a country that oppresses black people and people of color. To me, this is bigger than football, and it would be selfish on my part to look the other way. There are bodies in the street and people getting paid leave and getting away with murder" (Hauser 2017, 223).

Kaepernick's actions stirred deep national divisions. President Donald J. Trump interpreted the act not as one of courage and conviction but as one of disrespect. In obvious reference to Kaepernick and numerous other players who followed his example, Trump asked, "Wouldn't you love to see one of these NFL owners, when somebody disrespects our flag, to say 'Get that son of a bitch off the field right now. Out! He's fired. He's fired!'" (Paulson 2017).

Kaepernick later accused NFL owners of conspiring against his efforts to find a new team and filed a lawsuit seeking appropriate damages; fellow protestor Eric Reid filed a similar grievance against the Cincinnati Bengals when they decided not to sign him after asking him whether he intended to continue his anthem protests. Although Kaepernick remained the subject of considerable criticism, in 2018 the shoe company Nike used his picture to launch a new advertising campaign based on the theme "Believe in something, even if it means sacrificing everything" (Creswell, Draper, and Maheshwari 2018). In 2019, the company suspended sales of a tennis shoe with the so-called Betsy Ross Flag on it. The decision was attributed both to Kaepernick's remarks associating it with an era during which millions of black Americans were enslaved and to reports that some white supremacists had appropriated the flag design as a favored symbol (Vile 2019).

On February 15, 2019, the lawyers representing Kaepernick and Reid announced that they had resolved their claims, but the settlement was subject to a confidentiality agreement and was thus not revealed (Newport 2019).

See also: African Americans; Sports Events.

Further Reading

Creswell, Julie, Kevin Draper, and Sapna Maheshwari. 2018. "Nike Nearly Dropped Colin Kaepernick Before Embracing Him." *New York Times*, September 26. https://www.nytimes.com/2018/09/26/sports/nike-colin-kaepernick.html.

Edelman, Marc. 2018. "Standing to Kneel: Analyzing NFL Players' Freedom to Protest during the Playing of the U.S. National Anthem." *Fordham Law Review* Online 86:1–15,

Hauser, Thomas. 2017. *There Will Always Be Boxing: Another Year Inside the Sweet Science*. Fayetteville: University of Arkansas Press.

Johnson, Martenzie. 2016. "Let's Take the National Anthem Literally, and the Songwriter at His Word." *The Undefeated*, August 30. https://theundefeated.com/features/lets-take-the-national-anthem-literally-and-the-songwriter-at-his-word.

Newport, Kyle. 2018. "Colin Kaepernick, Eric Reid Settle Grievances with NFL in Collusion Case." *Bleacher Report*, February 15. https://bleacherreport.com/articles/2820996-colin-kaepernick-eric-reid-settle-grievances-with-nfl-in-collusion-case.

Paulson, Ken. 2017. "NFL Protests: Your Boss Can Tell You to Stand for the Anthem. Trump Can't." *First Amendment Encyclopedia*, Free Speech Center, Middle Tennessee State University, October 2. https://mtsu.edu/first-amendment/post/57/nfl-protests-your-boss-can-tell-you-to-stand-for-the-anthem-trump-can-t.

Vile, John R. 2019. "Americans Should Reclaim the Betsy Ross Flag Instead of Abandoning It." *Tennessean*, July 8. https://www.tennessean.com/story/opinion/2019/07/08/betsy-ross-flag-nike-controversy/1675249001.

Key, Francis Scott

Francis Scott Key (1779–1843) was the American attorney who authored "The Star Spangled Banner," the song that Congress designated in 1931 as the national anthem.

Key was born in Frederick (now Carroll) County, Maryland, to John Ross Key and Ann Pheobe Dagworthy Charlton Key in 1779. He graduated from St. John's College in Annapolis, where he was known for his antics but later played an influential role in saving the institution. Key read law under his uncle Philip Barton Key, who had been a Loyalist during the Revolutionary War but had returned to Maryland after America gained its independence and remained well respected in his community.

In 1802 Francis Scott Key married Mary Tayloe Lloyd, who was usually called Polly. They had eleven children, a number of whom predeceased their parents. Key, meanwhile, became a well-respected lawyer who argued numerous cases before the U.S. Supreme Court, was elected as president and recorder for the Georgetown Board of Alderman in 1808, and was appointed in 1833 to be the U.S. attorney for the District of Columbia. Key was also an amateur poet and songwriter, although the only songs that he is known to have written were religious in nature.

Key had been among those who had opposed the War of 1812 because of concerns that it stemmed primarily from the desire to incorporate Canada into the United States rather than to rectify wrongs that the English had inflicted on American sailors. This view, however, did not keep him from serving with the hapless group of militia volunteers who unsuccessfully attempted to defend the nation's capital from the British invasion at the Battle of Bladensburg. Key's service was based on his belief that, whatever the justifications for again taking up arms against the British, the war was now tied to the defense of the American homeland. Soon thereafter, Key was authorized to visit the British in an attempt to secure the release of Dr. William Beanes, a sixty-five-year-old medical doctor whom the British had captured from his house after he had facilitated the capture of renegade British troops who had raided one of his farms.

FRANCIS SCOTT KEY

Francis Scott Key is the author of the poem "The Star-Spangled Banner." Key wrote the words while negotiating a prisoner release with the British in the War of 1812. His words would later be set to music and finally officially adopted as the U.S. national anthem in 1931. (Library of Congress)

Key boarded a ship, probably the *President*, to make contact with the British fleet that was imprisoning Beanes. With the help of John Stuart Skinner, a government official who had brought letters from British soldiers telling how American doctors had dressed their wounds, Key succeeded in securing an agreement for Beanes's release. Because the British feared that Key and his companion knew too much about their plans to attack Baltimore, they insisted that they stay aboard ship during their attack on Fort McHenry.

The night of September 13, 1814, that Key spent aboard the *President* formed the backdrop for "The Star-Spangled Banner." Although the British had plans for an attack by both land and sea, the former largely faltered with the death of commander John Ross at the Battle of North Point, stormy weather, and the presence of a large number of militiamen defending the coast against a British landing.

This left a flotilla of five fearsomely named British war ships—*Devastation, Terror, Volcano, Aetna*, and *Meteor*—to launch the attack against Fort McHenry. These ships are believed to have fired about fifteen hundred mortars within a twenty-four-hour period, some of which were two hundred pounds (Leepson 2014, 61–62). Army Major George Armistead, who commanded U.S. forces at the fort, had ordered two flags from Mary Young Pickersgill to fly over the compound. One was a storm flag, measuring seventeen by twenty-five feet, which was probably flown during the night of shelling and rain. The other, which measured thirty by forty-two feet, was probably the one hoisted the next morning to symbolize Fort McHenry's fighting spirit. The latter flag is the one that has been designated as the Star-Spangled Banner. Consistent with legislation that had been adopted in 1794 (later revised), the flag had both fifteen stars (recognizing the new states of Kentucky and Vermont) and fifteen stripes—today's has fifty stars and thirteen stripes.

As dawn broke, Key scanned the ramparts on the early morning of September 14, 1814, of Fort McHenry to see whether Americans under the command of George Armistead had abandoned or surrendered. To his great relief, he saw the flag through the mists and wrote the lyrics to what was originally titled "Defence of Fort M'Henry" and is today known as "The Star-Spangled Banner." These lyrics were soon thereafter published as a broadside and then in a Baltimore newspaper.

In a letter that Chief Justice Roger Taney, Key's son-in-law, wrote in 1856, Taney recalled his father-in-law's account of his experiences that fateful night and morning:

> [Key] told me, that under the excitement of the time he had written a song and handed me a printed copy of 'The Star-Spangled Banner.' I asked him how he had found time in the scenes he had been passing through to compose a song? He said he commenced it on the deck of their vessel, in the fervor of the moment when he saw the enemy hastily retreating to their ships, and looked at the flag he had watched for so anxiously as the morning opened: that he had written some lines or brief notes that would aid him in calling them to mind upon the back of a letter, which he happened to have in his pocket, and for some of the lines as he proceeded he was obliged to rely altogether on his memory, and that he finished it in the boat on his way to the shore and wrote it out as it now stands at the hotel on the night he reached Baltimore, and immediately after he arrived; he said that on the next morning he took it to Judge Nicholson to ask him what he thought of it, that he was so much pleased with it that he immediately sent it to a printer, and directed copies to be struck off in hand-bill form. (Shippen and Taney 1898, 324–25)

Key described his sentiments in a letter to his eccentric longtime friend Congressman John Randolph of Roanoke, who had also initially opposed the war. Noting that his fears had been heightened by reports that the British planned to burn Baltimore if they won at Fort McHenry, and by observations of "illiberal, ignorant and vulgar" behavior by British officers, Key gave a vivid description of the attack on Fort McHenry:

> The heavens aglow were a seething sea of flame, and the waters of the harbor, lashed into an angry sea by the vibrations, the Minden [ship] rode and tossed as though in a tempest. It is recorded that the houses in the city of Baltimore, two miles distant, were shaken to their foundations. Above the tempestuous roar, intermingled with its hubbub and confusion, were heard the shrieks and groans of the dying and wounded. But alas! They were from the direction of the fort. What did it mean? For over an hour the pandemonium reigned. Suddenly it ceased—all was quiet, not a shot fired or sound heard, a deathlike stillness prevailed, as the darkness of night resumed its sway. The awful stillness and suspense were unbearable. (City-On-A-Hill 2012)

As an attorney, Key dealt with cases both to secure the freedom of slaves and to recover them for their owners. He was a key supporter of the American Colonization Society, which opposed abolitionists. Many abolitionists, meanwhile, thought that Colonization Society members were attempting to deport freedmen whom they feared might otherwise provoke or aid in emancipation. Key was responsible for the prosecution of an abolitionist who had moved to the capital and, in Key's judgment, had contributed to slave unrest (Vile 2019).

As a pious man who had considered becoming an Episcopal priest, Key helped found and support a number of churches. He was a member of the American Bible Society, the American Tract Society, and a leader in the Sunday school movement, and he used the office of U.S. attorney to combat the vices of gambling and prostitution, as well as to defend a number of high-profile defendants, including Sam Houston, who had caned a member of Congress. St. John's Church in Georgetown has a commemorative marker that notes that Key was one of its founders and a tablet that contains the epitaph that Key wrote for the church's first rector. Christ Church in Georgetown, the current structure of which was built in 1885, contains a stained glass window of Miriam (sister of Moses and Aaron) dedicated to Key (Roberts 2011). The Washington Cathedral dedicated a bronze table to the memory of Key at a ceremony in April 1931 (Svejda 2005, 411).

Key was a loyal supporter of President Andrew Jackson and a member of an unofficial group of advisors known as Jackson's "kitchen cabinet." In 1833, Jackson appointed him as U.S. attorney for the District of Columbia.

Although Key is far more remembered for his authorship of "The Star-Spangled Banner" than for his legal work, he had relatively little to say about the song later in life. In a speech he gave on August 6, 1834, though, Key indicated that it was "peculiarly gratifying to me, to know that, in obeying the impulse of my own feelings, I have awakened yours." He also observed that the song "came from the heart, and it has made its way to the hearts of men whose devotion to their country and the great cause of freedom I know so well" (Leepson 2014, 161):

I saw the flag of my country waving over a city—the strength and pride of my native state—a city devoted to plunder and desolation by its assailants. I witnessed the preparation for its assaults. I saw the array of its enemies as they advance to the attack. I heard the sound of battle; the noise of the conflict fell upon my listening ear, and told me that 'the brave and the free' had met the invaders. (161)

Key said that after seeing "the stars of that banner" on the next morning, his heart spoke, and he asked, "Does not such a country, and such defenders of their country, deserve a song?" (162). Seeking to share the credit, Key said that he had been overcome with inspiration. "Let the praise, then, if any be due, be given, not to me, who only did what I could not help doing: not to the writer, but to the inspirers of the song!" (162). Similarly, in a poem, "To Miss ____" that he penned for a friend of Mrs. Sarah Gayle, the wife of an Alabama governor, Key wrote:

Not even thy praise can make me vainly deem
That 'twas the poet's power, and not his theme,
That woke thy young heart's rapture, when from far

His song of vict'ry caught thy fav'ring ear:
That victory was thy country's, and his strain
Was of that starry banner that again
Had waved in triumph on the battle plain.

Key died of pneumonia in 1843 at the age of sixty-three. The Walters Art Museum in Baltimore, Maryland, has a portrait of Key, believed to have been painted about 1825, that is attributed to Joseph Wood. C. Gregory Stapko painted another portrait that is in St. John's Church in Georgetown Parish in Washington, DC. Tim O'Brien has done a more modern portrait of Key featuring clouds at sunrise in the background and an American flag directly behind him.

Two bridges have been named after Key. One crosses the Potomac River and links Arlington, Virginia, and Washington, DC, and was opened in 1923. The other, which is also called the Outer Harbor Bridge, opened in 1977 and crosses the Patapsco River in Baltimore.

In 1966, the U.S. Navy launched submarine USS *Francis Scott Key*, which remained in operation until being decommissioned in 1993. The United States had a liberty ship by the same name during World War II and has also issued coins and stamps that honor Key and "The Star-Spangled Banner." Every year since 1972, the U.S. Coast Guard has placed a red, white, and blue buoy to mark the spot where Key's ship is believed to have been anchored during the bombardment of Fort McHenry (DeMetrick 2018).

There are a number of memorials to Francis Scott Key. One, which is now operated by the National Park Service, is located in Rock Creek Park, which is located at Thirty-Fifth and M Street NW, near Key's Georgetown home in Washington DC, and includes a bronze bust of Key and a description of the U.S. flag from 1814.

There is a far more impressive memorial to Key at the Golden Gate Park in San Francisco. Commissioned by James Lick and dedicated in 1887, the marble and bronze monument was executed by William W. Story. The top of the monument has a bronze of a woman (probably Columbia, a symbol of America) holding an American flag, while the center of the monument has a bronze of a youthful Francis Scott Key sitting on a chair. A tablet identifies Key as the "Author of the National Song The Star-Spangled Banner."

Another impressive monument is located at Eutaw Place in Baltimore. Financed by a gift of $25,000 by Charles Marburg (1842–1907) of Baltimore, the monument was executed by Marius Jean Antonin Mercie (1845–1916) of France and completed in 1911. It too portrays a female figure, highlighted in gold leaf and holding a flag, at the top and a depiction in bronze of Key standing aboard a small boat being paddled by a companion. After being splashed with red paint and the words "Racist Anthem" in September 2017, the monument was restored but city officials surrounded it with a chain link fence (Johns Hopkins, n.d.).

The oddest monument to Key may be the twenty-four-foot bronze statue of Orpheus, the Greek poet, musician, and singer, which is called "Orpheus with the Awkward Foot," and is on the grounds of Fort McHenry Park. It was executed by Charles H. Niehaus (1855–1935) for centennial celebrations of the Battle of

Baltimore and the writing of "The Star-Spangled Banner" but, because of World War I, was not completed until 1922. William G. Harding dedicated the statue, his remarks the first by a president to be broadcast via the radio. Orpheus is covered with nothing but a headband and a fig leaf and is holding a lyre. A fifteen-foot cylindrical marble base contains carvings of numerous other classical figures with a medallion portraying Key and giving the years of his birth and death. Once located near the entrance to the fort, the monument was moved to a less prominent location on the site in 1962 (Browne 2012).

Originally buried at Old St. Paul's Church in Baltimore, as per his previously expressed wishes, Key was moved twenty years later to the Mount Olivet Cemetery in Frederick, Maryland, where a large monument, raised in part from contributions by school children, replaced his initial gravestone. It was designed by Pompeo Coppini (1870–1957), an Italian immigrant, and dedicated in 1898. The top of the monument is a bronze statue of Key pointing to a flag with one hand and holding his hat in the other. The base has a bronze of Columbia, flanked by one boy holding a sword, representing war, and the other a lyre, representing the arts. Near the base is a button that visitors can push to hear "The Star-Spangled Banner" (Wood 2014).

Another monument to Key can be found at Terra Ruba, in northcentral Maryland, close to the Pennsylvania border and at the site where Key spent his childhood; the original home was damaged in a storm and has been replaced. A tall white marble marker with an inscribed waving flag and Key's name and date of birth indicates that it was dedicated in 1915 (Meyer 1995, 73–74).

One of the monuments to Key that has not survived is the house that he occupied in Georgetown for almost thirty years. Opened in 1907 as a museum, it was unable to secure sufficient funding and was demolished in 1947 to make way for the Whitehurst Freeway. Although the materials were initially saved for possible reconstruction, they eventually disappeared and the opportunity was lost (Miller 2017, 29–30). There is a painting of this house by John Ross Key, one of Key's grandsons, in one of the Diplomatic Reception Rooms at the U.S. Department of State, and another in the museum of Roger Taney in Frederick, Maryland (Meyer 1995, 31).

See also: African Americans; Armistead, George; Baltimore, Maryland; Beanes, William; Francis Scott Key House; "Hymn for the Fourth of July, 1832"; Indian Queen Hotel (Baltimore); Pickersgill, Mary Young; War of 1812.

Further Reading

Browne, Allen. 2012. "Orpheus" *Landmarks* (blog), November 3. http://allenbrowne.blogspot.com/2012/11/orpheus.html.

City-On-A-Hill. "Francis Scott Key – Letter to John Randolph." 2012. *Virtue, Liberty, and Independence* (blog), April 10. http://liberty-virtue-independence.blogspot.com/2012/04/francis-scott-key-letter-to-john.html.

Delaplaine, Edward S. 1998. *Francis Scott Key: Life and Times.* Stuarts Draft, VA: American Foundation Publications. First published 1937.

DeMetrick, Alex. 2018. "Historic Francis Scott Key Buoy Placed for Season." *WJZ 13, CBS Baltimore,* June 8. https://baltimore.cbslocal.com/2018/06/08/historic-francis-scott-key-buoy-placed-for-season.

Ferris, Marc. 2014. *Star-Spangled Banner: The Unlikely Story of America's National Anthem*. Baltimore: Johns Hopkins University Press.

Gelb, Norman. 2004. "Francis Scott Key, the Reluctant Patriot." *Smithsonian Magazine* (September). https://www.smithsonianmag.com/history/francis-scott-key-the-reluctant-patriot-180937178.

Gelles, Auni. 2016. "Orpheus with the Awkward Foot: Francis Scott Key in Allegorical Form." Baltimore Heritage (website), December 17. https://explore.baltimoreheritage.org/items/show/570.

"Golden Gate Park—Francis Scott Key." 2012. *Public Art and Architecture from Around the World* (blog), February 18. https://www.artandarchitecture-sf.com/golden-gate-park-san-francisco-february-18-2012.html.

Johns Hopkins, n.d. "Battle Monument." Explore Baltimore Heritage (website). https://explore.baltimoreheritage.org/items/show/2.

Johns Hopkins, n.d. "Francis Scott Key Monument." Explore Baltimore Heritage (website). https://explore.baltimoreheritage.org/items/show/105.

Leepson, Marc. 2014. *What So Proudly We Hailed: Francis Scott Key, A Life*. New York: Palgrave/Macmillan.

Meyer, Sam. 1995. *Paradoxes of Fame: The Francis Scott Key Story*. Annapolis, MD: Eastwind.

Miller, Marla R. 2018. "The U.S. Flag in America's Historic-House Museums." In *The American Flag: An Encyclopedia of the Stars and Stripes in U.S. History, Culture, and Law*, edited by John R. Vile, 19–32. Santa Barbara, CA: ABC-CLIO.

Molotsky, Irvin. 2001. *The Flag, the Poet and the Song: The Story of the Star-Spangled Banner*. New York: Dutton.

Roach, David. 2018. "Writer of 'Star Spangled Banner' Helped Evangelize West thru Sunday School Movement." *God Reports* (blog), July 4. https://blog.godreports.com/2018/07/writer-of-star-spangled-banner-helped-evangelize-west-thru-sunday-school-movement.

Roberts, Jay. 2011. "Finding Francis Scott Key: His Churches in Georgetown." *Jaybird's Jottings* (blog), December 2. https://jay.typepad.com/william_jay/2011/12/finding-francis-scott-key-his-churches-in-georgetown.html.

Shafer, Leah. 2013. "Francis Scott Key and the Complex Legacy of Slavery." *A Blog of History*, U.S. Capitol Historical Society, June 14. https://uschs.wordpress.com/2013/06/14/francis-scott-key-and-the-complex-legacy-of-slavery.

Shippen, Rebecca Lloyd, and R. B. Taney. 1898. "The Star-Spangled Banner." *Pennsylvania Magazine of History and Biography* 22:321–25.

Smith, F. S. Key. 1909. "A Sketch of Francis Scott Key, with a Glimpse of His Ancestors." *Records of the Columbia Historical Society* 12:71–88.

Svejda, George J. 2005. *History of the Star Spangled Banner from 1814 to the Present*. Honolulu, HI: University Press of the Pacific. First published in 1969 by Division of History, Office of Archeology and Historic Preservation, U.S. Department of the Interior, National Park Service.

Vile, John R. 2019. "Trial of Reuben Crandall (1835–1836)." In *First Amendment Encyclopedia*, Free Speech Center, Middle Tennessee State University. https://mtsu.edu/first-amendment/article/1606/trial-of-reuben-crandall.

Winter, Aaron McLean. 2009. "The Laughing Doves of 1812 and the Satiric Endowment of Antiwar Rhetoric in the United States." *PMLA* 124 (October): 1562–81.

Wood, Pamela. 2014. "Francis Scott Key Legacy Lives on in Frederick." *Baltimore Sun*, August 14. https://www.baltimoresun.com/news/maryland/bs-md-40-key-memorial-20140813-story.html.

Knowledge of the National Anthem

One criticism of "The Star-Spangled Banner" is that it is difficult to sing; another is that few people know the words, especially those beyond the first verse. Shortly after Congress designated "The Star-Spangled Banner" as the national anthem in 1931, a newspaper cartoon in the (*Baltimore*) *Sun* depicted a puzzled-looking Uncle Sam under the caption, "I Wonder If They'll Make Me Learn the Words Now?" (Svejda 2005). In 1932, just a year after Congress declared "The Star-Spangled Banner" to be the national anthem, Congressman Claude A. Fuller of Arkansas proposed making knowledge of the anthem a condition for civil service employment (Svejda 2005, 415). Such a requirement, however, would likely have excluded a great many applicants. By the 1940s, for example, the lack of knowledge of the anthem had become a source of humor. One oft-told story concerned an American sentry who, upon hearing a voice in the night, shouted, "Halt! Who goes there?" After receiving the response, "An American," the sentry commanded, "Advance, and give the second verse of *The Star Spangled Banner*." When greeted with the response, "I don't know it," the sentry reported replied, "Proceed American" (Delaplaine 1944/1945, 21–22).

Knowledge of the lyrics of "The Star-Spangled Banner" does not appear to have improved over time. In 2005 the *American Music Teacher* reported that a Harris poll had found that 61 percent of Americans could not complete the opening line of the anthem: "O say, can you see, by the dawn's early light . . ." ("Losing Their Voices," 84). It further reported that about 38 percent of teens could not identify the nation's official song by name (84). A survey conducted of first-time visitors to the National Museum of American History, which houses the flag that Key saw flying over Fort McHenry, reported that only one in ten first-time visitors knew that the flag displayed there was the one that had inspired Key (Bielick et al. 1998, iv).

In an effort to combat this illiteracy, the Music Teachers National Association joined forces with the National Association for Music Education and other groups to promote a project entitled "The National Anthem Project: Restoring America's Voice." They attributed the lack of knowledge of the anthem to cuts in music education and to the difficulty individuals had in singing it. They offered practical suggestions for teaching the anthem in schools ("Losing Their Voices," 84).

See also: Criticisms and Defenses of "The Star-Spangled Banner"; Singing "The Star-Spangled Banner."

Further Reading

Bielick, Stacey, Zahava D. Doering, Anne Kazimirski, and Andrew J. Pekarik. 1998. *Public Perception of the Star-Spangled Banner: Background Studies for the National Museum of American History.* Report 98-6. Washington, DC: Smithsonian Institution.

Davis, Hank. 2016. "The Star Spangled Banner: Just What Are We Singing About?" *Psychology Today*, May 10. https://www.psychologytoday.com/us/blog/caveman-logic/201605/the-star-spangled-banner-just-what-are-we-singing-about.

Delaplaine, Edward S. 1944/1945. "Francis Scott Key and the National Anthem." *Records of the Columbia Historical Society* 50th Anniversary Volume: 13–26.

Guerrini, Susan C., and Mary C. Kennedy. 2009. "Cross-Cultural Connections: An Investigation of Singing Canadian and American Patriotic Songs." *Bulletin of the Council for Research in Music Education*, no. 182 (Fall): 31–49.

"Losing Their Voices: The Struggle for a Nation's Anthem and Its People." 2005. *American Music Teacher* 54 (April/May): 84–85.

Svejda, George J. 2005. *History of the Star Spangled Banner from 1814 to the Present.* Honolulu, HI: University Press of the Pacific. First published in 1969 by Division of History, Office of Archeology and Historic Preservation, U.S. Department of the Interior, National Park Service.

Williams, Ian. 2018. "Anthems." In *Memory*, edited by Philippe Tortell, Mark Turin, and Margot Young, 165–71. Vancouver, BC: Peter Wall Institute for Advanced Studies.

"La Marseillaise"

One way to understand "The Star-Spangled Banner" is to compare it to the anthems of other nations. In 1794, almost twenty years prior to when Francis Scott Key wrote "The Star-Spangled Banner," Claude Joseph Rouget de Liste (1760–1836) wrote his "Chant de guerre pour l'armee du Rhin," which became the national anthem of France. He composed the song at the home of Baron Phillippe-Frederic de Dietrich, the mayor of Starsbourg, as Prussian and Austrian forces advanced on France to crush the French Revolution. The song acquired its current name after a battalion from Marseille entered Paris singing it. Although it was subsequently repealed on a number of occasions (such as during the reign of Napoleon), it became the French national anthem on July 14, 1795, and was reestablished in 1879 (Crawford 2011, 24).

In terms of lyrics, the first verse of the French anthem is fairly characteristic of the anthem as a whole:

Arise children of the fatherland
The day of glory has arrived
Against us tyranny's
Bloody standard is raised
Listen to the sound in the fields
The howling of these fearsome soldiers
They are coming into our midst
To cut the throats of yours sons and consorts
To arms citizens
Form your battalions
March, march
Let impure blood
Water our furrows.

The lyrics of the third verse of "The Star-Spangled Banner," which have been criticized for their militarism, seem almost tame by comparison. In seeking to make further comparisons of the two anthems in her master's thesis, Katlyn Crawford observed that whereas the American anthem celebrates a battle already won, "La Marseillaise" calls citizens to arms prior to an anticipated battle (2011, 30). She further noted that the French anthem "is full of bloody images of war and of ideas of vengeance" (31), whereas the battle in the American anthem "is used not as a battle, but as a light source" (32). Admitting that her analysis is something of a "surmise," Crawford observes that "this detachment from the violence of war is perhaps inherent American non-military mindsets toward wars in general—idealizing war, hoping for the best, but displaying an overall ignorance of its realities" (32). She further contrasts the perspectives of Key as "a lawyer/poet" with that of Liste who was a "soldier/poet" (33) and notes that whereas the French anthem only mentions God in passing, the U.S. anthem specifically gives him praise for victory. The American anthem celebrates "a war of defense against attackers" whereas the French celebrates "a war of revolution" (32).

Crawford believes that both anthems have been effective in stirring emotions of patriotism. She notes that both are prominent at sporting events within their respective countries and references the way that the French Resistance was able to use the French anthem against the Nazi occupation during World War II.

In the early part of the Civil War, partly because of the influence of the French in New Orleans, which had been part of an earlier French colony, Southerners used "La Marseillaise" as a rallying song (Stone 1941, 545).

See also: Anthem; Confederate National Anthem; Criticisms and Defenses of "The Star-Spangled Banner"; Patriotism; War and the National Anthem.

Further Reading

Crawford, Katlyn Marie. May 2011. "France and the United States: Borrowed and Shared National Symbols." Master's thesis, University of North Texas.

"'La Marseillaise' Lyrics: The Meaning and Translation of the French National Anthem." 2015. *Evening Standard*, November 17. https://www.standard.co.uk/news/world/la-marseillaise-lyrics-the-meaning-and-translation-of-the-french-national-anthem-a3116306.html.

Mattfeld, Julius. 1919. "The Use of Some National Anthems in Music." *Art & Life* 11 (July): 27–30.

Stone, James. 1941. "War Music and War Psychology in the Civil War." *Journal of Abnormal and Social Psychology* 36 (October): 543–60.

"Land of the Free and the Home of the Brave"

The last two lines of each of the four verses of "The Star-Spangled Banner" resemble a chorus in that each refers both to the "star-spangled banner" and to "the land of the free and the home of the brave." Apart perhaps from the opening "O say, can you see," the last two lines are likely the most recognizable and the lines that audience members are most likely to join in singing.

On the surface, the self-congratulatory lines are fairly easy to understand. America is a land of freedom and its people are brave, which enables them to stand up against any foes who might seek to take their freedom away. Alex Marshall, a British writer who studies national anthems throughout the world, believes that this line is the emotional heart of the song that is most meaningful to Americans. After interviewing Babatunde Ogunnaike, the dean of engineering at the University of Delaware and a naturalized citizen who wrote Nigeria's national anthem before he came to America, Marshall asserted that Ogunnaike and other immigrants associate this line with "the American Dream," that an individual can come to the United States with almost nothing but the ability to work and succeed in building a better life (2015, 87).

Although critics point out that "The Star-Spangled Banner" author Francis Scott Key was a slaveholder and that slavery was pervasive throughout the American South, Key and fellow whites could boast that they were free both because they were no longer colonists but also because they had created a representative government. They viewed the war as a way of maintaining their freedom against a country seemingly intent on denying their rights, especially on the high seas. Moreover, those who opposed slavery and saw the contradiction between the American ideal and the reality of chattel slavery could still view the lines as aspirational. America would only achieve its full greatness when the freedom enjoyed by whites was extended to all.

Although they had foreign help in the earliest wars in their nation's history, Americans prided themselves on having earned their liberty through heroic struggle. How else could one explain the success of the American colonies against the world's strongest power other than as an example of divine providence (also referenced in the last verse of "The Star-Spangled Banner") and self-help?

Unfortunately, barely a month before Key wrote his anthem, when confronted by British bayonets and rockets, American militiamen had ingloriously run at the Battle of Bladensburg, which became known as the "Bladensburg races," leaving the capital defenseless. With this rout still fresh in his mind, Key must have been particularly anxious about whether Americans at Fort McHenry would be able to withstand one of the greatest naval bombardments in history to that date. The sight of the Star-Spangled Banner flag was not only a sign that the fortress remained in American hands but that American resolve had not been broken. The heirs of the American Revolution could rightfully claim their place with their intrepid fathers. Even though the War of 1812 largely ended in stalemate, Americans' confidence in their own ability to defend themselves was further bolstered by Andrew Jackson's conclusive victory over British troops at the Battle of New Orleans, which had occurred after the signing of the treaty of peace but before this news had traveled to America.

There is always the danger that American exceptionalism, or triumphalism, will justify unjust actions, but Key arguably attempted to guard against this. He did so in two ways. First, he phrased the last two lines of the first verse as a question, thus arguably provoking an introspective patriotism. Second, just before the last two lines of the last verse, Key linked American victory to circumstances in which "our cause it is just."

Tying his phrase to Jacksonian ideology, Key later linked it to freedom from corporate power. At a speech in Frederick, Maryland, Key thus warned:

> But if ever forgetful of her past and present glory, she shall cease to be "the land of the free and the home of the brave," and become the purchased possession of a company of stock jobbers and speculators, if her people are to become the vassals of a great moneyed corporation, and to bow down to her pensioned and privileged nobility: if the patriots who shall dare to arraign her corruptions and denounce her usurpations, are to be sacrificed upon her gilded altar; such a country may furnish venal orators and presses but the sound of national poetry will be gone. That muse will, "Never bow the knee in mammon's fane [shrine]." (Smith 1909, 78)

Since Key penned his famous song, however, a number of critics of American policies have beseeched the United States and its citizenry to do a better job of living up to the words of the anthem. In 1844, Robert Dale Owen (1801–1877), a utopian member of the U.S. House of Representatives from Indiana, claimed that as a naturalized citizen from Scotland, he had the same rights as did those who were natural born. In answering a native-born critic, he said, "The world admits America's own claim to be 'the land of the free, and the home of the brave.' The free claim this for their country. I, foreign born, though I be—I rightfully claim it for my country. It is mine by free selection, by deliberate preference; the gentleman's by accident only" (Prothero 2012, 218).

In 1846, the African American abolitionist Frederick Douglass claimed that the people of Dublin, Ireland, had treated him better than his own countrymen: "Whatever may be said of the aristocracies here, there is none based on the color of a man's skin. This speech of aristocracy belongs preeminently to 'the land of the free and the home of the brave'" (Prothero 2012, 219).

Over time, an increasing number of Americans came to believe that slavery was unjust and that the nation could not forever remain half free and half slave. Lincoln thus cited the biblical admonition that "a house divided against itself shall not stand." His wise leadership during the Civil War, and the bravery of those who fought for the Union cause (including many African Americans), eventually eliminated slavery in America—and brought the nation closer to embodying the values championed in "The Star-Spangled Banner."

Sometime the words of the anthem could take a strange term. In 1879, an editorial in the *Chicago Tribune* favoring greater restrictions on Chinese immigrants, criticized those who "assuming this country to be the 'land of the free and the home of the brave,' . . . are inclined to think its mission is to open all its doors to all who knock, without any regard to the welfare of those who are already in possession" (Prothero 2012, 219). In a speech reminiscent of Key's address in Frederick, Maryland, U.S. Senator John James Ingalls of Kansas sought to apply the words of the anthem to the issue of income inequality when noting that "we are accustomed to speak of this as the land of the free and the home of the brave. It will soon be the home of the rich and the land of the slave" (Prothero 2012, 220).

Long after slavery ended, meanwhile, African Americans continued to endure brutality, discrimination, and disenfranchisement at the hands of whites in the Jim Crow South. These conditions prompted the rise of the civil rights movement in the 1950s and 1960s—a movement that demanded that Americans acknowledge that it was failing to live up to the principles enshrined in "The Star-Spangled Banner" and other foundational documents and statements of national purpose. When civil rights activist Fannie Lou Hamer called for African American delegates from the Mississippi Freedom Democratic Party to be seated at the Democratic National Convention of 1964, she asked, "Is this America, the land of the free and the home of the brave, where we have to sleep with our telephones off the hooks because our lives be threatened daily, because we want to live as decent human beings, in America?" (Prothero 2012, 220).

Leonard Pitts, Jr., a newspaper columnist addressing graduates of Wake Forest University, further reflected on the world after the 9/11 terrorist attacks and what he considered to be the nation's willingness to give up civil liberties for security when he said, "It is time all of us grew a spine. Because, there is one undeniable truth about being the land of the free and the home of the brave; if you do not have the guts to be the one, you will soon cease to be the other (Prothero 2012, 221).

In a comparative study of national anthems, Alex Marshall has noted the increased popularity of country musician Lee Greenwood's "God Bless the USA" and its use in naturalization ceremonies. Although he thinks that it is "one of the schmaltziest, most emotionally manipulative pieces of music" he has ever heard (Marshall 2015, 94), Greenwood's references to a land "where at least I know I'm free" and his praise of those "who died" to give "that right to me," is actually quite similar to the references in the "The Star-Spangled Banner" to "the land of the free and the home of the brave."

See also: Fort McHenry; Immigrants; "In God Is Our Trust"; Lyrics of "The Star-Spangled Banner"; Slavery; War of 1812.

Further Reading

Marshall, Alex. 2015. *Republic or Death! Travels in Search of National Anthems.* London: Random House.

Prothero, Stephen. 2012. *The American Bible: How Our Words Unite, Divide, and Define a Nation.* New York: HarperOne.

Smith, F. S. Key. 1909. "A Sketch of Francis Scott Key, with a Glimpse of His Ancestors." *Records of the Columbia Historical Society* 12:71–88.

Latino National Anthem

Just as African Americans have adopted "Lift Every Voice and Sing" as an anthem, so too some Latinos have imbued the folk song "De Colores" ("All the Colors") as a song of particular meaning and importance to Latino Americans. In addition to being quite popular among Spanish-speaking audiences, Cesar Chavez and other members of the United Farm Workers Union used the song during their marches in the 1960s and 1970s for better wages and working conditions in California.

If adopted as an official anthem, it would be one of the least aggressive of the genre. The song stresses that the fields (flowers), birds, and the rainbow all come in many colors. At least implicitly, these colors are also reflected in the "mixed racial, cultural, and historical heritage" (Bordas 2018) of the Spanish-speaking peoples. Juana Bordas (2018), an activist and leadership and diversity consultant who advocates adopting "De Colores" as the Latino national anthem, said, "This moment in history when the Latino community is coming of age is also the time when our multicultural national and global community is rapidly emerging. Leaders must ensure that people of different races, ages, nations, sexual orientations, religions and cultures work and live peacefully together."

Like many folk songs, there are alternative verses to the song, some focusing on the sounds of roosters and baby chicks, which might be especially appreciated by children, and another that specifically references Christ as the King who does not die.

Given the criticism that has sometimes been directed to political demonstrations in the United States that involved waving the Mexican flag, "De Colores" would likely be less divisive than a song like the Mexican national anthem that specifically emphasizes another national identity.

See also: English Language and "The Star-Spangled Banner"; "Lift Every Voice and Sing"; Mexican National Anthem.

Further Reading

Bordas, Juana. 2018. "It's Time for a National Anthem for Latinos." Juana Bordas (website), September 15. https://www.juanabordas.com/its-time-for-a-national-anthem -for-latinos.

[Scott, Terry?]. n.d. "The UFW: Songs and Stories Sung and Told by UFW Volunteers." Farmworker Movement Documentation Project (website). https://libraries.ucsd .edu/farmworkermovement/media/Scott/INTRODUCTIONTOSONGSAND COMMENTARY(FINAL).pdf.

LGBTQ Community

After years of discrimination, members of the lesbian, gay, bisexual, transgender, and queer (LGBTQ) community have not only eliminated laws that made gay sex illegal, but they have also secured protections against discrimination in employment and the right to same-sex marriage. The latter movement culminated with the U.S. Supreme Court decision in *Obergefell v. Hodges* (2015).

Legal analyst Jeffrey Toobin observed that when members of the movement celebrated in front of the U.S. Supreme Court, they did not choose a traditional protest song (as, for example, "We Shall Overcome") but instead sang "The Star-Spangled Banner." He saw this as a sign that members of this group "want to participate in American society more than they want to transform it" (Toobin 2015). He further attributed the success of the movement to what he identified as this conservative approach. Harvey Milk (1980–1978), a member of the San Francisco Board of Supervisors, pioneered this approach in a keynote address on June 25, 1978, while reminding the audience about American values: "On the Statue of Liberty it says: 'Give me your tired, your poor, your huddled masses yearning to breathe free.' In the Declaration of Independence it is written: 'All men are created equal and they are endowed with certain inalienable rights.' And in our national anthem it says "Oh, say does that star-spangled banner yet wave o'er the land of the free'" (Hall 2011, 48).

In 2016, the San Diego Gay Men's Chorus was humiliated when, after they came on the field to play before a San Diego Padres game, an audio of a girl singing the anthem was played instead. This appeared to have been a mistake rather than an intentional slight, however, and a year later, they were invited back and joined by other groups (Zeigler 2017).

In kicking off a U.S. Gay Pride Parade rally in New York in 2013, the entertainer Lady Gaga clutched a gay pride flag as she sang the national anthem. She also altered the words to say "Oh say does that spar-spangled banner flag of pride yet wave" ("Lady Gaga" 2013).

Further Reading

Hall, Simon. 2010. "The American Gay Rights Movement and Patriotic Protest." *Journal of the History of Sexuality* 29 (September): 536–62.

Hall, Simon. 2011. *American Patriotism, American Protest: Social Movements since the Sixties.* Philadelphia: University of Pennsylvania Press.

Kelen, Christopher (Kit). 2015. "Putting a Queer Shoulder to the Wheel: Irony, Parody, and National Devotion." *Interdisciplinary Literary Studies* 17 (1): 110–36.

"Lady Gaga Sings US National Anthem at Gay Pride Rally." 2013. *Telegraph*, July 1. https://www.telegraph.co.uk/news/worldnews/northamerica/usa/10152332/Lady-Gaga-sings-US-national-anthem-at-Gay-Pride-rally-2013.html.

Obergefell v. Hodges, 576 U.S. _____ (2015).

Toobin, Jeffrey. 2015. "Why Gay Marriage Victory Anthem Was 'Star Spangled Banner.'" *CNN*, June 30. https://www.cnn.com/2015/06/26/opinions/toobin-same-sex-marriage-scotus/index.html.

Zeigler, Cyd. 2017. "San Diego Gay Men's Chorus Sings National Anthem a Year after Padres Blunder." *Outsports*, April 25. https://www.outsports.com/2017/4/25/15431714/san-diego-padres-gay-chorus-anthem.

Liberian National Anthem

One way of putting the claim of "The Star-Spangled Banner" in context is to recognize that, although it proclaimed the United States to be "the land of the free," many Americans had arrived in the United States from Africa in chains. Moreover, some former slaves left the United States for the shores of Africa and established Liberia in 1821. Indeed, Francis Scott Key, who wrote "The Star-Spangled Banner," was a leading member of the American Colonization Society, which favored the return of freed slaves to Africa.

The Liberian flag resembles the U.S. flag with a single white star in the blue canton and eleven alternating red and white stripes. The seal features a ship sailing back to the homeland, under a dove and the proclamation "The Love of Liberty Brought Us Here." Liberia's capital Monrovia was named after James Monroe, America's fifth president.

Daniel B. Warner (1815–1880), who eventually became the third president of Liberia, composed the anthem, while Cleveland Olmsted Lucas (1826–1869), an African American pianist, composed the music while living in Liberia from 1861 to 1864. The longest verse, undoubtedly looking back to the nation's origins, includes the words "We'll shout the freedom / Of a race benighted."

Whereas the U.S. national anthem hails the U.S. flag, the Liberian anthem begins by hailing the nation. Not unexpectedly, its central theme is liberty. Like the final verse of the U.S. national anthem, a good portion of the Liberian national anthem attributes liberty to "God's command." Although praising the nation's "powers," the emphasis is on defense. One verse thus proclaims:

With heart and hand
Our country's cause defending
We'll meet the foe
With valor unpretending.

See also: Key, Francis Scott; Slavery.

Further Reading
Massah, Lloyd. 2016. "Origin of Liberia's National Anthem." *Bush Chicken*, July 28. https://www.bushchicken.com/origin-of-liberias-national-anthem.
National Anthems of the World Organisation. n.d. "Sheet Music: Liberia National Anthem." http://www.national-anthems.org/anthems/country/LIBERIA.

"Lift Every Voice and Sing"

One of the more problematic aspects of "The Star-Spangled Banner" is that it was written by a slaveholder, who used the third verse to condemn British foes for enlisting African Americans in the War of 1812. Although the song refers to a collective people, it is not clear that this people included African Americans.

By contrast, a school principal named James Weldon Johnson, who had been asked to address a group assembled in Jacksonville, Florida, in 1899 to celebrate Abraham Lincoln's birthday, wrote a poem entitled "Lift Every Voice and Sing." His brother, John Rosamond Johnson, transformed this poem into a song, which has since been designated as the black national anthem. A year after it was composed, the song was performed by a group of five hundred school children at the Lincoln celebration (Schmidt 2018). It was subsequently included in a number of church hymnals and was adopted by the National Association for the Advancement of Colored People as its official song.

The song has three stanzas. The opening stanza, like that of "The Star-Spangled Banner," evokes voices singing as well as the image of the sky and the sea:

Lift ev'ry voice and sing,
'Till earth and heaven ring,
Ring with the harmonies of Liberty;
Let our rejoicing rise
High as the list'ning skies,
Let it resound loud as the rolling sea.
Sing a song full of the faith that the dark past has taught us,
Sing a song full of the hope that the present has brought us;
Facing the rising sun of our new day begun,
Let us march on 'til victory is won.

The second stanza moves from focus on years of pain and sorrow to the hope of a bright future, that is signaled by "the white gleam of our bright star":

Stony the road we trod,
Bitter the chastening rod,
Felt in the days when hope unborn had died;
Yet with a steady beat,
Have not our weary feet
Come to the place for which our fathers sighed?

We have come over a way that with tears has been watered,
We have come, treading our path through the blood of the slaughtered,
Out from the gloomy past,
'Til now we stand at last.
Where the white gleam of our bright star is cast.

The final stanza, like that of "The Star Spangled Banner," is also the most devout, attributing deliverance to God:

God of our weary years,
God of our silent tears,
Thou who has brought us thus far on the way;
Thou who has by Thy might
Led us into the light,
Keep us forever in the path, we pray.
Lest our feet stray from the places, our God, where we met Thee,
Lest, our hearts drunk with the wine of the world, we forget Thee;
Shadowed beneath Thy hand,
May we forever stand,
True to our God,
True to our native land.

Some NBA teams have played the song at their games during February, which is Black History Month. In 2017, some New York Police Department officers joined Colin Kaepernick, who had refused to stand for the national anthem as a protest against societal racism and alleged police brutality in communities of color, in singing "Lift Every Voice and Sing" (Schmidt 2018).

In 2008, the jazz singer Rene Marie was invited to sing the national anthem at the State of the City address in Denver, Colorado, which was anticipating the nomination of Barack Obama at the Democratic National Convention that the city was hosting. Marie surprised the platform party and the audience by substituting the words of the black national anthem while utilizing the tune of "The Star-Spangled Banner," in a move that led to considerable discussion (Redmond 2015).

Some African Americans have rejected the idea of calling the song a black national anthem. Timothy Askew, an English professor from Clark Atlanta University, for example, said, "To sing the 'black national anthem' suggests that black people are separatist and want to have their own nation. This means that everything Martin Luther King, Jr., believed about being one nation gets thrown out the window" (Schmidt 2018).

See also: African Americans; Kaepernick, Colin.

Further Reading

Johnson, James Weldon. n.d. "Lift Every Voice and Sing." Poetry Foundation. https://www.poetryfoundation.org/poems/46549/lift-every-voice-and-sing.

McKenna, Dave. 2008. "The Other National Anthem." *Washington City Paper*, September 26. https://www.washingtoncitypaper.com/arts/theater/article/13036334/the-other-national-anthem.

Perry, Imani. 2018. *May We Forever Stand: A History of the Black National Anthem*. Chapel Hill: University of North Carolina Press.

Redmond, Shana L. 2015. "Indivisible: The Nation and Its Anthem in Black Musical Performance." *Black Music Research Journal* 35 (Spring): 97–118.

Schmidt, Samantha. 2018. "'Lift Every Voice and Sing': The Story Behind the 'Black National Anthem' That Beyonce Sang." *Washington Post*, April 16. https://www.washingtonpost.com/news/morning-mix/wp/2018/04/16/lift-every-voice-and-sing-the-story-behind-the-black-national-anthem-that-beyonce-sang.

Linthicum, John Charles

J. Charles Linthicum (1867–1932) served consecutively as a Democrat representative from Maryland to the U.S. House of Representatives from 1911 until his death in 1932. A graduate of the Maryland State Normal School (the predecessor of today's Towson State University) and the law department of Johns Hopkins University, he had previously served as a member of the Maryland House of Delegates and the state Senate and as a judge advocate general for Governor Austin L. Crothers.

Linthicum, who led efforts to repeal national prohibition on alcohol during the 1920s, was also notable for his effort to designate and preserve Fort McHenry as a national monument. With the encouragement of Mrs. Reuben Ross Holloway of the Maryland Society of the United States Daughter of 1812, he introduced resolutions from 1918 through 1931 to designate "The Star-Spangled Banner" as the national anthem of the United States. He was joined in this effort by Senator Millard E. Tydings, who also represented Maryland.

In introducing the hearings that would lead to the adoption of "The Star-Spangled Banner" as the national anthem, Linthicum said, "There have been suggestions at various times for some other song or poem to be adopted as the national anthem, but national anthems can not be written at any time—they are inspired. It has become dear to the hearts of the people. There must be an inspiration, there must be background for the creation of a national anthem" ("Legislation" 1930, 2). He further observed that "no other anthem, no other poem, no other author, could ever get the setting which Key got when at old Fort McHenry when his country's fate hung in the balance and, when that song, that poem, was written by him, everybody began to sing it. It seemed to unite the forces of the South and of the North; it seemed to bring to this country something which it had never had—a national anthem, which meant everything to patriotism and everything to the future of our country" (3).

In 1932, Linthicum introduced a resolution that would enable the United States to pay some of the expenses of the Permanent Court of International Justice (Hudson 1932).

See also: Congress and "The Star-Spangled Banner"; Holloway, Mrs. Reuben Ross.

Further Reading

Hudson, Manley O. 1932. "The Linthicum Resolution on the World Court." *American Journal of International Law* 26 (October): 794–96.

Knox, Felicity. 2014. "The Fight for the Anthem." *Towson University History*, TU Special Collections and University Archives, June 30. https://wp.towson.edu/spcoll/2014/06/30/the-fight-for-the-anthem.

"Legislation to Make 'The Star-Spangled Banner' the National Anthem." 1930. Hearings before the Committee on the Judiciary, House of Representatives, Seventy-First Congress, Second Session on H.R. 14. Washington, DC: Government Printing Office.

Lyrics of "The Star-Spangled Banner"

Although there are few occasions where Americans sing more than the first verse, "The Star-Spangled Banner" consists of four verses, each of eight lines, and with nine rhymes. It was written by Francis Scott Key and set to the tune of the "To Anacreon in Heaven," which had been composed by Ralph Tomlinson for the London Anacreontic Society in honor of a Greek lyric poet and set to the music of John Stafford Smith.

"The Star-Spangled Banner" is deeply rooted in a specific historical event, as Key, restricted aboard a ship, anxiously awaited the outcome of the British siege of Baltimore during the War of 1812 by focusing his eyes to see whether the American flag was still flying from the ramparts of Fort McHenry, a major bulwark of defense for the city. If the U.S. flag, which Key dubbed the Star-Spangled Banner, were no longer flying, it would signal that the British had defeated American forces and forced their surrender. If it remained flying above the fort, it would indicate that both it and the city had survived the onslaught. Despite the song's origin in a specific battle of a specific war, it does not specifically refer to the British or any of its commanders by name (Hildebrand 2014). Moreover, as long as the republic endures, contemporary singers can affirm, with Key, that the flag still waves.

The primary image of the song is that of the "star-spangled banner," or flag, which in turn highlighted the contrast between light and darkness. The "dawn's early light," in the opening line of the first stanza is set against "the twilight's last gleaming" in the following line. Two lines later, Key evokes "the rocket's red glare, the bomb bursting in air," which periodically revealed the flag as it waved "through the night." It is unclear whether Key's original use of "rocket's" and "bomb" was intentionally designed to accent each bomb and each rocket blast (or perhaps the specific type of rocket or bomb) or whether they were grammatical mistakes. In any case, it is much more common for contemporary versions of the song to say "rockets'" and "bombs'" rather than use the singular construction. In terms of light and darkness, the second stanza again evokes that which is "dimly seen," half revealed and half concealed, until the flag "catches the gleam of the morning's first beam."

The contrast between light and darkness is further highlighted by the contrast between the great turbulence signaled by the "rockets' red glare" and "the bomb bursting in air" (which would have produced sound as well as light) and Key's own joy and tranquility upon seeing the U.S. flag the next morning. Edward Green likens this imagery to the turbulence of "the storm scene in King Lear," which provided the King with insight (Siegel and Green 2014, 34).

The opening line of the first and fourth stanzas both begin with the word "O," which is also called the vocative O. Linguist Arika Okrent (2014) explains that it is used to "indicate that someone or something is being directly addressed." It has parallels in such songs as "O Christmas tree" and "O Canada." By contrast, the word "Oh," which is sometimes printed in the lower case, and which is sometimes found in contemporary printings of the anthem, is an interjection that overlaps with "O" but generally indicates "pain, surprise, disappointment, or really any emotional state" (Okrent 2014).

The opening four lines of the first three verses all end in questions, whereas those of the last end with an explanation mark. The first two stanzas essentially focused on the "what" (can you see the flag?), while the third focuses on asking where the British hirelings and slaves have gone and indicates that they have either fled or died.

The opening line of the first verse is the only one to use the second person ("O say, can you see"), thus involving the listener (it may also have referred to Key or one of his companions aboard the ship) from the very beginning. Most of the other verses are worded in the first person plural ("we hail'd"), with some third-person references. While the use of "we" and "us" gives the song a collective element, the third verse suggests that certain American residents, most notably slaves, are not part of this collective people.

Although it would not be uncommon to refer to the banner as a personification, Key referred to it in the third person. The penultimate line of the second stanza thus says, "O long may it wave," rather than, as some subsequent iterations, "long may she wave." Recognizing that the flag is a collective symbol, Key refers to it in the sixth line of the first verse as "our flag."

The primary imagery of the song consists of the flag, which is usually described as in motion ("streaming," "wave," "blows,"), almost as though it were a living being. Key consistently identified it as a "star-spangled banner" rather than a mere flag. This imagery plays to the idea, embodied within the flag, that the United States of America constituted a new and growing constellation (Shalev 2011). Although it is today more common to refer to the "stars and stripes," Key refers to the flag's "broad stripes and bright stars." The only color that Key mentions in the lyrics is the "red glare" of the rockets, although the references to twilight and dawn might further evoke images of blue (or black) skies and white stars that are found in the canton of the flag.

Key associated the flag with a number of national ideals. The country that the flag represents is a free nation of brave citizens. Each stanza's concluding line refers to "the land of the free and the home of the brave." The fourth line of the first stanza further says that the flag itself was "gallantly" waving at sunset. Consistent with the idea of civic republicanism, the link between bravery and freedom suggests that freedom is likely to be something that a nation has to fight for rather than something that is bestowed upon it. A nation that lacks brave men and women may, by implication, be unable to preserve such freedom.

The first line of the last stanza affirms that the star-spangled banner should wave as long as "freemen shall stand." Freemen defend their homes and their liberties. It would appear that the flag does not embrace American slaves, whom

British had recruited in their fight. The "slave" is thus grouped with the "hireling" in the unsettling third verse, whose fate is said to be either "the terror of flight or the gloom of the grave." Unlike the Declaration of Independence, Key does not in this song evoke notions of human equality, other than perhaps that of "freemen." That gendered term, in turn, reflects the reality of American political life prior to woman's suffrage.

The words "land" and "home" are inextricably linked together in the last line of each stanza. The second line of the fourth verse further contrasts the "lov'd home" of freemen against "war's desolation." These terms serve as reminders that the British are the invading forces. The third line of verse three ties the ideas of "A home and a Country" together. Line two of the fourth stanza further refers to "the heav'n rescued land," while line four draws a tie to the "nation." These terms all refer to what political scientists identify as the "nation" (a group of people bound together by common ties of identity like raced, language, beliefs, etc.) rather than as the "state," or form of government. Although he was a lawyer, Key does not specifically reference republicanism, democracy, separation of powers, checks and balances, or other dimensions of American constitutionalism.

Invocations of land and country typically evoke patriotism, which generally consists both of love of and pride in one's country and its symbols. The second line of the first verse thus refers to the banner as that "so proudly we hail'd." Lest this pride become destructive, Key uses the second and third verses to contrast it with haughtiness. Line two of the second stanza thus refers to "the foe's haughty host," whereas the first line of the third verse suggests that the British had "vauntingly" sworn to take away both home and country. This is a case, described in both Greek notions of hubris and Christian prophecy, in which the enemy's pride preceded its defeat.

The flag is also associated with "triumph" and "vict'ry" over foreign foes, in this case, one that has invaded. Such triumph is, in turn, linked in the third line of the fourth stanza to "peace." One reason that the song was initially so popular was that it represented one of the nation's victories in a war that had witnessed many defeats.

Less prominent, but no less important, is the link on line five of the fourth and final stanza between the flag and justice. This stanza portrays the necessity of victory "when our cause it is just," and not, as in some corruptions of the song, "for our cause it is just" or "since our cause it is just" (Lichtenwanger 1972, 97). The justice of the American cause is highlighted by the fact that it is defending itself against a marauding foreign foe.

Although the primary imagery of the song is that of the star-spangled banner, the next most vivid imagery comes from the controversial third stanza, which features what one critic described as "embarrassingly blood-soaked phrases" (Dennis 2014, 296). Referring to British hirelings and slaves, this verse says that "Their blood has wash'd out their foul footstep's pollution," which is followed two lines later with "the terror of flight or the gloom of the grave." The idea of transgressors' blood washing away their own "pollution" is certainly a contrast to the Christian belief that the blood of Jesus takes away individuals' sins.

Although one might tie Key's references to twilight and dawn to creation, and thus at least indirectly to a Creator, it is only in the last stanza that Key, who was a religious man, evoked God, to whom he attributes the victory. The nation becomes "the heav'n rescued land." The stanza further praises "the power that hath made and preserv'd us a nation!" Just as the Bible evokes God as the creator and preserver of the universe (and of the Jewish nation), so too, Key saw God as the creator and preserver of the American nation. Whatever personal bravery and sacrifice might have been involved, long before the term was inscribed on American currency, Key identified the nation's "motto" as "In God is our trust." As David Hildebrand, director of the Colonial Music Institute, was quoted as saying, "It's a hymn of redemption. It's a hymn of, 'We've been saved! The fact I can see the flag means the fort has not been taken.' It's the ultimate statement of relief with a capital R, and that emotion gives the song a really strong appeal" (Marshall 2014).

The last verse ends, as the three before it, with evocations of "the star-spangled banner" waving "o'er the land of the free and the home of the brave." Although a few other national flags could easily be described both as "star-spangled" and as having "broad stripes and bright stars," one of the fascinating aspects about "The Star-Spangled Banner" that distinguished it from some of its eventual rivals for national anthem status is that it nowhere specifically mentions either America or the United States of America. Nor does it mention Columbia, a name that was sometimes used for the nation in other contemporary songs that were considered as alternative anthems. After pointing out that "the flags of Uzbekistan, New Zealand, and Cape Berde also have both stripes and stars," philosophy professor Theodore Gracyk observes that since Key is known to be the song's author and he refers to the flag as "our flag," "a 'semantic pragmatics' for indexicals says that the words of this *song* refer to the flag of the United States," even though someone might sing it for another (2013, 26).

In the last half century or so, performers have presented the song in new genres and contexts, as when Jimi Hendrix used "guitar pyrotechnics" to imitate "bombs bursting in air," or when he interrupted the ending by playing "Taps," with apparent reference to those who had died in Vietnam (Gracyk 2013, 28). Gracyk also explains, although the "semantics" of the song have been relatively constant, the "pragmatics" have generated "differing meanings by different performances" (Gracyk 2013, 23).

See also: "Battle of Baltimore, The"; "In God Is Our Trust"; Key, Francis Scott; "To Anacreon in Heaven."

Further Reading

American Historama. 2014. "Star Spangled Banner Lyrics." United States History for Kids. http://www.american-historama.org/1801-1828-evolution/star-spangled -banner-lyrics.htm.

Blackstone, Jerry, Mark Clague, and Andrew Thomas Kuster. 2014. "A Star-Spangled Bicentennial: A Conversation with Jerry Blackstone, Mark Clague, and Andrew Kuster." *Choral Journal* 54 (April): 6–17.

Dennis, Matthew. 2014. "Reflections on a Bicentennial: The War of 1812 in American Public Memory." *Early American Studies* 12 (Spring): 269–300.

Gracyk, Theodore. 2013. "Meanings of Songs and Meanings of Song Performances." *Journal of Aesthetics and Art Criticism* 72 (Winter): 23–33.

Hildebrand, David K. 2014. "Bicentenary Essay: Two National Anthems? Some Reflections on the Two Hundredth Anniversary of 'The Star-Spangled Banner' and Its Forgotten Partner, 'The Battle of Baltimore.'" *American Music* 32 (Fall): 253–71.

Lichtenwanger, William. 1972. "Star-Spangled Bibliography." *College Music Symposium* 12 (Fall): 94–102.

Marshall, Alex. 2014. "Why 'The Star-Spangled Banner' Is the Perfect Insight into America's Soul." *Guardian*, August 11. https://www.theguardian.com/music/musicblog/2014/aug/11/malcolm-gladwell-star-spangled-banner-america-200th-anniversary.

Okrent, Arika. 2014. "What's the Difference between 'O' and 'Oh'?" *Mental Floss*, May 7. http://mentalfloss.com/article/56582/whats-difference-between-o-and-oh.

Shalev, Eran. 2011. "'A Republic Amidst the Stars': Political Astronomy and the Intellectual Origins of the Stars and Stripes." *Journal of the Early Republic* 31 (Spring): 39–73.

Siegel, Eli, and Edward Green. 2014. "'The Star-Spangled Banner' as a Poem." *Choral Journal* 55 (November): 218–35.

Madama Butterfly

Madama Butterfly is an opera by Giacomo Puccini (1858–1925) that premiered in 1904 and highlights differences between East and West. It is based on a short story, "Madame Butterfly," that was written by John Luther Long (1861–1927) in 1898 and premiered as a one-act play, *Madame Butterfly: A Tragedy of Japan*, in 1900. Long in turn based his story on a tale his sister, Jennie Correll, the wife of a Methodist missionary, had told him. It involves the relationship between a U.S. naval officer, Lieutenant Benjamin Franklin Pinkerton, and Ciocio-san, a fifteen-year-old Japanese girl whose name means butterfly.

Planning to take advantage of liberal Japanese divorce laws, Pinkerton marries Ciocio-san but envisions a marriage that will only last a month, while his bride is so deeply in love with him that she renounces her Japanese gods for his and is cast out of her family. Pinkerton subsequently leaves and returns some three years later after marrying an American woman who comes to claim Ciocio-san's child. Ciocio-san, in turn, commits suicide.

One of the most notable aspects of the opera is that it uses the tune of "The Star-Spangled Banner" to highlight Pinkerton's American background even though the song had not yet been designated as the American national anthem (Groos 2016, 52). Elsewhere in the play, the arrival of the Imperial Commissioner is signaled by the playing of "Kimigayo," the Japanese national anthem (57).

See also: Congress and "The Star-Spangled Banner."

Further Reading

Atlas, Allan W. 1990. "Crossed Stars and Crossed Tonal Areas in Puccini's *Madama Butterfly*." *19th-Century Music* 14 (Autumn): 186–96.

Groos, Arthur. 2016. "*Madama Butterfly* between East and West." In *Giacomo Puccini and His World*, edited by Arman Schwartz and Emanuele Senici, 49–84. Princeton, NJ: Princeton University Press.

Madison, James

James Madison (1751–1836) was one of America's most important founding fathers. Born on a Virginia plantation, Madison was largely educated by private tutors prior to attending the College of New Jersey (today's Princeton), where he studied under its president, John Witherspoon, the only clergyman to sign the Declaration of Independence.

Madison, who studied but never practiced law, went back to Virginia where he became involved in the movement for American independence and remained in politics for most of his life. He was a member of the committee who successfully proposed that the Virginia Declaration of Rights, which was largely written by George Mason, should include protections for the "free exercise" of religion, a phrase that was later incorporated with the First Amendment of the U.S. Constitution. Madison also worked to adopt the Virginia Statute for Religious Freedom, which Thomas Jefferson had largely authored to disestablish the state church.

Madison served in Congress under the Articles of Confederation as well as his state legislature, and he was an advocate for creating a stronger national government. He was among those who attended the Annapolis Convention that called for what became the Constitutional Convention of 1787, which met in Philadelphia, Pennsylvania. As a delegate to the Constitutional Convention from Virginia, Madison is believed to have been the primary author of the Virginia Plan, which called for establishing three branches of government and for a bicameral Congress with increased powers in which states would be represented according to population in both branches. In addition to being an influential debater at the convention, Madison also kept the most comprehensive notes of its proceedings. He also joined with Alexander Hamilton and John Jay to author the *Federalist Papers*, which explained and advocated for the ratification of the proposed Constitution. Madison also played a major role at the Virginia Ratifying Convention, which met in Richmond.

After being elected to the first Congress under the new Constitution, Madison led the way for the adoption of the first ten amendments (today known as the Bill of Rights), which largely focused on the protection of individual rights rather than, as some Anti-Federalists had hoped, in strengthening states' rights. As Secretary of State Alexander Hamilton and other members of the Federalist Party pushed for increased powers, some of which were not specifically delineated within the Constitution, Madison and his friend Thomas Jefferson helped establish the Democratic-Republican Party, which won the presidency in the election of 1800, with Jefferson as its head.

Madison loyally served as Jefferson's Secretary of State throughout Jefferson's two-term presidency and was in this position when the United States purchased the Louisiana Territory. He supported Jefferson's decision to try to avoid a war and embargo American shipping to Britain rather than engage the British, who were impressing American sailors into their service. Even though this measure was extremely unpopular, especially in the Northeast where it took a significant toll on the shipping industry, Madison was elected to succeed Jefferson as president and was barely through his first of two terms when pressure from congressional war hawks like Henry Clay and John C. Calhoun led him to ask Congress to declare war. The nation would have undoubtedly been far better prepared for this conflict had Madison and Jefferson not been as committed as they were to fiscal conservativism, which had included low military budgets.

The war did not initially go well for the United States, and its hopes to capture British Canada were quickly dashed by early defeats that would only later be partly compensated by some naval victories on the Great Lakes and the high seas. John Armstrong Jr. (1813–1814) proved to be a weak Secretary of State who did not adequately prepare for the possibility that the British might seek to attack the nation's capital and Baltimore. On April 2, 1811, Madison replaced him with James Monroe, who would succeed Madison as president.

Whereas potential conflict with France had led the administration of John Adams to adopt the repressive Alien and Sedition Acts, Madison did not seek laws to repress criticisms of his policies, and he gained some praise after his popular wife, Dolley, was able to save the painting of George Washington that had been hanging in the White House prior to the time that the British burned it. The Battle of Baltimore, which inspired Francis Scott Key to write "The Star-Spangled Banner," was one of the war's turning points. It was followed by an even greater military victory by Andrew Jackson at the Battle of New Orleans. Jackson's triumph actually occurred after diplomats had already signed a treaty of peace that largely restored the status quo prior to the war but the news of which had not yet reached America.

Whatever setbacks the nation had faced during the War of 1812, it stirred American patriotism. Contemporaries would classify the war as a second American Revolution that further established that America would be free from its former mother country. This sentiment is undoubtedly expressed in the hope of "The Star-Spangled Banner" that America would remain "the land of the free and the home of the brave."

By the time of his death in 1836, Madison was the last surviving individual who had attended the Constitutional Convention. As he aged, Madison was increasingly worried about rising sectional divisions within the United States that would eventually challenge whether the states, whose stars were portrayed on the flag that Francis Scott Key had celebrated, would stay together or divide.

See also: War of 1812.

Further Reading

Borneman, Walter R. 2009. *1812: The War That Forged a Nation.* New York: HarperCollins.

Cheney, Lynn. 2015. *James Madison: A Life Reconsidered.* New York: Penguin.

Howard, Hugh. 2012. *Mr. and Mrs. Madison's War: America's First Couple and the Second War for Independence.* New York: Bloomsbury Press.

Meyers, Marvin, ed. 1972. *The Mind of the Founder: Sources of the Political Thought of James Madison.* Indianapolis: Bobbs-Merrill.

Vogel, Steve. 2013. *Through the Perilous Fight: From the Burning of Washington to the Star-Spangled Banner; The Six Weeks That Saved the Nation.* New York: Random House.

Mennonite National Anthem

Mennonites and Jehovah's Witnesses generally do not salute the flag or participate in singing the national anthem. Thus, in 2011, Goshen College, a Mennonite College in Indiana, dropped the practice of playing the national anthem, which it had done for a year, after students and alumni expressed fears that the song was too militaristic and unwelcoming to foreign students (St Clair and Hamilton 2011; Schloneger 2011). Generally, Mennonites fear that either the flag or the anthem could become an object of idolatry and believe that both are inconsistent with their advocacy of pacifism.

It is therefore somewhat ironic that despite the Mennonite tradition that usually also eschews instrumental music, the song "Praise God From Whom All Blessings Flow" has been unofficially designated as the Mennonite national anthem. Indeed, after being printed as number 606 in the 1969 edition of the Mennonite Hymnal, this song became so widely known that it is often referred to simply as "606."

Unlike the doxology that may be sung in other churches, the Mennonite version has separate parts for various voices. Musicologist Austin Juhnke (2017) explains, "Unlike most hymns, in which the voice parts move more or less in the rhythm, in 606 the soprano, alto, tenor, and bass voices jump in and out unpredictably. One example of this is right at the beginning of the hymn. Here the soprano and tenor voices begin singing 'Praise God from whom' in duet. Not until a measure later do the alto and bass voices join in, singing a compressed rhythm to catch up to the other voices by the end of the first musical phrase."

Juhnke (2017) believes that "it is precisely because it is difficult for outsiders to join in that the hymn works as a musical identity marker. For those who are able to sing along, 606 is a powerful auditory and embodied experience of Mennonite community, yet this insider experience is predicated on musical stumbling blocks that produce outsiders in the act of performance."

Just as "The Star-Spangled Banner" has been criticized for being both racist and sexist, so too some critics of the Mennonite anthem fear that it has become exclusionary. Rebecca Slough, the academic dean at the Associated Mennonite Biblical Seminary in Elkhart, Indiana, thus wrote a paper in which she concluded that although the hymn was widely embraced by white Mennonites with roots in Western Europe, it was less popular among Spanish-speaking and other Mennonites. She concluded that "I would not want '606' to go by the wayside anytime soon, . . . but it is not the Mennonite hymn for all" (Groff 2008, 14). Bradley Kauffman, who is chair of the music department at Hesston College in Kansas, asked a question that has sometimes been raised with respect to "The Star-Spangled Banner," namely, "If the vitality of '606' is fading, broadly or narrowly—intentionally or otherwise—what are we replacing it with?" (Groff 2008, 15).

See also: African Americans; Singing "The Star-Spangled Banner"; Women.

Further Reading

Groff, Anna. 2008. "606: When, Why and How Do Mennonites Use the Anthem?" *Mennonite* (March 18): 14–15.

Juhnke, Austin McCabe. 2017. "Rethinking 606, the 'Mennonite National Anthem.'" *Mennonite*, December 5. https://themennonite.org/opinion/rethinking-6060-mennonite-national-anthem.

Scholneger, Mark. June 26, 2011. "My Faith: Why I Don't Sing the 'Star-Spangled Banner.'" *CNN Belief Blog*, June 26. http://religion.blogs.cnn.com/2011/06/26/my-faith-why-i-dont-sing-the-star-spangled-banner.

St. Clair, Stacy, and Brian Hamilton. 2011. "Goshen College Sparks a Fight over National Anthem." *Chicago Tribune*, August 25. https://www.chicagotribune.com/news/ct-xpm-2011-08-25-ct-met-star-spangled-banner-boycott-20110825-story.html.

Mexican National Anthem

Three countries inhabit the North American continent, and each has its own anthem with its own history. Although some individuals have criticized "The Star-Spangled Banner" for being too militaristic, it appears relatively tame when compared to that of its neighbor to the south.

Mexico did not achieve its independence from its Spanish motherland until 1821. This was eleven years after Father Miguel Hidalgo y Costilla (1753–1811) issued a call to arms. It would undergo a major revolution from 1910 to 1920 when the current system of government was established.

During the administration of General Santa Anna, the general who had lost much of his country to its U.S. neighbor to the north, a contest was sponsored for a suitable anthem, and it was won in 1853 by the poet Francisco Gonzalez Bocanegra (1824–1861). His reluctance to enter the contest was apparently overcome by his fiancée, Guadalupe Gonzalez del Pino, who reportedly locked him in a room until he wrote one.

Originally set to the music of Giovanni Bottesini of Italy, a new competition was launched for another score, which was also won in 1853 by Jaime Nuno (1824–1908), whom Santa Anna had met while in exile in Cuba and subsequently named head of his military bands. Nuno, however, entered his own composition anonymously. The tune was first performed on September 15, 1854.

Nuno later moved to the United States and died in Buffalo, New York. In 1942 his remains were exhumed and moved to Mexico, where they were placed beside those of Bocanegra in the Rotunda of Illustrious Men in Mexico City.

The song was officially adopted as the Mexican anthem in 1943 by the order of President Manuel Avila Camacho. By that time, it had been stripped of complimentary references to Santa Anna and to former Mexican emperor Agustin de Iturbide. In an interesting twist that has not been adopted by Mexico's northern neighbor in regard to its own national anthem, the law imposed jail terms on individuals who attempted to alter the structure or violate the rules related to its proper performance (Gurza 2018).

The chorus of the anthem highlights its martial nature:

Mexicans, at the cry of war,
Prepare the steel and the stead,
And may the earth shake at its core
In the resounding roar of the cannon

Although the first stanza of the song urges the nation to gird "your crown with olive" and describes the nation's destiny as having been written "in the heavens by the hand of God," as the song continues, it warns any foe that would set foot on the nation:

War, without truce to any who dare
to tarnish the country's coat-of-arms!
War, war! Take the national pennants

and soak them in waves of blood.
War, war! In the mountain and valley,
thunder the cannons in horrid unison
And the resonant echoes
with the voices of
Union,
Liberty!

Similarly the rest of the anthem expresses the hope that "your fields may be watered in blood" and "your temples, palaces and towers collapse" before "your children bow to the yoke" of invading forces (Inside Mexico, n.d.).

After the poem was set to the music of Nuno, a critic commented that the work was a winsome combination of "Italian floridity, German vigor, and American grandiosity" (Gurza 1018). Unlike "The Star-Spangled Banner," the Mexican anthem makes no reference to its flag.

See also: Criticisms and Defenses of "The Star-Spangled Banner"; "O Canada."

Further Reading

Carey, Lydia. 2018. "Everything You Need to Know about the Mexican National Anthem." Culture Trip, March 31. https://theculturetrip.com/north-america/mexico/articles/everything-you-need-to-know-about-the-mexican-national-anthem.

Chen, Yu. 2010. "An Empirical Study of Hispanic American National Anthems." University of Texas at Austin. http://lanic.utexas.edu/project/etext/llilas/ilassa/2010/chen.pdf.

Gurza, Agustin. 2018. "Himno Nacional Mexicano: The Long and Winding History of Mexico's National Anthem." *Strachwitz Frontera Collection of Mexican and Mexican American Recordings* (blog), January 22. http://frontera.library.ucla.edu/blog/2018/01/himno-nacional-mexicano-long-and-winding-history-mexico%E2%80%99s-national-anthem.

Inside Mexico. n.d. "Mexican National Anthem. El Himno Nacional Mexicano." https://www.inside-mexico.com/reference-info/national-anthem.

Military Regulations

Long before Congress adopted and President Herbert Hoover signed the law making "The Star-Spangled Banner" the official national anthem, military authorities had made a number of decisions that had elevated the song to near official status. It was natural that the military would be particularly vested in a song that was born from an important battle and that glorified the flag under which members of the military fought.

Dr. George Svejda, who worked for the National Park Service, has included many of these orders and regulations in the appendices of his history of "The Star-Spangled Banner." The first was General Order No. 374 that Secretary of the Navy Benjamin Franklin Tracy, a successful advocate for a strong modern navy, issued on July 26, 1889, for ships and naval stations. It specified that when bands were present, they would play "The Star-Spangled Banner" at morning colors and "Hail Columbia" at evening colors. It further provided that all navy personnel who were able to do so "will please face towards the colors and salute as the ensign reaches the peak or truck in hoisting, or the taffrail or ground in haling down" (Svejda 2005, 470).

Accompanying regulations that the navy issued as Article 157 in 1893 provided that bands would preface the music of "The Star-Spangled Banner" with "three rolls and three flourishes" and that it would be played at both morning and evening ceremonies. It also provided that sailors "shall stand facing the ensign and shall salute when it reaches the peak or trunk." These rules were further codified in Section 158 of rules issued by the navy in 1896 (Svejda 2005, 471–72).

On December 16, 1907, the War Department issued General Order No. 246. It specified that all military men would stand at attention for "The Star-Spangled Banner." It further provided that when a band was present, it would play "The Star-Spangled Banner" as the flag was being lowered.

In 1916, President Woodrow Wilson, who by virtue of his office was commander in chief of the armed forces, issued an executive order specifying that "The Star-Spangled Banner" would be the official anthem of the U.S. armed forces.

See also: Code for the National Anthem; Congress and "The Star-Spangled Banner"; Wilson, Woodrow.

Further Reading

Cooling, B. Franklin. 1972. "The Making of a Navalist: Secretary of the Navy Benjamin Franklin Tracy and Seapower." *Naval War College Review* 25 (September–October): 83–90.

Svejda, George J. 2005. *History of the Star Spangled Banner from 1814 to the Present.* Honolulu, HI: University Press of the Pacific. First published in 1969 by Division of History, Office of Archeology and Historic Preservation, U.S. Department of the Interior, National Park Service.

Monroe, Lucy

Lucy Monroe (1906–1987) was a gifted singer who became known as the "Star-Spangled Soprano." A descendant of President James Monroe, she was the daughter of Anna Laughlin Monroe, an actress who played Dorothy in the original stage production of *The Wizard of Oz*, and Dwight Monroe, a diamond merchant who courted Anna after becoming enchanted with her performances.

After Lucy's father died in 1925, Lucy joined the Ziegfeld Follies and began appearing on such radio programs as the *American Album of Familiar Music* and *Circus Night*. She also sang for a number of opera companies and orchestras.

Monroe began singing the national anthem at an American Legion Convention that was held in New York City in 1937 and subsequently took part in the "American Jubilee" program at the New York World's Fair in 1940 where, after both opening and closing the show with renditions of the anthem, she became known as "The Star-Spangled Banner Girl." She was also the official soloist for the American Legion and the Veterans of Foreign Wars and RCA Victor's director of patriotic music.

In 1941 Monroe's rendition of "The Star-Spangled Banner" was recorded at Philadelphia's Constitution Hall, where she was accompanied by the National Symphony Orchestra. That same year, she participated in "I Am an American Day" at Central Park in New York and at an Independence Day rally at the Washington Monument, the latter of which was attended by thirty thousand people who sang the chorus to the anthem as they lit matches. Committed to the U.S. war effort, she led a community sing sponsored by the Treasury Department at the Lincoln Memorial in 1942, which forty thousand people attended. In 1943 she sang at the War Bond Jubilee Game at the New York Polo Grounds. One year later she performed at Fort McHenry to commemorate the 130th anniversary of Key's song, and in 1948 she celebrated the fiftieth anniversary of the Francis Scott Key Museum in Frederick, Maryland.

She frequently performed for American troops but rarely sang the anthem for them because of her stated belief that "the men are living it" (Belkin 1987). She also became a fixture at Yankee Stadium, performing the anthem at each home season opener and at all World Series in which the New York Yankees participated between 1945 and 1960 (Folkart 1987).

Altogether, she is believed to have performed "The Star-Spangled Banner" more than five thousand times. Monroe married a New York lawyer, Harold M. Weinberg, in 1961 and became a widow in 1977. They had no children.

See also: Sports Events.

Further Reading

Belkin, Lisa. 1987. "Lucy Monroe Dies; a Celebrated Singer of National Anthem." *New York Times*, October 16. https://nytimes/29zQiTh

Folkart, Burt A. 1987. "Obituaries: Lucy Monroe; Singer Noted for 'Star-Spangled Banner.'" *Los Angeles Times*, October 17. Latimes.com/archives/la-xpan-1987-10-17-mn-3484-story.html

Vitty, Cort. "Lucy Monroe." https://sabr.org/node/50381.

Vitty, Cort. 2010. "The Star Spangled Soprano." Metropolitan Washington Old Time Radio Club. http://www.mwotrc.com/rr2010_06/soprano.htm.

Movie Theaters

Contemporary Americans are probably most likely to hear the national anthem played at school events (particularly graduations) and sports competitions. There was a time, however, when it was common for "The Star-Spangled Banner" to be played in movie theaters.

Early in the twentieth century, during the silent-film era, many theaters installed Wurlitzer organs, which would play the anthem before movies began. Indeed, for a number of years, the Smithsonian Institution housed such an organ in front of its display of the flag that flew over Fort McHenry during the British bombardment and inspired Francis Scott Key to write the national anthem (Miller 2002).

Theaters were particularly good venues for military recruiting during World War I, and the government accordingly produced prowar newsreels as well as patriotic shows and speakers (Melnick 2012, 142). Indeed, during silent-era newsreels of the firing of big guns, theaters were urged to use "a simultaneous crash of cymbals and then a rumble on the organ with the biggest pipes we have" (148). It seems likely that most theatergoers would have stood for the anthem. Indeed, two theological students who refused to stand for it in a Chicago theater in 1942 were each fined $200 (Day 2016).

It is still common for the anthem to be performed prior to movies on military bases. In 2004, base movie theaters in South Korea agreed that they would play both the South Korean and U.S. national anthems before showing movies, partly as a way to placate public opinion after a U.S. armored vehicle ran over two local girls (Giordono and Song-Won 2004). In early 2018, the Supreme Court of India modified an earlier ruling that had made standing for its national anthem mandatory prior to film screenings.

See also: Code for the National Anthem; State and Municipal Laws and Ordinances.

Further Reading

Day, Meagan. 2016. "It Used to be Illegal to Not Stand for the National Anthem." *Timeline*, September 13. https://timeline.com/illegal-stand-national-anthem-2227 75e14f93.

Giordono, Joseph, and Choe Song-Won. 2004. "S. Korea Anthem to Co-Star with 'Star-Spangled Banner' at U.S. Base Movie Theaters." *Stars and Stripes*, April 2. https:// www.stripes.com/news/s-korea-anthem-to-co-star-with-star-spangled-banner-at -u-s-base-movie-theaters-1.18313.

Melnick, Ross. 2012. *American Showman: Samuel "Roxy" Rothafel and the Birth of the Entertainment Industry, 1908–1935*. New York: Columbia University Press.

Miller, Mary K. 2002. "It's a Wurlitzer." *Smithsonian Magazine* (April). https://www .smithsonianmag.com/history/its-a-wurlitzer-61398212.

PTI New Delhi. 2018. "Playing of National Anthem in Cinema Halls Optional: Supreme Court." BusinessLine, January 9. https://www.thehindubusinessline.com/news /playing-of-national-anthem-in-cinema-halls-optional-supreme-court/article1002 1703.ece.

Muck, Karl (see German-American Composers during World War I)

Murals

There are at least three murals in the United States that depict Francis Scott Key. The earliest appears to have been painted by George Gray, or Grey (born about 1908), of Harrisburg, Pennsylvania, and is entitled *'Tis the Star-Spangled Banner*. It was officially dedicated on September 1939 and depicts Key and his companions, under apparent guard by British soldiers, looking toward the flag flying above Fort McHenry.

Originally painted for Hotel Rennert in Baltimore, this mural was subsequently moved to Fort McHenry, possibly in 1939, the year that the government redesignated the fort as a National Monument and Historic Shrine (Bronstein 1995). The mural now hangs in one of the second floor offices at Fort McHenry (Taylor 2018).

The Francis Scott Key Hotel, which opened in Frederick, Maryland, on January 8, 1923, and stayed open for more than fifty years, also appears to be the site of a mural that was painted by R. McGill Mackall (1889–1982). Like Gray's mural, it pictured Key as he witnessed the bombardment of Fort McHenry. It was apparently commissioned in 1965 by the Loyola Federal Savings and Loan (later Crestar Bank) when it purchased the first floor of the hotel (Walker 1999). In 1995, the mural was at the Homewood Retirement Center in what was previously the Francis Scott Key Hotel (Meyer 1995, 37).

Yet a third mural for an apartment complex in Baltimore is an outdoor painting that depicts three famous individuals from Baltimore—Edgar Allen Poe, Francis Scott Key, and Billie Holiday—and was painted by Jeff Huntington of Annapolis. The three notable individuals from Baltimore are portrayed in black and white against depictions of the flags of the United States and of Baltimore that are in color.

See also: Baltimore, Maryland; Fort McHenry; Visual Arts.

Further Reading

Bronstein, Hugh. 1995. "Hotel Owners Mark Their 10th Year." *Morning Call*, June 19. http://articles.mcall.com/1995-06-19/news/3029917_1_murals-count-zinzendorf-fort-mchenry.

"Fort McHenry National Monument and Historic Shrine." 1961. United States Department of the Interior National Park Service. Washington, DC: Government Printing Office.

Lynch, Kevin. 2017. "Anthem House Adding New Key Highway Mural Honoring Edgar Allen Poe, Francis Scott Key, and Billie Holiday." SouthBmore.com, June 8. https://www.southbmore.com/2017/06/08/anthem-house-adding-new-key-highway-mural-honoring-edgar-allen-poe-francis-scott-key-and-billie-holiday.

Meyer, Sam. 1995. *Paradoxes of Fame: The Francis Scott Key Story.* Annapolis, MD: Eastwind.

Taylor, Blaine. 2018. "The Rockets' Red Glare: Francis Scott Key's 'Star-Spangled Banner.'" *Warfare History Network*, November 7. https://warfarehistorynetwork.com/daily/military-history/the-rocket.

Walker, Julie Summers. 1999. "Remembering the Francis Scott Key Hotel." *Frederick News-Post*, March 26. https://www.fredericknewspost.com/archive/remembering-the-francis-scott-key-hotel/article_ccb5bceb-d09b-509d-b223-8a2f4e34d1bb.html.

"My Country, 'Tis of Thee" ("America")

Of all the songs that might have been designated as the national anthem instead of Francis Scott Key's "Star-Spangled Banner," none may have been more worthy of consideration than "My Country, 'Tis of Thee," which was often simply designated as "America." Although it was not ultimately chosen, it remains a patriotic favorite.

The song was composed in 1831 by Samuel Francis Smith (1808–1895), who was a graduate of Harvard. At the time, he was a student at Andover Theological

Marian Anderson sings to a packed crowd at the Lincoln Memorial in 1939, after the Daughters of the American Revolution refused to allow her to perform at Constitution Hall because of her race. (Library of Congress)

Seminary, where he was training to be a Baptist minister. Tasked by a professor Lowell Mason, who would later become the first school Superintendent of Music in Boston, to look through a book of German songs that a friend had given to him, Smith found a patriotic tune that he liked and decided to write lyrics more appropriate to America. He did so apparently unaware that the tune was also that of the British National anthem "God save the Queen." Smith drew in part from an earlier song "The Children's Independence Day," which he had written for an Independence Day celebration the previous year. This version had included the phrases "Freedom's holy light" and "Let music float on every breeze" (Branham and Hartnett 2002, 58).

Although Smith did not immediately realize the song's potential, Mason included it in a children's presentation at Boston's Park Street Church for Independence Day in 1831. Altogether the verse had five stanzas, the first and last of which remain the best known.

The first verse is as follows:
My country! 'tis of thee,
Sweet land of liberty—
    Of thee I sing;

Land, where my fathers died;
Land of the pilgrim's pride;
From every mountain-side
    Let freedom ring.

One of the most notable aspects of this verse is that it begins in the first person ("my" and "I"), allowing individual singers to claim the song for their own. The song highlights the value of liberty and evokes proud forebears (especially the Pilgrims who settled in New England)—albeit possibly at the cost of not connecting as well to non-native-born immigrants who came to America from other countries (Hahner, 2017, 113). The last line of this song was effectively used by Dr. Martin Luther King, Jr. in his famous "I Have a Dream" civil rights speech in Washington, DC, in 1963.

The second verse continues with the same emphasis on the "native country," with further attention to its geographical features:

My native country! Thee—
Land of the noble free—
    Thy name I love.
I love thy rocks and rills,
The woods and templed hills;
My heart with rapture thrills,
    Like that above.

Smith later expressed reservations about his third verse, which was long omitted from many published versions. It bears some similarity to the third verse of "The Star-Spangled Banner" and has been similarly criticized for stirring up negative feelings against what was once the mother country:

No more shall tyrants here
With haughty steps appear,
    And soldier-bands:
No more shall tyrants tread
Above the patriot dead—
No more our blood be shed
    By alien hands.

The reference to tyrants "above the patriot dead" is a reference to the British occupation of the Copp's Hill Burying Ground in Boston (Branham and Hartnett 2002, 58).

The fourth verse specifically focuses on the power of song and seems reminiscent of Jesus's words during his entry into Jerusalem in which he proclaimed that had the people not shouted out their praises, the rocks would have done so:

Let music swell the breeze,
And ring from all the trees
    Sweet freedom's song.

Let mortal tongue awake—
Let all that breathe partake—
Let rocks their silence break—
   The sound prolong.

As is the case with the final stanza of "The Star-Spangled Banner," the last verse is the most religious, transferring the glory that some monarchies would give to their human rulers to God himself, who remains identified as the God of forebears:

Our fathers' God! To Thee—
Author of liberty,
   To thee we sing:
Long may our land be bright
With freedom's holy light—
Protect us by Thy might,
   Great God, our King!

Smith lived a long life, and in 1889, he added another verse celebrating the centenary of George Washington's inauguration:

Our joyful hearts today,
Their grateful tribute pay,—
   Happy and free.
After our toils and fears,
After our blood and tears,
Strong with our hundred years,
   God to Thee.

Unlike "The Star-Spangled Banner," Smith's song does not mention the flag, which had become an increasing object of veneration in America culture. Despite its popular accolades and its easy-to-sing melody, some individuals did not think it was appropriate for America to use the same tune for its national anthem as the British did for theirs. In 1889, the *New York Times* thus editorialized that "'America' should be ignored by all persons who do not wish to be classed as receivers of stolen goods," while Professor Thomas Lounsbury of Yale later wrote that "there is nothing more impudent in the history of plagiarism than our appropriation of 'God Save the King' and calling it 'America'" (Branham and Hartnett 2002, 14).

Sometimes having two such anthems to the same tune created confusion. It is thus reported that when the British novelist Charles Dickens was visiting Philadelphia in 1863, he stood to the tune of "America" thinking that the band was complimenting his country. The audience, in turn, thought that Dickens was complimenting the United States (Scholes 1954, 198).

"America" gained considerable impetus through its promotion in public schools (Massachusetts was the first state to establish a system of public schools in 1827), which used it and other tunes to promote national pride, especially among children of immigrants. Bostonians became known for saying, *"Amoris patriae nutric carmen,"* meaning "song is the nourisher of patriotism" (Branham and Hartnett 2002, 67). From the beginning, the song was also often associated with the temperance movement (71–83) .

Writing about the song before the nation had chosen "The Star-Spangled Banner" as its national anthem, musicologist Oscar Sonneck observed that "America" was "perhaps too hymnlike and devotional in character for a national anthem, and possibly is pervaded too much by a peculiar New England flavor" (1909, 76). He noted, however, that it was "appropriate for all occasions and professions, for old and young and for both sexes," adding the somewhat unusual comment, "It does not sound odd from the mouth of a woman as does, for instance, 'The Star-Spangled Banner'" (1909, 76–77).

In 1932, a year after Congress designated "The Star-Spangled Banner" as the national anthem, it adopted a resolution commending the singing of Smith's song on Independence Day of that year, which it apparently thought was its centennial. Part of the tune of the song is incorporated in composer Rick Kirby's (1945–) "An American Fanfare."

In 1939, in her famed concert on Easter Sunday at the Lincoln Memorial, African American singer Marian Anderson (1897–1993), who had been excluded from the hall of the Daughters of the American Revolution, altered the words of the song to say "To thee we sing" rather than "Of thee I sing." In the words of Scott Sandage, a rhetoric professor, she was thus "painting 'land of liberty' as more aspiration than description and catching both the communalism and conflict of the day she sang at the Lincoln Memorial" (1993, 136).

See also: Alternatives to the National Anthem; Children; Public Schools.

Further Reading

Branham, Robert James, and Stephen J. Hartnett. 2002. *Sweet Freedom's Song: "My Country 'Tis of Thee" and Democracy in America.* New York: Oxford University Press.

Collins, Ace. 2003. *Songs Sung Red, White, and Blue: The Stories Behind America's Best-Loved Patriotic Songs.* New York: HarperCollins.

Hahner, Leslie A. 2017. *To Become an American: Immigrants and Americanization Campaigns of the Early Twentieth Century.* East Lansing: Michigan State University Press.

Maginty, Edward A. "'America': The Origin of Its Melody." *Musical Quarterly* 20 (July): 259–66.

Sandage, Scott A. 1993. "A Marble House Divided: The Lincoln Memorial, the Civil Rights Movement, and the Politics of Memory, 1939–1963." *Journal of American History* 80 (June): 135–67.

Scholes, Percy A. 1954. *God Save the Queen! The History and Romance of the World's First National Anthem.* New York: Oxford University Press.

Sonneck, Oscar George Theodore (compiler). 1909. *Report on "The Star-Spangled Banner," "Hail Columbia," "America," "Yankee Doodle."* Washington, DC: Government Printing Office (Library of Congress).

National Anthem Contest

In part because many hymns were used as patriotic songs prior to Congress's specific adoption of "The Star-Spangled Banner" as the national anthem in 1931, questions remained as to whether it was suitable. Although it had the advantage of expressing public opinion at a pivotal moment in U.S. history, the range of the music was difficult for amateurs to master, and as the Civil War approached, it had not even been clear whether it was a Union or a Confederate song.

Apparently prompted in part by the lack of a national anthem and the rise of the role of "Dixie" in the South (Hutchinson 2007, 620), in 1861 a number of New Yorkers, chaired by Richard Grant White, a scholar of Shakespeare who later wrote an account of the committee's work, formed a National Hymn Committee to find an official national hymn. It offered a prize of $500 for the winning entry.

The first guideline for the contest, which would seem to exclude songs like "The Star-Spangled Banner," required that "the hymn . . . be purely patriotic, adopted to the whole country—not a war-song, or only appropriate to the present moment" (White 1861, 65). A second guideline required the hymn to consist of from sixteen to forty lines, exclusive of the chorus. A third criterion, likely pointing to what the committee considered to be existing deficiencies in "The Star-Spangled Banner," required that "it should be of the simplest form and most marked rhythm; the words easy to be retained by the popular memory, and the melody and harmony such as may be readily sung by ordinary voices" (White 1861, 65).

Although the widely advertised campaign solicited over twelve hundred entries, the committee ultimately concluded that none were worthy of the prize. Ironically, Julia Ward Howe provided something of a Northern anthem when she adopted the tune of "John Brown's Body" to what became "Battle Hymn of the Republic." Moreover, once the war ended, and especially during the Spanish-American War of 1898, both Northerners and Southerners embraced the flag and "The Star-Spangled Banner" that celebrated it as symbols of national unity and pride.

A scholar who has examined the contest believes that its most important product was a parody of possible anthems. This study was authored by Robert Henry Newell, whose pen name was Orpheus C. Kerr, in the style of various contemporary poets for the *Sunday Mercury* and was titled "The Rejected 'Anthems.'" (Eby 1960, 403–9). Writing in 1869, the Reverend Elias Nason scoffed at the idea that money could create such an anthem: "Money, some years ago, was offered for a national hymn. Futility! Money may buy machinery—sometimes in the form of men—but inspiration, never" (12).

In February of 1895, at its so-called Continental Congress in Washington, DC, the Daughters of the American Revolution devoted a special program, complete with the U.S. Marine Band, to come up with a new national hymn. Writing about this contest, Miss Janet E. Hosmer Richards observed that "with all deference to the composers of these songs, to the committee of 'Daughters' who arranged this entertaining programme, and to the charming young ladies who rendered it, I think it may be safely affirmed that not one person present remembered a word of one of those productions, or recalled a line of the accompanying airs, half an hour after the audience dispersed" (1895, 538). Richards concluded that "The Star-Spangled Banner" remained the obvious choice: "In this soul-stirring hymn we have embodied a sentiment which will serve all true Americans for all occasions. In times of peace, dear flag, we hail thee! In time of danger, inspired by this anthem, we will gladly rally to thy defense and shed our life's blood, if necessary, in order that we may proudly proclaim after the heat and hardship of the struggle, 'Our Flag is still there!'" (1895, 539–40).

At the end of 1925, the magazine *Musical America* initiated a contest to award $3,000 for an epic American rhapsody. It ultimately awarded the prize to Ernest Bloch, a Jewish immigrant from Switzerland, for his composition entitled "America." Critics, however, almost immediately attacked "America," often employing seemingly contradictory arguments and criticisms. Some charged that it was "artificially sentimental and old-fashioned" and others claimed that it was "an egregious example of over-wrought ultramodernism" (Brotman 1998, 418). It had consisted of three movements, dealing successively with British colonization of the land of the Indians, the American Civil War, and America's future as it moved deeper into the twentieth century (433–34). Critics further found his portrayals to be overly idealized with a past "bleached to perfection, its future fixed upon a prediction of a utopian role of leadership" (Moicz 2011, 177).

In 1926, the National Federation of Music Clubs held a contest to come up with new music for "America the Beautiful." It also offered a $500 prize "to the American-born composer whose setting best expresses the love, loyalty and majesty its lines express" (Sherr 2001, 66). Again, however, the committee found all the entries lacking, and it did not award the prize.

In 1929, the Brooks-Bright Foundation offered $6,000 in prizes for a better composition. Although it awarded $1,000 of the money, it did not select a new anthem (Spiegel 1998, 33). Somewhat more successfully, *Liberty* magazine sponsored a contest in 1938 for a song for the Army Air Corps, which resulted in the submission of a song by Robert Crawford, now titled "The U.S. Air Force" (Corbeil 2017).

In recent years a number of contests have been held to determine who would be chosen to sing the national anthem at major sports and other events.

See also: "America the Beautiful"; "Battle Hymn of the Republic"; Mexican National Anthem.

Further Reading
Brotman, Charles. 1998. "The Winner Loses: Ernest Bloch and His America." *American Music* 16 (Winter): 417–47.

Corbeil, Shannon. 2017. "7 Air Force Song Facts That Will Make You Want to Go Off into the Wild Blue Yonder." *We Are the Mighty*, September 19. https://www .wearethemighty.com/music/7-air-force-song-facts-that-will-make-you-want-to-go -off-into-the-wild-blue-yonder.

Eby, Cecil D., Jr. 1960. "The National Hymn Contest and 'Orpheus C. Kerr.'" *Massachusetts Review* 1 (Winter): 400–9.

Guenter, Scot M. 1990. *The American Flag, 1777–1924: Cultural Shifts from Creation to Codification.* Cranbury, NJ: Associated University Presses.

Gurza, Agustin. 2018. "Himno Nacional Mexicano: The Long and Winding History of Mexico's National Anthem." *Strachwitz Frontera Collection of Mexican and Mexican American Recordings* (blog), January 22. http://frontera.library.ucla.edu/blog /2018/01/himno-nacional-mexicano-long-and-winding-history-mexico%E2%80 %99s-national-anthem.

Hutchison, Coleman. 2007. "Whistling 'Dixie' for the Union." *American Literary History* 19 (Autumn): 603–28.

Kowalewski, Albin J. 2011. "The Star Spangled Bummer." *Opinionator* (blog), *New York Times*, August 25. https://opinionator.blogs.nytimes.com/2011/08/25/the-star-spangled-bummer.

Moicz, Klara. 2011. "The Birth of a Nation and the Limits of the Human Universal in Ernest Bloch's America." *American Music* 29 (Summer): 168–202.

Nason, Elias. 1869. *A Monogram on Our National Song.* Albany, NY: Joel Munsell.

Richards, Janet E. Hosmer. 1895. "The National Hymn." *American Monthly Magazine* (December): 536–40.

Rips, Michael D. 1986. "Freedom, in Song and Literature: Let's Junk the National Anthem." *New York Times*, July 5.

Sherr, Lynn. 2001. *America the Beautiful: The Stirring True Story Behind Our Nation's Favorite Song.* New York: Public Affairs.

Spiegel, Allen D., and Marc B. Spiegel. 1998. "Redundant Patriotism: The United States National Anthem as an Obligatory Sports Ritual." *Culture, Sport, Society* 1 (1): 24–43.

White, Richard Grant. 1861. *National Hymns: How They Are Written and How They Are Not Written. A Lyric and National Study for the Times.* New York: Rudd & Carleton.

National Anthem Day

Although Francis Scott Key wrote "The Star-Spangled Banner" in September 1814, Congress did not declare the song to be the national anthem until March 3, 1931.

Marc Ferris, the author of *Star-Spangled Banner: The Unlikely Story of America's National Anthem*, who lives in Greenwich, Connecticut, wants the national government to set aside this date as National Anthem Day.

Such a designation would neither mandate nor preclude a national observance on this day.

In the meantime, a number of civic and patriotic groups have already unofficially designated March 3 as National Anthem Day.

See also: Commemorations of "The Star-Spangled Banner"; Congress and "The Star-Spangled Banner."

Further Reading

Dunne, Susan. 2015. "Greenwich Author Says 'Star-Spangled Banner' Deserves a National Anthem Day." *Hartford Courant*, March 2. https://www.courant.com /entertainment/arts/hc-star-spangled-banner-book-0303-20150302-story.html.

Ferris, Marc. 2014. *Star-Spangled Banner: The Unlikely Story of America's National Anthem*. Baltimore: Johns Hopkins University Press.

National Anthem Project

Educators have fretted for many years about both student and citizen ignorance of the lyrics to "The Star-Spangled Banner" and the inability of many of them to sing it. In March 2005 the Music Educators National Conference, today known as the National Association for Music Education, responded to this state of affairs by launching a campaign called the National Anthem Project. Its purpose was to "restore America's voice through music education" (Abril 2007, 81).

To this end, the organization created a traveling show that operated from a tractor-trailer and carried tents where individuals could learn the national anthem. The organization also created a website with teaching materials related to the song and named September 14 as National Anthem Project Day.

Professor Deborah Bradley (2009), however, criticized the National Anthem Project on a number of grounds. She thought that "positioning of the 'Star-Spangled Banner' within the music education advocacy argument locates the anthem as the means to an end, or what Adorno refers to as 'a propagandistic device or an ideological export article'" (66). She further criticized the images used to promote the program as too homogeneous, noting that the statement of the National Anthem Project "assumes a monolithic American identity and a single American culture." Like other critics of the lyrics of the anthem, she also considered them to be too "warlike" (67, 69).

Estelle R. Jorgensen (2007) of Indiana University expressed a number of similar reservations. Arguing that "at the very least, we cannot simply forward this one song" (153), she said, "We shall want to choose songs to sing that are singable by the great majority of people rather than just a few musicians. . . . We need to teach the nation songs that promote a love of tranquility over unbridled violence, law over brute force, and an informed grasp of social obligations over a simplistic world view in which our particular notions of justice prevail" (153–54). Considering such songs as "America the Beautiful" and "America," however, she also found them to be too monotheistic and male. Jorgensen suggested, "Questioning our own national anthem, asking if we need new songs to express our attachment to home and this land, and teaching the nation to sing these songs can prompt us to wonder collectively how we might once again join not only with each other across this country but with many around the world who would willingly sing with us" (156).

Yet another critic was concerned that the National Anthem Project fostered militarism and that it "endangers music education as it threatens to divert financial resources to counterproductive conflicts while creating an educational climate in which technical skills are favored while the liberal and performing arts are under-appreciated" (Hebert 2015, 82). Other educators were likely pleased with a program designed both to enhance knowledge of the national anthem and enhance the ability of students to sing it.

See also: Criticisms and Defenses of "The Star-Spangled Banner"; Knowledge of the National Anthem.

Further Reading

Abril, Carlos R. 2007. "Functions of a National Anthem in Society and Education: A Sociocultural Perspective." *Bulletin of the Council for Research in Music Education*, no. 172 (Spring): 69–87.

Bradley, Deborah. 2009. "Oh, That Magic Feeling! Multicultural Human Subjectivity, Community, and Fascism's Footprints." *Philosophy of Music Education Review* 17 (Spring): 56–74.

Hebert, David G. 2015. "Another Perspective: Militarism and Music Education." *Music Educators Journal* 101 (March): 77–84.

Jorgensen, Estelle R. 2007. "Songs to Teach a Nation." *Philosophy of Music Education Review* 15 (Fall): 150–60.

"Schools Celebrate National Anthem Anniversary." 2005. *Music Educators Journal* 92 (November): 10–13.

Wilson, Michael. 2006. "Project Reteaches National Anthem." *New York Times*, March 14. https://www.nytimes.com/2006/03/14/us/project-reteaches-national-anthem.html.

National Peace Jubilee

No conflict in U.S. history has been bloodier or more divisive than the Civil War. The carnage stirred hopes, however, that with the elimination of slavery a new era of peace might sweep over the nation. Such aspirations were reflected in "Battle Hymn of the Republic" and in other songs of the era.

In 1869, Boston was the site of a National Peace Jubilee, which lasted from June 15 through June 19. The Jubilee was largely the brainchild of Pat Gilmore (1829–1892), who had previously staged a musical extravaganza in New Orleans in 1864. Gilmore was a flamboyant Irish-born bandleader who had immigrated to Boston in 1848 and served early in the Civil War in the band of the Twenty-Fourth Massachusetts Volunteers. He became known for his grand concerts and for writing "When Johnny Comes Marching Home" under the pen name of Louis Lambert (Cipolla 1988, 286). The Jubilee was housed in a wood coliseum, known as the Temple of Peace, which was built especially for the occasion and was capable of seating thirty thousand people, plus a chorus of ten thousand and an orchestra of one thousand—two of the event's greatest features that included violinists Ole Bull and Carl Rosa and singers Parepa-Rosa and Adelaide Phillips. One hundred Boston firemen, each with his own hammer and anvil, participated in the "Anvil Chorus" (from Verdi's *Il Trovatore*). President Ulysses S. Grant attended the event, as did Admiral David Farragut.

Although the nation had not yet adopted an official national anthem, two patriotic songs that are known to have highlighted the festivities were "The

Star-Spangled Banner" and "America," also known as "My Country, 'Tis of Thee." The performances of both were accompanied by the ringing of bells and the firing of a battery near the coliseum.

Horowitz (2005) says that twenty-five hundred base singers began "The Star-Spangled Banner." They were joined by twenty-five hundred tenors and, on the chorus, by all ten thousand singers. Sopranos and altos began the second verse with "organ, drum corps, bells," and cannon from outside reinforced the third verse. Horowitz further reports that "the audience demanded, and received, a repeat performance" (17).

An article in the June 16, 1869, issue of the *Worcester Daily Spy* further noted that "the numbers that most effectually aroused the enthusiasm of the people were the Star Spangled Banner and the Anvil Chorus from 'Il Trovadore.' Tempestuous applause and ten thousand waving handkerchiefs greeted both these stirring performances, and encores followed" (Svejda 2005, 209).

The Jubilee was well attended and resulted in a profit, which apparently went to Gilmore. He sponsored a much less successful World Peace Jubilee in Boston in 1872.

See also: "My Country, 'Tis of Thee" ("America").

Further Reading

Celebrate Boston. n.d. "National Peace Jubilee (1869)." http://www.celebrateboston.com /events/national-peace-jubilee.htm.

Cipolla, Frank J. 1988. "Patrick S. Gilmore: The Boston Years." *American Music* 6 (Autumn): 281–92.

Horowitz, Joseph. 2005. "The Grand Peace Jubilee." In *Classical Music in America: A History of Its Rise and Fall*, 16–18. New York: W.W. Norton. http://wesclark.com /jw/peace_jubilee.html.

Humphreys, Jere T. 1987. "Strike Up the Band! The Legacy of Patrick S. Gilmore." *Music Educators Journal* 74 (October): 22–26.

Svejda, George J. 2005. *History of the Star Spangled Banner from 1814 to the Present*. Honolulu, HI: University Press of the Pacific. First published in 1969 by Division of History, Office of Archeology and Historic Preservation, U.S. Department of the Interior, National Park Service.

Nationalism versus Internationalism

Sociologist Karen Carulo says, "National symbols—in particular, national anthems and flags—provide perhaps the strongest, clearest statement of national identity. In essence, they serve as modern . . . signs that bear a special relationship to the nations they represent, distinguishing them from one another and reaffirming their identify boundaries" (1993, 244). Flags and anthems provide a mechanism both to teach national values to young people and to demonstrate solidarity with other citizens. In the United States, the national anthem is frequently played at naturalization ceremonies.

Sometimes displays of loyalty to the U.S. flag and the national anthem are used not only to affirm one's own nation but also to cast aspersions on those of others.

Indeed, in 1844, an incident involving a flag led to a series of riots in Philadelphia. This violence, including widespread fires and other forms of property destruction, was aimed at ethnic communities that were identified as un-American by the mob. In 1849, a number of nativists formed the secretive Order of the Star-Spangled Banner. This anti-immigrant organization later developed into the Know-Nothing Party, which ran candidates for the U.S. presidency during the 1850s.

Although individuals might show respect by standing or remaining silent during renditions of anthems of other countries, they are more likely to be emotionally involved in renditions of their own. Group identities are often established not only by a process of inclusion but of exclusion. Americans who are justly proud of being "free," might look with disdain, if not on the people, at least on governments that do not recognize similar freedoms. It is ironic that at a time when millions of African Americans were enslaved, Francis Scott Key not only proclaimed that the flag flew "o'er the land of the free," but he excoriated the British for employing the "hireling and slave."

Patriotism, or love of country, is often equated with nationalism, which can often manifest itself in a form of mindless triumphalism or chauvinism, such as that of Nazi Germany or the Soviet Union. It can be used as an excuse to conquer rather than as a call to set an example of national values.

One of the main concerns expressed about adopting "The Star-Spangled Banner" as the national anthem was that it celebrated a U.S. military victory. The first stanza, with its evocations of "the rockets' red glare, the bombs bursting in air," is especially graphic and warlike. Moreover, the third verse, expressed strong anglophobic sentiments, albeit against individuals who were regarded as invaders.

Born in war, "The Star-Spangled Banner" is thought to be especially effective in rallying citizens during similar times of peril. Moreover, compared to the French "La Marseillaise," the Mexican national anthem, and some others, "The Star-Spangled Banner" hardly stands out as especially militaristic. The anthem was actually written by a member of the Federalist Party who had opposed American incursions into Canada and celebrated a defensive victory rather than an offensive operation.

When the National Association for Music Education launched the National Anthem Project to teach the anthem in U.S. schools, Professor Estelle Jorgensen suggested that it should include other songs. She advocated what she called "a measured approach that eschews fundamentalism, rampant militarism, and excessive patriotism, embraces musically the tensions between internationalism, nationalism, and localism, and expresses a sensitive world-view through the choice of songs that cultivate and express liberal and democratic ideals and foster peace internationally" (2007, 150). Yet another critic suggested that it might be time to move "beyond restrictive racial, ethnic, and national identities . . . to an international globalization that transforms everyday consciousness and identities" to include "global concerns" (Bradley 2009, 58).

See also: Anthem; Anti-British Sentiments; Children; Criticisms and Defenses of "The Star-Spangled Banner"; Immigrants; "La Marseillaise"; "Land of the Free and the Home of the Brave"; Mexican National Anthem; National Anthem Contest; Patriotism; Slavery.

Further Reading

Anderson, Benedict. 2006. *Imagined Communities*. New York: Verso.

Bradley, Deborah. 2009. "Oh, That Magic Feeling! Multicultural Human Subjectivity, Community, and Fascism's Footprints." *Philosophy of Music Education Review* 17 (Spring): 56–74.

Cerulo, Karen A. 1993. "Symbols and the World System: National Anthems and Flags." *Sociological Forum* 8 (June): 243–71.

Jorgensen, Estelle R. 2007. "Songs to Teach a Nation." *Philosophy of Music Education Review* 15 (Fall): 150–60.

Marshall, Alex. 2015. *Republic or Death! Travels in Search of National Anthems*. London: Random House.

Native American Indians

Native Americans may be citizens both of the United States, which recognized them as such in 1924, and of their own tribes, which exercise at least some degree of sovereignty. Like African Americans, however, through much of American history they were regarded first as a separate people and then as second-class citizens, if citizens at all.

Native Americans have long incorporated the American flag, the primary subject of "The Star-Spangled Banner," into their artwork. At times they identified it with magical powers (Schmittou and Logan 2002). At other times, they portrayed flags flying upside down, at half-staff, or with different colors, which might have intended to convey feelings of distress, mourning, or mistreatment (Logan and Schmittou 2007).

Whereas one of the primary criticisms of "The Star-spangled Banner" has been that it is too warlike, this might actually enhance its appeal among Native Americans who have what Felicia Fonseca (2017) describes as "an enduring regard for warriors," and for whom "serving in the military and protecting one's homeland is considered a continuation of warrior traditions." In fact, Fonseca points out that Americans of Native American heritage have served in the U.S. armed forces at higher rates per capita than any other ethnic group. "I'll stand [for the national anthem]," said Arny Zah of the Navajo Nation. " I'll do whatever I think is appropriate to honor them first, and then over there, I can debate about whether the country is living up to its side of the deal when it comes to treaty rights, water rights, social issues that affect a lot of the tribes" (Fonseca 2017).

Native Americans do have their own national anthems, or flag songs, which they sing at events such as powwows. They contain such lines as "The president's flag will stand forever," "Our country, our land is the most powerful country in the world," and "Under the nation's flag, generations will stand forever. So do I" (Fonseca 2017).

An editorial in the *Native Sun News* does recount an incident during a Lakota Nation Invitational game in the 1970s in which Native Americans refused to stand for "The Star-Spangled Banner," and white spectators refused to stand for the Sioux national anthem (2017).

See also: African Americans; Criticisms and Defenses of "The Star-Spangled Banner."

Further Reading

Fonseca, Felicia. 2017. "In Indian Country, Honoring Flag Might Mean Different Anthem." *Denver Post*, November 25. https://www.denverpost.com/2017/11/25 /taking-a-knee-native-american-persepective.

Logan, Michael H., and Douglas A. Schmittou. 2007. "Inverted Flags in Plains Indian Art: A Hidden Transcript." *Plains Anthropologist* 52 (May): 209–27.

Native Sun News Today Editorial Board. 2017. "To Stand or To Kneel for the National Anthem." *Native Sun News Today*, October 6. https://www.indianz.com/News /2017/10/06/native-sun-news-today-editorial-to-stand.asp.

Schmittou, Douglas A., and Michael H. Logan. 2002. "Fluidity of Meaning: Flag Imagery in Plains Indian Art." *American Indian Quarterly* 26 (Autumn): 559–604.

Nicholson, Joseph Hopper

Joseph Hopper Nicholson (1770–1817) was a lawyer who served in the U.S. House of Representatives from 1799 to 1806. During his time in Congress he led the impeachment proceedings against U.S. District Judge John Pickering, who was removed from office after a subsequent Senate trial, and against U.S. Supreme Court Justice Samuel Chase, who was not. Nicholson subsequently served as chief justice of Maryland's sixth judicial district and as associate justice of the Maryland Court of Appeals from 1806 to 1817.

Nicholson helped raise volunteers to man Fort McHenry against the attack by the British fleet, which Francis Scott Key witnessed, during the War of 1812. Nicholson was Key's brother-in-law, and he actively encouraged him to publish his work. He may have even suggested to Key that he set his song to the music of "To Anacreon in Heaven" (Davis 2019, 39; Anonymous 1914, 12). Years later, Nicholson's granddaughter, Rebecca Lloyd Nicholson, was among those who arranged for the publication of the music to "Maryland, My Maryland," which some considered to be a Confederate alternative (Davis 2019, 39).

Nicholson may have been the individual who penned the words that originally prefaced "the Defence of Fort M'Henry" (today's "The Star-Spangled Banner"), which are written in the third person and did not identify Key by name:

> The annexed song was composed under the following circumstances—A gentleman had left   Baltimore, in a flag of truce for the purpose of getting released from the British fleet, a friend of his who had been captured at Marlborough.—He went as far as the mouth of the Patuxent, and was not permitted to return lest the intended attack on Baltimore should be disclosed. He was therefore brought up the Bay to the mouth of the Patapsco, where the flag vessel was kept under the guns of a frigate, and he was compelled to witness the bombardment of Fort M'Henry, which the Admiral had boasted that he would carry in a few hours, and that the city must fall. He watched the flag at the Fort through the whole day with an anxiety that can be better felt than described, until the night prevented him from seeing it. In the night he watched the Bomb Shells, and at early dawn his eye was again greeted by the proudly waving flag of his country. ("Defence of Fort M'Henry" 1814)

In any event, Chief Justice Roger Taney, another of Key's sons-in-law, confirmed that Key had shown his composition to Nicholson who "was so pleased with it that he immediately sent it to a printer, and directed copies to be struck off in hand-bill form" (Shippen and Taney 1898, 325).

See also: Civil War; "Defence of Fort M'Henry"; Key, Francis Scott; "To Anacreon in Heaven."

Further Reading

Anonymous. 1914. "Captain Joseph Hopper Nicholson." *Patriotic Marylander* 1 (September): 11–13.

Davis, James A. 2019. *Maryland, My Maryland: Music and Patriotism during the American Civil War.* Lincoln: University of Nebraska Press.

"Defence of Fort M'Henry." 1814. Maryland Historical Society. http://www.mdhs.org /digitalimage/defence-sic-fort-mhenry.

Shippen, Rebecca Lloyd, and R. B. Taney. 1898. "The Star-Spangled Banner." *Pennsylvania Magazine of History and Biography* 22:321–25.

"O"

"O," the opening word of the opening line of "The Star-Spangled Banner," requires some explanation, especially since some versions of the song, interpreting the word simply as an old-fashioned spelling of "Oh," have changed it to the latter spelling in error.

In fact, the word "O" is what is known as a vocative O; it may also be called a "poetic apostrophe" ("O" vs. "oh"). This "O" indicates that it is addressing an individual person or thing. This form of the word is found in Walt Whitman's "O Captain, my captain," in "O Pioneers," in "O Canada," in "O Come All Ye Faithful," and "O Christmas Tree," among other places. "The Star-Spangled Banner" addresses itself to an individual—"you"—as well (Okrent 2014). This second-person reference probably has something of a double meaning. It may very well have been Francis Scott Key's own question to his companions as they bore witness to the British attack on Fort McHenry, but the second-person reference also seems to direct itself to the reader or singer; the questions seems not only appropriate for the dawn that followed the attack on Fort McHenry but for the present day: Is the American Flag still flying "o'er the land of the free and the home of the brave?"

By contrast to "O," the term "Oh," which is not necessarily capitalized, is an interjection generally used to "indicate pain, surprise, disappointment, or really any emotional state" (Okrent 2014). However, some individuals used the words interchangeably, and their meanings sometimes overlap. Scholar Arika Okrent observed, for instance, that when Juliet asks, "O Romeo, Romeo, wherefore art thou Romeo" in William Shakespeare's famous play, *Romeo and Juliet,* it is difficult to know whether she is "addressing him in her imagination or sighing with emotion" (Okrent 2014).

See also: Lyrics of "The Star-Spangled Banner."

Further Reading

Grammarist. n.d. "O vs. Oh." https://grammarist.com/usage/o-oh.

Okrent, Arika. 2014. "What's the Difference between 'O' and 'Oh'?" *Mental Floss*, May 7. http://mentalfloss.com/article/56582/whats-difference-between-o-and-oh.

"O Canada"

Although they are on the same continent, Canada and the United States have very different histories. The thirteen colonies that were settled in North America largely by the British declared their independence from Great Britain in 1776 and succeeded in winning their war for independence in 1781. The colonies to the North, originally settled by France, were ceded to the British at the end of the French and Indian War (1754–1763) but long continued their association with Britain. In fact, Britain's monarch remains the ceremonial chief-of-state in Canada, even though Britain acknowledged Canadian independence in the British North American Act on July 1, 1867.

Although Canadians have their own sense of national identity, the nation is often defined in terms of its relationship to the mother country and to its very powerful neighbor on its southern border—a neighbor that was interested in incorporating it as late as the War of 1812, during which Francis Scott Key wrote "The Star-Spangled Banner." Both Canada and the United States are democracies, but Canada has a parliamentary system whereas the United States has a presidential system of separated powers.

The origins of the Canadian national anthem can be traced back to Calixa Lavallee (1842–1891), a French-Canadian-American musician who had served in the Union army as a band musician during the Civil War. He was commissioned in 1880 to compose the music for a poem that Adolphe-Basile Routhier (1839–1920), a Canadian judge and lyricist had composed. It was first performed in the city of Quebec for the National Conference of French Canadian at the Saint-Jean Baptiste Day celebrations of June 24, 1880. Although it was initially well received, many Canadians probably first heard it when schoolchildren sang it for the Duke and Duchess of Cornwall when they toured in 1901.

It took some time, however, for "O Canada" to receive official designation as a national anthem. The Parliament accomplished this in 1980, fifteen years after formally adopting the red maple leaf flag as the national flag, when it adopted the National Anthem Act. Although there are a number of versions, the one that the Canadian Parliament adopted was written by lawyer Robert Stanley Weir in 1908 after *Collier's Weekly* held a competition for new English lyrics. In 2018, Parliament adopted further language designed to give parity to male and female references in the song, thus referring to "in all of us" rather than "in all thy sons." Because Canada, which was settled by two European powers, recognizes both their languages, the song may be sung in either English or French or a combination of the two. It is more common for Canadian school children to sing the anthem in school rather than saluting the flag (as used to be common in American classrooms).

Like "The Star-Spangled Banner," "O Canada" begins with a vocative O, which instead of being addressed to "you" is directly addressed to the nation itself.

The first, and most commonly sung English stanza, is as follows:

O Canada! Our home and native land!
True patriot love in all of us command.
With glowing hearts we see thee rise,
The True North, strong and free!
From far and wide, O Canada,
We stand on guard for thee.
God keep our land glorious and free!

O Canada, we stand on guard for thee.
O Canada, we stand on guard for thee.

As the lyrics reveal, this verse makes no reference to the flag but identifies the nation by place ("The True North") and by size ("far and wide"). The song portrays the nation as worthy of the love and protection of its citizens. The French version makes specific reference to the people's knowledge of how to "wield the sword" and "carry the cross."

The second stanza is similar to "America the Beautiful" in that it refers to the nation's beautiful natural resources. In the case of the Canadian anthem, the lyrics in the second stanza highlight "pines and maples," "great prairies," "lordly rivers," and a "broad domain, / From East to Western sea." Like the last line of "The Star-Spangled Banner," the last line of the second verse portrays a nation "strong and free." A third verse again references "From East to Western sea."

As with "The Star-Spangled Banner," the last verse of "O Canada" is the most religious and is in the language of a prayer:

Ruler supreme, who hearest humble prayer,
Hold our Dominion within thy loving care;
Help us to find, O God, in thee
A lasting, rich reward,
As waiting for the better Day,
We ever stand our guard.

One impetus for the practice of playing and/or singing the national anthem before ball games appears to have originated when U.S. and Canadian hockey teams met at a time when Canada had entered World War II as a British ally before the United States had joined the conflict. At these games, both nations played their respective anthems (Clague 2015, 220).

See also: "America the Beautiful"; "God Save the Queen"; "O"; Sports Events; War of 1812.

Further Reading

Clague, Mark, and Andrew Kuster, eds. 2015. *Star Spangled Songbook: A History in Sheet Music of "The Star-Spangled Banner."* Ann Arbor, MI: Star Spangled Music Foundation.

Cook, Sharon Anne. "'Patriotism, Eh?' the Canadian Version." *Phi Delta Kappan* 87 (April): 589–93.

Government of Canada. 2018. "Full History of 'O Canada.'" Last modified on October 24, 2018. https://www.canada.ca/en/canadian-heritage/services/anthems-canada/history-o-canada.html.

Guerrini, Susan C., and Mary C. Kennedy. 2009. "Cross-Cultural Connections: An Investigation of Singing Canadian and American Patriotic Songs." *Bulletin of the Council for Research in Music Education*, no. 182 (Fall): 31–49.

Reed, W. L., and M. J. Bristow, eds. 1985. *National Anthems of the World*, 6th ed. Poole, UK: Blandford Press.

O'Connor, Sinead

Sinead O'Connor (1967–) is a pop singer from Ireland who is known for such controversial actions as being ordained as a priest by an independent Catholic group, tearing up a picture of the pope on an October 3, 1992, performance of *Saturday Night Live* to protest against sexual abuse of children by Catholic priests, and eventually converting to Islam in October 2018, after which she changed her name to Shahada' Davitt.

She stirred controversy in 1990 when she refused to appear onstage at the Garden State Arts Center in New Jersey until officials canceled plans to play "The Star-Spangled Banner" prior to her appearance. She explained, "I sincerely harbor no disrespect for America or Americans, but I have a policy of not having any national anthems played before my concerts in any country, including my own, because they have nothing to do with music in general" (Anderson 1990).

The singer Frank Sinatra was among those who criticized her actions. He referred to them as "unforgiveable" and urged fans to boycott her subsequent performances. Some northeastern radio stations, which received numerous unsolicited phone calls, subsequently refused to play her recordings, and some even smashed her records on the air.

See also: Controversial Performances.

Further Reading

Anderson, Dale. 1990. "Singer's Anthem Antics Hit Sour Note." *Buffalo News*, August 29. https://buffalonews.com/1990/08/29/singers-anthem-antics-hit-sour-note-flag -waving-planned-for-sinead-oconnor-concert.

"Listeners Angered by Sinead O'Connor." 1990. *Washington Post*, August 27. https:// www.washingtonpost.com/archive/lifestyle/1990/08/28/listeners-angered-by-sinead -oconnor/b0b89b89-3ec1-4ad8-8978-4dd80513f342.

"Ode to the Star-Spangled Banner"

In December 1932, the year after Congress had designated "The Star-Spangled Banner" as the official national anthem, Ferde Grofe, Jr., (1892–1972) led his orchestra in the premier performance of "Sept. 13, 1814," which has subsequently become known as the "Ode to the Star-Spangled Banner," at Radio City Music Hall in New York City.

Grofe, who composed "The Grand Canyon Suite" and also arranged George Gershwin's famous "Rhapsody in Blue," wrote the piece for impresario A. F. Rothafel, the man responsible for building Radio City Music Hall. Grofe wrote the song to recall the British bombardment of Fort McHenry that had inspired Francis Scott Key to write "The Star-Spangled Banner" (Brown 2014). Although Grofe's jazz orchestra had subsequently played scaled-down versions of the piece, it was essentially lost to history until William S. Grauer, who had attended with his father the 1932 concert when he was a freshman at Johns Hopkins University, found a copy of the program at his house. With the help of Dr. Charles Limb, a Hopkins otolaryngologist, and Nicholas Alexander Brown at the Library of

Congress, the original score for the "Ode to the Star-Spangled Banner" was rediscovered in Grofe's papers.

Ferde Grofe, Jr., granted permission for the Baltimore Symphony Orchestra to replay the piece for the one hundredth anniversary of the composition of Key's anthem, and it was prepared for printing and performed on September 20, 2014. The performance was accompanied by footage from a History Channel docudrama about the War of 1812 that it had aired ten years earlier (Brown 2014).

See also: Key, Francis Scott.

Further Reading

Brown, Nicholas A. 2014. "'Ode to the Star-Spangled Banner' and #SSB200." *In the Muse* (blog), Library of Congress, July 1. https://blogs.loc.gov/music/2014/07/ode-to-the -star-spangled-banner-and-ssb200.

Grauer, Neil A. 2014. "Rediscovering the 'Ode to the Star-Spangled Banner.'" *Johns Hopkins Magazine* (Winter). https://hub.jhu.edu/magazine/2014/winter/grofe-ode-to -star-spangled-banner.

Smith, Tim. 2014. "'Banner' a Hit Song with Staying Power." *Baltimore Sun*, September 8. https://www.baltimoresun.com/entertainment/arts/artsmash/bs-ae-national -anthem-20140906-story.html.

"O'er the Ramparts"

This line from "The Star-Spangled Banner," which refers to the American flag flying over the walls of Fort McHenry during a British attack, has been used as the title for at least two musical performances designed to highlight the battles during the War of 1812 that led to the writing of "The Star-Spangled Banner."

The first was composed and performed in 1989 for the 175th anniversary of the events. Combining drama and music, it was written by Richard Byrd and F. Scott Black, with the music by William Watson (Grauer 1989).

The second of these was a collaboration of two professors at the Community College of Baltimore County (CCBC), Anne Lefter and William Watson, the latter of whom had also been involved in the earlier performance. They composed their performances for the bicentennial of "The Star-Spangled Banner" anthem in 2014.

Among the unique aspects of the latter production was that it focused on the Battle of North Point on September 12, 2014, that had preceded the attack on Fort McHenry. The clash at North Point had thwarted a land attack on Baltimore by British forces but gradually became an historical afterthought of sorts as attention shifted to the Battle of Fort McHenry, in part because that latter clash was immortalized in Key's "The Star-Spangled Banner." The 2014 performance, which was accompanied by the Baltimore Symphonic Band, also sought to highlight the role of African Americans like Grace Wisher, who served as an indentured servant to Mary Pickersgill, who sewed the giant flag now designated as the Star-Spangled Banner.

There was at least one musical production, described by musicologist George Svejda (1985) as a "nautical peace play" and entitled "The Star-Spangled Banner," that was performed at least twice in the nineteenth century. It was performed at the National Theatre in New York from February 13–15, 1837, and at the Bowery Theatre in the same city on May 8, 1846 (158).

See also: Baltimore, Maryland; Commemorations of "The Star-Spangled Banner"; Fort McHenry; Pickersgill, Mary Young; War of 1812.

Further Reading

BWW News Desk. 2014. "Experience the War of 1812's 'Battle of North Point' at CCBC's O'er the Ramarts This Weekend." *Broadway World*, September 12. https://www .broadwayworld.com/baltimore/article/Experience-the-War-of-1812s-Battle-of -North-Point-at-CCBCs-OER-THE-RAMPARTS-912-14-20140911.

Grauer, Neil A. 1989. "Seeking the Old Glory of Fort McHenry." *Washington Post*, September 7. https://www.washingtonpost.com/archive/local/1989/09/07/seeking-the -old-glory-of-fort-mchenry/3bf272e6-a8ae-4dfd-89a5-2c32147e8244.

Svejda, George J. 2005. *History of the Star Spangled Banner from 1814 to the Present.* Honolulu, HI: University Press of the Pacific. First published in 1969 by Division of History, Office of Archeology and Historic Preservation, U.S. Department of the Interior, National Park Service.

Olympic Protest (1968)

Colin Kaepernick, the quarterback for the San Francisco 49ers football team, started a movement and initiated considerable controversy when, in 2016, he sat (and, in later games, took a knee) during the playing of the national anthem prior to play. Years before, at the 1968 Summer Olympic Games in Mexico City, Tommie Smith and John Carlos, who were respectively being honored for winning the gold and bronze medals for the two-hundred-meter race, had registered a similar protest during the playing of the American national anthem that also garnered nationwide attention. Their symbolic protest against racism in American society was captured in a powerful photograph by John Dominis.

As the American flag was being raised and the national anthem was being played in their honor, they raised clinched gloved fists above their heads in a gesture widely recognized as an expression of support for the Black Power movement, which was far more assertive of African American rights than traditional civil rights protestors. Sportswriter David Davis (2008) explains that the symbolism went even further, with black socks without shoes to symbolize African American poverty and a scarf and beads in memory of lynching victims. They were apparently also deeply affected by the Mexican government's killing of political protestors ten day before the Olympic Games (Blakemore 2018). Although he did not raise his own hand, the silver medal winner, Australian Peter Norman, who had his own concerns about racial tensions within his own nation, also stood in solidarity with them and wore a button for the Olympic Project for Human Rights (Blakemore 2018).

All three competitors were disciplined by the Olympic Games authorities. The Americans were suspended and kicked out of the Olympic Village, and the Australians excluded Norman from future competitions. Although their actions were widely considered to be symbols of the Black Power movement, this movement itself was alternatively interpreted as a sign of black empowerment, solidarity, pride, and militancy. Smith actually told Carlos that "the national anthem is sacred to me, and this can't be sloppy. It has to be clean and abrupt" (Henderson 2013, 97). One scholar has said that "the expression of black pride and strong group identity simultaneously with the playing of 'The Star-Spangled Banner' powerfully expressed a double consciousness" (103).

Some of the concern that the salute generated stemmed from the belief that sports, especially Olympic events, should be free of political protests, although the Olympic Committee apparently took no action when the Czech gymnast Vera Caslavska turned her head away from the flag of the Soviet Union, which had invaded her country two month prior to the Olympics, during her appearances (Henderson 2013, 100). American politicians feared that the Smith and Carlos protest would hurt America's image during the Cold War.

In the decades since their famous protest, however, many Americans—especially those of color—have come to see the symbolic protest registered by Smith and Carlos at the 1968 Games as a landmark in social protest. In 2005, San Jose State built a statue on campus commemorating the event, and in 2008, the two athletes were given an Arthur Ashe Award for Courage (Henderson 2013, 112).

See also: African Americans; Kaepernick, Colin; Olympic Protest (1972); Sports Events.

Further Reading

Bass, Amy. 2002. *Not the Triumph But the Struggle: The 1968 Olympics and the Making of the Black Athlete.* Minneapolis: University of Minnesota Press.

Blakemore, Erin. 2018. "How the Black Power Protest at the 1968 Olympics Killed Careers." *History Stories*, History Channel (website), February 22. https://www.history.com/news/1968-mexico-city-olympics-black-power-protest-backlash.

Davis, David. 2008. "Olympic Athletes Who Took a Stand." *Smithsonian Magazine* (August). https://www.smithsonianmag.com/articles/olympic-athletes-who-took-a-stand-593920.

Henderson, Simon. 2013. *Sidelined: How American Sports Challenged the Black Freedom Struggle.* Lexington: University Press of Kentucky.

Thomas, Damion L. 2012. *Globetrotting: African Americans Athletes and Cold War Politics.* Champaign: University of Illinois Press.

Olympic Protest (1972)

Just as American sprinters Tommie Smith and John Carlos had been suspended from the 1968 Olympic Games in Mexico City, so too, Avery Brundage, the president of the International Olympic Committee, suspended two four-hundred-meter sprinters from the 1972 games in Munich, Germany. They were Vincent Matthews, a gold medalist, and Wayne Collett, a silver medalist. Both were African American athletes from UCLA.

Whereas Smith and Carlos had raised their fists in a salute to Black Power at the 1968 Games, Matthews and Collett had used the playing of the national anthem to strike a casual pose, one with bare feet and a hand on his hip and the other appearing to stroke his chin—a stance that journalist Roy Tomizawa (2016) says approximated the attitude of someone waiting at a bus stop; Collett had, however, also given a Black Power salute (Carlson 2010). This incident was captured in an iconic black and white photo that was published by the Associated Press.

The U.S. coach, Bill Bowerman, thought the athletes had behaved inappropriately but did not think they deserved to be suspended. He sought to have them reinstated, but they had already been sent from Olympic Village, and Bowerman had to pull the American team from the 4 × 400 relay team, which had been widely expected to win. Clifford Buck, who headed the U.S. Olympic Committee, explained that they deserved expulsion because "they insulted the American flag" (Tomizawa 2016). Collett, however, later explained, "I love America. I just don't think it's lived up to its promise. I'm not anti-American at all. To suggest otherwise is to not understand the struggles of blacks in America at the time" (Tomizawa 2016).

See also: African Americans; Kaepernick, Colin; Olympic Protest (1968); Sports Events.

Further Reading

Carlson, Michael. 2010. "Wayne Collett: Athlete Who Staged a Black Power Protest at the 1972 Olympic Games." *Independent*, April 28. https://www.independent.co.uk /news/obituaries/wayne-collett-athlete-who-staged-a-black-power-protest-at-the -1972-olympic-games-1956018.html.

Tomizawa, Roy. 2016. "Vincent Matthews and Wayne Collett: A Most Casual Protest with Most Striking Consequences." *The Olympians*, November 18. https://the olympians.co/2016/11/18/vincent-matthews-and-wayne-collett-a-most-casual -protest-with-most-striking-consequences.

Paintings of the Bombardment of Fort McHenry

The naval bombardment of Fort McHenry was, with the burning of Washington, DC, one of the more dramatic events of the War of 1812. In addition to the engraving executed by John Bower in 1814, there are at least two paintings of this historic event, which is best known for inspiring Francis Scott Key to write "The Star-Spangled Banner."

One painting by Alfred Jacob Miller (1810–1874), believed to have been painted from 1828 to 1830, shows the flag flying over the fort, which is enveloped by rising smoke as ships fire at it against a dark sky. Fort McHenry is on the left, and Forts Babcock and Covington on the right. The piece is owned by the Maryland Historical Society.

Another painting completed in 2014 by Peter Rindlisbacher (1956–) for the two hundredth anniversary celebration of the successful defense of Fort McHenry is entitled *Perilous Night: Naval Attack on Fort McHenry*. It pictures bombs exploding over the fort from the perspective of British boats that drew near while a group of soldiers on nine barges was mounting a land attack.

Dr. George Svejda, who is one of the chief experts on the anthem, has a copy of yet another sketch entitled *Bombardment of Fort McHenry*, which was believed to have been painted contemporaneously with the event (2005, 465–66). It mostly portrays a multitude of ships presumably gathering for the attack.

See also: "View of the Bombardment of Fort McHenry."

Further Reading

Miller, Alfred Jacob. 1828–1830. *Bombardment of Fort McHenry*. Maryland Historical Society. http://www.mdhs.org/digitalimage/bombardment-fort-mchenry.

Rindlisbacher, Peter. 2014. "Fort McHenry—A 200 Year Star Spangled Banner Celebration—Baltimore, Maryland." *Skipjack's Nautical Living* (blog), September 28. http://skipjacksnauticalliving.blogspot.com/2014/09/fort-mchenry-200-year-star-spangled.html.

Rindlisbacher, Peter. 2014. *Perilous Night: Naval Attack on Fort McHenry*. Original oil painting. Skipjack Nautical Wares. http://www.skipjackmarinegallery.com/perilous-night-naval-attack-on-fort-mchenry-original-oil-painting-by-peter-rindlisbacher.html.

Svejda, George J. 2005. *History of the Star Spangled Banner from 1814 to the Present*. Honolulu, HI: University Press of the Pacific. First published in 1969 by Division of History, Office of Archeology and Historic Preservation, U.S. Department of the Interior, National Park Service.

Panamanian National Anthem

One of the Central American nations that has been most closely linked to the United States is Panama. During the 1901–1909 administration of President Theodore Roosevelt, the United States took advantage of a secessionist movement in the present nation of Panama against the Columbian government, which was resisting the terms of an American treaty to permit the United States to build a canal between the Atlantic and Pacific Oceans and to exercise sovereignty over the resulting Canal Zone. As Panama declared its independence in 1903, the United States recognized the new government and sent ships to prevent Columbian intervention. It then secured Panamanian consent to a treaty highly favorable to the United States, in part by threatening to withdraw support if it did not comply (Conniff 2012, 69–70).

In 1914 the United States completed the Panama Canal, which was regarded as one of the engineering marvels of modern times. The United States maintained sovereignty within the Panama Canal Zone until the 1980s. Panama adopted a flag with four quadrants. One is solid red, one is solid blue, one is white with a blue star, and the other is white with a red star.

The Panamanian anthem, known as "Himno Istmeno," or the "Isthmian Hymn," was authored by Jeronimo de law Ossa (1847–1907) in 1903, and set to music by Santos A. Jorge (1870–1991) that same year. It was officially adopted in 1906.

The first verse refers to victory "in the happy field of union" of a "new nation." The second suggests that it is "necessary to veil with a curtain / The Calvary and Cross of the past." The third verse refers to the two oceans that bound the nation, with the next referencing the "flower covered soil," and the "brotherly love" that has replaced "warlike clamour." The last appears to glorify the common laborer with the following exhortation, which might have specifically envisioned work on the canal:

Ahead, with spade and stone-mason's hammer!
To work, without more delay!
In this way we shall be the honour and glory
Of this fertile land of Columbus.

The last line would, of course, be at least an indirect reference to the mother country of Columbia.

Seeking to stifle revolutions that might interfere with business on the canal, the United States played a key role in Panamanian affairs through much of the twentieth century. In 1979, the United States abolished the Canal Zone, in 1989 it deposed dictator Manuel Noriega (1934–2017), and in 1999 turned full control of the Panama Canal to Panama.

See also: Nationalism versus Internationalism.

Further Reading

Conniff, Michael L. 2012. *Panama and the United States: The End of the Alliance.* Athens: University of Georgia Press.

Link on Learning. n.d. "Panama National Anthem." http://www.linkonlearning.com /public/anthems/countries/panama.htm.

Parodies

Numerous school children have undoubtedly sung, "O say, can you see, any bed-bugs on me" to the tune of the opening line of "The Star-Spangled Banner." They might also have sung "Jose, do you see?" as they thought of a Spanish boy or man. In so doing, they have joined many more sophisticated adults who have also used other lyrics to parody the song.

One of America's most famous patriotic songs, "Yankee Doodle," attempted to reverse a gross British stereotype of Americans, while "Battle Hymn of the Republic" sought to add sophistication to the lyrics of "John Brown's Body." "My Country, 'Tis of Thee," which is to the tune of the British national anthem, has been the subject of numerous parodies; indeed some scholars have asserted that "'America' has been sung for the past two hundred and sixty years mostly as a vehicle of protest" (Branham and Hartnett 2002, 200). Professor Christopher Kelen (2015) described the Marx Brother's 1933 comedy film *Duck Soup*, which included a very short anthem designed to point to the manner in which anthems try to touch on the same sentiments of self-congratulation and patriotism:

> Hail, hail Freedonia
> Land of the brave and free. (120)

Kelen's work also covers Lydia Huntley Signourney, who wrote "God Save the Plough" in 1847, which used the tune of Britain's "God Save the Queen" to suggest that the real benefactors of the nation were those who worked in the fields (151). Similarly, the Russian performing group Pussy Riot, performed a song in Moscow's Cathedral of Christ the Savior, entitled "Mother of God, Cast Putin out" (128).

It is important to remember that the tune of "The Star-Spangled Banner" was not original but had been appropriated from Britain. Francis Scott Key had himself used the tune on a previous occasion to praise American heroes of the war against pirates in Tripoli. It had also served as the tune for campaign songs for both John Adams and Thomas Jefferson.

As it originated in eighteenth-century England, a parody song was a song that took a familiar tune and set it to different words. Just as Americans transformed the words of "God Save the King" into "God Save America," so too Key used the key to the Anacreontic song of an English musical society to laud the U.S. flag. Scholar Myron Gray (2017) pointed out that "music made good propaganda, amplifying the sentiment and broadening the appeal of political ideology. And if the music was already popular, then it did this work all the more quickly and cheaply" (2). He further noted, "Parody songs circumvented the laborious process of printing musical notation and the need for consumers to read it. They were a more convenient and accessible alternative to even the simplest music sheets. Because of this, and because secular music was rarely printed in the United States before 1793, the majority of early American parody songs appeared in typographic media like broadsides, newspapers, pamphlets, and songsters" (2). Notably, the first printing of "The Star-Spangled Banner" was in the form of a broadside that specifically stated the tune to which it was to be sung.

Just as Key had borrowed the tune to "The Star-Spangled Banner," so too both abolitionists and prohibitionists sought to use "The Star-Spangled Banner" to garner support for their causes. Oliver Wendell Holmes, Sr., added an antislavery verse that "became an all-but-official fifth verse" in many Northern publications (Clague and Kuster 2015, 132). The *Camp-Fire Songster* of 1862 printed a song, "The Union Must and Shall Be Preserved," to the tune of "The Star-Spangled Banner" (Lawrence 1975, 338). Prohibitionists authored at least three parodies of the song in their attempt to call attention to the evils of hard drink (Lindsay 2004).

The Civil War era proved a particularly fertile time to parody "The Star-Spangled Banner," which the Confederate states no longer saw as representing them. Historian Robert Bonner observes that Key's words were "endlessly mimicked, parodied, or rejected" (2002, 61). He thus noted that one version asked, "Oh! Say has the Star-Spangled Banner become / The flag of the tory and the vile Northern scum?" (61). He observes that "one composer depicted how 'the Star Spangled Banner dishonored is streaming O'er bands of fanatics / Their swords are now gleaming'" (62).

After a contest was held in the Northern states in 1861 to come up with a national anthem, Robert Henry Newell wrote parodies of "The Star-Spangled Banner" in the style of various contemporary poets in an article for the *Sunday Mercury* entitled "The Rejected Anthems" (Eby 1960, 403–9).

The line between parody and innovation is not always easy to discern, and some modern performers who have genuinely attempted to update the musical accompaniment rather than the lyrics have sometimes encountered considerable backlash. Others, however, have received acclaim for original interpretations. As is often the case, responses to these different renditions vary depending on the musical tastes of individual audience members.

The internet provides an outlet for creative minds to come up with their own parodies. A group called Airfarcewon thus wrote a parody entitled "The Lard Fangled Fannies" that mocked Americans for being obese. There were numerous parodies of Stacy ("Fergie") Ferguson's much-criticized rendition of the national anthem at the 2018 NBA All-Star Game.

In 2012, Indiana state senator Vaneta Becker introduced legislation that would impose a twenty-five-dollar fine on individuals who parodied "The Star-Spangled Banner" at an event at a public school or university. The law was designed only for intentional parodies rather than for those who merely flubbed lines, and it would also have required schools to maintain recordings of such performances for inspection (Carbone 2012). Although Massachusetts and Michigan have laws that ban embellishments on the anthem, it is doubtful that they would survive First Amendment scrutiny.

See also: Atlee, E. A.; "Battle Hymn of the Republic"; Confederate National Anthem; Early Printings; "God Save the Queen"; Temperance Movement; "When the Warrior Returns"; "Yankee Doodle."

Further Reading
Airfarcewon. n.d. "The Lard Fangled Fannies." AMiRight. http://www.amiright.com /parody/misc/nationalanthem2.shtml.

Bonner, Robert E. 2002. *Colors and Blood: Flag Passions of the Confederate South.* Princeton, NJ: Princeton University Press.

Branham, Robert James, and Stephen J. Hartnett. 2002. *Sweet Freedom's Song: "My Country 'Tis of Thee" and Democracy in America.* New York: Oxford University Press.

Carbone, Nick. 2012. "Watch Out, Weird Al: 'Modifying' National-Anthem Lyrics Could Get You Fined." *Time*, January 9. http://newsfeed.time.com/2012/01/09/watch-out -weird-al-modifying-national-anthem-lyrics-could-get-you-fined.

Clague, Mark, and Andrew Kuster, eds. 2015. *Star Spangled Songbook: A History in Sheet Music of "The Star-Spangled Banner."* Ann Arbor, MI: Star Spangled Music Foundation.

Eby, Cecil D., Jr. 1960. "The National Hymn Contest and 'Orpheus C. Kerr.'" *Massachusetts Review* 1 (Winter): 400–9.

Gray, Myron. 2017. "A Partisan National Song: The Politics of 'Hail Columbia' Reconsidered." *Music & Politics* 11 (Summer): 1–20.

Kelen, Christopher (Kit). 2015. "Putting a Queer Shoulder to the Wheel: Irony, Parody, and National Devotion." *Interdisciplinary Literary Studies* 17 (1): 110–36.

Lawrence, Vera Brodsky. 1975. *Music for Patriots, Politicians, and Presidents: Harmonies and Discords of the First Hundred Years.* New York: Macmillan.

Lindsay, Bryan. 2004. "Anacreon on the Wagon: 'The Star-Spangled Banner' in the Service of the Cold Water Army." *Journal of Popular Culture* 4 (Winter): 595–603.

Patriotic Holidays

It is common to associate particular musical compositions with holidays. In addition to religious compositions, many American Christmas celebrations are adorned with such beloved and well-known songs as "Jingle Bells," "I'm Dreaming of a White Christmas," "Feliz Navidad," and others. New Year's Day is often rung in to the tune of "Auld Lang Syne." Few American birthday celebrations would not be complete without singing "Happy Birthday."

Similarly, there are a number of patriotic holidays that remain particularly associated with music about America in general and renditions of "The Star-Spangled Banner" in particular.

The most obvious national holiday is Independence Day, which is celebrated on July 4 to mark the adoption of the Declaration of Independence. Because it describes rockets fired during a battle at night, "The Star-Spangled Banner" is a particularly appropriate selection to be played during the firework exhibitions that are often the highlight of such celebrations. Dr. George Svejda, with the National Park Service, has painstakingly documented occasions where the song was played on Independence Day ceremonies in various cities in 1815, 1817, 1818, 1819, 1820, 1821, 1822, 1826, 1828, 1829, and 1830. He believes it "took an established place among the many national airs," after which he believed performances lagged but experienced another revival during the Civil War" (2005, 145).

Because the national anthem is so closely associated with American veterans, "The Star-Spangled Banner" is also frequently played at Memorial Day celebrations on the last Monday in May and for Veterans Day on November 11. These

At Arlington Cemetery in Arlington, Virginia, spectators rise to sing "The Star-Spangled Banner" at the Memorial Day services in the amphitheater. This ceremony took place in May 1943. (Library of Congress)

occasions are also often marked by a medley of service songs for each of the five branches of the U.S. military. There is often a tension displayed between the idea of solemnly commemorating such events and the leisure activities that often accompany the holidays (Albanese 1974).

Maryland has designated September 12 as Defenders' Day to recognize those who fought against the British during the Battle of North Point and the Bombardment of Fort McHenry and for the writing of "The Star-Spangled Banner." Many of these celebrations are marked by fireworks accompanied by "The Star-Spangled Banner" and other patriotic songs. There have been particularly spectacular celebrations on major anniversaries of this event.

The song may also be played for Martin Luther King Day on the second Monday in January, a time in which "Lift Every Voice and Sing," which is sometime dubbed the black national anthem, might also be appropriate. Other appropriate holidays include Presidents' Day (the third Monday in February), Labor Day (the first Monday in September), and Columbus Day (the second Monday in October). Although it is not a holiday, commemorations of the September 11, 2001, terrorist attacks on U.S. soil also often include performances of the national anthem.

Similarly, although not currently an official national holiday, March 3 is the day on which President Herbert Hoover signed the congressional law designating "The Star-Spangled Banner" as the national anthem. Now known as National Anthem Day, this is certainly also an appropriate time to play the song.

The melody of "The Star-Spangled Banner" has often been adapted to presidential campaign songs. The song is often frequently sung at political conclaves and conventions, and at presidential inaugurations, that take place on January 20 every fourth year.

The song is also appropriate for the commemorations of military victories, especially those like the Battle of New Orleans at the end of the War of 1812.

See also: Commemorations of "The Star-Spangled Banner"; Fireworks; "Lift Every Voice and Sing"; Patriotism; Presidential Campaigns; Songs of the U.S. Armed Forces; War of 1812.

Further Reading

Albanese, Catherine. 1974. "Requiem for Memorial Day: Dissent in the Redeemer Nation." *American Quarterly* 26 (October): 386–98.

Gelles, Aunaleah V. 2015. "Commemorating the Defense of Baltimore, 1815–2015." Master's thesis, University of Maryland, Baltimore County.

Hay, Robert Pettus. "'Thank God We Are Americans': Yankees Abroad on the Fourth of July." *Indiana Magazine of History* 63 (June): 115–23.

O'Connell, Frank A. 2014. *National Star-Spangled Centennial Baltimore, Maryland, September 6 to 13, 1914.* Baltimore: National Star-Spangled Banner Centennial Commission.

Svejda, George J. 2005. *History of the Star Spangled Banner from 1814 to the Present.* Honolulu, HI: University Press of the Pacific. First published in 1969 by Division of History, Office of Archeology and Historic Preservation, U.S. Department of the Interior, National Park Service.

Patriotism

At least for those without religious scruples against doing so, saluting the flag and standing and singing during the playing of the national anthem and other songs extolling America, are widely recognized as ways of expressing love of country, or patriotism. This love is, in turn, often tied to the idea of nationalism.

Although love of country can be distorted into a belief in the superiority of one's race over others, as it was in Germany under Adolf Hitler in the 1930s, it is more typically associated with love of one's homeland and its people and with the principles for which it stands. However far the principle was from the reality of a nation that still held people in bondage, from its inception in 1776, America and its flag have been associated with a commitment to the principles enshrined in the Declaration of Independence that "all men are created equal" and that they are equally entitled to the rights of "life, liberty, and the pursuit of happiness."

In time, these principles became enshrined in the U.S. Constitution and its amendments, most notably the first ten amendments, now generally referred to as the Bill of Rights. They are also embodied in the post-Civil War constitutional amendments that outlawed involuntary servitude, sought to guarantee privileges and immunities, equal protection, and due process to all, and prohibited discrimination in voting on the basis of race (to which the Nineteenth Amendment, ratified in 1920, added sex).

Americans have historically sought to express and pursue unity in symbols. Few countries express the same devotion to their flags as does the United States, and relatively few make the flag the central theme of their national anthems. It is significant that during the U.S. Civil War (1861–1865), Americans were more divided than united by song. Just as the Confederate states adopted their own flag, so too many who adhered to this cause preferred songs like "Dixie" that stressed their regional identity and rejected "The Star-Spangled Banner" and "Battle Hymn of the Republic," which they associated with the Union.

This anthem also highlights American freedom. The consensus, which has been affirmed in U.S. court decisions, is that this freedom upholds the right of individuals who choose neither to salute the flag nor to honor the anthem when it is performed or sung. The last fifty years have also witnessed increased tolerance for entertainers who choose to sing or perform the song in new musical arrangements.

Although Americans encounter displays of flags far more frequently than they hear the national anthem, many likely learned "The Star-Spangled Banner" and other patriotic songs in grade school. Throughout the nineteenth and early twentieth centuries, teaching "The Star-Spangled Banner" and other songs was understood to be an effective tool for socializing immigrants into America.

Before American televisions stations maintained twenty-four-hour broadcast schedules, they ended programing each night with a rendition of "The Star-Spangled Banner" against the backdrop of a flag waving in the breeze. Most Americans are also likely to hear the anthem at school musical performances; at a variety of college and professional ball games; in places of worship; at commemorations of patriotic holidays like Independence Day, Flag Day, and Defenders' Day (Maryland); at political rallies and conventions; at presidential inaugurations; at naturalization ceremonies; at the funerals of military personnel and American leaders; and elsewhere. Members of the military are likely to hear the anthem at the beginning and end of each day.

Mothers often sing lullabies to their children, and the sound of tunes, especially those that have been learned in one's youth, serve as what Lincoln called in his first inaugural address, "mystic chords of memory" (Vile 2018, 22). Because songs evoke not only intellectual but also emotional commitments, political leaders sometimes use them to advance their own partisan agendas.

See also: Patriotic Holidays; Places of Worship; Sports Events; Veterans.

Further Reading
Huddy, Leonie, and Nadia Khatib. 2007. "American Patriotism, National Identity, and Political Involvement." *American Journal of Political Science* 51 (January): 63–77.

Pei, Minxin. 2003. "The Paradoxes of American Nationalism." *Foreign Policy*, no. 136 (May–June): 30–37.

Vile, John R., ed. 2018. *The Civil War and Reconstruction Eras: Documents Decoded.* Santa Barbara, CA: ABC-CLIO.

Vile, John R. 2019. *The Declaration of Independence: America's First Founding Document in U.S. History and Culture.* Santa Barbara, CA: ABC-CLIO.

Patty, Sandi

"The Star-Spangled Banner" is the musical equivalent to such material symbols as the U.S. flag, the Liberty Bell, and the Statue of Liberty. As the nation was celebrating the centennial of the Liberty Bell in 1986, the ABC television network closed its broadcast by using a recording of Sandi Patty (1956–) singing the national anthem. Patty had originally recorded the song for the Ellis Island Foundation on a record entitled *They Come to America.* This broadcast provided exposure to a much wider audience of a singer who had previously traveled with gospel singers Bill and Gloria Gaither (respectively born in 1936 and 1942) and won a Dove Award for gospel music. She was soon invited to be a guest on *The Tonight Show* and *ABC World News Tonight* and was featured in *USA Today* (Bream 1986).

Gifted with a powerful voice, Patty continued to focus chiefly on Christian music, singing the anthem only for special events and for military audiences. After a divorce from her manager in 1992, Patty's standing within the gospel music community was tarnished, but she confessed her own part in the divorce and has largely rebuilt her reputation not only through her singing but also through a number of books and movie roles.

After winning five Grammy Awards and forty Dove Awards, Patty announced in 2015 that she was retiring from the music circuit.

Further Reading

Bream, Jon. 1986. "Televised Anthem Brings Sandi Patti [sic] Liberty." *Chicago Tribune*, September 25. https://www.chicagotribune.com/news/ct-xpm-1986-09-25-8603 110651-story.html.

Merritt, Jonathan. 2015. "After Winning 5 Grammy and 40 Dove Awards, Sandi Patty Will Call It Quits." *Religion News Services*, September 28. https://religionnews .com/2015/09/28/grammy-winner-sandi-patty-announces-retirement-reflects-on -sins-and-successes.

Sandy Patti (website). n.d. "Bio." https://www.sandipatty.com/bio.

Philippine National Anthem

The Philippine national anthem, "Lupang Hinirang," was born in 1899 as the islands anticipated independence from Spanish rule. Jose Palma (1876–1903), a soldier who wrote for *La Independencia*, wrote the lyrics to a poem in Spanish that composer Julian Felipe (1861–1944) subsequently set to music. The words focus on the "Land of the Morning," which is also described as a "land dear and holy." Somewhat like "America the Beautiful," the song references geographical features such as its skies, its hills, and the sea (Santamaria 2012). In lines reminiscent of "The Star-Spangled Banner," it also refers to the Philippine flag, which consists of the sun and three yellow stars against a white triangular canton that bisects a strip of blue and one of red:

Thy banner, dear to all our hearts,
Its sun and stars alight.
O never shall its shining field
Be dimmed by tyrant's might.

The last line of the song further proclaims:

But it is glory ever, when thou art wronged,
For us, thy sons to suffer and die.

Unlike "The Star-Spangled Banner," the song makes no explicit reference to God.

Ironically, instead of achieving immediate independence, the Philippines traded one colonial ruler for another. Indeed, after receiving the islands from Spain after America's victory in the Spanish-American War (1896–1898), the United States assumed control of the Philippines and banned the playing of the anthem until 1919 (Santamaria 2012). The hymn was translated into Filipino during Japanese occupation during World War II. One year after that war concluded, on July 4, 1946, the United States formally granted the Philippines its independence. The song was revised by Felipe Padilla de Leon (1912–1992) in the 1950s. Philippine law now requires that the song be sung in Filipino.

In 2018, moviegoers in the Philippines were arrested for refusing to stand, as required by law, for the playing of the anthem (Tulabong 2018).

See also: "America the Beautiful."

Further Reading

Santamaria, Carlos. 2012. "PH National Anthem: Lost in Translation." *Rappler*, June 11. https://www.rappler.com/move-ph/campaigns/149-independence-day/6549-the-original-spanish-lyrics-of-the-philippine-national-anthem.

Talabong, Rambo. 2018. "34 Arrested for Sitting Out National Anthem at 'The Hows of Us' Screening." *Rappler*, September 6. https://www.rappler.com/nation/211293-persons-arrested-sitting-out-national-anthem-hows-of-us-showing.

Pickersgill, Mary Young

In addition to being the subject of song, flags are physical objects. Prior to mechanization, flags were sewn by hand, and this job was more frequently associated with women than with men. Betsy Ross of Philadelphia probably remains the most famous flag maker in America, but while historians are increasingly skeptical of claims that George Washington and other Founding Fathers met with her to commission the first U.S. flag, there is little doubt that the "star-spangled" flag that Francis Scott Key observed over the ramparts on the morning of September 14, 1814, was made by Mary Young Pickersgill (1776–1857), who was herself the daughter of another Philadelphia flag maker by the name of Rebecca Young. There has, however, been some confusion over which of the two flags that Pickersgill made for Colonel George Armistead was the one that Francis Scott Key likely observed.

Although Mary had grown up in Philadelphia, she moved to Baltimore after the death of her husband John Pickersgill in 1805. Since during the early nineteenth century, flags were more frequently flown at sea than on land, Baltimore, which was known for building clipper ships that could be used for privateering, would have been a good place for a flagmaker to locate.

Armistead actually ordered two flags from Pickersgill, who is believed to have been aided by her daughter Caroline, nieces Eliza and Margaret Young, and an African American indentured servant named Grace Wisher. One was a fifteen-by-twenty-five-foot storm flag that Key would likely have observed at night as it was lit by the British bombs and rockets that rained down on Fort McHenry on that famous September evening. The other is the better-known thirty-by-forty-two-foot flag that Armistead and his men would have raised the next morning; Armistead wanted it to be "so large that the British will have no difficulty seeing it from a distance" (Sheads 1986, 104). This flag, which has been meticulously preserved, is the one that was passed down through the Armistead family and is now displayed at the Smithsonian Institution.

Although there were eighteen states in the Union in 1812, the last time Congress had altered the flag was in 1895 when Vermont and Kentucky had entered the Union. Since Congress had not yet decided to limit the number of stripes, the flag contained fifteen stars and fifteen stripes. It was so large that Pickersgill had laid it out on the floor of the nearby Claggertt's Brewery's malt house. The government paid Pickersgill $495 for the large flag and $168.50 for the storm flag. Each star and each stripe on the larger flag was about two feet tall, and the blue material against which each star had been set was cut out in the back so that the stars could be seen from both sides.

Pickersgill's legacy is commemorated at her house, which is now called the Star-Spangled Banner Flag House. In addition to her work as a seamstress, Pickersgill was president of the Impartial Female Humane Society from 1828 to 1851 and was active in other social causes.

The Star-Spangled Banner Flag House included a painting by Robert McGill Mackall, painted about 1962, entitled *Placing the Stars on the Flag that Inspired Francis Scott Key to Write Our National Anthem*. It depicts the Pickersgill household and Commodore Joshua Barney, General John Stricker, and Colonel George Armistead, who commissioned the flag. The house has drawn in a ghost figure to represent Grace Wisher's relatively unknown contribution to this enterprise (Yuen and Boakyewa 2014).

See also: Armistead, George; Baltimore, Maryland; Key, Francis Scott; Ross, Betsy; Star-Spangled Banner Flag; Star-Spangled Banner Flag House.

Further Reading

America Comes Alive. n.d. "Mary Pickersgill: Maker of the Star-Spangled Banner." https://americacomesalive.com/2015/03/27/mary-pickersgill-maker-of-the-star -spangled-banner.

Griffin, Martin I. J. "The Flag 'Just Growed.'" *American Catholic Historical Researches* 8 (April): 179–80.

Grove, Tim. 2014. "Mary, Not Betsy." In *A Grizzly in the Mail and Other Adventures in American History*, 73–87. Lincoln: University of Nebraska Press.

Johnston, Sally, and Pat Pilling. 2014. *Mary Young Pickersgill: Flag Maker of the Star-Spangled Banner*. Bloomington, IN: AuthorHouse.

Miller, Marla R. 2018. "The U.S. Flag in America's Historic-House Museums." In *The American Flag: An Encyclopedia of the Stars and Stripes in U.S. History, Culture, and Law*, edited by John R. Vile, 19–32. Santa Barbara, CA: ABC-CLIO.

Sheads, Scott S. 1986. *The Rockets' Red Glare: The Maritime Defense of Baltimore in 1814*. Centreville, MD: Tidewater.

Yuen, Helen, and Asantewa Boakyewa. 2014. "The African American Girl Who Helped Make the Star-Spangled Banner." *O Say Can You See?* (blog), Smithsonian National Museum of American History, May 30. http://americanhistory.si.edu /blog/2014/05/the-african-american-girl-who-helped-make-the-star-spangled -banner.html.

Places of Worship

Individuals who attend places of worship typically bring their patriotic sentiments with them, and it is common for churches, especially those that are evangelical, to fly both a Christian, or denominational, flag and the U.S. flag (Vile 2018, 120–23). Although there are a few denominations like Mennonites, Amish, and Jehovah's Witnesses who oppose saluting the flag either because they view that action as a form of idolatry or an expression of antipacifist militarism, many Christian liturgies and hymnbooks also have patriotic selections.

Even though the American Episcopal Church grew from the Anglican Church, which was the official church of England, its national convention in America resolved in 1786 that "the Fourth of July shall be observed by this church forever, as a day of Thanksgiving to almighty God for the inestimable blessings of Religious and Civil Liberty vouchsafed to the USA" (Boorstein 2018). At that time, of course, Francis Scott Key had not yet penned "The Star-Spangled Banner," but it has since been incorporated into numerous patriotic services with relatively little dissent and has been especially popular during times of war. In the Civil War, churches began displaying flags on their property, and many congregations began singing national anthems, including "The Star-Spangled Banner" (Fahs 2001, 69). It is therefore hardly surprising that the Veterans of Foreign Wars took issue with David Greer, the Episcopal bishop of New York, when in 1917 he banned "The Star-Spangled Banner" from the Cathedral of St. John the Divine in Manhattan because he thought the tune was too militaristic (Connor 2017, 47).

Francis Scott Key was a religious man. The most appropriate verse of "The Star-Spangled Banner" for most houses of worship is the last verse, which specifically attributes the success of the American defenders of Fort McHenry to God and proposes the words "In God is our trust" as the national motto.

A survey by LifeWay Research, which was released in 2016, found that while two-thirds of American churches include patriotic music in services around the Independence Day holiday, the national anthem ranks fourth among the top choices, some of which are more explicitly religious. The others in order (skipping the fourth) are "America the Beautiful" (Jatgarine Lee Bates); "Mine Eyes Have Seen the Glory" (Julia Ward Howe); "My Country, 'Tis of Thee" (Samuel Francis Smith); God Bless the USA" (Lee Greenwood); "God Bless America Again" (Billy McVay); "May God Bless America" (Weldon C. Kennedy); "God of Our Fathers" (Daniel Crane Roberts and George William Warren); "A Patriotic Salute" (Linda Spevacek); and "America" (Chris Tomlin) (Shellnut 2018).

A study of Jews in America notes that they often celebrate American holidays, including Independence Day, Columbus Day, the births of George Washington and Abraham Lincoln, and Thanksgiving. The study's author observes that their Thanksgiving services often include "the singing of the national anthem and other patriotic hymns" along with "traditional psalms and prayers" (Wenger 2008, 370).

A survey of Roman Catholics in the United States released in 2017 reveals that 85 percent reported having sung a patriotic song at Mass. While 49 percent of respondents thought that this was appropriate, 42 percent expressed concern that singing such songs might detract from one's experience with God (Gallagher 2017).

In a review of denominational hymnals, historian Chris Gehrz (2016) has further identified the five most patriotic songs. They are as follows: "America" (Smith); "God Bless Our Native Land" (Mahlmann); "Battle Hymn of the Republic" (Howe); "America the Beautiful" (Bates); and "The Star-Spangled Banner" (Key). The first of these was, however, found in 1,685 hymnals whereas the last was only found in 376. Moreover, Gehrz notes that with the exception of "America," it was relatively uncommon for hymnals to contain patriotic songs at the beginning of the twentieth century. There was a revived interest in such songs in the 1920s, during the bicentennial of the nation's independence in 1976, and the 1990s.

Just as political scientists have often attempted to distinguish between patriotism and more militant strains of nationalism (Pei 2003; Huddy and Khatib, 2007), so too some pastors and theologians have expressed concern about identifying religious beliefs too closely to those of the nation. Thus, although the First Baptist Church of Dallas (which is headed by Robert Jeffress, who is also an advisor to President Donald J. Trump) performed a hymn entitled "Make America Great Again" (Boorstein 2018), theologian Richard Mouw observed, "Patriotic songs also contain many dangerous teachings. Take, for example, the 'eschatological' verse of 'America the Beautiful.' Themes that in the book of Revelation are used to describe the Holy City are here applied to the United States: 'alabaster cities,' 'undimmed by human tears,' the 'shining sea.' As if the United States will become the promised New Jerusalem" (Shellnutt 2018).

Katherine Meizel has observed that Lee Greenwood's "God Bless the USA" and Irving Berlin's "God Bless America" have increasingly "both been assigned substitutional or supplemental roles in contexts that might conventionally call for the official national anthem" (2006, 498).

See also: "America the Beautiful"; "Battle Hymn of the Republic"; "God Bless America"; "In God Is Our Trust"; Jehovah's Witnesses; "My Country, 'Tis of Thee" ("America").

Further Reading

Boorstein, Michelle. 2018. "The 'Star-Spangled Banner' in Church? Some Christians Are Questioning the Mix of Patriotism and God." *Washington Post*, July 1. https://www .washingtonpost.com/news/acts-of-faith/wp/2018/07/01/star-spangled-banner -in-church-sunday-christians-debating-god-and-country-anew.

Connor, Joseph. 2017. "Off Key." *American History* 51 (February): 42–51.

Fahs, Alice. 2001. *The Imagined Civil War: Popular Literature of the North and South, 1861–1865.* Chapel Hill: University of North Carolina Press.

Gallagher, Patrick. 2017. "Are Patriotic Songs Mass-Appropriate?" *U.S. Catholic* 82 (September): 31–35. https://www.uscatholic.org/articles/201709/are-patriotic-songs -mass-appropriate-31138.

Gehrz, Chris. 2016. "A Brief History of Patriotic Hymns." *Pantheos*, July 5. https://www .patheos.com/blogs/anxiousbench/2016/07/a-brief-history-of-patriotic-hymns.

Gehrz, Chris. 2017. "A (Brief) Religious History of the Star-Spangled Banner." *Pantheos*, September 26. https://www.patheos.com/blogs/anxiousbench/2017/09/religious-history -star-spangled-banner.

Huddy, Leonie, and Nadia Khatib. 2007. "American Patriotism, National Identity, and Political Involvement." *American Journal of Political Science* 51 (January): 63–77.

Meizel, Katherine. 2006. "A Singing Citizenry: Popular Music and Civil Religion in America." *Journal for the Scientific Study of Religion* 45 (December): 497–503.

Pei, Minxin. 2003. "The Paradoxes of American Nationalism." *Foreign Policy*, no. 136 (May–June): 30–37.

Shellnutt, Kate. 2018. "Make Worship Patriotic Again? The Top 10 Songs for Fourth of July Services." *Christianity Today*, June 29. https://www.christianitytoday.com/ct /2018/june-web-only/make-worship-patriotic-again-top-10-songs-fourth-of-july .html.

Vile, John R. 2018. *The American Flag: An Encyclopedia of the Stars and Stripes in U.S. History, Culture, and Law.* Santa Barbara, CA: ABC-CLIO.

Wenger, Beth S. 2008. "Rites of Citizenship: Jewish Celebrations of the Nation." In *The Columbia History of Jews and Judaism in America*, edited by Marc Lee Raphael. New York: Columbia University Press.

Wispelwey, Seth. 2018. "The NFL Is a Fundamentalist Church. And the Anthem Is Its Worship Song." *Sojourners*, June 1. https://sojo.net/articles/nfl-fundamentalist -church-and-anthem-its-worship-song.

Pledge of Allegiance

For many Americans, the Pledge of Allegiance occupies a place in our hearts and minds similar to that of "The Star-Spangled Banner." Both focus on the U.S. flag, and both are typically taught in schools, where the rendition of the song often accompanies the raising or introduction of the flag. Both are surrounded by similar etiquette protocols, which typically call for individuals to stand and face the flag and put a hand across their hearts or salute (if the individual is a member of the military). It is common for writers to express concern over how well Americans know or understand either the pledge or the national anthem.

The first pledge written by George Thacher Balch, an auditor for New York schools, in the 1880s proclaimed, "We give our Head!—and our Hearts!—to God! And our Country! One Country! One Language! One Flag." It was especially designed to help introduce the children of immigrants to American ideals.

The majority of the current pledge was composed by Francis Bellamy, a Baptist preacher who embraced socialism, in the 1890s as part of the celebration of the four hundredth anniversary of Columbus's discovery of America. His original pledge said, "I pledge allegiance to my flag, and to the republic for which it stands, one nation with liberty and justice for all." In 1923, the words "my flag" were replaced with "the flag of the United States," and in 1924, the words "of America" were added. In 1954, Congress further added the words "under God" to the pledge, in part to highlight the higher moral plane on which the United States operated in comparison with the Soviet Union and other communist nations.

This latter addition arguably furthered the hope that Francis Scott Key had expressed in the final verse of "The Star-Spangled Banner" that the national motto would be "In God is our Trust." This phrase is generally considered a mild form of ceremonial deism in that it does not identify a particular god or denomination, which would likely violate the establishment clause of the First Amendment.

Because both the pledge and the anthem profess beliefs, the cases prohibiting public schools from forcing children with religious convictions from saluting the flag are generally also thought to prohibit schools from forcing children to sing the anthem or even stand during its playing. The leading case on compulsory flag salutes is *West Virginia State Board of Education v. Barnette* (1943). A U.S. district court applied this reasoning to compulsory standing for "The Star-Spangled Banner" anthem in *Sheldon v. Fannin* (1963).

The pledge is shorter than any of the four original verses of the anthem and is less tied to a specific event than the anthem is tied to the defense of Fort McHenry. The pledge is also arguably more affirmative than the anthem, which employs a number of questions. Whereas the anthem refers to "the land of the free and the home of the brave," the anthem refers to the flag as a representative of a "republic," or representative, form of government. The pledge's emphasis on the fact that the nation is "indivisible" is an obvious reference to the controversy that led to the Civil War, which postdated Key's writing of the national anthem.

See also: Code for the National Anthem; "In God Is Our Trust"; *Sheldon v. Fannin* (1963).

Further Reading
Baer, John W. 1992. *The Pledge of Allegiance: A Centennial History, 1892–1992.* Annapolis, MD: Free State Press.
Ellis, Richard J. 2005. *To the Flag: The Unlikely History of the Pledge of Allegiance.* Lawrence: University Press of Kansas.
"Losing Their Voices: The Struggle for a Nation's Anthem and Its People." 2005. *American Music Teacher* 54 (April/May): 84–85.

Moser, A. C., and Bert B. David. 1936. "I Pledge a Legion." *Journal of Educational Sociology* 9 (March): 436–40.

Teachout, Woden. 2009. *Capture the Flag: A Political History of American Patriotism.* New York: Basic Books.

Vile, John R. 2018. *The American Flag: An Encyclopedia of the Stars and Stripes in US. History, Culture, and Law.* Santa Barbara, CA: ABC-CLIO.

Political Theory

Perhaps because it is a song rather than a government document, scholars have rarely given the political theory of "The Star-Spangled Banner" the same kind of scholarly analysis to which they have subjected the Declaration of Independence, the U.S. Constitution, and other early American documents.

Francis Scott Key, who authored the anthem, was a member of the Federalist Party. He had initially joined other Federalists as well as his eccentric friend, Congressman John Randolph of Virginia, in opposing America's entrance into the War of 1812 with Britain. He had even hypothesized that God might use the war to inflict judgment on the nation. In writing "The Star-Spangled Banner," however, Key was witnessing a defensive operation against a foreign foe, which consisted in part, as he noted in his notorious third verse, of "the hireling and slave" neither of which would have the same links to the nation as the freemen who he referenced in the fourth stanza. Key was writing as a citizen rather than as a Federalist partisan, and had the public understood the song as a partisan document, it is unlikely that it could ever have become the national anthem.

It is important to remember that Francis Scott Key was a lawyer and that lawyers, especially those in the Anglo tradition, took seriously the idea that law was essential not only to public order but also to individual freedom. These ideas arguably come together best in the anthem's last stanza where the idea of "vict'ry and peace" are connected to the security of national freedom. There are at least three additional strands of political thought that are evident in Key's verses.

There is, of course, its emphasis on freedom in the last two lines of each stanza. However inconsistent the freedom of whites was in contrast with the institution of slavery, the ideal of freedom found fertile soil in the classical liberal thought of John Locke of England and other social contract philosophers. They had stressed the manner in which individuals left the state of nature (which the English philosopher Thomas Hobbes had described as a state of war) in order to secure their life, liberty, and property, all of which the British invasion during the War of 1812 had threatened. Americans generally understood freedom to be a freedom under law through elected representatives and had, at least since the writing of Thomas Paine's *Common Sense*, generally contrasted such government to governments built on the divine right of kings and hereditary privilege. It is important to keep in mind that many U.S. leaders considered the War of 1812 to be a second American revolution assuring that Britain would not continue treating Americans as second-class citizens, whom the British navy could impress into military service.

One prominent strain in early American thought was known as civic republicanism, which dated at least as far back as the Italian philosopher Niccolo

Machiavelli (1469–1527) and continued through *Cato's Letters*, a popular work in early American history written by John Trenchard and Thomas Gordon of Britain, which was first published from 1720 to 1723 (Vile 2016, 746–47). It stressed the need for citizen "virtue," which was generally associated with a willingness to engage in civic activity, especially the defense of one's home and homeland. Notably, Key closely associated freedom with bravery, and although the Fort whose defense he had observed was partly manned by professional military, both it and the forces that had fought at North Point (like those at the disastrous Battle of Bladensburg) were largely manned by militiamen. This lent further justice to a cause in which the enemy was employing "the hireling and slave." To the extent that Key was attempting to equate the "hireling" with mercenary soldiers, he would be suggesting that the invaders had less civic attachment and virtue than those whom they are attacking. Civic republican thinkers were strong opponents of standing armies because they feared that they threatened representative government. This would have further underscored their foreignness.

Elements of Christianity have influenced American thought at least since the time of the Puritans and others who came to America seeking political and religious freedom. The Puritans often brought with them a sense of national destiny, perhaps best expressed by John Winthrop's early vision of his colony as serving on a "city upon a hill" (Vile 2015, 21). This was, in turn, tied to the idea that Americans were, like ancient Jews, a covenant people who owed their continuing existence and prosperity not only to their own patriots but also to divine providence. To the extent that the people had covenanted with God to engage in certain virtuous behaviors and to abstain from others that were sinful, God's blessings might depend in part on how well they had kept this covenant. This would lend particular significance to the idea that "conquer we must, when our cause it is just." Just as God might reward a just cause, so too he might punish one that was unjust.

The depth of Key's third stanza, the vitriol of which "Their blood has wash'd out their foul footstep's pollution" seems at odds with the tenor of most of the other verses, may further signal Christian warnings against the sins of pride and arrogance. Key notes that the enemy "vauntingly swore" to take away Americans' home and country. He thought that enemy soldiers with such proud and evil intentions are likely to encounter not only the displeasure of those whom they are attempting to subvert but of God himself. Exhibiting little sympathy, Key said that nothing could save them "from the terror of flight or the gloom of the grave," almost as though he were consigning them to hell (as religions sometimes do to unbelievers).

As is well known, the First Amendment to the U.S. Constitution prohibits an "establishment" of religion. But Key's verses reflected a widespread societal sentiment that a nation whose people had forsaken God, like those who are deficient in other patriotic virtues, might suffer adverse consequences. Based on the lyrics of the fourth stanza, in which Key proclaimed that the national motto should be "In God is our trust," Key would appear to be among those who believed that a nation could be broadly committed to God without having a state church that would violate the establishment clause of the First Amendment.

See also: "In God Is Our Trust"; Key, Francis Scott; Patriotism; Slavery; War of 1812.

Further Reading
Coleman, William. 2015. "'The Music of a Well Tun'd State': 'The Star Spangled Banner' and the Development of a Federalist Musical Tradition." *Journal of the Early Republic* 35 (Winter): 599–629.
Vile, John R., ed. 2015. *Founding Documents of America: Documents Decoded.* Santa Barbara, CA: ABC-CLIO.
Vile, John R. 2016. *The Constitutional Convention of 1787: A Comprehensive Encyclopedia of America's Founding.* 2 vols. Revised 2nd edition. Clark, NJ: Talbot Publishing.

Popular Opinion

Although Congress designated "The Star-Spangled Banner" as the national anthem in 1931, this did not stop individuals from arguing either for a new song or for the adoption of another song in its place. Such arguments usually centered on either finding a song that was less militaristic or one that was easier to sing. The former criticism has sometimes become an asset during times of war when the present anthem might do better at stirring patriotic feelings.

Polls of American public opinion on the subject are contradictory. In a 1977 readers' poll conducted by the *Boston Globe,* 493 respondents favored adopting "America the Beautiful" while only 220 favored keeping the existing anthem (Spiegel and Spiegel 1998, 33). After publishing a pro and con article on the subject in 1986, the newspaper *USA Today* found that of more than four thousand respondents, 64 percent favored the existing anthem, 38 percent favored "America the Beautiful," and about six hundred people favored a variety of other songs (Spiegel 1998, 34). In 1989, 81 percent of 389,000 respondents to a survey by *Parade Magazine* favored "America the Beautiful" over the current anthem. A *Time/CNN* telephone poll subsequently found that 67 percent of one thousand people favored the current anthem (Spiegel and Spiegel 1998, 34).

One reason for the adoption of "The Star-Spangled Banner" was its embrace by the American Legion and the Daughters of the American Revolution. It also had strong support in Maryland and surrounding areas where it was written.

It is important to recognize, however, that the popularity of the song transcends regional boundaries. Writing for *The Guardian* in 2014, Alex Marshall began a story by recounting a criticism by writer Malcolm Gladwell about the song's alleged militarism. After interviewing a variety of people, Marshall concluded, "When you know its history—or speak to the people who have been most affected by it—you get a different picture."

See also: Criticisms and Defenses of "The Star-Spangled Banner"; Regional Appeal.

Further Reading
Marshall, Alex. 2014. "Why 'The Star-Spangled Banner' Is the Perfect Insight into America's Soul." *Guardian*, August 11. https://www.theguardian.com/music/musicblog/2014/aug/11/malcolm-gladwell-star-spangled-banner-america-200th-anniversary.

Spiegel, Allen D., and Marc B. Spiegel. 1998. "Redundant Patriotism: The United States National Anthem as an Obligatory Sports Ritual." *Culture, Sport, Society* 1 (1): 24–43.

Presidential Campaigns

Although modern presidential campaigns are largely carried out through advertising over the air waves, nineteenth-century campaigns were highly participatory events. During the presidency of Andrew Jackson (1829–1837), many states expanded the franchise to almost all white males, opening the door to increased sloganeering, torchlight parades, political rallies, political conventions, and other forms of party participation, most of which continued well into the twentieth century.

Just as Francis Scott Key appropriated "To Anacreon in Heaven" to express patriotic sentiments, so too candidates used the same tune to stir political enthusiasm. Indeed, even before Key wrote his song, supporters of the Federalist Party rallied around a song to the later tune of "The Star-Spangled Banner" entitled "Adams and Liberty" while Democratic-Republicans responded with their own "Jefferson and Liberty."

One of the most raucous campaigns was that of 1840 in which Whig Party war hero William Henry Harrison, running on the slogan "Tippiecanoe and Tyler Too" (the site of one of Harrison's battle victories and the name of his vice-presidential running mate), successfully challenged incumbent Democrat Martin Van Buren. One sign of the growing popularity of "The Star-Spangled Banner" is that a collection of songs of that year entitled *The Harrison Medal Minstrel* included eight different selections, most praising Harrison, to its tune (Svejda 2005, 124). Other songs followed suit. One song entitled "Our Harrison" had four verses, each of which ended with a variant of the first verse:

> It is the name of our HARRISON—long will it flame
> In letters of light on the banner of Fame! (126)

That election was but a portent of things to come. In the election of 1844, which pitted Democrat James K. Polk against the Whig candidate Henry Clay, at least two songs to the tune of "The Star-Spangled Banner" extolled Clay (Svejda 2005, 127). A weekly publication in Nashville, Tennessee, that supported Polk was entitled *The Star Spangled Banner* (158), and the Polk and Dallas Minstrel sang "The Star-Spangled Banner of the Democrats" for Polk (Spofford 1904, 220):

> Oh say, can you see, through fierce faction's dark night,
>> The flag of Democracy gallantly gleaming,
> Whose stars never shed a more beautiful light,
>> Than now o'er Dallas and Polk mildly beaming!
> Oh! Thus it e'er when our party shall stand
>> Between, these great States and the Whigs' desolation,
> Blest with freedom and peace, may the well-governed land
>> Join the party whose zeal wrought this great reformation!

Let us sing the gold day when in battle array,
  We triump o'er both Frelinghuysen and Clay;
And bright shall the flag of Democracy wave
  O'er the land and the people 'tis destined to save!

In 1848, a campaign song for Whig candidate Zachary Taylor entitled "Our Brave Rough and Ready" highlighted his victories in the Mexican War (Svejda 2005, 127).

Although Whig candidate Winfield Scott lost to Democrat Franklin Pierce, the 1852 presidential campaign included another song to Key's tune called "Old Winfield, the Brave" (Svejda 2005, 127), and Democrat James Buchanan's successful 1856 presidential campaign included a song, to Key's tune, entitled the "National Club Song" (128). Each of the four stanzas ended with a variant of the first:

'Twas the flag of our Club, boys!— we saw it still wave
O'er the heads of the free, and hearts of the brave!

In the presidential election of 1860, there were at least two songs written to the tune of "The Star-Spangled Banner." One was a song called "The Banner of Freedom," which was written for Republican Abraham Lincoln, and the other, for the Constitutional Union Party candidates, was simply called "Bell and Everett" (Clague and Kuster 2015, 172–77). The chorus for the Lincoln song, which proclaimed, "Oh, long may that ban-ner tri-um-phant-ly wave—"O'er the land of the free and the home of the brave," was fairly close to the original, whereas the one for the Constitutional Union Party ended with a play on words, namely, "It calls us, all fac-tion and wrong to op-pose, And its call will be heed-ed where E-ve-rett goes!" (172–77). "The Star-Spangled Banner" was played shortly after Lincoln was inaugurated in 1861 (Svejda 2005, 165).

In the presidential election of 1864, Democrat George B. McClellan, a general who wanted to bring the Civil War to a negotiated end, challenged Abraham Lincoln unsuccessfully for the presidency. McClellan highlighted the fact that his vice-presidentual running mate, George H. Pendleton, was married to the daughter of Francis Scott Key (Svejda 2005, 194).

A song in the 1880 presidential campaign entitled "Garfield and Our Flag" was also sung to the tune of "The Star-Spangled Banner," as was "The Starry Old Flag" in the election of 1884, in which the Prohibition Home Protection Party had a similar song entitled "The Foe of Church and Freedom" (Svejda 2005, 216). By 1900, both parties were using "The Star-Spangled Banner" as a campaign song (266), and the song is now a staple at conventions and rallies held by all parties.

Although thus used by both parties, the martial nature of the song probably makes it best suited to candidates, especially former war heroes, with strong military credentials. It may not be surprising that the theme song of Theodore Roosevelt's Progressive Party was "Battle Hymn of the Republic," which he wanted the nation to adopt as its own anthem (Stauffer 2015, 140).

In 1916, President Woodrow Wilson exercised his power as commander in chief to proclaim "The Star-Spangled Banner" to be the national anthem for the armed forces. When Congress subsequently adopted legislation to extend its status to the anthem of the country as a whole, President Herbert Hoover signed this bill into legislation in 1931.

It is common for the White House to host musical performances. When Soviet Premier Nikita S. Khrushchev visited the White House in 1959, the national anthems of both countries were played. Apparently, during the rendition of "The Star-Spangled Banner," a man in the audience began singing and was joined by the audience in what was apparently an emotional display of American patriotism (Trott 2012, 16).

In recent years, presidential candidates from both major parties have elicited the support of musicians to draw support for their election (De Sola 2004). Musicians were particularly active in the 2004 campaign where many were particularly critical of President George W. Bush (Wissner 2016). In the 2016 political conventions, Republicans relied chiefly on recordings and the rock band directed by G. E. Smith whereas Democrats brought in many more performers with star power. James Deaville (2017) said their performances of the national anthem at the conventions also varied:

> One piece of music always performed by a singer onstage is the national anthem, which allows the respective parties to showcase noncelebrity talent while affirming their political and patriotic agendas. Trump's singers were young white musicians from northern Ohio who performed at ball games and other sporting events, in keeping with his populist ideology and the "wholesome" image the RNC wished to communicate (one singer was blind, and another was the daughter of a former senator from Massachusetts, Scott Brown). In contrast, Clinton demonstrated her and her party's inclusiveness through a racially and ethnically mixed lineup of youthful singers: on successive days, they featured a local African American choirboy, a blind music student, a Latino mariachi singer, and a online sensation from Florida, none professional singers and none over thirty-five years old. (454)

The performance of "The Star-Spangled Banner" has become a regular feature of modern presidential inaugurations as well. Thus sixteen-year-old Jackie Evancho, the second place winner of the television show *America's Got Talent*, was both praised by Trump's supporters and criticized by those who opposed him for agreeing to sing the anthem at President Donald J. Trump's 2017 inauguration (Gorzelany-Mostak 2017).

See also: "Adams and Liberty"; "To Anacreon in Heaven."

Further Reading
Clague, Mark, and Andrew Kuster, eds. 2015. *Star Spangled Songbook: A History in Sheet Music of "The Star-Spangled Banner."* Ann Arbor, MI: Star Spangled Music Foundation.

De Sola, David. 2004. "The Politics of Music: Musicians Mobilize For and Against President Bush." *CNN*, August 30. http://edition.cnn.com/2004/ALLPOLITICS/08/29/gop.music/index.html.

Deaville, James. 2017. "The Unconventional Music of the Democratic and Republican National Conventions of 2016." *American Music* 35 (Winter): 4446–66.

Gorzelany-Mostak, Dana. 2017. "Hearing Jackie Evancho in the Age of Donald Trump." *American Music* 35 (Music and the 2016 U.S. Presidential Campaign, Winter): 467–77.

"Presidential inauguration performers through the years." January 21, 2017. Newsday. com Staff. https://www.newsday.com/entertainment/music/presidential-inaugura tion-performers-through-the-years-1.12962245.

Spofford, Ainsworth R. 1904. "The Lyric Element in American History." *Records of the Columbia Historical Society* 7:211–36.

Stauffer, John. 2015. "'The Battle Hymn of the Republic': Origins, Influence, Legacies." In *Exploring Lincoln: Great Historians Reappraise Our Greatest President*, edited by Harold Holzer, Craig L. Symonds, and Frank J. Williams, 123–45. New York: Fordham University Press.

Svejda, George J. 2005. *History of the Star Spangled Banner from 1814 to the Present*. Honolulu, HI: University Press of the Pacific. First published in 1969 by Division of History, Office of Archeology and Historic Preservation, U.S. Department of the Interior, National Park Service.

Trott, Donald. 2012. "Choral Music in the White House." *Choral Journal* 52 (June and July): 8–17.

Troy, Gil. 1992. "Stars, Stripes, and Spots." *Design Quarterly*, no. 157 (Autumn): 2–10.

Wissner, Reba. 2016. "Not Another Term: Music as Persuasion in the Campaign against the Re-Election of George W. Bush." Trax on the Trail, October 5. https://www.traxonthetrail.com/2020/02/05/not-another-term-music-as-persuasion-in-the-campaign-against-the-re-election-of-george-w-bush.

Public Schools

Contrary to popular misconceptions, there is no national law that requires public school children to sing "The Star-Spangled Banner" each day, although it is not uncommon for many students to begin the day with a salute to the U.S. flag.

Among patriotic songs, "The Star-Spangled Banner" has a wider vocal range, thus making it more difficult to teach and sing than many others. Judith Kogan of National Public Radio believes that it has become less common in general to teach patriotic songs in school than in the nineteenth century, when teaching patriotic songs was considered to be a way of creating unity and teaching ideals associated with freedom and democracy. Teachers in Massachusetts, which led the way for universal public education, were known for saying "*Amoris patriae nutric carmen*," meaning "song is the nourisher of patriotism" (Branham and Hartnett 2002, 67).

In 2018, on the seventeenth anniversary of the September 11, 2001, airplane hijackings and terrorist attacks against the United States, school children across the nation were again encouraged to sing the first verse of the national anthem beginning at 1:00 p.m. Eastern time in a "National Anthem Sing-A-Long" sponsored by the American Public Education Foundation. The organization further encouraged schools to make this part of a program of at least thirty minutes. The organization included a website that included access to curricular materials written by Marie Basiliko Davis under the direction of Mia Toschi.

The U.S. Supreme Court has ruled, most notably in *West Virginia State Board of Education v. Barnette* (1943), that public schools cannot force individuals with

In Lancaster County, Pennsylvania, around 1938, the children in Martha Royer's school sing "The Star-Spangled Banner." (Library of Congress)

religious objections to salute the U.S. flag, and they would almost certainly apply similar principles to schools that try to compel students either to salute the flag or to stand at attention for the playing of "The Star-Spangled Banner" at athletic or other events (Cohen 2017; Underwood 2017). In *Sheldon v. Fannin* (1963), a U.S. district court affirmed the right of Jehovah's Witnesses to remain seated during renditions of the national anthem at their school.

See also: Knowledge of the National Anthem; *Sheldon v. Fannin* (1963); Sports Events.

Further Reading

Branham, Robert James, and Stephen J. Hartnett. 2002. *Sweet Freedom's Song: "My Country 'Tis of Thee" and Democracy in America*. New York: Oxford University Press.

Cohen, David S. 2017. "What the Supreme Court Says about Sitting Out the National Anthem." *Rolling Stone*, October 6. https://www.rollingstone.com/politics/politics-features/what-the-supreme-court-says-about-sitting-out-the-national-anthem-199512.

Davis, Marie Basiliko, and Mia Toschi. 2015. "Embracing the Star-Spangled Banner: A Cross Curricular Approach." Curricular supplement developed for the American Public Education Foundation. https://docs.wixstatic.com/ugd/991d30_3b3a0783f9ea46268c6230179b1974ca.pdf.

Kogan, Judith. 2016. "As Patriotic Songs Lose Familiarity in Public Schools, Do They Still Hold Value?" *Weekend Edition*, National Public Radio, July 3. https://www

.npr.org/2016/07/03/484563018/as-patriotic-songs-lose-familiarity-in-public
-schools-do-they-still-hold-value.

McCrea, Nick. 2015. "National Anthem to be Sung in Schools across US on 9/11." *Bangor Daily News*, September 5. https://bangordailynews.com/2015/09/05/news/nation /national-anthem-to-be-sung-in-schools-across-us-on-911.

Schuster, Sarah J. 1914. "The Star Spangled Banner: The Friday Afternoon Club in the Rural School." *Journal of Education* 80 (August 27): 157–59.

Underwood, J. 2017. "Kneeling During the National Anthem: At Schools, It's Protected Speech." *Phi Delta Kappan*, September 28. https://www.kappanonline.org /kneeling-during-the-national-anthem-at-schools-its-protected-speech.

Punctuation in the National Anthem

Attentive readers of "The Star-Spangled Banner" will find that the first stanza contains two question marks. The first, which occurs after the fourth line, asks whether an individual (addressed as "you"—perhaps Key, one of his companions aboard ship, or those singing the song) can "see" the flag. The second occurs at the end of the first stanza, where Key asks:

O say, does that star-spangled banner yet wave
O'er the land of the free and the home of the brave?

Educational specialist Megan Smith (2013) notes that the inclusion of this question mark highlights the situation in which Francis Scott Key found himself the morning after the British bombardment of Fort McHenry because it "captures the mix of fear, patriotism, and anxiety that Key felt throughout the long rainy night of the battle. Does that Star-Spangled Banner yet wave? Would he have a country to return home to?" Smith further explains that one strength of this question is that it can prompt contemporary reflection "on whether we are upholding the ideals embodied in the vision of America as the land of the free and the home of the brave."

Writing from a somewhat different perspective, law professor Robert A. Ferguson emphasizes that "the crucial first stanza opens and closes with the questions of a consuming anxiety. The proud hailing of the symbol of America, its flag, has taken place in the last gleaming of a previous twilight, but that affirmation is now lost in the temporal moment of the stanza, the approach of another dawn. Key's embracing questions are 'Can you see?' and 'Does it wave?'" (2009, 250). Tying these questions to the hymn's four refrains, Ferguson says, "'The Star-Spangled Banner' appears first in the interrogative mood (does it wave?), next in the subjunctive (may it wave) and imperative (it shall wave) of stanzas three and four" (251). He further observes that Key emphasizes the need for bravery to defend freedom: "True republicans stand armed and vigilant 'between their lov'd home, and the war's desolation.' When they conquer in a just cause, the spangled flag, symbol of triumph, both receives and reflects their achievement" (251).

There are two other question marks in subsequent verses. The third and fourth lines of the second verse thus ask:

> What is that which the breeze, o'er the towering steep,
> As it fitfully blows, half conceals, half discloses?

Similarly, the first three lines of the often-ignored third stanza ask:

> And where is that band who so vauntingly swore,
> That the havoc of war and the battle's confusion
> A home and a country should leave us no more?

When it comes to the last two lines of each of the last three stanzas, however, none end with this punctuation. The last two lines of the second stanza are worded as a wish, or even a prayer, that ends (like the second and fourth lines of the fourth stanza) in an exclamation mark:

> 'Tis the star-spangled banner—O long may it wave
> O'er the land of the free and the home of the brave!

The last two lines of the third stanza are more like an affirmation:

> And the star-spangled banner in triumph doth wave
> O'er the land of the free and the home of the brave.

The last two lines of the fourth and final stanza, which, in context, may rest on the nation's continuing dependence on God—the words that Key proposes for the nation's motto, "In God is our trust," are the only ones within quotation marks—can be interpreted as prophecy, hope, or affirmation:

> And the star-spangled banner in triumph shall wave
> O'er the land of the free and the home of the brave.

See also: English Language and "The Star-Spangled Banner"; Lyrics of "The Star-Spangled Banner"; Writing of "The Star-Spangled Banner."

Further Reading

Ferguson, Robert A. 1989. "'What Is Enlightenment?': Some American Answers." *American Literary History* 1 (Summer): 245–72.

Ruane, Michael E. 2014. "Francis Scott Key's Anthem Keeps Asking: Have We Survived as a Nation?" *Washington Post*, September 11. https://www.washingtonpost.com/local/francis-scott-keys-anthem-keeps-askinghave-we-survived-as-a-nation/2014/09/11/4061854c-39b3-11e4-9c9f-ebb47272e40e_story.html.

Smith, Megan. 2013. "You Asked, We Answered: Why Is There a Question Mark at the End of the National Anthem?" *O Say Can You See?* (blog), Smithsonian National Museum of American History, June 14. http://americanhistory.si.edu/blog/2013/06/you-asked-we-answered-why-is-there-a-question-mark-at-the-end-of-the-star-spangled-banner.html.

Radio, Television, and Satellite Transmissions

One of the great ironies of the current controversy over athletes who take a knee in protest of police brutality during the playing of "The Star-Spangled Banner" is that, more often than not, television and radio stations cut to commercials during such renditions, suggesting that the profit motive might be more important than acknowledgement of the flag and the nation that it represents.

At a time before radio stations regularly broadcast programming twenty-four hours a day and seven days a week, it was common for them to sign off (usually at midnight) with the playing of the national anthem. The practice may have originated overseas. In a letter that she wrote to the chairman of the Federal Communications Commission in 1935 (just four years after Congress adopted "The Star-Spangled Banner" as the national anthem), Representative Virginia E. Jenckes of Indianapolis formally requested that regulations be instituted requiring radio stations to sign off with "The Star-Spangled Banner," expressing admiration for other nations that followed the practice: "It is most impressive, for instance, at the end of a broadcast from Great Britain to hear the majestic rendition of 'God Save the King,'" and "Likewise, the 'Marseillaise' thunders through from Paris, and the German national anthem from Berlin" (Jacobs 2019).

American television subsequently copied the practice in its formative years, with many local stations airing footage of a flag flying as the anthem played.

Perhaps because of this lack of conformity, Republican Congressman John W. Wydler of New York introduced a resolution on August 8, 1963, that would have required all radio and television stations to play the anthem when they signed off for the day (Svejda 2005, 444).

On July 10, 1962, NASA launched the Telstar I satellite for AT&T. In its first day of orbit, it transmitted a video of the U.S. flag blowing in the wind to the music of "The Star-Spangled Banner" to a receiving station in France (Omer-Man 2011). On July 26, 1963, the Syncon II communications satellite received "The Star-Spangled Banner" and transmitted it back to earth (Svejda 2005, 444).

The national anthem is so ubiquitous that many television series have used it at one time or another. One controversial use took place in the summer of 2017 when Comedy Central ran a series called *Hood Adjacent*, in which in the very first episode ("Ruin Your Life"), comedian James Davis says, "The national anthem represents everything this country was founded on—white entitlement" after which he did a "rap music" version of the song, designed to critique prevailing cultural norms (Buckman 2017). Presented in rap, the anthem may have sent mixed messages, as one reviewer said, "In fact, it wasn't especially disrespectful of the song at all, which is to say that the video was not in conformity with Davis's disapproval of the anthem. Or at least that's how it felt to me" (Buckman 2017).

In October 2019, Gray Television, with 145 television stations, announced that it was reinstituting the practice of playing the national anthem in early morning at the time that marks the technical end to one day's broadcast and the beginning of the next. CBS's corporate-run station and the Nexstar Media Group announced that they would follow suit (Jacobs 2019). Hilton H. Howell, Jr., who is Gray's chief executive, tied renewal of the practice toward that of promoting national unity and "bringing back a great tradition of television" while further indicating that "this is a purely nonpolitical statement by our company" (Jacobs 2019).

The clip, which runs one minute and forty-five seconds, features numerous scenes from nature as well as a picture of a serviceman giving a flag salute. It features a powerful rendition of the anthem by a preteen girl, Reina Ozbay, from Parkland, Florida, who has performed in musical theater.

See also: Early Recordings; Movie Theaters; Sports Events.

Further Reading

Buckman, Adam. 2017. "No One Will Be Shocked When Comedian Slams National Anthem." *TVBlog*, Media Post, June 28. https://www.mediapost.com/publications/article/303568/no-one-will-be-shocked-when-comedian-slams-nationa.html.

CBS4. 2019. "Meet Reina Ozbay, the Powerhouse Voice behind the National Anthem On CBS4." *CBSN Denver*, October 11. https://denver.cbslocal.com/2019/10/11/reina-ozbay-voice-national-anthem.

Jacobs, Julia. 2019. "Local TV Revives a Bygone Tradition: Airing the National Anthem." *New York Times*, October 30.

MeTV Staff. 2016. "10 Awesome TV Station Sign-offs from the Era of Dead Air." MeTV, October 4. https://www.metv.com/stories/10-awesome-vintage-tv-station-sign-offs.

Omer-Man, Michael. 2011. "This Week in History: Satellites Connect the World." *Jerusalem Post*, July 16. https://www.jpost.com/Features/In-Thespotlight/This-Week-in-History-Satellites-connect-the-world.

Svejda, George J. 2005. *History of the Star Spangled Banner from 1814 to the Present.* Honolulu, HI: University Press of the Pacific. First published in 1969 by Division of History, Office of Archeology and Historic Preservation, U.S. Department of the Interior, National Park Service.

Regional Appeal

One way to trace knowledge of, and possible appreciation for, "The Star-Spangled Banner" is to follow its publication history. Another essay in this volume traces this early history in newspapers and sheet music. Yet another approach is to trace the number and geographic distribution of songsters (collections of songs) that included the anthem.

Dr. George Svejda (2005) observed that such songsters were published in Hagerstown, Maryland, in 1814; in Philadelphia in 1815, 1818, 1827, 1829, 1835, and 1837; in Wilmington, Delaware, in 1816; in Pittsburgh in 1818; in New York in

1818, 1820, 1840, 1842, and 1845; in New Haven, Connecticut in 1819; in Richmond, Virginia in 1824; in Hartford, Connecticut in 1826; in Baltimore in 1831; in Newark, New Jersey, in 1834; and in Cincinnati in 1836.

Although some of these cities were larger than neighboring ones, one of the most notable aspects of this list is that, with the exception of New Haven and Hartford, none were published in New England. New England had, of course, been the center of opposition to both the embargos that the United States had imposed on Britain during the Jefferson administration and the War of 1812. This later opposition was particularly prominent during the Hartford Convention, which had met from December 15, 1814, to January 5, 1815.

As the Civil War split the nation into North and South, at least some Southerners attempted to keep "The Star-Spangled Banner" as an anthem (Svejda 2005, 166), but the tune was largely appropriated by Union forces, with Southern forces more typically singing or playing "Dixie." Moreover, J. W. Davies & Sons, of Richmond, Virginia, published a piece of sheet music by Francis Hundley entitled "Farewell to the Star Spangled Banner" (Filby and Howard 1972, 146, 149). Ironically noting that the Southern states would not submit like slaves, the song ended with the lines:

> No longer shall wave o'er the land of the free.
>> But we'll unfurl to the broad breeze of
>>> Heaven
>> Thirteen bright stars round the Palmetto
>>> tree.

During the Civil War, "The Star-Spangled Banner" became considerably more popular in the New England states as well as in the Midwest. Svejda (2005) believes that New Englanders preferred "My Country, 'Tis of Thee" as a national anthem, in part because a Bostonian, Samuel Francis Smith, had composed it. New Englanders also probably appreciated the song's reference to the Pilgrims.

One of the reasons that "The Star-Spangled Banner" triumphed over rival tunes to be designated as the national anthem in 1831 is that, because it was so firmly rooted in a specific historical event that took place in Baltimore, it had the solid support of the Maryland congressional delegation as well as descendants of those who had fought in the War of 1812.

See also: Baltimore, Maryland; Early Printings; Early Recordings; War of 1812.

Further Reading

Filby, P. W., and Edward G. Howard (compilers). 1972. *Star-Spangled Books: Book, Sheet Music, Newspapers, Manuscripts, and Persons Associated with "The Star-Spangled Banner."* Baltimore: Maryland Historical Society.

Svejda, George J. 2005. *History of the Star Spangled Banner from 1814 to the Present.* Honolulu, HI: University Press of the Pacific. First published in 1969 by Division of History, Office of Archeology and Historic Preservation, U.S. Department of the Interior, National Park Service.

Ripley Cartoon

In 1929, Robert L. Ripley (1890–1949) published a cartoon as part of his *Believe It or Not* series. It pictured a rotund man joyfully lifting a wine glass at what appears to be a pub or tavern (others there appear to be drinking from mugs) and singing, "LONG MAY THE SONS OF ANACREON ENTWINE THE MYRTLE OF VENUS WITH BACCHUS'S VINE." Further proclaiming that "AMERICA HAS NO NATIONAL ANTHEM!" the cartoon expounded on the situation by noting, "THE U.S.A. (BEING A DRY COUNTRY) HAS BEEN USING—WITHOUT AUTHORIZATION—A VULGAR OLD ENGLISH DRINKING SONG." The cartoon further observed that as recently as 1914, Congress had refused to endorse the anthem, which was to the music of an English pub favorite called "To Anacreon in Heaven." When readers complained to Ripley about his irreverent cartoon, he suggested that they should direct their attention not to him but to Congress. The furor over this incident may have led to the petition signed by five million Americans that prompted Congress finally to act and make Francis Scott Key's "The Star-Spangled Banner" the country's official anthem (Rinaldi, n.d.).

In point of fact, Congress did adopt, and President Herbert Hoover did sign, a law in 1931 making "The Star-Spangled Banner" the national anthem, but support for the measure was hardly new, and the influence of some determined members of American patriotic organizations and Maryland congressmen probably had as much, if not more, impact as the petition. Moreover, it is not at all clear that Ripley's depiction of "The Star-Spangled Banner" as "a vulgar old English drinking song" would have been likely to encourage its adoption as the national anthem.

See also: Congress and "The Star-Spangled Banner"; "To Anacreon in Heaven."

Further Reading

Daily Dose. n.d. "March 3, 1931: 'The Star Spangled Banner' Finally Becomes the Official National Anthem for the United States." http://www.awb.com/dailydose/?p=1949.

Rinaldi, Sierra. n.d. "10 Things You Didn't Know About 'The Star-Spangled Banner.'" *Readers' Digest.* https://www.rd.com/culture/star-spangled-banner-national-anthem-facts.

"Rockets' Red Glare"

One of the most striking images in "The Star-Spangled Banner," and the only one specifically to mention a color, is that of the "rockets' red glare."

This imagery was used to describe the distinctive trail of the so-called Congreve rockets that British ships fired on Fort McHenry on September 13, 1814, in a failed attempt to seize the port city of Baltimore during the War of 1812. Both rockets and fireworks, their pyrotechnic predecessors, originated in China and India, but had been refined for the English by William Congreve (1772–1828), who was most interested in standardizing the production and discharge of such

Congreve rockets were developed by Sir William Congreve and used in war for the first time in 1806. The rockets were inaccurate and largely ineffective in the War of 1812, despite their spectacular and intimidating appearance. (Congreve, Sir William, c. 1814.)

weapons so as to minimize dependence on individual artisans and shipmen (Werrett 2009). These rockets were mounted on sticks with incendiary explosives in their cones and did not have the recoil of cannon and other weaponry.

The British use of such rockets against Fort McHenry followed their use against Copenhagen in 1807 and was followed by later engagements at Leipzig in 1818, and then against Barbary pirates and in India (Werrett 2009, 48). Although Congreve never patented his rocket, he benefited considerably from royal patronage and was elected in 1811 to the Fellowship of the Royal Society.

Rockets could travel between two thousand and two thousand five hundred yards, making it possible for British vessels firing the rockets at Fort McHenry to launch most of them beyond the range of the fort's own cannon. There were two types of Congreve rockets: "the case-shot rocket employed as a substitute for artillery or auxiliary thereto, and the rocket loaded with inflammable material designed to start conflagrations" (Robinson 1945, 1). The former type contained carbine balls that exploded in a manner similar to shrapnel when a combustible powder housed behind the balls was lit by a fuse (1–2).

During the attack, the weather was stormy and the sky was filled with clouds, which would undoubtedly have reflected the bursts of the bombs and rockets, probably making them seem even more terrifying. Congreve rockets had been particularly effective against American troops during the Battle of Bladensburg on August 24, which immediately preceded the burning of Washington, DC, when the British had used them in place of artillery (Robinson 1945, 3). Interestingly, contemporaries questioned whether such rockets or torpedoes were humane instruments of warfare (5–6).

See also: "Bombs Bursting in Air"; Fort McHenry.

Further Reading

"Congreve Rockets." 1848. *Scientific American* 3 (September 16): 411.

McNamara, Tom. 2017. "What Is the 'Red Glare' in the Star Spangled Banner?" *Popular Science*, September 4. https://www.popsci.com/what-are-rockets-red-glare-in-star -spangled-banner.

Robinson, Ralph. 1945. "The Use of Rockets by the British in the War of 1812." *Maryland Historical Magazine* 40 (March): 1–6.

Werrett, Simon. 2009. "William Congreve's Rational Rockets." *Notes and Records of the Royal Society of London* 63 (March 20): 35–56.

Ross, Betsy

Few females are more widely celebrated in American history than Betsy Ross (1752–1836), a Philadelphia seamstress who made flags. Ever since her grandson William J. Canby read a paper entitled "The Origin of the American Flag" before the American Historical Society in 1870, she has been widely credited with designing the first American flag for General George Washington and members of a committee of Congress. This meeting between Ross and Washington and his cohorts has been celebrated in a number of paintings and prints, and her house has long been a popular tourist attraction in Philadelphia.

In truth, Canby attributed Ross's actions to a time prior to that in which Congress had authorized a design for the flag, and there is no evidence that she met with General Washington on the subject. The best evidence suggests that it was Francis Hopkinson (1737–1791), a signer of the Declaration of Independence who also helped design the official shield of the United States, who created the original

In this 1932 painting by Jean Leon Gerome, Betsy Ross reportedly shows Major Ross and Robert Morris how she cut the stars for the American flag; George Washington sits in a chair on the left. The story of Ross sewing the first U.S. flag is mythical. (Library of Congress)

design of the U.S. flag, with its distinctive stars and stripes, that (in somewhat modified form) Francis Scott Key would have observed on the morning of the day that he authored "The Star-Spangled Banner."

Ross was, however, an interesting historical figure. Raised as a Quaker, she had been expelled from that religious community after she married John Ross, who was not a Quaker and who died during the Revolutionary War. Her second husband, Joseph Ashburn, died in a British jail after being captured for privateering. He was incarcerated with John Claypoole, who later became Betsy Ross's third husband.

However confused some of the facts surrounding Ross may be, she highlights the role that women like Mary Young Pickersgill, herself the daughter of another Philadelphia flag maker, played in early American flag making. Although her name is less widely known, Pickersgill and members of her family sewed both the storm flag that likely flew over Fort McHenry during the night of the Battle of Baltimore as well as the larger "Star-Spangled Banner" flag that Key likely saw on the morning after the battle.

See also: Key, Francis Scott; Pickersgill, Mary Young.

Further Reading

Crews, Ed. 2008. "The Truth About Betsy Ross." *Colonial Williamsburg Journal* (Summer). https://www.history.org/foundation/journal/summer08/betsy.cfm.

Harker, John B. 2005. "Betsy Ross: An American Legend and Patriot Revisited." *Raven: A Journal of Vexillology* 12:87–99.

Menezes, Joann. 1997. "The Birthing of the American Flag and the Invention of an American Founding Mother in the Image of Betsy Ross." In *Narratives of Nostalgia, Gender, and Nationalism*, edited by Jean Pickering and Suzanne Kehde, 74–87. Washington Square: New York University Press.

Miller, Marla. 2011. *Betsy Ross and the Making of America*. New York: Henry Holt.

Ross, Robert

Major General Robert Ross (1766–1814) was one of the most important individuals in the events leading up to the Battle of Baltimore that occasioned the writing of "The Star-Spangled Banner."

Born in Ireland and educated at Trinity College in Dublin, he enlisted in the British army in 1789 and served in the Napoleonic Wars before being assigned to take charge of British troops fighting in America during the War of 1812. In this capacity, he was among those who visited the home of Dr. William Beanes in Upper Marlboro, Maryland, on August 22 and 23 before leading British troops to victory over American militiamen at the Battle of Bladensburg. From there he marched to Washington, DC, where he and his troops carried out orders to burn the White House and other governmental buildings, while sparing civilian residences. After Francis Scott Key and Colonel John S. Skinner met with him and Admiral Alexander Cochrane aboard his ship to negotiate the release of Dr. Beanes, they were detained and effectively provided with a front row seat to the subsequent attack on Fort McHenry.

On September 12, 1814, Ross landed at North Point with the intention of capturing the city of Baltimore. Indeed, when his host for breakfast asked whether he intended to return for dinner, he colorfully replied, "No. I'll eat in Baltimore tonight—or in hell" (Rasmussen 2011).

As Ross rode ahead of his troops, American marksmen, possibly privates Henry Gough McComas and Daniel Wells who were soon killed in a firefight, fired on him and delivered a mortal wound. Ross's death dispirited his men, whose advance was later halted by further fighting and stormy weather. The failure to capture Baltimore by land led to the naval attack on Fort McHenry, after which Francis Scott Key observed the huge U.S. flag that still proudly flew over the fort.

Ross's body was stored in a barrel of rum—a fact wryly noted in a contemporary American song "The Battle of Baltimore"—and buried in the Old St. Paul Burying Ground in Nova Scotia (Rasmussen 2011). This may have thwarted consideration of an American plan to burn Ross's family home and village in Rostrevor in Northern Ireland (Graham 2014).

Ross's memory has been commemorated by a large granite obelisk in Northern Ireland and by a monument at St. Paul's Cathedral in London, England. It reads:

ERECTED AT THE PUBLIC EXPENSE TO THE MEMORY OF MAJOR GENERAL ROBERT
ROSS WHO HAVING UNDERTOOK AND EXECUTED AN ENTERPRISE AGAINST THE
CITY OF WASHINGTON, THE CAPITOL OF THE UNITED STATES OF AMERICA WHICH
WAS CROWNED WITH COMPLETE SUCCESS WAS KILLED SHORTLY AFTERWARDS
WHILE DIRECTING A SUCCESSFUL ATTACK UPON A SUPERIOR FORCE NEAR THE CITY
OF BALTIMORE ON THE 12TH DAY OF SEPTEMBER 1814

See also: "Battle of Baltimore, The"; Beanes, William; Key, Francis Scott; War of 1812.

Further Reading

Graham, Claire. 2014. "Robert Ross: The NI Man Who Started the White House Fire 200 Years Ago." *BBC News*, August 24. https://www.bbc.com/news/uk-northern -ireland-28897646.

Kendrick, Josephus. 1821. "Monument to Major General Robert Ross." Art and Architecture, Conway Collections, Courtauld Institue of Art. http://www.artandarchitecture .org.uk/images/conway/ff823138.html.

Lord, Walter. 1972. *The Dawn's Early Light.* New York: W.W. Norton.

McGavitt, John, and Christopher T. George. 2016. *The Man Who Captured Washington: Major General Robert Ross and the War of 1812.* Norman: University of Oklahoma Press.

Rasmussen, Frederick N. 2011. "British General Meets His End at Battle of North Point." *Baltimore Sun*, October 23. https://www.baltimoresun.com/maryland/bs-md -robert-ross-backstory23-20111023-story.html.

Scholarship

In 1972, William Lichtenwanger, who was head of the Music Division at the Library of Congress, sought to alert his colleagues to what he thought was a major lacuna in music scholarship. Referring to "The Star-Spangled Banner" as "a musical work that has been completely neglected (so far as I am aware) by university scholars and their students despite the fact that it is the most often performed, most problem-ridden, and today the most controversial piece of American music, bar none" (94), he went on to argue that this topic offered one of the greatest challenges "to multidisciplinary study" (94). He concentrated much of the rest of his essay to fairly arcane studies of the origins of the tune of the anthem.

These studies included one that would likely head almost anyone's list, namely Dr. George Svejda's *History of the Star Spangled Banner from 1814 to the Present*, which he prepared for the Division of History for the National Park Service in 1969 and has subsequently been reprinted.

Concerned as he was with studies of the text, Lichtenwanger justly commended P. W. Filby and Edward G. Howard's compilation of *Star-Spangled Books* (1972) as well as Oscar George Theodore Sonneck's *"The Star Spangled Banner"* (1914), which was a revised edition of a yet earlier study of several tunes that were being considered as a national anthem. There are several great treatments of some of the airs that were possible rivals to "The Star-Spangled Banner." Robert James Branham and Stephen J. Hartnett's *Sweet Freedom's Song*, which focused on the composition and history of "My Country, 'Tis of Thee," is among them.

Had Lichtenwanger been writing about scholarship just three years later, he might have included Vera Brodsky Lawrence's *Music for Patriots, Politicians, and Presidents* (1975), which, although it does not concentrate on "The Star-Spangled Banner," does much to put it into context. Lichtenwanger was also particularly complimentary of the works of Richard (Dick) Hill, not all of which were published (see, however, Hill 1951), with respect to the origins of the tune (Lichtenwanger 1972, 97–99).

Lichtenwanger did more than complain about the alleged dearth of good scholarship about Francis Scott Key's famous song. In the late 1970s he authored two fairly seminal articles, each of which sought chiefly to resolve questions about the writing and composition of the tune.

There is more than enough contemporary scholarship for those who are interested in "The Star-Spangled Banner." Professor Mark Clague has done much to clear away many of what he calls the "mythconceptions" surrounding the national banner while joining with Andrew Kuster to produce the *Star Spangled Songbook*

(2015) and an accompanying CD, *Poets and Patriots*. Indeed, the years leading up to the bicentennial of the War of 1812 and the writing of "The Star-Spangled Banner" led to a flurry of illuminating writings by Clague and other scholars. There is, of course, considerably more knowledge of the U.S. flag than in the past. Although this encyclopedia has largely concentrated on the anthem rather than the flag, it rests on an earlier encyclopedia that I compiled on the latter (Vile 2018). That volume in turn rests on such classics as Scot Guenter's *The American Flag, 1777–1924* (1990), Marc Leepson's *Flag: An American Biography* (2005), and Woden Teachout's *Capture the Flag* (2009). It also profited from the scholarship of Eran Shalev, particularly his article on the origin of the flag (2011), and on publications connected to recent flag restorations (Taylor, Kendrick, and Brodie 2008).

The bicentennials of the War of 1812 and of the composition of "The Star-Spangled Banner" have produced several popular works that center either on the anthem, the flag, or both. These include Marc Ferris's *Star-Spangled Banner* (2014) and Irvin Molotsky's *The Flag, the Poet and the Song* (2001). Marc Leepson, whose work on the flag has already been mentioned, has added a good biography of Francis Scott Key that supplements several from earlier decades, most notably those of Victor Weybright (1934) and Edward S. Delaplaine (1998 [1937]).

Although most individuals who are interested in Fort McHenry will likely turn to Merle T. Cole and Scott S. Sheads's serviceable *Fort McHenry and Baltimore's Harbor Defenses* (2001), scholars will want to be sure to examine a report prepared by Patrick Sullivan in 2013 on the fort.

There are a number of highly readable books on the War of 1812 including Walter Lord's classic *The Dawn's Early Light* (1972), A. J. Langguth's *Union 1812* (2006), Donald Hickey's *The War of 1812: The Forgotten Conflict* (2012), Walter Borneman's *The War That Forged a Nation* (2009), and Steve Vogel's *Through the Perilous Fight* (2014). Scott S. Sheads has added a number of volumes that help fill in gaps, most notably *The Rockets' Red Glare* (1986). The bicentennial of the War of 1812 has been a particularly productive time for historians to revisit the primary causes of this conflict.

Most of the legal issues involving the star-spangled banner center on pledges to the flag rather than to the national anthem, so there are not as many articles in law journals addressing the anthem, although there are a number of relevant congressional hearings and reports. In addition, there are a plethora of modern articles on the anthem, again, many undoubtedly stimulated by the bicentennials of the War of 1812 and of the anthem. Numerous articles on the anthem that have been written in the last ten years are assessable through Journal Storage (JSTOR) and Google Scholar.

The same is true of stories on the Internet. In addition to controversies generated by players who have chosen to sit or kneel during renditions of "The Star-Spangled Banner" at sports events, numerous newspaper and magazine articles have highlighted individualistic renditions of the national anthem and its use in holiday celebrations like Independence Day and Defenders' Day. Just as visual artists have increasingly experimented with portrayals of the U.S. flag, so too, performance artists have continued to push boundaries, which are often the subject of contemporary news reports.

For individuals seeking information on the anthem, a visit to Fort McHenry is almost a must. There are also numerous monuments and markers throughout the park and the city of Baltimore.

See also: Clague, Mark; Sonneck, Oscar George Theodore; Svejda, George J.

Further Reading

Borneman, Walter R. 2009. *1812: The War That Forged a Nation.* New York: HarperCollins.

Branham, Robert James, and Stephen J. Hartnett. 1996. "'Of Thee I Sing': Contesting 'America.'" *American Quarterly* 48 (December): 623–52.

Branham, Robert James, and Stephen J. Hartnett. 2002. *Sweet Freedom's Song: "My Country 'Tis of Thee" and Democracy in America.* New York: Oxford University Press.

Clague, Mark, and Andrew Kuster, eds. 2015. *Star Spangled Songbook: A History in Sheet Music of "The Star-Spangled Banner."* Ann Arbor, MI: Star Spangled Music Foundation.

Cole, Merle T., and Scott S. Sheads. 2001. *Images of America: Fort McHenry and Baltimore's Harbor Defenses.* Charleston, SC: Arcadia.

Delaplaine, Edward S. 1998. *Francis Scott Key: Life and Times.* Stuarts Draft, VA: American Foundation Publications. First published 1937.

Ferris, Marc. 2014. *Star-Spangled Banner: The Unlikely Story of America's National Anthem.* Baltimore: Johns Hopkins University Press.

Filby, P. W., and Edward G. Howard (compilers). 1972. *Star-Spangled Banner Books, Sheet Music, Newspapers, Manuscripts, and Persons Associated with "The Star-Spangled Banner."* Baltimore: Maryland Historical Society.

Hickey, Donald R. 2012. *The War of 1812: A Forgotten Conflict.* Bicentennial edition. Urbana: University of Illinois Press.

Hill, Richard S. 1951. "The Melody of 'The Star-Spangled Banner' in the United States before 1820." In *Essays Honoring Lawrence C. Wroth,* edited by Lessing J. Rosenwald Collection (Library of Congress), 151–92. Portland, ME: Anthoensen Press.

Langguth, A. J. 2006. *Union 1812: The Americans Who Fought the Second War of Independence.* New York: Simon & Schuster.

Lawrence, Vera Brodsky. 1975. *Music for Patriots, Politicians, and Presidents: Harmonies and Discords of the First Hundred Years.* New York: Macmillan.

Leepson, Marc. 2005. *Flag: An American Biography.* New York: St. Martin's Press.

Leepson, Marc. 2014. *What So Proudly We Hailed: Francis Scott Key, A Life.* New York: Palgrave/Macmillan.

Lichtenwanger, William. 1972. "Star-Spangled Bibliography." *College Music Symposium* 12 (Fall): 94–102.

Lichtenwanger, William. 1977. "The Music of 'The Star-Spangled Banner': From Ludgate Hill to Capitol Hill." *Quarterly Journal of the Library of Congress* 34 (July): 136–70.

Lichtenwanger, William. 1978. "The Music of 'The Star-Spangled Banner': Whence and Whither?" *College Music Symposium* 18 (Fall): 34–81.

Lord, Walter. 1972. *The Dawn's Early Light.* New York: W.W. Norton.

Molotsky, Irvin. 2001. *The Flag, the Poet and the Song: The Story of the Star-Spangled Banner.* New York: Dutton.

Shalev, Eran. 2011. "'A Republic Amidst the Stars': Political Astronomy and the Intellectual Origins of the Stars and Stripes." *Journal of the Early Republic* 31 (Spring): 39–73.

Sheads, Scott S. 1986. *The Rockets' Red Glare: The Maritime Defense of Baltimore in 1814.* Centreville, MD: Tidewater.

Sonneck, Oscar George Theodore. 1914. *"The Star Spangled Banner" (Revised and Enlarged from the "Report" on the Above and Other Airs, Issued in 1909).* Washington, DC: Government Printing Office (Library of Congress).

Sullivan, Patrick. 2013. *Fort McHenry National Monument and Historic Shrine: Administrative History.* New South Associates Technical Report 2256. Stone Mountain, GA: New South Associates for the National Park Service.

Svejda, George J. 2005. *History of the Star Spangled Banner from 1814 to the Present.* Honolulu, HI: University Press of the Pacific. First published in 1969 by Division of History, Office of Archeology and Historic Preservation, U.S. Department of the Interior, National Park Service.

Taylor, Lonn, Kathleen M. Kendrick, and Jeffrey L. Brodie. 2008. *The Star-Spangled Banner: The Making of an American Icon.* New York: Smithsonian Institution in conjunction with HarperCollins.

Teachout, Woden. 2009. *Capture the Flag: A Political History of American Patriotism.* New York: Basic Books.

Vile, John R. 2018. *The American Flag: An Encyclopedia of the Stars and Stripes in U.S. History, Culture, and Law.* Santa Barbara, CA: ABC-CLIO.

Vogel, Steve. 2013. *Through the Perilous Fight: From the Burning of Washington to the Star-Spangled Banner; The Six Weeks That Saved the Nation.* New York: Random House.

Weybright, Victor. 1934. *Spangled Banner: The Story of Francis Scott Key.* New York: Farrar & Rinehart.

Sheldon v. Fannin (1963)

In addition to widely publicized U.S. Supreme Court decisions affirming the right of students to refuse to salute the U.S. flag for religious reasons, a U.S. district court ruled in *Sheldon v. Fannin* (1963) that students have a similar right to refuse to stand for the national anthem because of the protections in the First and Fourteenth Amendments.

The case arose in Arizona when students and their parents who were Jehovah's Witnesses sought and eventually received injunctive relief after Pinetop Elementary School expelled the students after they refused to stand for the anthem. Their refusal led school officials to charge them with truancy and delinquency. The students justified their refusal by citing the example of Shadrach, Meshach, and Abednego, recounted in the Bible's book of Daniel, who had refused to bow down to an image at the sound of musical instruments by order of King Nebuchadnezzar of Babylon.

Because the expulsion resulted from the actions of the local board of trustees, rather than from an explicit state law requiring children to stand, there was some question, reflected in an earlier decision by a three-judge district court, as to whether the actions of the trustees constituted state action subject to judicial review. Seemingly acting somewhat reluctantly, the court decided that the decision in *Monroe v. Pape* (1961) had provided a broad enough definition of state action that it included the acts of the trustees.

Thus reviewing the First and Fourteenth Amendments as well as the Supreme Court decision in *West Virginia State Board of Education v. Barnette* (1943), which had invalidated compulsory flag salutes, the court concluded that the right to the free exercise of religion, at least when nondisruptive, typically outweighed more general laws and regulations. Indeed, its statement remains relevant to a host of subsequent controversies: "Clearly, then, if the refusal to participate in the ceremony attendant upon the singing or playing of the national anthem had not occurred in a public-school classroom, but in some other public or private place, there would be not the slightest doubt that the plaintiffs were free to participate or not as they choose. Every citizen is free to stand or sit, sing or remain silent, when the Star Spangled Banner is played" (774).

Rejecting the idea that "the National Anthem contains words of prayer, adoration and reverence for the Deity, and that a State's prescription of participation therein amounts to a prohibited 'establishment of religion,'" the court explained that "the singing of the National Anthem is not a religious but a patriotic ceremony, intended to inspire devotion to and love of country. Any religious references therein are incidental and expressive only of the faith which as a matter of historical fact has inspired the growth of the nation" (*West Virginia State Board of Education v. Barnette* 1943, 774). Suggesting that the plaintiffs appeared inconsistent in being willing to stand for the Pledge of Allegiance but not for the national anthem, it concluded that "the Constitution fortunately does not require that the beliefs or thoughts expressed be reasonable, or wise, or even sensible" (774). It further refused to inquire into the sincerity of such beliefs.

The court distinguished this case from those where student conduct might be "disorderly" or where students might "materially disrupt the conduct and discipline of the school (*West Virginia* 1943, 775).

See also: First Amendment; "In God Is Our Trust"; Jehovah's Witnesses; Public Schools; State and Municipal Laws and Ordinances.

Further Reading
Monroe v. Pape, 365 U.S. 167 (1961).
Sheldon v. Fannin, 221 F. Supp. 766 (D. Ariz. 1963).
West Virginia State Board of Education v. Barnette, 319 U.S. 624 (1943).

Singing the National Anthem in Public Spaces

One principle that has guided contemporary interpretations of the First Amendment is that of content neutrality. It is the idea that government has the right to control the time, place, and manner of speaking on public property, but if it recognizes such a forum for one such activity, it cannot restrict it in the case of others.

This rule, which is designed to promote public safety while preventing the government from arbitrarily allowing for the expression of some speech over that of others, can sometimes result in some bizarre consequences.

In 2010, a group of students attending a leadership conference in Washington, DC, sponsored by the Young America's Foundation were told that they could not sing the national anthem at the Lincoln Memorial although they could have done so outside the monument. Apparently, they sang anyway in what was described as an impromptu act of civil disobedience (Starnes 2010).

By contrast, when a middle school choir from North Carolina was stopped from a similar performance on the plaza of the 9/11 Memorial in Manhattan, their teacher reported that "we very reverently and quietly stopped what we were doing and complied with his request and quietly exited the park" (Associated Press 2016). Moreover, when visitor Star Swain sang the national anthem at the Lincoln Memorial in June 2016, her performance was widely shared on social media.

In another incident, a flight attendant told Pamela Dee Gaudry of Georgia that it was against the policy of Delta Airlines for a passenger to sing the anthem, which Gaudry had encouraged fellow passengers to do after she learned that the plane they were flying to Atlanta was carrying the body of a fallen soldier. The attendant had told Gaudry that the airline had this policy in place in order not to offend any foreigners who might be aboard. After learning of the incident, however, the company said that the attendant was mistaken and that it did not have such a policy. In December 2018, travelers passing through the Nashville airport stopped to sing the national anthem to children of fallen servicemen who were headed toward a trip to Disneyland (Richardson 2018). Clearly, performances of the national anthem in public spaces, whether done spontaneously or not, can elicit strong emotions.

See also: First Amendment; Patriotism.

Further Reading

Associated Press. 2016. "Guard Stops Students from Singing National Anthem at 9/11 Memorial." *New York Times*, April 25. https://www.nytimes.com/2016/04/26/nyregion/guard-stops-students-from-singing-national-anthem-at-9-11-memorial.html.

"Delta Airlines Prevented Woman from Singing National Anthem on Flight with Fallen Soldier, She Claims." 2017. *Fox News*, October 16. https://www.foxnews.com/travel/delta-airlines-prevented-woman-from-singing-national-anthem-on-flight-with-fallen-soldier-she-claims.

Richardson, Matt. 2018. "Nashville Airport Travelers Stop to Sing National Anthem for Children of Fallen Service Members, Viral Video Shows." *Fox News*, December 10. https://www.foxnews.com/travel/nashville-airport-travelers-stop-to-sing-national-anthem-for-children-of-fallen-service-members-viral-video-shows.

Starnes, Todd. 2010. "Students at Lincoln Memorial Told to Stop Singing National Anthem." *Fox News*, August 9. Updated November 30, 2015. https://www.foxnews.com/us/students-at-lincoln-memorial-told-to-stop-singing-national-anthem.

"Woman Performs Stunning Rendition of the National Anthem at Lincoln Memorial." 2016. *Fox News Insider*, July 2. https://insider.foxnews.com/2016/07/02/woman-sings-national-anthem-lincoln-memorial-video-goes-viral.

Singing "The Star-Spangled Banner"

One enduring criticism of "The Star-Spangled Banner" is that it is too difficult for most individuals who have not been professionally trained to sing well. Not only are the lyrics more complex than those of a typical song or poem, but the music has a range of an octave and a half, making the high notes particularly difficult for low or untrained voices to reach.

When debates were being held in 1931 over the song's suitability as a national anthem, the *Herald Tribune* referred to "words that nobody can remember to a tune nobody can sing" while journalist Poultney Bigelow observed that "no one with a normal esophagus can sing [it] without screaming" (Connor 2017, 48).

An unidentified individual attempted to illustrate the difficulty with two verses of parody, the first of which is as follows (Jones 1918; Connor 2017, 48):

> Oh, say, can you sing from the start to the end,
> What so proudly you stand for
> When the orchestras play it;
> When the whole congregation, in voices that blend,
> Strike up the grand hymn
> And then torture and slay it?
> How they bellow and shout
> When they're first starting out,
> But 'the dawn's early light' finds them
> Floundering about.
> 'Tis the Star Spangled Banner'
> They're trying to sing
> But they don't know the words
> Of the precious old thing.

The second verse continued (Connor 2017, 48):

> Hark! The 'twilight's last gleaming'
> Has some of them stopped.
> But the valiant survivors press forward serenely
> To 'the ramparts we watched,'
> Where some others are dropped
> And the loss of the leaders is manifest keenly;
> Then 'the rockets' red glare'
> Give the bravest a scare
> And there's a few left to face
> The 'bombs bursting in air'
> 'Tis a thin line of heroes that manage to save
> The last of the verse
> And 'the home of the brave.'

One commonly employed solution to this problem at public events is to have the anthem played or sung by a professional musician, sometimes alone and sometimes joined by the crowd. One advantage of the custom of standing and facing the flag with one's hand over one's heart (or at attention if one is a member of the military) is that it gives individuals reluctant to join in the singing a way to participate. Some individuals, most notably Lucy Monroe (1906–1987), who was known as the "Star-Spangled Soprano" for her countless performances of the national anthem as the official soloist for the Veterans of Foreign Wars and American Legion, have virtually made their careers on their renditions of the song.

One fascinating aspect about the difficulty of singing "The Star-Spangled Banner" is that some of its proponents actually cited this difficulty as a reason to make it the national anthem. An editorial in the *New York World* of February 3, 1930, said, "The truth is that 'The Star-Spangled Banner' is one of those things which are quite unsingable, except by professionals, and probably there is nothing to do about it. And is this so very regrettable? Not to our thinking. As we have already pointed out, it saves our anthem from being worn threadbare by many repetitions; it is reserved for ceremonial occasions, when it is performed by competent musicians; thus it retains a suggestion of dignity and glamor. That, we submit, is as it should be" (Weybright 1934, 165).

After asking, "What if school children could sing it?," another *World* editorial from March 31, 1930, observed that under those circumstances, "We should be so sick of it by now that we could not endure the sound of it, as the French are sick of the 'Marseillaise.' The virtues of 'The Star-Spangled Banner' are that it does require a wide compass, so that school children cannot sing it, and that it is in three-four time so that parades cannot march to it. So being, it has managed to remain fresh, not frayed and worn, and the citizenry still hear it with some semblance of a thrill, some touch of reverence" (Weybright 1934, 166–67).

During World War I some German-American conductors expressed reluctance to perform the "The Star-Spangled Banner" at American concerts because they claimed that it did not rise to the level of high art. Defenders of the song countered by arguing that its difficulty did, in fact, lift it to that category. Musicologist Matthew Mugmon thus noted that "the injection of 'The Star-Spangled Banner' into a national debate about its performance by an eminent symphony orchestra subtly transformed these well-established concerns about its melodic difficulty into a point of pride about the sophistication of American music" (Mugmon 2014, 21).

See also: Criticisms and Defenses of "The Star-Spangled Banner"; German-American Composers during World War I.

Further Reading

Connor, Joseph. 2017. "Off Key." *American History* 51 (February): 42–51.

Hardy, Kathryn (Katie) Macko. 2014. "Why Is the National Anthem so Hard to Sing?" *O Say Can You See?* (blog), Smithsonian National Museum of American History, May 14. http://americanhistory.si.edu/blog/2014/05/why-is-the-national-anthem-so -hard-to-sing.html.

Jones, Edna D. 1918. *Patriotic Pieces from the Great War.* Philadelphia: Penn Publishing.

Mugmon, Matthew. 2014. "Patriotism, Art, and 'The Star-Spangled Banner' in World War I: A New Look at the Karl Muck Episode." *Journal of Musicological Research* 33:4–26.

Weybright, Victor. 1934. *Spangled Banner: The Story of Francis Scott Key.* New York: Farrar & Rinehart.

Skinner, John Stuart

John Stuart Skinner (1788–1851) was born in Calvert County, Maryland, and educated at Charlotte-Hall, a notable classical academy, before reading law and entering
that profession. During the War of 1812, President James Madison appointed Skinner
to oversee packets of communication between the Americans and the British coming
out of Annapolis and to negotiate the exchange of hostages during the conflict.

As British troops advanced toward Washington, DC, Skinner rode ninety miles
to warn the government, and he accordingly became known as "Maryland's Paul
Revere." Madison subsequently appointed him to join Francis Scott Key on the
mission to release Dr. William Beanes from British custody. Skinner and Key
brought letters with them from British soldiers telling how American doctors had
tended to their wounds, and these were likely responsible for the British decision
to release Dr. Beanes.

Because Skinner, Key, and Beanes were all privy to British plans to attack Fort
McHenry, they were kept aboard the ship of truce during the bombardment of the
fort—the survival of which became the inspiration for "The Star-Spangled Banner." Skinner reported, "It was from her deck in view of Fort McHenry, that we
witnessed through an anxious day and night, 'The rockets red glare, the bombs
bursting in air,' and the song which was written [by Key] the night after we got
back to Baltimore, in the hotel then kept at the corner of Hanover and Market
streets, was but a versified and almost literal transcript of our expressed hopes and
apprehensions, through that ever-memorable period of anxiety to all but never of
despair" (Svejda 2005, 72).

Although there are conflicting accounts, Skinner may have been the individual,
or among the individuals, who took Key's lyrics to the press and had them published (Svejda 2005, 72, 78–79). In a letter to the Baltimore *Gazette* of May 23,
1849, Skinner observed that in addition to getting Dr. Beanes released, his mission
"ended happily in giving us one national song, that will be as imperishable as the
naval renown it will forever serve to celebrate and to cherish" (71).

After the war, Madison appointed Skinner as the postmaster of Baltimore,
where he served until 1837. In 1819, Skinner also began publishing *The American
Farmer*, which would continue for ten years, after which he began *The American
Tuft Register and Sporting Magazine*. Still later, he would edit the *Farmer's
Library and Monthly Journal of Agriculture* and *The Plough, the Loom, and the
Anvil*. In time, the Marquis de Lafayette selected Skinner to manage twenty thousand acres of land that Congress had granted him (Poore 1854, 11). Skinner also
served as a member of the Board of Visitors for West Point and as one of the direc-
tors of the Bank of Baltimore (Poore 1854, 12–13).

In March of 1851, Skinner fell down the steps of the post office in Baltimore
and died of his injuries.

See also: Baltimore, Maryland; Beanes, William; Key, Francis Scott; War of 1812; Writing of "The Star-Spangled Banner."

Further Reading

Bishko, Lucretia Ramsey. 1972. "John S. Skinner Visits the Virginia Springs, 1847." *Virginia Magazine of History and Biography* 80 (April): 158–92.

Poore, Ben Perley. 1954. "Biographical Notice of John S. Skinner." *The Plough, the Loom, and the Anvil* 7 (July): 1–20.

Svejda, George J. 2005. *History of the Star Spangled Banner from 1814 to the Present.* Honolulu, HI: University Press of the Pacific. First published in 1969 by Division of History, Office of Archeology and Historic Preservation, U.S. Department of the Interior, National Park Service.

Slavery

Deeply entangled in debates about whether symbolic protest actions undertaken during the playing of the national anthem are justified or disrespectful is the issue of whether the anthem, which Francis Scott Key penned in 1814, contains racist lyrics and tacitly endorsed slavery.

Rarely does the public sing, or hear, more than the first verse of the song, which, like the three successive verses that follow, end with references to "the land of the free and the home of the brave." Moreover, the first line of the fourth verse specifically refers to occasions "when freemen shall stand."

The reality of early nineteenth-century Maryland, of course, was that it was a slave-holding society. Key himself owned slaves, and the family of Key's wife once owned the famous black slave-turned-abolitionist Frederick Douglass. As a lawyer, Key both defended and prosecuted slaves who were seeking their freedom, and he vigorously prosecuted Reuben Crandall, a doctor and botanist who had come from Connecticut for having abolitionist literature in his possession (Kramer 1980; Asch and Musgrove 2017, 80–81). Key was also quite active in the American Colonization Society, which favored recolonization of free blacks back to Africa (Delaplaine 1998, 447–50). Key explained his attitude toward slavery when responding in 1838 to a questionnaire by Reverend Benjamin Tappan. He indicated that he did not believe that the Bible either mandated or prohibited slavery, that individuals holding slaves should do so while abiding by the biblical Golden Rule ("Do unto others as you would have them do unto you"), that he thought abolitionist literature had been detrimental to attempts to free slaves, and that blacks constituted "a distinct and inferior race of people, which all experience proves to be the greatest evil that afflicts a community" (448–49).

Key is hardly, however, the only early American to have owned slaves. Indeed, this was true of four of the first five presidents, including Thomas Jefferson, who had written the words of the Declaration of Independence declaring that "all men are created equal," and James Madison, who is often called the father of the U.S. Constitution.

The central question relative to the anthem is not, therefore, whether Key owned slaves or favored slavery but whether he incorporated such sentiments into "The Star-Spangled Banner." This is where the little-known third verse of the anthem comes into play:

And where is that band who so vauntingly swore,
That the havoc of war and the battle's confusion
A home and a country should leave us no more?

Their blood has wash'd out their foul footstep's pollution.
No refuge could save the hireling and slave
From the terror of flight or the gloom of the grave,
And the star-spangled banner in triumph doth wave
O'er the land of the free and the home of the brave.

This is by far the weakest verse of the anthem in part because it is so personal. Whatever implications the conflict may have had for slavery, the War of 1812 was not directed against American slaves but against Great Britain, their colonists in Canada, and the Native Americans with whom they were allied. The first three lines of the third verse clearly refer to the British, and explain why the War of 1812 is sometimes called the second American Revolution. As Key, who had originally opposed the war, observed British deprecations on the coast, the burning of the nation's capital, and the bombardment of Fort McHenry, he came to see British actions as designed to take back the freedom that Americans had gained during the American Revolution. At least from his perspective, the British did not want Americans to have their own "home" and "country." Thus, even though he had initially opposed the war, Key could not help but think that the British invasion of his country was a form of pollution that was rightly washed away by their own blood.

The next two lines seem to widen the net of Key's ire:

No refuge could save the hireling and slave
From the terror of flight or the gloom of the grave.

At least on the surface, the verse seems to be glorying in the death of slaves. In context, however, it appears that Key is not lauding the death of slaves in general but the deaths of both mercenaries and slaves who were part of the British invasion.

In point of fact, the British had followed the example of a number of colonial governors (most notably, Virginia's John Murray, the Fourth Earl of Dunmore) who had, during the Revolutionary War, offered freedom to slaves who would fight on their behalf. Alexander Cochrane, who led the British naval attacks against the U.S. in the War of 1812, further recruited black regiments from the Caribbean in hopes that they would help entice American blacks to seek their freedom. He and other British commanders often found, however, that African Americans considered themselves superior to African- or Caribbean-born blacks (Millett 2012, 188, 193). At the end of the war, the British evacuated several thousand former American slaves to Halifax, Canada, and to the Caribbean (199).

Key tied the British strategy of recruiting slaves to fight or rebel to that of hiring mercenaries (who they had also employed during the Revolutionary War), or "hirelings," to do their fighting for them. One of the American grievances against the British, which made their promises of freedom to U.S. slaves seem hollow, was that they had practiced their own form of involuntary servitude by impressing U.S. sailors into their navy (Eustace 2012, 170). Under the circumstances, some observers believe that it was not particularly bloodthirsty or racist of Key to hope that forces allied with the British invasion of his homeland would either die or flee.

At the end of the Civil War in 1865, the United States adopted the Thirteenth Amendment, which abolished slavery. Three years later, in 1868, the Fourteenth Amendment bestowed citizenship on all people born or naturalized in the United States.

Christopher Wilson (2016), the Director of Experience Design at the Smithsonian's National Museum of American History, observed that "every time Jackie Robinson stood on the baselines as the anthem was played, or when Civil Rights Movement activists had the flag ripped out of their hands as they peacefully marched, or when my dad saluted the flag at a segregated army base in Alabama fighting for a nation that didn't respect him, the song became less Key's and more ours." Rashad Jennings, an African American player for the New York Giants, put it somewhat differently when he said, "I figure if it was the intention of our Founding Fathers to keep America a nation of slaves, then it wouldn't have chosen a song where all four verses end with 'the land of the free and the home of the brave' instead of 'land of the free, home of the slave'" (Stepman 2016).

See also: African Americans; Key, Francis Scott; Lyrics of "The Star-Spangled Banner"; Sports Events; War of 1812.

Further Reading

Asch, Chris Myers, and George Derek Musgrove. 2017. *Chocolate City: A History of Race and Democracy in the Nation's Capital.* Chapel Hill: University of North Carolina Press.

Delaplaine, Edward S. 1998. *Francis Scott Key: Life and Times.* Stuarts Draft, VA: American Foundation Publications. First published 1937.

Eustace, Nicole. 2012. *1812: War and the Passions of Patriotism.* Philadelphia: University of Pennsylvania Press.

Kramer, Neil S. 1980. "The Trial of Reuben Crandall." *Records of the Columbia Historical Society* 50:123–39.

Millett, Nathaniel. 2012. "Slavery and the War of 1812." *Tennessee Historical Quarterly* 71 (Fall): 184–205.

Morley, Jefferson. 2013. "Francis Scott Key and the Slavery Question." *Globalist*, July 5. https://www.theglobalist.com/francis-scott-key-and-the-slavery-question.

Morley, Jefferson. 2017. "It Is Time to Examine the Words and the Origins of Our National Anthem, Another Neo-Confederate Symbol." *Salon*, August 27. https://www.salon.com/2017/08/27/it-is-time-to-examine-the-words-and-the-origins-of-our-national-anthem-another-neo-confederate-symbol_partner.

Olson, Walter. 2017. "History of the National Anthem: Is 'The Star-Spangled Banner' Racist?" *National Review*, September 15. https://www.cato.org/publications/commentary/star-spangled-banner-racist.

Schwarz, Jon. 2016. "Colin Kaepernick Is Righter Than You Know: The National Anthem Is a Celebration of Slavery." *The Intercept*, August 28. https://theintercept.com/2016/08/28/colin-kaepernick-is-righter-than-you-know-the-national-anthem-is-a-celebration-of-slavery.

Stepman, Jarrett. 2016. "Unlike the NFL's Colin Kaepernick, Frederick Douglass Loved 'The Star-Spangled Banner.'" *Daily Signal*, August 29. https://www.dailysignal

.com/2016/08/29/unlike-the-nfls-colin-kaepernick-frederick-douglass-loved-the
-star-spangled-banner.

Wilson, Christopher. 2016. "Where's the Debate on Francis Scott Key's Slave-Holding
Legacy?" *Smithsonian Magazine*, July 1. https://www.smithsonianmag.com
/smithsonian-institution/wheres-debate-francis-scott-keys-slave-holding-legacy
-180959550.

Smith, John Stafford

Although the issue was long a matter of contention, it now appears fairly well
established that John Stafford Smith (1750–1836) composed the tune to "To Anacreon in Heaven," which was, in turn, appropriated as the melody for "The Star-
Spangled Banner." The key piece of evidence is a diary entry written by London
composer Richard John Samuel Stevens (1757–1837). After noting that Ralph
Tomlinson, an attorney who served for a time as president of the Anacreontic
Society, had written "the Poetry of the Anacreontic Song," Stevens observed that
it has been Stafford Smith who had "set [it] to Music" (Lichtnewanger 1978, 54).

Smith was born to Martin and Agrilla Stafford Smith and baptized on March
30, 1750, at Gloucester Cathedral. He studied music under his father, who was the
organist for the cathedral, and under William Boyce, whose daughter, Elizabeth,
he would later marry. In addition to becoming an organist, he was made a Gentleman of the Chapel Royal and served as a lay-vicar at Westminster Abbey, where
he was installed in 1786 (Lichtenwanger 1978, 56).

Smith composed both sacred and secular works, and scholars believe that he
can rightfully be considered one of the early musicologists (Lichtenwanger 1978,
57). Although Smith had an interest in ancient music, in composing the Anacreontic tune he "achieved a melody that is surely *sui generis* [unique, or one of a kind]"
(57). Smith's own position in the ranks of English society further contradicts the
claim that the melody was simply that of an English drinking song.

See also: Drinking Song; "To Anacreon in Heaven."

Further Reading

Lichtenwanger, William. 1977. "The Music of 'The Star-Spangled Banner': From Ludgate
Hill to Capitol Hill." *Quarterly Journal of the Library of Congress* 34 (July):
136–70.

Lichtenwanger, William. 1978. "The Music of 'The Star-Spangled Banner': Whence and
Whither?" *College Music Symposium* 18 (Fall): 34–81.

Smith, Samuel

One of the largely unsung heroes of the battle to save Baltimore during the War of
1812 was Major General Samuel Smith (1752–1839). Smith, who was born in Car-
lisle, Pennsylvania, later came with his family to Baltimore. As commander of
Baltimore's militia during the war, he refused to relinquish his command to Brigadier General William Winder, who had failed to defend the U.S. Capitol against
British forces, which subsequently burned most of its public buildings.

Smith had gained military experience during the Revolutionary War before becoming one of Baltimore's leading merchants and one of Maryland's most influential members of Congress. Long an advocate of greater military preparedness in a party (Democratic-Republican) that often put greater emphasis on keeping the federal budget under control, Smith was able to get support for his efforts after Rear Admiral George Cockburn's British fleet sailed into the Chesapeake Bay (Cassell 1969, 351).

In addition to increasing the number of troops at Fort McHenry and adding cannons that could be directed against British ships, Smith mobilized his militia, prepared to sink ships to prevent the British from sailing past the fort into Baltimore's inner harbor, aided in the construction of a battery at what became Fort Covington, and created a line of breastworks and other defenses that ultimately thwarted the British attack at North Point. In Maryland, "He was the integrating force that meshed Baltimore's will to survive with the practical necessity of obtaining trained men, arms, and fortifications," wrote one biographer. "The battle of Baltimore was won as much in 1812 as in 1814, and from first to last it was singularly Smith's victory" (Cassell 1969, 360). Without Smith's efforts, it seems unlikely that Fort McHenry would have been able to withstand the onslaught of the world's greatest navy.

Funds were raised during the 1914 centennial celebration of the Battle of Baltimore for the commissioning of an imposing bronze statue of Smith by Hans Schuler (1874–1951). It was dedicated on Independence Day in 1918. After several moves, it is now located on Federal Hill, where it overlooks Baltimore's inner harbor. An inscription on the monument reads:

> MAJOR-GENERAL SAMUEL SMITH, 1752–1829 / UNDER HIS
> COMMAND THE ATTACK OF THE BRITISH UPON BALTIMORE
> BY LAND AND SEA SEPTEMBER 12–14, / 1814 WAS REPULSED.
> MEMBER OF CONGRESS FORTY SUCCESSIVE YEARS. /
> PRESIDENT U.S. SENATE, SECRETARY OF THE NAVY, MAYOR
> OF BALTIMORE. / HERO OF BOTH WARS FOR AMERICAN
> INDEPENDENCE—LONG ISLAND—WHITE / PLAINS—
> BRANDYWINE—DEFENDER OF FORT MIFFLIN—
> VALLEY FORGE— / MONMOUTH—BALTIMORE. / ERECTED
> BY THE NATIONAL STAR-SPANGLED BANNER
> CENTENNIAL (SHEADS 2013).

Smith was later elected major of Baltimore. Like Francis Scott Key, Smith favored colonizing freed African American slaves abroad.

See also: Baltimore, Maryland; Commemorations of "The Star-Spangled Banner"; Fort McHenry; War of 1812.

Further Reading

Cassell, Frank A. 1969. "Baltimore in 1813: A Study of Urban Defense in the War of 1812." *Military Affairs* 33 (December): 349–61.

Cassell, Frank A. 1971. *Merchant Congressman in the Young Republic: Samuel Smith of Maryland, 1742–1839.* Madison: University of Wisconsin Press.

Howard, Hugh. 2012. "War of 1812: Big Night in Baltimore." *HistoryNet*, January 6. https://www.historynet.com/war-of-1812-big-night-in-baltimore.htm.

Sheads, Scott S. 2013. "Major General Samuel Smith Monument at Federal Hill." Baltimore Heritage (website), February 12. Updated on May 7, 2019. https://explore .baltimoreheritage.org/items/show/190.

Songs of the U.S. Armed Forces

Although U.S. troops no longer go into battle to the sound of military bands, each division of the U.S. armed forces has adopted its own anthem to inspire its members. In addition to playing "The Star-Spangled Banner" and other patriotic songs at Memorial Day, it is also common to introduce a medley of the service hymns during which veterans from each of the services stand at attention while their respective anthem is being played.

The earliest of the songs that was composed for this purpose was the "Marines' Hymn." The music appears to have been from an aria entitled "Genevieve de Brabant" in the opera composed by Jacques Offenbach (1819–1880) of France. As the reference in the first line of the song to "the Halls of Montezuma" suggest, the song appears to have originated in the U.S. war with Mexico in 1846–1848. The officer who wrote the song has not been identified, but it has been used as the U.S. Marines anthem since 1929.

In addition to highlighting the many places in which the marines have fought (Mexico, Tripoli, "far-off Northern lands," and "sunny tropic scenes)," the hymn expresses obvious pride in this branch of the armed forces. Each of the three stanzas closes with the name of the branch. The last branch, undoubtedly written in the spirit of rivalry observes that:

> If the Army and the Navy
> Ever look on Heaven's scenes.
> They will find the streets are guarded
> By the United States Marines.

Much as in "The Star-Spangled Banner," the beginning of the second verse claims that "Our flag's unfurled to every breeze," but the flag is probably that of the corps itself (American forces initially fought under regimental colors more frequently than they did the U.S. flag). Like "The Star-Spangled Banner," the song evokes both "dawn" and "setting sun."

The U.S. Navy's "Anchors Aweigh" anthem appears to have been the second of the service hymns to be written. Composed by Lieutenant Charles A. Zimmerman (1861–1916), a U.S. Navy bandmaster, and Midshipman Alfred Hart Miles (1883–1956), it was initially designed as a fight song in 1906 to inspire the football team of the U.S. Naval Academy in its annual game against the U.S. Army team from West Point, and to honor the class of 1907. The image of "anchors aweigh" is that of pulling up the anchor to be ready for action. Consistent with its origins, the initial verse urged the army to "steer shy," as navy rolled up the score to "Sink the Army, sink the Army grey!"

These lyrics were revised by George D. Lottman in 1926 to caution the "vicious foe" to steer shy. A further change made by John Hagan in 1997 changed the lines "Farewell to college joys," which would not be applicable to all members of the navy, to "Farewell to foreign shores." The song does not contain any direct reference to the U.S flag.

Although the U.S. Army was established in 1775, its anthem was not written until more than a century later. "The Army Goes Rolling Along," which was originally known as "The Caisson Song," actually arose during the American occupation of the Philippines, which it gained from Spain as a result of the Spanish-American War of 1898. Composed by Lieutenant Edmund L. "Snitz" Gruber (1879–1941), who during a long march heard an officer shout, "Come on! Keep 'em rolling!" to those who were pulling a caisson (a field cart), the lyrics were especially adaptable to marching.

The first verse of the song identifies the army as:

First to fight for the right,
And to build the nation's might
And the Army goes rolling along.

The second verse identifies with "Valley Forge, Custer's ranks, San Juan Hill and Patton's tanks," with the next verse providing further allusions to the suffering at Valley Forge. Although none of the verses refer specifically to the U.S. or U.S. Army flags, the last verse ends with:

Faith in God, then we're right,
And we'll fight with all our might,
As the Army keeps rolling along.

Captain Francis S. Van Boskerck (1868–1927) wrote the words to the U.S. Coast Guard hymn "Semper Paratus," meaning "always ready," aboard a ship outside Savannah, Georgia, in 1922. He wrote the music while stationed in the Aleutian Islands five years later.

Although the Coast Guard is probably most frequently associated with coastal defense, the opening lines of their anthem cite locations "From Aztec shore to Arctic zone, to Europe and Fair East." In what appears to be a direct reference to the American flag, the second line further notes, "The Flag is carried by our ships in times of war and peace."

A second verse cites the names of various ships that the Coast Guard has commanded. The third verse is most clearly tied to the song's title:

Aye, we've been "Always Ready,"
To do, to fight, or die
Write glory to the shield we wear,
In letters to the sky.
To sink the foe or saved the maimed,

Our mission and our pride,
We'll carry on 'til Kingdom Come,
Ideals for which we've died.

Similarly, the last two lines of the chorus proclaim:

"Semper Paratus" is our guide,
Our fame, our glory too,
To fight to save or fight and die!
Aye! Coast Guard we are for you!

The last of the military songs to be written for a branch of the armed forces was submitted as part of a contest sponsored by *Liberty* magazine to find a song for the U.S. Army Air Corps, which eventually became the U.S. Air Force. It was selected from more than 750 entries and written by Robert MacArthur Crawford (1899–1961), a graduate of Princeton University and a teacher at the Juillard School of Music who was known as "The Flying Baritone" for flying around the country to give concerts.

The most distinctive lines of the song are probably the first two:

Off we go into the wild blue yonder,
    Climbing high into the sun.

The first verse also refers to "one helluva roar," which radio and television stations often changed to "terrible roar" instead (Corbeil 2017).

Although "The Air Force Song" exalts in flight, and identifies the atmosphere as "the wild blue yonder," it does not refer to the "stars and stripes" or any other common appellations for the U.S. flag. In 1971, Air Force Colonel David R. Scott and Lieutenant Colonel James B. Irwin carried the first page of Crawford's score to the moon aboard Apollo 15 (Corbeil 2017).

In addition to individual service songs, soldiers have often been inspired by more popular tunes that they share in common not only with the other services but with the American people. "Yankee Doodle" and "Battle Hymn of the Republic" have been among the most popular. "Dixie" was an inspiration to soldiers fighting for the Confederacy in the Civil War.

See also: "Battle Hymn of the Republic"; Confederate National Anthem; War and the National Anthem; "Yankee Doodle."

Further Reading

Arlt, Gustave O., and Chandler Harris. 1944. "Songs of the Services." *California Folklore Quarterly* 3 (January): 36–49.

Concannon, Mike. n.d. "US Armed Forces Service Songs & Lyrics." Military Officers Association of America, Western New York Chapter. http://wnymoaa.org/index_htm_files/Service%20Songs%20and%20History.pdf.

Corbeil, Shannon. 2017. "7 Air Force Song Facts That Will Make You Want to Go Off into the Wild Blue Yonder." *We Are the Mighty*, September 19. https://www.wearethemighty.com/music/7-air-force-song-facts-that-will-make-you-want-to-go-off-into-the-wild-blue-yonder.

"Memorial Day Music Class: The History of Armed Service Songs." 2014. *Musicnotes* (blog), May 25. https://www.musicnotes.com/blog/2014/05/25/armed-service-songs.

U.S. Department of Veterans Affairs. n.d. "Celebrating America's Freedom: Military Songs Inspire Troops, Preserve Tradition." https://www.va.gov/opa/publications /celebrate/militarysongs.pdf.

Sonneck, Oscar George Theodore

Much of what we know about "The Star-Spangled Banner" and other patriotic American songs is the work of generations of scholars, many of whom worked prior to the time when few Americans understood the importance of such studies.

One of the most important of these scholars was Oscar George Theodore Sonneck (1873–1928). Although he was born in the United States, he went to Germany as a child and received most of his musical education there. In addition to attending the University of Heidelberg and the University of Munich, he received private instruction from a number of leading musicians, after which he did some research at libraries in Italy before returning to the United States.

After Sonneck offered to the Library of Congress his *Bibliography of Early Secular American Music* (1905), which he had largely compiled through research into multiple newspapers, he made such an impression that even though he ended up privately publishing the piece (later republished in 1945), he was offered a job as chief of its music division. He held this position from 1902 to 1917. He was credited with creating one of the most important music collections in the world. Moreover, the library published his *Report on "The Star-Spangled Banner," "Hail Columbia," "America," "Yankee Doodle"* (1909), which remains a standard in the field, as well as his subsequent revised and enlarged edition of the section on "The Star-Spangled Banner" (Kinkeldey 1953, 30). Sonneck published numerous books that also established him as an expert on American opera and on German composer Ludwig van Beethoven. A review of Sonneck's work on American patriotic songs, which notes how such songs are often "enshrouded in pseudo-history or in absolute fiction" credited him with the ability to sift "the false from the true" and with having "cleared the field of its many errors" (Elson 1910, 625).

In 1917, Rudolph Schirmer, a music publisher, hired Sonneck as its director of publications, where he helped launch *The Musical Quarterly*, which remains influential within the field of musicology. In time, he was promoted to vice-president of the company.

See also: Scholarship.

Further Reading

Elson, Louis C. 1910. "Report on 'The Star-Spangled Banner,' 'Hail Columbia,' 'America,' 'Yankee Doodle' by Oscar George Theodore Sonneck." *American Historical Review* 15 (April): 625–26.

Kinkeldey, Otto. 1953. "Oscar George Theodore Sonneck (1873–1928)." *Notes* 11 (December): 25–32.

"Oscar George Theodore Sonneck." 1936. In *Dictionary of American Biography*. New York: Charles Scribner's Sons.

Sousa, John Philip

Few individuals have been more influential in the history of American music, and especially that of marching tunes, than composer and conductor John Philip Sousa (1854–1932), a consummate performer who is often dubbed "The March King." After having left the U.S. Marine Band, which he had joined in his youth in 1868, he returned to conduct the band in 1880 before forming his own in 1892 and leading performances throughout the United States and the world. In addition to his many other works, he wrote and composed "The Stars and Stripes Forever," which has been designated as America's national march.

Motivated by a desire to promote standardization in the way that Americans welcomed foreign dignitaries, in 1889 Navy Secretary Benjamin Franklin Tracy ordered Sousa to compose a collection of patriotic tunes. Sousa subsequently produced a collection entitled *National Patriotic and Typical Airs of All Lands*. He produced a version for voice and piano and another for bands, and it quickly became "the first widely recognized version of the piece" (Warfield 2018, 271). Sousa had previously written an orchestral fantasia *The International Congress*, which included "The Star-Spangled Banner," "Yankee Doodle," and other tunes, for the centennial of the Declaration of Independence in Philadelphia in 1876.

Complaining to the *New York Times* in 1889 that "Yankee Doodle" was set to a foreign tune that was difficult to sing, he said that "when our national anthem is written it will have to be within an octave and to have a swing and dash about it which will commend it to even the most unmusical persons" (Warfield 2018, 277). In 1891, he was further quoted by the *Daily Nebraska State Journal* as favoring "Hail Columbia" over "The Star-Spangled Banner" (276). In 1909, however, Sousa incorporated the theme of "The Star-Spangled Banner" into his operetta entitled *The Glassblowers*, which was also known as *The American Maid* (Mattfeld 1919, 30) and centered on a couple who had united in their fight against Spain in the Spanish-American War (Winship 2002).

During World War I, Sousa was appointed to a committee with the task to create a standardized version of "The Star-Spangled Banner." This task ultimately proved to be a hopeless endeavor due to differences of opinion within the committee. By this time, however, Sousa had changed his mind about the song's suitability as a national anthem. He told the Philadelphia *Inquirer* in August 1917 that "I have played [The] Star Spangled Banner in nearly every country on the earth . . . and if the American people could have witnessed all the remarkable demonstrations over it as I have, there would not be any complaint about this music or any demand for a new national anthem" (Warfield 2018, 306–7). In July 1918 he told a newspaper in Dayton, Ohio, "We salute only one flag, and we should rise for only one song. . . . Just as a man should have but one sweetheart, so we should keep 'The Star Spangled Banner' sacred above all other songs of our country" (Warfield 2018, 307). When German-born conductor Karl Muck became involved in a controversy over his willingness to play "The Star-Spangled Banner," Sousa was quoted by the *Detroit Journal* on November 19, 1917, as saying, "He had better get back to Germany where he belongs" (Warfield 2018, 308). During the late 1920s, Sousa became more ambivalent about designating Key's famous song as the national anthem, but advocates of adopting "The Star-Spangled Banner" continued to cite him as a supporter (Warfield 2018, 307n85). It helped that Sousa refused to lobby for his own song, "The Stars and Stripes Forever," a piece that was sometimes mentioned as a candidate for national anthem status.

See also: German-American Composers during World War I; "Hail Columbia"; "Star-Spangled Banner, The," Official Version; "Stars and Stripes Forever, The."

Further Reading
Mattfeld, Julius. 1919. "The Use of Some National Anthems in Music." *Art & Life* 11 (July): 27–30.

Warfield, Patrick. 2018. "Educators in Search of an Anthem: Standardizing 'The Star-Spangled Banner' during the First World War." *Journal of the Society for American Music* 12:268–316.

Winship, Frederick M. 2002. "Forgotten John Philip Sousa Opera Revived." *United Press Internationl,* April 29. https://www.upi.com/Forgotten-John-Philip-Sousa-opera -revived/91571020085200.

Sports Events

Other than learning about the national anthem in school, more Americans probably hear the singing or playing of "The Star-Spangled Banner" at sports events than at any other venue. Some scholars have even classified such events as "quasi-religious rituals" that "are uniquely constitutive of American national identity" (Butterworth 2005, 108). Moreover, sports are often associated with key American values, including physical conditioning, teamwork, meritocracy, and sportsmanship (Kaufman and Wolff 2010), with which the flag might be appropriately associated.

Although Congress did not specifically designate "The Star-Spangled Banner" as the national anthem until 1931, the military had been using the song for ceremonial occasions since 1893. Attention to the song that now serves as the national anthem stems in large part from its close association with the American flag. Just as the anthem was born from Francis Scott Key's anxiety over whether he would continue to see the flag after the Battle of Baltimore during the War of 1812, so too the identification of the flag with the Union was cemented during the Civil War, and again heightened during the Spanish-American War and subsequent world wars.

Early performances of "The Star-Spangled Banner" at sports events often coincided with war or threats of war. The first documented occasion where "The Star-Spangled Banner" was played at a professional sporting event was a May 15, 1862, baseball game in Brooklyn, New York (Clague 2015, 146). In a development that has been tied to patriotism generated by the Spanish-American War, the opening day of the 1896 baseball season at the New York City Polo Grounds was also marked by a band performance of "The Star-Spangled Banner" (Guenter 1990, 167).

The 1903 World Series pitted Boston against Pittsburgh. The band hired by the Boston team played such patriotic songs as "The Star-Spangled Banner" in part to

In 2018, members of the Colorado Rockies stand at attention for the American national anthem at a spring training Major League Baseball game at Salt River Fields stadium in Scottsdale, Arizona. (Carol M. Highsmith Archive, Library of Congress, Prints and Photographs Division, Library of Congress)

highlight the team's designation as the "Boston Americans" or "Amerks" (Clague 2015, 146). Playing the anthem at professional games became fairly standard practice during World Wars I and II, and by 1931 was also apparently a fairly standard feature of most college games (Phillips 1931, 137).

The idea of playing the anthem before every game actually originated with hockey, where the practice of playing both the American and Canadian anthems became standard practice whenever teams from the two countries met (Clague 2015, 220). Perhaps the idea was also fueled by the Olympics, which began playing the national anthem of the gold winner for each event in 1924—a practice that was unsuccessfully challenged in 1968 by Prince George William of Hanover, who thought that it promoted undue nationalism (Murtha 2018).

Conductor Jerry Blackstone observes that the practice of having "The Star-Spangled Banner" performed before each game required "two technologies to make it economically feasible: recording and loud speaker" (2014, 11). Prior to these developments, performances were typically by bands.

After Japan surrendered to the United States at the end of World War II, Elmer Layden, the commissioner of the National Football League (NFL), favored continuation of the practice and said, "The national anthem should be as much a part of every game as the kickoff" (Barker 2017). The beginning of the Cold War with the Soviet Union that almost immediately followed World War II, undoubtedly provided motive for continuing a tradition that was thought to foster patriotism.

Not all were convinced, however. In a January 1955 issue of *Sports Illustrated*, novelist William Faulkner openly wondered:

> Just what a professional hockey-match, whose purpose is to make a decent and reasonable profit for its owners, had to do with our National Anthem. What are we afraid of? Is it our national character of which we are so in doubt, so fearful that it might not hold up in the clutch, that we not only dare not open a professional athletic contest or a beauty-pageant or a real-estate auction, but we must even use a Chamber of Commerce race for Miss Sewage Disposal or a wildcat land-sale, to remind us that liberty gained without honor and sacrifice and held without constant vigilance and undiminished honors and complete willingness to sacrifice at need, was not worth having to begin with? (Wilson 2016)

Recent years have witnessed controversies over both how the anthem is performed and how team members react to it. Canadian-born Robert Goulet was critiqued for flubbing the lines at a heavyweight boxing title match in Lewiston, Maine, in 1965; Jose Feliciano's folk rendition of the tune was questioned in 1969; Marvin Gaye's performance at an NBA All-Star Game was criticized in 1983; and Roseanne Barr's parody of the anthem at a game in 1990, which included grabbing her crotch and spitting, was so crass that it became known as the "Barr-Bungled" or "Barr-Mangled Banner" (Ferris 2014, 242). At Super Bowl XLV in 2011, pop singer Christina Aguilera flubbed some of the lines by singing, "What so proudly we watched / At the twilight's last reaming."

In 1950, a Guatemalan military band, attempting to emphasize its anti-colonialism, played the dance tune "La Borinquena" instead of "The Star-Spangled Banner," when the Puerto Rican color guard took its place at the Central American Olympic Games. After American protests, the band played the American national anthem after Puerto Rican athletes won the high jump (Svejda 2005, 427–28).

In 1968, African American track stars, Tommie Smith and John Carlos, who had respectively won gold and silver medals, defiantly raised their fists in a Black Power salute during the playing of the U.S. national anthem at Mexico City, and were subsequently ousted from the Games. They were not protected by the First Amendment because the penalty was not inflicted by the government (Paulson 2017). Similarly the Olympics barred track stars Vince Matthews and Wayne Collett from the Munich games in 1972 after they neither faced the flag nor appeared to be at attention.

In the 1970s, the Philadelphia Flyers hockey team began alternating the playing of "The Star-Spangled Banner" and "God Bless America" at their games, with many players and fans believing that the latter brought them better luck.

In 1996, Mahmoud Abdul-Rauf of the Denver Nuggets basketball team was heavily criticized after refusing to stand for the national anthem, which he believed conflicted with his Islamic beliefs (Ferris 2014, 245). Similar criticism followed the decision in 2016 of African American quarterback Colin Kaepernick, of the San Francisco 49ers, to take a knee during the playing of the national anthem as a way to protest racism in American society. This movement, led by players who were particularly concerned about reports of unarmed blacks being killed in confrontations with police officers, spread to a number of teams. In September 2017,

President Trump further roiled the waters when he asked: "Wouldn't you love to see one of these NFL owners, when somebody disrespects our flag, to say 'Get that son of a bitch off the field right now. Out! He's fired. He's fired!'" (Paulson 2017). In part because of Kaepernick's choice to take a knee, rather than raise a fist, he also had his defenders. Even though he was unable to get his contract renewed or find a new position within the NFL, Nike, best known for its sports-related tennis shoes, decided to feature Kaepernick in its "Just Do It" advertising campaign in 2018. The advertisement featured his picture and the words: "Believe in something. Even if it means sacrificing everything" (Cobb 2018). Reactions to the decision were mixed, with at least one writer questioning whether playing the national anthem at such events was necessary and suggesting that "leisure needs no patriotic commendation, and when we kick off a sporting event in the same manner as a graduation ceremony at the Air Force Academy, perspective is lost" (Fleming 2018).

In addition to the playing of the national anthem, many sports events have included flyovers, the display of huge flags, flying eagles, and the use of other patriotic symbols. In a variant of "pay to play," in 2015 Senators John McCain and Jeff Flake, both from Arizona, revealed that the Department of Defense had spent $6.8 million between 2012 and 2015 to sponsor patriotic events at professional sports games, which seemed to call the sincerity of some of these events into question (Kight 2017).

In recent years, a number of critics have complained that the version of "The Star-Spangled Banner" that has been played at the Olympics and other international games has been subpar, substituting minor for major chords. This version was apparently altered, along with many other such anthems, by Philip Sheppard of the London Philharmonic Orchestra prior to the 2012 London games, in part to shorten each of them to seventy seconds or less (Segal 2016).

See also: Advertising; Congress and "The Star-Spangled Banner"; "God Bless America"; Kaepernick, Colin; Olympic Protest (1968); Olympic Protest (1972); War and the National Anthem; World Wars I and II.

Further Reading

Barbash, Fred, and Travis M. Andrews. 2016. "A Brief History of 'The Star-Spangled Banner' Being Played at Games and Getting No Respect." *Washington Post*, August 30. https://www.washingtonpost.com/news/morning-mix/wp/2016/08/30/a-brief-history-of-the-star-spangled-banner-being-played-at-games-and-getting-no-respect.

Barker, Barbara. 2017. "National Anthem: Why We Play It Before We Play." *Newsday*, September 30. https://www.newsday.com/sports/columnists/barbara-barker/national-anthem-why-we-sing-it-before-we-play-1.14307117.

Bass, Amy. 2002. *Not the Triumph But the Struggle: The 1968 Olympics and the Making of the Black Athlete.* Minneapolis: University of Minnesota Press.

Blackstone, Jerry, Mark Clague, and Andrew Thomas Kuster. 2014. "A Star-Spangled Bicentennial: A Conversation with Jerry Blackstone, Mark Clague, and Andrew Kuster." *Choral Journal* 54 (April): 6–17.

Butterworth, Michael L. 2005. "Ritual in the 'Church of Baseball': Suppressing the Discourse of Democracy after 9/11." *Communication and Critical/Cultural Studies* 2:107–29.

Clague, Mark, and Andrew Kuster, eds. 2015. *Star Spangled Songbook: A History in Sheet Music of "The Star-Spangled Banner."* Ann Arbor, MI: Star Spangled Music Foundation.

Cobb, Jelani. 2018. "Behind Nike's Decision to Stand by Colin Kaepernick." *New Yorker*, September 4. https://www.newyorker.com/news/daily-comment/behind-nikes-decision-to-stand-by-colin-kaepernick.

Duffy, Thomas. 2016. "Man Sings National Anthem While Painting Patriotic Picture before ECHL Game." *Bleacher Report*, October 23. https://bleacherreport.com/articles/2671342-man-sings-national-anthem-while-painting-patriotic-picture-before-echl-game.

Epstein, Adam. 2011. "Religion and Sports in the Undergraduate Classroom: A Surefire Way to Spark Student Interest." *Southern Law Journal* 21:133–47.

Ferris, Marc. 2014. *Star-Spangled Banner: The Unlikely Story of America's National Anthem*. Baltimore: Johns Hopkins University Press.

Fleming, Colin. 2018. "NFL Should Just Dump the National Anthem and Get on with Playing Football." *USA Today*, August 2. https://www.msn.com/en-us/sports/nfl/nfl-should-just-dump-the-national-anthem-and-get-on-with-playing-football/ar-BBLorK1.

Friedersdorf, Conor. 2017. "Kneeling for Life and Liberty Is Patriotic." *Atlantic*, September 26. https://www.theatlantic.com/politics/archive/2017/09/kneeling-for-life-and-liberty-is-patriotic/540942.

Guenter, Scot M. 1990. *The American Flag, 1777–1924: Cultural Shifts from Creation to Codification*. Cranbury, NJ: Associated University Presses.

Kaufman, Peter, and Eli A. Wolff. 2010. "Playing and Protesting: Sport as a Vehicle for Social Change." *Journal of Sport and Social Issues* 34 (2): 154–75.

Kight, Stef W. 2017. "The History of Singing the National Anthem before NFL Games." Axios, September 26. https://www.axios.com/the-history-of-singing-the-national-anthem-before-nfl-games-1513305769-97a4edd0-6748-432d-b1cc-2b377848e712.html.

Kooijman, Jaap. 2013. *Fabricating the Absolute Fake: America in Contemporary Pop Culture*. Amsterdam, Holland: Amsterdam University Press.

Molotsky, Irvin. 2001. *The Flag, the Poet and the Song: The Story of the Star-Spangled Banner*. New York: Dutton.

Murtha, Ryan. 2018. "An Olympics without Anthems." *Slate*, February 7. https://slate.com/culture/2018/02/fifty-years-ago-the-olympics-almost-banned-national-anthems-and-flags.html.

Paulson, Ken. 2017. "NFL Protests: Your Boss Can Tell You to Stand for the Anthem. Trump Can't." *First Amendment Encyclopedia*, Free Speech Center, Middle Tennessee State University, October 2. https://mtsu.edu/first-amendment/post/57/nfl-protests-your-boss-can-tell-you-to-stand-for-the-anthem-trump-can-t.

Phillips, Robert. 1931. *The American Flag: Its Uses and Abuses*. Boston: Stratford.

Segal, David. 2016. "At Rio Olympics, the National Anthem Sounds . . . Sad?" *New York Times*, August 11. https://www.nytimes.com/2016/08/12/sports/olympics/usa-national-anthem-rio-games.html.

Sherr, Lynn. 2001. *America the Beautiful: The Stirring True Story Behind Our Nation's Favorite Song*. New York: Public Affairs.

Spiegel, Allen D., and Marc B. Spiegel. 1998. "Redundant Patriotism: The United States National Anthem as an Obligatory Sports Ritual." *Culture, Sport, Society* 1 (1): 24–43.

Staples, Brent. 2018. "African-Americans and the Strains of the National Anthem." *New York Times*, June 9. https://www.nytimes.com/2018/06/09/opinion/african-americans-national-anthem-protests.html.

Svejda, George J. 2005. *History of the Star Spangled Banner from 1814 to the Present.* Honolulu, HI: University Press of the Pacific. First published in 1969 by Division of History, Office of Archeology and Historic Preservation, U.S. Department of the Interior, National Park Service.

Vile, John R. 2018. *The American Flag: An Encyclopedia of the Stars and Stripes in U.S. History, Culture, and Law.* Santa Barbara, CA: ABC-CLIO.

Wilson, Clyde. 2016. "Allegiances." *Abbeville Blog*, Abbeville Institute, September 28. https://www.abbevilleinstitute.org/blog/allegiances.

Star Spangled Music Foundation

The Star Spangled Music Foundation, is a 501(c)(3) nonprofit charitable association that a group of musicians and educators created on September 14, 2012, in anticipation of the bicentennial anniversary of the composition of the song by Francis Scott Key. Its website, updated in November 2015 after it had sponsored its Star-Spangled Music Day the previous September 12, lists its purpose as fostering "deeper understanding of the historical and cultural significance of music in the political dialogue of the United States through scholarly research, education, performance, and media."

The organization has published a songbook entitled the *Star Spangled Songbook*. It has also produced a CD entitled *Poets & Patriots: A Tuneful History of "The Star-Spangled Banner,"* with thirty-seven different tracks of patriotic songs. The association offers an exhibit on the national anthem entitled "Banner Moments" for displays at schools, libraries, and museums. The foundation also serves as a platform for a blog that includes a list of "mythconceptions" about "The Star-Spangled Banner," authored by Mark Clague, who is a musicologist at the University of Michigan.

See also: Clague, Mark.

Further Reading

Hawkins, Sydney. 2016. "U-M Professor Debunks Famous 'Star-Spangled Banner' Myths." *Michigan News*, June 30. https://arts.umich.edu/news-features/star-spangled-banner-mythconceptions-series-debunks-famous-rumors.

Star Spangled Music Foundation. n.d. "About." http://starspangledmusic.org/sample-page.

Star-Spangled Banner Flag

When a U.S. flag is present, protocol specifies that individuals should turn toward this flag during the playing or singing of "The Star-Spangled Banner." Although this term has thus become one of several designations for the U.S. flag, when Francis Scott Key wrote "The Star-Spangled Banner," he was

In 1914, the flag flown over Fort McHenry during the war of 1812 was put on display at the Smithsonian Castle, Washington, DC, in celebration of the one hundredth anniversary of the Battle of Baltimore. It is now on display in the National Museum of American History. (Library of Congress)

recalling the specific flag that he saw waving over Fort McHenry on the dawn of September 14, 1814.

That flag, which is arguably America's most sacred object, had been commissioned by Major George Armistead, who commanded the fort during the British bombardment. He had ordered it from a local flag maker by the name of Mary Young Pickersgill. Designed to make a clear statement to the British and any other foreign intruders, it was originally thirty by forty-two feet (its length is now ten feet shorter because of early souvenir hunters). Consistent with the most recent legislation on the subject, it had both fifteen stars and fifteen stripes, thus recognizing the entry of Kentucky and Vermont into the Union. Although Tennessee, Ohio, and Louisiana had also entered, legislation had not yet been passed to add stars to the flag in recognition of their statehoods.

The flag that Key is believed to have observed being illumined by the bursting rockets and bombs during the night of September 13–14 was probably a smaller storm flag, still formidable at seventeen by twenty-five feet, that would better have been able to withstand the heavy winds and storms of the Atlantic coast. The flag that he observed on the morning of September 14, though, would have been the larger one that the Americans would have flown as the British attackers sailed away.

This larger flag was passed down through the Armistead family. It was displayed on a few special occasions, such as the visit by the Marquis de Lafayette (the Frenchman who had fought beside Americans during the Revolutionary War) to Baltimore in 1824, a visit by president-elect William Henry Harrison in 1841, and on annual Defenders' Day celebrations. Unfortunately, it was common for a number of years following the war to cut out pieces of the flag to give out as souvenirs, including one of the giant stars, the whereabouts of which is still unknown. Armistead's wife, Louisa, had also sewn a red chevron in the shape of the letter A on one of the white stripes near the bottom of the flag (Vile 2018, 301).

Armistead's daughter, Georgiana Armistead Appleton, sent the flag to George Henry Preble, a prominent scholar of the flag. He had canvas backing stitched to it to help preserve it. The first known photograph was taken of the flag in 1873 as it hung from the side of a building in the Boston Naval Yard. After taking a trip to the Centennial Celebration in Philadelphia in 1876, the flag was returned to Georgiana, whose son, Eben Appleton, kept it locked in a safe before loaning it to the Smithsonian Institution in 1907, and then gifting it to the Smithsonian in 1912. The Smithsonian subsequently commissioned Amelia Flower of Boston and her assistants to add a linen backing that required 1.7 million stitches. It was long displayed in a case in the Arts and Industries Building in Washington, DC, before being transported to a warehouse outside Luray, Virginia, for safekeeping in 1942. It was returned to the capital in 1944.

The Smithsonian transferred the flag to the Museum of History and Technology (today's National Museum of American History) in 1964, where it was displayed vertically until 1998. After this, it underwent years of painstaking and expensive restoration, largely financed by designer Ralph Lauren, that included removing the flag backing that Amelia had added and replacing it with a lighter polyester material known as Stabiltex. It is currently displayed in dim light at the Smithsonian in a largely horizontal position.

See also: Armistead, George; Pickersgill, Mary Young.

Further Reading
Grove, Tim. "Mary, Not Betsy." In *A Grizzly in the Mail and Other Adventures in American History*, 73–87. Lincoln: University of Nebraska Press.

Hatchett, Louis, and W. K. McNeil. 2005. "There's a Star-Spangled Banner Waving Somewhere." In *Country Music Goes to War*, edited by Charles K. Wolfe and James E. Akenson, 33–42. Lexington: University Press of Kentucky.

Poole, Robert M. 2008. "Star-Spangled Banner Back on Display." *Smithsonian Magazine* (November). http://www.smithsonianmag.com/history/star-spangled-banner-back -on-display-83229098.

Svejda, George J. 2005. *History of the Star Spangled Banner from 1814 to the Present*. Honolulu, HI: University Press of the Pacific. First published in 1969 by Division of History, Office of Archeology and Historic Preservation, U.S. Department of the Interior, National Park Service.

Taylor, Lonn. 2000. *The Star-Spangled Banner: The Flag That Inspired the National Anthem*. New York: National Museum of American History, Smithsonian Institution, in association with Harry N. Abrahms.

Taylor, Lonn, Kathleen M. Kendrick, and Jeffrey L. Brodie. 2008. *The Star-Spangled Banner: The Making of an American Icon.* New York: Smithsonian Institution in conjunction with HarperCollins.

Vile, John R. 2018. *The American Flag: An Encyclopedia of the Stars and Stripes in U.S. History, Culture, and Law.* Santa Barbara, CA: ABC-CLIO.

Wu, Corinna. 1999. "Old Glory, New Glory: The Star-Spangled Banner Gets Some Tender Loving Care." *Science News* 144 (June 16): 408–10.

Star-Spangled Banner Flag House

In the popular mind, many Americans closely associate the American flag itself with Francis Scott Key's "The Star-Spangled Banner," which has since 1931 officially served as the U.S. national anthem.

Thus, although one might expect that the house located at 844 E. Pratt Street in Baltimore, Maryland, and designated as the Star-Spangled Banner Flag House might be that of Francis Scott Key, who authored the anthem, it instead commemorates the home and business of flag maker Mary Pickersgill. She was the seamstress who created the huge flag that Key saw from the ramparts of Fort McHenry the morning after the British had attacked it during the War of 1812.

This house in Baltimore, Maryland, was the home of Mary Young Pickersgill, who in 1813 sewed the flag that flew over Fort McHenry during the Battle of Baltimore. (Library of Congress)

Pickersgill, who lived in the house from 1806 until her death in 1857, is believed to have been helped in making that famous flag by both her daughter, Mary, and Grace Wisher, an African American indentured servant.

Purchased by the city of Baltimore in 1929, the house has been designated as a National Historic Landmark. In 1953, Baltimore built a one-and-a-half story building behind the house for a museum.

See also: Francis Scott Key House; Key, Francis Scott; Pickersgill, Mary Young.

Further Reading

Miller, Marla R. 2018. "The U.S. Flag in America's Historic-House Museums." In *The American Flag: An Encyclopedia of the Stars and Stripes in U.S. History, Culture, and Law*, 19–32. Santa Barbara, CA: ABC-CLIO.

National Park Service. 2019. "Star-Spangled Banner Flag House." Last updated July 17, 2019. https://www.nps.gov/places/star-spangled-banner-flag-house.htm.

Star-Spangled Banner Pageant

Although many of the events surrounding the centennial of the writing of "The Star-Spangled Banner" were concentrated in Baltimore, Maryland, they were not limited to this vicinity. In October 1914, residents of Madison, Wisconsin, held a pageant at Capitol Park in which they recounted the events that had led to the composition of the song.

The pageant consisted of seven episodes, most of which were recreated fairly accurately, as to the story of Francis Scott Key's experiences during the British shelling of Fort McHenry in September 1814—experiences that inspired him to write the song that eventually became America's national anthem. The pageant featured the singing of numerous songs from both the English and American sides and included a living flag featuring hundreds of school children. It also featured an individual playing the role of Francis Scott Key who read the first stanza of his anthem, as well as symbolic figures dressed as "Columbia, Liberty, Peace, Justice, Law and Progress with her spirits History, Art, Music, Literature, Science, Invention, and Commerce" (Rockwell 1914, 35, 37). It ended as representatives of various industries in Madison followed the living flag as they sang "The Star-Spangled Banner" and marched from the grounds (39).

As in naturalization ceremonies, the pageant seemed designed in part to make sure that immigrants shared in the new national identity. Thus, as children came on stage dressed in costumes of their native countries and doing a folk dance, they clasped hands in what one historian described as a symbolic gesture emphasizing "that in America the German, the English, the French, the Irish, the Italian, the Greek, the Jew, the Norwegian, the Swede, and all other nationalities represented, have become united into the American with all of the old-world prejudices forgotten" (Rockwell 1914, 37).

See also: Children; Immigrants.

Further Reading
Rockwell, Ethel T. 1914. *Star-Spangled Banner Pageant: Staged in the Capitol Park at Madison, Wisconsin, in Celebration of the One-Hundredth Anniversary of the Writing of This National Song by Francis Scott Key.* N.p.: Ethel Theodora Rockwell.

"Star-Spangled Banner, The," Official Version

Although the official U.S. flag has not varied in pattern since Hawaii entered the Union as the fiftieth state in 1960, artists like Jasper Johns and others have continued to portray the flag in unique ways. So too, musical artists have experimented with "The Star-Spangled Banner." And even as "The Star-Spangled Banner" became the official anthem of the United States in 1931, early printings varied, and the resolution itself did not specify which such variant was the "official" one. Nor has it done so to this day.

There have been at least two major efforts to devise a standardized, or official, version of "The Star-Spangled Banner." The first was prompted when Elsie M. Shawe, the director of music for the St. Paul Public Schools, wrote to President Theodore Roosevelt in 1907 asking for a national edition of the song. This desire for standardization was a product of the Progressive movement as well as the mass singing movement, which was aimed at building citizenship through such renditions (Warfield 2018, 280–82).

Shawe's note helped inspire Oscar Sonneck's significant compilation of a history of various patriotic tunes (1909). In the meantime the National Education Association (NEA) appointed a committee in 1908 to draw up a resolution of "the Uniformity of National Songs"; the committee consisted of Shawe, Arnold Gantvoort, and Powell G. Fithian. This resolution in turn resulted in the creation of another committee that consisted of Gantvoort (as chair), Shawe, and Osbourne McConathy, who supervised music in the public schools of Chelsea, Massachusetts. After this committee split, a ten-person committee was established to pursue standardization efforts for songs associated with the nation's history. In the meantime, the National Conference of Music Supervisors printed a pamphlet entitled "18 Songs for Community Singing," which had been compiled by a committee chaired by Peter W. Dykema at the University of Wisconsin (Warfield 2018, 288, 291).

In time, the NEA appointed yet another committee consisting of Will Earnhart (chair), Arnold Gantvoort, Oscar Sonneck, John Philip Sousa, and Walter Damrosch (Warfield 2018, 296). This committee took existing arrangements of "The Star-Spangled Banner" and attempted to come up with a consensus version that was largely completed by Damrosch. Subject to intense criticism, this version seemed to point to the futility of the entire process, and no officially sanctioned version was accepted.

It is not clear whether he knew about these earlier efforts or not, but in the 1950s, Congressman Joel Broyhill of Virginia proposed that Congress settle on an official version of the national anthem, and he notified the National Music Council

The original manuscript of Francis Scott Key's "The Star-Spangled Banner." (Library of Congress)

of his resolution. It set up a committee that attempted to focus on "the words, the melody, the rhythm, and the harmony" (Hill 1957, 34).

In looking at the words, the committee largely took its cue from the original manuscript that Key penned. The committee thought it was appropriate to keep his "O" in the opening line rather than the more formal "Oh," and to omit the explanation point that later editors had sometimes added after the word "say" (Hill 1957, 35). It believed that it was appropriate to replace Key's curlicue with an "and" rather than an ampersand and that it could substitute e's for the apostrophes in the words "hail'd" and "watch'd" (35). The committee also thought it was important in the last verse of the anthem to keep the original words "when our cause it is just," rather than, as some publishers had substituted, "since our cause is just" (35). It also recommended using the singular of rocket and bomb in line five of the first stanza rather than the more commonly used plural form and using the words "in the stream" rather than "on the stream" in verse two (35–36).

In addressing the melody, the committee followed suggestions of two earlier committees. Both had suggested beginning with a "descending triad" rather than with the initially published identical notes (Hill 1957, 37–38).

As to rhythm, it recommended following the Service Version of the song "in dotting the first quarter-note in the three repetitions" of "proudly we," "ramparts we," and "proof through the" (Hill 1957, 38–39). With regard to harmony, the committee concluded, "There seems to be no question that this should employ the traditional chord progressions of the 19th century" (40).

Dr. Mark Clague (2014), an associate professor of musicology at the University of Michigan School of Music, has observed that no standardized version has ever been adopted. Noting that the *Poets & Patriots* recording included thirty-seven different variants of the song, Clague said his takeaway was that "'The Star-Spangled Banner' must be performed with sincere and artful intent, not just repeated as a cliché."

As time has passed, and it has become increasingly common to perform the anthem at ball games, the anthem has become not only the subject of protest but also the object of very individualistic performances, a few of which have provoked considerable criticism by their deviations from more standard arrangements. Many scholars of the subject would probably agree with Warfield's view that "it is the flexibility of the national anthem that allows it to thrive" (2018, 312).

See also: Broyhill, Joel; Congress and "The Star-Spangled Banner"; Controversial Performances; Flubbed Performances.

Further Reading

Clague, Mark. 2014. "Spangled Mythconception #7: An Official Version of 'The Star-Spangled Banner' Exists." *Star Spangled Music*, June 14. Star Spangled Music Foundation. http://starspangledmusic.org/spangled-mythconception-7-an-official-version-of-the-star-spangled-banner-exists.

Hill, Richard S. 1957. "A Proposed Official Version of the Star Spangled Banner." *Notes* 14 (December): 33–42.

Sonneck, Oscar George Theodore (compiler). 1909. *Report on "The Star-Spangled Banner," "Hail Columbia," "America," "Yankee Doodle."* Washington, DC: Government Printing Office (Library of Congress).

Warfield, Patrick. 2018. "Educators in Search of an Anthem: Standardizing 'The Star-Spangled Banner' during the First World War." *Journal of the Society for American Music* 12:268–316.

Star-Spangled Banner: Anthem of Liberty

On Flag Day of 2014, David Clark Inc. and Blue Mountain Film Associates Inc. released a twenty-three-minute three-dimensional film that was distributed by Giant Screen Films and entitled *Star-Spangled Banner: Anthem of Liberty.* The film depicts the British bombardment of Fort McHenry that inspired Francis Scott Key to write "The Star-Spangled Banner."

The film, which debuted at the Maryland Science Center, was filmed using a reconstructed British war ship called the *Niagara* on Lake Erie, as well as modern computer graphics (Franciotti 2014). In justifying such computer-generated pyrotechnics, park ranger Vince Vaise noted, "It was a scientific bombardment, I mean with the British bombs and rockets, and you'll see those in the movie with the computer-generated graphics. Historically, those were the most scientifically advanced weapons of their age" (Franciotti 2014).

See also: "Bombs Bursting in Air"; "Rockets' Red Glare."

Further Reading

Franciotti, Jennifer. 2014. "200-Year-Old Battle Comes to Life on IMAX Screen." *WBAL TV11*, June 13. https://www.wbaltv.com/article/200-year-old-battle-comes-to-life -on-imax-screen/7087550#!ZLIgg.

Giant Screen Cinema Association. n.d. "Film Details: *Star-Spangled Banner: Anthem of Liberty.*" https://www.giantscreencinema.com/Films/Film-Database/FilmDatabase DetailView/movieid/2529.

Star-Spangled National Historic Trail

Although Fort McHenry and the Visitor and Education Center that serves as a focal point for tourists and scholars are well designed to explain the history of the fort during the War of 1812—and especially its pivotal role in spiriting Francis Scott Key to write "The Star-Spangled Banner"—the bombardment that Key witnessed was only a small part of the larger war with the British, much of which took place in the Chesapeake area. It had been preceded by British attacks on border cities and towns, the disastrous Battle of Bladensburg, the burning of the U.S. Capitol, and other events that are not so easily encapsulated within a single site or set of exhibits.

After Senator Paul Sarbanes introduced and Congress adopted the Star-Spangled Banner National Historic Trail Study Act of 1999, the National Park Service conducted an extensive feasibility study, which it published in 2004. In 2008, Congress designated a 560-mile land and water route encompassing sites in Maryland, Virginia, and the District of Columbia as a National Historic Trail to help visitors understand the wider war context in which Fort McHenry came under attack in September 1814. It is one of nineteen designated trails in the National Trails System, and one of only two in the mid-Atlantic region—the other being the Captain John Smith Chesapeake National Historic Trail. The trail enables visitors to trace the movements of both British and American troops and provides signs directing individuals to nearby historic sites, parks, and museums. It includes five National Historical Landmarks, four National Park Service parcels, thirty-seven properties on the National Register of Historic Sites, two National Natural Landmarks, and thirty-nine Chesapeake Bay "Gateways" (a collection of parks, museums, water trails, wildlife refuges, and other notable sites in the region).

See also: Fort McHenry; Fort McHenry Visitor and Education Center; War of 1812.

Further Reading

Brown, DeNeen L. 2004. "Star-Spangled Banner Historic Trail Follows War of 1812 Battles." *Washington Post*, June 19.

National Park Service. 2015. "Star-Spangled Banner National Historic Trail." Last updated March 1, 2015. https://www.nps.gov/stsp/learn/historyculture/index.htm.

National Park Service, Northeast Region. 2004. *Star-Spangled Banner National Historic Trail Feasibility Study and Environmental Impact Statement.* Philadelphia: U.S. Department of the Interior.

"Stars and Stripes Forever, The"

Although Congress designated "The Star-Spangled Banner" as the national anthem in 1931, in 1987 it also designated composer John Philip Sousa's "The Stars and Stripes Forever" as the nation's official march.

Few figures have had the impact on music, and especially military music, than the talented and charismatic John Philip Sousa. Born to a military family in 1854, Sousa joined the U.S. Marine Band in 1868, spent some time in a theatrical orchestra before becoming head of the band in 1880, where his high standards quickly made it one of the best in the nation. It became known as the President's Own Band. Sousa himself cut a striking figure with a full beard and mustache and a uniform bedecked with many medals. He became known as "The March King" and composed many of the band's marches, including "Semper Fidelis" (which would later become the official march of the U.S. Marines), "The Liberty Bell," "El Capitain," "The Washington Post," and many others.

In 1892, Sousa retired from the marine band and formed his own band, which was managed by his friend Robert Blakely. After a series of tours, Sousa decided to vacation in Europe with his wife in 1896 as the band continued playing under Blakely's leadership. While in Europe, however, he received a telegram informing him that Blakely had died. Sousa made plans to return to the United States to continue the band's scheduled tour. It was on this return journey that he developed the music that would become "The Stars and Stripes Forever." Sousa later explained the circumstances under which he composed the song:

> As the vessel steamed out of the harbor I was pacing the deck, absorbed in thoughts of my manager's death and the many duties and decisions which awaited me in New York. Suddenly, I began to sense the rhythmic beat of a band playing within my brain. It kept on ceaselessly, playing, playing, playing. Throughout the whole tense voyage, that imaginary band continued to unfold the same themes, echoing and re-echoing the most distinct melody. I did not transfer a note of that music to paper

while on the steamer, but when we reached shore, I set down the measures that my brain-band had been playing for me. (Warfield 2013, 264)

On his return, Sousa first wrote out a pencil version of "The Stars and Stripes Forever." He then put an ink version to paper that he dated Christmas Day of 1896.

The piece formally debuted in Philadelphia on May 14, 1897, although he had probably played it as an encore two weeks earlier at a band performance in Augusta, Maine (Warfield 2013, 264). A near instant success, at least in part because Sousa unveiled it at the beginning of the Spanish-American War, when patriotic sentiment was very high, the bandleader incorporated it into a "Grand International Spectacle" of band songs that he called the "Tropping of the Colors" (267). The tune became especially popular during World War I. A reviewer observed that the work was "stirring enough to rouse the American eagle from his crag and set him to shriek exultantly while he hurls his arrows at the aurora borealis" (267). It was the last song Sousa conducted on March 6, 1932, the day of his death (Collins 2003, 156).

Like "The Star-Spangled Banner" and "You're a Grand Old Flag," Sousa's song highlights the American flag, through which he hoped to unite all regions of the nation. The first verse proclaims:

> Let martial note in triumph float
> And liberty extend its mighty hand
> A flag appears 'mid thunderous cheers,
> The banner of the Western land.
> The emblem of the brave and true
> Its folds protect no tyrant crew;
> The red and white and starry blue
> Is freedom's shield and hope.

Sousa was quite aware that other nations had their flags, but he unapologetically (perhaps chauvinistically) lauded the flag of the United States as the best:

> Other nations may deem their flags the best
> And cheer them with fervid elation
> But the flag of the North and South and West
> Is the flag of flags, the flag of Freedom's nation.

The chorus borrows an analogy from "Columbia, the Gem of the Ocean" and connects the flag both to the nation's might and to its adherence to "right" standards:

> Hurrah for the flag of the free!
> May it wave as our standard forever,
> The gem of the land and the sea,
> The banner of the right.

Let despots remember the day
When our fathers with mighty endeavor
Proclaimed as they marched to the fray
That by their might and by their right
It waves forever.

Like Key, Sousa evoked the breeze to portray the flag as a moving, living object. He also referenced the American eagle. His song tied the flag not only to liberty but also to light, which for some might trigger the image of the Statue of Liberty holding a torch:

Let eagle shriek from lofty peak
The never-ending watchword of our land;
Let summer breeze waft through the trees
The echo of the chorus grand.
Sing out for liberty and light,
Sing out for freedom and the right.
Sing out for Union and its might,
O patriotic sons.

Given its popularity, Sousa's song might have been a contender for the national anthem, but he did not lobby for it. He explained in a 1915 letter, "If the Stars and Stripes Forever ever becomes a national air it will be because the people want it and not because of any congressional decree" (WQXR Staff 2016).

One fascinating aspect to Sousa's march is that, like "The Star-Spangled Banner" itself, it has been subject to parody, most notably "Be Kind to Your Web-Footed Friends," attributed to Fred Allen, and often played by Mitch Miller (1911–2010) on his NBC television program from 1961 to 1964 entitled *Sing Along with Mitch*. It implores:

Be kind to your web-footed friends.
For a duck may be somebody's mother.
They live all alone in the swamp,
Where the weather is cold and damp.

The melody of "The Stars and Stripes Forever" is probably better known than the words (indeed the words to the parody might be better known), which, consistent with its format as a march, are more assertive than the central question ("O say, can you see?) that highlights "The Star-Spangled Banner." The song was triggered by a specific loss in Sousa's own life, unlike Key's famous song, which was inspired by the British attack on Fort McHenry during the War of 1812.

Sousa was buried in Washington's Congressional Cemetery with other marines, in a grave featuring a tombstone that includes engravings of the first measures of "The Stars and Stripes Forever."

See also: Alternatives to the National Anthem; "Columbia, the Gem of the Ocean"; Parodies; Sousa, John Philip; "You're a Grand Old Flag."

Further Reading

Collins, Ace. 2003. *Songs Sung Red, White, and Blue: The Stories Behind America's Best-Loved Patriotic Songs.* New York: HarperCollins.

Lovrien, David. 2012. "The Stars and Stripes Forever." SousaMusic.com, June 13. http://sousamusic.com/the-stars-and-stripes-forever.

Warfield, Patrick. 2013. *Making the March King: John Philip Sousa's Washington Years, 1854–1893.* Urbana-Champaign: University of Illinois Press.

WQXR Staff. 2016. "How John Philip Sousa Almost Authored Our National Anthem." *WQXR Features,* June 29. https://www.wqxr.org/story/how-john-philip-sousa-almost-authored-our-national-anthem.

State and Municipal Laws and Ordinances

Even before Congress designated "The Star-Spangled Banner" as the national anthem, some states and localities had begun to adopt legislation designed to regulate behavior surrounding its performance.

In 1916, the city of Baltimore adopted a law prohibiting its "musical desecration." According to journalist Meagan Day, the ordinance prohibited "'indiscriminate renditions' such as medleys and ragtime performances—the song should be played in full, and without embellishments. The law also stipulated that musicians should stand for the song, although it said nothing of the audience" (Day 2016).

Even though Baltimore was the birthplace of the anthem, the ordinance encountered severe opposition, especially from people who incorrectly thought that it mandated audience members to stand. One person objected in a letter that the ordinance "smacks of German militarism." Another asked, "Can it be true that in this twentieth century a handful of men can come together and dictate to more than half a million people when they shall stand, sit, lie down, or perform any other act under penalty of a heavy fine for failure to comply?" (Day 2016).

In the same year that Congress designated "The Star-Spangled Banner" as the national anthem, Michigan adopted a law defining the performance of the anthem as follows:

> How played—The national hymn or anthem, "The Star Spangled Banner," shall not be played, sung or otherwise rendered in this state in any public place nor at any public entertainment, nor in any theatre, motion picture hall, restaurant or café, except as an entire and separate composition or number and without embellishments of national or other melodies; nor shall "The Star Spangled Banner" or any part thereof or selection from the same, be played as a part or selection of a medley of any king; nor shall "The Star Spangled Banner" be played at or in any of the places mentioned herein for dancing or as an exit march. (Rall 2015)

Massachusetts adopted a similar law, with a fine of up to $100. There must have been similar laws elsewhere since two theological students who sat through a rendition of the anthem at a movie theater in Chicago, Illinois, in 1942 were each fined $200 (Day 2016).

Citing Supreme Court decisions related to saluting the flag and other religious activities, in 1963 a U.S. district court in Arizona ruled in *Sheldon v. Fannin* that public schools could not expel children who were Jehovah's Witnesses who had cited their religious beliefs in refusing to stand for the anthem.

In *Cotto v. United Technologies Corp.* (1999), the Connecticut Supreme Court upheld the right of a private employer to fire an individual for refusing to display a flag at his private workplace (Schwartz 2017).

In 2017, Republican state representative Milo Smith of Indiana proposed a law that was not adopted that would require the Indianapolis Colts to refund money for football games up until the end of the first quarter in the event that members of the team kneeled during the playing of the anthem (Bodden 2017).

See also: Baltimore, Maryland; Code for the National Anthem; Congress and "The Star-Spangled Banner"; Sports Events.

Further Reading

Bowden, John. 2017. "Indiana Bill Would Force Colts to Refund Fans Offended by Anthem Protests." *The Hill*, December 28. https://thehill.com/blogs/blog-briefing -room/news/366722-indiana-bill-would-force-colts-to-offer-refunds-to-fans.

Cotto v. United Technologicies Corp. 251 Conn. 1 (1999).

Day, Meagan. 2016. "It Used to Be Illegal to Not Stand for the National Anthem." *Time-line*, September 13. https://timeline.com/illegal-stand-national-anthem-222775 e14f93.

Rall, Laura. 2015. "You May Have Been Illegally Singing the National Anthem Your Whole Life." *Star Spangled Music* (blog). Star Spangled Music Foundation, December 4. http://starspangledmusic.org/you-may-have-been-illegally-singing -the-national-anthem-your-whole-life.

Schwartz, Daniel. 2017. "All Rise (or Not)! A Flag, the National Anthem & Connecticut Law." *Connecticut Employment Law Blog*, October 12. https://www .ctemploymentlawblog.com/2017/10/articles/can-you-be-required-to-display-flag -at-work.

State Songs and Anthems

Although "The Star-Spangled Banner" serves as an official national anthem, the United State is a nation of fifty states and a number of territories, each with its own state and regional identity. One of the nation's mottos, the Latin phrase "E Pluribus Unum" (which translates to "From Many, One"), celebrates its desire to create one national entity from many individual units.

Just as states have their own flags, many also have a state flower, a state bird, a state animal, a state tree, and the like. Notably, many state songs either take the name of the state or include the name of the state within their titles. It is no surprise that the famous musical show tune "Oklahoma" by Rogers and Hammerstein was adopted by that state as its official song. Song names can sometime be deceptive, however, as a bandleader in New York found when, in what he intended to be a tribute to a visiting delegation from Georgia, he struck up "Marching Through Georgia," which instead of celebrating the glories of the state, described Union General William Tecumseh Sherman's destructive march through Georgia during the Civil War in which his troops burned Atlanta (Page 1996).

Some states have a number of officially recognized songs; Tennessee heads the list with nine official songs. At least one state, Virginia, has retired a song ("Carry Me Back to Old Virginny") to emeritus status for reflecting racial stereotypes of an earlier era (it included lines like "There's where the old darke'ys heart am longed to go" and references to "Massa and missis") and replaced it with "Our Great Virginia."

Iowa appears to be the earliest state to have adopted an original song when it officially recognized "The Song of Iowa" in 1911. But like "The Star-Spangled Banner," many of the songs were written years, if not decades, before they were adopted. Stephen Foster (1826–1864) was thus the author of both "My Old Kentucky Home," which serves for its namesake, and "Old Folks at Home," also known as "Suwanee River," which is one of three songs that Florida claims. John Denver not only wrote and performed "Rocky Mountain High," which Colorado adopted as its anthem, but also West Virginia's "Take Me Home Country Roads."

Connecticut is the only state that has claimed a tune that was once under consideration as a candidate for designation as America's national anthem, "Yankee Doodle." Americans throughout the United States probably associate Ray Charles with "Georgia on my Mind," but although he made it a hit with his 1960 album *The Genius Hits the Road*, it was actually written by Hoagy Carmichael and Stuart Gorrell in 1930. Many also know "Home on the Range," which is one of the official songs of Kansas (and is a symbol of the prairies more generally), and Louisiana's "You Are My Sunshine," which was cowritten by Jimmy Davis, a former governor of Louisiana, and Charles Mitchell. Tennessee has embraced "Tennessee Waltz," "Rocky Top," and other tunes, while Oklahoma has adopted "Swing Low, Sweet Chariot" as its official state gospel song. Apparently New Jersey considered adopting native-son Bruce Springsteen's "Born to Run," despite its passages of yearning for the open road and distant places (Page 1996). Indiana's "On the Banks of the Wabash, Far Away" was among the most popular songs of the nineteenth century.

Fans of the University of Wisconsin may think either of its athletic teams or the state as a whole when singing either the original or a modified version of "On, Wisconsin!"

Just as "The Star-Spangled Banner" focused chiefly on the U.S. flag, so too Alaska has adopted "Alaska's Flag," which focuses on its flag, as its state song. Like the canton of the U.S. flag, the Alaska flag features stars, in its case the Big Dipper and the North Star set against a night sky.

Maryland's official song, "Maryland, My Maryland," is not only sung to the tune of "O Tannenbaum (Christmas Tree)," a distinction it shares with "The Song of Iowa," but it was actually written by an individual hoping that the state would join the Confederate cause. Confederate forces sang the song on their way to the famous Battle of Gettysburg in Pennsylvania but never adopted it because it referred to a specific state that never joined the Southern cause.

Washington state's official folk song is Woody Guthrie's "Roll On, Columbia, Roll On," which was his attempt to support federal efforts to generate hydroelectric power in the state. Guthrie is also known for composing "This Land Is Your Land," which has sometimes been suggested as a national anthem.

U.S. territories also have their own official songs, including the "Virgin Islands March" and Puerto Rico's anthem "La Borinquena."

See also: Regional Appeal; "Yankee Doodle."

Further Reading

Bentancourt, David. 2016. "As Puerto Rican Superhero Makes Debut, Her Writer Brings 'The Power of the People' to Comics." *Washington Post*, May 11. https://www.washingtonpost.com/news/comic-riffs/wp/2016/05/11/as-puerto-rican-superhero-makes-debut-her-writer-brings-the-power-of-our-people-to-comics.

Hladczuk, John, and Shanon Schnieder Hladcuk. 2000. *State Songs: Anthems and Their Origins*. Lanham, MD: Scarecrow Press.

Marshall, Alex. 2008. "And the Winning Anthem Is." *The Guardian*, August 10. https://www.theguardian.com/music/2008/aug/11/olympics2008.

Page, Tim. 1996. "National Fight Songs." *Washington Post*, July 28. https://www.washingtonpost.com/archive/lifestyle/style/1996/07/28/national-fight-songs/012f9c4b-c0f7-4413-b5aa-e809d884f76b.

"Steamroller Music Box"

One of the most unusual artistic attempts to raise questions about American history and identity is that of Dave Cole (1975–), who produced an exhibit for the Cleveland Institute of Art in 2012 entitled *The Music Box*. It has since been exhibited elsewhere.

Consisting of a sculpture composed of a giant refabricated Ohio Caterpillar steamroller with prongs that strike tines on a giant attached music box, the exhibit plays a cacophonous version of "The Star-Spangled Banner." Curtis Aric, who worked with Cole in installing his exhibit at the Fitchburg Art Museum in 2018, said, "It's about as subtle as a chain saw—brutal to the eyes and horrible to the ears" (Shea 2018). He further noted, "It plays it in this discordant, kids banging on trash cans kind of way. It's slightly slow, slightly off-key. And all of that's totally intentional" (Shea 2018).

Although Cole's primary objective is to engage the audience, he observed that "on one hand, it is this solid piece of Manifest Destiny, road-building, Caterpillar, steel, American iron, rolling proudly forward into the future playing the national anthem, right? It's also something that's designed to crush things" (Shea 2018).

Other works by Cole have included two John Deere excavators that knit a twenty-foot-wide American flag at the Massachusetts Museum of Contemporary Art and three baby rattles made to resemble World War II–era grenades.

See also: Visual Arts.

Further Reading

Shea, Andrea. 2018. "'Brutal to the Eyes, Horrible to the Ears': The National Anthem, as Played by a Steamroller Music Box." *The ARTery*, February 19. https://www.wbur .org/artery/2018/02/19/national-anthem-steamroller.

Stetson, Augusta E.

In 1922, Miss Augusta E. Stetson (1842–1927), founder of the First Church of Christ, Scientist in New York, published lengthy advertisements in the *New York Tribune*, the *(Baltimore) Sun*, and the *Washington Post* opposing recognition of "The Star-Spangled Banner" as the national anthem. Her arguments appear to be based almost solely on those that Kitty Cheatham, a fellow member of the Christian Science Church denomination, had voiced a few years earlier.

One of Stetson's advertisements, for example, declared that the "spiritual ideals" of figures like Leif Ericson, George Washington, and Abraham Lincoln "can never be voiced through a song whose music was not written by an American, but was borrowed from a ribald, sensual drinking song, 'Anacreon in Heaven,' and whose words express vicious hatred of our natural brother and Anglo-Saxon comrade, Britain" (Friends of Irish Freedom 1922, 7).

Echoing Cheatham's earlier criticisms, Stetson also decried "the evil influence exerted upon their children, as well as upon themselves, by 'The Star Spangled Banner'" with its references in the third verse to "the havoc of war," "their foul footsteps' pollution," the "hireling and slave." She rhetorically asked, "Do these phrases fittingly express the spirit of America, the nation to whom the longing world looks today for moral and spiritual Leadership, with Christ at the head?" (Friends of Irish Freedom 1922, 7). In answer she asserted, "The spirit of America is not suitably expressed by hatred, nor by the horrors of war, which all nations today are praying may be abolished. America's national anthem, which should be composed, as well as written, by Americans, should express the same noble animus as that which Washington voiced, when he said, 'Let us raise a standard, to which the wise and honest can repair'" (7).

The Memorial and Executive Committee of the Grand Army of the Republic meeting in the Bronx borough of New York City responded to Stetson with a indignant statement of its own: "We protest this pernicious anti-American campaign against our long standing National song, the poetic expression of our patriotic spirit, and we call upon whosoever may be the proper law officers to take such action as may be best to stop further attempts to degrade this poetic story which so soulfully sings of a glorious past and the future hopes of our Republic" (Svejda 2005, 361).

See also: Cheatham, Kitty.

Further Reading

Friends of Irish Freedom, National Bureau of Information. 1922. *News Letter of the Friends of Irish Freedom* 4, no. 2 (July 8): 6–7.

Gray, Christopher. 2004. "Streetscapes/The First and Second Churches of Christ, Scientist; A Tale of 2 Warring Churches, and of One Woman." *New York Times*,

February 15. https://www.nytimes.com/2004/02/15/realestate/streetscapes-first-second-churches-christ-scientist-tale-2-warring-churches-one.html.

Svejda, George J. 2005. *History of the Star Spangled Banner from 1814 to the Present.* Honolulu, HI: University Press of the Pacific. First published in 1969 by Division of History, Office of Archeology and Historic Preservation, U.S. Department of the Interior, National Park Service.

Stravinsky, Igor

Igor Stravinsky (1882–1971) was a gifted Russian-born composer who immigrated to the United States from France in 1939. By that time, he had already made arrangements of the "Song of the Volga Boatmen," the post-Czarist anthem, and a violin arrangement of "La Marseillaise," which was the French national anthem. He gave the Charles Eliot Norton lectures at Harvard in the 1939–1940 school year, became the conductor of the Boston Symphony, and applied for U.S. citizenship.

At the time, the most common arrangement for the harmonization of "The Star-Spangled Banner" was one by Walter Damrosch (1862–1950). Although Stravinsky had led performances of this arrangement, he was living during a time when there was continuing criticism of the anthem on both musical and lyrical grounds and even calls for a new one (Slim 2008, 325).

Stravinsky's own arrangement, which he described as being arranged as a sacred chorale, premiered in Los Angeles under the direction of conductor James Sample on October 14, 1941, and later performed in San Francisco; Washington, DC; and Baltimore. His work received mixed reviews, perhaps fed by fears that Stravinsky was somehow trying to subvert an American icon at a time when the United States was engaged in a battle for its own survival. Marie Hummel, a Los Angeles violinist, wrote a letter to the *Los Angeles Times* asking, "Why do we need anyone to change our national anthem? [Is a] melody we all have cherished since childhood and sung in school, and in these perilous times, when every vestige of patriotism is necessary, and played at almost every public performance, to be distorted away from pure harmonic structure, such as it was last night?" (Slim 2006, 352).

His scheduled performance of his new arrangement in St. Louis in December 1941 was, however, cancelled (Stavinsky played the standard arrangement instead), but while the audience attempted to join in singing at his performance of the anthem in Boston on January 14, 1944, most gave up trying to sing what one reviewer called "the odd, somewhat dissonant harmonies" (Slim 2006, 364). When Stravinsky prepared for a subsequent performance to be broadcast by radio, Boston authorities told him that a state law made it illegal for him to play anything other than the standard version, and Stravinsky did not test it. Later, false reports that he had been arrested stemmed from a picture of the composer that resembled a police mug shot but was actually the visa picture he had taken for residence in the United States. Stravinsky did later record his own arrangement in the 1960s.

Despite the attacks that came his way, Stravinsky became a naturalized citizen in 1945 and frequently spoke with patriotic pride about the United States. "I love America . . . and Americans, and I like very much the American spirit" (Slim 2006, 400). He sent out Christmas cards with the opening notes of the anthem and the words "May the U.S.A. be victorious" and purchased large numbers of war bonds (Slim 2006, 401).

Although Congress has never endorsed an arrangement of the national anthem as official, Stravinsky's experience suggests that Americans often regard any tampering with traditional arrangements as threatening, especially when introduced by an individual who is foreign-born.

See also: Broyhill, Joel; Immigrants.

Further Reading

Slim, H. Colin. 2006. "Stravinsky's Four Star-Spangled Banners and His 1941 Christmas Card." *Musical Quarterly* 89 (Summer–Fall): 321–447.

Stilwell, Blake. 2018. "A Famous Russian Composer Re-arranged the Star-Spangled Banner." *We Are the Mighty*, August 13. https://www.wearethemighty.com/music/stravinsky-national-anthem.

Svejda, George J.

Although there are some good biographies of Francis Scott Key and numberous accounts of his writing of "The Star-Spangled Banner," there is no single better source for information about the national anthem than Dr. George J. Svejda's *History of the Star Spangled Banner from 1814 to the Present*. The National Park Service first published this book in 1969. In both its original and republished forms, it resembles a dissertation as much as it does a book, with close to five hundred pages of double-spaced typing, footnotes in which titles are underlined rather than italicized, and no index. Dealing both with the American flag and "The Star-Spangled Banner" anthem, the book includes information on their history, message, music, popularity, reception during the Civil War through the end of the nineteenth century, uses by branches of the U.S. armed forces, efforts to adopt the song as the national anthem, and criticisms.

Although he subsequently became a U.S. citizen, Svejda was born in Horni Vilimex, which was then part of Czechoslovakia in 1927. He attended Masaryk College in Ludwigsburg, Germany, prior to transferring to St. Procopius College (today's Illinois Benedictine University) where he earned his bachelor's degrees. He subsequently obtained a PhD at Georgetown University and did postdoctoral work at the University of Pennsylvania before being employed by the National Park Service in 1962.

In addition to his work on "The Star-Spangled Banner," Dr. Svejda has also published reports for the National Park Service on immigration and issues related to the army at Morristown during the Revolutionary War.

See also: Scholarship.

Further Reading

"George J. Svejda." Contemporary Authors Online, Gale, 2001. Gale in Context: Biography. https://link.gale.com/apps/doc/H1000096671/BIC?y=tel_middleten&sid=BIC&xid=5875cf67.

Svejda, George J. 2005. *History of the Star Spangled Banner from 1814 to the Present.* Honolulu, HI: University Press of the Pacific. First published in 1969 by Division of History, Office of Archeology and Historic Preservation, U.S. Department of the Interior, National Park Service.

Temperance Movement

Just as abolitionists appropriated the Liberty Bell as a symbol in opposition to slavery, so too various causes have attempted to utilize the "The Star-Spangled Banner" for their own purposes.

Professor Bryan Lindsay (2004) has found at least three parodies of the song that served to promote alcohol prohibition. The first, published in 1843 in the *Temperance Annual and Cold Water Magazine*, began with the lines:

Oh! Who has not seen by the dawn's early light,
Some poor bloated drunkard to his home weakly reeling.

The song may be most notable for the last couplet in its third verse:

And the temperance banner in triumph shall wave,
O'er the land of the free and the home of the brave.

Another such parody was published in a collection called *The Washington Choir* in 1843. After portraying "the dark mental night" brought about by drunkenness, the song ends with:

'Tis the bright star of Temperance, long may it shine,
Enlight'ning the soul with its radiance divine.

Yet another is found in *The Boston Temperance Glee Book* from 1851. Titled "Ye Sons of Columbia," the song ends by evoking the joys of water:

Be water, pure water, bright sparkling with glee,
That flows like our life's blood, unfettered and free.

Musicologist George J. Svejda (2005) further observed that the Prohibition Home Protection Party used a song entitled "The Foe of Church and Freedom" in 1884 to the tune of "The Star-Spangled Banner" (216). Yet another temperance collection of songs published in 1889 contained the song "The Star of Temperance," which was designed to be sung to the tune of "The Star-Spangled Banner" as well (131).

Lindsay finds the appropriation absurd because of the melody's origin in the Anacreontic Society, in which participants appeared to have enjoyed alcohol as well as music. Lindsay thus observes, "One can imagine the use of 'Bringing in the Sheaves,' or 'The Old Rugged Cross,' as the vehicle for a brandy commercial almost as easily as one can envision the function of a classical English glee" (2004, 602). He suggested that "Jose Feliciano's restructuring of the tune during the 1968 World Series is a far cry from the travesty perpetrated upon this venerable old drinking song by the charming little old ladies and hellfire-and-damnation preachers of the *Temperance Annual and Cold Water Magazine*" (2004, 602).

Perhaps, however, this criticism is equivalent to saying that it was sacrilegious for Francis Scott Key to attempt to capture the sentiment of the American nation after the successful defense of Baltimore with an *English* song of mirth. The use of the tune "Yankee Doodle" would suggest that such expropriation has a fairly long history. Moreover, "The Star-Spangled Banner" was but one of many tunes that the temperance movement utilized (Ewing 1971).

See also: "To Anacreon in Heaven."

Further Reading

Ewing, George W. 1971. "The Well-Tempered Lyre: Songs of the Temperance Movement." *Southwest Review* 56 (Spring): 139–55.

Lindsay, Bryan. 2004. "Anacreon on the Wagon: 'The Star-Spangled Banner' in the Service of the Cold Water Army." *Journal of Popular Culture* 4 (Winter): 595–603.

Svejda, George J. 2005. *History of the Star Spangled Banner from 1814 to the Present.* Honolulu, HI: University Press of the Pacific. First published in 1969 by Division of History, Office of Archeology and Historic Preservation, U.S. Department of the Interior, National Park Service.

"That Star-Spangled Banner"

The title of the national anthem, as well as one of its most striking phrases, refers to "that star-spangled banner," and this term is one of several endearing phrases that people use to describe the flag.

The term "banner" may be used both to describe flags in general and the U.S. flag in particular. Frederick Edwin Church has thus executed an oil painting entitled *Our Banner in the Sky,* which portrays a sky reflecting the stars and stripes of the flag. Other nicknames for the American flag, which have been incorporated into a number of song titles, include "The Red, White, and Blue," "Old Glory," the "Old Flag," the "Grand Old Flag," and the "Stars and Stripes" (Vile 2018, 242–43). The Pledge of Allegiance simply refers to "the flag of the United States of America."

The term "star-spangled" is arguably a richer, albeit somewhat disputed, term. Famed playwright William Shakespeare used the term in both *A Midsummer Night's Dream* ("by spangled star-light sheen") and *The Taming of the Shrew* ("what stars do spangle heaven with such beauty"). Francis Scott Key had previously used the term in the third verse of "When The Warrior Returns," a poem later set to music, in which, in honoring American heroes of the war in Tripoli, he had referred to "The Star Spangled flag of our nation."

Because the chief definition of a spangle is a small shining object, some critics have charged that the term was lacking in sufficient gravity for Key to use in describing the American flag. Protesting against its use, a writer for the Charleston, South Carolina, *Courier* on July 4, 1821, said that the term reminded him of the ornaments on the shoes of opera dancers or of tawdry dresses. "To connect a star, a mighty luminous orb, a world of light and beauty, with a Spangled, diminutive, insignificant tinsel, worthless ornament of a dirty kid slipper—to bring together one of the glories of the firmament, and the trodden refuse of a country dance, is a most degrading association," he declared. "Let us maintain, if we can, the elevation of the stars, but God deliver us from the objections of the spangles" (Svejda 2005, 139).

This phrasing had many defenders, though. They argued, for example, that the designation points to the manner in which the U.S. flag was originally designed to represent a new political, republican constellation of states that would no longer be dominated, like many European predecessors, by a single monarch (Shalev 2011).

See also: Star-Spangled Banner Flag; "When the Warrior Returns."

Further Reading

Linderman, Juliet. 2014. "Do You Know 'The Star-Spangled Banner'?" *Smithsonian Tween Tribune*, September 14. https://www.tweentribune.com/article/tween56/do-you-know-star-spangled-banner.

Shalev, Eran. 2011. "'A Republic Amidst the Stars': Political Astronomy and the Intellectual Origins of the Stars and Stripes." *Journal of the Early Republic* 31 (Spring): 39–73.

Svejda, George J. 2005. *History of the Star Spangled Banner from 1814 to the Present*. Honolulu, HI: University Press of the Pacific. First published in 1969 by Division of History, Office of Archeology and Historic Preservation, U.S. Department of the Interior, National Park Service.

Vile, John R. 2018. *The American Flag: An Encyclopedia of the Stars and Stripes in U.S. History, Culture, and Law*. Santa Barbara, CA: ABC-CLIO.

"This Land Is Your Land"

One of the songs that has risen to near-anthem status in the United States in a song by Woody Guthrie (1912–1967) now known as "This Land Is Your Land" but originally titled "God Blessed America."

Apparently stimulated in part by Guthrie's disgust with Irving Berlin's "God Bless America," which Guthrie thought painted too rosy a picture of the nation, Guthrie penned the song in 1940 but did not record it until 1944. In addition to describing America as a beautiful nation, Guthrie originally included a reference to "dust clouds rolling" (an image from the Dust Bowl), a stanza questioning private property, and another depicting individuals lined up at a relief office. Many subsequent printed versions of the song have omitted these lines.

After his mother had a mental breakdown and the family moved from Okemah, Oklahoma, to Pampa, Texas, when he was still in his teens, Guthrie began street entertaining, riding the rails, and encountering many refugees from the Dust Bowl

This sheet music of "The Anacreontic Song as sung at the Crown & Anchor Tavern in the Strand," published c. 1790 in London, shows Ralph Tomlinson, Esq., as the song's lyricist. (Library of Congress)

during the Great Depression. Later in New York, he encountered similar poverty in the Bowery.

Many sources believe that the Carter Family's recording of "When the World's on Fire" provided the tune on which Guthrie based his famous song (Spitzer 2012), while others believe the origins were more complex (Jackson 2007, 26). One advantage of the song is that, in contrast to "The Star-Spangled Banner," its range is a single octave, making it easier for most people to sing (Jackson 2007, 26).

Each stanza of the original lyrics ended with "God blessed America for me," before Guthrie changed them to "This land was made for you and me." The song is particularly popular among critics of entrenched economic privileges. Over time, opponents of the Vietnam War, individuals concerned about environment degradation, and others have adapted the lyrics to their causes. Folk music legend Pete Seeger, who was also known for coauthoring with Lee Hays "If I Had a Hammer," which emphasized themes of justice, freedom, and love, was among the other singers who helped popularize Guthrie's song.

See also: "God Bless America."

Further Reading

Jackson, Mark Allan. 2007. *Prophet Singer: The Voice and Vision of Woody Guthrie.* Oxford: University Press of Mississippi.

Spitzer, Nick. 2012. "The Story of Woody Guthrie's 'This Land Is Your Land,'" *The NPR 100*, National Public Radio, February 15. https://www.npr.org/2000/07/03/1076186/this-land-is-your-land.

"To Anacreon in Heaven"

Although the words to "The Star-Spangled Banner" originated with Francis Scott Key, the tune did not. It is the same as that for a song entitled "To Anacreon in Heaven," often known as "The Anacreontic Song," which was the constitutional song of the London Anacreontic Society (Hildebrand 2014, 258). This organization was founded in about 1766 and met at the Crown and Anchor Tavern in London. The song was named in honor of Anacreon of Teos, a Greek poet from the sixth century BC, who was known as a poet of wine and love (Montgomery 1948, 30). The lyrics to "To Anacreon in Heaven" are as follows:

> To Anacreon in heav'n, where he sat in full Glee,
>   A few Sons of Harmony sent a Petition;
> That He their Inspirer and Patron would be;
>   When this Answer arriv'd from the Jolly Old Grecian
>   "Voice," Fiddle, and Flute,
>   No longer be mute.
> I'll lend you my Name, and inspire you to boot,
> And besides, I'll instruct you like me, to intwine,
> The Myrtle of Venus with Bacchus's Vine.
> And, besides, I'll instruct you like me, to entwine,
> The Myrtle of Venus with Bacchus's Vine.

The Society consisted of a group of amateur musicians who would first attend a concert performed by an invited musician or group of musicians and then feast together. The song, which had first been published in 1778, was particularly popular in army camps. It is believed the words were written by Ralph Tomlinson, an early president of the Anacreontic Society, while the musical arrangement has been generally attributed to John Stafford Smith (Lichtenwanger 1978).

Despite its origin in the upper echelons of society, the song appears to have been widely known. A poem that Key wrote in 1805 entitled "When the Warrior Returns" to honor American heroes of the war in Tripoli had been set to the same tune.

Opposition to designating "The Star-Spangled Banner" as the national anthem included the somewhat contradictory charges that it was both elitist and a well-known drinking song.

See also: Criticisms and Defenses of "The Star-Spangled Banner"; Drinking Song; Key, Francis Scott; "When the Warrior Returns."

Further Reading

Hildebrand, David K. 2014. "Bicentenary Essay: Two National Anthems? Some Reflections on the Two Hundredth Anniversary of 'The Star-Spangled Banner' and Its Forgotten Partner, 'The Battle of Baltimore,'" *American Music* 32 (Fall): 253–71.

Lichtenwanger, William. 1977. "The Music of 'The Star-Spangled Banner': From Ludgate Hill to Capitol Hill." *Quarterly Journal of the Library of Congress* 34 (July): 136–70.

Lichtenwanger, William. 1978. "The Music of 'The Star-Spangled Banner': Whence and Whither?" *College Music Symposium* 18 (Fall): 34–81.

Montgomery, Henry C. 1948. "Anacreon and the National Anthem." *Classical Outlook* 26 (December): 30–31.

Tomlinson, Ralph

Less is known about Ralph Tomlinson (1744–1788), who authored the words "To Anacreon in Heaven" (or "The Anacreontic Song"), than about John Stafford Smith (1750–1836), who actually composed the tune to this song to which Francis Scott Key's "The Star-Spangled Banner" would later be set.

Tomlinson was an attorney, probably a solicitor rather than a barrister, who likely learned his trade by reading law or apprenticing in a law office (Lichtenwanger 1977, 142). He composed the words to the poem honoring the Greek poet for the London Anacreontic Society, of which he served for a time as president. The gentleman's society met for musical entertainment and meals, first at a London Coffee House on Ludgate Hill and then, as its membership expanded, at the Crown and Anchor Tavern.

A visiting musician by the name of Richard John Samuel Stevens (1757–1837), who recorded his visit to the London Anacreontic Society in a diary entry under the general date of 1777, provides much of what is known about Tomlinson. Stevens wrote, "The President was Ralph Tomlinson Esq[re], very much of a Gentleman, and a sensible, sedate, quiet man: I believe that he was a Solicitor in Chancery. He wrote the Poetry of the Anacreontic Song; which Stafford Smith set to Music: this Song was sung by Webster, when I first attended the Society" (Lichtenwanger 1977, 148).

Tomlinson's obituary further reported that he was a bachelor, and his death at a relatively young age suggests that he died suddenly. The only other work for which he is known is "A Slang Pastoral: Being a Parody on a Celebrated Poem of Dr. Byron's," which was printed in 1780 (Lichtenwanger 1977, 142).

See also: Anacreon; Smith, John Stafford; "To Anacreon in Heaven."

Further Reading
Lichtenwanger, William. 1977. "The Music of 'The Star-Spangled Banner': From Ludgate Hill to Capitol Hill." *Quarterly Journal of the Library of Congress* 34 (July): 136–70.

Tracy, Benjamin Franklin

Benjamin Franklin Tracy (1830–1915) was the Secretary of the Navy from 1889 to 1893. He issued General Order No. 374 on July 26, 1889, which provided that when navy bands were aboard men-of-war at naval stations, they would play "The Star Spangled Banner" when the flag was raised in the morning and "Hail Columbia" when it was lowered at night. This order further provided that "all persons present, belonging to the Navy, not so employed as to render it impracticable, will please face towards the colors and salute as the ensign reaches the peak or truck in hoisting, or the taffrail or ground in haling down" (Svejda 2005, 470).

Tracy issued this order and its accompanying instructions on proper flag etiquette prior to the time in 1916 that President Woodrow Wilson would declare "The Star-Spangled Banner" to be the official anthem for U.S. armed forces and

Congress's passage of a bill, signed by President Herbert Hoover in 1931, making it the nation's official anthem.

Tracy was a practicing lawyer who was elected to the New York State Assembly prior to serving in the Union army during the Civil War. After performing valiantly in combat, he was appointed as commander of a prisoner-of-war camp in Elmira, New York. He was active in Republican politics, part of Thomas C. Platt's Republican state machine, and served for a time as a member of the New York Court of Appeals.

Although he had little knowledge of naval affairs when Benjamin Harrison appointed him to be Secretary of the Navy, he was a quick learner. He joined with Alfred Thayer Mahan (1840–1914) and Rear Admiral

Benjamin Franklin Tracy, c. 1897. (Library of Congress)

Stephen B. Luce (1827–1917) in touting the importance of naval power to America's future. He accordingly proposed an aggressive policy of ship building at a time when the U.S. Navy lagged behind that of other major nations, and he encouraged industrialist Andrew Carnegie to manufacture ship armor. Largely due to the poor health of Secretary of State James G. Blaine (1830–1893), he was able to lead fairly aggressive naval actions during his time in office (Cooling 1972, 88).

In early U.S. history, flags were far more ubiquitous on land than on sea, and it is possible that Tracy chose "The Star-Spangled Banner" for morning colors in part because of its focus on the flag. In an attempt to standardize the way that American welcomed foreign dignitaries, Tracy also ordered John Philip Sousa to compose a collection of patriotic tunes, which resulted in the publication of *National Patriotic and Typical Airs of All Lands* in 1890.

See also: Code for the National Anthem; Congress and "The Star-Spangled Banner"; Sousa, John Philip; War and the National Anthem; Wilson, Woodrow.

Further Reading

Cooling, B. Franklin. 1972. "The Making of a Navalist: Secretary of the Navy Benjamin Franklin Tracy and Seapower." *Naval War College Review* 25 (September–October): 83–90.

Cooling, B. Franklin. 1973. *Benjamin Franklin Tracy.* Hamden, CT: Shoe String Press.

Svejda, George J. 2005. *History of the Star Spangled Banner from 1814 to the Present.* Honolulu, HI: University Press of the Pacific. First published in 1969 by Division of History, Office of Archeology and Historic Preservation, U.S. Department of the Interior, National Park Service.

Trump, Donald J.

Donald J. Trump (1946–), who succeeded Barack Obama as president in 2017, has energized his right-wing Republican base by raising fears of immigrants and appealing to patriotic symbols. He ran on the slogan "Make America Great Again."

A study of the presidential nominating conventions of 2016 observed that Republicans relied more on recordings and the live music performed by a rock band directed by G. E. Smith, whereas Democrats relied more heavily on live performance by star artists to entertain convention attendees. This contrast was evident in performances of the national anthem as well: "Trump's singers were young white musicians from northern Ohio who performed at ball games and other sporting events, in keeping with his populist ideology and the "wholesome" image the RNC wished to communicate . . . In contrast, Clinton demonstrated her and her party's inclusiveness through a racially and ethnically mixed lineup of youthful singers: on successive days, they featured a local African American choirboy, a blind music student, a Latino mariachi singer, and a viral sensational from Florida, none professional singers and none over thirty-five years old" (Deaville 2017, 454).

Trump's inauguration festivities featured country music and a special appearance by Lee Greenwood, who sang "God Bless the USA," a song that had also been performed at the inaugurations of each of three prior Republican presidents (Blim 2017, 482). The concert also featured Toby Keith singing "American Soldier," "Made in America," "Beer for My Horses," and "Courtesy of the Red, White, and Blue" (Blim 2017, 482–83).

The only person who has ever become president without previously holding a political office or serving in the military, Trump also sought to improve public perceptions of his patriotism by casting himself as a staunch defender of the American flag and the national anthem. He harshly criticized prominent NFL players and other athletes who knelt during renditions of the national anthem as a form of social protest. He made his most strident criticism against Colin Kaepernick, a quarterback for the San Francisco 49ers, who first sat, and later took a knee, during pregame performances of the anthem in protest of police brutality. Trump later criticized Megan Rapinoe, the co-captain of the U.S. women's soccer team, after she participated in similar protests (Nugent 2019).

In January 2018, a video of Trump singing along to "The Star-Spangled Banner" at a football game appeared to suggest that he was not fully conversant with the words of the anthem. The footage made him the target of considerable mockery (Emery 2018). Similarly, Trump gave a speech on July 4, 2019, in which after mentioning Valley Forge and Yorktown, two famous military sites of the

American Revolutionary War, turned to the War of 1812. In his remarks, Trump claimed that the American army had "manned the air (unintelligible), it rammed the ramparts. It took over the airports. It did everything it had to do. And at Fort McHenry, under the rockets' red glare, it had nothing but victory. And when dawn came, their star-spangled banner waved defiant" (Associated Press 2019). Trump White House officials later asserted that Trump's odd suggestion that the fight at Fort McHenry that inspired Francis Scott Key to write "The Star-Spangled Banner" somehow involved an airport was the result of a teleprompter malfunction.

See also: Kaepernick, Colin; Presidential Campaigns.

Further Reading
Associated Press. 2019. "AP Fact Check: Trump's Tangle on American History." *WTOP News*, July 5. https://wtop.com/white-house/2019/07/ap-fact-check-trumps-tangle-on-american-history.

Blim, Dan. 2017. "Party Politics: Ideology and Musical Performance at Donald Trump's Inaugural Celebration." *American Music* 35 (Winter): 478–89.

Deaville, James. 2017. "The Unconventional Music of the Democratic and Republican National Conventions of 2016." *American Music* 35 (Winter): 4446–66.

Emery, David. 2018. "Does Donald Trump Not Know the Words to the National Anthem?" *Snopes*, January 10. https://www.snopes.com/fact-check/trump-words-national-anthem.

McLaughlin, Timothy, and Casey Quackenbush. 2019. "Hong Kong Protesters Sing 'Star-Spangled Banner,' Call on Trump to 'Liberate' the City." *Washington Post*, September 9.

Nugent, Ciara. 2019. "Trump Says It's Inappropriate for U.S. Soccer Star Megan Rapinoe to Protest during the National Anthem." *Time*, June 25. https://time/com/5613766/trump-says-inappropriate-megan-rapinoe-national-anthem-protest.

Paulson, Ken. 2017. "NFL Protests: Your Boss Can Tell You to Stand for the Anthem. Trump Can't." *First Amendment Encyclopedia*, Free Speech Center, Middle Tennessee State University, October 2. https://mtsu.edu/first-amendment/post/57/nfl-protests-your-boss-can-tell-you-to-stand-for-the-anthem-trump-can-t.

Unity

One beauty of song is that it unites individuals, often of diverse backgrounds, in a common endeavor. One indication of this is the way that almost all churches begin with congregational or choral singing. As much as any nation, the United States has sought to create one nation from many states and nationalities, as symbolized in its motto "E Pluribus Unum" ("From Many, One"). One function and goal of the national anthem is to unite Americans, particularly in times of war, economic crisis, or other threat. It is common for individuals to sing or play the national anthem at naturalization ceremonies as well.

America has historically prided itself on the hope that individual interests would be either subsumed in wider national interests, or that the system of representative government on which it is founded would seek to refine and enlarge opinions so that they had a more national cast.

One of the principles that is dear to Americans is that of individual self-expression, which the First Amendment of the U.S. Constitution protects. Although there are guidelines for saluting the flag and singing the national anthem (civilians typically put their right hand over their heart and stand as the anthem is being playing), individual citizens thus have the right to refuse to salute the flag or to stand for the anthem. One of the most visible, if arguably counterproductive, methods of bringing attention to protests that might call American policies into question (American involvement in foreign wars or police conduct toward minority citizens, for example) is to burn the flag or to refuse to stand during the anthem.

When such actions become widespread, they may disrupt the unity that one expects an anthem to inspire or detract from the entertainment (sports events, for example) that people came to enjoy. Although private employers may enact sanctions (this often depends on individual contracts), the First Amendment prohibits the government from doing so.

In "The Star-Spangled Banner," Francis Scott Key, who had initially opposed the War of 1812, sought to convey a sense of unity in invoking the protection of the homeland in the face of an invading enemy. He also sought to rally Americans around the common symbol of the flag and a common love of freedom. The final verse further evoked American civil religion in suggesting that the nation's motto should be "In God is our trust."

In recent years, a number of foreign countries have arrested and punished individuals who chose not to stand for their anthem or sang it to a different tune or in a different language. One reason that the United States has long resisted doing so is the belief that such actions are part of what it means to live in "the land of the free."

See also: English Language and "The Star-Spangled Banner"; Sports Events.

Further Reading

Day, Darla. 2017. "Dear America: A National Anthem for Unity." YouTube, May 6. https://www.youtube.com/watch?v=2KrQPnwXy_4.

Rosenberger, Peter. 2017. "Our National Anthem, Once a Source of Unity, Now Rings with Discord and Dissonance." *Fox News*, September 25. https://www.foxnews.com/opinion/our-national-anthem-once-a-source-of-unity-now-rings-with-discord-and-dissonance.

Very Visionary Star-Spangled Sidewalk

One of the more visual representations of the national anthem is the Very Visionary Star-Spangled Sidewalk, which is found outside the American Visionary Art Museum in Baltimore, Maryland. The sidewalk was colorfully designed by Lee T. Wheeler and painted with the help of volunteers in April 2013 in connection with Maryland's Star Spangled National Bicentennial Celebration of the next year.

Wheeler patterned the sidewalk to the lyrics of the first verse of the anthem. In illustrating the opening words, "O say, can you see," the mural begins with a picture of Chief Tecumseh of the Shawnee tribe who was believed to have the gift of seeing into the future, including the New Madrid earthquakes of 1811 and 1812. It continues with "By the dawn's early light" and a boat moving backward up the Mississippi River during one of the earthquakes, along with a picture of a giant wheel of imported cheese that was presented to President James Madison at the end of the war. Pictures of Uncle Sam and Lady Liberty intervene before the line "What so proudly we hailed" (Wheeler, n.d.).

As the sidewalk gets to "At the twilight's last gleaming," it portrays Key as he looks toward Fort McHenry with Congreve rockets fired from attacking British ships and bursting in the distance. As the lyrics continue, Wheeler depicts a rooster crowing during the bombardment of Fort McHenry and a picture of the newspaper that first published "The Star-Spangled Banner." Other images portray a slave, a tree with a poem describing national divisions during the War of 1812, the impressment of American seamen, which had led to the war, and Chief Tecumseh again. The mural also includes the flags of the United States, Canada, and Great Britain.

See also: Baltimore, Maryland; Visual Arts.

Further Reading

Wheeler, Lee T. n.d. "A Guide to American Visionary Art Museum's A Very Visionary Star-Spangled Sidewalk." American Visionary Art Museum (website). http://www.avam.org/exhibitions/pdf/Star-Spangled-Sidewalk-Guide.pdf.

Veterans

Of all the groups in America, those who are serving or who have served in the military are often among the citizens who show the most reverence for the U.S. flag and songs like "The Star-Spangled Banner" that reference it. "The Star-Spangled Banner" anthem was inspired by the waving of the flag in the aftermath of an 1814 battle to defend Fort McHenry and the nearby city of Baltimore from British forces during the War of 1812. Each branch of the military has its own song, and military bands use music like the national anthem and "Battle Hymn of the Republic" to motivate and inspire troops in defense of their nation.

Although early military units generally marched under regimental colors, this began to change during the Mexican-American War from 1846–1848, when they began going into battle under the U.S. flag (Vile 2018, 233). This flag, and the songs that lauded it, received further impetus during the Civil War, when Southerners marched to a different flag and to rival tunes. Long before Congress voted to designate "The Star-Spangled Banner" as the national anthem, military officials required the tune to be played first at the raising of the flag, and later at both its raising and lowering. When in uniform, members of the military are instructed to stand at attention, face the flag, and salute while the anthem is being played. Groups like the American Legion and Veterans of Foreign Wars were influential in getting "The Star-Spangled Banner" adopted as the national anthem.

Veterans are, however, far from monolithic on this subject with some veterans choosing to view the flag as a symbol of First Amendment freedoms of speech and expression—including protest actions undertaken when the flag is being recognized or celebrated. In 2016, a diverse group of veterans signed an open letter supporting the decision by San Francisco 49ers quarterback Colin Kaepernick to take a knee during playing of the national anthem as a way of underscoring his concerns with alleged police brutality and racial discrimination in African American communities. After reviewing past instances of athletes who had taken political stances, the letter said, "The right for those athletes, and all Americans, to protest is one we all pledged to defend with our lives if necessary. Far from disrespecting our troops, there is no finer form of appreciation for our sacrifice than for Americans to enthusiastically exercise their freedom of speech" (Walker 2016). The letter further noted, "While we would not all personally choose to protest in a manner identical to Kaepernick, we respect and honor his choice" (Walker 2016). John Middlemas, a ninety-seven-year-old veteran from World War II, was thus photographed taking a knee in support of this right (Jacobo 2017).

Renditions of the national anthem gain added poignancy when veterans perform them. In November of 2018, Robert McClintock of the U.S. Army Air Corps, a veteran of World War II who was just about to celebrate his one hundredth birthday, joined U.S. Air Force Sergeant Sonya Bryson to sing the anthem at the Tampa Bay Lightning Military Appreciation Night prior to a game with the New York Islanders (Calicchio 2018).

See also: Code for the National Anthem; Congress and "The Star-Spangled Banner"; Kaepernick, Colin; Native American Indians; Songs of the U.S. Armed Forces; Sports Events.

Further Reading
Calicchio, Dom. 2018. "WW2 Veteran, Turning 100 Soon, Belts Out National Anthem before NHL Game." *Fox News*, November 8. https://www.foxnews.com/sports /ww2-veteran-turning-100-soon-belts-out-national-anthem-before-nhl-game.

Fonseca, Felicia. 2017. "In Indian Country, Honoring Flag Might Mean Different Anthem." *Denver Post*, November 25. https://www.denverpost.com/2017/11/25 /taking-a-knee-native-american-persepective.

Jacobo, Julia. 2015. "Veterans Take a Knee in Support of National Anthem Protests." *ABC News*, September 25. https://abcnews.go.com/US/veterans-knee-support-national -anthem-protests/story?id=50075609.

Vile, John R. 2018. *The American Flag: An Encyclopedia of the Stars and Stripes in U.S. History, Culture, and Law*. Santa Barbara, CA: ABC-CLIO.

Walker, Rhiannon. 2016. "An Open Letter from American Military Veterans in Support of Colin Kaepernick." *The Undefeated*, September 2. https://theundefeated.com /features/an-open-letter-from-american-military-veterans-in-support-of-colin -kaepernick.

Vietnam War

Of all the wars in U.S. history, few were as unpopular as the Vietnam War, in which the United States sought to defend South Vietnam against the communist North from 1955 to 1975. Domestic opposition to the war mounted as U.S. military and Vietnamese civilian casualties rose, as stories emerged of American participation in the massacre of civilians, and as evidence mounted that American political and military leaders had been portraying the outlook for victory more optimistically than circumstances warranted.

The war created fault lines between college students, many of who had student deferments from the military draft, and others. In 1970, four students were killed by National Guard troops during an antiwar demonstration at Kent State University in Ohio. The war marked a time when protestors sometimes burned the U.S. flag or their draft cards or flew the flag of the North Vietnamese enemy. Indeed, Congress adopted a law prohibiting the burning of draft cards that was upheld by the U.S. Supreme Court in *United States v. O'Brien* (1968). Laws against flag burning were eventually invalidated as violations of the First Amendment right of speech in *Texas v. Johnson* (1989) and *United States v. Eichman* (1990). Returning servicemen were sometimes reviled for their service, and it became commonplace to hear stories of servicemen who upon completing their tour of duties and returning home were called baby-killers and other names rather than being celebrated for their service.

Interestingly, because selective service provided a number of exemptions, the National Football League (NFL) was able to keep all but two of its players out of the draft, often by having them enrolled in the National Guard and reserves (Jenkins 2018). Ironically, during this same period, teams were displaying their patriotism as in the first flyover of military planes at Super Bowl II in 1968.

In another sport, heavyweight boxing champion Muhammad Ali was stripped of his title in 1967 after he refused to serve in Vietnam because of his religious convictions. In 1969, Jimi Hendrix's rendition of the national anthem at the Woodstock music festival, which highlighted the bombs and rockets, was generally interpreted as an antiwar performance (Clague 2014). In 1971, Donald Sutherland, Jane Fonda, and others toured the country performing antiwar skits and songs at coffeehouses and other venues near U.S. military bases. One of the skits featured people refusing to stand for the national anthem.

See also: Feliciano, Jose; Hendrix, Jimi; Olympic Protest (1968); Sports Events; War of 1812.

Further Reading

Clague, Mark. 2014. "'This Is America': Jimi Hendrix's Star Spangled Banner Journey as Psychedelic Citizenship." *Journal of the Society for American Music* 8:435–578.

Jenkins, Sally. 2018. "The Roots of the NFL's National Anthem Controversy Stretch to the 1960s and Vietnam." *Washington Post*, May 27. https://www.washingtonpost .com/sports/the-roots-of-the-nfls-national-anthem-controversy-stretch-to-the -1960s-and-vietnam/2018/05/27/933efcbe-61d1-11e8-a69c-b944de66d9e7_story .html.

Remnick, David. 2017. "Vietnam War Resistance in the Age of Trump." *New Yorker*, September 24. https://www.newyorker.com/news/daily-comment/recalling-muhammad -alis-vietnam-war-resistance-in-the-age-of-trump.

Texas v. Johnson, 491 U.S. 397.

United States v. Eichman, 496 U.S. 310 (1990).

United States v. O'Brien, 391 U.S. 367 (1968).

"View of the Bombardment of Fort McHenry"

The War of 1812 took place before the advent of photography, which is one reason that Francis Scott Key's vivid descriptions of "the rockets' red glare" and the "bombs bursting in air" are so striking.

There is an aquatint print by John Bower and believed to have been published in 1814 (although at least one scholar believes the date was 1819), which depicts the scene on the morning of September 13, 1814, when British ships attacked Fort McHenry outside Baltimore. The color print portrayed the attacking ships in the background, lodging round bombs arching into the fort near the center of the print. There are two houses, some trees, and some fields in the foreground and dark clouds in the sky. An American flag is depicted flying above the fort.

The print, an original of which is owned by the Maryland Historical Society, has been frequently reproduced and photographed. It is labeled in large letters at the bottom with "A VIEW of the BOMBARDMENT of Fort McHenry." A text in script continues with "taken from the observatory under the command of Admirals Cochrane & Cockburn, on the morning of the 13th of Sept. 1814 which lasted 24 hours & thrown from 1500 to 1800 shells in the night attempted to land by forcing a passage up the ferry branch, but were repulsed with great loss."

According to the National Museum of American History, John Bower was an engraver who worked from 1809 to 1819 in Philadelphia, another port city ("Printing Plate," 1811).

There is another color print entitled "FIRST VIEW of the BATTLE of PATAPSCO NECK," which was published in Baltimore within two weeks of the incident (Hunter 1951, 236). It depicts British and American forces at the time of the shooting of General Robert Ross. It was designed by Corporal Andrew Duluc, who

"A View of the Bombardment of Fort McHenry," by John Bower, c. 1819. (Library of Congress)

claimed to have been an eyewitness and who acknowledged receiving help from Captain Boulden, a surveyor. This may be viewed online at the Library of Congress website.

See also: Paintings of the Bombardment of Fort McHenry; Visual Arts.

Further Reading

Bower, John. 1814. "A View of the Bombardment of Fort McHenry." Maryland Historical Society. http://www.mdhs.org/digitalimage/view-bombardment-fort-mchenry -near-baltimore-british-fleet-taken-observatory-under-com.

Duluc, Andrew. 1814. "First View of the Battle of Patapsco Neck Dedicated to Those Who Lost Their Friends in Defence of Their Country, Septr. 12, 1814." Library of Congress. https://www.loc.gov/resource/pga.05972.

Hunter, Wilbur H., Jr. 1951. "The Battle of Baltimore Illustrated." *William and Mary Quarterly* 8 (April): 235–37.

"Printing Plate." 1811. Smithsonian National Museum of American History. http://ameri canhistory.si.edu/collections/search/object/nmah_315317.

Visual Arts

The American flag has been the subject of numerous artists, including such luminaries as Jasper Johns, Childe Hassam, and Robert Longo. "The Star-Spangled Banner" is itself an attempt to pay tribute to the flag through music.

Although the flag is itself a more frequent subject for artists than the anthem that describes its enduring presence in the face of the British attack on Fort McHenry in 1814, there are a number of artists who have sought to celebrate the song as well. Many of these are described in a photographic essay published by *Smithsonian Magazine*.

One is a cartoon by R. O. Blechman entitled "The Midwife Midshipman" in which he portrays Francis Scott Key, author of "The Star-Spangled Banner," encountering writer's block aboard a ship. He begins writing when a fellow passenger asks, "Sir, can you see there by the dawn's early light? Your flag, it's still there!"

Another is a painting by Tim O'Brien of a youthful looking Francis Scott Key staring directly at the viewer. The painting portrays sunlight shining on clouds in the background and a streaming American flag directly behind him.

Yet another painting by Peter Halley, which the Smithsonian refers to as a "flowing photomontage," portrays three flags with bright red, white, and blue colors swirling. Clearly inspired by the words of "The Star-Spangled Banner," Halley observes, "In a way the stars and stripes get equated with streaming and bursting." The tie to the song is further enhanced by capitalized letters with the first line of the song on some of the red and white stripes.

Daniel Libeskind, a Polish immigrant who is also known for incorporating bells into his work, has combined a framed picture of a flag on the left with lines of music engraved on steel and aluminum on the right. He designed these metals to illustrate the flag's (and the song's) resilience.

John Bower was the engraver of a fairly primitive print of Fort McHenry entitled "View of the Bombardment of Fort McHenry," which was published fairly contemporaneously with the event. Brad Holland (1943–), who was raised near Fort Stephenson, which was also attacked by the British, has also painted a beautiful color picture of Fort McHenry the day after the battle. Bright clouds dominate the background against which the star-spangled banner is flying and what appears to be a very peaceful fort in the foreground looking deceptively calm and unfortified.

See also: Cartoons and the National Anthem; Paintings of the Bombardment of Fort McHenry; Ripley Cartoon; "View of the Bombardment of Fort McHenry."

Further Reading

Hartvigsen, Kenneth. 2018. "The Flag in American Art." In *The American Flag: An Encyclopedia of the Stars and Stripes in U.S. History, Culture and Law*, edited by John R. Vile, 45–53. Santa Barbara, CA: ABC-CLIO.

"These Artistic Interpretations of the Star-Spangled Banner Call Out the Inner Patriot." 2014. *Smithsonian Magazine* (June). https://www.smithsonianmag.com/arts-cul ture/these-artistic-interpretations-star-spangled-banner-call-out-inner-patriot -180951536.

War and the National Anthem

Although it was based on a popular English tune known as "To Anacreon in Heaven," which was more commonly associated with love and wine than with war, "The Star-Spangled Banner" was conceived in the aftermath of a battle during the War of 1812. Moreover, it gained increased recognition during the Civil War and others that followed. Over the decades it has been both praised for stirring patriotism during times of war and danger, and criticized as bellicose.

In contrast to other songs that were composed during the War of 1812, Francis Scott Key's song managed to convey the intensity of conflict—"the rockets' red glare, the bombs bursting in air"—without glorifying it. Apart from the controversial third verse (which is usually omitted), which wished "the terror of flight or the gloom of the grave" on enemies whom the author identified as "the hireling and slave," Key further refused to personalize the conflict by naming specific individuals in the conflict. Moreover, the final verse links victory not to further conflict but to "peace." As a whole, the song glorifies the flag, rather than war or conflict, even speaking in the last verse of "war's desolation."

Perhaps because the tune is so stirring, military authorities ordered the playing of "The Star-Spangled Banner" during flag raisings and lowerings and President Woodrow Wilson designated it as the anthem for U.S. armed forces long before Congress chose the song as the anthem for the entire nation in 1931.

Prior to the U.S. entry into World War I, Katherine D. Blake, a pacifist suffragist, penned an alternative that stressed peace over war:

O say can you see, you who glory in war,
All the wounded and dead
Of the red battle's reaping
Can you listen unmoved to their agonized groans
Hear the children who starve,
And the pale widows weeping?
Henceforth let us swear,
Bombs shall not burst in air,
Nor war's desolation wreck all that is fair.
But the star spangled banner by workers unfurled
Shall give hope to the nations
And peace to the world.

American entry into the war resulted in the increasing incorporation of "The Star-Spangled Banner" into concert performances and athletic events, many of the

This envelope from the Civil War shows an eagle atop arrows and a drum with the American flag, cannon, and rifles along with the words "The Star Spangled Banner Must Be Upheld." Envelopes such as these were used as propaganda on both sides. (Library of Congress)

latter of which are also closely associated in the American imagination with traditional ideals of manhood and combat. For many years, television stations also ended their day by airing "The Star-Spangled Banner."

As momentum began to build to declare "The Star-Spangled Banner" the nation's anthem, the chief opposition came from those who thought the song was too warlike (with some critics especially concerned about its effect on children) and others who asserted that the song's roots in an English drinking song made it unsuitable. Augusta E. Stetson and Kitty Cheatham, both prominent members of the Christian Science Church, were among those who thought the song was too militaristic. Columbia Professor Clyde R. Miller complained that the song linked patriotism "with killing and being killed, with great noise and clamor, with intense hatreds and fury and violence" (Connor 2017, 48). Strong support for designating Key's song as the nation's official anthem, however, came from Maryland and surrounding states (since the song came from a historical event that took place in the region), as well as from such organizations as the American Legion, Veterans of Foreign Wars, and Daughters of the American Revolution. Moreover, lack of consensus on an alternative eventually led to the official congressional recognition of the anthem in 1931. It is far from the only national anthem that focused on war ("This Is My Fight Song" 2017).

During the Vietnam War, some antiwar protestors burned the American flag in protest of U.S. involvement in the conflict. In recent years, however, the practice of flag burning as a form of social protest has become exceedingly rare—in large part because of perceptions that such actions are counterproductive in terms of building support for the cause or protest action in question.

See also: Cheatham, Kitty; Civil War; Code for the National Anthem; Congress and "The Star-Spangled Banner"; Military Regulations; Songs of the U.S. Armed Forces; Sports Events; Stetson, Augusta E.; Veterans; Vietnam War; War of 1812; World Wars I and II.

Further Reading

Booth, Wayne C. 2005. "War Rhetoric, Defensible and Indefensible." *JAC* 25:221–44.

Connor, Joseph. 2017. "Off Key." *American History* 51 (February): 42–51.

"This Is My Fight Song—Seven National Anthems Inspired by Bloodshed, Battles and War." 2017. *Military History Now,* June 20. https://militaryhistorynow.com/2017/06/20/this-is-my-fight-song-seven-national-anthems-inspired-by-bloodshed-battles-and-war.

Wilson, Carl. 2014. "Proudly Hailed: 'The Star-Spangled Banner' Is Militaristic, Syntactically Garbled, and Impossible to Sing. It's Perfect." *Slate,* July 3. https://slate.com/culture/2014/07/the-star-spangled-banner-four-reasons-it-shouldnt-be-the-national-anthem-but-always-will-be.html.

War of 1812

"The Star-Spangled Banner" was composed by Francis Scott Key after he witnessed the British bombardment of Fort McHenry just outside Baltimore during the War of 1812.

That war, sometimes dubbed as America's second war for independence, is probably best known for the unsuccessful attempt by the United States to capture Canada; by a series of American naval victories, mostly on the Great Lakes, against British naval forces; by the British burning of most public buildings in Washington, DC; by the successful defense of Baltimore that "The Star-Spangled Banner" celebrates; and by Andrew Jackson's celebrated victory over the British in the Battle of New Orleans.

The thirteen colonies had declared their independence from the British mother country in 1776 and secured recognition of this independence in the Treaty of Paris in 1783. Even after the United States replaced its Articles of Confederation with a more powerful government in 1789, however, it was affected by European conflicts, especially those involving Napoleonic France and Britain, both of which attempted to restrict U.S. trade to the other side. During the administration of John Adams, the second U.S. president, the United States came close to an undeclared war with France, but many Americans felt greater affinity to French ideals of "liberty, fraternity, and equality" than to British monarchism.

During the administration of Thomas Jefferson, the United States enforced its own embargoes against Britain and France in largely unsuccessful, and highly unpopular (especially in New England) attempts to influence their policies. When James Madison became president in 1809, the French proved more adept at promising to end deprecations against American shipping than the British, who further angered Americans by stopping U.S. ships and impressing (seizing for military service) seaman whom they suspected of being British deserters. In 1807, the HMS *Leopard* attacked an American vessel called the *Chesapeake* and removed four sailors, one of whom it hanged. In 1811, the USS *President* had fired on the British *Little Belt* and exacted casualties in a battle that was also precipitated by fears of British impressment.

Although the issues of freedom of the seas and impressment were significant, much of the impetus for the War of 1812 is attributable to American "war hawks" like Henry Clay of Kentucky and John C. Calhoun of South Carolina, who believed that British support through Canada of Native Americans was hindering America's settlement of the western frontier. There is continuing dispute as to whether they wanted to annex the land that Americans had helped the British capture from France during the French and Indian War as a bargaining chip, or whether they intended to incorporate it into the United States (Hatter 2012).

Although Britain repealed its Orders in Council, which had embargoed U.S. goods, on June 16, 1812, the action came too late to avert war. The U.S. House of Representatives had already voted to go to war on June 4, 1812, by a vote of seventy-nine to one, and the Senate had followed with a vote of nineteen to thirteen on June 17 (Langguth 2006, 154). Five months later, James Madison was elected to a second term as president.

Initial hopes that Americans would be welcomed with open arms into Canada proved largely illusory. American commanders, most notably Brigadier General William Hull, the governor of the Michigan Territory, suffered a number of embarrassing defeats. In time, Commodore Oliver Perry did win a number of naval battles on Lake Erie, just as the USS *Constitution* would distinguish itself on the high seas. Moreover, Americans killed Tecumseh, the Native American Indian who successfully led a coalition of tribes in alliance with Britain, at the Battle of Thames in 1813.

Elsewhere, American General Andrew Jackson carried out a brutal but effective war against the Creek Indians, who were also allied with the British, in 1814. That same year, however, the British defeated Napoleon, allowing them to divert more resources to North America, where British ships under the command of Admiral George Cockburn had been blockading American ports and destroying towns like Frenchtown and Havre de Grace—but where American privateers, many of which were based in Baltimore, Maryland, had, in turn, been preying on British ships. After British troops defeated American militiamen at the Battle of Bladensburg on August 24, 1814, British troops advanced to a largely undefended U.S. capital and burned the Capitol Building and the White House. The First Lady, Dolley Madison, emerged as something of a heroine during this assault, as she saved a large portrait of George Washington by Gilbert Stuart from destruction before fleeing from the White House. The British then set their sights on Baltimore with the intention of inflicting severe damage on that city as well. They used American arson of some public buildings in York, the provincial capital of Ontario (today's Toronto), in 1813 as justification for these actions.

In a subsequent attack on North Point, however, General Robert Ross was killed by American sharpshooters, which frustrated an attempt to invade Baltimore by land and led to the naval bombardment of Fort McHenry. Largely due to the efforts of U.S. Senator Samuel Smith, who also commanded Maryland's third militia division, it had been significantly fortified the previous year (Cassell 1969, 349–50). During the bombardment, the British kept Francis Scott Key aboard the ship of truce on which he had come to negotiate the release of Dr. William Beanes, a medical doctor whom the British had captured for what they believed to have been his duplicity. The battle was especially notable for the British use of Congreve rockets and huge bombs, which they launched at the fort from their ships.

The Battle of Baltimore, which took place on September 13 and 14, 1814, was full of sound and fury but proved unsuccessful in forcing the Americans to surrender. On the morning of September 14, Key was filled with great relief when he saw the gigantic American flag still flying from the ramparts in the early dawn light. British forces under the direction of Admiral George Cockburn subsequently withdrew from the Chesapeake Bay and headed for New Orleans, where under the direction of Major General Sir Edward Pakenham, they met American forces led by General Andrew Jackson, who was joined by privateer Jean Lafitte. On January 8, 1815, the American forces, who were much more familiar with the topography of the area and were entrenched in defensive positions, won the Battle of New Orleans, exacting a heavy toll on their British attacks. More than 140 years later, in 1959, Johnny Horton authored a popular song called "The Battle of New Orleans" celebrating this victory.

Both the Battle of Baltimore and the victory at New Orleans did much to boost American pride, but although the participants did not know it, the latter battle actually occurred after the Americans and British had signed the Treaty of Ghent, which essentially ended the war and restored the two nations to their prewar status quo. American negotiators included John Quincy Adams, Henry Clay Albert Gallatin, James Bayard, and Jonathan Russell. Because of the memory of those two big military triumphs in the conflict's final weeks and the early popularity of "The Star-Spangled Banner," the public memory of the war tended "to exaggerate the United States' triumph and overstate its martial and global power. . . . Retroactively the war quickly became an emblem and trophy of national feeling, unity, strength, and expansion" (Dennis 2014, 271).

The War of 1812 had witnessed atrocities on all sides, which helps explain the venom that Key directed to British hirelings and slaves in the third verse of the anthem, which Americans seldom sing today. Although James Madison's initial appointees, especially Secretary of the Army John Armstrong and Secretary of the Navy William Jones, had proven woefully unsuccessful in preparing for war—and especially in appreciating the vulnerability of the capital—Madison was lauded for preserving civil rights and liberties during the conflict.

Largely as a result of its opposition to the war, the Federalist Party, which was strongly based in New England and whose members had participated in the Hartford Convention, which had discussed the possibility of secession and had proposed a number of changes in the U.S. Constitution, largely died out. After a brief period known as "The Era of Good Feelings," under the Presidency of James Monroe, who had served as Madison's Secretary of State and Secretary of War, in time the Whig Party replaced it.

See also: Baltimore, Maryland; Beanes, William; Fort McHenry; Key, Francis Scott; Madison, James; Ross, Robert; Smith, Samuel; Star-Spangled National Historic Trail; War and the National Anthem.

Further Reading

Borneman, Walter R. 2009. *1812: The War That Forged a Nation.* New York: HarperCollins.

Cassell, Frank A. 1969. "Baltimore in 1813: A Study of Urban Defense in the War of 1812." *Military Affairs* 33 (December): 349–61.

Dennis, Matthew. 2014. "Reflections on a Bicentennial: The War of 1812 in American Public Memory." *Early American Studies* 12 (Spring): 269–300.

Green, Emma. 2014. "The Series of Improbable Events That Gave Us 'The Star Spangled Banner.'" *Atlantic,* July 8. https://www.theatlantic.com/national/archive/2014/07 /we-luh-ya-war-of-1812/374056.

Hatter, Lawrence B. A. 2012. "Party Like It's 1812: The War at 200." *Tennessee Historical Quarterly* 71 (Summer): 90–111.

Hickey, Donald R. 2012. *The War of 1812: A Forgotten Conflict.* Bicentennial edition. Urbana: University of Illinois Press.

Hildebrand, David K. 2014. "Bicentenary Essay: Two National Anthems? Some Reflections on the Two Hundredth Anniversary of 'The Star-Spangled Banner' and Its Forgotten Partner, 'The Battle of Baltimore.'" *American Music* 32 (Fall): 253–71.

Howard, Hugh. 2012. *Mr. and Mrs. Madison's War: America's First Couple and the Second War for Independence.* New York: Bloomsbury Press.

Langguth, A. J. 2006. *Union 1812: The Americans Who Fought the Second War of Independence.* New York: Simon & Schuster.

Lord, Walter. 1972. *The Dawn's Early Light.* New York: W.W. Norton.

Vogel, Steve. 2013. *Through the Perilous Fight: From the Burning of Washington to the Star-Spangled Banner; The Six Weeks That Saved the Nation.* New York: Random House.

"When the Warrior Returns"

In 1805, Francis Scott Key composed a poem for an event honoring Stephen Decatur and Charles Stewart, two heroes of the war in Tripoli, who were being feted at McLaughlin's Tavern in Georgetown. The poem, entitled "When the Warrior Returns," was later set to the music of "To Anacreon in Heaven," which was also the tune to which "The Star-Spangled Banner" was later set (Leepson 2014, 68).

The song is significant for a number of reasons. First, as stated above, it was written by the same author and set to the same tune as the national anthem. Second, like "The Star-Spangled Banner," it focused on battle. Third, it specifically mentioned the "Star Spangled flag of our nation." Finally, the concluding line of each verse references the "brave."

"When the Warrior Returns" is composed of five verses. The first notes the appropriateness of welcoming the warrior "To the home and the country he nobly defended." Welcoming the heroes to "the feast-flowing board," participants throng:

Where, mixed with the olive, the laurel shall wave,
And form a bright wreath for the brows of the brave.

The second verse identified the heroes as "Columbians" and a "band of your brothers" who had crossed the ocean and the dessert: "To a far distant shore, to the battle's wild roar."

The third verse mentioned "the war's desolation." It further observed:

And pale beamed the Crescent, its splendor obscured
By the light of the Star Spangled flag of our nation.
Where each radiant star gleamed a meteor of war,
And the turbaned heads bowed to its terrible glare.

At least one writer has criticized the national anthem for originating in these lines, which he believes to be anti-Muslim (Husseini 2016). One might just as simply describe the lines as opposing the payment of forced tribute to any nation.

The fourth verse attempted to tie the bravery of those who had gone to Tripoli with those of the Founding Fathers, while identifying the Tripoli foes as "infidels":

Our fathers, who stand on the summit of fame,
Shall exultingly hear of their sons the proud story:
How their young bosoms glow'd with the patriot flame,
How they fought, how they fell, in the blaze of their glory.
And triumphant they rode over the wondering flood,
And stained the blue waters with infidel blood.

The final verse, like the first, largely welcomes the warrior heroes home again and rejoices that their "perils are ended" and that their fame rolls along.

See also: Key, Francis Scott; Pickersgill, Mary Young; "To Anacreon in Heaven."

Further Reading

Husseini, Sam. 2016. "Why We Should All Remain Seated: The Anti-Muslim Origins of 'The Star-Spangled Banner.'" *Counterpunch*, August 30. https://www.counter punch.org/2016/08/30/the-anti-muslim-origins-of-the-star-spangled-banner.

Key, Francis Scott. 1805. "When the Warrior Returns." Memorial Day Tribute. http://www.thememorialdaytribute.com/memorial-day-songs/when-the-warrior-returns.html.

Leepson, Marc. 2014. *What So Proudly We Hailed: Francis Scott Key, A Life*. New York. Palgrave/Macmillan.

"Whose Broad Stripes and Bright Stars"

Although the national anthem is best known for identifying the U.S. flags as the star-spangled banner, it is also associated with another nickname for the flag, namely the stars and stripes. Francis Scott Key's reference in "The Star-Spangled

Banner" to "whose broad stripes and bright stars" indicates that the current order for distinguishing the two main elements of the flag was not at that time standard. Key's further use of the word "whose," which usually references a person rather than a thing, is also arguably the anthem's only explicit time where the anthem personifies the flag by giving it human qualities.

The flag that Key is believed to have seen through the mists on the morning after the bombardment of Fort McHenry had been ordered by Colonel George Armistead from Mary Pickersgill and was quite large. Although its length has subsequently been shortened by early souvenir hunters after 1814, it measured thirty by forty-two feet so that, even from a distance, the stripes would have appeared to have been "broad."

The national march is John Philip Sousa's "The Stars and Stripes Forever."

See also: Key, Francis Scott; Star-Spangled Banner Flag; "Stars and Stripes Forever, The."

Further Reading

Vile, John R. 2018. *The American Flag: An Encyclopedia of the Stars and Stripes in U.S. History, Culture, and Law*. Santa Barbara, CA: ABC-CLIO.

Wilson, Woodrow

Thomas Woodrow Wilson (1856–1924), who commonly used his middle name, served as president from 1913 to 1921. In 1916, he followed up on earlier actions by Secretary of the Navy Benjamin Franklin Tracy, who had made "The Star-Spangled Banner" the official song for flag raisings in the navy, by mandating that it would now be used as the official anthem of all U.S. armed forces.

Wilson, who was born in Virginia, is the only U.S. president to have had a PhD. He earned it at Johns Hopkins University, where he wrote a dissertation on congressional government and expressed great admiration for the British parliamentary system of government. After publishing numerous books, he went on to serve as president of Princeton, and then, from 1911 to 1913, as governor of New Jersey.

In 1912, Wilson won the Democratic nomination for president of the United States. In the general election that November, he defeated incumbent Republican William Howard Taft and former president Theodore Roosevelt, who was running as the candidate of the Progressive "Bull Moose" Party. Despite his well-documented racism, Woodrow's own New Freedom agenda was considered to be progressive. He largely won reelection in 1916 by stressing how he had kept America out of World War I, which erupted across Europe in 1914. Shortly after his reelection, however, Wilson was goaded to action by attacks of German U-boats (submarines) on American shipping. On April 2, 1917, he asked Congress for a declaration of war against Germany and its allies in what he described as "a war to end all wars." In retrospect, his attempt to establish an official national anthem for the military might have been in preparation for this eventuality.

In 1916, the same year that Wilson recognized the flag as the official anthem of the armed forces, he issued the first presidential proclamation recognizing June 14 as Flag Day:

> With special patriotic exercises, at which means shall be taken to give significant expression to our thoughtful love of America, our comprehension of the great mission of liberty and justice to which we have devoted ourselves as a people, our pride in the history and our enthusiasm for the political programme of the nation, our determination to make it greater and purer with each generation, and our resolution to demonstrate to all the world its vital union in sentiment and purpose, accepting only those as true compatriots who feel as we do the compulsion of this supreme allegiance. (Vile 2018, 164–65)

During the war, Wilson's attorney general, A. Mitchell Palmer (1872–1936), led a series of raids against American leftists and antiwar activists, showing little regard for their civil rights or liberties. Wilson himself had little sympathy for those who expressed opposition to his war policies. As the war ended, Wilson pushed his so-called "14 points," through which he hoped to bring about a permanent global peace, but he failed to secure Senate support for one of the key elements of this policy, namely the League of Nations (a type of precursor to today's United Nations), and during whistle-stop trips to secure support for this, he suffered a debilitating stroke that further limited his effectiveness.

In 1918, Columbia Records released a recording of Wilson's daughter, Margaret, singing "The Star-Spangled Banner." The sales were used to benefit the Red Cross.

After World War I, support for making "The Star-Spangled Banner" the national anthem for the entire country continued to grow. In 1931, Republican President Herbert Hoover (1874–1964), who was at that time presiding over the devastating economic downturn known as the Great Depression, signed congressional legislation that designated "The Star-Spangled Banner" as the national anthem. It is quite possible that both Congress and Hoover considered that the adoption of such an anthem might help instill pride in a nation that was suffering from severe unemployment.

See also: Tracy, Benjamin Franklin.

Further Reading

Kampion, Helen. 2008. "Star-Spangled Presidents." Our White House: Looking In, Looking Out (website). National Children's Book and Literary Alliance. http://our whitehouse.org/star-spangled-presidents.

Vile, John R. 2018. *The American Flag: An Encyclopedia of the Stars and Stripes in U.S. History, Culture, and Law.* Santa Barbara, CA: ABC-CLIO.

Women

A survey of national anthems by editors of *The Guardian* (2015) reveals that "The Star-Spangled Banner" is one of the least sexist. In the entire four stanzas, there is only one direct reference to gender, when the fourth verse proclaims "thus be it ever, when freemen shall stand / Between their loved home and the war's desolation!" Although the term man or men was sometimes contemporaneously used to include members of both sexes, given the complexion of military forces of the time it seems likely that Key was primarily thinking that men would be fulfilling this role.

Other references to "you" in the first line of the first verse, as well as later references to "we" and "our" would include both sexes, as would references to "the land of the free and the home of the brave." Indeed, at the time Key was writing, visions of home might more often have included women than men.

At the time, it was not uncommon to refer to nations and their flags as gendered, as in "fatherland" or "motherland"; Key passed up the opportunity of personification and refers to the star-spangled banner as an "it" rather than as a "he" or "she."

Just as some religious denominations have sought to purge their hymnbooks of masculine pronouns, so too a number of nations, including Canada, have changed their national anthem to include both genders. Britain's anthem, which is directed to the monarch rather than to the flag, calls on God to save the "King" or "Queen," depending on the gender of the current individual on the throne.

Beginning in the mid-nineteenth century, the women's suffrage movement had a number of protest songs including one based on "My Country, 'Tis of Thee" that was as follows:

Our country, now from thee,
Claim we our liberty,
In freedom's name
Guarding home altar fires,
Daughter of patriot sires,
Their zeal our own inspires,
Justice to claim.

U.S. suffragists made liberal use of the American flag during their protests for the right to vote, and they made similar use of patriotic songs. After a major parade in Washington, DC, in 1913, women played "The Star-Spangled Banner" prior to staging a pageant at the Treasury Building featuring representations of Columbia, Charity, Justice, Liberty, Peace, and Hope (Harvey 2001). The modern women's movement has had a number of songs that are sometimes classified as women's anthems. These include Aretha Franklin's iconic "Respect," Helen Reddy's "I Am Woman," and "I Can't Keep Quiet," which was used during the Women's March on Washington in 2017.

One of the central concerns about "The Star-Spangled Banner," which makes references to the "hireling" and "slave" in the third verse, in addition to the above-mentioned "freemen," has centered more on whether the song, which was written by a slaveholder, was racist. Lawrence Johnson, who is concerned both about perceived racism and sexism in "The Star-Spangled Banner," has launched an online petition to change the national anthem to "America the Beautiful."

See also: "America the Beautiful"; "God Save the Queen"; Lyrics of "The Star-Spangled Banner"; "O Canada"; Slavery.

Further Reading

Harvey, Sheridan. 2001. "Marching for the Vote: Remembering the Woman Suffrage Parade of 1913." Library of Congress. https://guides.loc.gov/american-women -essays/marching-for-the-vote.

Hayward, Nancy. n.d. "Brief Overview of Protest Songs." National Women's History Museum. https://www.womenshistory.org/resources/general/brief-overview-protest -songs.

Johnson, Lawrence. n.d. "Change America's National Anthem from 'The Star-Spangled Banner' to 'America the Beautiful.' (A Civil Rights Issue)." Petition to Chairman of the Congressional Black Caucus Cedric Richmond. Change .org. https://www .change.org/p/the-congressional-black-caucus-change-america-s-national-anthem -from-the-star-spangled-banner-to-america-the-beautiful-a-civil-rights-issue.

Nardelli, Alberto, and Ami Sedghi. 2015. "Which Is the Most Sexist National Anthem?" *The Guardian*, February 25. https://www.theguardian.com/news/datablog/2015 /feb/25/how-sexist-is-canadas-national-anthem-compared-with-others.

Vile, John R. 2018. *The American Flag: An Encyclopedia of the Stars and Stripes in U.S. History, Culture, and Law.* Santa Barbara, CA: ABC-CLIO.

World Wars I and II

"The Star-Spangled Banner" was written in the aftermath of the British bombardment of Fort McHenry in 1814 during the War of 1812. Although this occurred during a time when most troops on land continued to fight under colors of their battalion, Francis Scott Key centered his anthem on the visibility of the U.S. flag over the fort throughout the blasts of bombs and rockets during the night and in the mists of the next morning. Ever since then, the popularity of the anthem has corresponded with the rise in affection for the flag as a national symbol.

This affection for both flag and anthem was certainly enhanced during both world wars. Shortly before World War I, President Woodrow Wilson issued an executive order making Key's song the official song of the U.S. military, which had already established regulations mandating that the song be played at flag raisings in the morning. The so-called "war to end all wars" also marked the period in which it became common to play the tune at baseball games. The flag that the song extolled was also increasingly used in art, as in the impressionist paintings by Childe Hassam. There were strong reactions to German-American composers, such as Karl Muck, who refused to play—or were perceived as refusing to play— "The Star-Spangled Banner" during the war years (Mugmon 2014).

Congress officially recognized "The Star-Spangled Banner" as the national anthem in 1931, between the two world wars. In the interim, Kate Smith stirred patriotic emotions with her renditions of Irving Berlin's "God Bless America." As the United States fought Nazism during World War II, American courts affirmed the rights of individuals not to salute the flag. This war also marked the releases of "There's a Star-Spangled Banner Waving Somewhere," as well as the iconic photograph of U.S. Marines raising an American flag over Mount Suribachi on Iwo Jima after a major victory over the Japanese. Miss Lucy Monroe furthered her reputation as the "Star-Spangled Soprano" during the war. Meanwhile,

Russian-born composer Igor Stravinsky received criticism for his 1944 performance of the anthem, which departed in a number of respects from more traditional renditions.

See also: Veterans; War of 1812; Wilson, Woodrow.

Further Reading

Mugmon, Matthew. 2014. "Patriotism, Art, and 'The Star-Spangled Banner' in World War I: A New Look at the Karl Muck Episode." *Journal of Musicological Research* 33:4–26.

United States World War One Centennial Commission. n.d. "The Star-Spangled Banner and World War One." https://www.worldwar1centennial.org/index.php/educate /places/the-star-spangled-banner-and-world-war-one.html.

Writing of "The Star-Spangled Banner"

Although some symbols emerge from the mists of history, Francis Scott Key's writing of "The Star-Spangled Banner" literally arose as his eyes tried to penetrate the physical mists connected to one of the most consequential battles of the War of 1812. The United States had declared this war against Great Britain in 1812 after a series of self-imposed blockades had failed to stop British imprecations against U.S. shipping, including the impressment of U.S. soldiers, whom the British believed (sometimes correctly) had deserted from their fleet.

Francis Scott Key was a fairly prominent Maryland-born attorney who largely practiced out of Georgetown but who, like many fellow Federalists of his day, had opposed American participation in the war. As British ships began burning towns along the Chesapeake Bay area where he lived, however, he was determined to resist and actually served for a brief time during the disastrous Battle of Bladensburg, after which the British burned most of the government buildings in Washington, DC.

During some of their sojourn in Maryland, General Robert Ross had lodged at the house of sixty-five-year-old Dr. William Beanes, where Beanes, a highly regarded local physician, treated his men and him hospitably and may even have taken an oath of good behavior. After they left, however, Beanes, who was a leading citizen of Upper Marlborough, had sought the arrest of a number of British soldiers who had returned and begun abusing his neighbors. Thinking that he had been betrayed, General Ross ordered Beanes's arrest, a process that was carried out with little regard to the doctor's dignity. Beanes's friends enlisted Key to help secure his release.

By this time, Ross was aboard ship with Beanes as a prisoner. Key received permission from President James Madison to seek Beanes's release. He was joined by Colonel John S. Skinner, who carried letters from British prisoners indicating that Americans were treating British officers and other soldiers that they had taken prisoner with humanity.

On September 7, a ship of truce (probably the *President*) carrying Key and Skinner caught up with Admiral Alexander Cochrane, who was aboard his flagship the *Tonnant*. Over a period of several days, the British were convinced to release Beanes, more because they appreciated American care for the wounded than out of conviction that Beanes deserved clemency. In the meantime, however, the British thought it unwise to release either the American emissaries or Dr. Beanes for fear that they would convey news of the pending British attack against Fort McHenry to their countrymen. The British initially transferred the men to the HMS *Surprise,* which Sir Thomas Cochrane (the admiral's son) commanded. They were then returned (apparently at Skinner's insistence) to their own ship still flying a flag of truce. It was from there that Key, anxious about the fate of Baltimore, witnessed the withering bombardment of Fort McHenry on the evening of September 13 that would become the focus of "The Star-Spangled Banner."

Writing about his experiences with Key in a letter to the *Baltimore Patriot and Commercial Gazette,* dated May 29, 1849, John Skinner reported that it was from the deck of their own ship "in view of Fort McHenry, that we witnessed through an anxious day and night, 'The rockets red glare, the bombs bursting in air,' and the song which was written the night after we got back to Baltimore, in the hotel then kept at the corner of Hanover and Market streets, was but a versified and almost literal transcript of our expressed hopes and apprehensions, through that ever-memorable period of anxiety to all, but never of despair" (Svejda 2005, 72).

Further evidence of what happened is found in a hearsay account by Key's brother-in-law, none other than U.S. Chief Justice Roger B. Taney, in a letter dated March 17, 1856, to Charles Howard of Baltimore, who had married Key's oldest daughter. Confirming much of what Skinner had said about Key's presence aboard ship during the bombardment of Fort McHenry, Taney reported that at dawn "their glasses [by which he presumably meant spyglasses] were turned to the fort, uncertain whether they should see there the stars and stripes, or the flag of the enemy. At length the light came, and they saw that 'our flag was still there'" (Key 1857, 25).

Taney summarized Key's response after Key handed Taney a printed copy of "The Star-Spangled Banner," and Taney asked him how he had found time to write the song amid the chaos:

> He said he commenced it on the deck of their vessel, in the fervor of the moment, when he saw the enemy hastily retreating to their ships, and looked at the flag he had watched for so anxiously as the morning opened; that he had written some lines or brief notes that would aid him in calling them to mind, upon the back of a letter which he happened to have in his pocket; and for some of the lines, as he proceeded, he was obliged to rely altogether on his memory; and that he finished it in the boat on his way to the shore, and wrote it out as it now stands, at the hotel, on the night he reached Baltimore, and immediately after he arrived. (Key 1857, 26)

Taney further reported that Key had taken the song the next morning to Judge Joseph Nicholson, who was so pleased that he took it to the printer (Skinner claimed to have done the same, so either one is mistaken or they took it together).

Key's song appears to have been first printed as a broadside by the Baltimore *American and Commercial Daily Advertiser* on September 17, 1814, under the title of the "Defense of Fort M'Henry." Samuel Sands, who would have been fourteen years old at the time, later said that he had set the type as an apprentice at the office of the *American* (Svejda 2005, 80–81). The text of the song was preceded with the following description, which was likely penned by Nicholson or Skinner:

> The annexed song was composed under the following circumstances—A gentleman had left Baltimore, in a flag of true for the purpose of getting released from the British fleet, a friend of his who had been captured at Marlborough.—He went as far as the mouth of the Patuxent, and was not permitted to return lest the intended attack on Baltimore should be disclosed. He was therefore brought up the Bay to the mouth of the Patapsco, where the flag vessel was kept under the guns of a frigate, and he was compelled to witness the bombardment of Fort McHenry, which the Admiral had boasted that he would carry in a few hours, and that the city must fall. He watched the flag at the Fort through the whole day with an anxiety that can be better felt than described, until the night prevented him from seeing it. In the night he watched the Bomb Shells, and at early dawn his eye was again greeted by the proudly waving flag of his country. ("Defence of Fort M'Henry" 1814)

Subsequent printings referred to the song by its current name.

Almost twenty years after he wrote the song, Key gave a speech on August 6, 1834, in which he described the circumstances that had given rise to the song. Recounting how, as a prisoner of the British, he had watched the preparations for battle with utmost anxiety, he further noted that "in the hour of deliverance, and joyful triumph, the heart spoke; and, Does not such a country, and such defenders of their country, deserve a song? was its question" (Key 1857, 198). Key observed that with the question came "an inspiration not to be resisted; and if it had been a hanging matter to make a song he must have made it" (158).

Key suggested, however, that if any praise for the song should go "not to the writer, but to the inspirers of the song" (1857, 198). He ended the speech by reiterating that "he was but the instrument in executing what they had been pleased to praise; it was dictated and inspired by the gallantry and patriotism of the sons of Maryland. The honor was due, not to him who made the song, but to the heroism of those who made him make it" (203). He ended by proposing a toast to "the real authors of the song, the defenders of the star spangled banner: What they would not strike to a foe, they will never sell to traitors" (203).

The greatest strength of Key's composition may well be that it grew from a specific threat to the United States that evoked not only colorful language but deep emotions that might better arise from the heat of the moment than from academic reflection. As one scholar wrote, "The idea of writing a national hymn to order in times of peace, without the inspiration of a nation's peril, or the fear of losing a people's liberty, seems to be as absurd as to suppose that the poet Bryant might have written Thanatopsis 'to order' as an obituary; or that Grey could have written his immortal Elegy as a funeral ode, in obedience to a royal mandate" (Richards 1895, 537).

See also: Baltimore, Maryland; Early Printings; Fort McHenry; Indian Queen Hotel (Baltimore); Key, Francis Scott; Smith, John Stafford; "To Anacreon in Heaven"; War of 1812; "When the Warrior Returns."

Further Reading

"Defence of Fort M'Henry." 1814. Maryland Historical Society. http://www.mdhs.org /digitalimage/defence-sic-fort-mhenry.

Key, Francis S. 1857. *Poems of the Late Francis S. Key, Esq., Author of "The Star-Spangled Banner."* Edited by Henry V. D. Johns. New York: Robert Carter & Brothers.

Magruder, Caleb Clarke, Jr. 1919. "Dr. William Beanes, the Incidental Cause of the Authorship of the Star-Spangled Banner." *Records of the Columbia Historical Society* 22:207–25.

Richards, Janet E. Hosmer. 1895. "The National Hymn." *American Monthly Magazine* (December): 536–40.

Svejda, George J. 2005. *History of the Star Spangled Banner from 1814 to the Present.* Honolulu, HI: University Press of the Pacific. First published in 1969 by Division of History, Office of Archeology and Historic Preservation, U.S. Department of the Interior, National Park Service.

Wyeth, N. C.

One of the paintings associated with the composition of "The Star-Spangled Banner" that is the most difficult to locate is one that illustrator N. C. Wyeth (1882–1945) was commissioned to paint for a new edition of *Poems of American Patriotism*, which Brander Matthew first published in 1882.

The collection included such patriotic favorites as Henry Wadsworth Longfellow's "Paul Revere's Ride," Julia Ward Howe's "Battle Hymn of the Republic," and Walt Whitman's "O Captain! My Captain!" It also included Francis Scott Key's "The Star-Spangled Banner."

Wyeth's illustration for the latter selection shows Francis Scott Key aboard a ship with two companions whose eyes are trained on the flag flying above Fort McHenry. It appears to be on the night of the bombardment because there is a lantern on the ship deck, and the sky above the fort is illumined by bright white and red clouds, presumably of smoke and the reflection from "the rockets' red glare."

See also: Baltimore, Maryland; Fort McHenry; Key, Francis Scott; Visual Arts.

Further Reading

National Park Service, Northeast Region. 2004. *Star-Spangled Banner National Historic Trail Feasibility Study and Environmental Impact Statement.* Philadelphia: U.S. Department of the Interior.

Troup, David. 2018. "N. C. Wyeth Exhibition: 'Poems of American Patriotism.'" *Wiscasset Newspaper*, June 2. https://www.wiscassetnewspaper.com/article/nc-wyeth-exhibition-poems-american-patriotism/102108.

"Yankee Doodle"

Of all the famous songs that conjure up feelings of national pride and patriotism, few are as intriguing as "Yankee Doodle." The song's origins are typically attributed to British troops (and specifically to a Dr. Richard Shuckburgh) who used it to ridicule Americans as country rubes but who, in turn, appropriated the song as a form of comic self-identification. Scholar J. A. Leo Lemay, however, points out that if he were the author, Shuckburgh had in fact come to America before 1735 and spent most of his adult life here. Moreover, Lemay believes that only an individual who was thoroughly Americanized could have written the song (1976, 441).

Unlike those who further attributed the origins of the song to either the French and Indian War in which Americans had fought alongside British regular troops or to the Revolutionary War, where they fought against them, Lemay believes that the original lyrics originated in a victory during King George's War of New Englanders led by William Pepperrell on June 16, 1745, at Fort Louisbourg on Cape Breton rather than a second engagement during the French and Indian War in 1758 (Lemay 1976, 443). He thus believes the original lyrics, which refer to a "Brother Ephraim" who sold a cow in order to get a British commission to fight against the French in Canada, was not satiric but ironic. He explains, "This ostensible satire of the provincial American militia is a perfect example of a dominant tradition of American humor. From the seventeenth century to the mid-twentieth, Americans have been keenly aware of English criticisms of their supposed barbarism. Colonial Americans learned to reply to English snobbery by deliberately posturing as unbelievably ignorant yokels. Thus, if the English believed the stereotype, they would be taken in by the Americans. And, of course, if they were taken in, the Americans had reversed the snobbery and proven that the English were credulous and foolish" (444–45). If Lemay is correct, and he musters strong evidence to support it, then "Yankee Doodle" originated as a New England folk song that was in oral circulation by the 1740s.

One elusive element about the tune is that it comes in many different versions. In addition to the version described above, Lemay cites two others. One is what he calls the "Corn Stalks" motif, which is a kind of "harvest-festival song," that describes activities surrounding corn husking (Lemay 1976, 448) and combines elements of poetry, music, and dance (451). Another is what Lemay calls the "Visit to Camp" motif (451), which describes a country bumpkin coming to an army camp and trying to explain drums, cannons, and other things that he has seen. There are, of course, many variants of the Revolutionary War version, including the one that may be the most popular:

> Yankee Doodle went to town,
> Riding on a pony,
> Stuck a feather in his cap,
> And called it macaroni.

Best-selling author Ace Collins believes this ditty, which originally referred to "Nankey Doodle," may actually date back to the British Civil War and was directed by British royalists (the Cavaliers) against the Cromwellian Parliamentary Roundheads, whose close-cropped hair was quite different than the long ringlets of the Cavaliers (2003, 204).

It seems clear that in the American contest, the term Yankee referred either generally to Americans or more specifically to New Englanders. During the Civil War, the term was used to refer to Union forces, whereas in contemporary lingo, many foreigners refer to Americans in general as Yankees.

The origin of the term is quite elusive. It might have been a Native American term for "English" or may have referred to an expression by a slow-witted but sharp-dealing farmer named Jonathon Hastings who was fond of telling customers that they were getting a "Yankee good deal" (Collins 2003, 207).

The derivation of the word "Doodle" is even more disputed. It may have been a synonym for "a silly or foolish fellow" (Davis 1938, 94), but it might also refer to a small penis (Abelove 2008, 14; Hildebrand 2014, 257). If so, much of the song might be interpreted as an extended phallic joke, with the doodle being a young unattached man with no female sexual outlets such as one might find among army recruits. John Picker (n.d.) cites one version of the song as follows:

> Two and two may go to Bed;
> Two and two together,
> And if there is not room enough,
> Lie one a top o'to'ther.

Whether the term "doodle" has a bawdy meaning or not, neither the simple tune nor the lyrics qualify as an "anthem." Nineteenth-century music critic Richard Grant White thus noted that "no sane person would ever dream of regarding it as a national hymn. Its words, as all know who have ever heard them, are mere childish burlesque; and its air, if air it must be called, is as comical as its words, and can hardly be regarded as being properly music" (1861, 19). In a similar fashion, the Reverend Elias Nason observed that "men laugh at "Yankee Doodle," yet they love it; they find all manner of fault with it, as with the romping, reckless, hoyden [boisterous] girl of the family; and yet they make the most of it. The world indeed has no tune like it" (1869, 27).

The latter association of the lyrics with a region of the country undoubtedly further worked against the song being designated as the national anthem.

Whatever its origins, the song was immensely popular. It was, for example, played at the surrender of British forces under Lord Cornwallis in Yorktown, Virginia, that effectively brought an end to the Revolutionary War. It was also played at the raising of "The Star-Spangled Banner" at Fort McHenry on the morning after its bombardment by the British (Sheads 1995, 41). It was often sung by northern troops during the Civil War. Ulysses S. Grant is reputed to have said, "I know only two tunes: one of them is 'Yankee Doodle' and the other isn't" (Gibbons 2008, 246). The tune was incorporated into Benjamin Carr's "Federal Overture," which was first performed in 1794, and in the Broadway play *The Yankee Doodle Boy*, or *I'm a Yankee Doodle Dandy*, which opened on Broadway in 1904, and was later transformed into a movie, *Yankee Doodle Dandy*, starring James Cagney. In 1978, Connecticut adopted "Yankee Doodle" as its official state song.

See also: Alternatives to the National Anthem; State Songs and Anthems.

Further Reading

Abelove, Henry. 2008. "Yankee Doodle Dandy." *Massachusetts Review* 49 (Spring–Summer): 13–21.

Browne, C. A. 1919. *The Story of Our National Ballads*. New York: Thomas Y. Crowell.

Collins, Ace. 2003. *Songs Sung Red, White, and Blue: The Stories Behind America's Best-Loved Patriotic Songs*. New York: HarperCollins.

Davis, Harold. 1938. "On the Origin of Yankee Doodle." *American Speech* 13 (April): 93–96.

Gibbons, William. 2008. "'Yankee Doodle' and Nationalism, 1780–1920." *American Music* 26 (Summer): 246–74.

Hildebrand, David K. 2014. "Bicentenary Essay: Two National Anthems? Some Reflections on the Two Hundredth Anniversary of 'The Star Spangled Banner' and Its Forgotten Partner, 'The Battle of Baltimore.'" *American Music* 32 (Fall): 253–71.

Lemay, J. A. Leo. 1976. "The American Origins of 'Yankee Doodle,'" *William and Mary Quarterly* 33 (July): 335–464.

Nason, Elias. 1869. *A Monogram on Our National Song*. Albany, NY: Joel Munsell.

Picker, John. n.d. "Two National Anthems." In *A New Literary History of America*, edited by Greil Marcus and Werner Sollors. http://www.newliteraryhistory.com/national anthems.html.

Sheads, Scott S. 1995. *Fort McHenry*. Baltimore: Nautical & Aviation Publishing Company of America.

Sonneck, Oscar George Theodore (compiler). 1909. *Report on "The Star-Spangled Banner," "Hail Columbia," "America," "Yankee Doodle."* Washington, DC: Government Printing Office (Library of Congress).

White, Richard Grant. 1861. *National Hymns: How They Are Written and How They Are Not Written. A Lyric and National Study for the Times*. New York: Rudd & Carleton.

"You're a Grand Old Flag"

Among America's patriotic songs, the one that arguably comes closest to "The Star-Spangled Banner" in highlighting the flag is "You're a Grand Old Flag." Composed by George M. Cohan (1878–1942) as part of a Broadway musical called *George Washington, Jr.*, it was first performed in 1906 and included a scene, later dropped, in which Cohan, who realized its symbolic appeal, wrapped himself in an American flag.

Cohan claimed to have been born on July 4 and said he was inspired to write "You're a Grand Old Flag" after giving a ride to a Civil War veteran who fondled a ragged piece of cloth from a flag that he had carried in the war and which he called "a grand old rag" (Collins 2003, 220–21). Cohan's original version contained this phrase, but he changed "rag" to "flag" after getting negative reactions from his audiences.

Much as in John Philip Sousa's "The Stars and Stripes Forever," Cohan sought to unite rival sections of the country, especially the North and South, by combining the sentiments expressed in "Yankee Doodle" with those of "Dixie." The result, as evidenced by the memorable lyrics of the first verse, lacks the more solemn dignity that is usually represented by an anthem:

> There's a feeling comes a-stealing
> And it sets my brain a-reeling
> When I'm list'ning to the music of a military band
> Any time like "Yankee Doodle"
> Simply sets me off my noodle
> It's the patriotic something
> That no one can understand
> "Way down South in the land of cotton"
> Melody untiring
> Ain't that inspiring!
> Hurrah! Hurrah! We'll join the jubilee
> And that's going some
> For the Yankees, by gum!
> Red, white and blue
> I am for you
> Honest, you're a grand old flag.

Like "The Star-Spangled Banner," the chorus, from which the song takes its title, directs primary attention to the American flag. Cohan's reference to "the home of the free and the brave" arguably borrows from "The Star-Spangled Banner," while his reference to the colors of the flag present an element that is not present in that work:

> You're a grand old flag,
> You're a high flying flag
> And forever in peace may you wave.
> You're the emblem of
> The land I love
> The home of the free and the brave.
> Ev'ry hearts beats true
> 'neath the Red, White and Blue,

Where there's never a boast or brag
Should auld acquaintance be forgot,
Keep your eye on the grand old flag.

Whereas the chorus eschews "a boast or a brag," the second stanza seems to glory in U.S. military might while again evoking the colors of the flag. It also evokes the symbol of Uncle Sam but again revels in popular language such as "hanky panky" and "square honest Yankee" that would probably exclude it from serious consideration as an anthem:

I'm a cranky hanky panky
I'm a dead square honest Yankee
And I'm mighty proud of that old flag
That flies for Uncle Sam
Though I don't believe in raving
Ev'ry time I see it waving
There's a chill runs up my back
That makes me glad I'm what I am
Here's a land with a million soldiers
That's if we should need 'em
We'll fight for freedom!
Hurrah! Hurrah! For ev'ry Yankee tar
And old G.A.R.
Ev'ry stripe, ev'ry star
Red, white and blue
Hats off to you
Honest, you're a grand old flag.

See also: Confederate National Anthem; "Yankee Doodle."

Further Reading

Collins, Ace. 2003. *Songs Sung Red, White, and Blue: The Stories Behind America's Best-Loved Patriotic Songs.* New York: HarperCollins.

McCabe, John. 1973. *George M. Cohan: The Man Who Owned Broadway.* Garden City, NY: Doubleday.

Whitmer, Mariana. 2005. "Songs with Social Significance: An Introduction." *OAH Magazine of History* 19 (July): 9–16, 22.

Appendix

For information on efforts to standardize the lyrics of "The Star-Spangled Banner," see the entry, "'Star-Spangled Banner, The,' Official Version," which includes an image of Francis Scott Key's original manuscript.

COMPLETE LYRICS OF "THE STAR-SPANGLED BANNER"

O say, can you see, by the dawn's early light,
What so proudly we hailed at the twilight's last gleaming?
Whose broad stripes and bright stars, through the perilous fight,
O'er the ramparts we watched, were so gallantly streaming!
And the rockets's red glare, the bombs bursting in air,
Gave proof through the night that our flag was still there:
O say, does that star-spangled banner yet wave
O'er the land of the free and the home of the brave?

On the shore, dimly seen through the mists of the deep,
Where the foe's haughty host in dread silence reposes,
What is that which the breeze, o'er the towering steep,
As it fitfully blows, half conceals, half discloses?
Now it catches the gleam of the morning's first beam,
In full glory reflected now shines on the stream:
'Tis the star-spangled banner! O long may it wave
O'er the land of the free and the home of the brave!

And where is that band who so vauntingly swore
That the havoc of war and the battle's confusion
A home and a country should leave us no more?
Their blood has washed out their foul footsteps pollution.
No refuge could save the hireling and slave
From the terror of flight, or the gloom of the grave:
And the star-spangled banner in triumph doth wave
O'er the land of the free and the home of the brave!

O thus be it ever, when freemen shall stand
Between their loved homes and the war's desolation!
Blest with victory and peace, may the heaven-rescued land
Praise the Power that hath made and preserved us a nation
Then conquer we must when our cause it is just

And this be our motto: "In God is our trust."
And the star-spangled banner in triumph shall wave
O'er the land of the free and the home of the brave!

Source: Fort McHenry National Monument and Historic Shrine. Available online at https://www.nps.gov/fomc/learn/historyculture/the-star-spangled-banner.htm.

Bibliography

ARTICLES

Abad-Santos, Alex. 2018. "Nike's Colin Kaepernick Ad Sparked a Boycott—and Earned $6 Billion for Nike." *Vox*, September 24. https://www.vox.com/2018/9/24/17895704/nike-colin-kaepernick-boycott-6-billion.

Abelove, Henry. 2008. "Yankee Doodle Dandy." *Massachusetts Review* 49 (Spring–Summer): 13–21.

Abril, Carlos R. 2007. "Functions of a National Anthem in Society and Education: A Sociocultural Perspective." *Bulletin of the Council for Research in Music Education*, no. 172 (Spring): 69–87.

Airfarcewon. n.d. "The Lard Fangled Fannies." AMiRight. http://www.amiright.com/parody/misc/nationalanthem2.shtml.

Aisen (Asen), Avrom. 1943. "The Star Spangled Banner in Yiddish." Museum of Family History. http://www.museumoffamilyhistory.com/yw-ssb.htm.

Albanese, Catherine. 1974. "Requiem for Memorial Day: Dissent in the Redeemer Nation." *American Quarterly* 26 (October): 386–398.

"Alexander Cochrane." n.d. War of 1812, Biography. American Battlefield Trust. https://www.battlefields.org/learn/biographies/alexander-cochrane.

Allen, Erin. 2012. "The Star-Spangled Banner." *LCM: Library of Congress Magazine* 14 (September/October): 14–15.

America Comes Alive. n.d. "Mary Pickersgill: Maker of the Star-Spangled Banner." https://americacomesalive.com/2015/03/27/mary-pickersgill-maker-of-the-star-spangled-banner.

American Public Education Foundation. n.d. "2018 National Anthem Sing-A-Long." https://www.theapef.org/national-anthem-sing-a-long.

Anderson, Dale. 1990. "Singer's Anthem Antics Hit Sour Note." *Buffalo News*, August 29. https://buffalonews.com/1990/08/29/singers-anthem-antics-hit-sour-note-flag-waving-planned-for-sinead-oconnor-concert.

Anonymous. 1914. "Captain Joseph Hopper Nicholson." *Patriotic Marylander* 1 (September): 11–13.

Araton, Harvey. 2017. "From the N.B.A., a Cautionary Tale on National Anthem Protests." *New York Times*, November 6. https://www.nytimes.com/2017/11/06/sports/basketball/anthem-nba-abdul-rauf-kaepernick.html.

Arlt, Gustave O., and Chandler Harris. 1944. "Songs of the Services." *California Folklore Quarterly* 3 (January): 36–49.

Armistead, George. 1814. "Official Account of the Bombardment of Fort McHenry. Copy of a Letter from Lieut. Colonel Armistead, to the Secretary of War." Smithsonian National Museum of American History (website). https://amhistory.si.edu/starspangledbanner/pdf/TRANSCRIPT%20Official%20Account%20of%20the%20Bombardment%20of%20Fort%20McHenry.pdf.

Aronson, Julian. 1942. "P.S. 2 Won the War: Back in 1917 We Pupils Memorized the National Anthem and Sold War Stamps in the Office Buildings." *Clearing House* 17 (October): 107–9.

Associated Press. 2016. "Guard Stops Students from Singing National Anthem at 9/11 Memorial." *New York Times*, April 25. https://www.nytimes.com/2016/04/26/nyregion/guard-stops-students-from-singing-national-anthem-at-9-11-memorial.html.

Associated Press. 2018. "Fergie Responds to 'Star-Spangled Banner' Criticism: 'I Honestly Tried My Best.'" *Newsday*, February 20. https://www.newsday.com/entertainment/celebrities/fergie-star-spangled-banner-nba-1.16863493.

Associated Press. 2019. "AP Fact Check: Trump's Tangle on American History." *WTOP News*, July 5. https://wtop.com/white-house/2019/07/ap-fact-check-trumps-tangle-on-american-history.

Atlas, Allan W. 1990. "Crossed Stars and Crossed Tonal Areas in Puccini's *Madama Butterfly*." *19th-Century Music* 14 (Autumn): 186–96.

Badger, Sylvia. 1994. "Jim McManus Honored for His Service to Humanity." *Baltimore Sun*, September 9. http://www.baltimoresun.com/news/bs-xpm-1994-09-1994252019-story.html.

Barbash, Fred, and Travis M. Andrews. 2016. "A Brief History of 'The Star-Spangled Banner' Being Played at Games and Getting No Respect." *Washington Post*, August 30. https://www.washingtonpost.com/news/morning-mix/wp/2016/08/30/a-brief-history-of-the-star-spangled-banner-being-played-at-games-and-getting-no-respect.

Barker, Barbara. 2017. "National Anthem: Why We Play It Before We Play." *Newsday*, September 30. https://www.newsday.com/sports/columnists/barbara-barker/national-anthem-why-we-sing-it-before-we-play-1.14307117.

Baron, Dennis. n.d. "Jose Can You See? The Controversy over the Spanish Translation of the Star-Spangled Banner." http://www.english.illinois.edu/-people-/faculty/debaron/essays/anthem.html.

Becker, Sam. 2018. "The Crazy Amount of Money the Military Gives to the NFL." *CheatSheet*, June 11. https://www.cheatsheet.com/money-career/amount-money-military-gives-nfl.html.

Belkin, Lisa. 1987. "Lucy Monroe Dies; a Celebrated Singer of National Anthem." *New York Times*, October 16.

Bentancourt, David. 2016. "As Puerto Rican Superhero Makes Debut, Her Writer Brings 'The Power of the People' to Comics." *Washington Post*, May 11. https://www.washingtonpost.com/news/comic-riffs/wp/2016/05/11/as-puerto-rican-superhero-makes-debut-her-writer-brings-the-power-of-our-people-to-comics.

Berry, Edmund. 1970. "The Poet of Love and Wine." *Mosaic: An Interdisciplinary Critical Journal* 3 (Winter): 132–43.

Billboard. 2018. "10 Worst National Anthem Performances Ever." *Billboard News*, February 2. https://www.billboard.com/articles/list/513562/10-worst-national -anthem-performances-ever.

Bishko, Lucretia Ramsey. 1972. "John S. Skinner Visits the Virginia Springs, 1847." *Virginia Magazine of History and Biography* 80 (April): 158–92.

Blackstone, Jerry, Mark Clague, and Andrew Thomas Kuster. 2014. "A Star-Spangled Bicentennial: A Conversation with Jerry Blackstone, Mark Clague, and Andrew Kuster." *Choral Journal* 54 (April): 6–17.

Blakemore, Erin. 2018. "How the Black Power Protest at the 1968 Olympics Killed Careers." *History Stories*, History Channel (website), February 22. https:// www.history.com/news/1968-mexico-city-olympics-black-power-protest -backlash.

Blanck, Jacob. 1966. "The Star Spangled Banner." *Papers of the Bibliographical Society of America* 60 (Second Quarter): 176–84.

Blim, Dan. 2017. "Party Politics: Ideology and Musical Performance at Donald Trump's Inaugural Celebration." *American Music* 35 (Winter): 478–89.

Blyler, Dorothea. 1960. "The Song Choices of Children in the Elementary Grades." *Journal of Research in Music Education* 8 (Spring): 9–15.

"'Bob Ross Meets Frank Sinatra.'" n.d. Joe Everson Art. https://www.joeeverson .com/about.

Boggs, Winthrop S. 1938. "Music and Stamps." *Musical Quarterly* 24 (January): 1–10.

Boorstein, Michelle. 2018. "The 'Star-Spangled Banner' in Church? Some Christians Are Questioning the Mix of Patriotism and God." *Washington Post*, July 1. https://www.washingtonpost.com/news/acts-of-faith/wp/2018/07/01 /star-spangled-banner-in-church-sunday-christians-debating-god-and -country-anew.

Booth, Wayne C. 2005. "War Rhetoric, Defensible and Indefensible." *JAC* 25:221–44.

Bordas, Juana. 2018. "It's Time for a National Anthem for Latinos." Juana Bordas (website), September 15. https://www.juanabordas.com/its-time-for -a-national-anthem-for-latinos.

Bowden, John. 2017. "Indiana Bill Would Force Colts to Refund Fans Offended by Anthem Protests." *The Hill*, December 28. https://thehill.com/blogs/blog -briefing-room/news/366722-indiana-bill-would-force-colts-to-offer -refunds-to-fans.

Bower, John. 1814. "A View of the Bombardment of Fort McHenry." Maryland Historical Society. http://www.mdhs.org/digitalimage/view-bombardment -fort-mchenry-near-baltimore-british-fleet-taken-observatory-under-com.

Bowles, Edmund A. 2007. "Karl Muck and His Compatriots: German Conductors in America during World War I (and How They Coped)." *American Music* 25 (Winter): 405–40.

Boyd, Malcolm. 1980. "National Anthems." In *New Grove Dictionary of Music and Musicians*, 46–70. London: Macmillan.

Bradley, Deborah. 2009. "Oh, That Magic Feeling! Multicultural Human Subjectivity, Community, and Fascism's Footprints." *Philosophy of Music Education Review* 17 (Spring): 56–74.

Branham, Robert James, and Stephen J. Hartnett. 1996. "'Of Thee I Sing': Contesting 'America.'" *American Quarterly* 48 (December): 623–52.

Bream, Jon. 1986. "Televised Anthem Brings Sandi Patti [sic] Liberty." *Chicago Tribune*, September 25. https://www.chicagotribune.com/news/ct-xpm-1986-09-25-8603110651-story.html.

Breig, James. 2014. "1914 Speech Saluted 'Star-Spangled Banner.'" Gettysburg Flag Works, August 21. https://www.gettysburgflag.com/blog/history-lessons/1914-speech-saluted-star-spangled-banner.

Bronstein, Hugh. 1995. "Hotel Owners Mark Their 10th Year." *Morning Call*, June 19. http://articles.mcall.com/1995-06-19/news/3029917_1_murals-count-zinzendorf-fort-mchenry.

Brooks, Albert. 2018. "Rewriting the National Anthem." YouTube, September 7. https://www.youtube.com/watch?v=xc79HAg8ZXo.

Brotman, Charles. 1998. "The Winner Loses: Ernest Bloch and His America." *American Music* 16 (Winter): 417–47.

Brown, DeNeen L. 2004. "Star-Spangled Banner Historic Trail Follows War of 1812 Battles." *Washington Post*, June 19.

Brown, Nicholas A. 2014. "'Ode to the Star-Spangled Banner' and #SSB200." *In the Muse* (blog), Library of Congress, July 1. https://blogs.loc.gov/music/2014/07/ode-to-the-star-spangled-banner-and-ssb200.

Browne, Allen. 2012. "Orpheus" *Landmarks* (blog), November 3. http://allenbrowne.blogspot.com/2012/11/orpheus.html.

Buckman, Adam. 2017. "No One Will Be Shocked When Comedian Slams National Anthem." *TVBlog*, Media Post, June 28. https://www.mediapost.com/publications/article/303568/no-one-will-be-shocked-when-comedian-slams-nationa.html.

Buhi, Jason. 1919. "A National Anthem Debate Led America to Reaffirm Freedom of Speech. Hong Kong Should Take Note." *South China Morning Post*, January 15. https://www.scmp.com/comment/insight-opinion/hong-kong/article/2181966/national-anthem-debate-led-america-reaffirm.

Buker, Alden. 1958. "National Anthems: National or International?" *Music Educators Journal* 44 (June–July): 46–48.

Burke, Timothy. 2018. "When Aretha Franklin's 'Star-Spangled Banner' Drew a Torrent of Racial Abuse." *Daily Beast*, August 18. https://www.thedailybeast.com/when-aretha-franklins-star-spangled-banner-drew-a-torrent-of-racial-abuse.

Butterworth, Michael L. 2005. "Ritual in the 'Church of Baseball': Suppressing the Discourse of Democracy after 9/11." *Communication and Critical/Cultural Studies* 2:107–29.

BWW News Desk. 2014. "Experience the War of 1812's 'Battle of North Point' at CCBC's O'er the Ramarts This Weekend." *Broadway World*, September 12. https://www.broadwayworld.com/baltimore/article/Experience-the

-War-of-1812s-Battle-of-North-Point-at-CCBCs-OER-THE
-RAMPARTS-912-14-20140911.

Calicchio, Dom. 2018. "WW2 Veteran, Turning 100 Soon, Belts Out National Anthem before NHL Game." *Fox News*, November 8. https://www.foxnews .com/sports/ww2-veteran-turning-100-soon-belts-out-national-anthem -before-nhl-game.

Cananaugh, Ray. 2016. "The Star-Spangled Banner: An American Anthem with a Very British Beginning." *Guardian*, July 4. https://www.theguardian.com /music/2016/jul/04/star-spangled-banner-national-anthem-british-origins.

Cantor-Navas, Judy. 2018. "Jose Feliciano to Sing 'Star-Spangled Banner,' Donate Guitar at Smithsonian Citizenship Ceremony: Exclusive." *Billboard News*, June 6. https://www.billboard.com/articles/columns/latin/8459567/jose -feliciano-sing-star-spangled-banner-donate-guitar-smithsonian-citizen ship-ceremony.

Carbone, Nick. 2012. "Watch Out, Weird Al: 'Modifying' National-Anthem Lyrics Could Get You Fined." *Time*, January 9. http://newsfeed.time.com/2012 /01/09/watch-out-weird-al-modifying-national-anthem-lyrics-could-get -you-fined.

Carey, Lydia. 2018. "Everything You Need to Know about the Mexican National Anthem." Culture Trip, March 31. https://theculturetrip.com/north-amer ica/mexico/articles/everything-you-need-to-know-about-the-mexican -national-anthem.

Carlson, Michael. 2010. "Wayne Collett: Athlete Who Staged a Black Power Protest at the 1972 Olympic Games." *Independent*, April 28. https://www .independent.co.uk/news/obituaries/wayne-collett-athlete-who-staged -a-black-power-protest-at-the-1972-olympic-games-1956018.html.

Cassell, Frank A. 1969. "Baltimore in 1813: A Study of Urban Defense in the War of 1812." *Military Affairs* 33 (December): 349–61.

CBS4. 2019. "Meet Reina Ozbay, the Powerhouse Voice behind the National Anthem On CBS4." *CBSN Denver*, October 11. https://denver.cbslocal.com /2019/10/11/reina-ozbay-voice-national-anthem.

Celebrate Boston. n.d. "National Peace Jubilee (1869)." http://www.celebrate boston.com/events/national-peace-jubilee.htm.

Cerulo, Karen A. 1989. "Sociopolitical Control and the Structure of National Symbols: An Empirical Analysis of National Anthems." *Social Forces* 68 (September): 76–99.

Cerulo, Karen A. 1993. "Symbols and the World System: National Anthems and Flags." *Sociological Forum* 8 (June): 243–71.

Christgau, Robert. 2019. "Jimi Hendrix's 'Star-Spangled Banner' Is the Anthem We Need in the Age of Trump." *Los Angeles Times,* August 13. https:// www.latimes.com/entertainment-arts/music/story/2019-08-13 /jimi-hendrixs-star-spangled-banner-is-the-anthem-we-need-in-the -age-of-trump.

Christie's. 2017. "THE STAR SPANGLED BANNER – Baltimore Patriot & Evening Advertiser, Baltimore: Munroe & French, No. 54 South Street, 21

September 1814." June 15, Sale 14376, Lot 274. https://www.christies.com
/lotfinder/Lot/the-star-spangled-banner-baltimore-patriot-6-details.aspx.

Cipolla, Frank J. 1988. "Patrick S. Gilmore: The Boston Years." *American Music*
6 (Autumn): 281–92.

City-On-A-Hill. "Francis Scott Key – Letter to John Randolph." 2012. *Virtue, Liberty, and Independence* (blog), April 10. http://liberty-virtue-independence
.blogspot.com/2012/04/francis-scott-key-letter-to-john.html.

[Clague, Mark] Usmusicscholar. 2013. "Star Spangled Cantata—Michael Gandolfi's Chesapeake: Summer of 1814." *O Say Can You Hear: A Music History
of American's Anthem* (blog), March 9. https://osaycanyouhear.wordpress
.com/2013/03/09/star-spangled-cantata-michael-gandolfis-chesapeake
-summer-of-1814.

Clague, Mark. 2014. "Spangled Mythconception #7: An Official Version of 'The
Star-Spangled Banner' Exists." *Star Spangled Music*, June 14. Star Spangled Music Foundation. http://starspangledmusic.org/spangled-mythconception-7-an-official-version-of-the-star-spangled-banner-exists.

Clague, Mark. 2014. "'This Is America': Jimi Hendrix's Star Spangled Banner
Journey as Psychedelic Citizenship." *Journal of the Society for American
Music* 8:435–578.

Clague, Mark. 2014. "To Be or Not: Is 'The Star-Spangled Banner' Really Based
on an Old English Drinking Song?" *Musicology Now* (blog), January 30.
American Musicological Society. http://musicologynow.org/2014/01/to-be
-or-not-is-star-spangled-banner.html.

Clague, Mark. 2016. "Abolitionist Star Spangled Banner—'Oh Say, Do You Hear?'
(1844)." *Star Spangled Music*, September 3. Star Spangled Music Foundation. http://starspangledmusic.org/abolitionist-star-spangled-banner-oh
-say-do-you-hear-1844.

Clague, Mark, and Jamie Vander Broek. 2014. "Banner Moments: The National
Anthem in American Life." Special Collections, University of Michigan
Library. https://deepblue.lib.umich.edu/bitstream/handle/2027.42/120293
/star_spangled_banner_14.pdf.

Cobb, Jelani. 2018. "Behind Nike's Decision to Stand by Colin Kaepernick." *New
Yorker*, September 4. https://www.newyorker.com/news/daily-comment
/behind-nikes-decision-to-stand-by-colin-kaepernick.

Cohen, David S. 2017. "What the Supreme Court Says about Sitting Out the
National Anthem." *Rolling Stone*, October 6. https://www.rollingstone
.com/politics/politics-features/what-the-supreme-court-says-about-sitting
-out-the-national-anthem-199512.

Coleman, William. 2015. "'The Music of a Well Tun'd State': 'The Star Spangled
Banner' and the Development of a Federalist Musical Tradition." *Journal
of the Early Republic* 35 (Winter): 599–629.

Coleman, [William] Billy. 2017. "Guest Post: Patriotism, Partisanship, and 'The
Star-Spangled Banner': A View from the Early Republic." *The Junto*, September 28. https://earlyamericanists.com/2017/09/28/guest-post-patriotism
-partisanship-and-the-star-spangled-banner-a-view-from-the-early-republic.

Collins, Cory. 2018. "Roseanne Barr's National Anthem: An Oral History of the Barr-Bungled Banner." *Sporting News*, May 29. http://www.sportingnews .com/us/mlb/news/roseanne-barr-national-anthem-video-padres-reds-oral -history-25th-anniversary/jf1o4z9qe1ai13otl1z0w58cl.

"Columbia the Gem of the Ocean." 2002. Song-Collection. Library of Congress. https://www.loc.gov/item/ihas.200000004.

Concannon, Mike. n.d. "US Armed Forces Service Songs & Lyrics." Military Officers Association of America, Western New York Chapter. http://wny moaa.org/index_htm_files/Service%20Songs%20and%20History.pdf.

"Congreve Rockets." 1848. *Scientific American* 3 (September 16): 411.

Conner, Eugene H. 1979. "Notes and Events." *Journal of the History of Medicine and Allied Sciences* 34 (April): 224–32.

Connor, Joseph. 2017. "Off Key." *American History* 51 (February): 42–51.

Cook, Sharon Anne. "'Patriotism, Eh?' the Canadian Version." *Phi Delta Kappan* 87 (April): 589–93.

Cooling, B. Franklin. 1972. "The Making of a Navalist: Secretary of the Navy Benjamin Franklin Tracy and Seapower." *Naval War College Review* 25 (September–October): 83–90.

Corbeil, Shannon. 2017. "7 Air Force Song Facts That Will Make You Want to Go Off into the Wild Blue Yonder." *We Are the Mighty*, September 19. https:// www.wearethemighty.com/music/7-air-force-song-facts-that-will-make -you-want-to-go-off-into-the-wild-blue-yonder.

Creswell, Julie, Kevin Draper, and Sapna Maheshwari. 2018. "Nike Nearly Dropped Colin Kaepernick Before Embracing Him." *New York Times*, September 26. https://www.nytimes.com/2018/09/26/sports/nike-colin -kaepernick.html.

Crews, Ed. 2008. "The Truth About Betsy Ross." *Colonial Williamsburg Journal* (Summer).

Criss, Doug, and Jill Martin. 2019. "Sports Teams Dump Kate Smith's 'God Bless America' because of Her Racist Songs." *CNN*, April 29. https://www.cnn .com/2019/04/19/us/kate-smith-yankes-flyers-god-bless-america-song -dropped-trnd/index.html.

Criss, Doug, Jill Martin, and Eric Levenson. 2019. "The Philadelphia Flyers Remove a Statue of Kate Smith over Her Racist Songs." *CNN*, April 21. www.cnn.com/2019/04/21/us/philadelphia-flyers-kate-smith-statue/index .html.

Croatto, Pete. 2013. "The All-Star Anthem." *Grantland*, February 16. http://grant land.com/features/the-marvin-gaye-national-anthem.

Cush, Andy. 2016. "Remember When Jimi Hendrix Protested the National Anthem on a National Stage?" *Spin,* September 12. https://www.spin.com/2016/09 /remember-when-jimi-hendrix-protested-the-national-anthem-on-a -national-stage.

Daily Dose. n.d. "March 3, 1931: 'The Star Spangled Banner' Finally Becomes the Official National Anthem for the United States." http://www.awb.com /dailydose/?p=1949.

Davis, David. 2008. "Olympic Athletes Who Took a Stand." *Smithsonian Maga-zine* (August). https://www.smithsonianmag.com/articles/olympic-athletes -who-took-a-stand-593920.

Davis, David. 2017. "The World Series National Anthem That Infuriated Amer-ica." *Deadspin*, October 6. https://deadspin.com/the-world-series-national -anthem-that-infuriated-americ-1819151571.

Davis, Hank. 2016. "The Star Spangled Banner: Just What Are We Singing About?" *Psychology Today*, May 10. https://www.psychologytoday.com /us/blog/caveman-logic/201605/the-star-spangled-banner-just-what-are-we -singing-about.

Davis, Harold. 1938. "On the Origin of Yankee Doodle." *American Speech* 13 (April): 93–96.

Davis, James A. 2005. "Hearing History: 'Dixie,' 'Battle Hymn of the Republic,' and Civil War Music in the History Classroom." In *Music and History: Bridging the Disciplines*, edited by Jeffrey H. Jackson and Stanley C. Pelkey, 200–19. Jackson: University Press of Mississippi.

Davis, James A. 2010. "Music and Gallantry in Combat during the American Civil War." *American Music* 28 (Summer): 141–72.

Day, Meagan. 2016. "It Used to Be Illegal to Not Stand for the National Anthem." *Timeline*, September 13. https://timeline.com/illegal-stand-national -anthem-222775e14f93.

Deaville, James. 2017. "The Unconventional Music of the Democratic and Repub-lican National Conventions of 2016." *American Music* 35 (Winter): 4446–66.

"Defence of Fort M'Henry." 1814. Maryland Historical Society. http://www.mdhs .org/digitalimage/defence-sic-fort-mhenry.

Delaplaine, Edward S. 1944/1945. "Francis Scott Key and the National Anthem." *Records of the Columbia Historical Society* 50th Anniversary Volume: 13–26.

"Delta Airlines Prevented Woman from Singing National Anthem on Flight with Fallen Soldier, She Claims." 2017. *Fox News*, October 16. https://www.fox news.com/travel/delta-airlines-prevented-woman-from-singing-national -anthem-on-flight-with-fallen-soldier-she-claims.

DeMetrick, Alex. 2018. "Historic Francis Scott Key Buoy Placed for Season." *WJZ 13, CBS Balitmore,* June 8.

Dennis, Matthew. 2014. "Reflections on a Bicentennial: The War of 1812 in Amer-ican Public Memory." *Early American Studies* 12 (Spring): 269–300.

De Sola, David. 2004. "The Politics of Music: Musicians Mobilize For and Against President Bush." *CNN*, August 30. http://edition.cnn.com/2004/ALLPOLI TICS/08/29/gop.music/index.html.

Donahue, Alice D. 2013. "*The Star-Spangled Banner* Weekend, September 7–9, 2012." *Public Historian* 35 (February): 100–4.

Duffy, Thomas. 2016. "Man Sings National Anthem While Painting Patriotic Pic-ture before ECHL Game." *Bleacher Report*, October 23. https://bleacher report.com/articles/2671342-man-sings-national-anthem-while-painting -patriotic-picture-before-echl-game.

Duluc, Andrew. 1814. "First View of the Battle of Patapsco Neck Dedicated to Those Who Lost Their Friends in Defence of Their Country, Septr. 12, 1814." Library of Congress. https://www.loc.gov/resource/pga.05972.

Dunaway, David King. 1987. "Music and Politics in the United States." *Folk Music Journal* 5:268–94.

Dunne, Susan. 2015. "Greenwich Author Says 'Star-Spangled Banner' Deserves a National Anthem Day." *Hartford Courant*, March 2. https://www.courant.com/entertainment/arts/hc-star-spangled-banner-book-0303-20150302-story.html.

Ebert, Joel. 2018. "As Super Bowl Looms, Blackburn Launching Radio Ads Encouraging Standing during National Anthem." *Tennessean*, January 25. https://www.tennessean.com/story/news/politics/2018/01/25/super-bowl-blackburn-launching-radio-ads-encouraging-people-stand-during-national-anthem/1067052001/.

Eby, Cecil D., Jr. 1960. "The National Hymn Contest and 'Orpheus C. Kerr.'" *Massachusetts Review* 1 (Winter): 400–9.

Edelman, Marc. 2018. "Standing to Kneel: Analyzing NFL Players' Freedom to Protest during the Playing of the U.S. National Anthem." *Fordham Law Review Online* 86:1–15.

Effron, Lauren, and Sheila Marikar. 2012. "Why Is 'The Star Spangled Banner' So Hard to Sing?" *ABC News*, July 11. https://abcnews.go.com/Entertainment/celebrities-flubbed-national-anthem-star-spangled-banner-hard/story?id=16756113.

Elson, Louis C. 1910. "Report on 'The Star-Spangled Banner,' 'Hail Columbia,' 'America,' 'Yankee Doodle' by Oscar George Theodore Sonneck." *American Historical Review* 15 (April): 625–26.

Emery, David. 2018. "Does Donald Trump Not Know the Words to the National Anthem?" *Snopes*, January 10. https://www.snopes.com/fact-check/trump-words-national-anthem.

Epstein, Adam. 2011. "Religion and Sports in the Undergraduate Classroom: A Surefire Way to Spark Student Interest." *Southern Law Journal* 21:133–47.

Epstein, Steven B. 1996. "Rethinking the Constitutionality of Ceremonial Deism." *Columbia Law Review* 96 (December): 2083–174.

Ewing, George W. 1971. "The Well-Tempered Lyre: Songs of the Temperance Movement." *Southwest Review* 56 (Spring): 139–55.

Fallis, Jeff. 2004/2005. "Marvin Gaye Sings 'The Star-Spangled Banner.'" *Iowa Review* 34 (Winter): 81–82.

Feloni, Richard. 2014. "Coke Had Americans Singing 'American the Beautiful' in Different Languages and a Bunch of People Hated It." *Business Insider*, February 2. https://www.businessinsider.com/coke-super-bowl-america-the-beautiful-ad-2014-2.

Ferguson, Robert A. 1989. "'What Is Enlightenment?': Some American Answers." *American Literary History* 1 (Summer): 245–72.

Filby, P. William. 1976. "Music in the Maryland Historical Society." *Notes* 32 (March): 503–17.

"First Edition of Star Spangled Banner Given to Library." 1968. *The Quarto* 80 (March): 1. https://clements.umich.edu/wp-content/uploads/2019/09/quarto1st-80.pdf.

Fisher, Louis, and Nada Mourtada-Sabbah. 2002. "Adopting 'In God We Trust' as the U.S. National Motto." *Journal of Church and State* 44 (Autumn): 671–92.

Fleming, Colin. 2018. "NFL Should Just Dump the National Anthem and Get on with Playing Football." *USA Today*, August 2. https://www.msn.com/en-us/sports/nfl/nfl-should-just-dump-the-national-anthem-and-get-on-with-playing-football/ar-BBLorK1.

Flood, W. H. Grattan. 1915. "'Britannia, the Pride of the Ocean': Origin of the Song and Tune." *Musical Times* 56 (March 1): 159.

Folkart, Burt A. 1987. "Obituaries: Lucy Monroe; Singer Noted for 'Star-Spangled Banner.'" *Los Angeles Times*, October 17.

Fong, Joss, and Estelle Caswell. 2018. "Does the USA Need a New National Anthem?" *Vox*, July 4. https://www.vox.com/2018/7/4/17531950/national-anthem-star-spangled-banner-hard-to-sing.

Fonseca, Felicia. 2017. "In Indian Country, Honoring Flag Might Mean Different Anthem." *Denver Post*, November 25. https://www.denverpost.com/2017/11/25/taking-a-knee-native-american-persepective.

Franciotti, Jennifer. 2014. "200-Year-Old Battle Comes to Life on IMAX Screen." *WBAL TV11*, June 13. https://www.wbaltv.com/article/200-year-old-battle-comes-to-life-on-imax-screen/7087550#!ZLIgg.

Friedersdorf, Conor. 2017. "Kneeling for Life and Liberty Is Patriotic." *Atlantic*, September 26. https://www.theatlantic.com/politics/archive/2017/09/kneeling-for-life-and-liberty-is-patriotic/540942.

Gallagher, Patrick. 2017. "Are Patriotic Songs Mass-Appropriate?" *U.S. Catholic* 82 (September): 31–35. https://www.uscatholic.org/articles/201709/are-patriotic-songs-mass-appropriate-31138.

Gavilanes, Grace. 2018. "Fergie Wasn't the First: The Most Controversial National Performances." *People*, February 19. https://people.com/music/controversial-national-anthem-performances.

Gehrz, Chris. 2016. "A Brief History of Patriotic Hymns." *Pantheos*, July 5. https://www.patheos.com/blogs/anxiousbench/2016/07/a-brief-history-of-patriotic-hymns.

Gehrz, Chris. 2017. "A (Brief) Religious History of the Star-Spangled Banner." *Pantheos*, September 26. https://www.patheos.com/blogs/anxiousbench/2017/09/religious-history-star-spangled-banner.

Gelb, Norman. 2004. "Francis Scott Key, the Reluctant Patriot." *Smithsonian Magazine* (September). https://www.smithsonianmag.com/history/francis-scott-key-the-reluctant-patriot-180937178.

Gelles, Auni. 2016. "Orpheus with the Awkward Foot: Francis Scott Key in Allegorical Form." Baltimore Heritage (website), December 17. https://explore.baltimoreheritage.org/items/show/570.

George, Alice. 2018. "For 50 Years, Jose Feliciano's Version of the National Anthem Has Given Voice to Immigrant Pride." *Smithsonian Magazine*, June 15. https://www.smithsonianmag.com/smithsonian-institution/for-50

-years-jose-felicianos-soulful-take-national-anthem-given-pride-immi grant-pride-180969380.

Geyser, A. F. 1918. "The Star-Spangled Banner / Vexillum Stellatum." *Classical Weekly* 11 (April 22): 191.

Giant Screen Cinema Association. n.d. "Film Details: *Star-Spangled Banner: Anthem of Liberty.*" https://www.giantscreencinema.com/Films/Film -Database/FilmDatabaseDetailView/movieid/2529.

Gibbons, William. 2008. "'Yankee Doodle' and Nationalism, 1780–1920." *American Music* 26 (Summer): 246–74.

Gilles, Bobby. 2012. "What Makes a Worship Song a Hymn?" *My Song in the Night* (blog), October 1. https://mysonginthenight.com/2012/10/01/what -makes-a-worship-song-a-hymn.

Giordono, Joseph, and Choe Song-Won. 2004. "S. Korea Anthem to Co-Star with 'Star-Spangled Banner' at U.S. Base Movie Theaters." *Stars and Stripes*, April 2. https://www.stripes.com/news/s-korea-anthem-to-co-star-with -star-spangled-banner-at-u-s-base-movie-theaters-1.18313.

"God Bless America." n.d. Irving Berlin (website). Irving Berlin Music Company. http://www.irvingberlin.com/god-bless-america.

"Golden Gate Park—Francis Scott Key." 2012. *Public Art and Architecture from Around the World* (blog), February 18. https://www.artandarchitecture-sf .com/golden-gate-park-san-francisco-february-18-2012.html.

Gonyea, Don. 2017. "'Hail to the Chief': Fanfare Sought by Some Presidents, Avoided by Others." *Weekend Edition*, National Public Radio, March 4. https://www.npr.org/2017/03/04/518333087/hail-to-the-chief-fanfare-sought -by-some-presidents-avoided-by-others.

Gorzelany-Mostak, Dana. 2017. "Hearing Jackie Evancho in the Age of Donald Trump." *American Music* 35 (Music and the 2016 U.S. Presidential Campaign, Winter): 467–77.

Government of Canada. 2018. "Full History of 'O Canada.'" Last modified on October 24, 2018. https://www.canada.ca/en/canadian-heritage/services /anthems-canada/history-o-canada.html.

Gracyk, Theodore. 2013. "Meanings of Songs and Meanings of Song Performances." *Journal of Aesthetics and Art Criticism* 72 (Winter): 23–33.

Graham, Claire. 2014. "Robert Ross: The NI Man Who Started the White House Fire 200 Years Ago." *BBC News*, August 24. https://www.bbc.com/news /uk-northern-ireland-28897646.

Grammarist. n.d. "O vs. Oh." https://grammarist.com/usage/o-oh.

Grauer, Neil A. 1989. "Seeking the Old Glory of Fort McHenry." *Washington Post*, September 7. https://www.washingtonpost.com/archive/local/1989/09/07 /seeking-the-old-glory-of-fort-mchenry/3bf272e6-a8ae-4dfd-89a5-2c32 147e8244.

Grauer, Neil A. 2014. "Rediscovering the 'Ode to the Star-Spangled Banner.'" *Johns Hopkins Magazine* (Winter). https://hub.jhu.edu/magazine/2014 /winter/grofe-ode-to-star-spangled-banner.

Gray, Christopher. 2004. "Streetscapes/The First and Second Churches of Christ, Scientist; A Tale of 2 Warring Churches, and of One Woman." *New York*

Times, February 15. https://www.nytimes.com/2004/02/15/realestate/street scapes-first-second-churches-christ-scientist-tale-2-warring-churches -one.html.

Gray, Myron. 2017. "A Partisan National Song: The Politics of 'Hail Columbia' Reconsidered." *Music & Politics* 11 (Summer): 1–20.

Green, Emma. 2014. "The Series of Improbable Events That Gave Us 'The Star Spangled Banner.'" *Atlantic*, July 8. https://www.theatlantic.com/national /archive/2014/07/we-luh-ya-war-of-1812/374056.

Greene, Andy. 2014. "Flashback: Marvin Gaye Reimagines 'The Star-Spangled Banner' in 1983." *Rolling Stone*, February 13. https://www.rollingstone .com/music/music-news/flashback-marvin-gaye-reimagines-the-star -spangled-banner-in-1983-117710.

Grewal, Zareena. 2007. "Lights, Camera, Suspension: Freezing the Frame on the Mahmoud Abdul-Rauf-Anthem Controversy." *Souls* 9 (2): 109–22.

Griffin, Martin I. J. "The Flag 'Just Growed.'" *American Catholic Historical Researches* 8 (April): 179–80.

Groff, Anna. 2008. "606: When, Why and How Do Mennonites Use the Anthem?" *Mennonite* (March 18): 14–15.

Groos, Arthur. 2016. "*Madama Butterfly* between East and West." In *Giacomo Puccini and His World*, edited by Arman Schwartz and Emanuele Senici, 49-84. Princeton, NJ: Princeton University Press.

Guerrini, Susan C., and Mary C. Kennedy. 2009. "Cross-Cultural Connections: An Investigation of Singing Canadian and American Patriotic Songs." *Bulletin of the Council for Research in Music Education*, no. 182 (Fall): 31–49.

Gurza, Agustin. 2018. "Himno Nacional Mexicano: The Long and Winding His- tory of Mexico's National Anthem." *Strachwitz Frontera Collection of Mexican and Mexican American Recordings* (blog), January 22. http:// frontera.library.ucla.edu/blog/2018/01/himno-nacional-mexicano-long -and-winding-history-mexico%E2%80%99s-national-anthem.

GWWO Architects. n.d. "Fort McHenry Visitor & Education Center." https:// www.gwwoinc.com/projects/fort-mchenry-visitor-education-center.

"Hail Columbia." https://www.liveabout.com/thmb/tQGn2tGS6t7W_3TruBlbwiG Fp9w=/768x0/filters:no_upscale():max_bytes(150000):strip_icc(): format(webp)/hailcolumbia-58b058ca3df78cdcd8805b39.jpg.

Hall, Roger Lee. n.d. "'The Star Spangled Banner': A Musical Salute." Center for American Music Preservation. www.americanmusicpreservation.com/The StarSpangledBanner.1814.htm.

Hall, Simon. 2010. "The American Gay Rights Movement and Patriotic Protest." *Journal of the History of Sexuality* 29 (September): 536–62.

Handel, Craig. 2018. "Jose Feliciano Paid a Price When He Sang National Anthem 50 Years Ago, but He Has No Regrets." *News Press*, October 5. https:// www.news-press.com/story/entertainment/2018/10/05/jose-feliciano-paid -price-when-he-sang-national-anthem-1968/1514370002.

Hardy, Kathryn (Katie) Macko. 2014. "Why Is the National Anthem so Hard to Sing?" *O Say Can You See?* (blog), Smithsonian National Museum of

American History, May 14. http://americanhistory.si.edu/blog/2014/05/why-is-the-national-anthem-so-hard-to-sing.html.

Harker, John B. 2005. "Betsy Ross: An American Legend and Patriot Revisited." *Raven: A Journal of Vexillology* 12:87–99.

Hartvigsen, Kenneth. 2018. "The Flag in American Art." In *The American Flag: An Encyclopedia of the Stars and Stripes in U.S. History, Culture and Law*, edited John R. Vile, 45–53. Santa Barbara, CA: ABC-CLIO.

Harvey, Sheridan. 2001. "Marching for the Vote: Remembering the Woman Suffrage Parade of 1913." Library of Congress. https://guides.loc.gov/american-women-essays/marching-for-the-vote.

Hatchett, Louis, and W. K. McNeil. 2005. "There's a Star-Spangled Banner Waving Somewhere." In *Country Music Goes to War*, edited by Charles K. Wolfe and James E. Akenson, 33–42. Lexington: University Press of Kentucky.

Hatter, Lawrence B. A. 2012. "Party Like It's 1812: The War at 200." *Tennessee Historical Quarterly* 71 (Summer): 90–111.

Hawkins, Sydney. 2016. "U-M Professor Debunks Famous 'Star-Spangled Banner' Myths." *Michigan News*, June 30. https://arts.umich.edu/news-features/star-spangled-banner-mythconceptions-series-debunks-famous-rumors.

Hay, Robert Pettus. "'Thank God We Are Americans': Yankees Abroad on the Fourth of July." *Indiana Magazine of History* 63 (June): 115–23.

Hayward, Nancy. n.d. "Brief Overview of Protest Songs." National Women's History Museum. https://www.womenshistory.org/resources/general/brief-overview-protest-songs.

Hebert, David G. 2015. "Another Perspective: Militarism and Music Education." *Music Educators Journal* 101 (March): 77–84.

Henry, H. T. 1913. "The Air of the 'Star-Spangled Banner.'" *Records of the American Catholic Historical Society of Philadelphia* 24 (December): 289–335.

Hevesi, Dennis. 2006. "Joel T. Broyhill, 86, Congressman Who Opposed Integration, Dies." *New York Times*, October 4. https://www.nytimes.com/2006/10/04/washington/04broyhill.html.

Hildebrand, David K. 2013. "New York in Song: The War of 1812." *New York History* 94 (Summer/Fall): 283–99.

Hildebrand, David K. 2014. "Bicentenary Essay: Two National Anthems? Some Reflections on the Two Hundredth Anniversary of 'The Star-Spangled Banner' and Its Forgotten Partner, 'The Battle of Baltimore.'" *American Music* 32 (Fall): 253–71.

Hill, Richard S. 1951. "The Melody of 'The Star-Spangled Banner' in the United States before 1820." In *Essays Honoring Lawrence C. Wroth*, edited by Lessing J. Rosenwald Collection (Library of Congress), 151–92. Portland, ME: Anthoensen Press.

Hill, Richard S. 1957. "A Proposed Official Version of the Star Spangled Banner." *Notes* 14 (December): 33–42.

"History of the Cylinder Phonograph." n.d. Inventing Entertainment: The Early Motion Pictures and Sound Recordings of the Edison Companies. Library of Congress. https://www.loc.gov/collections/edison-company-motion

-pictures-and-sound-recordings/articles-and-essays/history-of-edison
-sound-recordings/history-of-the-cylinder-phonograph.

Hogan, Liam. 2015. "Slave Market of America: An Anti-Slavery Broadside (1836)." *Medium*, July 21. https://medium.com/@Limerick1914/slave-market-of-america-an-anti-slavery-broadside-1836-1b6bc7f37e03.

Howard, Hugh. 2012. "War of 1812: Big Night in Baltimore." *HistoryNet*, January 6. https://www.historynet.com/war-of-1812-big-night-in-baltimore.htm.

Huddy, Leonie, and Nadia Khatib. 2007. "American Patriotism, National Identity, and Political Involvement." *American Journal of Political Science* 51 (January): 63–77.

Hudson, Manley O. 1932. "The Linthicum Resolution on the World Court." *American Journal of International Law* 26 (October): 794–96.

Humphreys, Jere T. 1987. "Strike Up the Band! The Legacy of Patrick S. Gilmore." *Music Educators Journal* 74 (October): 22–26.

Hunter, Wilbur H., Jr. 1951. "The Battle of Baltimore Illustrated." *William and Mary Quarterly* 8 (April): 235–37.

Hunter-Hart, Monica. 2017. "Could the United States Actually Change Its National Anthem?" *Inverse*, June 29. https://www.inverse.com/article/33437-how-could-the-united-states-change-its-national-anthem.

Husseini, Sam. 2016. "Why We Should All Remain Seated: the Anti-Muslim Origins of 'The Star-Spangled Banner.'" *Counterpunch*, August 30. https://www.counterpunch.org/2016/08/30/the-anti-muslim-origins-of-the-star-spangled-banner.

Hutchison, Coleman. 2007. "Whistling 'Dixie' for the Union." *American Literary History* 19 (Autumn): 603–28.

Iglehart, Ken. 2012. "200 Years: The War of 1812." *Baltimore Magazine*. https://www.baltimoremagazine.com/2012/6/1/200-years-the-war-of-1812.

"In God We Trust. 1892." *American Journal of Numismatics, and Bulletin of the American Numismatic and Archaeological Society* 26 (April): 83.

Jacobo, Julia. 2015. "Veterans Take a Knee in Support of National Anthem Protests." *ABC News*, September 25. https://abcnews.go.com/US/veterans-knee-support-national-anthem-protests/story?id=50075609.

Jacobs, Julia. 2019. "Local TV Revives a Bygone Tradition: Airing the National Anthem." *New York Times*, October 30.

Jenkins, Sally. 2018. "The Roots of the NFL's National Anthem Controversy Stretch to the 1960s and Vietnam." *Washington Post*, May 27. https://www.washingtonpost.com/sports/the-roots-of-the-nfls-national-anthem-controversy-stretch-to-the-1960s-and-vietnam/2018/05/27/933efcbe-61d1-11e8-a69c-b944de66d9e7_story.html.

Johns Hopkins. n.d. "Battle Monument." Explore Baltimore Heritage (website). https://explore.baltimoreheritage.org/items/show/2.

Johns Hopkins. n.d. "Francis Scott Key Monument." Explore Baltimore Heritage (website). https://explore.baltimoreheritage.org/items/show/105.

Johnson, James Weldon. n.d. "Lift Every Voice and Sing." Poetry Foundation. https://www.poetryfoundation.org/poems/46549/lift-every-voice-and-sing.

Johnson, Latrise P., and Elizabeth Eubanks. 2015. "Anthem or Nah? Culturally Relevant Writing Instruction and Community." *Voices from the Middle* 23 (December): 31–36.

Johnson, Lawrence. n.d. "Change America's National Anthem from 'The Star-Spangled Banner' to 'America the Beautiful.' (A Civil Rights Issue)." Petition to Chairman of the Congressional Black Caucus Cedric Richmond. Change.org. https://www.change.org/p/the-congressional-black-caucus-change-america-s-national-anthem-from-the-star-spangled-banner-to-america-the-beautiful-a-civil-rights-issue.

Johnson, Martenzie. 2016. "Let's Take the National Anthem Literally, and the Songwriter at His Word." *The Undefeated*, August 30. https://theundefeated.com/features/lets-take-the-national-anthem-literally-and-the-songwriter-at-his-word.

Johnston, Arthur. 1919. "America's National Songs." *High School Journal* 2 (May): 152–53.

Jorgensen, Estelle R. 2007. "Songs to Teach a Nation." *Philosophy of Music Education Review* 15 (Fall): 150–60.

Juhnke, Austin McCabe. 2017. "Rethinking 606, the 'Mennonite National Anthem.'" *Mennonite*, December 5. https://themennonite.org/opinion/rethinking-6060-mennonite-national-anthem.

Junior Research Seminar. 2016. "The National Anthem Effect on 'The Star Spangled Banner.'" Music in Twentieth Century American History, Villanova University. https://historyrocks.library.villanova.edu/music-history/national-anthem.

Kaplan, James. 2018. "The Complicated DNA of 'God Bless America,'" *New York Times*, November 9. https://www.nytimes.com/2018/11/09/opinion/irving-berlin-god-bless-america.html.

Kaufman, Peter, and Eli A. Wolff. 2010. "Playing and Protesting: Sport as a Vehicle for Social Change." *Journal of Sport and Social Issues* 34 (2): 154–75.

Kelen, Christopher (Kit). 2015. "Putting a Queer Shoulder to the Wheel: Irony, Parody, and National Devotion." *Interdisciplinary Literary Studies* 17 (1): 110–36.

Kendrick, Josephus. 1821. "Monument to Major General Robert Ross." Art and Architecture, Conway Collections, Courtauld Institue of Art. http://www.artandarchitecture.org.uk/images/conway/ff823138.html.

Kenney, Kirk. 2015. "Roseanne Barr's Anthem Still Anathema." *San Diego Union-Tribune*, July 24. https://www.sandiegouniontribune.com/sports/padres/sdut-roseanne-barr-butcher-padres-anthem-25th-years-ago-2015jul24-htmlstory.html.

Kerr-Kineen, Luke. 2017. "How Whitney Houston's Iconic National Anthem Set-off a Pointless Controversy." *For the Win* (blog), *USA Today Sports*, February 2. https://ftw.usatoday.com/2017/02/whitney-houston-national-anthem-video-super-bowl-51-2017.

Kight, Stef W. 2017. "The History of Singing the National Anthem before NFL Games." Axios, September 26. https://www.axios.com/the-history-of

-singing-the-national-anthem-before-nfl-games-1513305769-97a4edd0
-6748-432d-b1cc-2b377848e712.html.

Kinkeldey, Otto. 1953. "Oscar George Theodore Sonneck (1873–1928)." *Notes* 11
(December): 25–32.

Kirk, Elise K. 1997. "'Hail to the Chief': The Origins and Legacies of an American Ceremonial Tune." *American Music* 15 (Summer): 123–36.

Knox, Felicity. 2014. "The Fight for the Anthem." *Towson University History*, TU
Special Collections and University Archives, June 30. https://wp.towson
.edu/spcoll/2014/06/30/the-fight-for-the-anthem.

Kogan, Judith. 2016. "As Patriotic Songs Lose Familiarity in Public Schools, Do
They Still Hold Value?" *Weekend Edition*, National Public Radio, July 3.
https://www.npr.org/2016/07/03/484563018/as-patriotic-songs-lose
-familiarity-in-public-schools-do-they-still-hold-value.

Kouwenhoven, John Atlee, and Lawton M. Patten. 1937. "New Light on 'The Star
Spangled Banner.'" *Musical Quarterly* 23 (April): 198–200.

Kowalewski, Albin J. 2011. "The Star Spangled Bummer." *Opinionator* (blog).
New York Times, August 25. https://opinionator.blogs.nytimes.com/2011
/08/25/the-star-spangled-bummer.

Kramer, Neil S. 1980. "The Trial of Reuben Crandall." *Records of the Columbia
Historical Society* 50:123–39.

Kreps, Daniel. 2018. "Watch Fergie's Disastrous National Anthem at NBA All-
Star Game." *Rolling Stone*, February 29. https://www.rollingstone.com
/music/music-news/watch-fergies-disastrous-national-anthem-at-nba-all
-star-game-203023.

"Lady Gaga Sings US National Anthem at Gay Pride Rally." 2013. *Telegraph*, July 1.
https://www.telegraph.co.uk/news/worldnews/northamerica/usa/10152332
/Lady-Gaga-sings-US-national-anthem-at-Gay-Pride-rally-2013.html.

LaLande, Jeff. 2018. "Jehovah's Witnesses Riots, 1942." *Oregon Encyclopedia*.
Last updated March 17, 2018.

"'La Marseillaise' Lyrics: The Meaning and Translation of the French National
Anthem." 2015. *Evening Standard*, November 17. https://www.standard.co
.uk/news/world/la-marseillaise-lyrics-the-meaning-and-translation-of-the
-french-national-anthem-a3116306.html.

Leepson, Marc. 2014. "'Our Good Frank's Patriotic Song.'" *American History*
(October): 44–47.

Lemay, J. A. Leo. 1976. "The American Origins of 'Yankee Doodle.'" *William
and Mary Quarterly* 33 (July): 335–464.

Levy, Lester S., and James J. Fuld. 1970. "Unrecorded Early Printings of 'The Star
Spangled Banner.'" *Notes* 27 (December): 245–51.

Lewis, Walker. 1981. "John Quincy Adams and the Baltimore 'Pirates.'" *American Bar Association Journal* 67 (August): 1010–14.

Lichtenwanger, William. 1972. "Star-Spangled Bibliography." *College Music
Symposium* 12 (Fall): 94–102.

Lichtenwanger, William. 1977. "The Music of 'The Star-Spangled Banner': From
Ludgate Hill to Capitol Hill." *Quarterly Journal of the Library of Congress* 34 (July): 136–70.

Lichtenwanger, William. 1978. "The Music of 'The Star-Spangled Banner': Whence and Whither?" *College Music Symposium* 18 (Fall): 34–81.

Linderman, Juliet. 2014. "Do You Know 'The Star-Spangled Banner'?" *Smithsonian Tween Tribune*, September 14. https://www.tweentribune.com/article/tween56/do-you-know-star-spangled-banner.

Lindsay, Bryan. 1970. "Anacreon on the Wagon: 'The Star-Spangled Banner' in the Service of the Cold Water Army." *Journal of Popular Culture* 4 (Winter): 595–603.

"Listeners Angered by Sinead O'Connor." 1990. *Washington Post*, August 27. https://www.washingtonpost.com/archive/lifestyle/1990/08/28/listeners-angered-by-sinead-oconnor/b0b89b89-3ec1-4ad8-8978-4dd80513f342.

Logan, Michael H., and Douglas A. Schmittou. 2007. "Inverted Flags in Plains Indian Art: A Hidden Transcript." *Plains Anthropologist* 52 (May): 209–27.

"Losing Their Voices: The Struggle for a Nation's Anthem and Its People." 2005. *American Music Teacher* 54 (April/May): 84–85.

Lovrien, David. 2012. "The Stars and Stripes Forever." SousaMusic.com, June 13. http://sousamusic.com/the-stars-and-stripes-forever.

Lynch, Kevin. 2017. "Anthem House Adding New Key Highway Mural Honoring Edgar Allen Poe, Francis Scott Key, and Billie Holiday." SouthBmore.com, June 8. https://www.southbmore.com/2017/06/08/anthem-house-adding-new-key-highway-mural-honoring-edgar-allen-poe-francis-scott-key-and-billie-holiday.

MacGregor, Robert M. 2003. "I Am Canadian: National Identity in Beer Commercials." *Journal of Popular Culture* 37 (November): 276–86.

Mackintosh, Barry. [1981] "The Loss of the Francis Scott Key House: Was It Really?" National Park Service Integrated Resource Management Applications Portal. https://irma.nps.gov/DataStore/DownloadFile/469096.

Maginty, Edward A. "'America': The Origin of Its Melody." *Musical Quarterly* 20 (July): 259–66.

Magruder, Caleb Clarke, Jr. 1919. "Dr. William Beanes, the Incidental Cause of the Authorship of the Star-Spangled Banner." *Records of the Columbia Historical Society* 22:207–25.

Marshall, Alex. 2008. "And the Winning Anthem Is." *The Guardian*, August 10. https://www.theguardian.com/music/2008/aug/11/olympics2008.

Marshall, Alex. 2014. "Why 'The Star-Spangled Banner' Is the Perfect Insight into America's Soul." *Guardian*, August 11. https://www.theguardian.com/music/musicblog/2014/aug/11/malcolm-gladwell-star-spangled-banner-america-200th-anniversary.

Martin, Sarah Jackson. 2017. "Katherine 'Kitty' Cheatham." In *Tennessee Encyclopedia*, October 8. http://tennesseeencyclopedia.net/entries/katherinecheatham.

Martinez, Albert J., Jr. 2008–2010. "The Palatinate Clause of the Maryland Charter, 1632–1776: From Independent Jurisdiction to Independence." *American Journal of Legal History* 50 (July 6): 305–25.

Mashon, Mike. 2014. "The Birth of the Star-Spangled Banner (Edison, 1914)." *Now See Hear! The National Audio-Visual Conservation Center Blog*,

September 11. Library of Congress. https://blogs.loc.gov/now-see-hear
/2014/09/the-birth-of-the-star-spangled-banner-edison-1914.

Massah, Lloyd. 2016. "Origin of Liberia's National Anthem." *Bush Chicken*, July 28. https://www.bushchicken.com/origin-of-liberias-national-anthem.

Mattfeld, Julius. 1919. "The Use of Some National Anthems in Music." *Art & Life* 11 (July): 27–30.

McCrea, Nick. 2015. "National Anthem to be Sung in Schools across US on 9/11." *Bangor Daily News*, September 5. https://bangordailynews.com/2015/09/05/news/nation/national-anthem-to-be-sung-in-schools-across-us-on-911.

McLaughlin, Timothy, and Casey Quackenbush. 2019. "Hong Kong Protesters Sing 'Star-Spangled Banner,' Call on Trump to 'Liberate' the City." *Washington Post*, September 9.

McMullen, Kim. 1990. "The Fiction of Correspondence: 'Letters' and History." *Modern Fiction Studies* 36 (Autumn): 405–20.

McNamara, Tom. 2017. "What Is the 'Red Glare' in the Star Spangled Banner?" *Popular Science*, September 4. https://www.popsci.com/what-are-rockets-red-glare-in-star-spangled-banner.

Mead, Lucia Ames. 1921. "A Vigorous Protest." *Journal of Education* 94 (October): 399–400.

Meizel, Katherine. 2006. "A Singing Citizenry: Popular Music and Civil Religion in America." *Journal for the Scientific Study of Religion* 45 (December): 497–503.

"Memorabilia of Francis Scott Key Recovered after a Museum Theft." 1978. *New York Times*, February 14.

"Memorial Day Music Class: The History of Armed Service Songs." 2014. *Musicnotes* (blog), May 25. https://www.musicnotes.com/blog/2014/05/25/armed-service-songs.

Menezes, Joann. 1997. "The Birthing of the American Flag and the Invention of an American Founding Mother in the Image of Betsy Ross." In *Narratives of Nostalgia, Gender, and Nationalism*, edited by Jean Pickering and Suzanne Kehde, 74–87. Washington Square: New York University Press.

Merritt, Jonathan. 2015. "After Winning 5 Grammy and 40 Dove Awards, Sandi Patty Will Call It Quits." *Religion News Services*, September 28. https://religionnews.com/2015/09/28/grammy-winner-sandi-patty-announces-retirement-reflects-on-sins-and-successes.

MeTV Staff. 2016. "10 Awesome TV Station Sign-offs from the Era of Dead Air." MeTV, October 4. https://www.metv.com/stories/10-awesome-vintage-tv-station-sign-offs.

Miller, Cait. 2014. "Printing 'The Star-Spangled Banner.'" *In the Muse* (blog), Library of Congress, September 15. https://blogs.loc.gov/music/2014/09/printing-the-star-spangled-banner.

Miller, Marla R. 2018. "The U.S. Flag in America's Historic-House Museums." In *The American Flag: An Encyclopedia of the Stars and Stripes in U.S. History, Culture, and Law*, edited by John R. Vile, 19–32. Santa Barbara, CA: ABC-CLIO.

Miller, Mary K. 2002. "It's a Wurlitzer." *Smithsonian Magazine* (April). https://www.smithsonianmag.com/history/its-a-wurlitzer-61398212.

Millett, Nathaniel. 2012. "Slavery and the War of 1812." *Tennessee Historical Quarterly* 71 (Fall): 184–205.

Mohrmann, G. P., and F. Eugene Scott. 1976. "Popular Music and World War II: The Rhetoric of Continuation." *Quarterly Journal of Speech* 62 (April): 145–56.

Moicz, Klara. 2011. "The Birth of a Nation and the Limits of the Human Universal in Ernest Bloch's America." *American Music* 29 (Summer): 168–202.

Montgomery, David. 2006. "An Anthem's Discordant Notes." *Washington Post*, April 28. http://www.washingtonpost.com/wp-dyn/content/article/2006/04/27/AR2006042702505.html

Montgomery, Henry C. 1948. "Anacreon and the National Anthem." *Classical Outlook* 26 (December): 30–31.

Morley, Jefferson. 2013. "Francis Scott Key and the Slavery Question." *Globalist*, July 5. https://www.theglobalist.com/francis-scott-key-and-the-slavery-question.

Morley, Jefferson. 2013. "Star-Spangled Confederates: How Southern Sympathizers Decided Our National Anthem." *Daily Beast*, July 4. https://www.thedailybeast.com/star-spangled-confederates-how-southern-sympathizers-decided-our-national-anthem.

Morley, Jefferson. 2017. "It Is Time to Examine the Words and the Origins of Our National Anthem, Another Neo-Confederate Symbol." *Salon*, August 27. https://www.salon.com/2017/08/27/it-is-time-to-examine-the-words-and-the-origins-of-our-national-anthem-another-neo-confederate-symbol_partner.

Morris, Athina. 2018. "Today in History: 'The Star Spangled Banner' Becomes the National Anthem." *WFLA*, March 3. https://www.wfla.com/national/today-in-history-the-star-spangled-banner-becomes-the-national-anthem/1030603400.

Moser, A. C., and Bert B. David. 1936. "I Pledge a Legion." *Journal of Educational Sociology* 9 (March): 436–40.

"Mrs. Holloway, Patriot, Is Dead." 1940. *Baltimore Sun*, December 1.

Mugmon, Matthew. 2014. "Patriotism, Art, and 'The Star-Spangled Banner' in World War I: A New Look at the Karl Muck Episode." *Journal of Musicological Research* 33:4–26.

Murtha, Ryan. 2018. "An Olympics without Anthems." *Slate*, February 7. https://slate.com/culture/2018/02/fifty-years-ago-the-olympics-almost-banned-national-anthems-and-flags.html.

Muskal, Michael. 2014. "'Star-Spangled Banner': Anthem Was Once a Song of Drinking and Sex." *Los Angeles Times*, September 13. https://www.latimes.com/nation/nationnow/la-na-nn-star-spangled-banner-200-anniversary-20140912-story.html.

Napolitano, Andrew. 2017. "Is Taking a Knee Protected Speech?" *RealClearPolitics*, October 12. https://www.realclearpolitics.com/articles/2017/10/12/is_taking_a_knee_protected_speech_135235.html.

Nardelli, Alberto, and Ami Sedghi. 2015. "Which Is the Most Sexist National Anthem?" *The Guardian*, February 25. https://www.theguardian.com /news/datablog/2015/feb/25/how-sexist-is-canadas-national-anthem -compared-with-others.

Nathan, Hans, and Daniel Decatur Emmett. 1949. "Dixie." *Musical Quarterly* 35 (January): 60–84.

National Anthems of the World Organisation. n.d. "Sheet Music: Liberia National Anthem." http://www.national-anthems.org/anthems/country/LIBERIA.

National Park Service. n.d. "Archeological Treasures at Fort McHenry." https:// www.nps.gov/fomc/learn/historyculture/upload/Archeological%20Trea sures.pdf.

National Park Service. 2015. "Star-Spangled Banner National Historic Trail." Last updated March 1, 2015. https://www.nps.gov/stsp/learn/historyculture /index.htm.

National Park Service. 2019. "Star-Spangled Banner Flag House." Last updated July 17, 2019. https://www.nps.gov/places/star-spangled-banner-flag-house .htm.

National Society United States Daughters of 1812. n.d. "Mrs. Reuben Ross Holloway." https://usdaughters1812.org/mrs-reuben-ross-holloway.

Native Sun News Today Editorial Board. 2017. "To Stand or To Kneel for the National Anthem." *Native Sun News Today*, October 6. https://www.indi anz.com/News/2017/10/06/native-sun-news-today-editorial-to-stand.asp.

Neal, Mark Anthony. 2019. "Gladys Knight Has Earned the Right to Sing the National Anthem at the Super Bowl." *CNN*, January 21. https://www.cnn .com/2019/01/21/opinions/gladys-knight-super-bowl-national-anthem-neal /index.html.

Newport, Kyle. 2018. "Colin Kaepernick, Eric Reid Settle Grievances with NFL in Collusion Case." *Bleacher Report*, February 15. https://bleacherreport .com/articles/2820996-colin-kaepernick-eric-reid-settle-grievances-with -nfl-in-collusion-case.

"New Study Finds 85% of Americans Don't Know All the Dance Moves to National Anthem." 2012. *The Onion*, July 4. https://www.theonion.com /new-study-finds-85-of-americans-dont-know-all-the-danc-1819573602.

Nix, Naomi. 2012. "Perfect Anthem? Dream On." *Chicago Tribune*, January 24. https://www.chicagotribune.com/news/ct-xpm-2012-01-24-ct-talk-national -anthem-0124-2-20120124-story.html.

NPR Staff. 2013. "For 'Star-Spangled Banner,' a Long Road from Song to Anthem." *Morning Edition*, July 4. https://www.npr.org/2013/07/04/198418605/for -star-spangled-banner-a-long-road-from-song-to-anthem.

Nugent, Ciara. 2019. "Trump Says It's Inappropriate for U.S. Soccer Star Megan Rapinoe to Protest during the National Anthem." *Time*, June 25. https:// time/com/5613766/trump-says-inappropriate-megan-rapinoe-national -anthem-protest.

Okrent, Arika. 2014. "What's the Difference between 'O' and 'Oh'?" *Mental Floss*, May 7. http://mentalfloss.com/article/56582/whats-difference -between-o-and-oh.

Olson, Walter. 2017. "History of the National Anthem: Is 'The Star-Spangled Banner' Racist?" *National Review*, September 15. https://www.cato.org/publi cations/commentary/star-spangled-banner-racist.

Omer-Man, Michael. 2011. "This Week in History: Satellites Connect the World." *Jerusalem Post*, July 16. https://www.jpost.com/Features/In-Thespotlight /This-Week-in-History-Satellites-connect-the-world.

Otte, Paul R. 1978. "The English Anthem." *Choral Journal* 18 (April): 16–24, 26–28.

"Our National Anthem." 1946. *Music Educators Journal* 32 (June): 40.

Page, Tim. 1996. "National Fight Songs." *Washington Post*, July 28. https://www .washingtonpost.com/archive/lifestyle/style/1996/07/28/national-fight -songs/012f9c4b-c0f7-4413-b5aa-e809d884f76b.

Paine, Robert Treat. 1798. "Adams and Liberty." *Poem of the Week.org*. http:// www.potw.org/archive/potw233.html.

Palmer, Jesse. 1998. "Using Songs as Original Sources in History and Government Classes." *Clearing House* 71 (March–April): 221–23.

Paulson, Ken. 2017. "NFL Protests: Your Boss Can Tell You to Stand for the Anthem. Trump Can't." *First Amendment Encyclopedia*, Free Speech Center, Middle Tennessee State University, October 2. https://mtsu.edu/first -amendment/post/57/nfl-protests-your-boss-can-tell-you-to-stand-for-the -anthem-trump-can-t.

Pei, Minxin. 2003. "The Paradoxes of American Nationalism." *Foreign Policy*, no. 136 (May–June): 30–37.

Peithman, Stephen. 2014. "America's Five National Anthems." *Capital Public Radio*, July 4. http://www.capradio.org/music/classical/2014/07/04/americas -five-national-anthems-1.

Picker, John. n.d. "Two National Anthems." In *A New Literary History of America*, edited by Greil Marcus and Werner Sollors. http://www.newliterary history.com/nationalanthems.html.

Pietras, Emily. 2017. "Oh, Say, Can You See—and Hear—the Patriotic Art of Joe Everson?" *Greenville Journal,* June 20. https://greenvillejournal.com/arts -culture/oh-say-can-see-hear-patriotic-art-joe-everson.

Plitt, Amy. 2014. "Why Baltimore Is Extra Patriotic This 4th of July." *Conde Nast Traveler*, June 30. https://www.cntraveler.com/galleries/2014-06-30/cele brate-star-spangled-banner-bicentenntial-all-summer.

Poole, Robert M. 2008. "Star-Spangled Banner Back on Display." *Smithsonian Magazine* (November). http://www.smithsonianmag.com/history/star -spangled-banner-back-on-display-83229098.

Poore, Ben Perley. 1954. "Biographical Notice of John S. Skinner." *The Plough, the Loom, and the Anvil* 7 (July): 1–20.

PTI New Delhi. 2018. "Playing of National Anthem in Cinema Halls Optional: Supreme Court." BusinessLine, January 9. https://www.thehindubusiness line.com/news/playing-of-national-anthem-in-cinema-halls-optional -supreme-court/article10021703.ece.

Rall, Laura. 2015. "You May Have Been Illegally Singing the National Anthem Your Whole Life." *Star Spangled Music* (blog). Star Spangled Music

Foundation, December 4. http://starspangledmusic.org/you-may-have-been-illegally-singing-the-national-anthem-your-whole-life.

Rasmussen, Frederick N. 2000. "She Wrapped Her Life in the Flag." *Baltimore Sun*, July 8. http://articles.baltimoresun.com/2000-07-08/features/0007 080044_1_ross-holloway-star-spangled-banner-reuben-ross.

Rasmussen, Frederick N. 2011. "British General Meets His End at Battle of North Point." *Baltimore Sun*, October 23. https://www.baltimoresun.com/mary land/bs-md-robert-ross-backstory23-20111023-story.html.

Redmond, Shana L. 2015. "Indivisible: The Nation and Its Anthem in Black Musical Performance." *Black Music Research Journal* 35 (Spring): 97–118.

Redway, Virginia Larkin. 1932. "The Carrs, American Music Publishers." *Musical Quarterly* 18 (January): 150–77.

Reich, Howard. 2000. "Faith Hill Puts Some Giddyap into National Anthem." *Chicago Tribune*, January 31. https://www.chicagotribune.com/news/ct -xpm-2000-01-31-0001310175-story.html.

Reilich, Gabriel, and Eric Pfeiffer. 2019. "Comedic Genius Bill Bailey Shows How the U.S. National Anthem Played in a Minor Key Makes It Sound Russian." *Good*, January 19. https://www.good.is/articles/star-spangled-banner -russia.

Remnick, David. 2017. "Vietnam War Resistance in the Age of Trump." *New Yorker*, September 24. https://www.newyorker.com/news/daily-comment /recalling-muhammad-alis-vietnam-war-resistance-in-the-age-of-trump.

Resnikoff, Paul. 2016. "Aretha Franklin Plays the Longest National Anthem in U.S. History." *Digital Music News*, November 25. https://www.digital musicnews.com/2016/11/25/aretha-franklin-longest-national-anthem.

Richards, Janet E. Hosmer. 1895. "The National Hymn." *American Monthly Magazine* (December): 536–40.

Richardson, Matt. 2018. "Nashville Airport Travelers Stop to Sing National Anthem for Children of Fallen Service Members, Viral Video Shows." *Fox News*, December 10. https://www.foxnews.com/travel/nashville-airport -travelers-stop-to-sing-national-anthem-for-children-of-fallen-service -members-viral-video-shows.

Riley, A. C. D. 1907. "Respect to Our National Hymn." *Journal of Education* 65 (May 2): 495.

Rinaldi, Sierra. n.d. "10 Things You Didn't Know About 'The Star-Spangled Banner.'" *Readers' Digest*. https://www.rd.com/culture/star-spangled-banner -national-anthem-facts.

Rindlisbacher, Peter. 2014. "Fort McHenry—A 200 Year Star Spangled Banner Celebration—Baltimore, Maryland." *Skipjack's Nautical Living* (blog), September 28. http://skipjacksnauticalliving.blogspot.com/2014/09/fort -mchenry-200-year-star-spangled.html.

Riordan, Liam. 2011. "'O Dear, What Can the Matter Be?' The Urban Early Republic and the Politics of Popular Song in Benjamin Carr's *Federal Overture*." *Journal of the Early Republic* 31 (Summer): 179–227.

Rips, Michael D. 1986. "Freedom, in Song and Literature: Let's Junk the National Anthem." *New York Times*, July 5.

Rissier, Tyler. 2014. "The Story Behind 'The Star-Spangled Banner': A Q&A with Author Marc Ferris." *American Songwriter*, December 2. https://american songwriter.com/2014/12/star-spangled-banner-qa-marc-ferris.

Roach, David. 2018. "Writer of 'Star Spangled Banner' Helped Evangelize West thru Sunday School Movement." *God Reports* (blog), July 4. https://blog .godreports.com/2018/07/writer-of-star-spangled-banner-helped-evan gelize-west-thru-sunday-school-movement.

Roberts, Jay. 2011. "Finding Francis Scott Key: His Churches in Georgetown." *Jaybird's Jottings* (blog), December 2. https://jay.typepad.com/william _jay/2011/12/finding-francis-scott-key-his-churches-in-georgetown .html.

Robin, William. 2014. "How the National Anthem Has Unfurled." *New York Times*, June 27. https://www.nytimes.com/2014/06/29/arts/music/the-star -spangled-banner-has-changed-a-lot-in-200-years.html.

Robin, William. 2016. "Colin Kaepernick and the Radical Uses of 'The Star-Spangled Banner.'" *New Yorker*, August 29. https://www.newyorker.com/ culture/culture-desk/colin-kaepernick-and-the-radical-uses-of-the-star-span gled-banner.

Robinson, Ralph. 1945. "The Use of Rockets by the British in the War of 1812." *Maryland Historical Magazine* 40 (March): 1–6.

Rodriguez, Cindy Y. 2013. "Mexican-American Boy's National Anthem Sparks Racist Comments." *CNN*, September 16. https://www.cnn.com/2013/06/12 /us/mexican-american-boy-sings-anthem/index.html.

Rosenberger, Peter. 2017. "Our National Anthem, Once a Source of Unity, Now Rings with Discord and Dissonance." *Fox News*, September 25. https:// www.foxnews.com/opinion/our-national-anthem-once-a-source-of-unity -now-rings-with-discord-and-dissonance.

Roth, Marty. 2000. "'Anacreon' and Drink Poetry; or, the Art of Feeling Very Very Good." *Texas Studies in Literature and Language* 42 (Fall): 314–45.

Ruane, Michael E. 2014. "Francis Scott Key's Anthem Keeps Asking: Have We Survived as a Nation?" *Washington Post*, September 11. https://www .washingtonpost.com/local/francis-scott-keys-anthem-keeps-askinghave -we-survived-as-a-nation/2014/09/11/4061854c-39b3-11e4-9c9f-ebb47272 e40e_story.html.

Saez, Diana. 2012. "Singing 'El Pendon Estrellado.'" *O Say Can You See?* (blog), Smithsonian National Museum of American History, September 26. http:// americanhistory.si.edu/blog/2012/09/singing-el-pend%C3%B3n-estrel lado.html.

Sandage, Scott A. 1993. "A Marble House Divided: The Lincoln Memorial, the Civil Rights Movement, and the Politics of Memory, 1939–1963." *Journal of American History* 80 (June): 135–67.

Sanders, Mary. 2016. "A Mighty Fortress Is Our Battle Hymn of the Republic: Episcopal Liturgy and American Civil Religion in the National Prayer Service on 14 September 2001." *Anglican and Episcopal History* 85 (March): 63–86.

Sandy Patti (website). n.d. "Bio." https://www.sandipatty.com/bio.

Santamaria, Carlos. 2012. "PH National Anthem: Lost in Translation." *Rappler*, June 11. https://www.rappler.com/move-ph/campaigns/149-independence -day/6549-the-original-spanish-lyrics-of-the-philippine-national-anthem.

Schmidt, Samantha. 2018. "'Lift Every Voice and Sing': The Story Behind the 'Black National Anthem' That Beyonce Sang." *Washington Post*, April 16. https://www.washingtonpost.com/news/morning-mix/wp/2018/04/16/lift -every-voice-and-sing-the-story-behind-the-black-national-anthem-that -beyonce-sang.

Schmitt, Pierre. 2017. "Representations of Sign Language, Deaf People, and Interpreters in the Arts and the Media." *Sign Language Studies* 18 (Fall): 130–47.

Schmittou, Douglas A., and Michael H. Logan. 2002. "Fluidity of Meaning: Flag Imagery in Plains Indian Art." *American Indian Quarterly* 26 (Autumn): 559–604.

Scholneger, Mark. 2011. "My Faith: Why I Don't Sing the 'Star-Spangled Banner.'" *CNN Belief Blog*, June 26. http://religion.blogs.cnn.com/2011/06/26 /my-faith-why-i-dont-sing-the-star-spangled-banner.

"Schools Celebrate National Anthem Anniversary." 2005. *Music Educators Journal* 92 (November): 10–13.

Schuster, Sarah J. 1914. "The Star Spangled Banner: The Friday Afternoon Club in the Rural School." *Journal of Education* 80 (August 27): 157–59.

Schwartz, Daniel. 2017. "All Rise (or Not)! A Flag, the National Anthem & Connecticut Law." *Connecticut Employment Law Blog*, October 12. https:// www.ctemploymentlawblog.com/2017/10/articles/can-you-be-required-to -display-flag-at-work.

Schwarz, Jon. 2016. "Colin Kaepernick Is Righter Than You Know: The National Anthem Is a Celebration of Slavery." *The Intercept*, August 28. https:// theintercept.com/2016/08/28/colin-kaepernick-is-righter-than-you-know -the-national-anthem-is-a-celebration-of-slavery.

[Scott, Terry?]. n.d. "The UFW: Songs and Stories Sung and Told by UFW Volunteers." Farmworker Movement Documentation Project (website). https:// libraries.ucsd.edu/farmworkermovement/media/Scott/INTRODUCTION TOSONGSANDCOMMENTARY(FINAL).pdf.

Segal, David. 2016. "At Rio Olympics, the National Anthem Sounds . . . Sad?" *New York Times*, August 11. https://www.nytimes.com/2016/08/12/sports /olympics/usa-national-anthem-rio-games.html.

Shafer, Leah. 2013. "Francis Scott Key and the Complex Legacy of Slavery." *A Blog of History*, U.S. Capitol Historial Society, June 14. https://uschs .wordpress.com/2013/06/14/francis-scott-key-and-the-complex-legacy-of -slavery.

Shalev, Eran. 2011. "'A Republic Amidst the Stars': Political Astronomy and the Intellectual Origins of the Stars and Stripes." *Journal of the Early Republic* 31 (Spring): 39–73.

Shea, Andrea. 2018. "'Brutal to the Eyes, Horrible to the Ears': The National Anthem, as Played by a Steamroller Music Box." *The ARTery*, February 19. https://www.wbur.org/artery/2018/02/19/national-anthem-steamroller.

Sheads, Scott S. 2013. "Major General Samuel Smith Monument at Federal Hill." Baltimore Heritage (website), February 12. Updated on May 7, 2019. https://explore.baltimoreheritage.org/items/show/190.

Sheads, Scott S., and Anna von Lunz. 1998. "Defenders' Day, 1815–1998: A Brief History." *Maryland Historical Magazine* 93 (Fall): 301–15.

Shellnutt, Kate. 2018. "Make Worship Patriotic Again? The Top 10 Songs for Fourth of July Services." *Christianity Today*, June 29. https://www.christianitytoday.com/ct/2018/june-web-only/make-worship-patriotic-again-top-10-songs-fourth-of-july.html.

Shippen, Rebecca Lloyd, and R. B. Taney. 1898. "The Star-Spangled Banner." *Pennsylvania Magazine of History and Biography* 22:321–25.

Shreve, Grant. 2017. "The Long, Winding History of the 'Battle Hymn of the Republic.'" *JSTOR Daily Newsletter*, October 20. https://daily.jstor.org/the-long-winding-history-of-the-battle-hymn-of-the-republic.

Siegel, Eli, and Edward Green. 2014. "'The Star-Spangled Banner' as a Poem." *Choral Journal* 55 (November): 218–35.

Slater, Joseph. 1957. "Early Light on Poetry." *College English* 18 (January): 214–18.

Slim, H. Colin. 2006. "Stravinsky's Four Star-Spangled Banners and His 1941 Christmas Card." *Musical Quarterly* 89 (Summer–Fall): 321–447.

Smith, Chuck. 2001. "The Persecution of West Virginia Jehovah's Witnesses and the Expansion of Legal Protection for Religious Liberty." *Journal of Church and State* 43 (Summer): 539–77.

Smith, F. S. Key. 1909. "A Sketch of Francis Scott Key, with a Glimpse of His Ancestors." *Records of the Columbia Historical Society* 12:71–88.

Smith, Gene A. 1999. "Armistead, George." In *American National Biography*, edited by John A. Garraty and Mark C. Carnes, 1:596–98. New York: Oxford University Press.

Smith, Tim. 2014. "'Banner' a Hit Song with Staying Power." *Baltimore Sun*, September 8. https://www.baltimoresun.com/entertainment/arts/artsmash/bs-ae-national-anthem-20140906-story.html.

Snyder, Edward D. 1951. "The Biblical Background of the 'Battle Hymn of the Republic.'" *New England Quarterly* 24 (June): 231–38.

Song and Praise. n.d. "God Save the Queen Lyrics." https://www.songandpraise.org/god-save-the-queen-hymn.htm.

Spiegel, Allen D., and Marc B. Spiegel. 1998. "Redundant Patriotism: The United States National Anthem as an Obligatory Sports Ritual." *Culture, Sport, Society* 1 (1): 24–43.

Spitzer, Nick. 2012. "The Story of Woody Guthrie's 'This Land Is Your Land,'" *The NPR 100*, National Public Radio, February 15. https://www.npr.org/2000/07/03/1076186/this-land-is-your-land.

Spofford, Ainsworth R. 1904. "The Lyric Element in American History." *Records of the Columbia Historical Society* 7:211–36.

Stanton, Zack. "When Aretha Franklin Rocked the National Anthem." 2018. *Politico*, August 16. https://www.politico.com/magazine/story/2018/08/16/aretha-franklin-controversial-national-anthem-219364.

Staples, Brent. 2018. "African-Americans and the Strains of the National Anthem." *New York Times*, June 9. https://www.nytimes.com/2018/06/09/opinion/african-americans-national-anthem-protests.html.

Star Spangled Music Foundation. n.d. "About." http://starspangledmusic.org/sample-page.

Starnes, Todd. 2010. "Students at Lincoln Memorial Told to Stop Singing National Anthem." *Fox News*, August 9. Updated November 30, 2015. https://www.foxnews.com/us/students-at-lincoln-memorial-told-to-stop-singing-national-anthem.

Starnes, Todd. 2018. "NFL Rejects Veterans Group's Super Bowl Ad Urging People to Stand for the Anthem." *Fox News*, January 23. https://www.foxnews.com/opinion/nfl-rejects-veterans-groups-super-bowl-ad-urging-people-to-stand-for-the-anthem.

Stauffer, John. 2015. "'The Battle Hymn of the Republic': Origins, Influence, Legacies." In *Exploring Lincoln: Great Historians Reappraise Our Greatest President*, edited by Harold Holzer, Craig L. Symonds, and Frank J. Williams, 123–45. New York: Fordham University Press.

St. Clair, Stacy, and Brian Hamilton. 2011. "Goshen College Sparks a Fight over National Anthem." *Chicago Tribune*, August 25. https://www.chicagotribune.com/news/ct-xpm-2011-08-25-ct-met-star-spangled-banner-boycott-20110825-story.html.

Stepman, Jarrett. 2016. "Unlike the NFL's Colin Kaepernick, Frederick Douglass Loved 'The Star-Spangled Banner.'" *Daily Signal*, August 29. https://www.dailysignal.com/2016/08/29/unlike-the-nfls-colin-kaepernick-frederick-douglass-loved-the-star-spangled-banner.

Stilwell, Blake. 2018. "A Famous Russian Composer Re-arranged the Star-Spangled Banner." *We Are the Mighty*, August 13. https://www.wearethemighty.com/music/stravinsky-national-anthem.

Stilwell, Blake. 2018. "How 'Hail to the Chief' Became the Presidential Anthem." *We Are the Mighty*, November 7. https://www.wearethemighty.com/history/hail-chief-presidential-anthem.

Stone, James. 1941. "War Music and War Psychology in the Civil War." *Journal of Abnormal and Social Psychology* 36 (October): 543–60.

Suiter Swantz Intellectual Property. 2017. "Who Owns the Copyright to the National Anthem?" https://www.suiter.com/the-national-anthem-and-copyright.

Talabong, Rambo. 2018. "34 Arrested for Sitting Out National Anthem at 'The Hows of Us' Screening." *Rappler*, September 6. https://www.rappler.com/nation/211293-persons-arrested-sitting-out-national-anthem-hows-of-us-showing.

Taylor, Blaine. 2018. "The Rockets' Red Glare: Francis Scott Key's 'Star-Spangled Banner.'" *Warfare History Network*, November 7. https://warfarehistorynetwork.com/daily/military-history/the-rocket.

"These Artistic Interpretations of the Star-Spangled Banner Call Out the Inner Patriot." 2014. *Smithsonian Magazine* (June). https://www.smithsonianmag

.com/arts-culture/these-artistic-interpretations-star-spangled-banner-call
-out-inner-patriot-180951536.

"This Is My Fight Song—Seven National Anthems Inspired by Bloodshed, Battles and War." 2017. *Military History Now*, June 20. https://militaryhistory
now.com/2017/06/20/this-is-my-fight-song-seven-national-anthems-in
spired-by-bloodshed-battles-and-war.

Thompson, Claude. 2018. "NFL Player Upset Media 'Ignore' His National Anthem
Demonstrations." *Washington Examiner*, December 29. https://www.washing
tonexaminer.com/news/nfl-player-upset-media-ignore-his-national
-anthem-demonstrations.

Thurmaier, David. 2014. "'When Borne by the Red, White, and Blue': Charles
Ives and Patriotic Quotation." *American Music* 32 (Spring): 46–81.

Tinsley, Justin. 2018. "The Players' Anthem: When Marvin Gaye Sang 'The Star-
Spangled Banner' at the 1983 All-Star Game." *The Undefeated*, February
13.   https://theundefeated.com/features/marvin-gaye-the-star-spangled
-banner-1983-nba-all-star-game-players-anthem.

Tischler, Barbara L. 1986. "One Hundred Percent Americanism and Music in
Boston during World War I." *American Music* 4 (Summer): 164–76.

Toobin, Jeffrey. 2015. "Why Gay Marriage Victory Anthem Was 'Star Spangled
Banner.'" *CNN*, June 30. https://www.cnn.com/2015/06/26/opinions/toobin
-same-sex-marriage-scotus/index.html.

Tomizawa, Roy. 2016. "Vincent Matthews and Wayne Collett: A Most Casual
Protest with Most Striking Consequences." *The Olympians*, November 18.
https://theolympians.co/2016/11/18/vincent-matthews-and-wayne-collett
-a-most-casual-protest-with-most-striking-consequences.

Trott, Donald. 2012. "Choral Music in the White House." *Choral Journal* 52 (June
and July): 8–17.

Troup, David. 2018. "N. C. Wyeth Exhibition: 'Poems of American Patriotism.'"
Wiscasset Newspaper, June 2. https://www.wiscassetnewspaper.com/arti
cle/nc-wyeth-exhibition-poems-american-patriotism/102108.

Troy, Gil. 1992. "Stars, Stripes, and Spots." *Design Quarterly*, no. 157 (Autumn):
2–10.

Underwood, J. 2017. "Kneeling During the National Anthem: At Schools, It's Protected Speech." *Phi Delta Kappan*, September 28. https://www.kappanon
line.org/kneeling-during-the-national-anthem-at-schools-its-protected
-speech.

United States World War One Centennial Commission. n.d. "The Star-Spangled
Banner and World War One." https://www.worldwar1centennial.org/
index.php/educate/places/the-star-spangled-banner-and-world-war-one
.html.

U.S. Department of Veterans Affairs. n.d. "Celebrating America's Freedom: Military Songs Inspire Troops, Preserve Tradition." https://www.va.gov/opa
/publications/celebrate/militarysongs.pdf.

Vacha, J. E. 1983. "When Wagner Was Verboten: The Campaign against German
Music in World War I." *New York History* 64 (April): 171–88.

Vaughn, Ashley. 2010. "Auction of First Edition of 'Star Spangled Banner' Tops $500,000." *CNN*, December 3. http://www.cnn.com/2010/US/12/03/new .york.star.spangled.banner/index.html.

Veltman, Chloe. 2017. "Why We Should Sing 'The Star-Spangled Banner's' Obscure Fifth Verse." *KQED*, March 2. https://www.kqed.org/arts/12822853/why -we-should-sing-the-star-spangled-banners-obscure-fifth-verse.

"Video: 7-Year-Old Girl Crushes National Anthem at LA Galaxy Game." 2018. ABC 7 Eyewitness News, September 24. https://abc7.com/sports/video -7-year-old-crushes-national-anthem-at-la-galaxy-game/4328455.

Vile, John R. 2019. "Americans Should Reclaim the Betsy Ross Flag Instead of Abandoning It." *Tennessean*, July 8. https://www.tennessean.com/story /opinion/2019/07/08/betsy-ross-flag-nike-controversy/1675249001.

Vile, John R. 2019. "Trial of Reuben Crandall (1835–1836)." In *First Amendment Encyclopedia*, Free Speech Center, Middle Tennessee State University. https://mtsu.edu/first-amendment/article/1606/trial-of-reuben-crandall.

Vitty, Cort. "Lucy Monroe." https://sabr.org/node/50381.

Vitty, Cort. 2010. "The Star Spangled Soprano." Metropolitan Washington Old Time Radio Club. http://www.mwotrc.com/rr2010_06/soprano.htm.

Vogel, Steve. 2012. "The Battle for Star-Spangled Coins." *Washington Post*, March 5. https://www.washingtonpost.com/blogs/federal-eye/post/star-spangled -coins-released/2012/03/02/gIQAz3TgnR_blog.html.

Wagner, Rodd. 2018. "The National Anthem Is Not a Company Song." *Forbes*, September 6. https://www.forbes.com/sites/roddwagner/2018/09/06/the -national-anthem-is-not-a-company-song.

Walker, Julie Summers. 1999. "Remembering the Francis Scott Key Hotel." *Frederick News-Post*, March 26. https://www.fredericknewspost.com/archive /remembering-the-francis-scott-key-hotel/article_ccb5bceb-d09b-509d -b223-8a2f4e34d1bb.html.

Walker, Rhiannon. 2016. "An Open Letter from American Military Veterans in Support of Colin Kaepernick." *The Undefeated*, September 2. https://the undefeated.com/features/an-open-letter-from-american-military-veterans -in-support-of-colin-kaepernick.

Warfield, Patrick. 2018. "Educators in Search of an Anthem: Standardizing 'The Star-Spangled Banner' during the First World War." *Journal of the Society for American Music* 12:268–316.

Wenger, Beth S. 2008. "Rites of Citizenship: Jewish Celebrations of the Nation." In *The Columbia History of Jews and Judaism in America*, edited by Marc Lee Raphael, 366–84. New York: Columbia University Press.

Werrett, Simon. 2009. "William Congreve's Rational Rockets." *Notes and Records of the Royal Society of London* 63 (March 20): 35–56.

Wheeler, Lee T. n.d. "A Guide to American Visionary Art Museum's A Very Visionary Star-Spangled Sidewalk." American Visionary Art Museum (website). http://www.avam.org/exhibitions/pdf/Star-Spangled-Sidewalk -Guide.pdf.

Whitmer, Mariana. 2005. "Songs with Social Significance: An Introduction." *OAH Magazine of History* 19 (July): 9–16, 22.

Williams, Ian. 2018. "Anthems." In *Memory*, edited by Philippe Tortell, Mark Turin, and Margot Young, 165–71. Vancouver, BC: Peter Wall Institute for Advanced Studies.

Williams, Liz. 2014. "Where Did Francis Scott Key Write the Song That Became Our National Anthem?" *O Say Can You See?* (blog), Smithsonian National Museum of American History, June 12. http://americanhistory.si.edu/blog /2014/06/where-did-francis-scott-key-write-his-famous-lines.html.

Williams, Susan. 1991. "Content Discrimination and the First Amendment." *University of Pennsylvania Law Review* 139 (January): 615–730.

Wilson, Carl. 2014. "Proudly Hailed: 'The Star-Spangled Banner' Is Militaristic, Syntactically Garbled, and Impossible to Sing. It's Perfect." *Slate*, July 3. https://slate.com/culture/2014/07/the-star-spangled-banner-four-reasons-it -shouldnt-be-the-national-anthem-but-always-will-be.html.

Wilson, Christopher. 2016. "Where's the Debate on Francis Scott Key's Slave-Holding Legacy?" *Smithsonian Magazine*, July 1. https://www.smith sonianmag.com/smithsonian-institution/wheres-debate-francis-scott-keys -slave-holding-legacy-180959550.

Wilson, Michael. 2006. "Project Reteaches National Anthem." *New York Times*, March 14. https://www.nytimes.com/2006/03/14/us/project-reteaches-national -anthem.html.

Winship, Frederick M. 2002. "Forgotten John Philip Sousa Opera Revived." *United Press Internationl*, April 29. https://www.upi.com/Forgotten-John -Philip-Sousa-opera-revived/91571020085200.

Winter, Aaron McLean. 2009. "The Laughing Doves of 1812 and the Satiric Endowment of Antiwar Rhetoric in the United States." *PMLA* 124 (October): 1562–81.

Wispelwey, Seth. 2018. "The NFL Is a Fundamentalist Church. And the Anthem Is Its Worship Song." *Sojourners*, June 1. https://sojo.net/articles/nfl -fundamentalist-church-and-anthem-its-worship-song.

Wissner, Reba. 2016. "Not Another Term: Music as Persuasion in the Campaign against the Re-Election of George W. Bush." Trax on the Trail, October 5. https://www.traxonthetrail.com/2020/02/05/not-another-term-music-as -persuasion-in-the-campaign-against-the-re-election-of-george-w-bush.

"Woman Performs Stunning Rendition of the National Anthem at Lincoln Memorial." 2016. *Fox News Insider*, July 2. https://insider.foxnews.com/2016/07 /02/woman-sings-national-anthem-lincoln-memorial-video-goes-viral.

Wood, Elizabeth Ingerman. 1967. "Thomas Fletcher: A Philadelphia Entrepreneur of Presentation Silver." *Winterthur Portfolio* 3:136–71.

Wood, Pamela. 2014. "Francis Scott Key Legacy Lives on in Frederick." *Baltimore Sun*, August 14. https://www.baltimoresun.com/news/maryland/bs -md-40-key-memorial-20140813-story.html.

WQXR Staff. 2016. "How John Philip Sousa Almost Authored Our National Anthem." *WQXR Features*, June 29. https://www.wqxr.org/story/how-john -philip-sousa-almost-authored-our-national-anthem.

Wu, Corinna. 1999. "Old Glory, New Glory: The Star-Spangled Banner Gets Some Tender Loving Care." *Science News* 144 (June 16): 408–10.

Yuen, Helen, and Asantewa Boakyewa. 2014. "The African American Girl Who Helped Make the Star-Spangled Banner." *O Say Can You See?* (blog), Smithsonian National Museum of American History, May 30. http://amer icanhistory.si.edu/blog/2014/05/the-african-american-girl-who-helped -make-the-star-spangled-banner.html.

Zeigler, Cyd. 2017. "San Diego Gay Men's Chorus Sings National Anthem a Year after Padres Blunder." *Outsports*, April 25. https://www.outsports.com /2017/4/25/15431714/san-diego-padres-gay-chorus-anthem.

BOOKS, BOOKLETS, THESES, AND DISSERTATIONS

Adams, Stephen J. 2018. *The Patriotic Poets: American Odes, Progress Poems, and the State of the Union*. Chicago: McGill-Queen's University Press.

Anderson, Benedict. 2006. *Imagined Communities*. New York: Verso.

Asch, Chris Myers, and George Derek Musgrove. 2017. *Chocolate City: A History of Race and Democracy in the Nation's Capital*. Chapel Hill: University of North Carolina Press.

Ashton, James Jackson. 2015. "Patriotic Sublime: Music and the Nation in America, 1790–1848." PhD diss., Johns Hopkins University.

Baer, John W. 1992. *The Pledge of Allegiance: A Centennial History, 1892–1992*. Annapolis, MD: Free State Press.

Bass, Amy. 2002. *Not the Triumph But the Struggle: The 1968 Olympics and the Making of the Black Athlete*. Minneapolis: University of Minnesota Press.

Bielick, Stacey, Zahava D. Doering, Anne Kazimirski, and Andrew J. Pekarik. 1998. *Public Perception of the Star-Spangled Banner: Background Studies for the National Museum of American History*. Report 98-6. Washington, DC: Smithsonian Institution.

Bonner, Robert E. 2002. *Colors and Blood: Flag Passions of the Confederate South*. Princeton, NJ: Princeton University Press.

Borneman, Walter R. 2009. *1812: The War That Forged a Nation*. New York: HarperCollins.

Bowman, Kent Adam. 1984. "The Muse of Fire: Liberty and War Songs as a Source of American History." PhD diss., North Texas State University.

Bradley, James, and Ron Powers. 2000. *Flags of Our Fathers*. New York: Bantam.

Branham, Robert James, and Stephen J. Hartnett. 2002. *Sweet Freedom's Song: "My Country 'Tis of Thee" and Democracy in America*. New York: Oxford University Press.

Browne, C. A. 1919. *The Story of Our National Ballads*. New York: Thomas Y. Crowell.

Cassell, Frank A. 1971. *Merchant Congressman in the Young Republic: Samuel Smith of Maryland, 1742–1839*. Madison: University of Wisconsin Press.

Castellan, James W., Ron van Dopperen, and Cooper C. Graham. 2016. *American Cinematographers in the Great War, 1914–1918*. Bloomington: Indiana University Press.

Cheatham, Kitty. 1918. *Words and Music of "The Star-Spangled Banner" Oppose the Spirit of Democracy which the Declaration of Independence*

Embodies: A Protest: [including] *Correspondence, Protest in Defense of Children, Excerpts from Letters.* N.p.

Chen, Yu. 2010. "An Empirical Study of Hispanic American National Anthems." University of Texas at Austin. http://lanic.utexas.edu/project/etext/llilas /ilassa/2010/chen.pdf.

Cheney, Lynn. 2015. *James Madison: A Life Reconsidered.* New York: Penguin.

Clague, Mark, and Andrew Kuster, eds. 2015. *Star Spangled Songbook: A History in Sheet Music of "The Star-Spangled Banner."* Ann Arbor, MI: Star Spangled Music Foundation.

Cole, Merle T., and Scott S. Sheads. 2001. *Images of America: Fort McHenry and Baltimore's Harbor Defenses.* Charleston, SC: Arcadia.

Collins, Ace. 2003. *Songs Sung Red, White, and Blue: The Stories Behind America's Best-Loved Patriotic Songs.* New York: HarperCollins.

Conniff, Michael L. 2012. *Panama and the United States: The End of the Alliance.* Athens: University of Georgia Press.

Cook, Jane Hampton. 2014. *America's Star-Spangled Story.* Raleigh, NC: Lighthouse Publishing of the Carolinas.

Cooling, B. Franklin. 1973. *Benjamin Franklin Tracy.* Hamden, CT: Shoe String Press.

Crawford, Katlyn Marie. 2011. "France and the United States: Borrowed and Shared National Symbols." Master's thesis, University of Texas.

Davis, James A. 2019. *Maryland, My Maryland: Music and Patriotism during the American Civil War.* Lincoln: University of Nebraska Press.

Delaplaine, Edward S. 1998. *Francis Scott Key: Life and Times.* Stuarts Draft, VA: American Foundation Publications. First published 1937.

Deman, John Watson. 1921. *Story of the Writing of the Star-Spangled Banner.* Benzonia, MI: Alice Van Deman.

Ellis, Richard J. 2005. *To the Flag: The Unlikely History of the Pledge of Allegiance.* Lawrence: University Press of Kansas.

Elson, Louis C. 1900. *The National Music of America and Its Sources.* Boston: L. C. Page.

Eustace, Nicole. 2012. *1812: War and the Passions of Patriotism.* Philadelphia: University of Pennsylvania Press.

Fahs, Alice. 2001. *The Imagined Civil War: Popular Literature of the North and South, 1861–1865.* Chapel Hill: University of North Carolina Press.

Ferris, Marc. 2014. *Star-Spangled Banner: The Unlikely Story of America's National Anthem.* Baltimore: Johns Hopkins University Press.

Filby, P. W., and Edward G. Howard (compilers). 1972. *Star-Spangled Books: Book, Sheet Music, Newspapers, Manuscripts, and Persons Associated with "The Star-Spangled Banner."* Baltimore: Maryland Historical Society.

Fischer, David Hackett. 2005. *Liberty and Freedom.* New York: Oxford University Press.

Fornas, Johan. 2012. *Signifying Europe.* Bristol, UK: Intellect.

Gamble, Richard M. 2019. *A Fiery Gospel: The Battle Hymn of the Republic and the Road to Righteous War.* Ithaca, NY: Cornell University Press.

Gelles, Aunaleah V. 2015. "Commemorating the Defense of Baltimore, 1815–2015." Master's thesis, University of Maryland, Baltimore County.

Grove, Tim. "Mary, Not Betsy." In *A Grizzly in the Mail and Other Adventures in American History*, 73–87. Lincoln: University of Nebraska Press.

Guenter, Scot M. 1990. *The American Flag, 1777–1924: Cultural Shifts from Creation to Codification*. Cranbury, NJ: Associated University Presses.

Hahner, Leslie A. 2017. *To Become an American: Immigrants and Americanization Campaigns of the Early Twentieth Century*. East Lansing: Michigan State University Press.

Hall, Simon. 2011. *American Patriotism, American Protest: Social Movements since the Sixties*. Philadelphia: University of Pennsylvania Press.

Hauser, Thomas. 2017. *There Will Always Be Boxing: Another Year Inside the Sweet Science*. Fayetteville: University of Arkansas Press.

Head, David. 2015. *Privateers of the Americas: Spanish American Privateering from the United States in the Early Republic*. Athens: University of Georgia Press.

Henderson, Simon. 2013. *Sidelined: How American Sports Challenged the Black Freedom Struggle*. Lexington: University Press of Kentucky.

Hickey, Donald R. 2012. *The War of 1812: A Forgotten Conflict*. Bicentennial edition. Urbana: University of Illinois Press.

Higgins, Edwin. 1898. *The National Anthem, 'The Star Spangled Banner,' Francis Scott Key, and Patriotic Lines*. Baltimore: Williams & Wilkins.

Hladczuk, John, and Sharon Schneider Hladczuk. 2000. *State Songs: Anthems and Their Origins*. Lanham, MD: Scarecrow Press.

Horowitz, Joseph. 2005. "The Grand Peace Jubilee." In *Classical Music in America: A History of Its Rise and Fall*, 16–18. New York: W.W. Norton. http://wesclark.com/jw/peace_jubilee.html.

Howard, Hugh. 2012. *Mr. and Mrs. Madison's War: America's First Couple and the Second War for Independence*. New York: Bloomsbury Press.

Hutchinson, Coleman. 2012. *Apples and Ashes: Literature, Nationalism, and the Confederate States of America*. Athens: University of Georgia Press.

Jackson, Mark Allan. 2007. *Prophet Singer: The Voice and Vision of Woody Guthrie*. Oxford: University Press of Mississippi.

Johnston, Sally, and Pat Pilling. 2014. *Mary Young Pickersgill: Flag Maker of the Star-Spangled Banner*. Bloomington, IN: AuthorHouse.

Jones, Edna D. 1918. *Patriotic Pieces from the Great War*. Philadelphia: Penn Publishing.

Key, Francis Scott. 1857. *Poems of the Late Francis S. Key, Esq., Author of "The Star-Spangled Banner."* Edited by Henry V. D. Johns. New York: Robert Carter & Brothers.

Kooijman, Jaap. 2013. *Fabricating the Absolute Fake: American in Contemporary Pop Culture*. Amsterdam, Holland: Amsterdam University Press.

Krythe, Maymie. 1968. *What So Proudly We Hail: All About Our American Flag, Monuments and Symbols*. New York: Harper & Row.

Langguth, A. J. 2006. *Union 1812: The Americans Who Fought the Second War of Independence*. New York: Simon & Schuster.

Lawrence, Vera Brodsky. 1975. *Music for Patriots, Politicians, and Presidents: Harmonies and Discords of the First Hundred Years*. New York: Macmillan.

Leepson, Marc. 2005. *Flag: An American Biography*. New York: St. Martin's Press.

Leepson, Marc. 2014. *What So Proudly We Hailed: Francis Scott Key, A Life*. New York: Palgrave/Macmillan.

"Legislation to Make 'The Star-Spangled Banner' the National Anthem." 1930. Hearings before the Committee on the Judiciary, House of Representatives, Seventy-First Congress, Second Session on H.R. 14. Washington, DC: Government Printing Office.

Lord, Walter. 1972. *The Dawn's Early Light*. New York: W.W. Norton.

Marshall, Alex. 2015. *Republic or Death! Travels in Search of National Anthems*. London: Random House.

McCabe, John. 1973. *George M. Cohan: The Man Who Owned Broadway*. Garden City, NY: Doubleday.

McConathy, Morgan, Mursell, Bartholomew, Bray, Miessner, and Birge. 1946. *New Music Horizons*. Fifth book. New York: Silver Burdett.

McGavitt, John, and Christopher T. George. 2016. *The Man Who Captured Washington: Major General Robert Ross and the War of 1812*. Norman: University of Oklahoma Press.

McWhirter, Christian. 2012. *Battle Hymns: The Power and Popularity of Music in the Civil War*. Chapel Hill: University of North Carolina Press.

Meacham, Jon, and Tim McGraw. 2019. *Songs of America: Patriotism, Protest, and the Music That Made a Nation*. New York: Random House.

Melnick, Ross. 2012. *American Showman: Samuel "Roxy" Rothafel and the Birth of the Entertainment Industry, 1908–1935*. New York: Columbia University Press.

Meyer, Sam. 1995. *Paradoxes of Fame: The Francis Scott Key Story*. Annapolis, MD: Eastwind.

Meyers, Marvin, ed. 1972. *The Mind of the Founder: Sources of the Political Thought of James Madison*. Indianapolis: Bobbs-Merrill.

Miller, Marla. 2011. *Betsy Ross and the Making of America*. New York: Henry Holt.

Molotsky, Irvin. 2001. *The Flag, the Poet and the Song: The Story of the Star-Spangled Banner*. New York: Dutton.

Morley, Jefferson. 2012. *Snow-Storm in August: Washington City, Francis Scott Key, and the Forgotten Race Riot of 1835*. New York: Doubleday.

Nason, Elias. 1869. *A Monogram on Our National Song*. Albany, NY: Joel Munsell.

National Park Service, Northeast Region. 2004. *Star-Spangled Banner National Historic Trail Feasibility Study and Environmental Impact Statement*. Philadelphia: U.S. Department of the Interior.

Newton, Merlin Owen. 1995. *Armed with the Constitution: Jehovah's Witnesses in Alabama and the U.S. Supreme Court, 1929–1946*. Tuscaloosa: University of Alabama Press.

O'Connell, Frank A. 2014. *National Star-Spangled Centennial Baltimore, Maryland, September 6 to 13, 1914.* Baltimore: National Star-Spangled Banner Centennial Commission.

Pedelty, Mark. 2012. *Ecomusicology: Rock, Folk, and the Environment.* Philadelphia: Temple University Press.

Perry, Imani. 2018. *May We Forever Stand: A History of the Black National Anthem.* Chapel Hill: University of North Carolina Press.

Peters, Shawn Francis. 2000. *Judging Jehovah's Witnesses: Religious Persecution and the Dawn of the Rights Revolution.* Lawrence: University Press of Kansas.

Phillips, Robert. 1931. *The American Flag: Its Uses and Abuses.* Boston: Stratford.

Prothero, Stephen. 2012. *The American Bible: How Our Words Unite, Divide, and Define a Nation.* New York: HarperOne.

Rainwater, Dorothy T., and Donna H. Felger. 1977. *American Spoons: Souvenir and Historical.* N.p.: Everybodys Press.

Reed, W. L., and M. J. Bristow, eds. 1985. *National Anthems of the World.* 6th ed. Poole, UK: Blandford Press.

Robbins, Karen E. 2013. *James McHenry, Forgotten Federalist.* Athens: University of Georgia Press.

Rockwell, Ethel T. 1914. *Star-Spangled Banner Pageant: Staged in the Capitol Park at Madison, Wisconsin, in Celebration of the One-Hundredth Anniversary of the Writing of This National Song by Francis Scott Key.* N.p.: Ethel Theodora Rockwell.

Salomone, Rosemary C. 2010. *True American.* Cambridge, MA: Harvard University Press.

Scholes, Percy A. 1954. *God Save the Queen! The History and Romance of the World's First National Anthem.* New York: Oxford University Press.

Sheads, Scott S. 1986. *The Rockets' Red Glare: The Maritime Defense of Baltimore in 1814.* Centreville, MD: Tidewater.

Sheads, Scott S. 1995. *Fort McHenry.* Baltimore: Nautical & Aviation Publishing Company of America.

Sheads, Scott S. 1999. *Guardian of the Star-Spangled Banner: Lt. Colonel George Armistead and the Fort McHenry Flag.* Baltimore: Toomey Press.

Sherr, Lynn. 2001. *America the Beautiful: The Stirring True Story Behind Our Nation's Favorite Song.* New York: Public Affairs.

Smith, Francis Scott Key. 1911. *Francis Scott Key, Author of The Star Spangled Banner, What Else He Was and Who.* Washington, DC: Key-Smith.

Smith, Herbert C., and John T. Willis. 2012. *Maryland Politics and Government.* Lincoln: University of Nebraska Press.

Smith, Kathleen E. R. 2003. *God Bless America: Tin Pan Alley Goes to War.* Lexington: University Press of Kentucky.

Sonneck, Oscar George Theodore (compiler). 1909. *Report on "The Star-Spangled Banner," "Hail Columbia," "America," "Yankee Doodle."* Washington, DC: Government Printing Office (Library of Congress).

Sonneck, Oscar George Theodore. 1914. *"The Star Spangled Banner" (Revised and Enlarged from the "Report" on the Above and Other Airs, Issued in*

1909). Washington, DC: Government Printing Office (Library of Congress).

Sousa, John Philip. 1890. *National, Patriotic and Typical Airs of All Lands with Copious Notes.* Philadelphia: H. Coleman.

Spener, David. 2016. *We Shall Not Be Moved / No nos moveran: Biography of a Song of Struggle.* Philadelphia: Temple University Press.

Stauffer, John, and Benjamin Soskis. 2013. *The Battle Hymn of the Republic: A Biography of the Song That Marches On.* New York: Oxford University Press.

Sullivan, Patrick. 2013. *Fort McHenry National Monument and Historic Shrine: Administrative History.* New South Associates Technical Report 2256. Stone Mountain, GA: New South Associates for the National Park Service.

Svejda, George J. 2005. *History of the Star Spangled Banner from 1814 to the Present.* Honolulu, HI: University Press of the Pacific. First published in 1969 by Division of History, Office of Archeology and Historic Preservation, U.S. Department of the Interior, National Park Service.

Taylor, Lonn. 2000. *The Star-Spangled Banner: The Flag That Inspired the National Anthem.* New York: National Museum of American History, Smithsonian Institution, in association with Harry N. Abrahms.

Taylor, Lonn, Kathleen M. Kendrick, and Jeffrey L. Brodie. 2008. *The Star-Spangled Banner: The Making of an American Icon.* New York: Smithsonian Institution in conjunction with HarperCollins.

Teachout, Woden. 2009. *Capture the Flag: A Political History of American Patriotism.* New York: Basic Books.

Thomas, Damion L. 2012. *Globetrotting: African Americans Athletes and Cold War Politics.* Champaign: University of Illinois Press.

"The Trial of Reuben Crandall, MD, Charged with Publishing Seditious Libels." 1836. John Bailey Pamphlet Collection (Library of Congress). New York: H. R. Piercy.

Vile, John R. 2015. *A Companion to the United States Constitution and Its Amendments.* 6th ed. Santa Barbara, CA: Praeger.

Vile, John R., ed. 2015. *Founding Documents of America: Documents Decoded.* Santa Barbara, CA: ABC-CLIO.

Vile, John R. 2015. *The Wisest Council in the World: Restoring the Character Sketches by William Pierce of Georgia of the Delegates to the Constitutional Convention of 1787.* Athens: University of Georgia Press.

Vile, John R. 2016. *American Immigration and Citizenship: A Documentary History.* Lanham, MD: Rowman & Littlefield.

Vile, John R. 2016. *The Constitutional Convention of 1787: A Comprehensive Encyclopedia of America's Founding.* 2 vols. Revised 2nd edition. Clark, NJ: Talbot.

Vile, John R. 2018. *The American Flag: An Encyclopedia of the Stars and Stripes in U.S. History, Culture, and Law.* Santa Barbara, CA: ABC-CLIO.

Vile, John R., ed. 2018. *The Civil War and Reconstruction Eras: Documents Decoded.* Santa Barbara, CA: ABC-CLIO.

Vile, John R. 2019. *The Declaration of Independence: America's First Founding Document in U.S. History and Culture*. Santa Barbara, CA: ABC-CLIO.

Vile, John R. 2020. *The Liberty Bell and Its Legacy: An Encyclopedia of an American Icon in U.S. History and Culture*. Santa Barbara, CA: ABC-CLIO.

Vogel, Steve. 2013. *Through the Perilous Fight: From the Burning of Washington to the Star-Spangled Banner; The Six Weeks That Saved the Nation*. New York: Random House.

Warfield, Patrick. 2013. *Making the March King: John Philip Sousa's Washington Years, 1854–1893*. Urbana-Champaign: University of Illinois Press.

Weybright, Victor. 1934. *Spangled Banner: The Story of Francis Scott Key*. New York: Farrar & Rinehart.

White, Richard Grant. 1861. *National Hymns: How They Are Written and How They Are Not Written. A Lyric and National Study for the Times*. New York: Rudd & Carleton.

CHILDREN'S BOOKS

D'Aulaire, Ingri, and Edgar Parin. 1942. *The Star Spangled Banner*. Garden City, NY: Doubleday.

Ingram, Scott. 2004. *The Writing of "The Star-Spangled Banner."* Milwaukee, WI: World Almanac Library.

Kroll, Steven. 1994. *The Story of the Star-Spangled Banner: By the Dawn's Early Light*. Illustrated by Dan Andreasen. New York: Scholastic.

Lyons, John Henry. 1942. *Stories of Our American Patriotic Songs*. New York: Vanguard Press.

Marquete, Scott. 2003. *America at War: War of 1812*. Vero Beach, FL: Rourke.

Rife, Douglas M. 1998. *The Star-Spangled Banner*. Carthage, IL: Teaching & Learning.

Sonneborn, Liz. 2004. *The Star-Spangled Banner: The Story Behind Our National Anthem*. Philadelphia. Chelsea Clubhouse.

COURT DECISIONS

Brown v. Board of Education, 347 U.S. 483 (1954).

Cotto v. United Technologies Corp., 251 Conn. 1 (1999).

Halter v. Nebraska, 265 U.S. 34 (1907).

McCreary County v. American Civil Liberties Union of Kentucky, 545 U.S. 844 (2005).

Minersville School District v. Gobitis, 310 U.S. 586 (1940).

Monroe v. Pape, 365 U.S. 167 (1961).

Obergefell v. Hodges, 576 U.S. _____ (2015).

Sheldon v. Fannin, 221 F. Supp. 766 (D. Ariz. 1963).

Texas v. Johnson, 491 U.S. 397 (1989).

United States v. Eichman, 496 U.S. 310 (1990).

United States v. O'Brien, 391 U.S. 367 (1968).

West Virginia State Board of Education v. Barnette, 319 U.S. 624 (1943).

RECORDINGS

Clague, Mark, Jerry Blackstone, Andrew Kuster, and Dave Schell. 2014. *Poets & Patriots: A Tuneful History of "The Star-Spangled Banner."* 2 compact discs. Ann Arbor, MI: Star Spangled Music Foundation. http://starspangled music.org/poets-patriots-recording-project.

Hildebrand, Mark. 2012. *Anthem*. Make Your Mark Media. Maryland Public Television. https://video.mpt.tv/video/mpt-specials-anthem.

Hildebrand, Mark, director. *Anthem: The Story Behind the Star-Spangled Banner.* DVD.

"The Star Spangled Banner." n.d. National Jukebox, Library of Congress. http://www.loc.gov/jukebox/recordings/detail/id/8141.

"'The Star-Spangled Banner' Early Recorded Version circa 1899 George J. Gaskin, Rare Cylinder." 2014. YouTube, December 14. https://www.youtube.com/watch?v=MN-0rBVoGxI.

"10 Hours of the USA National Anthem (The Star-Spangled Banner)." [Instrumental Music]. YouTube. https://www.youtube.com/watch?v=VrbRMK 8krtM.

"A World Premiere Recording of 'The Star-Spangled Banner'?" 2013. *Star Spangled Music* (blog), Star Spangled Music Foundation, January 18. http://starspangledmusic.org/a-world-premiere-recording-of-the-star-spangled -banner.

TEACHING MATERIALS

American Historama. 2014. "Star Spangled Banner Lyrics." United States History for Kids. http://www.american-historama.org/1801-1828-evolution/star -spangled-banner-lyrics.htm.

"An Anthem, a Flag, and Individual Liberties." Bridge the Divide eLesson. Bill of Rights Institute. https://billofrightsinstitute.org/anthem-flag-individual -liberties.

Davis, Marie Basiliko, and Mia Toschi. 2015. "Embracing the Star-Spangled Banner: A Cross Curricular Approach." Curricular supplement developed for the American Public Education Foundation. https://docs.wixstatic.com /ugd/991d30_3b3a0783f9ea46268c6230179b1974ca.pdf.

Hays, Judy Meyer. 2016. "The Star-Spangled Banner." Lesson plan. Illinois Comprehensive Musicianship through Performance Project. https://illinoiscmp .weebly.com/uploads/4/1/0/7/41075753/star-spangled_banner_cmp_plan _final.pdf.

Kampion, Helen. 2008. "Star-Spangled Presidents." Our White House: Looking In, Looking Out (website). National Children's Book and Literary Alliance. http://ourwhitehouse.org/star-spangled-presidents.

Maryland Humanities Council. *The Defense of a Nation: Maryland's Role in the War of 1812*. Teacher's Resource Guide. https://www.nps.gov/balt/learn /education/upload/1812_Guide_1-21.pdf.

National Park Service. "'The Rockets' Red Glare': Francis Scott Key and the Bombardment of Fort McHenry." Lesson plan. Teaching with Historic

Places. U.S. Department of the Interior. https://www.nps.gov/subjects
/travelbaltimore/upload/Twhp-Lessons_FortMcHenryRocketsRedGlare20
09_508compliant-5.pdf.

"'The Star-Spangled Banner'—ASL Translation." 2011. YouTube, September 19.
https://www.youtube.com/watch?v=CFPpJzLCs98.

"Understanding the American National Anthem for English Language Learners."
2017. *Grammarly* (blog). https://www.grammarly.com/blog/understanding
-the-american-national-anthem-for-english.

Wilson, Clyde. 2016. "Allegiances." *Abbeville Blog*, Abbeville Institute, September 28. https://www.abbevilleinstitute.org/blog/allegiances.

Index

Note: Page numbers in **bold** indicate the location of main entries. Page numbers in *italics* indicate images.

About the Author

John R. Vile, PhD, is professor of political science and dean of the University Honors College at Middle Tennessee State University. In addition to writing numerous reviews and articles, he has written, edited, and coedited a variety of books on legal issues, the U.S. Constitution, and the American Founding period. They include the following: *The Liberty Bell and Its Legacy: An Encyclopedia of an American Icon in U.S. History and Culture* (2020); *More Than a Plea for a Declaration of Rights: The Constitutional and Political Thought of George Mason of Virginia* (2019); *A Constellation of Great Men: Restoring the Character Sketches of Dr. Benjamin Rush of Pennsylvania of the Signers of the Declaration of Independence* (2019); *The Declaration of Independence: America's First Founding Document in U.S. History and Culture* (2019); *The American Flag: An Encyclopedia of the Stars and Stripes in U.S. History, Culture, and Law* (2018); *Essential Supreme Court Decisions*, 17th ed. (2018); *The Civil War and Reconstruction Eras* (2018); *Governmental Responses to Natural Disasters in the U.S.: A Documentary History* (2018); *Constitutional Law in Contemporary America*, 2 vols. (2017); *The Jacksonian and Antebellum Eras* (2017); *Encyclopedia of the First Amendment*, rev. online ed. (2017); *The Constitutional Convention of 1787: A Comprehensive Encyclopedia of America's Founding*, 2 vols., 2nd ed. (2016); *Conventional Wisdom: The Alternative Article V Mechanism for Proposing Amendments to the U.S. Constitution* (2016); *The Early Republic* (2016); *American Immigration and Citizenship* (2016); *Founding Documents of America: Documents Decoded* (2015); *Encyclopedia of Constitutional Amendments, Proposed Amendments, and Amending Issues, 1789–2015*, 4th ed. (2015); *The United States Constitution: One Document, Many Choices* (2015); *A Companion to the United States Constitution and Its Amendments*, 6th ed. (2015); *The Wisest Council in the World: Restoring the Character Sketches by William Pierce of Georgia of the Delegates to the Constitutional Convention of 1787* (2015); *Re-Framers: 170 Eccentric, Visionary, and Patriotic Proposals to Rewrite the U.S. Constitution* (2014); *The Men Who Made the Constitution: Lives of the Delegates to the Constitutional Convention of 1787* (2013); *Encyclopedia of the Fourth Amendment* (2013); *The Writing and Ratification of the U.S. Constitution: Practical Virtue in Action* (2012); *James Madison: Philosopher, Founder and Statesman* (2008); *The Encyclopedia of Civil Liberties in America* (2005); *Great American Judges: An Encyclopedia* (2003); *Great American Lawyers: An Encyclopedia* (2002);

Tennessee Government and Politics (1998); *Constitutional Change in the United States* (1994); *The Theory and Practice of Constitutional Change in America* (1993); *Contemporary Questions Surrounding the Constitutional Amending Process* (1993); *The Constitutional Amending Process in American Political Thought* (1992); *Rewriting the United States Constitution* (1991); and *History of the American Legal System: Interactive Encyclopedia* (CD-ROM, 2000).